This Strange Illness

This Strange Illness
Alcoholism and Bill W.

JARED C. LOBDELL

ALDINE DE GRUYTER
New York

About the Author

Jared C. Lobdell is author or editor of a dozen books in history and criticism and a number of articles in those fields; in alcohol studies; and in economic and systems analysis. He was Kirk Fellow at the Center for Alcohol and Addiction Studies and the John Hay Library at Brown University in 2001–2002 and 2003–2004. He is Lecturer at Millersville University of Pennsylvania and Adjunct Professor at Elizabethtown College; as well as coordinator of the weekend program at the Harrisburg Area Community College. He lives in Elizabethtown with his wife Jane Starke Lobdell—who worked with him on this book—their German Shepherd, Lolci, and six cats.

Copyright © 2004 Walter de Gruyter, Inc., New York

ALDINE DE GRUYTER
A division of Walter de Gruyter, Inc.
200 Saw Mill River Road
Hawthorne, New York 10532

This publication is printed on acid free paper ∞

Library of Congress Cataloging-in-Publication
Lobdell, Jared, 1937–
    This strange illness : alcholism and Bill W. / Jared C. Lobdell.
        p. cm.
    Includes bibliographical references.
    ISBN 0-202-30738-7 (cloth : alk. paper) — ISBN 0-202-30739-5 (pbk. : alk.
paper) 1. Alcoholism. 2. Alcoholism—Treatment. 3. Alcoholics—Rehabilitation. 4.
Alcoholics Anonymous. 5. Twelve-step programs—Religious aspects. I. Title.

    HV5035.L79 2004
    362.292—dc22
                                                                                2003020359
Manufactured in the United States of America

10 9 8 7 6 5 4 3 2 1

For my wife
Jane Starke Lobdell

and for my mother
Jane Hopkins Lobdell

Contents

Foreword

Jared Lobdell's *This Strange Illness* is an important book that arrives at an important time in the history of alcoholism and its treatment. There is a darkness that this book seeks to illuminate. That darkness comes not from the toll alcoholism exacts on individuals, families and communities, which is exorbitant, but from the stigma and shadows within which this disorder continues to be shrouded. For more than two centuries, America has vacillated between compassion and contempt in her response to alcoholism and the alcoholic. A reform movement of the late eighteenth and nineteenth centuries conceptualized chronic drunkenness (inebriety) as a disease—what Lobdell calls Alcoholism (1)—and generated a network of American inebriate homes and asylums. This movement collapsed in the early twentieth century as America lost faith in the potential for recovery and briefly courted the idea that alcoholism could be resolved by legally banishing the seed from which it was thought to grow.

In the mid-twentieth century, a "modern alcoholism movement" rose from the ashes of prohibition to claim again that alcoholism was a disease and that the alcoholic was a sick person who should be treated rather than punished. The image of the alcoholic as skid row wino was replaced by an image of the alcoholic as one's family member, neighbor, and coworker. This movement peaked in the 1970s as federal and state legislation dotted the American landscape with alcoholism treatment programs. Stereotypes (the alcoholic as the skid row wino) and stigma declined as Americans from all walks of life, including First Lady Betty Ford, stepped out of the shadows to declare their successful and sustained recovery from alcoholism.

The 1980s and 1990s witnessed the erosion of the modern alcoholism movement. The core concept of alcoholism gave way to chemical dependency, substance abuse, and addiction concepts that first merged alcoholism and illicit drug dependence and then added a host of other problems within their rubric. The commercialization of these broadened concepts by a rapidly expanding private treatment industry and the ensuing abuses within that industry led to a financial backlash that eroded insurance coverage for alcoholism and led to the closure of many treatment programs. There was also an ideological backlash that challenged the core ideas of the modern alcoholism movement. This countermovement proclaimed: (1) addiction is a myth, (2) excessive alcohol and drug consumption is a choice, not a disease, (3) Alcoholics Anonymous and alcoholism/addiction treatment are ineffective and potentially harmful, and (4) addiction treatment is a failed social experiment that should be defunded.

By the mid-1990s, it was clear that alcoholism and the broader cluster of problems with which it was now grouped were being restigmatized, demedicalized, and recriminalized. Severe alcohol and other drug-related problems were again being described within the province of morality rather than medicine; cultural ownership of these problems shifted from systems of care to systems of punishment and control. This trend has triggered the rise of a new recovery advocacy movement—grassroots organizations of recovering people and their families and allies who are seeking to change public attitudes and public policies by offering themselves as living proof of the reality and fruits of long-term recovery from alcoholism and other addictions. There is in this movement a recognition that the achievements and lessons of the modern alcoholism movement could be lost. It is in this context that Jared Lobdell's new book arrives. But it has not arrived alone.

There is an increased interest in the history of alcoholism and recovery, as evidenced by the publication of new books on the history of A.A. and Twelve Step recovery (*The Collected Ernie Kurtz*), A.A. cofounder Bill Wilson (*Bill W.; Bill W. and Mr. Wilson*), key A.A. figures (*How It Worked: The Story of Clarence H. Snyder; Mrs. Marty Mann: The First Lady of Alcoholics Anonymous;* and *Silkworth: The Little Doctor who Loved Drunks*), and the larger story of treatment and recovery (*Slaying the Dragon: The History of Addiction Treatment and Recovery in America*). Also in evidence is a dramatic increase in history-themed conferences related to addiction and recovery. This is the context in which Jared Lobdell's *This Strange Illness* arrives.

Lobdell's expansive essay contributes to the study of alcoholism, sobriety, and Alcoholics Anonymous in at least seven ways. First, it establishes a "scientific research program" (in the sense of those words used by the philosopher of science Imre Lakatos) within which this and further studies can take place. Second, it provides a sweeping narrative of the history of alcoholism and our social and therapeutic responses to it. Third, it recounts the history of Alcoholics Anonymous and how this fellowship came to conceptualize alcoholism as a disease of the mind, body and spirit. Fourth, it explores the long history of alcoholism typologies—efforts to describe varying patterns of alcoholism and their etiological roots. Fifth, it details in successive chapters what we know about the psychological, biological and spiritual dimensions of alcoholism, maintaining the validity of Bill W.'s original insight through current research and the congruence of treatment for the threefold illness. Sixth, it explicates the history and content of the Twelve Steps and Twelve Traditions of Alcoholics Anonymous. And seventh, the concluding chapter (entitled "Paradigm Regained") attempts to define that which must not be lost from both the collective experience of alcoholism recovery and the scientific study of alcoholism— and that which must indeed be further examined.

A growing number of observers believe that the backlash against the foundational ideas of the modern alcoholism movement and the backlash in response to abuses within the addiction treatment industry threaten to throw the baby out with the bath water. Lobdell's *This Strange Illness* marks the beginning of a new genre of literature that seeks to define and save the best within the modern history of alcoholism recovery. That effort alone would make this book a worthy contribution even if there were no more to it. But there is.

William L. White
Senior Research Associate
Chestnut Health Systems
Bloomington, Illinois

Introduction

ONE DOES NOT WISH TO BEGIN BY PUSHING READERS AWAY, but one wishes also to be honest. It is my belief that, in this world, complex questions have complex answers, indeed that the "simple" truth about almost anything one cares to name is frequently an oversimplification of necessary complexity. The subject of this book is complex enough: indeed, it is at least a fourfold subject, with the folds further enfolded among themselves. As briefly as I can put it here, the questions the book is designed to answer are these: What is the "disease" (or "illness" or what are the "diseases" or "illnesses") called alcoholism? Who was this Bill W. who founded Alcoholics Anonymous? What is this Alcoholics Anonymous (A.A.) that claims success in the treatment of alcoholism (and how does it connect with other, especially previous, treatments)? What *is* this success and how *can* A.A. be successful? The answers—and they are incomplete—will take us the next 170,000 words or so, more than most people will care to read, including (I would guess) most if not all those who are members of Alcoholics Anonymous. But for all that, I think the questions worth asking, and worth trying to answer. Admittedly, this book is only a first swerve at an answer, or even at providing a framework (a "scientific research program") within which and by which to seek an answer. In the final chapter, we will look briefly at work yet to be done.

The history of alcoholism goes back quite a long time (albeit not perhaps quite as long as generally thought—which is, in Bill W.'s phrase, since man first crushed grapes)—and the history of attempts to treat the condition go back for more than two centuries (many years before there was such a word as "alcoholism"). But it would appear that one particular mode of treatment for this condition offers a good chance of overcoming the "disease" in all its three aspects of mind, body, and spirit (or, as some might say, its two intersecting aspects of body and spirit, intersecting *in* the mind, or *as* the mind). This is the mode first proposed by the co-founders (Bill W. and Dr. Bob S.) and other early members and friends of the fellowship called Alcoholics Anonymous (A.A.) and it can be justified

1

both practically and theologically. (And psychologically, also, for those who may believe psychology is not practicality, or that justification cannot be purely utilitarian—"It works.")

We ought to try to clear up one point immediately. There is a great deal in this book that is technical—technical discussion of the mind and of psychology and psychiatry, technical discussion of the body, the brain and the neuronal system, and (oddest of all for the year 2004) technical discussion of theology. My attempt has been to find an interlinked theory or set of theories ("scientific research program") that would enable us to describe an illness of mind, body, and spirit, without allowing the assumptions underlying the way we look at one area of illness (say, the mind) to contradict the assumptions underlying the way we look at another (say, here, body—or spirit).

One need not accept the implicit Cartesian view of Mind found in Freudian or Jungian psychiatry (or in its most severe form, in Mary Baker Eddy) to accept the practical validity of what Freud and Jung did (or Mrs. Eddy) or recommended, but one had better not be working from a view inconsistent with the possibility of their achievements. Contrariwise, one need not accept the idea of heritable illness in order to get sober—at least, so it would appear—but if one accepts the real existence of the body, one had better take that into account in one's view of Mind, and in writing about alcoholism one had better also take into account explanations of alcoholism that involve biogenetics. And especially, one had better have a theology (science of spiritual action) that does not make nonsense of one's views of mind and body. I do not claim that our mix in this book of Johannine theology, modern psychology (especially Jung, Sandór Radó, and Harry Stack Sullivan), and recent research in biochemistry and genetics gives us a true unified field theory of alcoholism and what A.A. does—but I do claim that it is self-consistent and provides us with a workable scientific research program, in the terms presented back in the 1960s by the philosopher of science Imre Lakatos (or, in slightly less exact Kuhnian terms, a workable paradigm).

In the book, I have not gone much into the technical analysis of history—periodization and all that—but it would appear that the fellowship of A.A. was founded at a golden moment. What is of particular interest for us in looking at its continuance from that golden moment is, first, that the cofounder most interested in A.A.'s institutional longevity (Bill W.) subsequently established a singular structure for the "governance" and continuity of the fellowship—a kind of attempt to prolong the golden moment—and, second, that our study of this structure and its "governing" documents suggests that, both practically and in theory, it is *all* necessary—even if not necessarily sufficient—for that continuance. It therefore turns out that, with everything else it is, this book is also a study in a particular realm of philosophy called teleology, from the Greek *telos*, meaning end in the sense of goal or purpose, as in "the ends justify the means." But before we come to any conclusions about the *telos* of sobriety, we need to do our work in biology, chemistry, genetics, psychology, history of thought, social history, decision sciences, and theology—to name only a few.

You see why I say the subject is complex. On the other hand, we must also remember that complexity is the progenitor of chaos—in the technical, if not in the ordinary sense. Let me explain what I mean by the technical sense. I have already noted that complex problems have complex solutions: but let us suppose we can reduce our complex problems to a series of simple problems. Will we then have a series of simple solutions? We may, but we need not, and probably will not. Let me take a mechanical example. As with a starting a pendulum swinging, where we find that a very slight change in the speed with which we start it may convert it from oscillating motion to rotating ("over-the-top") motion, so in any number of problems, the solution may have a *sensitive dependence on initial conditions*. When we feed certain initial values into an iterative ("repeated-calculation") process for determining a solution to our problem, the values themselves may change and converge on (but never quite reach) certain other and different values. The final result is that, although there appears to be some set of rules of order for our solutions, we can never predict which (of a finite number of solutions at convergent points in our decision-space) will be *our* solution. To put it briefly, we can make good qualitative predictions, not quite so good quantitative predictions, and anecdotal evidence suddenly becomes more important than we had thought (because anecdotal evidence can be good qualitative evidence).

Human behavior represents a dynamical system or (better) set of dynamical systems (so likewise genetics, as we will see). The mathematics of dynamical systems is that area within chaos theory called fractal geometry, and it is important that, although this chaos is an ordered chaos, our attempts at solutions, even for our hypothetical series of simple problems, are likely to be probabilistic at best. That is, our simple problems will themselves have complex solutions. As a result, we must be careful not to think we can reduce our subject to simple equations and arrangements of statistical data, and get sure and certain answers from them. We can and will make use of statistical studies—not as proofs but as indications of possible underlying reality. But our model has been formed from qualitative observation (ours and others), and not merely from statistical tests. The paradox of chaos theory is that our best evidence is anecdotal (though from many anecdotes) rather than statistical. (I must make it entirely clear that this does not mean it has been formed from observation *at* A.A. meetings: even A.A. members at meetings are told and told again that what they hear and see there, stays there.)

A few more words here on the idea of the *telos*. By *telos* we mean an ultimate goal toward which a system—whether the whole universe or an individual human being or a group of human beings—is moving. In Christian theology, this is generally taken as the fulfillment of God's plan. The teleological (goal-seeking) aspect of Christianity, and of the Judaism from which it came, distinguishes both Christianity and Judaism from a number of other faiths, though not all. Zoroastrianism and Northern Paganism both have something of this same teleological character. As we will see later, a linear teleological character also inheres in the Jungian psychology of individuation—a point worth at least a brief mention here—and it may not be accidental that Jung occupies a unique place in the annals of Alcoholics Anonymous, as we shall also see.

Another part of the subject of our study (toward the end of this book) is the creation, history, and governance (or "ordering") of Alcoholics Anonymous as a *koinonia* (fellowship, gathering, or assembly) providing a locus for this mental and spiritual treatment of the condition of alcoholism. Our study here involves the threefold division of the arenas of human decision-making into the *agora* (the market), the *polis* (the state), and the *koinonia* (the community), and also involves the "Invention of Tradition" and "Theory of Committees" as areas of study particularly relevant to *koinonia* decision-making. It happens that, for whatever reason, these are areas in which I have concentrated a good deal of study: indeed, A.A. was called to my attention by a theorist of spontaneous order (in systems) as an example of precisely that.

When we come to medical and biochemical considerations (primarily in Chapters 3 and 4), we argue essentially that there is more than one type—indeed, more than two types—of alcoholism, which may be in fact genotypes as well as phenotypes; that these may have developed for different reasons in different human lineages; that alcoholism is at least analogous to an immune system condition or allergy; and that, unless one is a biological "sport"—which does sometimes happen—one is not an alcoholic except by inheritance (and note that even the sport may be the result of ordered chaos in genetic transmission). Some of the implications of genotypic alcoholism are suggested *seriatim* in the book. One has to do with a question of whether the fundamental condition with which we are concerned is alcoholism or addiction. It is the view taken here that alcoholism is a disease, allergy, or predisposition that some have and some do not, while addiction as a disease (though not *active* addiction) is more or less a general human condition. A general study of alcoholism in one book is thus, we believe, within human possibilities (though this, of course, may not be that book): a general study of addiction as a disease, and thus of all mankind, is almost certainly not.

One apparent oddity might be noted in places throughout the book. There occurs from time to time (has already, in fact, occurred above) reference to the name of Mrs. Mary Baker (Glover) Eddy (1821–1910), "Founder and Discoverer" of Christian Science. In no way may she be profitably— or correctly—considered as being in the line of direct development of Alcoholics Anonymous. And yet—she was virtually the only person presenting the possibility of a spiritual treatment for alcoholism in the 1890s, so she appears briefly in Chapter 1. Bill W. went to a Christian Science practitioner about his drinking before he got sober in the 1930s, and read and studied *Science and Health with Key to the Scriptures* and so she appears briefly in Chapter 2. Her view of the opposition of Matter and Spirit— opposed to the Johannine theology of the Incarnation—is relevant in Chapter 6. And her creation of a church is the road not taken by Bill W. in Chapter 8, and highly relevant there. And, of course (also in Chapter 1), William James, of *The Varieties of Religious Experience*, himself went to a Christian Science practitioner (L. C. Strang). At least as much as the Washingtonians, Mary Baker Eddy plays a kind of counterpoint to Bill W.'s Alcoholics Anonymous.

Briefly, the process of the book is this. First, in this introduction, we will go over what we are going to do. In Chapter 1, we look at the history of alcoholism—or rather, a few documented episodes in the history of alcoholism—and then at (even fewer) episodes in conversion and in the history of treatment for alcoholism, bringing us up roughly to 1934–35 (right after the end of Prohibition in the United States), when Alcoholics Anonymous was founded. We look at Shakespeare's Michael Cassio (in *Othello*, 1604) and at Nicolas Herrmann (Brother Lawrence, 1614–91). We look at episodes in conversion (working from William James, *The Varieties of Religious Experience*): these include John Bunyan (1622–88), Henry Alline (1748–84), and Samuel Hopkins Hadley (1842–1906). We consider the Jamesian distinction between volitional conversion and conversion by self-surrender, which has come down into the traditional lore of Alcoholics Anonymous pretty much as the distinction between an "educational" and a "white light" spiritual experience. Some clues as to what we should look at were given by the cofounder of Alcoholics Anonymous, who is called in these pages (following A.A. convention) Bill W. (In the decisive article on Alcoholics Anonymous in the *Saturday Evening Post* in March 1941 he was called William Griffith, but the convention of first name or nickname and last initial has by now taken firm hold and is used here.)

On the matter of treatment, we look, of course, at the Washington Temperance Society (and briefly at the Alcoholic Republic that spawned it). In the early days of Alcoholics Anonymous, Bill W. had his attention called to the Washingtonians (by an early A.A. member from North Carolina, I am told, but I have been unable to check that): he thereafter used the Washingtonians as a primary example of an antecessor of A.A. that had gone wrong in ways Bill W. did not want to see A.A. go wrong. We also look at something of the institutional treatment of inebriety (not yet alcoholism, except in a few publications in Germany), and at the first popular so-called medical treatment, the Keeley cure. We touch on Jerry McAuley's Water Street Mission in New York City, and more on the program instituted by Elwood Worcester at Emmanuel (Episcopal) Church in Boston, which gave rise eventually to the (unsuccessful) treatment popularized by "Dr." Richard Peabody, who seems to have died drunk at forty-two, and to the first lay therapist for alcoholism, Courtenay Baylor, who died sober years later. We mention Charlie Towns and the Towns cure. And we briefly examine the various anti-alcoholism programs supported by John D. Rockefeller, Jr., before looking (again briefly) at the book that brought the word "alcoholic" to the public consciousness—*John Barleycorn* (serialized in the *Saturday Evening Post* and then published in book form in 1913)—by Jack London, who died drunk, from complications of alcoholism, three years later, at the age of forty.

This brings us to Chapter 2, where we look at the history of the formation of Alcoholics Anonymous, in what I have called the golden moment—though, in fact, it lasted roughly from 1935 to 1940. The first part of this chapter concentrates particularly on Bill W. and a few more of the first one hundred members, and then on "this strange illness of mind, body, and spirit" (in the words of Bill W., the cofounder)—an heritable genetic condition (or allergy, or predisposition, or even perhaps disease), a mental illness (possibly connected with other mental illnesses), and a spiritual disorder. After looking a little at Bill W.'s life before he got sober in late 1934, to see (a little) what manner of man he was, we reprint much of his last published testimony on how he got sober and how A.A. was founded (presented in 1969 to a subcommittee of the U.S. Congress). The chapter also includes testimony by several other early members of A.A., Fitz M. (from A.A.'s "Big Book," all four editions), Jim B. (partly from the "Big Book," second, third, and fourth editions), and Clarence S. (partly from the "Big Book," first, second, and third editions). We also look at some of the nonalcoholic founders of A.A.—the Rev. Samuel M. Shoemaker (of Calvary Mission and the Oxford Group), Father Edward Dowling, S.J. William Duncan Silkworth, M.D. (of the Towns Hospital), perhaps Carl Jung (and thus Rowland H. and "Ebby" T.), and other early "friends" of Alcoholics Anonymous—including the enigmatic figure of Charlie Towns. We note especially that the information that seemed to make things work, that in fact came to these alcoholics as a message of hope, was the information that alcoholism was an illness, not a matter of moral willpower.

Chapter 3 discusses—primarily—the typology of alcoholisms and secondarily some modes of genetic transference (inheritance) and the possible origins of alcoholism as a leap into the adjacent possible. (Some readers will remark on the influence of work at the Santa Fe Institute on this formulation.) Further suggestions along this line are to be found in Chapter 9. We consider E.M. Jellinek's fivefold typology of alcoholisms, Cloninger's and Babor's dichotomies, and what we believe a promising approach first suggested in the 1980s by Robert Zucker. We examine the processes of natural selection, noting that these processes conduce to the preservation of those organisms best suited to preservation—a tautology and a truism, to be sure, but nonetheless important for us here. Here we make use of Darwin's principle that the system of evolutionary change must be based on three components of change: (1) overpopulation of the organism beyond environmental support, (2) subsequent competition among offspring for survival, and (3) inheritable variations in phenotype. This third component makes it possible for offspring with the phenotypic variant most suited to survival to be most likely the offspring to survive. In other words, surviving phenotypic variants survive because of the survival value of the variation—as I say, a tautology and a truism, but useful.

In our typological study, we suggest a combination of Jellinek's typology with Zucker's, believing this will provide a basis for examining genotypic variants of alcoholism. We come up with four principal variants, what might be called phenotypic variants, though I believe they reflect genotypes: (1) primary sociopathic alcoholism (phenotype Psa), (2) secondary depressive alcoholism (phenotype Sda), (3) primary cumulative alcoholism (phenotype Pca), and (4) primary episodic alcoholism (phenotype Pea). We look at Zucker's four types, (1) antisocial alcoholism, (2) developmentally limited alcoholism, (3) negative affect alcoholism, and (4) primary alcoholism. He subdivides type (4) into (a) isolated, (b) episodic, and (c) developmentally cumulative primary alcoholism. Like the Jellinek alpha and beta subtypes, Zucker type-2 drinkers seem to fall into the alcohol abuse rather than the alcohol dependence category.

This epsilon drinker does not specifically appear in the Zucker typology, except as a subset within type-1, antisocial alcoholism, and here Zucker may have misspecified an alcoholic type. But it should be noted that we are modifying the range of type in Jellinek epsilon to include all instantaneous drinkers in a binge pattern. We are thus in effect arguing that they are full-blown binge alcoholics (type epsilon) from the start, and suggesting the possibility that antisocial personality disorder (ASPD) is simply a characteristic of this type of alcoholism. This leaves hanging the question of whether their alcoholism is progressive. Jellinek indeed wondered whether epsilon alcoholics were really alcoholics, as their condition did not seem to be progressive, but this may have represented a false conflation of what we call Alcoholism(1) and Alcoholism(2).

Jellinek gamma drinkers (endogenous symptomatic drinkers, including those in which alcoholism is subsidiary to a major psychiatric disorder) would seem to include Zucker type-1 drinkers (antisocial alcoholism) and Zucker type-3 drinkers (negative affect alcoholism), which may be principally differentiated from each other by gender. Jellinek delta drinkers seem to fit within the bounds of Zucker's developmentally cumulative primary alcoholics (type 4-c). The area in which the Jellinek typology may be more exact and more useful than the Zucker typology is in the Jellinek definition of the epsilon drinker (as here modified), the "primary" or "true" alcoholic who is virtually an "instantaneous" alcoholic from the first drink. Anecdotal evidence from conversations with members of A.A. seems to support the existence of these drinkers.

Because there is a possibility—even probability—of genetic ordering, we look at recent investigations into how chaotic change in genetics or inheritance might be ordered. This involves the Santa Fe work on the co-construction of new diversity when communities of agents evolve to an edge of chaos, where a push into novelty (new diversity) may be formalized mathematically as passage into the adjacent possible of effective phase-space for the community. This links with the so-called Fourth Drive, present in other animals besides humans. Siegel's Fourth Drive—the drive to intoxication—is acquired rather than innate, but still a "natural" drive, which he finds virtually throughout the animal kingdom, so that intoxication must have adaptive value in evolution, or else its pursuit is a side effect of a beneficial gene or genes. In this case, we suggest a link between speech genes and alcoholism, after spending some time on the question whether there may in fact be genes for speech or reading. I should add that this almost certainly is of secondary interest to most of those for whom sobriety is a matter of life and death, but it should be of value here.

Chapter 4 addresses the illnesses of the mind—that is, its subject is psychology and alcoholism. What is mental illness, what is mind, and how did it get that way? Here we construct a research program that is not based on but seems to be consistent with the conclusions suggested more than a quarter-century ago by Julian Jaynes, to wit, the proposition that consciousness (that is, consciousness of self) occurs relatively recently in human history. Specifically, that it occurs, say, three thousand or so years ago, as part of a process that began with the invention of language, say ten times as long ago, and carried through the invention of nouns, say eight thousand to ten thousand years ago. As a corollary, there could be no philosophy, let alone psychology, until the invention or discovery of the self: it is not necessary (though it would be consistent) to accept Jaynes's idea of the bicameral person as part of our research program. (After all, most of what is explicit in Jaynes may be though implicit in that 1946 volume from the University of Chicago, *Before Philosophy*.) We do, however, suggest that transcendent experience through intoxication may have had something to do with the invention of language.

After what may seem to some of our readers a walk in the byways, we begin our look at psychiatric treatment—indeed at psychiatry—by looking at Freud, then a little at Adler and Jung, and then we take a first glance at the neglected American founder of group therapy, Harry Stack Sullivan (1894–1949). From there we return briefly to Siegel, chaos, and intoxication, passing on to the evolution of pattern in the brain, and then to the (neuronal) linkage of brain and body (including memory). A glance aside at Mrs. Eddy leads us into that other product of Boston and Cambridge, George Vaillant's *Natural History of Alcoholism* (1983) and *Natural History of Alcoholism Revisited* (1996a), from which we go to manic depression, antisocial personality disorder, other comorbidities known with alcoholism, with a note on the Cousins effect, wherein laughter is indeed the best medicine. From laughter as therapy (outside the bounds of A.A. or indeed of alcoholism), we go on to look at therapy relevant for alcoholism as suggested by Freud, Sullivan, and Hans Kohut. Here again we look at His Majesty the Baby, or as another might put it, the regressive narcissism of the alcoholic. This leads us into some considerations of the principal mode of therapy implicit within the social system of Alcoholics Anonymous.

Harry M. Tiebout, Sandór Radó, Harry Stack Sullivan, all used what we would now define as a species of narratization therapy—psychodynamic narrative, if you like, or psychotherapeutic narrative. (And as we also note in this chapter, this has strong ties to John Bowlby's Attachment Theory.) The outcome may be conceived as syntaxic reformulation from parataxic distortion by the therapist's (or sponsor's) consensual validation (this is Sullivan), or it may be conceived in Kohut's narratization terms. The therapy may include Tiebout's frequent use of explanatory (real-world) narrative based on dream-interpretation, or the practice in A.A. in some areas of starting the First Step with a life-story—which becomes part of the story of the recovery. The important point we should carry away from this discussion of alcoholism and the mind is that Bill W. was right in speaking of alcoholism as an illness of the mind—and the treatment, however defined and delimited, involves the use of narrative.

Chapter 5 deals with the illness of the body—specifically with the biology and genetics of alcoholism, not so much the disease concept of alcoholism as alcoholism as a disease, allergy, or predisposition. Among doctors may be mentioned C. Dudley Saul and A. Wiese Hammer of Philadelphia, and we are fortunate to have a brief reminiscence by a patient of Saul—Johnny L.—who got sober in 1938 and died, still sober, in 1983. What is of particular interest is that the doctors who recognized and diagnosed a medical or psychiatric condition recognized also the limitations of medicine and psychotherapy, and discovered the effectiveness of fellowship and spiritual recovery. I have summarized this chapter at fairly considerable length here, (1) because it is in some ways the kernel of the book's eventual conclusions on the *telos* of sobriety as well as on the underpinnings of the A.A. system, and (2) because the news that alcoholism was both a mental and a bodily illness was what freed early members of A.A. from their hopelessness. It is important to establish that the good news was in fact true. Dr. Silkworth, who treated Bill W.'s alcoholism in the early 1930s, was responsible for resurrecting the view that alcoholism includes an allergy—a view that such later observers as Barry Leach and Jack Norris accepted as in keeping with A.A.'s practical approach, while suggesting that it was not technically accurate. But our conclusions tend toward a reinvigoration of that definition. In any case, biochemical and biogenetic research shows—I believe—that the good news, the hopeful news, was true.

When we talk about allergy we are generally talking about improper reaction of the immune system. Pretty obviously, alcoholism is not an allergy in the usual sense of the word: alcohol is not, for alcoholics, an allergen producing extraordinary unfortunate results, like ragweed to a hay-fever sufferer. But it is an allergen in the sense that it produces extraordinary and idiosyncratic reactions among a group with special sensitivity to it. That the alcoholic's reactions to alcohol are initially pleasurable is the problem, and is what distinguishes them from the allergic reaction to ragweed. Here also we review the current state of knowledge primarily on biological phenotypes, under the following subheadings: (1) neurotransmitter-related systems, (2) enzyme systems, (3) cognition, response to stress, and electrophysiology, and (4) response to alcohol challenge, with some consideration of psychosocial phenotypes. Note that these areas of biological research fall into two broad categories: signal systems and breakdown systems, the way alcohol sends signals to the brain, and the way it alters the body, though these areas overlap in certain respects. The first is, in our view, incomparably the more important for our study.

Let us briefly define two terms here, so the reader will have them in mind throughout: *phenotype* and *genotype* (we will define them at least once more). By a phenotype we mean the visible properties of an organism produced by the interaction of the genotype and the environment. By genotype we mean all or part of the genetic constitution of an individual or a group. The phenotype of an organism is contrasted with its genotype on the grounds that the *phenotype* concerns the organism's concrete existence in the observer's domain or domains, whereas the *genotype* concerns the genetic makeup that the organism inherited and that accounted for its embryogenesis and development. An example may help to make the matter a little clearer. There are different kinds of corn—niblet, shoepeg, white—and these are genotypes. Plant the corn and grow the crop, and you get specific examples according to the soil, rainfall, sunlight, amount of labor expended—in short, the corn's concrete existence in the observer's domain, determined by interaction of the genotype and the environment. These are the phenotypes.

Obviously, as we note, if all offspring were phenotypically identical, survival would be solely a matter of chance. But because of phenotypic variation, some of the offspring will be better suited to survival than others. And if the phenotypic variations arise from differences in genotype, then the advantages given by these characteristics would propagate through the species through better survival rates. That is, to quote Alan Dean in *Chaos and Intoxication*, "those more suited to a specific environment by virtue of a phenotypic advantage which was grounded in a genetic change would have better rates of survival. Over time, the adapted variety would tend to increase in proportion to the non-adapted variety" (p. 34). Thus, to take modern examples, there are mosquitoes resistant to DDT, viruses resistant to penicillin, and so on.

We go on to look briefly at the mechanics of heritable diseases, allergies, or predispositions, a kind of primer on genetics and the development of pattern in the brain. Our primer on genetics is primarily historical in nature. With peas, the nineteenth-century monk Gregor Mendel could control pollination and develop highly inbred varieties that bred true and that had clearly defined and clearly observable traits (phenotypes). It was Mendel who first discussed dominant and recessive heritable characteristics. Then, by 1914, the British physician Archibald Garrod had shown that certain human metabolic maladies obeyed Mendel's paradigm and eventually suggested that each malady was the result of the loss of a different metabolic step, arguably because of a particular enzyme deficiency. We note that nothing yet has contradicted the assumption that all genetic systems, regardless of organism, work in fundamentally the same way and through the same set of molecules. So those doing genetic research have worked with the fruit fly *Drosophila melanogaster*, with the nematode *Caenorhabditis elegans*, and with mice. That is why, in discussing the genetics of alcoholism, we will find ourselves talking about flies, worms and mutant mice.

Of course, there are always possibilities of biological "sports"—that is, of a parent or parents possessing newly appearing characteristics (not previously evident in either genetic line) that can be passed on to the child. It is thus possible that a child could be an alcoholic even though alcoholism did not appear in either parental family. Not that it wasn't, in some sense, *there*, but it did not *appear*. If there is such a thing as chaotic ordering in genetics, as we believe there is, the process would simply have moved from tending toward one convergent variable ("attractor") in its result to another. The point is that in chaos theory, the progress of certain values (which may include genetic values) is heavily dependent upon initial conditions, giving rise to a system (meaning a system described in nonlinear equations) where solutions determining the values can only be determined iteratively (that is, by repetition), and where there are multiple "correct" solutions.

Finally we come to our suggested human phenotypes associated with alcoholism. As noted above, we are suggesting four types of alcoholism: primary sociopathic alcoholism (phenotype Psa), which is Jellinek epsilon alcoholism (modified) and Zucker type-1 revised with some Zucker 4-b; secondary depressive alcoholism (phenotype Sda), which is Jellinek gamma (subset) alcoholism and Zucker type-3; primary cumulative alcoholism (phenotype Pca), Jellinek delta alcoholism and Zucker type 4-c, which may include some Zucker type 4-b; primary episodic alcoholism (Pea) representing a separate phenotype from Psa, but nonetheless Jellinek epsilon (modified). It may be suggested that the same principle of parsimony (Occam's Razor) that would lead to substituting Zucker type-1 Revised for Zucker type-1 would also lead to including primary episodic alcoholism within the Psa phenotype—but this does not seem to be the case.

If we can identify chromosomal regions determining "alcoholic" response to alcohol, then alcoholism is not only a complex disease but a complexly genetic (heritable) disease, as we believe it is. And, since alcoholics marry other alcoholics, and have alcoholic children, we will have in effect recombinant inbred (RI) lines with a high degree of homozygosity, suggesting that genotypes will alter over the years. With recombinant inbred populations, if the parents differ significantly in genotype, the phenotypes of the children will show more extreme variation. Heterozygous hybrids are likely to show neither the dominant allele nor the recessive allele but lie somewhere in between. I have not yet seen it worked out how this conflates with chaos theory, but it suggests a kind of chaos system operating through genetic codes.

Chapter 6 deals with the theological underpinnings of our inquiry (as I understand them) and thus serves as a link with an eventual conclusion on the *telos* of sobriety as a model for the *telos* of salvation. This chapter can be skipped by those who are content with not trying to understand why A.A. works *sub specie aeternitatis* or who are not interested in talking about the *process* of salvation—which very likely includes most of the members of A.A. in the first case, and almost all in the second case. And this for the good and sufficient reason that discussion of why something works is at best tangential for those for whom its working is both a matter of faith and a matter of life and death. Nevertheless, those who skip the discussion will probably find themselves not entirely comfortable with some of our conclusions, and I think we had better summarize a little of this chapter here—though not in so great detail as we have summarized Chapter 5. But that is, essentially (or perhaps I should say, at least in part), because biogenetic analysis is currently pushing our frontiers of knowledge forward—so that much of this is new—while there have not been significant advances in theological analysis for quite a while.

Still, it is worth pointing out that the well-known partial origins of A.A. in the Oxford Group ("First-Century Christianity") have significant implications in several respects—at least one of which is closely tied in with A.A.'s partial origins in the office of Carl Jung. First off, the Oxford Group defined sin as spiritual disease—what we may call the *disease concept of sin*—which has, therefore, certain obvious (but neglected) links with the disease concept of alcoholism. We go at some depth into this concept as it appears in Christian doctrine in the first century, concentrating on the doctrine promulgated by St. John the Evangelist—what is called the Johannine doctrine of the Incarnation. Moreover, we look in some detail at the doctrine of Grace and of the sacrament of the Word by which prevenient Grace can become efficacious grace (the terms are explained in the chapter). This carries us forward (from the first century)—or back (from ours)—to theologians such as Augustine, Thomas Aquinas, Duns Scotus, and Alexander of Hales. We note that Jung's statement that in sobriety it is a case of *spiritus contra spiritum* and his whole doctrine of individuation both have close ties with Johannine theology generally, and especially with the Johannine process called *theosis* or *theopoiesis*—which in turn leads us to some of the Greek theologians (and a few saints) who followed after John.

We also pay some attention here to the triadic nature of spiritual percepts, as well as to an attempt to explain (in what we might call more modern terms) what I understand of the Johannine theology of the Incarnation. All this might seem to be unnecessary, even perhaps confusing and boring, but Linda Mercadante's recent study of the theology of Alcoholics Anonymous (*Victims and Sinners: Spiritual Roots of Addiction and Recovery*, 1996, titled as a study of the theology of Twelve-Step addiction-recovery programs) has essentially asserted that the A.A. model is at best paradoxical—at worst self-contradictory. The common insistence in A.A. that the alcoholic "can't get anyone but himself [or herself] sober"—the emphasis on anniversaries—the saying "I'm not a bad person trying to get good: I'm a sick person trying to get well"—all these (it is argued) lead to a kind of emphasis on self, accompanied by an abnegation of self-responsibility for actions while in the grip of alcoholic drinking. Moreover, the emphasis on alcoholism as a condition of self-will run riot suggests that what the alcoholic has is simply a problem of exercising his (or her) own will rather than

God's (Mercadante, pp. 136ff). In other words, the program of Alcoholics Anonymous seems both to affirm and deny free will, and to promote as well as decry an emphasis on the self. But the answer should be fairly clear, after what we have said. It would seem that alcoholism is to sobriety almost precisely as sin is to salvation. Both are inherited tendencies toward going wrong (that is, in St. James's terms, off the path), and the answer to both comes through grace, and—we should add—the humility that Grace produces. (We go more fully into the matter of humility in considering the Twelve Steps, and particularly Step Seven, in Chapter 7.)

In Chapter 7, we look at how A.A. works, or at least at how A.A. appears to us to work, concentrating on the Twelve Steps. Essentially, we make use of the "Big Book" (*Alcoholics Anonymous*, 1939, 1955, 1976, 2001, not including the stories that make up most of each edition) and the *12&12* (*Twelve Steps and Twelve Traditions*, 1952/3). Both of these were written by Bill W., with some help and editing (especially in the "Big Book"). We have also made some use of an early Akron pamphlet, *Table Talk*, to show how the steps were regarded in the very early days, two separate lists of the "original" Six Steps (one from Akron, one from New York), and research on the Rev. Samuel Moor Shoemaker, who was credited by Bill W. with being one of the founders of A.A. Also, we have used what some might call church history, and some theological history, especially on the questions of amends and humility.

For those who do not have the Twelve Steps at their fingertips or committed to memory, here they are (they are also, of course, included in Chapter 7):

> (1) We admitted we were powerless over alcohol—that our lives had become unmanageable; (2) Came to believe that a Power greater than ourselves could restore us to sanity; (3) Made a decision to turn our will and our lives over to the care of God *as we understood Him*; (4) Made a searching and fearless moral inventory of ourselves; (5) Admitted to God, to ourselves, and to another human being the exact nature of our wrongs; (6) Were entirely ready to have God remove all these defects of character; (7) Humbly asked Him to remove our shortcomings; (8) Made a list of all persons we had harmed, and became willing to make amends to them all; (9) Made direct amends to such people wherever possible, except when to do so would injure them or others; (10) Continued to take personal inventory, and when we were wrong, promptly admitted it; (11) Sought through prayer and meditation to improve our conscious contact with God as *we understood Him*, praying only for the knowledge of His will for us and the power to carry that out; (12) Having had a spiritual awakening as the result of these steps, we tried to carry this message to alcoholics, and practice these principles in all our affairs. (Printed by permission of A.A. World Services)

In Chapter 7, we are looking at the Twelve Steps, in order, as presented in the "Big Book" and in the *12&12*, including the summaries in the front

(Contents) of the *12&12*. When we do this, we find some interesting differences between what Bill W. wrote in 1938/39 and what he wrote in 1952/53. The "Big Book" is, in general, the more immediately practical of the two, the *12&12* more philosophical—at least on Steps One through Five, Eight and Nine, and that part of Step Twelve concerned with what in A.A. is known as "carrying the message." On the other hand, on Steps Six and Seven (which take up a minuscule portion of the "Big Book"), Ten and Eleven, and the rest of Step Twelve, the practical advice (and for Six and Seven pretty much the only coverage beyond the—highly important— Seventh Step prayer) is in the *12&12*. Why? And what happened to turn Bill W. in a new direction on the Steps? The answer we suggest (it is no more than a suggestion) is that the difference is akin to the difference between *volitional conversion* and *conversion by self-surrender* in William James's *Varieties of Religious Experience*, the difference between Catholic spiritual exercises (Ignatius Loyola, for example, or Brother Lawrence) and Protestant instantaneous conversion.

Bill W. was converted to sobriety as a result, apparently, of a "white-light" or "Road to Damascus" spiritual experience—of which there are earlier examples given in William James. As a result, he saw Steps Six and Seven ("Were entirely ready to have God remove all our defects of character" and "Humbly asked Him to remove our shortcomings") as following immediately and without significant difficulty upon moral inventory (self-examination) and (auricular) confession. That was when he was four years sober. By the time he was eighteen years sober, and possibly as a result of dealing with alcoholics who had not been stricken on the Road to Damascus, had not fallen on the ground like the Prophet Daniel—and certainly as a result of the wise counsel of the Jesuit Father Edward Dowling—he had come to see that for most alcoholics things were not that simple or easy. Hence the more detailed consideration of process on Steps Six and Seven in the *12&12*.

Similarly, he expanded his consideration of the practical process involved in Steps Ten and Eleven (continuing to take personal inventory and maintaining conscious contact with a Higher Power)—though this, I think, may have come mostly from his own internal experience. I would say here that, to me, it appears that the Tenth Step would be the most difficult of all the Twelve Steps, as it seems, on Bill W.'s showing, to involve virtually continuous and automatic self-examination until one has achieved something like Brother Lawrence's continual practice of the presence of God. On the Eleventh Step, we may note that Bill W. enjoyed writing prayers: his advice on meditation comes in part from the practice of the Emmanuel Movement, but many of the prayers he used (including those in the "Big Book") were his own creation.

The discussion of the Twelfth Step in the *12&12*, as noted, concentrates on the spiritual awakening that comes through the Twelve Steps, and on practicing these principles in all the alcoholic's affairs—which is a matter of spiritual practice. All the Twelve Steps, in one or both of the books, are indeed spiritual exercises. They provide a spiritual answer to a physical and mental illness—as we have remarked, and as is clear throughout the book. Earlier ages (even the nineteenth century) would have called it a religious answer, and, of course, the ordinary course of the explorer who has found a new religious territory (or a new religious answer) is to found a church. Unless, like Francis of Assisi (or Ignatius Loyola), he founds a society or a company. That is what Bill W. did, and that is what Chapter 8 is (at least partly) about.

That is, Chapter 8 discusses Alcoholics Anonymous as a fellowship (*koinonia*) and reviews the threefold distinction of the human being acting in the *agora* or marketplace, in the *polis* or voting place, and in the *koinonia*, the assembly or fellowship—and looks into the theories of bounded rationality that underlie this approach. This threefold distinction, which comes from work in political economy, has strong implications for cognitive psychology and rational decision-making. Note that we are discussing these three, the *agora*, the *polis*, and the *koinonia*, as subsystems of the overall social system: in so doing, we can make use of systems theory, particularly general systems theory, and especially the work of Henry Teune and Zdravko Mlinar in a much-neglected book, *The Developmental Logic of Social Systems*. The principal point to be noted here is that social systems, being developmental systems, must change (by creating new internal diversity in response to new exogenously created diversity). The chapter also looks specifically at the "Invention of Tradition" (a field generally connected with the study of literature, particularly of the Celtic Revival of the nineteenth century) and at the "Theory of Committees" (as ideally suited to the governance of the *koinonia*—a field generally connected with political and decision sciences). But principally the chapter deals with the Twelve Traditions as the means of preserving the *koinonia*.

Societies, as J.G.A. Pocock has taught us, exist in time and conserve images of themselves as continuously so existing. An essential feature of society is tradition—the handing on of formed ways of acting. Traditions of this kind are immemorial, prescriptive, and presumptive. What stands outside tradition is charismatic, whether postulating timeless existence or sacred origin (which includes creative origin). The criticism—but thus the affirmation—of tradition is history. All classical (as opposed to romantic) social systems are of this traditionalist sort. But because societies necessarily—in order to be societies—conserve images of themselves as existing (and acting in a certain way) *nemo meminisse contradicente*, there is necessary conservatism in the very idea of a society. These images appeal to tradition and are thus traditional (or traditionary). They conserve tradition and are thus conservative, even if the tradition they conserve is not a conservative tradition—as in Romanticism, and (I think) Alcoholics Anonymous.

So we look at the Twelve Traditions as well as at the dual nature of *koinonia* (as social system and, roughly, church). The Twelve Traditions (they are listed again in Chapter 8) are as follows:

(1) Our common welfare should come first; personal recovery depends upon A.A. unity; (2) For our group purpose there is but one ultimate authority—a loving God as he may express Himself in our group conscience. Our leaders are but trusted servants; they do not govern; (3) The only requirement for A.A. membership is a desire to stop drinking; (4) Each group should be autonomous except in matters affecting other groups or A.A. as a whole; (5) Each group has but one primary purpose—to carry its message to the alcoholic who still suffers; (6) An A.A. group ought never endorse, finance, or lend the A.A. name to any related facility or outside enterprise, lest problems of money, property, and prestige divert us from our primary purpose; (7) Every A.A. group ought to be fully self-supporting, declining outside contributions; (8) Alcoholics Anonymous should remain forever non-professional, but our service centers may employ special workers; (9) A.A., as such, ought never be organized; but we may create service boards or committees directly responsible to those they serve; (10) Alcoholics Anonymous has no opinion on outside issues; hence the A.A. name ought never be drawn into public controversy; (11) Our public relations policy is based on attraction rather than promotion; we need always maintain personal anonymity at the level of press, radio, and films; (12) Anonymity is the spiritual foundation of all our traditions, ever reminding us to place principles before personalities. (Reprinted by permission of A.A. World Services)

Traditions should provide "responses to novel situations which take the form of reference to old situations, or which establish their own past by quasi-obligatory repetition" (Hobsbawm and Ranger 1981). The key words may be *old* and *past*, though certainly there is quasi-obligatory repetition of the Twelve Traditions at many A.A. meetings. We can (and do) look at these Traditions as a kind of social engineering for a *koinonia* ordered (appropriately) through a committee structure. Bill W.'s emphasis on committee consensus rather than majority vote may be seen as a way of avoiding the pitfalls of intransitivity of social choice. The emphasis on the primary purpose or singleness of purpose may be seen as a way of ensuring single-peaked preferences so as to permit Condorcet solutions and avoid the necessity for mechanistic De Borda solutions or the log-rolling of Dodgson solutions. Whether or not he knew what he was doing in the terms we would use now, I believe he knew what he was doing. Not for nothing did Aldous Huxley call him the greatest social engineer of the twentieth century. Not for nothing did *Time* magazine's end-of-the-century poll rank him in the top one hundred men and women of the century. But in the end, the social engineering was based on a spiritual insight, and with all the safeguards of the Twelve Traditions, it looks to us as though A.A. will function well as a *koinonia* in the social-systems sense pretty well to the degree it functions well as a *koinonia* in the spiritual-assembly sense. That would appear to be the lesson in particular of the Twelfth Tradition.

But for all that we have said here, it is obvious that, however brilliantly (in our analysis) Bill W. handled the "social-systems" problem of creating Alcoholics Anonymous, he believed he was creating a spiritual fellowship, a "company" in the same sense the Round Table was a company. We know he learned something from Alexis de Tocqueville's *Democracy in America*. So far as we know he did not specifically study social-systems theory beyond that. His references to the "Society of Alcoholics Anonymous" make me wonder if he did not have in his mind a kind of pun on the French word for company in the ordinary business sense—*Societé Anonyme*—with collective not individual responsibility for actions (and, of course, limited personal liability). When he speaks of the "Fellows" of Alcoholics Anonymous, one can even see him with a (humorous) picture in his mind of recovered alcoholics putting F.S.A.A. after their names, as Fellows of the Society of Antiquaries put F.S.A. A pretty picture, if a trifle improbable.

In Chapter 9, we try to tie it all together, and suggest some areas for possible future study. That is, we link the threefold nature of the malady, what we know of the nature of the mind and how it links with the body, what we know of the nature of the mind and how it links with the spirit (or the spiritual), the possible origins and transmission of alcoholism in the human neuronal and genomic systems, and the curious congruence of treatment of mind, of body, and of spirit. Here we should emphasize one particular point: when we are talking about treatment for bodily alcoholism we are mostly not talking about treatment for *alcoholismus chronicus* in the sense that phrase was used by Magnus Hoff in 1848. We are not speaking of treating the physical results of prolonged drinking (though that may be involved, with detoxification, for example, as a necessary preliminary for future treatment). What we are talking about treating is the behavior (alcoholic behavior) incident on the alcoholic precondition—what we call Alcoholism(2) rather than Alcoholism(1). We reject the view that the precondition toward alcoholism justifies alcoholic behavior (though it may make it harder to escape), and we are not convinced that forced choice (through medical or genetic manipulation) provides a fully satisfactory outcome, though it may (as with Antabuse) provide a kind of time cushion for change.

Because this is a study deriving from Bill W.'s vision of the threefold illness and its congruent treatment, we have concentrated our study on the background to the vision, the founding of A.A. in answer to the vision, the essential truth of Bill's paradigm of the threefold illness and its congruent treatment (following that truth to the present day), considering mind, body, and spirit in separate chapters. Then we have looked at the process of sobriety in Alcoholics Anonymous, and the path Bill W. followed to keep Alcoholics Anonymous as a fellowship short of a church and separated from a government. We are only very slightly interested in Bill W.'s personality and his personal life; we are very interested indeed in the truth of his vision and his creation of a fellowship for its preservation. We are also interested in some of the other founders of A.A., even some (like Johnny L.) not usually considered in that category.

We look therefore at Bill W.'s vision, particularly at his vision at the point of the mind/body interface, at psychology and chemical reactions and genetics, in understanding individual alcoholisms. We look at the nature of fellowship (*koinonia*) in both the theological and the organizational sense (where it is opposed to *agora* or *polis*) in understanding how A.A. continues as a (mutual-help) society, and at the implicit theology of A.A., as well as at Bill W.'s practical work toward preserving the fellowship. We look at the congruence of treatments for the threefold illness, their mental, physical, and theological (or metaphysical) underpinnings. To quote here from the end of the book, "We believe—at least we have adopted as our scientific research program the belief—that the syntaxic development of psychotherapeutic narrative, the reentrant extended phenotypic training of neuronal group selection, and the Sacrament of the Word (in accordance with the Johannine doctrine of the Incarnation) are congruous, indeed congruent, indeed joined together in Bill W.'s formulation—which no one had put together before, and which is the gift of Alcoholics Anonymous as he set it up. . . . Along the way, we have met quite a number of interesting people . . . but we believe the necessary, indeed the indispensable, connecting thread is provided by one man . . . And that is Bill W." Whether A.A., judged from the outside, is carrying out the vision, we cannot say in the present state of our research, and it would be presumptuous to sit in judgment on that in any case, with any amount of research. (We do, however, note some cases in which Traditions seem to be given current meanings differing from what may have been intended by Bill W.) Whether A.A., judged from the inside, is carrying out the vision, no one of those outside can possibly say, and those inside (as I understand from the Traditions) will pretty much keep their opinions inside.

Nevertheless, we hope this book will be of interest to both, and will suggest some lines along which future research on alcoholism and A.A. may be carried out. There is, in any case, a point I should make here about our complex model, a point introduced above with the observation that to many members of Alcoholics Anonymous much of this book will be irrelevant. From early days, the injunction "Keep it simple!" has been ingrained in the literature and folklore of Alcoholics Anonymous. Indeed, those words are reported to have been the parting injunction of one of the cofounders to the other at their last meeting in November 1950: one might almost call them a deathbed command. Members tell each other at their meetings "This is a simple program." And there is another injunction amongst the members of the fellowship, less used but still common: "Utilize, don't analyze." Doubtless all this is well said for those who have a simple and unconditional faith in God and Alcoholics Anonymous. Doubtless they should use the system as it was set up, not analyze it—if it can remain as it was set up.

This book is not written for them. It is written for me, and for others who may want to explore the (I think heritable) complex condition called alcoholism, the more complex matter of treatment for the condition, and the yet more complex matter of why (some would say, why or whether) A.A. works (and what we mean by "works"), and what all this may tell us about how God (or the Universe) works—or, as members of A.A. frequently say, how their Higher Power works. This business of how the Higher Power works is what brings me—reluctantly—into the unfashionable and unpopular realm of technical theology in Chapter 6.

In the end, perhaps even those with the necessary simple faith will find some use for what is in this book. There is a pledge sometimes said by members of A.A.—"When anyone, anywhere, reaches out for help, I want the hand of A.A. always to be there—and for that, I am responsible." I take it this is a pledge to keep A.A. working. In which case, it may not be entirely without value to try to see—at least to suggest reasons—why it has (apparently) been working since 1935.

1 ～

Alcoholism and Treatment for Alcoholism from Early Times to the Repeal of Prohibition

THERE WAS A MAN—some say he was sent from God—named Bill W., who was the driving force behind the creation of Alcoholics Anonymous, a man with a vision of how alcoholism might be treated. Much of this book is about that vision. Bill W. wrote once that the condition of alcoholism had existed, apparently, since man had first crushed grapes (*Twelve Steps and Twelve Traditions*, 1952/53:22). The echoes of that phrase are certainly biblical, and in the *Book of Genesis* there is a description of the Patriarch Noah who, after the flood, planted a vineyard, then "drank of the wine and was drunken and he lay uncovered in his tent" (9:21). One wonders if it may be significant that Noah, who voyaged (albeit in the ark), rather than staying at home, should be the patriarch who got drunk. There are also some relevant Old Testament passages in *The Song of Songs*, about looking on the wine when it is red.

Likewise, there is the biblically derived self-description of a sober alcoholic, going back to the Washingtonians in the 1840s (and even before, in *The Intemperate and the Reformed* in 1833) and forward to the present day in Alcoholics Anonymous—"clothed and in my right mind." To be sure, this is based not on Noah's drunkenness, but on the spirits whose name is Legion and the Gadarene swine, in *Mark* 5:15 and *Luke* 8:35: the connection is in the ancient linking of nakedness, drunkenness, madness, and shame. Also, in a traditional society, those who stay at home are subject to the traditions and mores of the society, while those who are not rooted in their home, far-travelers, wayfarers, vagabonds, soldiers, are rootless, or rooted in the contrary traditions of the open road or of war, or of travel and wayfaring.

There is one generally overlooked description of a (quite literally) raging alcoholic in a novel (for want of a better word) written about the time of Christ, and known—for reasons clearer two thousand years ago than they are today—as the *Third Book of Maccabees* (conveniently in the *New Oxford Annotated Bible*, 2001:306–19). The raging alcoholic is Ptolemy IV Philopator, king of Egypt 221–204 B.C.E., who of course had nothing whatever to do with the Maccabees. The picture of Philopator has, I believe, a considerable significance for our look at the evolution of alcoholism—how there came to be alcoholics—in connection with our look at the evolution of the brain and mind, in Chapters 3–5. Briefly, Philopator visits the Jewish temple, wants to go into the Holy of Holies, is told he cannot, says in effect, "But don't you understand, look who I am?" and persists, until finally, on attempting to enter the sanctuary, he lurches from side to side, shaken "on this side and that as a reed is shaken by the wind, so that he lay helpless on the ground and, besides being paralyzed in his limbs, was unable even to speak" (2:35:309).

Philopator, thinking the Jews had cast spells on him, vows vengeance and summons his elephants, planning a massacre of the Jews by trampling. The king passes from drunken feast to drunken feast, his mahout gets the elephants drunk, but they all pass out before the king can give the word: the next day, it is hard to rouse the king—and when he is roused, he simply returns to drinking and asks (drunkenly) why the Jews are still alive. Follows a repeat performance of the night before, and in the morning the king has forgotten what he was planning and asks his councillors why everyone is there. There follows another night of drunken revels, and this time, in the morning, the king sets the stage again for the massacre—and then suddenly veers over and begins praising the Jews. Their troubles are over for the moment, and that is where the novel (or novella) ends. The author credits the Most High God of Israel and the steadfastness of the Jews. But Philopator is quite clearly a drunk and at least arguably, on the evidence, an alcoholic (and after all, he is the descendant of one of Alexander the Great's generals and heirs). He is also a dévoté—quite literally— of the god Dionysios. The importance of this will become more evident, I hope, in the later chapters. And now to somewhat later times.

We have some records of wayfaring life through the ages, and particularly from Elizabethan England—fragmentarily from the Roman Empire and the Middle Ages. We have records of far-travelers from earliest times and particularly, in the Middle Ages, of pilgrims—but most of these are from those who intended to return home, and they are chiefly of value to us for their occasional glimpses of the life of the roads. What we have in abundance is records of the actions and attitudes of soldiers—from both the soldiers and commanders on the one hand, and those they victimized on the other. From earliest recorded history, certainly throughout the Middle Ages and into the Renaissance, and in more modern times, soldiers have celebrated victories (and even excoriated defeats) with riotous and drunken behavior, and have whiled away the hours of garrison life and other boring assignments by getting drunk. Freed from restraints of home and church, living a sporadically violent life, seeking companionship in isolated places far from the customary skies, they have turned to bottle or wineskin or beer-mug, or more than their portion of grog at sea.

MICHAEL CASSIO AND NICOLAS HERRMANN

That much is well-known. What has been less examined (partly because of insufficient evidence left from the past) is the degree to which professional armies of the past—which means, in effect, all armies until the *levée en masse* of Revolutionary France in 1792–93—were armies of alcoholics. Nevertheless, we may look to the records of these armies, and their soldiers—and any contemporary literary evidence—for any discussion of alcoholism (and, if we are lucky, recovery) in earlier ages. Our immediate purpose here, however, is not to examine these records, but to take one dramatic presentation of an alcoholic soldier in fiction and one life of a soldier turned holy man to see where they lead us. We begin with the alcoholic soldier in fiction.

Othello's lieutenant, Michael Cassio, in Shakespeare's *Othello: The Moor of Venice*, is recognizably an alcoholic. Iago invites him to drink, and he responds, "Not tonight, good Iago. I have very poor and unhappy brains for drinking" (act II, scene iii, lines 34–35). Iago (who is trying to get Cassio in trouble) argues "But one cup; I'll drink for you" (lines 38–39). To which Cassio answers, "I have drunk but one cup tonight, and that was craftily qualified too, and behold what innovation it makes here. I am unfortunate in the infirmity and dare not task my weakness with any more" (lines 40–43). But he cannot stop with one: Iago persuades him to have another (it does not take much persuasion), and soon he's drunk again. Here, in a mercenary army, in a late sixteenth-century (or early seventeenth-century) context, is a picture of the alcoholic as we know him. The play goes on to describe Cassio's carouse and drunkenness, which may be of interest here, as evidence of understanding of what we call alcoholism around 1600, as well as putative evidence that Shakespeare himself (who died from hypothermia when he fell drunk in a ditch celebrating his fifty-second birthday) may well have been an alcoholic—thus writing of alcoholism from the inside. (It is told by John Ward that he died after a night of celebratory drinking with Michael Drayton and the ruddy and corpulent—and heavy-drinking if not alcoholic—Ben Jonson.)

Iago has full knowledge of Cassio's "weakness"—when asked if Cassio is always thus (that is, drunk at night), he remarks that "'T is evermore the prologue to his sleep. He'll watch the horologe a double set [all day and all night], if drink rock not his cradle" (act II, scene iii, lines 134–36). Just before this, Cassio has taken the drink Iago has enticed him to, commenting favorably on the English drinking songs sung by Iago's "gentlemen"—"And let me the cannikin clink, clink, / And let me the cannikin clink. / A soldier's a man, / O, man's life's but a span, / Why then let a soldier drink!"—and then the ballad "Bell My Wife" (lines 73–103). Then he says, tipsily (lines 117–20), "Do not think, gentlemen, I am drunk. This is my ancient [ensign, Iago], this is my right hand, and this is my left. I am not drunk now. I can stand well enough and I speak well enough." But shortly thereafter he is pursuing Roderigo, crying, "A knave teach me my duty? I'll beat the knave into a twiggen bottle" (lines 155–56). And when Montano intervenes (lines 161–62), saying, "I pray you, Sir, hold your hand" (which seems reasonable enough), Cassio responds, "Let me go sir, or I'll knock you o'er the mazard." (Those who have drunk wine from a bottle encased in wicker have drunk from a "twiggen bottle"—and "mazard" is slang for "head.")

And on the morning after (lines 300–302), "O thou invisible spirit of wine, if thou hast no name to be known by, let us call thee devil!" Iago asks (lines 303–304), "What was he that you followed with your sword? What had he done to you?" To receive the response (line 305), "I know not." He asks (line 306), "Is 't possible?" Then (lines 307–12), "I remember a mass of things, but nothing distinctly; a quarrel, but nothing wherefore. O God! That men should put an enemy in their mouths to steal away their brains! That we should with joy, pleasance, revel, and applause transform ourselves into beasts!" And when Iago comments that he seems well enough now, and asks how he recovered, comes the answer (lines 315–17), "It hath pleased the devil drunkenness to give place to the devil wrath. One unperfectness shows me another, to make me frankly despise myself." Iago counsels him disingenuously (lines 320–21), "I could heartily wish this had not so befallen. But since it is as it is, mend it for your own good." And Cassio responds that he will ask Othello for his place (as Lieutenant) again, but (lines 322–27) "he shall tell me I am a drunkard! Had I as many mouths as Hydra, such an answer would stop them all. To be now a sensible man, by and by a fool, and presently a beast! O, strange! Every inordinate cup is unblessed, and the ingredient is a devil!"

In brief, he needs to drink in order to sleep; he cannot stop drinking when he wants to; he has blackouts; the morning after, he is angry with himself, indeed despises himself; alcohol is his devil, but he cannot let it go. Recalling that there is no dramatic need specifically for Cassio's fault to have been drunkenness, and recalling that Shakespeare was himself both soldier and traveler (as circuit lawyer's clerk, strolling player, and even perhaps as writer-for-hire), it seems likely that Cassio's experience is from his own, even if not his very own (though I rather think it is). Now, let us look in this same context (and in the seventeenth century) to see if we can find a recovering or recovered alcoholic. I believe we can. It is from the ranks of former soldiers in a bloody war that we might hope to find the first record of spiritual recovery from alcoholism, if such there was before the word *alcoholic* was coined.

A good candidate might be Nicolas or Nicholas Herrmann or Herman, born in the Duchy of Lorraine in 1614, a soldier in the army of Lorraine (then an independent principality) from 1632 to 1634/1635, then a footman to a Treasurer of France, then a hermit, and from 1642 until his death nearly a half-century later (1691), a Carmelite friar under the name Brother Lawrence of the Resurrection.

His *Practice of the Presence of God*, first published in 1692, is a spiritual handbook suggesting steps to the absolute abandonment of one's will to God. Now, we do not know that Brother Lawrence was a recovered alcoholic, and in fact we know very little about him. It is even possible that what we "know" is misleading. We do know, however, that he had at least one mystical experience in his early years, specifically

> while he was still in the [secular] world, when he was eighteen [1632]. He told me that one day while looking at a tree stripped of its leaves, and reflecting that before long its leaves would appear anew, then its flowers and fruits would bloom, he received an insight into the power of God which was never erased from his soul; that this insight had completely detached him from the world. (Herrmann 1996:1)

But in fact it was at eighteen he became a soldier in the forces of Lorraine in the Thirty Years' War: thereafter he was captured by enemy troops, charged with being a spy, and threatened with hanging, before convincing his captors that he was innocent. He was released and rejoined the army, then was soon after wounded in a skirmish with Swedish forces at Rambersville(?) in Lorraine. Then he served as a footman—a common enough position for released soldiers—to Guillaume(?) de Fieubet, treasurer of King Louis XIII of France, in which position he described himself as "a clumsy lummox who broke everything." It was not until 1640 (after a time in seclusion, perhaps as a hermit) that he applied as a lay brother at the monastery of the Discalced Carmelites on the Rue de Vaugirard in Paris: he was professed in 1642. He worked in the kitchen for many years, then as a cobbler—two professions common enough in the army in those days (ibid.:xx–xxii). He was also sometimes employed in buying wine for the monastery, in which position, apparently, he did not taste the wine but merely looked at the casks (ibid.:9)—noting that he did not let the task bother him. (The name of Nicholas Hermann's master is given in all the sources I have seen as William or Guillaume, but the *trésorier de l'Épargne* (the King's personal "savings account") under Louis XIII was in fact *Gaspard* de Fieubet, 1577–1647, Siegneur de Cendrey and Baron de Launac, butler in ordinary to the king (*maître de hôtel ordonnaire du Roi*), Councillor of State, not the sort one would expect to employ a "clumsy lummox" of an ex-soldier from Lorraine. One is tempted to see some influence at work here from someone higher up.)

As I say, we do not know whether Nicholas Hermann was an alcoholic, though the comment about not letting his buying the wine bother him may be revealing. We do know that (like Bill W. at age twenty-one in Winchester Cathedral—see page 1 in the "Big Book") he had a spiritual experience, at age eighteen, that had no immediate effect. We know that he was remarkably quiet—indeed secretive—about his background. We know that he had an uncle who was a Carmelite. We know that he wrote decent French: he was apparently a literate man, though a blunt and gruff man with a rough exterior. We know that he said he sought the life of a religious "thinking that by doing so he would be censured for his clumsiness and faults and so would sacrifice his life and all his pleasures to God; but that God had outwitted him and in his religious life he had found nothing but satisfaction; that this had often made him say to God: 'You have outwitted me'" (ibid.:2). An A.A. member of my acquaintance has suggested that this comment is in keeping with what she called the A.A. sense of humor (but this is, of course, purely anecdotal evidence). We know that he was wounded by Swedish soldiers at a time when France and Sweden were allies, just about the time when Charles IV, Duke of Lorraine, was compelled by France—that is, by Richelieu—to resign his Principality to his brother François-Nicolas de Lorraine Vaudémont (in 1634). We know he went first into service (possibly below his station?) to Treasurer Fieubet, then into seclusion. One would be hard put not to see him as a rootless soldier and ex-soldier with a mystical bent and a life suggesting a secret at its base—and there is that comment about buying the wine. (The fact that he, like John Bradford of "There goes John Bradford, but for the Grace of God," were both soldiers involved with money transactions in occupied territory *may*—of course—be only a coincidence.)

That being said, we should look at this "practice of the presence of God," which brought Brother Lawrence out of all his checkered past and in which God "outwitted" him by making him happy. The principle is not very different from George Herbert's "Who sweeps a room to the Glory of God / Makes that [the room] and the action fine!" Briefly, he has six "ways of acquiring the presence of God":

(1) The first way is great purity of life. (2) The second is a great faithfulness to the practice of His presence, and an interior gaze on God which should always be quiet, humble and loving, without succumbing to any difficulties or disquietude. (3) It is necessary to take particular care to begin, if only for a moment, your exterior actions with this interior gaze and that you do the

same while you are doing them and when you have finished them. . . . (4) It would be pertinent for those who undertake this practice to make up interiorly short ejaculations such as: "My God, I am all yours," "God of love, I love you with all my heart," "Lord, make me according to Your heart," and any such words that love may beget on the spur of the moment. But they must be careful that the mind does not wander and return again to worldly things . . . (5) This presence of God, though a bit painful in the beginning, works secretly in the soul and . . . leads it insensibly to . . . that loving sight of God everywhere, which is the most holy, the most solid, the most efficacious manner of prayer. (6) Notice, if you please, that to attain this state you must take for granted the mortification of the senses . . . since to be with God requires complete rejection of worldly things. (Herrmann [1692] 1996:91–93)

This is, of course, largely what the twentieth-century theologian Charles Williams defined as the Way of Rejection (or the Way of Rejection of Images). We shall come to that much later when we look at the Disease and Recovery of the Spirit. In the meantime we may note that Brother Lawrence's devotion to instructing all who came to him in this practice of the presence of God drew wide attention, particularly in the decade before his death. But even if he was an alcoholic (which I think likely) and even if this was his highly successful way of dealing with his problems, it could not be codified, as Bill W. codified the A.A. approach in the "Big Book" of Alcoholics Anonymous, until the time was ripe—and certainly not until the word "alcoholic" had been invented. Nor, without substantial adaptation, could it be made practicable for those still in the world—which, of course, sobriety through A.A. must be. It may (or may not) be noteworthy that Brother Lawrence was suspected of various heresies, particularly Quietism and Jansenism, because his exercises in spirituality got mixed up in the religious controversies of the day. It is certainly noteworthy that Lawrence's *Practice of the Presence of God* was highly regarded not only by the Oxford Groups, but also—particularly—by Emmet Fox, whose *Sermon on the Mount* the early A.A. member Jim B. considered to be one of the primary influences on Bill W. We do not know that Brother Lawrence was a recovered alcoholic any more than we know Francis of Assisi was a recovered alcoholic, though both may have been—and certainly Francis of Assisi was considered an "hereditary degenerate" by some in the days of William James ([1903] 1961:29)—which is a term not unknown for alcoholics in the nineteenth century.

VARIETIES OF RELIGIOUS CONVERSION

To consider conversion of this sort generally (though not necessarily conversion from alcoholism) in the period up to 1800, we may look (as this suggests) at another of the books to which Jim B. traced Bill's understanding of the problems of alcoholism, and what might be done about them. This is William James, *The Varieties of Religious Experience* ([1903], 1961). In Lecture Nine, on conversion, James is discussing the conclusions of James Leuba, "Studies in the Psychology of Religious Phenomena" in *American Journal of Psychology* (1896). Leuba

> subordinates the theological aspect of the religious life almost entirely to its moral aspect. The religious sense he defines as "the feeling of unwholeness, of moral imperfection, of sin, to use the technical words, accompanied by the yearning after the peace of unity." The word "religion" he says "is getting more and more to signify the conglomerate of desires and emotions springing from a sense of sin and its release," and he gives a large number of examples, in which the sin ranges from drunkenness to spiritual pride, to show that the sense of it may beset one and crave relief as urgently as does the anguish of this sickened flesh or any form of physical misery. (James [1903] 1961:168–69)

Professor James suggests that this nonintellectual regeneration ("springing from a sense of sin and its release") corresponds to a subjectively centered form of morbid melancholy of which John Bunyan (1622–88) of *The Pilgrim's Progress* (1678, 1684) provides a striking seventeenth-century example and the Nova Scotia evangelist Henry Alline (1748–84) a notable eighteenth-century case. Let us look, by way of introduction, at one further remark by Brother Lawrence: "I regard myself as the most wretched of all men, stinking and covered with sores, and as one who has committed all sorts of crimes against his King. Overcome by remorse, I confess all my wickedness to Him . . ." (Herrmann [1692] 1996:43). That is exactly the note struck by Bunyan in his *Grace Abounding to the Chief of Sinners* (1666):

> Nay, thought I, now I grow worse and worse. . . . Sometimes I would tell my condition to the people of God, which, when they heard, they would tell of the Promises. . . . Oh, how gingerly did I then go, in all I did or said! . . . But my original and inward pollution, that was my plague and my affliction. By reason of that, I was more loathsome in my own eye than was a toad . . . Sin and corruption, I said, would as naturally bubble out of my heart as water would bubble out of a fountain. . . . I was both a burthen and a terror to myself; nor did I ever so know, as now, what it was to be weary of my life, and yet afraid to die. How gladly would I have been anything but myself! Anything but a man! And in any condition but my own. (quoted in James [1903] 1961:136–37)

And in the next century, young Henry Alline, of Puritan stock out of Boston, living in Nova Scotia, wrote in his journal:

Everything I saw seemed to be a burden to me; the earth seemed accursed for my sake: all trees, plants, rocks, hills, and vales seemed to be dressed in mourning and groaning, under the weight of the curse . . . When I waked in the morning, the first thought would be, Oh, my wretched soul, what shall I do, where shall I go? . . . I awoke morning after morning with a horrible dread at the pit of my stomach, and with a sense of the insecurity of life that I never knew before, and that I have never felt since . . . for months I was unable to go out in the dark alone. (quoted in James [1903] 1961:137–38)

But then on March 26, 1775:

As I was about sunset wandering in the fields lamenting my miserable lost and undone condition . . . the following impressions came into my mind, like a powerful but still small voice. You have been seeking, praying, reforming, laboring, reading, hearing, and meditating, and what have you done by it towards your salvation? . . . I cried out within myself, O Lord god, I am lost, and if thou, O Lord, dost not find some new way I know nothing of, I shall never be saved . . . these discoveries continued until I went into the house and sat down . . . and almost in an agony, I turned very suddenly round in my chair, and seeing an old Bible . . . I caught hold of it in great haste; and opening it without any premeditation, cast my eyes on the 38th psalm, which was the first time I ever saw the Word of God . . . I . . . continued praying in the words of the psalm, "Oh help me, help me!" Cried I . . . At that instant of time, when I gave up all to him to do with me as he pleased, and was willing that God should rule over me at his pleasure . . . the burden of guilt and condemnation was gone, darkness was expelled . . . and my whole soul . . . was now filled with immortal love, soaring on the wings of faith, freed from the chains of death and darkness . . . Looking up, I thought I saw the same light [he had on more than one occasion seem subjectively a bright blaze of light], though it appeared different. (quoted in James [1903] 1961:180–81)

James's subsequent comments are worth summarizing here. In fact, they may be worth quoting *in extenso*:

Now there are two forms of mental occurrence in human beings, which lead to a striking difference in the conversion process . . . You know how it is when you try to recollect a forgotten name. Usually you help the recall by working for it, by mentally running over the places, persons, and things with which the word was connected. But sometimes this effort fails: you feel then as if the harder you tried, the less hope there would be, as though the name were *jammed*, and pressure in its direction only kept it all the more from rising. And then the opposite expedient often succeeds. Give up the effort entirely; think of something altogether different, and in half an hour, the lost name comes sauntering into your mind, as Emerson said, as carelessly as if it had never been invited. . . . A certain music teacher, says Dr. Starbuck [in his *Psychology of Religion*], says to her pupils, after the thing to be done has been clearly pointed out, and unsuccessfully attempted, "Stop trying, and it will do itself!" There is thus a conscious and voluntary way and an involuntary and unconscious way in which mental results may get accomplished; and we find both ways exemplified in the history of conversion, giving us two types, which Starbuck calls the *volitional type* and the *type by self-surrender* respectively. (ibid.:172)

Of course, as James points out, most self-surrender has volitional aspects, and most volitional conversion has aspects of self-surrender (ibid.:174).

Nevertheless, the distinction may be important as we view the first sustained U. S. efforts toward a mental or spiritual "cure" for what we will here (to avoid anachronism) call *inebriety*. But before looking toward the Washingtonians and the "cure," let us first look at what Dr. Rorabaugh (1979) has called the Alcoholic Republic. If the proposed cure was Temperance (however defined), what was the perceived problem? In one sentence, "Americans between 1790 and 1830 drank more alcoholic beverages per capita than ever before or since." (ibid.:ix)

ALCOHOLISM IN THE ALCOHOLIC REPUBLIC

Now, Rorabaugh goes on to say, "drinking customs and habits [are] not random, but reflective of a society's fabric, tensions, and inner dynamics, and the psychological sets of its people" (ibid.:xii) and—though he unfortunately neglects the point (perhaps the one principal flaw in his otherwise brilliant study, in my opinion)—reflective of the genetic inheritance of its people. For this plays a part in the psychological set, as well as in what has been called the development of an extended phenotype (which we discuss in Chapter 4). With this *caveat* in mind, let us look at the reasons Rorabaugh finds for this period of extreme intemperance.

They are in part connected with what we have said about the far-travelers and soldiers. Briefly, until the time of the American Revolution, there was land to be had on the Atlantic shore. But that land grew scarce, and once the Alleghenies were crossed, the land was on rivers communicating not to the Atlantic but to the Gulf (ibid.:77). Those who stayed on the coastal lands, or in the cities, were farmhands or other laborers having no ownership in the land—in that sense rootless—while those on the expanding frontier might be rooted in their new land, but they were cut off from their former roots (ibid.:127–28). Also, many of those in the first expansion were Irish or Scots-Irish—to take two famous examples, both alcoholism and manic depression were common in the family of Meriwether Lewis (1774–1809), and alcoholism at least in the family of William

Clark (1770–1838). Of course, both Lewis and Clark grew up in a frontier society—but we should also note that at the beginning of the eighteenth century, Americans "like Englishmen and Europeans, universally believed that rum, gin, and brandy were nutritious and helpful," and that before 1750, "nearly all Americans of all social classes drank alcoholic beverages in quantity, sometimes to the point of intoxication" (ibid.:25). But then, why was it 1790–1830 rather than (say) 1710–50 that represented the apex of American drinking?

Rorabaugh suggests that the change from daily (but more or less controlled) drinking to episodic binge drinking represented a way of relieving loneliness on the frontier (whether in private or communal binges), of relieving anxiety about failure in an expanding world, of furthering ideas of independence and democracy, and as an indication (for those above the "common level" as viewed from that level) of *largesse*—this last not very different from the old Celtic or Saxon tradition of drinking at the lord's expense on festivals or even the drinking around the lord's fire at night in the days of Cuchulainn or of Niall of the Nine Hostages (which would be ca. 300 c.e.). We will see later how this and the story of Philopator, and other historical evidence, can suggest *why* alcoholism developed and was passed on. Also, of course, reasons for this episodic binge drinking on the frontier were not so very different from many of the reasons for binge-drinking on college campuses right now (or, I suppose, of high school students on weekends). And, on what may be a more mundane level, the price of drinks went steadily down from 1750 to 1790, and there were uprooted country men who fought in the War of the Revolution, and then carried their fighting out onto the frontiers.

Genotypically, it is doubtful the people had changed—or indeed that they have changed much now. Phenotypically? Well, just as the prevalence of mind-altering drugs in the 1960s and 1970s may have altered alcoholic phenotypes (based on alcoholic interaction with the environment), so the prevalence of cheap distilled spirits may have done the same in the period from 1790 to 1830. It is perhaps noteworthy that what some (certainly not all) have considered the first effective "Temperance" movement came from a rapidly growing Eastern port city (Baltimore), and that the six founders seem to have been of Scottish descent (Anderson and Campbell), Scots-Irish (McCurley, possibly Mitchell), English (Steers), and German (Hoss), stay-at-home city artisans or clerks from the ethnic groups that populated the first trans-Allegheny West (but I do not think Baltimore was their original home, so they too were in a sense rootless). The whole Washingtonian phenomenon has been mostly examined by those with an interest in Alcoholics Anonymous, as a precursor in whose lack of eventual success there are lessons for A.A.—but it is also of significant interest for us here as an example of views on alcoholism (or inebriety) and its treatment at the middle of the nineteenth century. Let us see if we can avoid the anachronism implicit in looking at the Washingtonians solely or even principally as exemplar for Alcoholics Anonymous. But before we look at the Washingtonians, we should look briefly at another strand in the history of alcoholism and its treatment.

Benjamin Rush, the first American man of medicine to look seriously at the problems of "inebriety" (in 1786), was advocating hospital care for drunkards in the very early 1800s,

> and the Connecticut State Medical Society proposed the establishment of an asylum for inebriates in 1830. (Of course, Rush did tend to think everything was a disease—excess of passion for liberty being the disease of *anarchia*, loyalists suffering from *revolutiona*, liars from the disease of lying, blasphemers from derangement of the principle of faith, and so on—it is not clear what asylums were to be suggested for these diseases.) Samuel Woodward, the patriarch of institutional psychiatry in North America, and also a temperance orator, published in 1838 the first widely read tract in support of specialized inebriate asylums. (Baumohl and Room 1987:135–36)

Since Benjamin Rush, physicians in America, England, and Europe had been suggesting that intemperance was a disease, a bodily condition that impaired the will (Porter 1985:385–96, cited in Baumohl and Room 1987:142). As a man sick with a disease that was like—but not the same as—insanity, the chronic inebriate required medical supervision and treatment. Woodward, for example (the medical superintendent of the Worcester State Lunatic Hospital in Massachusetts), had formed "the fullest conviction, that a large portion of the intemperate in a well-conducted institution would be radically cured, and would go again into society with health re-established, diseased appetites removed, with principles of temperance well grounded and thoroughly understood, so that they would afterwards be safe and sober men" (Woodward 1838, quoted in Baumohl and Room 1987:142).

TEMPERANCE IN THE ALCOHOLIC REPUBLIC

At the same time, the temperance movement, in both the United States and the United Kingdom, was shifting from moderation to complete abstinence (or "teetotalism"), putting it more in line with the doctors who supported special asylums for the inebriate—a kind of consciousness that "inebriety" was a disease, like insanity. The most concise summary of the significance of this shift is found in an English local study:

Once the temperance movement had adopted the reclaiming of drunkards as its leading objective, it had to transform its local structure. Regular meetings alone could keep the drunkard out of the drinking place [and] provide him with the companionship he had sacrificed. . . . Only by regular visitation, by "pairing off" with reformed drunkards, and by creating a new framework of life for its members could the teetotal movement secure the ground it had gained. (Harrison 1969:115–16, quoted in Baumohl and Room 1987:137–38)

This may be the place to introduce one of the earliest documents showing the redirection of the American Temperance Movement from "saving the sober" to the "recovery of the drunkard"—this being the "Letter from Gerrit Smith to Edward C. Delavan, Esq., on the Reformation of the Intemperate," published both separately and in Lydia H. Sigourney's tract *The Intemperate and the Reformed* (1833), with the further subtitle, *Shewing the Awful Consequences of Intemperance, and the Blessed Effects of the Temperance Reformation*. Gerrit Smith (1797–1874) was, of course, something of a crank and a visionary—he wound up financing John Brown at Harper's Ferry in the cause of Abolition—but for all that, he was a shrewd observer, not least of alcohol ("ardent spirits") and alcohol abuse ("intemperance") in the village of Peterborough, New York, where he lived. In his letter, he provides Edward Delavan with the life histories of thirty-eight men of Peterborough who have become sober through church or temperance society, noting *inter alia* that whereas in 1819 more than half the men in the village were drunkards, now there is only one, and that from 1821 to 1833 there were ninety-four cases brought before the town magistrate—and eighty-eight of them involved drunkards (or, as we might say, alcohol abusers).

What Gerrit Smith does not do—could not do, viewing the problem from outside—is to say how the reformation takes place. It is, however, possible to read between the lines, and to suggest that it was the meeting of the reforming drunkards *in the temperance society* that was decisive. The temperance societies were formed by the churches, but church membership without membership in a society did not work (*viz*, the next-door neighbor in Smith's case no. 3, 1833:28–29). Implicitly, if not explicitly, what seemed then to work toward sobriety is one drunk talking to another, or at least to others. But Peterborough, New York, may have been extraordinary, as a glass-blowing town where the glass-blowers had a high incidence of hard-drinking, and where more than half the adult male population came into the societies as drunkards. Mrs. Sigourney's tract (besides showing how a "geographical cure" did not work) details the life of a family man turned solitary drunkard, providing further suggestive evidence that fellowship was thought to be highly significant in reform. Nevertheless, this was essentially church-*directed* or church-*centered* reform.

THE WASHINGTONIANS

The creation of inebriate asylums—and any efforts at medical cure—waited nearly half a century, except, as it happens, for those associated with the Washingtonians, to whom we now return. Our principal source for the founding and original principles and practices of these Washingtonians is a brief (less than seventy-page) account entitled *The Foundation, Progress and Principles of the Washington Temperance Society of Baltimore* (Zug 1842, apparently not yet reprinted in a scholarly edition). The author is not identified but as the book was entered in the Clerk's Office of the District Court of Maryland by John Zug, he may reasonably be considered the author.

> On the evening of [April 5, 1840], half a dozen men met in the bar-room of a tavern in Baltimore. They had often met there before, spent their hours in friendly converse, and mingled in the mutual drowning of care in the bowl. . . . And now they had met there as before, to drink together from the poisonous cup, to which they were all too much addicted. Without having become outcasts or sots, they had all confessedly suffered severely from the frequent and intemperate use of intoxicating drinks. . . . They were the *victims*, the *unwilling victims*, rather than merely the *votaries* of the pleasures of the bowl. . . . They knew it was wrong. They saw the evil; they felt it; they lamented it; and times without number did they promise wife and friend and self, that they would drink no more. They were sincere. They meant to be sober. But at some fatal hour, they would take *one glass* again, *"just one glass,"* and they found themselves as powerless and debased as ever. (ibid:7–10)
>
> Previous to the evening on which the society was formed, we have intimated that the subject of reformation had been in contemplation among them for several days. . . . it was resolved among themselves, that they would place the temperance cause, so far as they were concerned, in the position of a *unit*: that the society, as such, was to recognize no creed of religion, nor party in politics; and that neither political nor religious action of any kind, should ever be introduced into the society's operations. *Personal abstinence* from all intoxicating drinks was to be the basis and *only requisite* of membership. Moral suasion was to be the only means by which they, as a body, were to induce others to adopt their principles. . . . Moreover, they determined that the regular meetings of the society should be meetings for the detail of personal experience . . . all temperance addresses were to be in the form of the individual experience of the several members . . . and the principle of *common honesty* was to direct them in all their movements. . . . When the individual was once within their hall, they regarded him as an easy convert. The *experience* of others who had been like him, and the good influence set to work upon him, soon led him to feel, think and act aright. . . . In the course of some months . . . the members . . . began to feel

better, to look better, and in every respect to be satisfied with the change in their habit. . . . The "experiences" of the members were now more and more interesting, and began to attract somewhat the attention of the public; and through their influence many of the most desperate and hopeless subjects of intemperance were redeemed (ibid.:13–17).

But it was just this public attention that seems to have been their downfall.

In six months after its formation, the society numbered eighty or ninety, many of whom were reformed drunkards (ibid.:17). In November 1840 they had their first public meeting. "Frequent public experience meetings now followed and were continued week after week during the entire winter. Public attention was now fully arrested (ibid.:18). The society was now "familiarly known by the expressive title of the *'Resurrection Society'*" (ibid.:19). In March 1841 a delegation went to New York, consisting of *"Messrs. Hawkins, Casey, Pollard, Shaw,* and subsequently President *Mitchell* himself" (ibid.:22). On April 5, 1841,

the anniversary of the formation of the original Washington Society was celebrated in Baltimore by a grand Procession. . . . It was estimated that at least six or eight thousand were in the ranks. . . . One of the "original six," Captain *John F. Hoss,* was the Chief Marshal of the day. President *William K. Mitchell* and the remaining four, in company with distinguished strangers, and the orator and chaplains of the day, rode in open barouches drawn each by four grey horses. (ibid.:23)

And then,

the Missionary operations of the society began to be developed on a large scale. Messrs. Hawkins and Wright in New England, and the Eastern and Middle States generally—Pollard and Wright in New York—Vickers in the valley of the Ohio—Carey, Stansbury, Morrison, Mules and Michael in various parts of Pennsylvania and Maryland—Carey in North and South Carolina—Michael in Virginia, with numerous others. (ibid.:24)

In short, what had been a successful endeavor by six men to keep themselves (and their friends) sober by telling each other their stories—which became better and more interesting as they stayed sober—became an organized temperance effort, indeed a missionary effort to spread the gospel by public meetings. A careful reading of Milton Maxwell's classic account strongly suggests that the villain (if that is the right word for a reformed drunkard and tireless temperance worker) was John H. W. Hawkins (1797–1858). For determining what brought the Washingtonians down, we are indebted Maxwell (1950), to which we now turn—with a brief introduction from Jerome Murray's *Ruminations of an Ex-Inebriate* (1879).

What happened to the Washingtonians? Their doctrines and principles, Murray says,

> were met by the *should-be* friends of temperance only with derision and contempt. . . . The movement [meaning, in Murray's context, the Temperance Movement as represented by the Washingtonians], based upon such liberal principles was, unfortunately, in advance of the intelligence and philanthropy of the age. At the zenith of success it was retired [note, not *it retired* but *it was retired*] within the portals of the church and behind the locked door, behind the secret pass-word and grip of a few temperance societies, where it remained in an almost dormant condition for nearly two-score years. (ibid.:76–77).

In short, though professional temperance reformers like Hawkins and John B. Gough—who were indeed Washingtonians but who were not present at the creation—went on being temperance reformers, and were even spoken of as Washingtonians (Maxwell 1950:425), the Washingtonian movement had pretty much disappeared from public sight by 1848. Maxwell's account of their history, supplemented by Murray's remarks (despite his very obvious biases), is highly instructive.

According to Maxwell the success of the Washingtonians, measured by numbers, showed its most dramatic strides,

> between the summers of 1841 and 1842, but apparently the peak of activity was reached in 1843. That year, [John] Gough was touring New England and Hawkins northern and western New York, as well as sections of Vermont, New Hampshire, and Maine. R. P. Taylor was doing effective work in Georgia. Late that autumn Hawkins campaigned in North and South Carolina and Georgia, stimulating great Washingtonian activity in that region. . . . [Then] May 28, 1844, in Boston [where Hawkins had brought the movement in April 1841], the Washingtonians were the sponsors of, and leading participants in, the largest temperance demonstration ever held, up to that time, with nearly 30,000 members of various temperance organizations participating. Governor George M. Briggs, William K. Mitchell and John B. Gough were the leading speakers. In the fall of 1845 Hawkins began one of his most intensive campaigns, in Ohio, Indiana and Illinois, winding up in the spring of 1846 with very successful meetings in New Orleans and Mobile. . . . [But in] Cincinnati [for example] in January 1845, Lyman Beecher wrote to John Marsh . . . that, "though the Washingtonians have endured and worked well, their thunder is worn out." (ibid.:424–25)

Perhaps a key lies in the report of the American Temperance Union, referring to Washingtonian missionary activity out of Cincinnati in 1842, with claims of one hundred thousand signatures (to the pledge) in Ohio, Kentucky, and Illinois: "Every seventh man is a reformed drunkard, and every fourth man a reformed tippler" (ibid.:425). Now John H. W. Hawkins himself, unlike the original six, was a prohibitionist, and with his preaching, and with its widespread extension, the movement lost something of its focus.

It was no longer Washingtonianism, as formulated by Anderson and Campbell and Hoss and McCurley and Mitchell and Steers: it was only Temperance.

We know about the public meetings that were reported in the press, and we know about the original meetings in Baltimore, but what went on at the regular meetings of the Washington Temperance Society? One clue I have found in what may seem a slightly surprising place, *The American Bicentennial Song Book, Volume I, The First Hundred Years* (1975:163–66), where we learn that in 1843 the Washingtonian Temperance Society of Harrisburg, Pennsylvania, borrowed the tune of the rollicking old drinking song, "Old Rosin, the Beau," for their social antidrinking song, "The Washington Badge." The words of the Harrisburg song are these:

> Come join in our temperance army
> And put on the Washington badge;
> I'm sure that it never will harm ye
> To give in your name to the pledge.
> We've done with our days of carousing,
> Our nights, too, of frolicsome glee;
> For now with our sober minds choosing,
> We've pledged ourselves never to spree. (ibid.: s.n. "Old Rosin")

The Harrisburg society almost certainly came up from Baltimore, as the societies in Philadelphia called themselves the Jeffersonians (Maxwell 1950:423). The implication I find in "The Washington Badge" (and its tune) is that, in Harrisburg at least (and I suspect, in Baltimore), the Washingtonians replaced the fellowship of the tavern with the fellowship of the Washingtonian meeting. This is quite in line with Brian Harrison's general sketch of the "teetotal" movement.

In fact, there is extant at least one set of directions for conducting a Washingtonian meeting, in the 1842 *Washingtonian Pocket Companion, Containing a Choice Collection of Temperance Hymns, Songs, etc.* (1842), though its place of publication (Utica, New York, far from Baltimore in 1840s measurement) and its contents both suggest that it represents the "missionary" aspect of Washingtonianism. Here are the suggestions on how to run a meeting:

> After the meeting has come to order, always open with a hymn or song. Transact the business of the society with the utmost order and dispatch.

... Then call for speakers. Let there be as many "experiences" as possible, interspersed with brief arguments, appeals, exhortations, news of the progress of the cause, temperance anecdotes, etc. Consult brevity, so as to have as many of the brethren speak as possible—the more the better. ... And always be sure to call for persons to take the pledge, when the audience feel in the right spirit. When the pledges are being filled up for delivery, pour out the warmest appeals, or sing the most interesting hymns or songs. (quoted from Maxwell 1950:435)

Despite the missionary tone—and the distance from Utica to Baltimore—it would seem clear that singing was an integral part of the Washingtonian meeting, in an era when singing was an integral part of American life.

There is another clue from Harrisburg on what happened to the Washingtonians. In 1858 there was in Harrisburg, a Washington Lodge, no. 107, of the Independent Order of Good Templars: "The organization numbers about three hundred members, and is very serviceable in the cause of temperance. It meets every Thursday evening, in the Sons of Temperance Hall, Second street ... [It] was instituted January 28, 1854 (Morgan 1858:323)— and I am reminded of Jerome Murray's comment that the movement disappeared behind the locked door and the secret password and grip. Was 1854 the date of that final disappearance, in Harrisburg at least? We may recall that in New York, the Washingtonians had been folded into the Sons of Temperance as early as the early 1840s (Maxwell 1950:425). The Independent Order of Good Templars was founded in 1852 (two years before it reached Harrisburg), "the largest fraternal temperance order of all" (ibid.:440), with Washingtonian Nathaniel Curtis as its first president. But the Washingtonians as a society did not entirely disappear. We know that they survived in Boston at least until 1860, and indeed it was Washingtonians (apparently) who founded the Boston Washingtonian Home in 1857 (still in existence in the twentieth century as the Washingtonian Hospital, and indeed until the 1980s). The Chicago Washingtonian Home was founded in 1863 by members of the International Order of Good Templars, who were almost certainly (as Maxwell suggests, ibid.:425–26) Washingtonians.

I believe that Murray has given us the clue, borne out by the Chicago Home and the Harrisburg "Washington Lodge." In the 1850s, the Washingtonians disappeared into the fraternal order of the International Order of Good Templars. But their ideal of a separate place set aside for recovering inebriates, in which they were in line with medical thinking of the time, survived. How appropriate their ideal of moral suasion was, we may come to see. Indeed, the medical thinking of the time, and especially the "psychiatric" thinking of the time, deserves some attention here.

NINETEENTH-CENTURY PSYCHOLOGY

Perhaps the clearest discussion I have seen is in Baumohl and Room's "Inebriety, Doctors and the State" (1987), from which (pp. 144–45) the following is taken, with some abridgments. Basically, early- and mid-nineteenth century American psychiatry held to a Cartesian view in which an eternal, immaterial, incorruptible Mind—God's presence in humankind—was entirely distinct from the body. Mind being eternal and incorruptible, disease necessarily lay in Mind's corporeal agent, the brain, or in the nervous system. Oddly, as asylum physicians practiced moral treatment—essentially psychological therapy—they subscribed to an etiology that was entirely somatic (that is, based on the body). If the irreducible innate ethical sense or "moral nature" could not be reached by reason, it could at least be touched by kindness and moral suasion, which is where institutional psychiatry and Washingtonianism touched. But the superintendents of insane asylums found it difficult to extend to drunkards the same kind of sympathy they extended to the mentally ill, and this for four reasons.

First, drunkards in an insane asylum were a nuisance. They were typically admitted while acutely intoxicated or in the throes of withdrawal or delirium tremens. But they were shortly restored to "perfect consciousness" and then resented association with the insane, became querulous and rebellious and liabilities to the institutional routine and harmony necessary to treatment by moral suasion.

Second, the superintendents were split on whether habitual drunkenness was in fact a disease. A disease ought (by the standards of the time) to have "anatomical correlates" evident to a pathologist. Some superintendents (as, for example, Henry Harlow of the Maine Insane Asylum) argued that loss of control over drinking implied a neurological defect, but, on the other hand, others argued that "the scalpel has never revealed" such a disease.

Third, some superintendents feared the social consequences of giving habitual drunkenness the status of a disease, because it would provide a license for viciousness. (Echoes of this view are still heard in debates over the misunderstood "disease concept of alcoholism.")

Fourth, by the eve of the American Civil War, the asylums were overcrowded, understaffed, and rapidly verging on being mere warehouses for chronic incurables.

It was at this point that the private Washingtonian facilities (homes rather than asylums) were established in Boston and Chicago and a similar foundation in San Francisco (1859), the Home for the Care of the Inebriate (Baumohl and Room 1987:146). (It has been suggested to me that the

San Francisco home may have been founded by a Washingtonian, perhaps even one of the original six.) The physicians associated with these homes were skeptical about the use of medicine in the treatment of inebriety, so that, in short, these "Washingtonian" establishments, though staffed with physicians, were committed to a regimen that was social, psychological, and spiritual—and only incidentally medical. In fact, the medical practices involved in moral treatment—such as they were—were relatively simple and straightforward. The diet was regulated, the bowels opened with gentle laxatives, and sedatives used to promote rest (ibid.:142). The psychological treatment, a matter of somewhat greater complexity, was carried out in a setting removed from previous environmental influences, based on reciprocal respect between patient and doctor, and patient treatment was individualized to the extent that "melancholics were cheered, maniacs were soothed, paranoiacs coaxed into trust by gentle denial of their fears, and so forth" (ibid.:142–43).

We may pause to look here at what was happening in the larger world at the end of the twenty years (1840–1860) which represent the great years of pre–Civil War temperance. First and most obvious, the American society was broken apart by the Civil War, but that was only the cataclysmic working out of earlier events. The twenty years before that war were a time not only for temperance agitation but for expansion, Manifest Destiny, Abolition, middle-class (or artisan) religious revival, early feminism, the idea of progress (with its millennial visions), and the great immigrations from Ireland and Germany. Mark Lender and James Kirby Martin (in their *Drinking in America*, New York 1982) call the period from 1860 to 1920 the time of a search for consensus on drinking, and subtitle their chapter on that period "The War Against Pluralism." And we recall the notorious words that may have cost Republican James G. Blaine the Presidency in 1884, when the Reverend Samuel Burchard called the Democrats the party of "Rum, Romanism, and Rebellion." I would break the period (so far as our subject is concerned) into two parts, say 1860–1900—a period of contending paradigms (in Thomas Kuhn's terms)—and 1900–20, when Prohibition marched from state to state until it seized the whole country with the Volstead Act and the Eighteenth Amendment.

THE STRUGGLE AGAINST INEBRIETY, 1864–1914

Five landmarks in the history of the struggle against inebriety came in 1864, 1870, 1872, 1874, and 1879/80. In the first of these years, just one year after the founding of the Chicago Washingtonian Home, came the first state inebriate asylum in Binghamton, New York. In 1870 the American Association for the Cure of Inebriates was formed. In 1872, the first "Skid Row" gospel mission was established in New York City. In 1874 Connecticut passed an "Inebriate Law" providing for compulsory commitment, and in 1879/80 the first "Keeley Cure" sanitarium was set up in Dwight, Illinois. The first state inebriate asylums seem to have attracted professionals, white-collar workers, and persons of the artisan class. Once there was compulsory commitment the mix changed, and reformers began to see a distressing tendency of the asylums to arrogate to themselves (and thus to "institutional medicine") the functions of penal institutions. The link between medicine and moral suasion, already weak, was broken, and the effect was to promote the moral suasion of the gospel mission, the medicine or pseudomedicine of such answers as the Keeley cure, and forced incarceration of those effectively considered incurable drunkards, as three separate approaches to the problem, none of them entirely satisfactory.

This brings us to the "Red and Blue Ribbon Movement" and the 1870s and 1880s, which attempted to preach temperance that was not "Gospel Temperance" and, if Jerome Murray is to be believed, designed to return in some degree to part of the original Washingtonian ideal:

> Gospel Temperance . . . however acceptable it may be to the religious portion of the community, is not designed to reach the man whose mind is prejudiced, and whose heart is seared with strong drink. . . . Gospel Temperance, properly construed, would only have for its advocates those who have been formally commissioned or *ordained* to preach the Gospel, and would thus exclude that most productive class of speakers (reformed men) whose labors have thus far been crowned with the greatest success. . . . No unconverted reformed man could essay to address a strictly Gospel Temperance meeting without compromising himself, and yet that same reformed man has by far the best access to a drunkard's mind and heart, because he best knows and can enter into all a drunkard's feelings. (1879:80–82)

One is indeed reminded of the distinction drawn in present-day A.A. parlance, between a spiritual program (in nineteenth-century terms, "religious") and a religious one (in nineteenth-century terms, "Gospel"). Here we may return to *The Varieties of Religious Experience*. The leading case used here as an example of spontaneous conversion is that of Samuel Hopkins Hadley (1842–1906), "who after his conversion became an active and useful rescuer of drunkards in New York" ([1903] 1961:169). William James quotes Hadley's account at length, and so will I (though at somewhat lesser length):

> "One Tuesday evening I sat in a saloon in Harlem, a homeless, friendless, dying drunkard. . . . I could not sleep unless I was dead drunk. I had not

eaten for days, and for four nights preceding I had suffered with *delirium tremens,* or the horrors, from midnight till morning. I had often said, 'I will never be a tramp. I will never be cornered, for when that time comes, if ever it comes, I will find a home in the bottom of the river.' But the Lord so ordered it that when that time did come, I was not able to walk one quarter of the way to the river. As I sat there thinking, I seemed to feel some great and mighty presence. . . . I walked up to the bar and pounded it with my fist till I made the glasses rattle. . . . I said I would never take another drink. . . . Something said, 'If you want to keep this promise, go and have yourself locked up.' I went to the nearest station house and had myself locked up. . . . [The Spirit] that came to me in the saloon was present, and said, Pray. I did pray, and though I did not feel any great help, I went on praying. . . . I was finally released . . . and toward [Sunday] evening it came into my head to go to Jerry McAuley's Mission. The house was packed, and with great difficulty I made my way to the space near the platform. There I saw the apostle to the drunkard and the outcast—that man of God, Jerry McAuley. He rose and amid deep silence told his experience. . . . I found myself saying, 'I wonder if God can save me?' I listened to the testimony of twenty-five or thirty persons, every one of whom had been saved from rum, and I made up my mind I would be saved, or die right there. . . . I said 'Dear Jesus, can you help me?' . . . Although up to that minute my soul had been filled with indescribable gloom, I felt the glorious brightness of the noonday sun shine into my heart. . . . From that moment until now I have never wanted a drink of whiskey." (ibid.:169–70, quoting Hadley, *Rescue Mission Work,* published at the Old Jerry McAuley Water Street Mission, New York, presumably after Jerry's death in order to raise funds)

The author, as noted above, was born in 1842 and died in 1906. His later and better-known book, *Down in Water Street,* was published in 1902: the date of his conversion I do not know, but Jeremiah (Jerry) McAuley, the "apostle to the lost," was born in 1839 and died in 1884—so the conversion was before 1884. This I take to be a "religious" conversion (Murray uses the word "religious" as opposed to "Gospel," in much the same way, as we have noted, that Alcoholics Anonymous was later to use the word "spiritual" as opposed to "religious")—but clearly not a "gospel" conversion. It is highly significant, I believe, that it is nevertheless a conversion very much like that of John Bunyan or Henry Alline. As we shall see in the next chapter, this apparently matches the "conversions" of some early members of A.A. (Jim B. and Fitz M.), though not all—and not even perhaps that of A.A.'s founder (or "cofounder") Bill W. (His was, perhaps, more akin to that of Nicholas Hermann, Brother Lawrence.)

Curiously, the next successful local effort at conversion from alcohol—and we should follow custom and call this one a clinic rather than a mission—was established by an *ordained* priest of the Episcopal Church, in Boston. (And the Calvary mission that was directly involved with Bill W's sobriety and the founding of Alcoholics Anonymous was also established by an *ordained* Episcopal priest, in New York.) The Emmanuel Movement was formally started in November 1906 at Emmanuel (Episcopal) Church in Boston, where Dr. Elwood Worcester had been Rector since July 1904. The formal beginning was marked by lectures on the relation of religion to medicine by such prominent speakers as James Jackson Putnam, Professor of Neurology at Harvard, and Dr. Richard C. Cabot, eminent internist and pioneer in the social aspects of medicine. By 1909 the movement, which combined religion and counseling in matters of mental health, and which led, among other creations, to the Nazarene Society and the Episcopal Church's Commission on Healing, had become conspicuously controversial in relation to Christian Science, whose "founder and discoverer" Mary Baker Eddy (1821–1910) still lived in Boston. I have been unable to find Mrs. Eddy's opinion of the Emmanuel Movement, but Father Worcester's appreciation of Mrs. Eddy seems to have included a strong comparison to first-century Christianity (see Powell 1930:36–37).

Mrs. Eddy had experience with inebriates, including her second husband, Dr. Daniel Patterson, and in the brief section on "Saving the Inebriate" in *Science and Health With Key to the Scriptures* (1875), remarks that the "drunkard thinks he enjoys drunkenness, and you cannot make the inebriate leave his besottedness, until his physical sense of pleasure yields to a higher sense. Then he turns from his cups, as the startled dreamer who wakens from an incubus incurred through the pains of distorted sense" (ibid.:322) Her recommended technique (in her chapter on "Christian Science Practice") is this:

> If a man is an inebriate, a slave to tobacco, or the special servant of any one of the myriad forms of sin, meet and destroy these errors with the truth of being—by exhibiting to the wrong-doer the suffering which his submission to such habits brings, and by convincing him that there is no real pleasure in false appetites. (ibid.:404)

But she acknowledges that this will work better if the inebriate is suffering in his body ["The healthy sinner is the hardened sinner" (ibid.)].

Wednesday night Christian Science meetings then practiced—and still practice—a form of "sharing" in which members of what is now the Church of Christ, Scientist, tell how Christian Science has given them healing and understanding. Some testimonies of this sort (but from letters in the period 1890–1900) are collected in the section of *Science and Health* called "Fruitage" and at least three (ibid.:643–45, 678–79, 693–94) deal with the effect of *Science and Health* on the desire to drink [which "simply disappeared" (p. 644)—or "disappeared" (p. 693) or on the "drink habit" (which "was removed")], while others (especially one on pp. 676–77) probably deal with the same thing. There was, however, a social stigma attached to drunkenness that might have inhibited "sharing" on that subject on Wednesday nights at the end of the nineteenth century. There is a hint in one of Mrs. Eddy's uncollected writings that she may have recognized this as a problem—though the passage may of course have other interpretations. But she did relax a ban on a practitioner's communicating one patient's experiences (anonymously) to another with the same problem (referred to in *Story of the Christian Science Church Manual*, New York 1934). I suspect this at least referred to problems that would not be part of the sharing of spoken testimonies.

William James, who supported Emmanuel and went to a Christian Science practitioner, was a longtime friend of James Jackson Putnam, who spoke at the formal opening meeting of Emmanuel—indeed James vacationed at Putnam's camp in the Adirondacks for many years—and as early as 1894 James had published in the *Boston Transcript* a letter supporting the practice of medicine by persons without medical degrees (Rosenzweig 1994:175–78, 313–34). It is not surprising that he favored the "lay therapy" of the Emmanuel Movement. Moreover, James was an avowed mystic whose opponents, being also opponents of the Emmanuel Movement, accused him of "using his professional authority to build up a modern occultism" (Witmer 1909:295, quoted in Rosenzweig, 1994:175–76). Cabot we will meet again in the next chapter, in connection with Charlie Towns and his treatment for alcoholism and drug addiction (and gambling, and other illnesses). But let us turn now to the Emmanuel Movement.

THE EMMANUEL MOVEMENT

Worcester and his assistant, Dr. Samuel McComb, operated what was called a free clinic at Emmanuel Church for something like twenty-three years, until Worcester retired in 1929. In 1913 a man named Courtenay Baylor began to work for the Emmanuel Clinic as a specialist in alcoholism, probably the first paid alcoholism therapist in the United States. Originally an insurance agent, he had come to Worcester in 1911 for help with his drinking problem. After a period of sobriety, he retired from the business world to become a paid "friendly visitor" in the church's Social Services Department. He remained at the church until Worcester's retirement, when, in effect, they took the clinic with them to the Craigie Foundation in Boston. Worcester died in 1940. In 1945, Baylor resumed his old job at the church. By all accounts, he died sober. He described his treatment technique in the book, *Remaking A Man* (1919). Alcoholics (Baylor may have been the first therapist to use that word customarily, at least in the United States) came to him from as far away as Santa Barbara, Denver, Mobile, Washington, and Philadelphia, "while New York is a suburb from which we have many commuters" (quoted in McCarthy 1984:47).

Though Courtenay Baylor died sober, the Emmanuel Movement's most significant "graduate" was a man named Richard Peabody, who apparently did not. But it was Peabody who set up a practice in New York based in part on the Emmanuel Movement and wrote a book called *The Common Sense of Drinking* (1931). He "treated" so many "patients" in his clinic at 24 Gramercy Park that he was frequently referred to as Dr. Peabody. We will come back to "Dr." Peabody, but first, let us look at Worcester's clinic in its first years. Once again, we are indebted to McCarthy's study for what follows.

Worcester and McComb were not alcoholics and their "therapeutic method" was originally designed to treat the condition then spoken of as *neurasthenia*—an assortment of neurotic symptoms, psychosomatic problems, phobias, extreme worry, anxiety, addiction, and various other conditions then considered nonorganic. In 1906–7, the first year the clinic was operating, Dr. Cabot reported that only 12 percent were alcoholics. A considerable majority of the nonalcoholic patients—and a majority of all the patients—were women. The alcoholic patients were mostly men. There were three rules relating to the acceptance of alcoholic patients: (1) They must come voluntarily from their own desire to stop drinking, not because of pressure from others. (2) They must be willing to accept the goal of total abstinence, inasmuch as "the attempt to convert a drunkard into a moderate drinker . . . cannot be done once in a thousand times." (3) They must be "dry" during the first interview and must pledge to be abstinent for one week.

Worcester believed that *all* diseases had physical, mental, and spiritual components. Some problems might be primarily physical, such as a broken leg, but the patients' attitudes could still advance or retard healing. "The realms of the body, mind, and spirit interacted in a delicate balance in each person; an improvement in one area might lead to improvements in another. Severe pain from an intractable physical ailment could be relieved by changes in attitude; the physical craving for alcohol or morphine could be eliminated by a more spiritual way of life. All nervous sufferers could be helped by redirecting their attention away from themselves to a life of service to others" (McCarthy 1984:49–50). Baylor, so far as we can tell, took his ideas on the unity of body, mind, and spirit from Worcester, and Worcester took them from Gustav Fechner, under whom he had studied at Leipzig. Fechner was well known for his work in experimental psychology, but he was better known for his attempt to meld the mystical and the scientific—the spiritual and the material—into a true *Geistwissenschaft*, a study that could express both worlds as part of a true science.

The Worcester-McComb therapy involved significant use of suggestion and autosuggestion, even extending to occasional hypnotism to keep alcoholics sober long enough to receive treatment. Generally, the patient was simply put in a state of relaxation, in a comfortable chair, in a dim and quiet room, with the therapist giving directions for systematically relaxing each limb and slowing down racing thoughts. Baylor, for example, would ask the patient to imagine that he was sailing in a small boat toward an island, at first quickly, then more slowly, until the patient ended up lying comfortably on a sunny shore. The therapist would then suggest to an alcoholic, for example (this is from Worcester's practice), that the desire to drink would soon pass, that he would sleep better, and that he could begin to make progress in life. In this way, the powerful healing forces of the *subconscious* (not *unconscious*) mind could be directed to support the patient's conscious desire to recover. Worcester saw the subconscious mind as a source of enormous strength, creativity, inherited memory (this begins to sound like Carl Jung), and communication with the spiritual realm (and this sounds like both Jung and William James). He saw the subconscious as the regulator of elementary physical processes such as heartbeat, circulation, respiration, and "time-keeping."

The redirection of attention away from self and toward the development of a spiritual life and service to others was a primary goal of Emmanuel therapy. The theological basis of Worcester's therapy, Katherine McCarthy suggests, was the Biblical injunction to "resist not evil" (*cf.* the use of this same injunction in Christian Science)—meaning (for Worcester) that constructive psychological change could be better promoted by building up a person's strengths than by directly attacking the problem itself. In later A.A. terms, this fits in with the idea that the problem is alcoholism rather than alcohol (and in Christian Science with the injunction, "Start with the truth and not the problem!").

Prayer was used as the essential vehicle for therapy, as (in Worcester's words) the "surrender implied in sincere prayer is always followed by the consciousness of peace and inner freedom." What follows is, in fact (in Katherine McCarthy's words) "a process of conversion" (McCarthy 1984:48) whereby (in Worcester's words) the "tendency about which [the patient] was concerned is robbed of its attractive quality and the thought of it finds no entrance to his imagination" (ibid.:52). Moreover, the Emmanuel Movement not only provided individual therapy, lectures, and reading (which may have included *The Varieties of Religious Experience*), but also established social hours after the weekly classes. At these social hours the patients were expected to talk to each other about their growth and progress—but not to dwell on what was wrong with them. This particular part of the Emmanuel program was supported by a church-sponsored club for alcoholics, founded in 1910 by a nonalcoholic parishioner, Ernest Jacoby.

The Jacoby Club held meetings in the church basement on Saturdays, and its space was used for socializing most other nights. Apparently, non-alcoholics also attended, but the evidence is that the club's purpose was to help newly abstinent patients reinforce each other's abstinence, helping themselves by helping others. The club moved out of the church basement in 1914, but apparently continued an amicable relationship with the Emmanuel Movement and the church, which continued to send it new members. The main focus of Worcester's work, however, remained on what we would call a holistic approach. He "had no doubt that alcoholism was both a disease and a moral problem. Addiction involved habit—a moral category—but he ranked alcoholism with tuberculosis, cancer, and syphilis as one of the four major diseases of his time" (McCarthy 1984:53–54). Moral suasion—indeed the whole question of the will—was not the point. Recovery must come both from surrender to an external force (that is, conversion) and from the healing capacities within the subconscious. Therapy with the latter, in effect, made the former possible. One point of interest in passing: in 1908, Worcester earned the equivalent of a year's salary in writing five articles for the *Ladies' Home Journal*, including one on alcoholism in women. But most of the alcoholic patients at the Emmanuel clinic were men.

Worcester was not an alcoholic, so far as we know. Courtenay Baylor was, and he revealed this to his alcoholic patients: indeed mutual confidentiality was a condition for therapy. "Before we get through," he used to say, "I shall have to reveal as much about myself as you do about yourself" (ibid.:54). His "interviews" with patients were "one hundred percent suggestion, direct or indirect" (ibid.:54). He believed that when the alcoholic took the drink which he knew (in his right mind) he shouldn't take, it was as a result of "wrong impulses and a wholly false, though plausible, philosophy" (ibid.:55) resulting from a condition of the brain "akin to physical tension" (ibid.) in which the brain did not sense "things as they really are" (ibid.) Of course, Baylor was a layman and a lay therapist, neither minister nor doctor, but alcoholic, and this is the language neither of theology nor medicine. But it appears pretty much congruent with both.

As an alcoholic, Baylor came to realize (*Emmanuel Church Yearbook*, 1916)

> that it is unwise to attempt to accomplish the work in a few interviews, and an agreement is made with those who come that they will abide by our instructions for a year. . . . Getting the man to stop drinking is only the first step in a very long march. All the negative traits induced by alcohol must be eliminated and the positive traits put in their places. Irritability, self-pity, fear, worry, criticism of friends, bitter hatred of enemies, lack of concentration, lack of initiative and action, all these must be worked out of the character. The entire mental process must be changed, a new sense must be grown, one that can recognize the soul; when this is accomplished, we have the man himself cured from alcoholism. (quoted in McCarthy 1984:57)

(We may note, in passing, that Baylor did not say "cured of alcoholism" but "cured from alcoholism"—there may well be a much more than semantic difference here.)

In other words, Baylor was practicing a kind of continuing psychotherapy, though radically different from what Freud practiced. In fact, when Freud visited the United States for the Clark University Vigentennial in 1909, he was asked about Worcester's claim to have cured cases of alcoholism, and he replied,

> The suggestive technique does not concern itself with the origin, extent, and significance of the symptoms of the disease, but simply applies a plaster-suggestion—which it expects to be strong enough to prevent the expression of the diseased idea. The analytical therapy, on the contrary, . . . concerns itself with the origin and progress of the symptoms of the disease. (quoted in Hale, *Freud and the Americans*, 1971, reference in McCarthy 1984:56)

Of course, this begs the question whether knowing the origin and progress of the symptoms of the disease carries us beyond the diagnosis-prognosis-bedside manner progress of medical treatment in the absence of curative medicines.

Freud's influence may have had some positive (even if transient) effects on alcoholism therapy in the 1940s and 1950s (as we shall see in Chapter 4), but there is no doubt the effect was severely negative earlier. The case in point is Richard Peabody (1894–1936). Peabody came to Emmanuel for help with his alcoholism in 1921–22. He was suffering from the breakup of his marriage with Caresse Crosby (as she was), niece of J. P. Morgan, in the wake of his heavy drinking and erratic behavior since his return from the War in 1919. He had somehow lost his share in the family shipping fortune during the period of his enlistment (which began with service on the Mexican border in 1916 right after his marriage), and had been hospitalized for acute depression more than once, most recently after his wife divorced him. Even at the time of his marriage in 1915, after his dropping out of Harvard, his wife's family was already worried about his drinking.

He attended the clinic and weekly health classes in 1921–22, and by 1924 he was listed as a volunteer in the Emmanuel Church Social Service Department (*Report of the Emmanuel Church Department of Community Service*, 1924). In the 1920s he established his own office on Newbury Street, gained credit for remarkable cures, and became known as "Dr." Peabody. In the 1930s, he was publishing articles on "his method" in *The New England Journal of Medicine, Mental Hygiene*, and *The American Mercury*; moreover, his book *The Common Sense of Drinking*, published in 1931, was republished by the Atlantic Monthly Press in 1935. But, although Peabody was a "graduate" of the Emmanuel program, and a volunteer there, he systematically eliminated from his terminology and concepts anything that hinted of the church and [in his words] "feather-decorated, painted medicine men." The acknowledgments in his book include Baylor and six physicians, but he did not mention the Emmanuel Church [which was, after all, a competitor until 1929]. . . . Since Peabody had no credentials [beyond his work with Emmanuel] and chose not to use his own experience as the basis of his claim to be a teacher [in fact, virtually never mentioned his own experience], he was in a difficult position to justify his fees.' (McCarthy 1984:35).

With virtually no doctors in the field (except perhaps William Duncan Silkworth at Towns Hospital in New York, and one or two, including Thomas Scuderi, working quietly—but he only from 1934—with Sister Mary Ignatia Gavin at St. Vincent's Hospital in Akron), the field was open to Peabody. (There was also, from 1937, Dr. Dudley Saul in Philadelphia, with the program that eventually worked into the Saul Clinic.) Peabody apparently justified himself as a kind of trained tutor for those trying to learn how to recover from their alcoholism. Unfortunately, he was not a competent tutor.

The problem seems to have been, in part, besides his unhealthy instinct for self-aggrandizement (and a raging egomania based on a notable inferiority complex), his severe avoidance of considerations of either morality or feeling. It was almost as though he tutored his students on how to conquer their alcoholism simply on the grounds that alcoholism promoted inefficiency (shades of Taylorism and Jack London!) and they must learn to be efficient. He cited as a major drawback of excessive drinking its "supreme stupidity." If we were to place Peabody within any group of therapists as we understand therapy in the year 2004, we might consider him a cognitive therapist (not a very good one). To his credit, Peabody reformulated some of Baylor's central ideas—surrender, relaxation, suggestion, and catharsis (particularly surrender and suggestion)—in ways more specific to and useful for the alcoholic than Baylor had thought necessary. Moreover, he formulated the need for surrender with particular urgency (on this, at least, he may have looked inside himself):

"The first step to sobriety is surrender to the fact that the alcoholic cannot drink again without bringing disastrous results" upon himself, and this surrender (is the absolute starting point . . . With surrender, halfway measures are of no avail. (quoted by McCarthy 1984:51–52)

Unfortunately, having left behind what he considered the religious baggage of Worcester and Baylor, Peabody did not make it very clear what exactly one would be surrendering *to*. Perhaps what Bill W. wrote in his copy (or perhaps one of his copies) of *The Common Sense of Drinking* is to the point here: "Dr. Peabody was as far as is known the first authority to state, 'once an alcoholic, always an alcoholic,' and he proved it by returning to drinking and by dying of alcoholism—proving to us that the condition is incurable" (quoted in McCarthy 1984:57). In the end, Peabody's significance lay neither in his successes nor his failures, but in his maintaining that alcoholism was a treatable condition (beyond "religious" treatment), and worthy of scientific research and investigation. As we will see in the next chapter, Peabody's influence, through a Peabody-trained therapist named Raymond McCarthy, lasted into the first great attempt at the scientific study of alcoholism and its treatment, with the Yale School of Alcohol Studies.

NINETEENTH-CENTURY MEDICAL TREATMENT

But for the moment, let us put Worcester and Baylor and Peabody (and McCarthy) aside, and look at the most popular "medical cure" for alcoholism in the period from Jerry McAuley to Courtenay Baylor. This is the "Keeley cure of "bi-chloride of gold," formulated by Dr. Leslie E. Keeley (1832?–1900) in the American Midwest in the mid-1870s, with the usual extravagant claims. Keeley had graduated from a medical college and been with the Union army in the American Civil War, after which he settled in Dwight, Illinois, about eighty miles south of Chicago (along present-day I-55) and come up with the famous "bi-chloride of gold" or "double chloride of gold" formula for "curing" addiction to tobacco ($5.00 a bottle), alcohol ("inebriety"—$9.00 a bottle), or morphine or opium ($10.00 a bottle). The prices given (in the parentheses) are for Dr. Keeley's mail-order business for those being "cured" at home, in the years up to 1895. It is not entirely clear why the bottles should have different prices— except, perhaps (in the words of W. S. Gilbert), to "lend an air of verisimilitude to an otherwise bald and unconvincing narrative."

The first Keeley Institute was established in Dwight in 1879–80 (by Keeley, in partnership with John Oughton and Major Curtis Judd), at which time Keeley proclaimed, "Drunkenness is a disease and I can cure it" (quoted in W. L. White, *Slaying the Dragon*, p. 5), although, as we will see, his original primary interest was in curing morphine addiction. The institute grew slowly in the 1880s, but rapidly enough that by 1890 it could not handle all the business that came its way, and Keeley sent up branch facilities—at which point, growth really took off. By 1894, there were 118 Keeley institutes in the United States. From 1892 to 1900, through satisfied clients and aggressive advertising, the Keeley Company had revenues of $2.7 million (for comparison, when Andrew Carnegie sold his steel company into U.S. Steel that year, he realized $30 million, making him one of

America's richest men). A Keeley Day was held in 1893 as part of the World's Fair and Columbian Exposition in Chicago.

In 1896, Keeley published his book on *The Non-Heredity of Inebriety*, which of course argued that anyone could be cured of inebriety by the Keeley cure. But already the seeds of disillusion and disappointment were sowed, and by the time Keeley died in his winter home in California on February 21, 1900, the handwriting was on the wall. Partly as a result of the increase of state Prohibition laws (as a result of popular agitation and the support of certain business leaders like John D. Rockefeller), partly perhaps from the increasing number of patients who did not want to get well but were sent by their families, the way from then on was all downhill. By 1916 only the Keeley Institute in Dwight remained strong, though a few others were dying slowly around the country; by 1925 they were dead and the "gold cure" had been given up even at Dwight. By the time the doors at Dwight were closed in 1966, A.A. had been for a number of years a central part of the program.

Nevertheless, for a brief time, in the 1890s, the "Keeley cure" had swept the country. What was this Keeley cure?

When a patient entered a Keeley institute he was given a set of rules and guidelines, and received four mandatory injections of the "gold cure" each day, attended all scheduled lectures, was given a tonic every two hours, required to refrain from smoking tobacco, and was allowed no fraternization with patients of the opposite sex. Alcoholic patients remained four weeks at the facility, drug patients six weeks. What the "gold cure" contained is still unknown, though it may have had some antabuse-like agent that would induce nausea if the patient did drink. One point of particular interest: in 1891, at Dwight, patients and alumni formed the first Keeley League for mutual support. The league spread with the other Keeley facilities, and by 1897 there were 370 chapters. The original league meetings (held daily at Dwight) featured the introductions of new patients and speeches from patients leaving (sharing *experience*, perhaps in somewhat the same way the original Washingtonians shared their experience). Seven national conventions were held (1891–97), and the League advertised itself as "the only organization in the world composed exclusively of men who confess themselves to have been drunkards and cured" (meaning, cured of being drunkards) (quoted in White, *Slaying the Dragon*, p. 57).

Recovering alcoholics and addicts were employed in the institutes, and one modern historian has estimated that more recovering physicians were employed in the Keeley institutes than in any program before or since. We might appropriately quote William White's assessment of the "Keeley cure" in his *Slaying the Dragon: The History of Addiction Treatment and Recovery in America*:

The Spirit of mutual support born within the Keeley Institute and formalized in the Keeley League was the source of many permanent recoveries. Keeley put together many elements . . . medically supported detoxification, conceptualization of addiction [including addiction to alcohol] as a disease, a milieu of mutual support among those being treated, the guided restoration of physical and emotional health, and, not insignificantly, a gimmick that engaged addicts' propensity for magical thinking and helped them through the early weeks and months of recovery . . . [it] was the healing power of the milieu, not the medicine, that was Dr. Keeley's greatest legacy. (1998:63)

But, of course, that leaves us with two questions, despite our rather tentative suggestions about Prohibition laws and unwilling patients, noted above: (1) Why didn't it go on working? (2) Had it in fact really worked, or were the "permanent" cures something less than permanent or even less than cures? (Both, of these questions, of course, require some agreed-upon definition of what is meant by a "cure"—though it seems likely Dr. Keeley meant a condition of permanent abstinence.) In any case, we have no particular evidence on either count, but one point raised by David Musto (1980:329) deserves some attention. Since the Keeley program covered alcohol, tobacco, and narcotics—and since Dr. Keeley did not believe there was a genetic or heritable component in alcoholism, differentiating "inebriates" from other patients—is it not likely that the collapse of the Keeley movement resulted in part from the fact that the experiences "shared" in League meetings were not in fact shared experiences? Also, of course, there is William White's reference to magical thinking—which could get the alcoholic (or, in this case, addict) through the early phases of recovery, but proved a slender support for the long haul. In short, we might fairly say that there was no spiritual changeover, no real personality change, and (very likely) a constantly diminishing sense of unity. Moreover, there would seem to be a huge difference between 370 chapters of the Keeley League, all over the country, and the sense of both unity and locality in the original Washingtonians (in Baltimore at least), and in the Emmanuel Movement and the Jacoby Club in Boston.

It is certainly worth repeating that Dr. Keeley's original chief concern was not alcohol but opium. In fact, when he published his first book, it was *The Morphine Eater, or, From Bondage to Freedom* (1881). One suspects that many of his patients (and many of the others whose stories he prints) were veterans from the American Civil War who had acquired the morphine habit during that war. It may also be worth noting that another method, that of J. B. Gray, involved the administration of a tonic every two hours, and while we do not have any recipes from Keeley, we have the contents of Gray's tonic from Gray himself (quoted in Lender and Kirby Martin 1982:122): twelve grains of chloride of gold and sodium; six grains muriate of ammonia, one grain nitrate of strychnia, one-quarter grain atropine, three ounces compound fluid extract of cinchona, one ounce each of glycerine, fluid extract of coca, and distilled water. Some kind of saline solution, murate of ammonia, strychnine, belladonna, quinine, and cocaine—now, there's a tonic for you. In the Keeley cure, the chloride of gold was the basic "curative," but it seems not unlikely that Keeley's every-two-hours tonic would have otherwise been much like Gray's every-two-hours tonic. And there is even a resemblance to the Towns preparation of belladonna.

CHARLIE TOWNS

In fact, as the Keeley cure declined, after Keeley's death (and even a little before), another player appeared on stage. This is the highly ambiguous figure of Charlie Towns (at whom we will look again in the next chapter. Like Leslie Keeley (though Towns was a generation younger), he was a super-salesman. Like Bill W. (though Towns was a generation older), he was a super-salesman and a stock analyst. He had come to Wall Street from Georgia (where he had been a superlative insurance salesman) at the turn of the century and made money in the Street, though the firm he was with failed (1901–4). But somehow, at the time of the Pure Food and Drug Law of 1905, Charlie showed a new interest in drug addiction and drug treatment—he later related that he was approached by a fellow who whispered, "I've got a cure for the drug habit—morphine, opium, heroin, codeine, any of 'em—we can make a lot of money out of it!" (quoted in David F. Musto 1999:80). Towns sought out his personal physician, who told him the claim was ludicrous—but he followed it up, perhaps just in case there might be something to it, and put advertisements in the papers seeking drug fiends who wanted to be helped.

In David Musto's words, "Trying his formula out on such persons and restraining them when they wanted to get out of the hotel rooms Towns used for his experiments, he perfected the treatment [so he said] so as to 'eliminate all the suffering'" (ibid.:81). Probably needless to say, Towns and his "cure" were initially shunned by the medical profession. But he somehow was able to interest Alexander Lambert of Cornell, Teddy Roosevelt's personal physician, in his "cure"—and through Lambert's influence, Towns presented his "cure" to the Shanghai Opium Commission in 1908. He was then (at least in America) widely praised as "an everyday American fighter" who had found an effective treatment for addiction.

What was the treatment? One part "fluid extract of prickly ash bark," one part "fluid extract of hyoscyamus," and two parts "a 15-percent tincture of belladonna." Before beginning with the specific, there must be a complete evacuation of the bowels, and half an hour before formula administration, the largest tolerable dose of the addicting substance was given "to bridge the patient over as long a period as possible without having to use the drug again" (in Musto 1980:81). Twenty-four hours later, after a second cathartic, a dose of the addicting drug was given, one-half to one-third of the previous amount. Twelve hours later a third cathartic was administered, and six to eight hours later a dose of one to two ounces of castor oil. This more or less concluded the treatment, though this summary does not include the small doses of strychnine necessary to combat patient exhaustion. "One of the cure's detractors later labeled it 'diarrhea, delirium, and damnation,' but it seemed very neat and scientific when presented in 1909 under the auspices of the federal government, Dr. Lambert, and the *Journal of the American Medical Association*" (ibid.:82). To be sure, Lambert later recanted his support; by 1920 the Towns "cure" had fallen into disrepute; and indeed the idea that any addiction could be cured had itself fallen into disrepute.

But in his heyday Towns published *Habits That Handicap: The Menace of Opium, Alcohol, and Tobacco, and the Remedy* (1915), with a preface by Richard C. Cabot of Harvard (whom we have met a little earlier) and an interesting appendix by Lambert, "The Relation of Alcohol to Disease" (but emphatically *not* on the "disease of alcoholism"). Still, Towns, like Keeley before and Peabody after, did believe that alcoholism and addiction were treatable medical conditions. Unlike Keeley and Peabody, he attempted what he apparently considered a purely medical treatment. Like Peabody's, Keeley's treatment was not truly medical—though doubtless strychnine, belladonna, and cocaine would have some medical effect—but in many ways managerial. Indeed, the Keeley patients who took the cure at home were required to send in report sheets on their activities every three days (and fill them out every day at the institute). And Peabody's method involved an even more highly detailed plan for time control.

> Before going to bed, the patient should write down on a piece of paper the different hours of the day. Then, so far as can be determined beforehand, he should fill in these hours with what he plans to do. Throughout the day notations should be made if exceptions have occurred in the original plans. . . . [The function of the time plan was to] (1) give the patient something concrete to do to change his condition, (2) provide the patient with "training in executing his own commands" and (3) prevent idleness. (McCarthy 1984:56)

Peabody's "time-cards" survived Peabody himself by some years. Of course, medicine has changed since Peabody's day—still more since Keeley's—and managerial understanding took a kind of quantum leap between Keeley and Peabody (with the advent of Taylor and Gilbreth and Scientific Management).

It is entirely possible, of course, that medicine (as we now understand it) and management techniques may be used to combat alcoholism, though these efforts are not cases in point. One thing is sure: Prohibition may have put the finishing touches on the Keeley cure. But Prohibition does not seem to have had any beneficial effect on the incidence of alcoholism. It does not appear that alcoholism is to be cured by removing alcohol from a list of legal substances. But removing it—nationwide in 1919—and returning it—in most states in 1933—did at least force a new look at inebriety, alcohol, and alcoholism. The rules of the game changed once more.

JOHN BARLEYCORN

Before we look at that rule change, we have one more literary document to examine, without which no study of alcoholism could even pretend to completeness. About the time Courtenay Baylor was beginning his treatment, America's most famous living writer was recording his struggles with alcoholism (which he denied he had), depression (which he called White Logic and believed was a clear and remorseless logic induced by alcohol), and his alcoholic dialogue with death ("the Noseless One") in *John Barleycorn* (1913). The writer was John Griffith ("Jack") London, and he had three years to live till he died an alcoholic death at forty in November 1916. If this book did nothing else, it revived the traditional name *John Barleycorn* (which Bill W. and other early A.A.s used, as London used it, to personify alcohol) and it provides us (I believe) with the first use of the word *alcoholic* outside of technical literature. It is a tragic—or at least an ironic—book, because it is the work of an obvious alcoholic telling us at length, in good style, and with no little ingenuity, that he is not really an alcoholic, that he has no need for John Barleycorn, and the White Logic and the Long Sickness have been laid away together. Perhaps the best comment on the book's use as support for Prohibition is what was said by Upton Sinclair, "That the work of a drinker who had no intention of stopping drinking should become a major propaganda piece in the campaign for Prohibition is surely one of the choice ironies in the history of alcohol" (quoted in London [1913] 2001:xxv).

But that was precisely what Jack London intended. He opens the book (ibid.:4) with a stylized conversation with his wife, Charmian (1871–1955). He has just (1911) voted for Women's Suffrage in California. Charmian, surprised, asks why. Jack, who is "lighted up, . . . feeling good, . . . pleasantly jingled," answers,

> "When the women get the ballot, they will vote for prohibition. . . . It is the wives, and sisters, and mothers, and they only, who will drive the nails into

the coffin of John Barleycorn—" "But I thought you were a friend to John Barleycorn," Charmian interpolated. "I am. I was. I am not. I never am. I am never less his friend than when he is with me and I seem most his friend. He is the king of liars. He is the frankest truth-sayer. He is the august companion with whom one walks with the gods. He is also in league with the Noseless One. His way leads to truth naked, and to death. He gives clear vision, and muddy dreams. He is the enemy of life, and the teacher of wisdom beyond life's vision. He is a red-handed killer, and he slays youth."

Then, after telling his life's story with John Barleycorn (the closest thing to an autobiography Jack London ever wrote), he returns to his first theme:

The women know. They have paid an incalculable price of sweat and tears for man's use of alcohol. Ever jealous for the race, they will legislate for the boys of babes yet to be born; and for the babes of girls, too, for they must be the mothers, wives, and sisters of these boys. And it will be easy. The only ones that will be hurt are the topers and seasoned drinkers of a single generation. I am one of these, and I make solemn assurance, based upon long traffic with John Barleycorn, that it won't hurt me very much to stop drinking when no one else drinks and when no drink is obtainable. On the other hand, the overwhelming proportion of young men are so normally non-alcoholic, that, never having had access to alcohol, they will never miss it. They will know of the saloon only in the pages of history, and they will think of the saloon as a quaint old custom similar to bull-baiting and the burning of witches. ([1913] 2001:206)

In the old line, "Sez you!" Or in current slang, sarcastically, "Right!" And this at the end of a book that remains one of our best accounts of the rituals of the drinking life, and of the long struggle of the alcoholic with John Barleycorn and his White Logic, his "argent messenger of truth beyond truth, the antithesis of life, cruel and bleak as interstellar space, pulseless and frozen as absolute zero, dazzling with the frost of irrefragable logic and unforgettable fact" (ibid.:xix). Of course, Jack. Of course, Prohibition will end drinking. Of course, alcoholics will fervently grasp their legally required sobriety and not miss their alcohol. Of course. Change the rules, and you change the man!

No, but change the rules, and you do at least change the rules.

2 ~

This Strange Illness of Mind, Body, and Spirit

SO THE RULES CHANGED. If we look back to the 1930s, a year or two after the repeal of Prohibition in 1933, we see a new concern with the problem of "alcoholism" and the beginnings of a new mode of treatment for this "alcoholism"—the society (sometimes called the fellowship) of Alcoholics Anonymous. Though Alcoholics Anonymous is self-described as the creation of its two "cofounders," Bill W. and Dr. Bob S., to an outside observer it would seem that Bill W. founded Alcoholics Anonymous, and Dr. Bob became the "cofounder" because he was the first person Bill himself boosted into sobriety. And also perhaps because Bill—a visionary who "could see further in the world than anyone [else] I have ever known," according to Dr. Bob's son (*A.A. Grapevine* 2001:37)—recognized the need for there to be more than one founder, even though "he could have very easily slipped into being *the* founder" (ibid.:43). Bill also gave a number of others honor as founders of A.A.—many of them nonalcoholics. One version of Bill W.'s story of the founding is a matter of public record, quite literally, and that is the one we will use here. But before we get to that, what manner of man was this Bill W. before he became sober? Here we have recourse to reminiscences taped by Bill W. in 1954, covering his life from birth to the beginnings of sobriety. These were recently published as *Bill W. My First 40 Years* (2000).

From them we can get at least the beginnings of a picture of a Vermont Yankee schoolboy with his full share of Yankee ingenuity, capable of immense and single-minded absorption in what he is doing, brought up by grandparents after his parents' marriage broke up, always needing to excel, always conscious of the superiority of the summer people, dogged, a craftsman rather than an artist (but at intervals a really fine craftsman), prone to long bouts of depression and debilitating fear, later a college dropout (nearly a high school dropout). He falls in love with a girl at his high school—the minister's daughter—who dies suddenly at the age of sixteen, plunging him into a severe depression, lasting through his senior year and into college, which he comes out of only when he meets his wife-to-be, Lois, who is five years his senior. Back at college he is flunking calculus, submerges himself in it till he can outargue the professor (but he's still flunking), enlists to avoid flunking out (or, in his word, "nongraduation," ibid.:37). He's commissioned into the Artillery in summer 1917, short of his twenty-first birthday, and "every third party" (which may have been just about every third day) he would "manage to pass out" (ibid.:44). He married Lois (in January 1918 at the Swedenborgian Church in Brooklyn), got through the war, and was unemployed.

He worked for the New York Central as a bookkeeper in the insurance office—and was fired. He worked "on one of the New York Central piers, driving spikes in planks" (ibid.:56)—and quit rather than join the union. He tested for a job at the Edison Laboratories at East Orange—and heard nothing. He went to work for the U.S. Fidelity & Guaranty Co. as a criminal investigator of defaults, studying law at night at the Brooklyn Law School. Then he was informed he'd passed the Edison test and "the old boy" wanted to hire him to do research with acoustics—and he turned it down. He says he graduated from the Brooklyn Law School—but was too drunk to pick up his diploma. And then he got a bright idea. He would travel around the country (with Lois, on a motorcycle) to find out what companies were good buys on the Stock Exchange—a kind of industrial detective work (or, as a less accommodating viewer might have said in later days, industrial espionage). He had the support of a friend, Frank Shaw, at J. K. Rice, and he had a motorcycle—and he and Lois began two years of travels in 1925, going on their first trip from Vermont (where his maternal grandfather had just died) to the General Electric plant at Schenectady. Lois wrote the trips up afterward, under the title *Diary of Two Motorcycle Hobos* (but not long enough afterward to be entirely honest about Bill's drinking, though in her final notes added after his death she did touch on the matter).

He had a gift for talking to people to find out what they were doing, a "stick-to-it-iveness" that was tied in with his single-minded pursuit of whatever interested him. He had, as we have said, a certain mechanical ingenuity, and it was important to him that he could make things work (particularly things that others could not make work), as well as that he could see things others could not. In a way, Bill W.'s trips around the country in 1925–27 (mostly on the motorcycle), talking to workers (and executives), finding out what made things tick, were the forerunner of the kind of investment research that became popular in the 1950s and 1960s. This is not, perhaps, the place to go very far into Bill's views on investment strategy, but it is interesting that he came down pretty much on the knife edge between the old New England view that a stock was a share of a business, bought for its intrinsic value based on future dividend flow, and the New York view that a stock was a piece of paper bought and sold for capital gains (or, less kindly, speculation). In 1929 he had virtually cornered the market on Penick & Ford (a pretty good stock, actually), but a corner on the Crash wasn't a good place to be, and he limped north to Montreal to rebuild his fortunes—and drank away his chances again. Back to New York in 1930, living with Lois's parents in Brooklyn Heights, drinking again, finding and losing a job with Stanley Statistics, haunting brokers' offices, living on Lois's job at Macy's—and drinking a bottle of gin a day. Then brief sobriety, ended by a rationalization that he had never tasted Jersey Lightning (ibid.:91–93)—and then it was "a tearful parting with Lois in the morning and at it again for the day. Two and three bottles of gin had become a routine" (ibid.:96).

BILL W. AND THE BEGINNINGS OF A.A.

It was at this point in his life that a "Wall Street friend" sent him to a Christian Science practitioner who gave him a copy of Mary Baker Eddy's *Science and Health With Key to the Scriptures* (authorized edition [1875] 1915 et seqq.). "My desperation was so great by now that I used to lie on my stomach in the sun in front of our camping place reading and rereading. Always, I used to say to myself, 'Yes, this would work if I could only believe it. But I can't believe'" (Bill W. 2000:97). This must have been around 1932. And then,

> at length my condition became so frightful that I began to be a regular visitor at Towns Hospital, 293 Central Park West. My visits there began, I think, in the fall of 1933, and though the pledge was pretty expensive, my brother-in-law came to the rescue, aided at the last by my mother, who was then told what the score was. (ibid.:104)

Then, in and out of Towns, under the care of Dr. Silkworth, and it may be useful to look here at Bill's descriptions of Charlie Towns and of William Duncan Silkworth.

Charlie Towns, in Bill W.'s words,

> was one of those American success stories. He had been a poor Georgia farm boy and later, banging around the world, his travels had taken him to China, where he'd seen belladonna applied to opium addicts [as we will discover, this may be "remembering with advantages"]. Later, he and the celebrated Dr. Lambert, expert on alcoholism [meaning our Alcoholism(1)] and the heart conditions that go with it, had founded the Charles B. Towns Hospital.

They began to use belladonna and whatever other stuff. They called it the Lambert Treatment for Alcoholism and Dope Addiction. Charlie stood about six-one, perfectly proportioned and, even in advanced years, was a physical prodigy. He radiated an animal vitality that hit people like a ton of bricks. . . . He was a great believer in gymnastics, spending about two hours a day at the New York Athletic Club himself. . . . Well, the subject of his lecture was this: no booze, plenty of exercise with the dumbbells, and muscle up the old willpower. Of course, anybody could stop if they really wanted to, once the poison was taken out of them by the famous Towns-Lambert treatment." (ibid.:106–7)

Obviously, Charlie Towns thought curing the symptoms of Alcoholism(1) meant curing alcoholism, though Bill W. notes that by this time, "in fairness . . . Charlie didn't talk too much about curing alcoholism. At one time their literature had used the word, but it had been dropped." And Dr. Silkworth? He was a neurologist who had

accumulated a small competence during the 1920s from private practice. In boom times a number of hospitals were built from public stock subscriptions, well watered for the most part. All of the little man's life savings went into one of these, and part of the sales talk carried the promise of a fine post for him on the staff of the hospital-to-be. His dream crashed in the tornado of 1929, and all his worldly goods were lost. In desperation he made a connection [in 1930] with Towns Hospital, where he was given the grandiose title of chief physician, or physician in chief. The pay was pitiful, something like forty dollars a week and board, I think. (ibid.)

"Silky" told Bill W. "how, seeing the miserable wreckage that floated through the place, he had resolved to try to do something about it." Even to Bill,

he admitted the great hopelessness of the situation so far as most of those afflicted went. But there were certain cases. . . . What could he do about alcoholism? . . . All those millions with this mysterious malady of *mind, emotions, and body* [my emphasis]. He'd formed, then, this theory of an allergy. Obviously there was a lessening tolerance to liquor in all these cases, and the obsession spoke to itself. It screamed on all sides. I listened to this little man, entranced. . . . This one understood. And he cared, too, in a deep special way. (ibid.:107–8)

So here we are with a confidence man playing doctor, and a doctor down on his luck whose training is in neurology playing allergist and psychologist, and a hopeless alcoholic going down for the last time. The malady is mental, emotional, and physical—not a word on the spiritual. And Bill W. has rejected the spiritual (at least, in the form of Christian Science) because he cannot believe. But, finally, the next year, in 1934, something happened. (It is interesting that the belief Bill W. eventually accepted, through the Oxford Groups, and the Christian Science belief he rejected were both proclaimed as returns to the Christian practice of the first century.) We have noted that the next part of the story is quite literally a matter of public record. In testimony before the Special Subcommittee on Alcoholism and Narcotics of the U. S. Senate Committee on Labor and Public Welfare, on July 24, 1969, Bill W. told the story in these words:

> Alcoholics Anonymous . . . had its start in the offices of one of the founders of modern psychiatry. I refer to Carl Jung, who in the early 1930s received a patient from America, a well-known businessman [Rowland H., the fifth of that name]. He had run the gamut of the cures of the time and desperately wanted to stop [drinking], and could get no help at all. He came to Dr. Jung and stayed with him about a year [note: work in the Hazard Papers at the Rhode Island Historical Society has cast some doubt on this chronology]. He came to love the great man. During this period the hidden springs of his motivation were revealed. He felt that now, with this new understanding, plus communication with this new and wonderful friend, he had really shed this strange illness of mind, body, and spirit. [Note here that "mind, body, and spirit" has replaced "mind, emotions, and body"—which is an indication of what happened to Bill W. in November and December 1934.]
>
> Leaving there, he was taken drunk, as we A.A.'s say, in a matter of a month, perhaps, and coming back, he said, "[Dr. Jung], what does all this mean?" Then [Dr. Jung] made the statement that I think led to the formation of A.A. It took a great man to make it. He said, "Rowland, up until recently I thought you might be one of those rare cases who could be aided and made to recover by the practice of my art. But like most who will pass through here, I confess that my art can do nothing for you."
>
> "What," said the patient, "Doctor, you are my port of last resort. Where shall I turn now? Is there no other recourse?"
>
> The Doctor said, "Yes, there may be. There is the off chance. I am speaking to you of the possibility of a spiritual awakening—if you like, a conversion."
>
> "Oh," said the patient, "but I am a religious man. I used to be a vestryman in the Episcopal Church. I still have faith in God, but he has little in me, I should think."
>
> Dr. Jung said, "I mean something that goes deeper than that, Rowland— not just a question of faith. I am talking about a transformation of spirit that can motivate you and set you free from this. Time after time, alcoholics have recovered by these means. The lightning strikes here and there, and no one can say why or how. All I suggest is that you expose yourself to some religious environment of your own choice."
>
> The patient went to England. He became associated with the group of that day in later years called Moral Re-Armament, and to his great surprise he began to feel released from this hideous compulsion. He returned to

America. He had a place in Vermont. There he ran into a friend of mine, a friend about to be committed, a friend we A.A.s lovingly call Ebby. Ebby, at the time a wealthy man, had just run his car through the house of a farmer, into the kitchen, pushing in the wall, and when he stopped, out stepped a horrified lady from inside, and [Ebby] said, "How about a cup of coffee?" This was the extent of his illness. . . . Rowland got hold of him, took him to New York, exposed him to the Oxford Groups, whose emphasis was upon hopelessness, in the sense [that] on one's unaided resources one could not go far. Another was on self-survey. Another was on a species of confession, and then there was restitution and belief in a Higher Power. That movement was rather evangelical, but A.A. owes it a great debt, in what to do and also in what not to do.

Then, thinking of me—and I was about at the end of my rope—my friend visited me. In the previous summer I had been at a drying-out emporium [Towns Hospital] in New York City, and there my doctor [William D. Silkworth, 1873–1951], who was to make a crucial contribution to A.A., had said to my wife, "Lois, I am afraid, my dear, that I can do nothing. I thought he might be one of those rare instances in which I could help him stay sober, but I am afraid not. He is the victim of a compulsion to drink against his will, and, as much as he desires, I don't think that compulsion can be broken; and this compulsion is coupled with what I call an allergy. It is a misnomer, but it is indicating that there is something wrong with this man physically. Therefore, the eternal dilemma has been this eternal compulsion to drink, to the point almost of lunacy, coupled with the physical allergy that guarantees insanity and death. I think you will have to lock him up."

After that treatment I came home, and a few months later, this friend appeared, sat across the kitchen table where there was a big pitcher of gin and pineapple juice. I was a solitary drinker of about two or three bottles of bathtub gin a day. The year is 1934. Enter this friend of mine whom I had known to be a very hopeless case. At once it struck me that he was in a state of release—this was not just another drunk on the wagon. Then he told me his story, how he had felt this relief—the moment he got honest with himself and adhered to their simple program, he began to feel this release—[and] how much more he had gotten through his friend, Rowland. . . . Finally, I put the question to him. I said, "Ebby, you say you don't want to drink—you are not drinking today. What does this mean?"

He said, "Well, I have got religion." I said, "Well, what brand is it?" So he revealed to me his story. I was deeply impressed, really, because here was somebody that I knew had lived in this strange world of alcoholism, where I too was a denizen. So this transmission [from Dr. Jung to Rowland to Ebby] of the fatal nature of this malady . . . struck me. I think it caused a great personal deflation and laid the ground for what was subsequently to happen.

My friend went off. I didn't see him for a few days. In no waking hour could I forget the face across the kitchen table. Yet I gagged on this concept of a Higher Power, even it its lowest denominator. So I finally decided I would go to the hospital, get detoxified. I appeared at the hospital. Dr. Silkworth began treatment. I announced I had found something new, I thought. I wanted to get sobered up. I could not have any emotional conversion. So after about three days' detoxification, I found myself falling into a terrible depression. I felt trapped. In other words, I was asking the impossible—to believe in a Higher Power, let alone cast my dependence on it, on the one side—and yet my guide to science [Dr. Silkworth] was saying, "But medically you are pretty hopeless." Out of this eventuated a very sudden spiritual awakening in which I was released from this compulsion to drink—a compulsion on my mind morning, noon, and night, for several years. I was suddenly released from it.

Mine was a rather spectacular experience. But it was . . . identical to what happens to any A.A. . . . . Their experiences are apt to take a longer time, and they are not so sensational, but we do get the transforming effect on motivation. With the experience came this thought: Why can't this be induced chain style? In other words, [if] I can identify myself with another alcoholic through this kinship of suffering, then why can't that deflate him, and perhaps he will be motivated and talk to another. I came out of the hospital, began to [work] feverishly . . . with alcoholics. We had a house full of them. I was so keyed up . . . I even thought I had a kind of divine appointment [for] all the alcoholics in the world. There was six months of complete failure. Finally, I went to Akron on a business trip to see if I could regain my fortunes. I was away from my friends. The business deal fell through. I had hardly carfare home, and all of a sudden the old desire to drink started to come back. I was frightened. Then I realized that in talking and trying to help other alcoholics, even though the cases had all been "put paid," this had a great deal to do with my staying sober. These were the elements of the process, and through a strange set of circumstances I was led to . . . the doctor in town [Akron] who was to become my partner in this thing [Dr. Bob S.]. He too, when the nature of his malady was revealed to him in medical terms, one alcoholic talking to another, achieved sobriety that he had long since thought impossible.

Shortly after that, in one of the Akron hospitals, number three got sober, and an A.A. group, the first one really, came into existence in June 1935 in Akron, Ohio. Then there was a return to New York, and a group started there. A few people in from Cleveland began to come to the group meetings in Akron. We grew very, very slowly, trial and error all along the line. If it seemed to work, "get with it!" If it failed, "discard it!" That was our practice until about four years later, [when,] after hundreds of failures, we found that we had a hundred people sober. At that time, having retired from the Oxford Groups, and yet having no name actually, we just called ourselves a nameless bunch of drunks trying to help each other get well. At that time we began to think in terms of a book, which, supported by case histories, would portray our approach. The book is called *Alcoholics Anonymous,* and it was published when we had a hundred members. Up to this time [1939], we had been virtually a secret society. Then we realized we would have to be publicized. We were very reluctant about this—what kind of people would come in?

We were publicized first by *Liberty* magazine, and flooded by 6700 inquiries into a post office box in New York. [This seems to represent an error in the transcript, as most accounts suggest the *Liberty* article led to 800 inquiries, and the later *Saturday Evening Post* article to the 6700.] We gave these inquiries to a few of our traveling people out of the small, established groups. Then came an experience in mass production of sobriety that I think is most relevant to any presentation here. Up until the fall of 1939, five years after I had sobered up, we had thought that the presentation of our case to other alcoholics was up to the founding fathers or the elder hierarchy or [whatever you call them]. We thought it was to be a very slow business indeed. The idea of a mass revival was very far from our minds. The Cleveland *Plain-Dealer* decided to publish a series of articles about us. There was a chap doing the articles who was himself an alcoholic. The poor devil never recovered, but he could talk our language. These articles were placed in a box on the editorial page every three or four days, and a supporting editorial was written. Then our friends of the press and the communications media began this benign process of bringing us customers. At this time the group in Cleveland numbered only about twenty people. They were suddenly confronted with hundreds of frantic telephone calls to hospitals, and people with or without money—people who were hospitalized this week next week were going with an older member to see somebody in the hospital. The thing pyramided so that in the succeeding year of 1940, these twenty had pyramided themselves into what turned out to be several hundred sound recoveries. (Bill. W. 1969)

This seems to be the last time Bill W. told this part of his story of the beginnings of Alcoholics Anonymous. It does not differ much from the story as he told it in a letter to Jung in 1961, though in that letter he goes on to mention the influence of William James in his *The Varieties of Religious Experience*:

Clear once more of alcohol [after the sojourn at Towns Hospital] I found myself terribly depressed. This was caused by my inability to gain the slightest faith. Edwin T. ["Ebby"] again visited me and repeated the simple Oxford Groups' formulas. Soon after he left me I became even more depressed. In utter despair, I cried out, "If there is a God, will He show himself?" There immediately came to me an illumination of enormous impact and dimension, something which I have tried to describe in the book *Alcoholics Anonymous*, and also in *A.A. Comes of Age*. . . . My release from the alcohol obsession was immediate. At once I knew I was a free man. Shortly following my experience, my friend Edwin came to the hospital, bringing me a copy of William James's *The Varieties of Religious Experience*. This book gave me the realization that most conversion experiences, whatever their variety, do have a common denominator of ego collapse at depth. (quoted in Leach and Norris, 1977:454)

SOME OTHER "FOUNDERS"

Neither the testimony nor the letter goes on to describe the dinner meeting set up by John D. Rockefeller, Jr., at the Union League Club on February 8,

1940, nor does either of them mention the *Saturday Evening Post* article by Jack Alexander in March 1941. To fill out the story a little, we can look at what Bill W. wrote in *A.A. Comes of Age* (1958, from internal evidence largely written before 1955). It begins with Dr. A. Wiese Hammer (and Dr. Dudley Saul) of Philadelphia, where an A.A. group had been established in late February and early March 1940, by Jim B. and Fitz M. (both of whom we will meet later on), with Bill W. in attendance at the first meeting. Dr. Hammer,

> already champion of A.A. in Philadelphia, had drawn our fellowship to the attention of Curtis Bok, one of the owners of the *Saturday Evening Post.* At first the editorial board of the *Post* was dubious. But Mr. Bok had seen some of our Philadelphia members and had heard about their recovery at first hand; he knew whereof he spoke. And the next thing we knew, Mr. Jack Alexander, a star feature writer for the *Post*, appeared at our Vesey Street office. Knowing the circulation and prestige of the *Saturday Evening Post*, we were thrown into great excitement. (1958:190–91)

(Jim B. later took some of the credit for getting coverage by the *Post*. I believe that a study currently in progress under the auspices of the Southeastern Pennsylvania Intergroup Association of A.A. is looking further into this.)

Bill goes on to say that Jack was

> an excellent reporter, and he by no means went overboard at once. The smell and taste of the Jersey rackets which he had just been investigating were still fresh to him. Seeing this, we gave him the most exhaustive briefing on Alcoholics Anonymous any writer has ever had. First he met our Trustees and New York people, and then we towed him all over the country. . . . The article appeared in the March 1, 1941, issue. Jack's extensive investigation and his remarkable capacity for sympathy and rapport with us produced a piece which had immense impact. (ibid.)

It was not the first, or second, or even third press report on Alcoholics Anonymous. The first was Morris Markey's piece in *Liberty* magazine, "Alcoholics and God" (1939). The second was the series of articles in the *Cleveland Plain-Dealer* (Davis 1939). The third (in 1940) was an article on Cleveland Indians catcher Rollie H. in *The Sporting News*. But it was the *Saturday Evening Post* article that really brought A.A. to national public attention, though I have been informed that, as late as 1947, there were still alcoholics finding A.A. through the article in *The Sporting News*.

With this, most of the players in the starting lineup are on the scorecard: Jung, Rowland H., Ebby T., Bill W. and his cofounder Dr. Bob S., Charlie Towns, Dr. Silkworth, Sam Shoemaker, John D. Rockefeller, Jr. (We will see shortly why John D. and some of his advisors should be considered part of the starting lineup.) Also, Fulton Oursler (the editor of *Liberty*), Willard Richardson (who was Rockefeller's advisor through whom Bill W. made his approach), a couple of other Oxford Group alcoholics, Shep C. and Cebra G.—and then, coming into the game in the early innings, we will find a number of the original "one hundred men and women" referred to in the subtitle of the first edition of A.A.'s "Big Book" (*Alcoholics Anonymous: The Story of How More Than One Hundred Men and Women Have Recovered from Alcoholism*). But there is one other man, not an alcoholic, who was closely connected to Alcoholics Anonymous, whose influence was great, and who is in fact largely responsible for the initial attention paid to the idea that alcoholism was a disease of the body, as well as of the mind (as the psychiatrists and psychologists tell us) and the spirit (as the Oxford Group believed). And not only a disease of the body, but both a progressive deterioration (a morbid condition), which we may call Alcoholism(1), and a precondition such that morbidity was likely to develop, which we may call Alcoholism(2). The man's name was Elvin Morton ("Bunky") Jellinek. (I am told the nickname means "little radish" in Hungarian, and was the "baby name" given Jellinek by his father.)

JELLINEK, SCIENCE AND SOCIETY, AND
PARADIGM SHIFT

The order in which Bill W. gives the three areas of the disease—mind, body, and spirit—is revealing. It is evident from his discussion of alcoholism as a disease (noted more fully at the end of this chapter), as well as from his locating the start of Alcoholics Anonymous in Jung's office, that when he discussed the medical problems of alcoholism, he was chiefly concerned with the medicine of the mind. The body, as it were, came after. Now there are those who believe that the body, including the brain, intersects in the mind with the spiritual world, however defined: they will of course argue that mental illness is precisely an intersection of physical and spiritual disease (or dis-ease), and reflects both. Though this may not be precisely the way I would put it by choice, it is at least pretty much consistent with Bill W.'s formulation in general, and ours here. We are arguing in this book (at least as the basis for a scientific research program) that there is a heritable precondition we call Alcoholism(2), the inborn tendency toward alcoholic drinking derived from the fact that those who have it react differently to alcohol from those who don't. We are arguing that this is distinct from Alcoholism(1)—chronic alcoholic drinking and its effects—and that this Alcoholism(2) is linked with both conditions of mental illness and conditions of what may be defined as spiritual disease. We are arguing precisely that alcoholism is indeed a "strange illness of mind, body, and spirit"—all three. In the early days of A.A., there seems to have been a tendency not to use the word *disease,* at least, not without qualifications. We will follow Bill W. and speak of illness.

In fact, the original "disease concept of alcoholism" seems to have been developed by Jellinek and others and pioneered by the National Council on Alcoholism from its founding in 1944 as the National Council for Education on Alcoholism. It included four elements:

(1) Alcoholism is a disease.
(2) Alcoholics gradually develop "loss of control" over drinking, so that once they begin drinking, they may be unable to stop.
(3) Alcoholism is a permanent and irreversible condition, so that alcoholics can never drink safely.
(4) Alcoholism is a progressive disease which, if untreated, can lead to insanity or death.

It is worth looking at the background for Jellinek's ideas. In the course of our look, we should come to see why John D. Rockefeller, Jr., and his associates should be considered as players here from the start. For what follows I am greatly indebted to the work of Richard Roizen, in his dissertation (1991) and a later paper (1993).

Briefly, Roizen suggests that the shift from a temperance paradigm to an alcoholism paradigm in the years immediately after repeal of Prohibition (1933) came from the continuing "wet/dry" debate that characterized the half-dozen years after repeal. In Roizen's view (and we see nothing to contradict it), the temperance paradigm for alcohol paralleled society's view of heroin use—that is, as no real distinction is made between addict and user, and concentration is on the substance not on the person using it, so the concentration was on alcohol and not on the alcoholic or on alcoholism. The "dry" view was that alcohol was an addictive and brutalizing poison unfit for human consumption; the "wet" view was that Prohibition created social problems worse than the problems it was designed to solve, and that citizens (of proper age and under proper circumstances) should have the personal liberty to drink if they wished. (Some may see a link here to present disagreements on "the war on drugs.")

Of course, in the very early days of the Temperance movement, *temperance* meant *moderation*—its classical meaning. Some observers (and notably Milton Maxwell [1950]) believe what we may call the abstinence model of temperance owes its rise to the Washington Temperance Society (Washingtonians) in the 1840s, though it had begun with Lyman Beecher's famous *Six Sermons* in 1825 (in which he defined intemperance not merely as drunkenness but as the daily use of ardent spirits). The *Six Sermons* were followed by the founding of the American Society for the Promotion of

Temperance (American Temperance Society) in 1826; and in 1836 the American Temperance Society was merged into the American Temperance Union, which took its stand for "total abstinence from all that can intoxicate" (quoted in Maxwell 1950:411). But it was not until the tremendous success of the Washingtonians in the very early 1840s that the goal of total abstinence became fixed (apparently for all time) as the goal striven for within the Temperance paradigm.

The Washingtonian movement has become part of the literature and folklore of Alcoholics Anonymous—a point we shall discuss in our consideration of the Twelve Traditions of A.A.—but its importance here is that it pretty much fixed the Temperance paradigm in place, so that the concentration was on alcohol, not alcoholism. Indeed, there was not yet a word for what we call alcoholism in either sense. The terms used by the American Temperance Union include "inebriates," "sots," "tipplers," "common tipplers," "tipplers in a fair way to become sots," "hard drinkers often drunken," "confirmed drinkers," "drunkards," "common drunkards," "confirmed drunkards"—which (though confused) suggest some concentration on the drinker as well as on the drink—but when "inebriate" and "inebriety" were eventually adopted as "scientific" (or "medical") terms, the concentration was firmly on the drink (Maxwell 1950:427ff.).

With repeal, Roizen argues (if not before), the paradigm shifted. Partly, the shift came from the obvious failure of Prohibition. Probably it came about also as a byproduct of a new attitude to medicine and science, as we shall see. (After all, it was at about this time that there began to be drugs that actually appeared to *cure* diseases, or at least stop their progress.) For our most immediate purposes here, the most significant point Roizen makes is this:

> One of the remarkable consistencies of the story of alcohol in the post-Repeal period is that nearly every new initiative we will examine . . . sought first to get funding from the Rockefeller establishment. And although none would succeed in achieving anything more than very modest support, the Rockefeller establishment provided an important target that, in turn, helped define how new proposals should be shaped. (1991:Chapter III, p. 1)

(The exception may in fact be Alcoholics Anonymous.) The ellipsis in the quotation covers Roizen's representative list of initiatives seeking Rockefeller funding—Everett Colby's Council for Moderation (1934–36), the Sponsoring Committee of the National Conference on Alcohol (SCNCA, 1937, and affiliated with the American Association for the Advancement of Science from December 1937), and the Research Council on the Problems of Alcohol (RCPA, also established in 1937, but begun in 1936, into which the SCNCA was folded, and which died in 1949).

The RCPA featured the work of Norman Jolliffe, chief of Medical Services of Bellevue Hospital's Psychiatric Division; one of its board members was Howard W. Haggard of Yale; and it was instrumental in establishing the *Quarterly Journal of Studies on Alcohol*. Jolliffe had, inter alia, a strong interest in a possible link between vitamin B deficiencies and alcohol-related pathologies. From 1938 until his death in 1959, Haggard was director of Yale's Laboratory of Applied Physiology (LAP), founded in 1920 by Yandell Henderson, who retired as director in 1938. The LAP's Section on Studies of Alcohol became the Yale Center of Alcohol Studies. This brief history may be compared to Bill W.'s version of these events:

I well remember Dr. H. W. Haggard of the Yale University faculty. In 1930, four years before I sobered up, this good physician was wondering what ailed drunks. He wanted to begin research—mostly a test tube project at the beginning to see what their chemistry was all about. This so amused some of his colleagues that no funds were forthcoming from the Yale treasury. But Dr. Haggard was a man with a mission. He put his hands in his own pockets and begged personal friends to do the same. His project launched, he and an associate, Dr. Henderson, began work. Later, in 1937, the renowned physiologist Dr. Anton Carlson and a group of interested scientists formed a subsidiary body called the Research Council on Problems of Alcohol. This was to be a more inclusive effort. Some of us early New York AAs went to their meetings—sometimes to cheer, and sometimes, I must confess, to jeer. (AA, you see, then thought it had a monopoly on the drunk-fixing business!)

Presently the Research Council took on a live wire, Dr. E. M. ["Bunky"] Jellinek. He wasn't an M.D., but he was a "doctor" of pretty much everything else. Learning all about drunks was just a matter of catching up on his back reading. Though a prodigy of learning, he was nevertheless mighty popular with us alcoholics. We called him a "dry alcoholic" because he could identify with us so well. . . . At length Bunky and Dr. Haggard joined forces and began in 1940 to publish the *Quarterly Journal of Studies on Alcohol,* which devoted itself to articles covering the total field of alcohol research and inquiry. . . . In 1943, Dr. Haggard and Bunky organized the Yale School for Alcohol Studies. It was seen that a laboratory and technical journal couldn't get far unless a wider audience was found. . . . A strangely assorted crowd turned up at the early sessions. I well remember the venerable Mr. Colvin, he who used to run on the Prohibition ticket for the U. S. presidency. At the other pole of violent opinion were certain representatives of the liquor industry. Sandwiched in between these were a sprinkling of clergymen, social workers, judges, cops, probation officers, educators, and a certain number of us drunks. Everybody had his own axe to grind. . . . It was out of this unpromising miscellany that Drs. Haggard and Jellinek had to bring order. . . . Bunky finally showed us that we had to face the actual facts together and be friendly about it besides. His was a stroke of diplomacy; it was perhaps the first beginning of a comprehensive and statesmanlike approach to the problem of alcohol in America. ([1957–58] 1989:187–89)

Note that the Council on Moderation, the SCNCA, the RCPA, the LAP, and the Yale Center—and indeed the *Quarterly Journal*—were all concerned, at least initially, with the older paradigm. When the RCPA received a Carnegie grant of $25,000 in May 1939, Jolliffe recruited Bunky Jellinek from the Worcester State Hospital in Massachusetts, where he was involved (as a "biometrician") with neuroendocrine research. Haggard offered to provide Jolliffe and the RCPA with the new journal, the *Quarterly Journal of Studies on Alcohol*. His motivation is obscure (though it may have been related to his participation in the Science & Society movement, centered in the American Association for the Advancement of Science, AAAS), but the Carnegie research provided the *Quarterly Journal* with a number of its early articles, and the Carnegie research provided Haggard with a coauthor, Jellinek, for his nontechnical book, *Alcohol Explored* (1942), as part of an AAAS series of popular monographs. Jellinek himself devoted major time and effort to evaluating what science could do in relation to alcohol problems. Haggard established the Yale Summer School of Alcohol Studies in 1943. And both Jellinek and Haggard faced the question—and, as Bill W. makes clear, got everyone else to face the question—What can science do to help us understand alcohol problems? (Note again that this was, in essence, part of the Science & Society movement.)

In essence, Jellinek's answer was that the problem of alcohol is really a series of complexly interrelated problems, and that science will help us understand their complexity and in some cases may help us find answers. Most important for our purposes, Jellinek believed the principal case where science might help was the problem of alcoholism. It may be remarked that one of the very early scientific products of the Yale program on alcohol studies was Anne Roe's 1945 study touching on alcoholic heredity, "Children of Alcoholic Parents Raised in Foster Homes." It may reasonably be said that Jellinek was part of the Science & Society movement in the 1930s and 1940s, seeking to find places where science could aid society—and if the problems of *alcohol* were too difficult and complex to disentangle, the problems of *alcoholism* (though still complex) seemed a promising candidate as a venue where this help might be provided. So, gradually, Jellinek looked less to alcohol and more to alcoholism as his field of study. But, as he realized (and indeed preached), if alcoholism is to be treated *scientifically* (in any usual sense of that word), it must in some sense be a disease. Remember (as we noted above) that we were just then, in the period 1938–44, at that watershed between the old days of medicine when the doctor's task was "diagnosis, prognosis, and a good bedside manner" and the present days of "miracle" drugs and "modern" medical care. Remember also that Silkworth took his medical degree before the turn of the century.

MEDICAL DEFINITIONS OF ALCOHOLISM

Although Jellinek is (properly) given credit for the disease concept of alcoholism, even though that concept may be misunderstood, he was not a medical doctor, and before his work there already existed a discussion of alcoholism as a medical phenomenon, by William Silkworth: "We believe . . . that the action of alcohol on these chronic alcoholics is a manifestation of an allergy . . . and unless [the alcoholic] can experience an entire psychic change there is very little hope of his recovery" (1939, 1955, 1976, 2001: "The Doctor's Preface"). He did not discuss the question whether the disease was progressive, but if the disease was an allergy, as A.A. members suggested in the "Big Book" and subsequently (and was indeed suggested as early as 1896), then it would arguably not be a progressive disease—unless we get into the question of defining threshold levels of sensitivity to alcohol as an "allergen." And then, even so, alcoholism as allergy could be progressive only if alcoholism goes against the pattern of most allergies, which decline over time. Symptoms, of course, could show progression, and so could their physical effects. But all this needs much more examination: what we talk about below is the value of looking at alcoholism as an overreaction of the immune system, which is what an allergy generally is thought to be.

It is only fair to note the comment by Leach and Norris that "the notion of alcoholism as an allergy had been set forth before, as early as 1896 (see Jellinek 1960), and was later published by Silkworth. Although it has been discredited scientifically, it continues to be used by A.A. members and by psychiatrists as an elucidating analogue, and 'probably is as good as or better than anything else for their purposes' (Jellinek 1960)" (1977:454, note). We will see a little later on that "discredited scientifically" may be an oversimplification, indeed an overstatement, and that in fact there are strong parallels between allergy and alcoholism, as hereditary preconditions—if we look at recent research on the nature of allergy.

The current medical definition of alcoholism, as approved by the Board of Directors of the National Council on Alcoholism and Drug Dependence, Inc. (NCADD), on February 3, 1990, and by the Board of Directors of the American Society of Addiction Medicine (ASAM, affiliated with the AMA) on February 25, 1990, is as follows:

> Alcoholism is a primary chronic disease with genetic, psycho-social, and environmental factors influencing its development and manifestations. The disease is often progressive and fatal. It is characterized by continuous or periodic impaired control over drinking, preoccupation with . . . alcohol, use of alcohol despite adverse consequences, and distortions in thinking, most notably denial. (quoted from "Facts and Information," www.ncadd.org)

The ellipsis signifies the omission of the words "the drug," which add nothing to the definition, in our view, except a tendentious affirmation of alcohol's status as a drug (like "other drugs"). We will consider this matter later, but for the moment, we note that the definition goes on to define the terms it uses.

By "primary" is meant that alcoholism is a disease entity separate from other pathophysiological states that may be associated with it, and is *not* a symptom of some other underlying disease state. By "disease" is meant an involuntary disability, which is the sum of the abnormal phenomena displayed by a group of individuals, by which they differ from the norm, and which places them at a disadvantage in relation to the norm. By "often progressive and fatal" is meant that the disease persists over time, and that physical, emotional, and social changes are often cumulative: also, the disease of alcoholism "causes premature death through overdose, organic complications involving the brain, liver, heart, and many other organs, and by contributing to suicide, homicide, motor-vehicle crashes, and other traumatic events"(NCADD "Definition of the Problem," n.d.) Note that the "progressivity" of the disease is here manifested by the progressive cumulative *results* of the alcoholism, not by changes in any disease or allergic/ allergenic threshold: Jellinek, however, seems to have believed there were such changes, as is evidenced by the Jellinek curve (see, most recently, *AA Grapevine*, November 2003). Note also that this, except for the "progressivity," is pretty much what we may call Alcoholism(2). But the progressivity is very clearly a part of Alcoholism(1), not so much of Alcoholism(2), unless perhaps we are referring to some kind of process of potentiation over time.

Or to the kind of "progressivity" that occurs when an alcoholic returns to drinking after a period of abstinence and finds his (or her) craving, reaction, behavior—entire condition—worse than it was at the time he (or she) stopped: part of this might be a "progressivity" in Alcoholism(2).

By "impaired control" is meant an inability to limit alcohol use, indicating excessive focused attention given to alcohol, its effects, and its use. By "adverse consequences" are meant alcohol-related problems or impairments in physical health, psychological functioning, interpersonal functioning, occupational functioning, and legal, financial, and spiritual problems. By "denial" is meant a range of psychological maneuvers designed to reduce the individual's awareness that alcohol is a cause of problems rather than their solution: the word is not used in the limited psychoanalytic sense of a single psychological defense mechanism disavowing the significance of particular events. To this 1990 definition may be added the 1971 statement by the House of Delegates of the American Medical Association:

> The American Medical Association identifies alcoholism as a complex disease with biological, psychological and sociological components, and recog-

nizes medicine's responsibility in behalf of affected persons. The Association recognizes that there are multiple forms of alcoholism [Jellinek's?], and that each patient should be evaluated and treated in an individualized and comprehensive manner. (quoted in Bill W., no date:22)

We will look a little later on at some of the physical characteristics that may help define the disease of alcoholism. In the meantime, we should consider a clue (however scientifically discredited) given us by the "Big Book"—that alcoholism may be looked at as an allergy. Allergies are generally understood as involving an adverse physical reaction of those suffering from the allergy to substances that are not toxic per se and are innocuous to other people: they are supposed to be the result of the immune system's overreaction to just about any normally innocuous foreign substance. Leaving aside for the moment the question whether alcohol falls into the category of a normally innocuous foreign substance, we can perhaps look at a possible truth behind the idea of alcoholism as an allergy by considering recent work on allergic reactions to drugs and biologic agents. It is true that we have suggested that alcohol should not be included with drugs in the AOD ("alcohol and other drugs") classification, (1) because this seems to beg the question whether alcoholics are addicts—a question that is likely to generate more heat than light—and (2) in line with our suggestion that the alcoholism may lie in the genotype and "other drug" usage in the phenotype. But on the question of allergy, we are looking not at drugs as understood by A.A. (or N.A.), but at chemical entities (CEs), and alcohol is clearly a CE. Allergic reactions are hypersensitive reactions, and allergy to CEs can produce skin reactions (including flushing), respiratory symptoms, organ dysfunction, and severe shock. In a nutshell, what we are talking about when we talk about allergy is improper (or at the very least "group-idiosyncratic") reaction of the immune system.

Among the prescribed CEs or BEs (biological entities) that have produced allergic reactions in patients are oral hypoglycemic agents (related to blood sugar contents), anticonvulsants, general anesthetics, enzymes (including chymopapain, asperaginase, and streptokinase), neuroleptics, Methyldopa (related to neurotransmission), Procainimide, antihistamines (related to ephedrine and epinephrine), and ACE inhibitors. Generally, children of parents allergic to certain CEs have a fifteen-fold greater relative risk for allergic reactions to those CEs than children without such histories. The reactions to hypoglycemic agents and insulin (also related to blood sugar levels), to anesthetics, enzymes, neuroleptics, Methyldopa, Procainimide, and antihistamines (which treat allergy symptoms and have some connections with norepinephrine), and to ACE inhibitors (including P substance inhibitors) would seem to be at least tangentially relevant to the question of "allergic" reactions to alcohol.

One difficulty in talking about alcoholism as a disease is precisely the question raised by Jellinek when he defines alcoholism as (1) a permanent and irreversible condition, so that alcoholics can never drink safely; and (2) as a progressive disease which, if untreated, can lead to insanity or death. Which one is the disease condition—the fact of being unable to drink safely [Alcoholism(2)], or the fact of irreversible damage from drinking and the progressivity of the disease [Alcoholism(1)]? The trench-coated bum with a bottle in a paper bag, sleeping under the railroad viaduct, may have both conditions, but this book is primarily about Alcoholism(2), the permanent condition of being unable to take a drink "like 'normal' people," or at least the preconditions—and treatment for the preconditions—for this disease condition. And, for that matter, treatment for the disease condition—though there is of course a question of whether they can be separated and, if so, which is being treated.

A word on the history of the words *alcoholic* and *alcoholism* may be in order here. In fact, in most of the nineteenth century, at least in English, there was no discussion of alcoholism, because there was no such word as "alcoholism." Before there could be *alcoholism*, there had to be such a person as an *alcoholic*, and, as we have noted below, the first use of the word *alcoholic* (in English) reported in the *Oxford English Dictionary* is in the phrase "chronic alcoholic" in an 1891 article published in the *Quarterly Journal of Inebriety*. Moreover, we should note that the next two uses (1907 and 1909) occur after the publication in 1903 of one of A.A.'s founding documents, *The Varieties of Religious Experience*, by the philosopher and psychologist William James. As we have also noted below, the *OED* gives credit for popularizing the word *alcoholic* to *Alcoholics Anonymous*, the "Big Book" of A.A. (1939). (But perhaps the credit should be given to the first popular literature to use the word—Jack London's *John Barleycorn* in 1913, serialized in the *Saturday Evening Post* in 1911–12.)

Before the word *alcoholic* was invented, *inebriety* was used with a variety of meanings, including what we now mean by *alcoholism*, and *inebriate* was used with a variety of meanings, including what we now mean by *alcoholic*. Accordingly, any discussion of alcoholism in the nineteenth century or before will be a discussion of inebriety or even drunkenness, meaning largely what we may call Alcoholism(1)—and that pretty much holds up to the time of the First World War (1914–18), or at least of *John Barleycorn* (London 1913). This had the natural effect of concentrating public attention not on the preconditions but on the outcomes—the irreversible damage. Also, it meant that alcoholism would be—and was—largely considered a disease of the will, through neglecting (or not knowing about) our Alcoholism(2).

A DISEASE OF THE SOUL?

It may be noted that the phrase "chronic alcoholic" occurs much earlier in German, in the phrase "alcoholismus chronicus" in 1852, and Marty Mann

(1951) traced it to a Swede (writing in German), Magnus Hoff, in 1848. The definition makes it clear that what is meant by "chronic alcoholism" is prolonged Alcoholism(1), the degenerated condition of the body after years of drinking—the condition of the chronic inebriate if you like, the American Temperance Union's "sots" or "confirmed drunkards." The "disease concept of alcoholism" seems to refer to both Alcoholism(1) and Alcoholism(2). But what is sometimes overlooked in discussions of the disease concept of alcoholism as expressed (if it is) in the literature of Alcoholics Anonymous is that A.A. had some of its origins in the Oxford Groups of the Rev. Frank Buchman, and that the Oxford Groups picked up an ancient Christian view we might call the disease concept of sin. If we go back to the first century—which is what Frank Buchman and his First-Century Christians (Oxford Groups) tried to do—we may note the statement of St. John's (and Polycarp's) friend Ignatius (Theophoros), that the *mysterion* (the sacrament) is *pharmaokon athanasias*, the medicine of immortality.

This is one of the first examples I have found (albeit an implied example) of the consideration of sin as illness, which is a part of the original Oxford Group disease concept of sin—or of alcoholism. The people who came into the Oxford Groups, or (to take its earlier name) the First Century Christian Fellowship, were seeking salvation. Those who came into A.A. were seeking sobriety. This book suggests that the search for sobriety may be considered—more baldly, is indeed—a model of the search for salvation—but this book is written in the year 2004, and we are talking about the years 1935–39. However, there is strong indication that Sam Shoemaker, at least, came to think of the alcoholic's struggle with alcoholism as a model for the human struggle with sin. The history of his connection with Alcoholics Anonymous is given in part in Dick B.'s *New Light on Alcoholism: The A.A. Legacy from Sam Shoemaker* (1998), and Shoemaker's own testimony is in his posthumously published "Those Twelve Steps as I Understand Them" in *The Grapevine,* January 1964 (Shoemaker [1964] 1986), "discussing what this program can mean to anyone who wrestles with a real problem" (ibid.:125).

It is widely documented that one principal problem in the early days of A.A. was the presence of agnostics or atheists who wanted to get sober, but didn't want to swallow "all this God stuff." "Official" A.A. history records (in several places) the case of Jim B. (also referred to in one place as "Ed"), who is supposed to be responsible for the insertion of "as we understood him" after the references to "God" in the Twelve Steps. (By "official" A.A. history, I mean A.A. history included in publications approved by A.A.'s General Service Conference, otherwise known as material that is "Conference approved.") We will spend at least a short time looking at Jim B. and what many have seen as a requirement that a recovering alcoholic must believe in God for A.A. to work. Obviously, Bill W. (with Dr. Bob's approval) would not have spread this step out so widely, into so many small steps [at least in part obeying the "(1) decide, then (2) do" rule], if

accepting dependence of God and requesting His guidance were not so
difficult for A.A.s in the first years.

JIM B., FITZ M., CLARENCE S.

In the story of Jim B., the principal relevant documents are his story in the
"Big Book" ("The Vicious Cycle," Bill W. et al. 1976:238–50), Bill W.'s
account of Jim B. (under the name "Ed") in *Twelve Steps and Twelve Traditions* (Bill W. 1952/53:143–45), backed by a few words in *Alcoholics Anonymous Comes of Age* (Bill W. 1958:163), and a brief article by Jim B. ([1968]
1999) in *The Grapevine*. I am told there are also tapes of talks Jim B. gave at
meetings of Alcoholics Anonymous, not only in Pennsylvania but also
later in New Mexico and California, but these I have not heard. There is
also a brief typescript "History of A.A. 1934–1941" by Jim B. (1946), a copy
of which has recently been provided to me by the archivist of A.A.'s Eastern Pennsylvania General Service Assembly Area 59. In addition, there is
a history of A.A. in Philadelphia that Jim B. wrote in 1946 (published in an
undated newsletter of the Allentown-Bethlehem-Easton Intergroup Association). Some of the typescript history is told from hearsay, since Jim B.
did not come into the fellowship of Alcoholics Anonymous until 1938, but
I believe it sheds considerable light on what was going on in New York,
just as the story of Clarence S. (noted later) sheds considerable light on
what went on in Akron and Cleveland.

First, Jim B., a traveling salesman, tells the story, how he got sober in
January 1938, made a nuisance of himself around A.A. in New York by his
taking "every opportunity to lambaste that 'spiritual angle'" ("Big Book"
1976:247) got drunk on a business trip to New England, called back to his
boss (Hank P., also in A.A.), and

> he fired me right then. This was when I really took my first good look at
> myself. My loneliness was worse than it had ever been before, for now even
> my own kind had turned against me. . . . My brilliant agnosticism vanished,
> and I saw for the first time that those who really believed, or at least honestly
> tried to find a Power greater than themselves, were much more composed
> and contented than I had ever been, and they seemed to have a degree of
> happiness which I had never known." (247–48 of the third [1976] edition)

Next, we have Bill W.'s account in his discussion of the Third Tradition
in *Twelve Steps and Twelve Traditions*:

> Ed got a sales job which took him out of town. At the end of a few days, the
> news came in. He'd sent a telegram for money, and everybody *knew* what

that meant. Then he got on the phone. In those days, we'd go anywhere on a Twelfth Step job [carrying the message], no matter how unpromising. But this time nobody stirred. "Leave him alone! Let him try it by himself for once: maybe he'll learn a lesson!" About two weeks later, Ed stole by night into an A.A. member's house, and, unknown to the family, went to bed. Daylight found the master of the house and another friend drinking their morning coffee.

A noise was heard on the stairs. To their consternation, Ed appeared.

A quizzical smile on his lips, he said, "Have you fellows had your morning meditation?" They quickly sensed he was quite in earnest. In fragments, his story came out. In a neighboring state, Ed had holed up in a cheap hotel. After all his pleas for help had been rebuffed, these words rang in his fevered mind: "They have deserted me. I have been deserted by my own kind. This is the end . . . nothing is left." As he tossed on his bed, his hand brushed the bureau near by, touching a book. It was a Gideon bible. Ed never confided any more of what he saw and felt in that hotel room. It was the year 1938. He hasn't had a drink since. ([1952/53] 1994:144–45)

But this is not all.

In an article in *The Grapevine*, Jim B. concluded in this way:

I do feel my experience was not in vain, for "God" was broadened to cover all types and creeds: "God as we understood Him." . . . For the new agnostic or atheist just coming in, I will try to give very briefly my milestones in recovery: (1) The first power I found greater than myself was John Barleycorn; (2) The AA Fellowship became my Higher Power for the first two years; (3) Gradually, I came to believe that God and Good were synonymous and were to be found in all of us; (4) And I found that by meditating and trying to tune in on my better self for guidance and answers, I became more comfortable and steady." ([1968] 1999:20–21, by permission of the *A.A. Grapevine*)

Now as historians we face a problem with our texts here: Bill W. describes a sudden conversion for Jim B., while Jim B. describes a gradual coming to terms with God and himself (reminiscent of what Bill W. wrote in the *Grapevine* in October 1948). Also, Jim B. here—as in his typescript history—claims credit for the insertion of "God as we understood him" into Steps 3 and 11, even though there is some doubt about that also: Ebby may have had it from Sam Shoemaker and Bill may have had it from both Ebby and Sam Shoemaker. (Though Jim B.'s version seems to be supported in Bill W. [1958:17]—but then, recollection might even play Bill W. false on occasion.) My reconstruction of what happened to Jim B. in his hotel room is relatively simple, though it requires taking the view that he deliberately downplayed the degree (and the suddenness) of his "conversion"—which would be in keeping with his sometimes controversial attitudes in his first ten years in A.A. I believe he opened the Gideon bible to a passage something like Luke 17:20–21, "The kingdom of God cometh not with observation: Neither shall they say, Lo here! or lo there! for behold, the kingdom of God is within you." Now it is certainly possible it might have been a passage like 1 Corinthians 3:16–17, "Know ye not that ye are the temple of God, and that the Spirit of God dwelleth in you? If any man defile the temple of God, him shall God destroy; for the temple of God is holy, which temple ye are." But whatever the passage may have been, it must fit with Jim B.'s later assertion that he came to believe God was to be found in all of us. To be sure, that's a Jungian point and he may have had that from Bill W. But it rings true to me, at least. I think one of these is the passage that "converted" Jim B.

I have gone into this at some length because the process of sobriety Jim B. is recounting is so clearly a charismatically inspired process of Jungian individuation, and the passages noted are precisely those quoted in a recent book discussing Jungian individuation and mystical Christianity—though I did not realize that until after I had picked them as the most probable passages for him to have read through Jim B.'s ([1968] 1999) *Grapevine* article (see Sanford 1996:273–78). It is not only the case that the "nonbeliever" Jung suggested sobriety must come through a spiritual awakening of the kind he called *individuation*. It is also the case that the militant agnostic who finally stayed sober, Jim B., seems to have followed A.A.'s process to that goal and with that result. It may also be the case that Jim B.'s process was very like Bill W.'s, without what Bill W. called his "white-light" experience—a flash, or flashes, of spiritual insight, kicking off the process of sobriety. Note—spiritual experience or experiences, but *not* the spiritual awakening mentioned in the Twelfth Step as *the* result of doing these steps (my emphasis—the N.A. preamble says only "a result"). Certainly, as we will discover, a kind of "white-light" experience was had by Fitz M., who brought Jim B. into the A.A. fold. Here, I believe it is time to quote from Jim B.'s "Evolution [or History] of Alcoholics Anonymous 1934–1941" (dated in his handwriting September 1947, but whether this was the date this copy was made or the original was written, I cannot say). This is quoted with the permission of the Archives of Eastern Pennsylvania General Service Area 59.

We begin with Ebby's visit to Bill, when he

greeted Bill with the words, "I've got religion." Bill says at the time he thought poor Ebby had gotten sober only to become balmy on religion. While still drinking, he listened to Ebby's story about having been converted some six months previously by the New York Oxford Group. He told Bill about the main idea of this group being one person helping another, and their other formulae. Bill said he listened to all this talk while he was in the process of keeping the jitters down by continuous drinking and probably smiling cynically to himself. When Ebby left a few hours later, he practically dismissed the incident—but he found later that this was not the case. Within five days he found himself wheeled into his old refuge, Towns Hospital, on Central Park West in New York, for the third time that year. On his arrival at the hospital with his wife Lois, he was greeted and put to bed immediately by his old friend, Dr. Silkworth, the Director.

Jim B. goes on:

Bill said that after he had been in there a short while, he heard the doctor talking to Lois by the door, saying that if her husband came out of this episode, and did drink again, he did not honestly believe he would live six months. Bill says that when he heard these words, he was immediately carried back to his talk with his friend, and could not dismiss the idea that although Ebby might be batty with religion, he *was* sober and he *was* happy. He kept turning this thing over in his mind, in a mild delirium, and came to a vague conclusion that maybe Ebby did have something in a man's helping others, in order to get away from his own obsessions and problems. A few hours later, when the doctor came in, he felt a tremendous elation and said, "Doc, I've got it!" At the same time, he felt he was on a high mountain and that a very swift wind was blowing through him, and despite the several weeks of drinking, he found he was completely relaxed and quiet. He asked Dr. Silkworth, "Am I going crazy with this sudden elation I have?" The doctor's answer was, seriously, "I don't know, Bill, but I think you better hold on to whatever you have."

While Bill was in the hospital,

Ebby and other Oxford Group people visited Bill and told him of their activities, particularly in the Calvary Mission. On Bill's release, while still shaky, he visited Dr. Shoemaker at Calvary, and made a decision to become very active in the Mission's work, and to try and bring other alcoholics from Towns to the Group. This resolution he put into effect, visiting the Mission and Towns almost daily for four or five months, and bringing some of the drunks to his home for rehabilitation.

There follows Jim B.'s recounting of the story of Bill W.'s trip to Akron, his meeting with Dr. Bob, and his sojourn in Akron until October 1, 1935.

Bill then returned to New York, where he continued his previous activities, with daily visits to Towns and Calvary Mission. During the latter part of October, Bill got his first real New York convert, Hank P. Hank later became one of the genuine inspirations of Alcoholics Anonymous, for he was a red-headed high pressure human dynamo. . . . From the time of their meeting and during the latter part of 1935, it was Hank and Bill who did all the ground work, but even they had but indifferent success until their next real convert, Paul R., came in about April 1936. (ibid.)

Then,

the next man to be pulled out of the mire, through Towns, was dear old Fitz M., who joined the others about November 1936. From this time on, the duet became a trio, Bill, Hank, and Fitz, and they were the spearheads in "drunk saving" for the Oxford Group in the New York area. However, they discovered, in September 1937, that despite all the wet-nursing, praying, and rehabilitation work done at Bill's house on Clinton Street, of approximately thirty-five or forty drunks, they were the only three men to come clear in almost two years. . . . In September 1937 the three concluded that perhaps their technique would be better if they would do their work with drunks outside of an affiliation with a religious organization. Having arrived at this decision, the trio formally resigned from the Oxford Group and concentrated all their efforts on working with alcoholics in Towns Hospital, using Bill's home as a de-fogging station. About this time the first completely alcoholic meeting were held in Bill's home on Tuesday evenings. Average attendance was about fifteen, including the drunks' families. Even though the trio had separated from the Oxford Group, they still retained a lot of their principles and utilized them in their discussions at these weekly meetings—but at the same time, more emphasis was placed on the disease of alcoholism as a psychological sickness. At the same time, they stressed spiritual regeneration and the understanding of one alcoholic for another. (ibid.)

Then Jim begins to tell the story from his own experience:

A few months after the break with the Oxford Group, the writer was brought into the New York fellowship, from Washington, by Fitz M., whom he had known since boyhood. I was enticed to New York by the existence of this new group and a small job Hank P. gave me in a little business Bill and he had gone into on the side. When I arrived in New York, I found myself thrust into this new group of three or four actively dry alcoholics, who at that time had no group name, or real creed or formula. Within the next two or three months, things really started popping. Hank, with his promotional ideas, started to push Bill into writing a formula and procedure for our Group. After many arguments and discussions, the trio finally decided a book should be written on our activities. This was in June 1938. Bill was naturally given the job of writing the book, for he was the only one who had made any real conclusive study of our problem. (ibid.)

On what was the book based?

From what I can remember, Bill's only special preparation for this was confined to the reading of four very well known books, the influence of which can clearly be seen in the A.A. book. Bill probably got most of his ideas from one of these books, namely James's *The Varieties of Religious Experience*. I have always felt this was because Bill himself had undergone such a violent spiritual experience. He also gained a fine basic insight of spirituality through Emmet Fox's *Sermon on the Mount*, and a good portion of the psychological approach of A.A. through Dick Peabody's *Common Sense of Drinking*. It is my opinion that a great deal of Bill's Traditions came from the fourth book, Lewis Browne's *This Believing World* [1929]. From this book I believe Bill attained a remarkable perception of possible future pitfalls for groups of our kind, for it clearly shows that the major failures of religions and cults in the past have been due to one of three things: too much organization, too much politics, and too much money or power.

We have already noted that Bill's copy (originally Jim B.'s wife's copy) of Peabody's book bears a notation that Peabody died drunk. Credit for a psychological approach belongs to Peabody (I would suggest), but credit for a successful psychological approach does not. One more passage from Jim B.'s history should be quoted here.

About this time [late 1938] we almost had a disaster in our still wobbly group, but it later turned out to be a god-send. Bill and Hank had distributed quite a few copies of the original manuscript to doctors, psychiatrists, and ministers, to get a last-minute reaction. One of these went to Dr. Howard, Chief Psychiatrist for the State of New Jersey. He became greatly interested and enthusiastic, but was highly critical of several things in the book, for after reading it he told us there was entirely too much "Oxfordism" and that it was too demanding. This is where the disaster nearly overtook us, for it nearly threw Bill into a terrific mental uproar to have his "baby" pulled apart by an outside "screwball" psychiatrist, who in our opinion knew nothing about alcoholism. After days of wrangling between Bill, Hank, Fitz, and myself, Bill was finally convinced that all positive and "must" statements should be eliminated, and in their place to use the word "suggest" and the phrase "we found we had to." Another thing that changed in this last rewriting was qualifying the word "God" with the phrase "as we understand him." (This was one of the writer's few contributions to the book.) In the final finishing, the fellowship angle was enlarged and emphasized.

(Jim B.'s contribution, apparently—but the idea may also have come from Sam Shoemaker, who meant by that phrase, "as much of God as we understand.")

Unfortunately, Fitz M. died (of cancer) in 1943, at the early age of forty-five, so the only account we have from him is in the first four editions of the "Big Book" of Alcoholics Anonymous. Like many of the stories in the first edition, it is somewhat overwritten, but it does contain information useful for reading Jim B.'s story. (Fitz's story is "Our Southern Friend," Bill

W. et al. 1976:497–507.) No, to say this is our only record is untrue, though it is our only record by Fitz: Bill W.'s version of the story is told in the "Big Book" (Bill W. et al. 1939, 1955, 1976, 2001:56–57 [in 1986]). Here is a part of the story as Bill tells it:

> One night, when confined in a hospital [Towns], he was approached by an alcoholic who had known a spiritual experience [one of Bill W.'s off-and-on drunks]. Our friend's gorge rose as he bitterly cried out: "If there is a God, He certainly hasn't done anything for me!" But later, alone in his room, he asked himself this question: "Is it possible that all the religious people I have known are wrong?" While pondering this answer, he felt as though he lived in hell. Then, like a thunderbolt, a great thought came. It crowded out all else: *"Who are you to say there is no God?"* (ibid.)

In Bill's telling, Fitz

> recounts that he tumbled out of bed to his knees. In a few seconds he was overwhelmed by a conviction of the presence of God. It poured over and through him with the certainty and majesty of a great tide at flood. . . . He stood in the Presence of Infinite Power and Love. He had stepped from bridge to shore. (ibid.)

And then Bill comments, "What is this but a miracle of healing? . . . Even so has God restored us all to our right minds. . . . When we drew near to Him, He disclosed Himself to us" (ibid.:57). (This is an echo of Bill W.'s favorite *Epistle General of St. James*, "Draw nigh to Him and He will draw nigh to you.") In Fitz's telling in his story four alcoholics were playing bridge in a smoke-filled room (at Towns Hospital). The other three leave the room, but one comes back. Here's the pivotal point of the story, in Fitz's words:

> He looks at me. "You think you are hopeless, don't you?" he asks.
>
> "I know it," I reply.
>
> "Well, you're not," says the man. "There are men on the streets of New York today who were worse than you, and they don't drink any more."
>
> "What are you doing here, then?" I ask.
>
> "I went out of here nine days ago, saying I was going to be honest, and I wasn't," he answers.
>
> A fanatic, I thought to myself, but I was polite. "What is it?" I enquire.
>
> Then he asks me if I believe in a power greater than myself, whether I call that power God, Allah, Confucius, Prime Cause, Divine Mind, or any other name. I told him that I believe in electricity and other forces of Nature, but

as for a God, if there is one, He has never done anything for me. Then he asks me if I am willing to right all the wrongs I have ever done to anyone, no matter how wrong I thought the others were. Am I willing to be honest with myself about myself and tell someone about myself, and am I willing to think of other people, of their needs instead of myself, in order to get rid of the drink problem?

"I'll do anything," I reply,

"Then all of your troubles are over," says the man and leaves the room. The man is in bad mental shape certainly. I pick up a book and try to read, but I cannot concentrate. I get in bed and turn out the light. But I cannot sleep. Suddenly a thought comes. Can all the worthwhile people I have known be wrong about God? Then I find myself thinking about myself, and a few things I had wanted to forget. I begin to see I am not the person I had thought myself, that I had judged myself by comparing myself to others, and always to my own advantage. It is a shock. Then comes a thought that is like a Voice, *"Who are you to say there is no God?"* It rings in my head: I can't get rid of it." (ibid.:502)

So he goes to the other man's room, and they talk some more. The other man says,

"The thing I do is to say, 'God, here I am, and here are all my troubles. I've made a mess of things and can't do anything about it. You take me, and all my troubles, and do anything you want with me.' Does that answer your question [about how to pray]?"

"Yes, it does," I answer. I return to bed. It doesn't make sense. Suddenly I feel a wave of utter hopelessness sweep over me. I am in the bottom of hell. And there a tremendous hope is born. It might be true. I tumble out of bed onto my knees. I know not what I say. But slowly a great peace comes to me. I feel lifted up. I believe in God. I crawl back into bed and sleep like a child. (ibid.)

There are pain and heartaches and desire to drink again still to come, but Fitz remains sober until his death. Here's how he sums up his experience.

I learn more of that foundation stone which is honesty. I learn that when we act upon the highest conception of honesty which is given us, our sense of honesty becomes more acute. I learn that honesty is truth, and that truth shall make us free. (ibid.)

Jim (who died sober in 1974) and Fitz (who died sober in 1943) are buried near each other in the cemetery of the church they attended when young, where Fitz's father was the minister.

One who got sober in Akron through Dr. Bob, but whose process of sobriety began in an odd way in New York and through Bill W., was a man named Clarence S. After living on the bum, homeless in New York City, where he had been dumped by his brother-in-law as the bad result of an attempt at a "geographical cure" for drinking, Clarence went back to Ohio, ran out from a meeting with Dr. Bob (being convinced Dr. Bob was a serial killer of bums), and went on the bum, homeless in Cleveland. How had he come to meet Dr. Bob in the first place? His sister-in-law in Yonkers had a doctor, L. V. Strong, whose brother-in-law was Bill W., who told him about A.A. and Dr. Bob. Clarence had held his last full-time job, with a finance company, drunk every day for three years, until he finally lost that and everything else. He was born December 26, 1902, and counted his sobriety from February 11, 1938, when he entered Akron City Hospital under the care of Dr. Bob: he was then thirty-five years old and (as he remembers it) the youngest male member of A.A.

Here is Clarence's much later recollection of his conversation with Dr. Bob on the day that Clarence was released from Akron City Hospital: Clarence asks Dr. Bob what the answer is to his drinking problem. Dr. Bob answers, "Well, young feller, we don't know about you. You're pretty young, and we haven't had any luck with these young fellows." According to Clarence, he shot back a reply, "What do I have to do to be ready? . . . I have no clothes, I have no money, I have no prospects. I have nothing. It's the middle of winter, and I'm in a strange town and you people say that I'm not ready yet." So Dr. Bob says, "Okay young feller, I'll give you the answer to this. Young feller, do you believe in God. Not *a* God, but God." Clarence answered, "Well, I guess I do." Dr. Bob responded, "There's no guessing about it. Either you do or you don't." So Clarence affirmed, "I do believe in God," and Dr. Bob believed him.

"Get down out of that bed," he said to Clarence, "You're going to pray." Clarence told the doctor, "I don't know anything about praying," to which Dr. Bob responded, "I don't suppose you do, but you get down there, and I'll pray. You can repeat it after me, and that will do for this time." They got down on their knees by the hospital bed. Clarence remembers the prayer as being something like this: "Jesus! This is Clarence. He's a drunk. Clarence! This is Jesus. Ask Him to come into your life. Ask Him to remove the drinking problem, and pray that He manage your life because you are unable to manage it yourself." They got up off their knees, and Dr. Bob told Clarence, "Young feller, you're going to be all right." And he was. He had been sober for forty-six years, one month and eleven days, when he died on March 22, 1984 (Clarence S. 1999: Chapter 3, p. 15).

But back then in 1938, it certainly didn't sound like the kind of prayer he remembered from his youth: Clarence was a Roman Catholic, and he said during his lifetime that one reason A.A. in Cleveland separated from the Oxford Groups was their process of public confession and their whole "Protestant" attitude. This is all an instructive contrast to Jim B. (and Fitz

M.) and Bill W. and the salvo, *as we understood Him*. Even if Clarence misremembered Dr. Bob's exact words, "Not *a* God, but God" is exactly in accord with everything I have been able to find out about Dr. Bob S. and the early days of A.A. in Akron. (A considerable body of work touching on this has been published by Dick B. [1998] in Hawaii.)

BILL W., PSYCHIATRY, AND MEDICINE

Quite possibly part of the difference in approach lies in the fact that Dr. Bob came to the Oxford Groups before he came into sobriety, while Bill W. became sober and then came to the Oxford Groups and the Calvary Mission. Part may lie in Bill's secondhand encounter with Jung and perhaps even a predisposition to accept psychiatry as a partner because his mother (Emily Stroebel) was a practicing Adlerian psychoanalyst (after she divorced Bill's father and left Vermont).

In the last chapter, we mentioned the broker and supersalesman Charles B. Towns, who had the "cure" for addiction that he sold to the 1908 Shanghai Opium Commission. After his fall from grace, Charlie Towns went on with the Charles B. Towns Hospital, and "as his standing in the medical world fell, his claims became more and more extravagant, and the substances he inveighed against multiplied to include tobacco, coffee, tea, bromides, marihuana, paraldehyde, etc., as well as opiates and alcohol" (Musto 1980:88). As late as 1932 he was claiming (in a little self-published book), that he "had *never had a negative result* in any case, free from disability," and in 1934 he administered the "belladonna treatment" to Bill W. David Musto likens the treatment to Benjamin Rush's "bleeding" in the late eighteenth century, and lobotomy in the early twentieth—but, though unpleasant, and possibly even "a harmful regimen within an accepted set of beliefs" (Musto 1980:89), the belladonna treatment was not generally so disastrous as bleeding or lobotomy. What may be more to our point is that Charlie Towns, though he was not a doctor (perhaps *because* he was not a doctor), continued to believe that addiction to drugs, alcohol, caffeine, or nicotine was a physical—indeed a physiological—condition.

Musto reports a possibly telling comment from Victor Heiser, Commissioner of Health in the Philippines in the first decade of the twentieth century, who had supported Towns's work there. When Musto interviewed Heiser in New York City, in March 1970, Heiser recalled that "Towns had an effective treatment of alcoholism at his hospital" (ibid.:334). One wonders whether this was the treatment before Bill W. or after, and it casts an interesting light on the attempt by Charlie Towns to get Bill W. to work for pay at the Towns Hospital as a lay therapist (recounted in *Bill W.* 1952/

53:136–38). Nevertheless, though the belladonna treatment may have been quackery, and though Charlie Towns was not above giving Towns Hospital credit for A.A.'s work, it is at least arguable that it was from Charlie Towns as much as from Silkworth's "allergy" and Bunky Jellinek's biometrics, that Bill W. gained his confidence that alcoholism was a disease of the body as well as the mind. (But that it was a spiritual disease came from Ebby and Sam Shoemaker.) We should look now at what it meant to Bill W. when he called alcoholism a disease of the body.

"A.A.," in Bill's words,

> is a synthetic concept—a synthetic gadget, as it were, drawing upon the resources of medicine, psychiatry, religion, and our own experience of drinking and recovery. You will search in vain for a single new fundamental. We have merely streamlined old and proven principles of psychiatry and religion into such forms that the alcoholic will accept them. And then we have created a society of his own kind where he can enthusiastically put these very principles to work on himself and other sufferers. (no date:25)

Then, in the same talk, a little later on, is a highly instructive comparison between what medicine tells the alcoholic and what religion tells the alcoholic. Recall that this is an address to the New York Medical Society Section on Neurology and Psychiatry. Recall also that it is 1944, at the very beginning of the era of "miracle drugs"—two years or so after the first successful use of penicillin on an adult patient (from Kent, Connecticut), six years after sulfa drugs were first used on an infant on the East Coast (the author). Here are the five points listed under "Medicine says":

> (1) The alcoholic needs a personality change. (2) The patient ought to be analyzed and should make a full and honest mental catharsis. (3) Serious "personality defects" must be eliminated through accurate self-knowledge and realistic adjustment to life. (4) The alcoholic neurotic retreats from life, is a picture of anxiety and abnormal self-concern; he withdraws from the "herd." (5) The alcoholic must find "a new compelling interest in life," must "get back into the herd." Should find an interesting occupation, should join clubs, social activities, political parties, or discover hobbies to take the place of alcohol. (ibid.:27–28)

And Bill goes on to say:

> We have torn still other pages from the Book of Medicine, putting them to practical use. It is from you gentlemen we learn that alcoholism is a complex malady; that abnormal drinking is but a symptom of personal maladjustment to life; that . . . our obsession guarantees that we shall go on drinking, but our increasing physical sensitivity guarantees that we shall go insane or

die if we do. When these facts, coming from the mouths of you gentlemen of science, are poured by an A.A. member into the person of another alcoholic, they strike deep—the effect is shattering. (ibid.:31)

In other words, what brings deflation (a spiritual remedy) to the alcoholic is the knowledge that, scientifically speaking, medically speaking, he has an identifiable and eventually fatal disease. But, paradoxically, that is apparently also what brings the alcoholic hope, through paradigmatic change. As Bill goes on to say, "That inflated ego, those elaborate rationalizations by which our neurotic friend has been trying to erect self-sufficiency on a foundation of inferiority, begin to ooze out of him" (ibid.). He is

reduced to a state of *complete dependence* on whatever or whoever can stop his drinking. He is in exactly the same mental fix as the cancer patient who becomes dependent, abjectly dependent if you will, on what you men of science do for cancer. Better still, he becomes "sweetly reasonable," truly open-minded, as only the dying can be. (ibid.)

In this time when (as we have noted) a doctor's care meant largely diagnosis, prognosis, and bedside manner, the scientific part of scientific medicine—the whole science of alcoholism as a disease, if you will—would be in the diagnosis (as, for example, by Jellinek's types of alcoholism) and the prognosis (the famous Jellinek Chart). The treatment would be either by religion—but religion would trace to William James and *The Varieties of Religious Experience,* so the "religious treatment" would be essentially psychological—or by medicine—but medicine, in this case, would mean psychiatry.

JOHNNY L.

We might look briefly here at the figure of Dr. Dudley Saul (and that of his colleague Dr. A. Wiese Hammer) in Philadelphia, and one of the first alcoholics to get sober in Philadelphia, Johnny L. Not much has been written on Dudley Saul in accounts of the history of treatment for alcoholism, even though his work antedated the development of A.A. in his city; perhaps some brief remarks by his patient Johnny L. may be relevant here.

I was introduced to AA in late winter or early Spring 1940 by C. Dudley Saul, M.D. Dr. Saul was our family physician and when my drinking reached the critical point in late 1938, my wife, Marie, called him in to see what he could do. . . . He told me, "John, you're an alcoholic." My reply was, "Yes?" "And," he added, "you are going to die or go crazy." "Is that all?" I asked. "That's all," he replied, "unless you're going to make up your mind never to take a drink again." I was in an emotional state where I was not inclined to quarrel with his diagnosis or his remedy, but what was interesting to me as I looked back on that experience, was that in seventeen years of drinking [he was 35] . . . [this was] the first time I had ever heard what was wrong with me.

Dr. Saul suggested going to a Turkish bath to get the alcohol out of my system—a mistaken program as we now know, but it seemed to make sense [then]. So I sweated at the bath for a couple of days and drank—at the doctor's suggestion—lots of liquids. Then I did what we tell AA prospects to do: I called my father, a clergyman who had been sorely grieved at my drinking, and told him that I was going to quit. He was delighted; he said nothing like "It's about time," as might be expected . . . There was no AA in Philadelphia, where my home was at that time, but Dr. Saul, in effect, had his own group. His patients—and there were others like me—were invited to come by his office (thus reminding ourselves that we were sick), say "hello" to him and report on how things were going, and chat with other patients in the waiting room. . . . And so I stayed dry, helped by the expression of confidence by the members of my church (of which my father was the pastor) who elected me a Ruling Elder. . . . After that, there were many times I wanted a drink very badly . . . but I just couldn't let those people down who had trusted me.

Early in 1940 Jimmy B. came over to Philadelphia from New York and, in effect, brought AA to the city. He got in touch with Dr. Saul and with another physician, Dr. A. Wiese Hammer, and told them about AA. The two doctors were on the staff of St. Luke's & Children's Medical Center and they invited the tiny new AA group to meet at the hospital. What this meant to AA was tremendous; it gave sponsorship and emphasized the AA message, that alcoholics are sick people. And Dr. Saul told me about the new group and advised me to go. (John P. L. no date; quoted by permission of Archives, Area 59, but available on at least one website)

On September 29, 1941, almost eight months after the Jack Alexander article appeared in the *Saturday Evening Post* (partly Saul's doing), the two doctors reported that the Philadelphia Alcoholics Anonymous Group had 113 active members, of whom eighty-three had been sober since their first meeting, five between two and four years, twenty-seven between one and two.

Johnny L. had at this time been sober for three years, so his was not the longest time, though preliminary research suggests he had the longest time of anyone who remained in Philadelphia and remained sober. He went on to be a member of the board of the Saul Clinic (established after World War II), a Class B Trustee of Alcoholics Anonymous, and died forty-five years sober in 1983 (though he left the Saul Clinic in 1958 and eventually settled in Albuquerque). It may be worth noting that he designed alcoholism programs for both the Presbyterian (his own) and the Episcopal church. His particular importance for us here is in part that for help with his drinking problem he came to his family physician, one of A.A.'s earliest friends among physicians, who diagnosed him as an alcoholic; he found a fellowship in the doctor's office (almost a kind of group therapy) before there was an A.A. group in Philadelphia, and found a spiritual answer to his physical problem. When Bill W. spoke of "this strange illness of mind, body, and spirit," what he had to say—if anything—that was new was not that it was an illness of mind, an illness of body, *and* an illness of spirit, but an illness of all three, together—and that the cure (as Johnny L. and Dr. Saul found) was spiritual, or at least had a kind of congruence with spiritual progress ("progress along spiritual lines").

JUNG

In his letter responding to Bill W., in 1961, Jung wrote that he was glad to hear again of Rowland H., remarking:

Our conversation . . . had an aspect of which he did not know. The reason that I could not tell him everything was that [in] those days I had to be exceedingly careful of what I said. . . . His craving for alcohol was the equivalent, on a low level, of the spiritual thirst of our being for wholeness, expressed in medieval language: the union with God. How could one formulate such an insight in a language that is not misunderstood in our days. The only right and legitimate way to such an experience is, that it happens to you in reality, and that it can only happen to you when you walk on a path which leads you to higher understanding. You might be led to that goal by an act of grace, or through a personal and honest contact with friends, or through a higher education of the mind beyond the confines of mere rationalism. . . . I am risking [giving you a full explanation] because I conclude from your very decent and honest letter that you have acquired a point of view above the misleading platitudes one usually hears about alcoholism. Alcohol in Latin is "spiritus" and you use the same word for the highest religious experience as well as for the most depraving poison. The helpful formula therefore is: *spiritus contra spiritum*. (quoted in Leach and Norris 1997:455)

The question naturally arises as to why Jung had to be careful, and why he was so much on guard against being misunderstood. Here a knowledge of events in Worcester, Massachusetts, on September 9 and 10, 1909, may be of value. The occasion is the only meeting of Jung, Sigmund Freud, and William James, at the Vigentennial Celebration of Clark University, under the auspices of its president, G. Stanley Hall. The subject at issue was the interpretation of dreams, on which Freud lectured on September 10. That evening, he walked with James (at the latter's request) to the railroad station, where James was to catch a train. On the way, James suffered an apparent heart attack and a period of mental fugue, possibly induced by the conversations with Freud.

In the conversations, James had learned that Freud was to go in two days to Putnam's Camp in the Adirondacks, a locale of extreme psychological significance for James—a significance that had worked itself out in dreams that he considered mystical, but that he knew Freud would (given that day's lecture) consider sexual. Freud and his followers (and Hall, though an old friend and colleague of James) attacked James for his mysticism, for his interest in faith-healing (including his visits to a Christian Science practitioner, L. C. Strang), for his association with the Emmanuel movement— in short, for his belief that religion (in whatever form) could cure physical ills—and for his mystical rather than sexual interpretation of dreams (see Rosenzweig 1994:esp. 79–119 and 171–98, on James and his day at the conference). Jung's belief in the collective unconscious came perilously close to the same mysticism (in the Freudian view): hence the need for care.

FAR OUT: PSYCHICAL RESEARCH, MANIC DEPRESSION

Indeed, by the 1930s, Jung was under severe Freudian attack for his own interpretation of dreams, in terms of the symbols and motifs of the collective unconscious. If he also fell afoul of Freud and his followers (or even Adler and his followers) by asserting the possibility of cure by religion, by a spiritual realignment, the acceptance (in Thomas Kuhn's later words) of a new paradigm, he would be still further discredited. What had happened with William James could not fail, I think, to be in his mind. G. Stanley Hall had made hay from James's involvement with the American branch of the Society for Psychical Research (even though Hall had also been involved with the Society, see Rosenzweig 1994:82–90).

One notes with a certain sense of the fitness of things that Bill W. was also strongly (and Dr. Bob somewhat) interested in psychical research (Wing 1992:55–57, 75–76). Nell Wing, his long-time secretary, tells the story of Bill W.'s visit to Nantucket in 1947. Bill got up early at his host's house his first morning, and "had lengthy conversations there with three Nantucketers who had lived more than a hundred years before: a whaler, a sailor who said his name was David Morrow and that he had been killed serving under Admiral Farragut at the battle of Mobile Bay, and a sea captain named Pettengill" (ibid.:56). He told his host the story, "making pointed reference to the names" (ibid.).

Next day Bill (with his host) looked at the Civil War Memorial on the main street—there was David Morrow—and went to the Whaling Museum, where he found a list of the masters of the old whaling vessels, including Pettengill. When J. B. Rhine at Duke was carrying out his 1950s research into ESP (extrasensory perception, second sight, sixth sense), Bill was an avid correspondent with him. This streak may help account for what some have seen as his almost mystical belief in his own destiny.

With the same sense of the fitness of things, one notes that both William James and Bill W. were depressives, and possibly, from the record, manic depressives. In fact, Bill described himself in those terms (Wing, ibid.:53), and Rosenzweig's account of James in *The Historic Expedition* (1994:191ff.) leaves little doubt in my mind that he could be described in like words. But then, as Kay Redfield Jamison (1993) has reminded us, manic depression lies insecurely hidden in many of the greatest English poets—not to mention a slew of American authors. It has been suggested that Bill W. was in a severely depressed state much of the time between his visit to California in 1943 (when he saw his mother, who finally found in A.A. something to praise him for) and about 1961 (when his mother, now widowed, moved in with him and his wife, Lois, in their house, Stepping Stones, in Bedford, New York). Certainly he was ill enough in 1945–46 not to be able to be flown to the reunion of old-time A.A.s at Camp Karephree in Minnesota, at the expense of the New Jersey insurance executive Joe F. (Dr. Bob and Earl T.—who brought A.A. to Chicago—and Arch T.—who brought A.A. to Detroit—were among those coming.) Or at least he told Joe F. that he was too ill—it has been suggested to me that he may simply not have wanted to go.

There is not much doubt in my mind (though my certainty does not come particularly from *The Varieties of Religious Experience*) that James had precisely the same kind of mystical experience himself that Bill had in 1934 (see Rosenzweig 1994:185ff.). In fact, throughout most of his career, William James found it necessary to deal with detractors who thought him not far removed from crackpot status on the question of spiritual healing. And, of course, as we will see in our next chapter, William James plays another part in our study, as the founder—at least the American founder—of the discipline (or study) of psychology. I do not think we risk tipping our hand on the matter of congruent treatment to suggest here that the closeness of the mental and "spiritual" in James to some extent induced the same closeness in Bill W., and even made possible his acknowledgment that alcoholism is a spiritual disease. That the closeness in James did induce the closeness in Bill W., and even induced that belated acknowledgment, is doubtless the case—but the congruence of treatment has roots much further back and much more complex than this.

3 ~

A Scientific Note: Typologies, Heredities, and the Adjacent Possible

THIS CHAPTER MAY SEEM TO BREAK THE FLOW OF THE BOOK, but there are some areas of scientific inquiry relevant to our overall "scientific research program" where a little additional groundwork may be necessary. Briefly, these are (1) the question of *types* of alcoholism we may want to be testing for or using in tests, (2) the question of the process of heredity—as it applies to Alcoholism(2) at least, and (3) the process of change itself and its preconditions.

The second question may be subdivided into what we ordinarily think of as heredity or genetics, or biogenetics, and what we are more likely to think of as human nature passed down in families ("He comes by that honestly; his grandfather was just like that!"), where we often doubt the presence of actual genes for certain character traits (poetic creation or reading ability, for example). This turns out to tie in with Stuart Kauffman's idea of the adjacent possible, a new and diverse realm (biosphere or econosphere) into which an agent can move when on the supercritical-subcritical edge. (What this means we shall see in good time; it is part of our analysis of the process of change.) First, on the *types* of alcoholism.

TYPES OF ALCOHOLISM

I am reminded that there is a well-known member of Alcoholics Anonymous who (it is commonly reported), in telling his story, refers to his "fine alcoholic mind" with the aside that an A.A. meeting is the only place where one hears much about the "fine alcoholic mind." Also that another well-known member of Alcoholics Anonymous frequently (I am told) uses the qualifier, "alcoholics of my type"—not meaning Jellinek types, or any other of the "scientific" typologies, but recognizing that there are different types of alcoholics. As a first step toward classifying alcoholics—and thereby (we believe) improving our chances for scientific study of alcoholics and alcoholism—we will accept his guidance and try to look at alcoholics by type of their (fine?) alcoholic minds.

We recall that William James (in *The Varieties of Religious Experience*) refers to different types of mentality. Moreover, Gerald Edelman remarks (1989; see also our Chapter 4) that, with secondary repertoires, environmental selection of the specific synaptic pathways occurs—individually—in behavioral engagement with the outside world. Henry Plotkin says that "once intelligence has evolved in a species, then thereafter brains have a causal force equal to that of genes" (1994:17). (This, if true—and we are accepting it as part of our research program—is obviously highly significant to the relationship between alcoholism and Alcoholics Anonymous.) Alan Dean (1997) suggests that at each stage of the ontogenesis of the individual there is so great an uncertainty with respect to outcomes that we may consider them as produced through individuality—begging, for the moment, the question of what constitutes individuality.

But many of those involved with the treatment of alcoholism seem to believe that, in the end, "one size fits all"—so, even with this weight of argument, should we bother to look at types of alcoholism, if in the end one mode of treatment treats all? For just one answer, though not the only one, it may be that part of the treatment works for one type and part for another, and we need to make sure therefore that all parts remain in force. Or it may be that the rules of genetics have so crossed and recrossed the types that there is a chance the old modes of treatment will not continue to work. Or it may be that genotypic variants remain relatively unchanged, with rapidly changing phenotypes. Or it may be important for quite different (even as yet unknown) reasons. Or it may be simply that we should pay attention to the alcoholics quoted above.

Or it may indeed be that the case is something entirely other that we have not even considered. But early observers, including alcoholics themselves, discovered different types of alcoholism (or of alcoholics), and it is at least worth looking at the question, Are these types valid and useful? Or, can they be used to make our research program better—more accurate and more useful? George Vaillant of Harvard, one of the leading experts in the field, has suggested that the deciding criterion for the validity of any typology is whether the classification is objective (i.e., distinguishes between or among different disease states with different underlying mechanisms and requiring different treatment), or subjective (i.e., distinguishes different symptom constellations without further relevance for etiology or treatment). Note that the difference between *objective* and *subjective* here lies partly in whether the distinctions help with treatment, not so much in whether they are accurate—that is, "really there." We will keep this in mind, even while noting that etiological differences (differences in disease origin and progress) may not necessarily imply differences in treatment, and even if they do, a given treatment combination may be sufficiently broad-ranging to cover these different patterns.

I should note also that Dr. Vaillant disagrees with me strongly on any advantage I see in looking at E. M. Jellinek's typology (whether modified or not), though agreeing that there are ambiguities in the results of studies on alcoholism thus far. I remain convinced, however, that we are missing a bet by not conducting (or interpreting) longitudinal studies using Jellinek's typology (modified), not only on genetic and biochemical questions generally but also and especially on the possible link between memory and alcoholism. For that reason, we will spend a few pages looking at typologies of alcoholism, beginning with Jellinek. In his classic book (1960) and in earlier articles, he divided alcoholism into five subtypes: alpha (α), beta (β), gamma (γ), delta (δ), and epsilon (ϵ), of which α and β subtypes were only implicit in his original 1941 classifications.

STARTING FROM JELLINEK

Briefly, it may be said that α alcoholism is a purely psychological continual dependence or reliance upon the effect of alcohol to relieve bodily or emotional pain. It would seem not to be progressive and would have no withdrawal symptoms in the event the "alcoholic" stopped drinking. Also, β alcoholism represents alcohol consumption leading to alcohol-related medical disorders, with neither physical nor psychological dependence, and no withdrawal symptoms. For Jellinek, the worst form of alcoholism was γ alcoholism, which led to "(1) acquired increased tissue tolerance to alcohol, (2) adaptive cell mechanism, (3) withdrawal symptoms and 'craving,' i.e., physical dependence, and (4) loss of control" (ibid.:37). This is the progressive fatal disease we usually think of as alcoholism—that is, our Alcoholism(1)—and to which Magnus Hoff gave the name *chronicus alcoholismus* in 1848.

Jellinek defined δ alcoholism as largely the same as γ alcoholism, but with inability to abstain in place of loss of control as the fourth symptom. Finally, he suggested a fifth species of alcoholism, what he called ϵ alcoholism, where periodic bouts of drinking could cause serious damage. Jellinek himself ruled out α (possibly) and β (definitely) as not truly the disease of alcoholism, while γ and δ both involved "adaptation of cell mechanism, and increased tolerance and the withdrawal symptoms, which bring about 'craving' and loss of control and ability to abstain" (ibid.:30). About ε alcoholism Jellinek reserved judgment (drawn in different ways by logic and instinct), having insufficient information. There remains significant uncertainty on ε alcoholism, and on its bounds. But Thomas Babor has made an interesting suggestion here.

The original (1941) Jellinek classifications were twofold. First there were (1) primary or true alcoholics, who were characterized by an immediate liking for alcohol's effects, rapid development of uncontrollable need for alcohol, and inability to abstain. Then there were (2) the secondary alcoholics, including (a) the steady endogenous symptomatic drinkers in whom alcoholism was secondary to a major psychiatric disorder, such as schizophrenia or syphilis; (b) the intermittent endogenous symptomatic drinkers who were distinguished by periodic drinking pattern but with development of the alcoholism secondary to a psychiatric disorder such as manic-depressive psychosis; and (c) the *stammtisch* drinkers, in whom alcoholism was precipitated by exogenous causes, the designation *stammtisch* coming from the table set aside for regular customers in a café. The α and β subtypes implicit in the 1941 classifications are characterized by biobehavioral dependence, while the γ and δ alcoholics are characterized by physical dependence.

In fact, according to Babor, himself a typologist of alcoholisms, the two groups of endogenous symptomatic drinkers in the 1941 classifications— 2(a) and 2(b), this last including manic-depressive periodic drinkers— were enfolded into the 1960 γ alcoholics (though some of the "primary" alcoholics may also have been enfolded there), while the more severe cases among the *stammtisch* drinkers became the 1960 δ alcoholics. On this showing, the γ alcoholics (1960 classification) are principally alcoholics whose alcoholism is secondary to a psychiatric disorder. Also according to Babor (this is the interesting suggestion referred to above), most of the "primary or true alcoholics" in the 1941 typology became a subclass of the ε drinkers in the 1960 typology—precisely those drinkers whose alcoholism Jellinek seemed to doubt.

On the one hand, this seems unlikely, since, as noted, Jellinek himself seemed not entirely convinced that ε alcoholics were really alcoholics at all. On the other hand—and this is Babor's point—for the "primary" alcoholics in the 1941 typology the disease was not developmental or progressive but instantaneous—and if instantaneous, and if periodic at the first instant, and if not progressive, it would thus, in many cases if not all, remain periodic. In this study we will refer to that class of alcoholics characterized by instantaneous alcoholic drinking in a binge pattern, and remaining binge drinkers (but not having antecedent psychiatric disorders), as Jellinek ε alcoholics (modified definition). There is no question, in our mind, that they are alcoholics, and quite possibly the original alcoholics. There are passages in the A.A. "Big Book" and personal stories (Bill W. et al. 1939, 1955, 1976, 2001:165ff) suggesting that quite a number of early members of A.A. fell into this pattern of drinking, not emphasized in early A.A. literature or in typologies of alcoholism.

Recently, Suzanne Hiller-Sturmhofel (1996) reported on a survey on Jellinek's typology among "leading researchers and clinicians" involved in studies of alcohol and alcoholism. They included Griffith Edwards (of the Edwards-Moss study in 1974); Harvey Skinner of the University of Toronto and the Addiction Research Foundation; George Vaillant of Harvard and Brigham-Women's Hospital, author of *The Natural History of Alcoholism* (1983) (and *The Natural History of Alcoholism Revisited*, 1996a) and now (March 2004) a Class A Trustee of Alcoholics Anonymous; C. Robert Cloninger (originator of a currently accepted type I and type II typology); LeClair Bissell, former president of the American Society of Addiction Medicine (ASAM); Marc Schuckit of UC-San Diego, the director of the Alcohol Research Center at San Diego V.A. Medical Center; and Enoch Gordis, former director of the National Institute on Alcohol Abuse and Alcoholism (NIAAA).

OTHER TYPOLOGIES

The Hiller-Sturmhofel survey asked three questions:

(1) How do alcohol researchers currently judge Jellinek's typology and its impact on the field of alcohol and alcoholism studies?
(2) How valid is Jellinek's classification of alcoholics after thirty-five years of further research?
(3) What is the future of alcoholism typology studies?

The author reports broad consensus among these "experts" that Jellinek's work was important, but also that the "details" of his classifications have not stood the test of time. She remarks that "Jellinek's five subtypes subsequently have been replaced by more detailed diagnostic categories based on sophisticated psycho-social approaches and the identification of biological markers, including molecular genetic markers" (quoted in Babor 1996 (20):10). But not on alcoholics' self-testimony.

We have mentioned Vaillant's criteria. His view is that Jellinek's classification is merely suggestive and in fact largely subjective. LeClair Bissell noted that, in her experience, no typology, including Jellinek's, plays or has played any significant role in treatment or in the administrative aspects of clinical practice. There have been attempts to match treatment to typology, and though these have not produced useful results, what is important here is that the question of whether Jellinek's typology is subjective (as Vaillant believes) is logically independent of the question of whether all Jellinek types can be treated in the same way—if we define "subjective" in the ordinary way. They could be objective (in the ordinary sense of that word) and have different etiologies, without different treatments being indicated.

In any case, although there was early and general acceptance of Jellinek's biometrical work, his typology stimulated little empirical research, nor did it inspire attempts to match subtypes to specific therapies. It may be that our study, building to some degree on Dean's *Chaos and Intoxication* (1997); and on more recent work expanding the paradigm and trying to apply a modified Jellinek typology to current research findings (believing his typology to be objective), will do more to stimulate this kind of research than Jellinek's own pioneering work. One hesitates to differ with George Vaillant on a question where I believe I may agree with his conclusions—essentially that one treatment, A.A., fits all. But it may be necessary to carry out at least an indicative research program before we see how (or if) our evidence supports him. We should note here (again) that Jellinek was not a medical doctor but a statistician, and that present definitions of alcoholism in the *Diagnostic and Statistical Manual of Mental Disorders* (DSM; American Psychological Association 1952, 1980, 1987, 1994) and the *Manual of the International Statistical Classification of Diseases, Injuries, and Causes of Death* (ICD 1903 et seqq.) are likewise definitions based on statistical study. The difference between Jellinek's and the other studies in typology is that Jellinek based his on self-identified alcoholics, while the others have used "clinical" definitions or court adjudications.

Because Jellinek was a statistician—biometrician—and not a medical man, his definitions were statistical, not diagnostic. William Duncan Silkworth, on the other hand, was a physician using anecdotal experience in his typology: we will consider more fully what he had to say in our discussion of alcoholism as disease, allergy, or predisposition. We begin our present discussion of diagnostic definitions of alcoholism as mental illness with DSM-I, DSM-II, and DSM-III (APA 1952, 1968, 1980). In these volumes, "alcoholism" was categorized as a subset within the set entitled Personality Disorders, Homosexuality, and Neuroses.

In response to perceived deficiencies in DSM-I and DSM-II, the Feighner criteria were developed in the early 1970s to establish a research base for diagnostic criteria for determining alcoholism. A little later on, Edwards and Gross (1976) focused on alcohol dependence: the essential elements of dependence were narrowing of the drinking repertoire, drink-seeking behavior, tolerance, withdrawal, drinking to relieve or avoid withdrawal symptoms, subjective awareness of the compulsion to drink, and return to drinking after a period of abstinence—these, of course, being symptoms of Alcoholism(2), in general. The Edwards-Gross study seems to have been connected with the fact that DSM-III (1980) dropped "alcoholism" in favor of the two possibly overlapping categories of Alcohol Dependence and Alcohol Abuse—overlapping categories, though not overlapping criteria. Then, in 1987, the *Third Edition Revised* (DSM-III-R) moved some of the symptoms that DSM-III placed under abuse into the dependence category—physiological symptoms, like tolerance and withdrawal, and behavioral symptoms, such as impaired control over drinking. Alcohol abuse became a residual category for "problem drinkers" not meeting all the dependence criteria. One begins to wonder if the increasing attempts to classify the condition are not a measure of desperation.

In 1994, DSM-IV, like its predecessors, provided what were to be considered nonoverlapping criteria for alcohol dependence and alcohol abuse. It provided for the subtyping of dependence according to the presence or absence of tolerance and withdrawal. The criteria for abuse were extended to include drinking despite recurrent social, interpersonal, and legal problems as the result of alcohol use. DSM-IV also highlighted the fact that symptoms of such disorders as anxiety and depression might be related to the use of alcohol or drugs. Briefly, in the DSM-IV (DSM-IV Text Revision, or DSM-IV-TR), there are five axes:

- Axis I, Clinical Disorders
- Axis II, Personality Disorders and Mental Retardation
- Axis III, General Medical Conditions
- Axis IV, Psychosocial and Environmental Problems (PEPs)
- Axis V, Global Assessment of Functioning (GAF)

Axis I is used to record what in the past were viewed as neuroses and psychoses, and Axis II is used to record what in the past were referred to as character disorders: briefly, Axis-I disorders can be changed through intervention, while Axis-II disorders cannot. In the current system, Axis I is used to record clinical disorders in the main section of the DSM-IV-TR (2000:39–729), while Axis II, as noted, is used for personality disorders and mental retardation (summarized in Munson 2001:69–76). Axis I and Axis II together are used to record the 340 disorders in the system, including substance-related disorders.

An overview of substance-related disorders suggests a certain ambivalence in the approach: as they are subject to intervention, they clearly belong on Axis I rather than Axis II, but they do not seem to be placed also (as we might expect) on Axis III, Mental Disorders Due to a General Medical Condition. The approach to diagnosis is a kind of odd-man-out in the DSM-IV-TR:

> Instead of having a discrete diagnosis for each class of substances, this section [on substance-related disorders] uses what Frances, First, and Pincus

(1995) have called a "mix and match approach," in which diagnosis starts with the name of the substance and then indicates the substance-related syndrome (dependence, intoxication, induced), and finally notes any specifiers that might apply. (APA 1995:147)

In other words, we do not initially diagnose the problem (the syndrome); we start by diagnosing the substance being used—which we know already.

These Substance-Related Disorders are divided into two groups: Substance-Use Disorders and Substance-Induced Disorders. Substance-Use Disorders are in turn divided into Substance Dependence and Substance Abuse. For Substance Dependence the "specifiers" are *With Physiological Dependence* and *Without Physiological Dependence*. The "course specifiers" (six in number, describing the stage of the condition) run from *Early Full Remission* to *In a Controlled Environment*. Substance-Induced Disorders are "quasi-divided" (ibid.:146) into Substance Intoxication and Substance Withdrawal, the specifiers being *With Onset During Intoxication* and *With Onset During Withdrawal*. The first of the eleven substances is alcohol. If the particular Substance-Induced Disorder is one appearing in some cases without the substance (delirium, persisting dementia, and so on), it is covered separately (in DSM-IV-TR) from disorders that are only substance-related. In fact, eight of these disorders are noted (Munson 2001:146): delirium, persisting dementia, persisting amnesic disorder, psychotic disorder, mood disorder, anxiety disorder, sexual dysfunction, and sleep disorder—any of which may be substance-induced, but all are discussed under their separate headings in DSM-IV-TR.

All these categorizations and definitions are those of the American Psychological Association, which publishes the manual. The World Health Organisation (WHO) in Geneva has developed its own diagnostic criteria published as part of the *Manual of the International Statistical Classification of Diseases, Injuries, and Causes of Death* (ICD, 1903). In ICD-8, published in 1967, WHO classified alcoholism with personality disorders and neuroses: this alcoholism included episodic excessive drinking, habitual excessive drinking, and alcohol addiction characterized by the compulsion to drink and excessive withdrawal symptoms when drinking was stopped. In ICD-9, published in 1977 (Vol. 1) and 1978 (Vol. 2), WHO published separate criteria for alcohol abuse and alcohol dependency, but continued to define them in terms of signs and symptoms. In ICD-10 (*The ICD-10 Classification of Mental and Behavioural Disorders: Clinical Descriptions and Diagnostic Guidelines*, Tenth Revision), alcohol dependence is defined by psychological symptoms, such as craving; physiological signs, such as tolerance and withdrawal; and behavioral indicators, such as the use of alcohol to relieve withdrawal discomfort. Instead of alcohol abuse, the ICD-10 creates the category Harmful Use, causing either physical or mental damage in the absence of dependence, thereby further complicating the matter of definition. In essence, current definitions for alcohol dependence (the term has succeeded alcoholism in technical literature), whether in ICD-10 or DSM-IV (or DSM-IV-TR), mirror the definitions of the Edwards-Gross study (1976) noted above.

The close definitional match between alcoholism and alcohol dependence is revealed, by the way, by the fact that the NIAAA itself uses "alcohol dependence" to refer to what, in the name of the institute, was called alcoholism. But overall definitions are not the only matters we need to be concerned with here: there have been a number of attempts to classify types of alcoholism, besides Jellinek's, and these attempts have had a considerable influence on research in the field, even if misdirected, or involving problems of misspecification.

TYPE I AND TYPE II

The first "scientific" binary typology of alcoholism, type I and type II, is associated with the name of C. R. Cloninger, and is derived from Swedish studies of alcoholism among children of alcoholic and nonalcoholic parents adopted shortly after birth (Cloninger et al. 1981). (There is an earlier but much-overlooked binary typology coming from Robert Knight at the Menninger Clinic in 1937—"essential alcoholics" and "reactive alcoholics"—which we will briefly note a little later on.) Type I alcoholism was identified in both men and women, usually starting at an early age, affecting individuals with few legal or social problems, and causing either mild or severe alcohol dependence. (This bifurcation of "mild or severe" within the same type seems to be a problem.) Type II occurred predominantly in men, among whom age at onset was earlier than among type I alcoholics: type II individuals were more likely to have social and legal problems, and dependence was usually moderate—also, type II alcoholism had a much higher heritability than type I. On the face of it, this study would seem likely to have odd results, and it would further seem that these odd results would mirror the oddity of the classification.

Among problems that have been noted with the Cloninger study are these two: (1) The diagnosis of alcohol abuse was based on information from adoption and other official records, rather than on interviews; and (2) the statistical bounds for type I were on both sides of the statistical bounds for type II. Bounds chosen for type I were either a single Temperance Board registration for drunkenness or four or more registrations with at least one hospital admission for alcoholism, while the bounds chosen for type II were two or three such registrations without hospital admission. In addition to suggested over-reliance on official records and the statistical delineation by which type I alcoholism is on both sides of type II alcoholism, it has been suggested that the model is not well suited to statistical tests directed at discovering a genetic component to alcoholism.

The Cloninger study has recently been replicated, warts and all, by the same investigators, using the same definitions and statistical model. The replication study found too few cases of alcoholism among women for in-depth analysis, so only the male data were analyzed in detail. The authors emphasize that their data are inconsistent with the analytical simplification that there are two clinical types of alcoholism, one of which (type II) is primarily hereditary, and one of which is not (type I). Moreover, a 1990 article by other investigators (Perrick et al. 1990:623–29) found that type I and type II alcoholism are not readily identifiable species of alcoholism in clinical populations, and, indeed, 90 percent of alcoholics seeking treatment have symptoms of both types.

Many of the problems noted with the Cloninger typology may be derived from the inclusion of severe dependence with mild abuse in type I, and putting all cases of moderate dependence (with some possible cases of severe nondependent abuse) in type II. It is perhaps unfortunate this typology should be so widely influential in determining the bounds of critical analysis of alcoholism, particularly in connection with possible genetic factors. It has been suggested that a type A/type B analysis proposed by Thomas Babor (1986) and his colleagues, which has some similarities to the Cloninger typology, may be better suited for further analytical study. In this typology, type A alcoholics are characterized by later onset of alcoholism, fewer childhood risk factors (such as conduct disorders or attention deficit disorders), less severe alcohol dependence, fewer alcohol-related problems, and lower degrees of psychopathology. Type B alcoholics are characterized by higher degree of childhood risk factors, a family history of alcoholism, early onset of alcohol-related problems, greater severity of dependence, multiple drug use (which may be phenotypical), a more chronic treatment history despite younger age, greater degrees of psychopathology, and more life stress. And if treated in or through treatment facilities, type B alcoholics are more likely to relapse into heavy drinking. (This last does not entirely agree with Vaillant [1983, 1996].)

Here perhaps we should look briefly at the early and forgotten typology of Robert Knight (1937). Knight's two types are "essential alcoholics" and "reactive alcoholics," and they seem to be divided according to whether they had achieved some success in life (reactives) or had not (essentials), whether fixated at the oral stage (essentials) or not (reactives), whether they had borderline character structure ("borderline personality disorder," essentials) or not (reactives), whether they were instantaneous alcoholics (essentials) or had developed alcoholism (reactives), and (though Knight in no way emphasized this) whether they had a genetic suscepti-bility to alcoholism (essentials) or not (reactives). It thus may be seen that Knight's essential alcoholics have much in common with Babor's type B, and that his reactive alcoholics much in common with Babor's type A.

ZUCKER'S TYPOLOGY AND BACK TO JELLINEK

Although Babor's typology is free of some of the Cloninger problems, it may still lump together too many different subtypes that are really types. A more fruitful approach may be one developed by Robert Zucker, ini-tially in an article in 1987 and subsequently presented in 1994. We will use this somewhat later version of the Zucker typology in our discussion here. This discussion may seem to be shortchanging Babor's typological contri-butions, but this is a natural outcome of what may be premature combi-nation of defining characteristics to form types. Babor's typology is based on the assumptions that heterogeneity among alcoholics is attributable to a complex interaction among genetic, biological, psychological, and socio-cultural factors, but that the seventeen different defining characteristics can in fact be combined into two predominant types. These are not subject to all the caveats suggested for the Cloninger type I and type II, but at this stage, we think the Zucker typology may be more fruitful.

In his 1994 study, Zucker defined four types of alcoholism: (1) Anti-social Alcoholism, (2) Developmentally Limited Alcoholism, (3) Negative Affect Alcoholism, and (4) Primary Alcoholism. He subdivides type (4) into (a) Isolated, (b) Episodic, and (c) Developmentally Cumulative Primary Alcoholism. Use of the word *primary* follows standard medical terminology: a disorder is primary when all other specific causes have been excluded from etiology—that is, from the origins of the morbid (life-threatening) condition. In other words, primary alcoholism is alcoholic disorder where, if there is another morbid condition, it comes after and because of the alcoholic condition. In Antisocial Alcoholism, Develop-mentally Limited Alcoholism, and Negative Affect Alcoholism, Zucker argues that the alcoholic condition is not primary: there is what is called strong *comorbidity* (presence of other *and earlier* life-threatening condi-tions). In fact, in our belief, this is true chiefly of alcoholism with manic-depressive psychosis—in which the manic-depressive psychosis is an anterior comorbid state—a variety of Jellinek's γ alcoholism.

Antisocial Alcoholism includes not only significant adult antisociality but early onset of alcohol-related symptoms, greater severity of symptoms, significant alcoholism in the family and apparently genetic predisposition to alcoholism, and (frequently) involvement with drugs. Developmentally Limited Alcoholism shows the same characteristics of antisociality, severe symptoms, and drug use, but seems to be specific to the stage of life we call adolescence, and does not have the same record of family alcoholism ("family history positive" or FHP) or genetic predisposition. Negative Affect Alcoholism is nonantisocial (at least by comparison with the first two types), is tied to anxiety, and is more common among females than males (unlike the first two). This, by the way, suggests a problem with the all-male studies underlying Vaillant's *Natural History of Alcoholism* (1983, 1996a).

The three subtypes of Primary Alcoholism—to which Zucker has given the names (a) Isolated, (b) Episodic, and (c) Developmentally Cumulative —are presumed to be the result of the same alcohol-specific factors, such as expectancies, tolerance, appetitive differences in preference, neural differences in the experience of intoxication (to which considerable attention should be paid), and differences in social and cultural norms. The differences in the three subtypes are in the number of occurrences. In subtype (a), though the etiology (origins) and symptoms are largely identical to the other subtypes, there is only one occurrence (the drinker reaches "the threshold of disorder" only once), and the condition would better be called *isolated alcohol abuse*. In subtype (b) we have a periodic clustering of occurrences: the clustering begins to approach a clinical syndrome. This is Zucker's Primary Alcoholism II: Episodic Alcoholism (which we may call type 4-b).

When the clustering continues (if it does), and the clusters come more and more together (if they do), other morbid (life-threatening) conditions develop (including antisocial activity or depression), and we get what Zucker calls Primary Alcoholism III: Developmentally Cumulative Alcoholism (which we may call type 4-c). Zucker notes that for more than half the alcoholic population, no comorbidity for drug abuse/dependence or other mental disorder exists, although this is based on studies now something like fifteen or twenty years old. In other words, the core causal framework for primary alcoholisms (Zucker types 4-a, 4-b, and 4-c) does not implicate comorbid etiology—which is why primary alcoholism is primary. However, alcoholics "whose symptomatic careers begin without comorbidity but then go on to develop it are potentially an etiologically very important sub-population" (Zucker 1994:279). That is, alcoholics who develop from "social drinking" to "alcoholic drinking" ought to be studied as showing a significant variety of alcoholism as they move from the noncomorbid to the comorbid subset.

This is in line with the developmental assumptions underlying the distinction between Primary Alcoholism II and Primary Alcoholism III— which may suggest a weakness in Zucker's approach, since we don't *know* whether Episodic Alcoholism develops into Developmentally Cumulative

Alcoholism (or, of course, whether it doesn't, or frequently doesn't, or infrequently doesn't). But even if this development is common, there remains another core developmental question of the extent to which comorbid intermingling leads to etiologic differentiation—the extent to which the fact that alcoholics develop other life-threatening disorders reflects different paths toward alcoholism.

Zucker suggests use of the phrase *alcohol dependence syndrome* in order to articulate the notion that a set of interdependent characteristics should be understood at the syndrome rather than the symptom level (ibid.)—that is, individual characteristics need to be viewed as part of a larger structure. Current definitions of alcoholism have led to such anomalous findings as (1) that the majority of alcoholics are from nonalcoholic families, and (2) that "severe and pathological alcoholic symptomatology occurs with greater frequency among non-alcoholic individuals" (ibid.) than among alcoholic individuals. Until we have a typology that will take these anomalous and counterintuitive (not to say ridiculous) findings into account, our research is likely to be somewhat flawed.

I believe we may reasonably build our future research in these areas on Zucker's typology (allowing for its developmental bias), but it is important to see how the other typologies fit with his, and indeed with each other. Because of the definitional problems noted with the Cloninger type I and type II analysis, and because whatever strengths that analysis has seem also to be found in the Babor type A and type B distinctions, we would principally restrict our inquiry here to Jellinek, the "Big Book" typology, Babor, and Zucker—but Babor (and the some extent the developmentally biased "Big Book" typology) may be largely subsumed into the more complex Jellinek-Zucker typology. We will, however, also take the DSM and ICD diagnostic definitions into account, and the NCADD/ASAM definition of the disease of alcoholism, which may in its turn also overemphasize the necessity for "progression" in symptoms. In this context, we should repeat that Zucker's study adopts a developmental paradigm, and thus may underemphasize the importance of instantaneous Jellinek type ε primary alcoholism.

It will be important to distinguish between alcoholic phenotype and alcoholic genotype. In order to do this, we will need to look more closely at the genetic process than has been generally done. The Jellinek α (mostly) and β subtypes seem to fall into the alcohol-abuse rather than the alcohol-dependence category, as do Zucker type 2 drinkers (developmentally limited alcoholics). Jellinek γ (endogenous symptomatic) drinkers, including, according to Babor, those in which alcoholism is subsidiary to a major psychiatric disorder, would seem to include Zucker type 1 (Antisocial Alcoholism) and Zucker type 3 (Negative Affect Alcoholism), which may be gender types. (We suggest below, however, that this may not be the most fruitful way to look at antisocial alcoholism.) The Jellinek δ drinkers seem to fit within the bounds of Zucker's developmentally cumulative primary alcoholics (type 4-c). Curiously, as we progress toward discovering or suggesting the origins of Alcoholism(2), we will see, I think, that these *stammtisch* drinkers are the true curiosities in the world of alcoholic types, the furthest from what we will suggest is the prototype (unless, of course, they preserve an autochthonic, pre–Indo-European, even pre–Cro-Magnon, set of traits).

The area in which the Jellinek typology may be more exact and more useful than the Zucker typology is the Jellinek definition of the ε drinker (as modified), the "primary" or "true" alcoholic who is virtually an instantaneous alcoholic from the first drink, who does not specifically appear in the Zucker typology, except as a subset within type 1, Antisocial Alcoholism. This is the point at which we think Zucker may possibly have misspecified a type. But note that we are modifying the range of alcoholism type in Jellinek ε to include all instantaneous drinkers in the binge pattern, arguing that they are full-blown binge alcoholics from the beginning (as opposed to the *stammtisch* process), and that ASPD (Anti-Social Personality Disorder) may simply be a characteristic of this type of alcoholism.

One problem is that Jellinek and Zucker use the word *primary* in slightly different ways: Zucker's primary alcoholics exhibit alcoholism before they exhibit any comorbid display—including as comorbid display "significant adult antisociality" (Zucker 1994:passim)—while Jellinek does not recognize "adult antisociality" as a comorbid state within the disease concept of alcoholism. Not comorbid but resulting from alcoholism. Thus Jellinek's primary alcoholics could—and presumably do—exhibit antisocial behavior patterns, but as a result (in his view) of their primary alcoholism. This divergence in typology could be bridged without difficulty if ASPD were restored to its earlier (Jellinek era) position as a part of alcoholism or at least of some "alcoholisms"—or, to put it another way, if it could be shown that what we now call ASPD is an integral part of both Antisocial Alcoholism, Zucker type 1, and Developmentally Limited Alcoholism, Zucker type 2. (Though the latter may not in fact be alcoholism within the definitions we are suggesting, any more than situational alcoholism, so called, may be alcoholism by our definition—though those who suffer it may consider themselves alcoholics.)

Within this suggested typology, the primary distinction between Zucker type 1 and Zucker type 2 would be that type 1 is pretty much a permanent condition with a genetic component, while type 2 is temporary with no apparent genetic component, which means, of course, that type 2 represents alcohol abuse rather than alcohol dependence or alcoholism. Also, if ASPD is an integral part of the alcohol dependence syndrome, then Zucker type 1 becomes a version of primary alcoholism, as it was for Jellinek (but possibly divided between γ and ε alcoholism). In addition, Zucker type 4-a, Isolated Primary Alcoholism (sometimes called situational alcoholism), moves into the category of alcohol abuse. We are left with Zucker type 1 Revised, which is Jellinek's primary alcoholism and perhaps his ε; Zucker type 3, Negative Affect Alcoholism, which is Jellinek's γ alcoholism (the subset with depressive comorbidity); Zucker type 4-b, Primary Episodic Alcoholism, which seems to be Jellinek ε alcoholism (*not* developing into type 4-c); and Zucker type 4-c, Primary Developmentally Cumulative Alcoholism—Jellinek's δ (or cumulative *stammtisch* drinkers).

One possible implication of Zucker's distinction between 4-b and 4-c is that episodes come closer and closer together, so that Primary Episodic Alcoholism becomes Primary Developmentally Cumulative Alcoholism, which would make 4-b an earlier stage of 4-c and thus of Jellinek δ alcoholism (eliminating his ε). In other words, episodic alcoholics ("periodics" or binge drinkers) would always develop cumulatively into daily drunks. This does not seem to be the case. If we incorporate ASPD as a characteristic of ε alcoholism (or ε alcoholism modified) then ε alcoholism matches not only with Zucker type 1 (Revised) and Zucker 4-b (if not cumulative), but with Silkworth's type 1 (psychopathic alcoholism). This would also bring it into line with Knight's essential alcoholism. Similarly, Zucker type 3 (Negative Affect) matches Jellinek γ alcoholism (subset) and Silkworth's type 4 (manic depressive). Zucker type 4-b (if cumulative) and 4-c become versions of Jellinek δ alcoholism.

The δ alcoholic is also Bill W.'s heavy drinker who becomes a true alcoholic if he goes on drinking. Bill W.'s three stages of "true" alcoholism all reflect types of individual reaction to the condition of γ alcoholism or δ alcoholism, but not instantaneous (ε or ε modified) alcoholism. Also in the "Big Book" is another Bill W. typology, in the chapter "To Wives," the types being (1) the heavy drinker, who is not a true alcoholic but may become one if he keeps on, (2) the real alcoholic who wants to want to stop, (3) the real alcoholic who wants to stop but cannot, and (4) the violent drunk who suffers *delirium tremens,* may have been institutionalized, and gets drunk on the way home from the institution. And Bill W. was not the only typologist of alcoholism in the "Big Book." Silkworth also ventured a few remarks on the classification of alcoholics: (1) the psychopath, (2) the type who is "unwilling to admit he cannot take a drink," (3) the type who believes that "after being entirely free from alcohol for a period of time he can drink without danger," (Bill W. et al.: 1939, 1955, 1976, 2001) and (4) the manic-depressive type.

These are all, of course, anecdotal rather than statistical types. They are of importance to us here because they show what the founders of Alcoholics Anonymous had in mind when the A.A. program was being put together. We should note here that Silkworth's second and third types are variations of each other, and Bill W.'s second, third, and fourth apparently represent stages in the disease in the same basic type, which is by definition progressive rather than instantaneous. (Once again, instantaneous periodic alcoholism seems the odd man out—or perhaps the "odd man in.")

HEREDITARY ALCOHOLISM: GENOTYPES, PHENOTYPES, QUANTITATIVE TRAIT LOCI

There is evidence, which we will be examining, that γ and ε (modified) alcoholism (Zucker type 3 and Zucker type 1 Revised with some Zucker 4-b) have an hereditary component. Evidence on δ alcoholism is somewhat less clear, perhaps because less looked for. If there is evidence for an hereditary (genetic) component here, or if we have misspecified our types so that δ is, in fact, a subset of γ or ε or both, then it may be (1) that alcoholism is distinguished from alcohol abuse *by the presence of a genetic component*, and (2) that Alcoholics Anonymous was set up in such a way that its program deals successfully through cognitive reconstruction (and other congruent means) with a genetic predisposition—and will not deal as successfully with alcohol abusers without that genetic predisposition. (This will be covered more fully when we look at the work of R. Plomin and G. M. Edelman, particularly as reported in Dean [1997]. Edelman's work we have already touched on in this chapter.) Passages in the "Big Book" describing alcoholism as an allergy may—given the 1930s understanding of allergy, or even ours—be closer to the mark than has been thought, certainly closer than suggested by Norris and Leach (1977; see Chapter 2). It all depends on just what one understands by the word *allergy*. One thing, of course, that one understands is that allergy is a hereditable precondition (discussed in Chapter 5). We should perhaps turn now to discussing the genetics of alcoholism.

We begin here by discussing human phenotypes associated with alcoholism. In so doing, we are looking at multiple domains, both biological and psychosocial (these including both chronicity on the one hand, and contextual, personality, and psychopathological variables on the other). Thus, if the Jellinek ε alcoholic (modified definition), or Zucker type 1 Revised existed in a time (temporal environment) before such drugs as marijuana or cocaine or heroin were readily available, he or she would not have used them. Now they are available, and in most cases may be used. The phenotype may have changed, but the genotype has not: the alcoholic remains an alcoholic even if a drug user. (Note, in this context, that "partying" in the late twentieth-century sense becomes part of an extended phenotype.) This phenotypical change and genotypical constancy is, as we will see in Chapter 8, a matter of importance in the *ordering* of (establishing an order for) A.A.

In our discussion of particular genotypes and phenotypes in what follows, the genotypes will be designated by italics, as *psa* (except for hypothetical founder "wildtypes" designated all capitals, no italics, as PSA), and the phenotypes by the same symbol as the genotype, but with the first letter capitalized and no italics, thus, Psa. This follows common style in plant pathology. Right now we should observe that our three or four suggested strong historical phenotypes may—and I believe they do—represent genotypes: I might even go so far as to suggest that the Psa phenotype (perhaps representing a PSA wildtype) will have variations in drug usage simply according to the availability of drugs. I would also suggest that drug usage among alcoholics depends in part on the phenotype.

What we are doing in part, in this chapter, is looking at apparent genetic components of alcoholism (largely the neuronal genetic components) so that we may eventually get a better idea of the biological components of alcoholism—that is, looking at alcoholic phenotypes (representing alcoholic genotypes) in order to understand more about the neurology and biology of alcoholism or, in other words, looking in a specific way at Alcoholism(1) to understand more about Alcoholism(2), and the other way 'round. Our genetic or genomic search involving alcoholism-associated phenotypes may be expected to show complex traits likely to be genetically heterogeneous, as is the case, for example, with asthma-associated phenotypes. In such cases, even working with founder populations with a relatively small number of independent genomes, susceptibility alleles at many loci may influence phenotypes, and these susceptibility alleles are likely to be common polymorphisms in the population. It follows that, if alcoholism is a polygenic condition (produced by combinations of genes), as indeed seems likely, research should seek quantitative trait loci (QTLs) for the condition.

Analysis of these QTLs will consider (1) the amount of trait variation controlled by a particular locus (on the genome), (2) the nature of the population being analyzed, and (3) the method used to analyze the population. We cannot, of course, breed alcoholics of various types as we breed plants for study, but there are indications that alcoholics marry other alcoholics, and have alcoholic children, so that we have in effect recombinant inbred (RI) lines with a high degree of homozygosity, suggesting that genotypes will alter over the years. In recombinant inbred populations, if parents differ significantly in genotype, the phenotypes of the children will show more extreme variation. (This may be of major importance if alcoholic types—in the Jellinek or Zucker sense—are in fact genotypes.) In particular, heterozygous hybrids are likely to show neither the dominant allele nor the recessive allele but somewhere in between. (So that a Jellinek type δ alcoholic marrying a Jellinek type γ alcoholic might have children showing what seems to be an alcoholism pure to neither type—but they will generally have an alcoholic predisposition.)

We suggest here that there may be at least three, more likely four, common present phenotypes useful for the study of alcoholism, rather than two, as with Cloninger type I and type II or Babor type A and type B or Knight essentials and reactives. We will designate the first three phenotypes as Primary Sociopathic Alcoholism (phenotype Psa), which is largely Jellinek ε alcoholism (modified) and Zucker type 1 Revised with some Zucker 4-b; Secondary Depressive Alcoholism (phenotype Sda), which is Jellinek γ (subset) alcoholism and Zucker type 3; and Primary Cumulative Alcoholism (phenotype Pca), which is Jellinek δ alcoholism and Zucker type 4-c, and may include some of Zucker type 4-b.

As we noted before, if Primary Episodic Alcoholism (Pea) represents a separate phenotype from Psa, research on the genetics of alcoholism will be greatly complicated: we believe this complication is necessary. We have modified Jellinek by treating primary instantaneous alcoholism as essentially episodic, although there may be a variety of instantaneous alcoholism that is not primary, if it is accompanied by a recognized disorder such as manic-depressive psychosis—in which case it becomes what we are calling Sda alcoholism. We have kept the division between Psa and Pea, even while recognizing that PEA, not PSA, may be the wildtype.

This may be a good place to discuss recent research on the question of phenotypes, and particularly the so-called *extended* phenotype. Here we appeal (although very briefly) to the paradigm-revising work of Richard Dawkins ([1982] 1999). I would like to quote Dawkins on the matter of genetic determinism. He is considering the view that "genetic determinism is determinism in the full philosophical sense of irreversible inevitability" (ibid.:10), and he suggests that some of those who hold this view

> are determinists in that they believe in a physical materialistic basis for all our actions. So am I. We would also probably . . . agree that human nervous systems are so complex that in practice we can forget all about determinism and behave as if we had free will. *Neurones may be amplifiers of fundamentally indeterminate physical events* [my emphasis]. The only point I wish to make is that, whatever view one takes on the question of determinism, the insertion of the word "genetic" is not going to make any difference. (ibid.:11)

That said, we can begin to look at the matter of Darwinian adaptation, and to what Dawkins calls the extended phenotype—extended, in some sense, to include alterations in the world around—not only in the interaction of genotype with that world but the actual creation of parts of that world. Before we do that, we may register an additional caveat, or series of caveats, on genes and genetics. Let us consider the problem of what Dawkins calls a *gene for reading*. The following is a summary of what he says (ibid.:23):

Reading is a learned skill of prodigious complexity, but that does not mean there cannot be a *gene for reading*. All we need to discover a "gene for reading" is to discover a gene for nonreading, say a gene that led to a brain lesion causing specific dyslexia. The dyslexic person might be normal and intelligent in all aspects except ability to read. No geneticist would be surprised if this dyslexia bred true in some Mendelian fashion. But the gene would only show its effect in an environment that included what we think of as normal education. In a prehistoric environment it might have had no detectable effect, or been known for a different effect. In our environment, it would properly be called a gene *for dyslexia*, since that would be its most salient effect. But it would establish a genetic component in reading ability. In fact, it follows from the ordinary conventions of genetic terminology that the wildtype gene at the same location, the gene the "nondyslexic" population has in double dose, would be called a gene *for reading*, in the same way there was a gene for *tallness* in Mendel's peas, the logic of the terminology being identical in the two cases.

EXTENDED PHENOTYPES

That is, in both cases what is of interest is a *difference*, and the difference only shows itself in some specified environment—as, in this case, a difference in reading ability can be shown only where there is something to read. However complex a given state of the world may be, the *difference* between that state of the world and some alternative state may be caused by something extremely simple. But Dawkins goes on to point out some further complications, using as his example the differences in hygienic behavior among two types of honeybees, Brown's and Van Scoy's:

> The hygienic behaviour of the Brown strain of honeybees involves the whole neuro-muscular system, but the fact that they perform the behaviour whereas Van Scoy bees do not is, according to Rothenbuhler's model, due to differences at two loci only. One locus determines the uncapping of cells containing diseased brood, the other locus determines the removing of diseased brood after uncapping. . . . Although the uncapping and removing genes of the Brown strain are rightly called genes for uncapping and removing, they are defined as such only because they have alleles whose effect is to prevent the behaviour from being performed. The mode of action of these alleles could be boringly destructive. They might simply cut some vital link in the neural machinery. I am reminded of [R. L.] Gregory's (1961) vivid illustration

of the perils of making inferences from ablation experiments on the brain: "the removal of any of several widely spaced resistors may cause a radio set to emit howls, but it does not follow that the howls are immediately associated with these resistors, or indeed that the causal relation is anything but the most indirect. In particular, we should not say that the function of the resistors in the normal circuit is to inhibit howling." (ibid.:25)

We will be defining our genetic terms more fully a little later. For the moment, we note that alleles are different forms or variants of genes found at the same place, or *locus* (pl. *loci*), on a chromosome. Now let us go on to the business of the *extended phenotype*. Here is Dawkins:

> Genes affect proteins, and proteins affect X which affects Y which affects Z which . . . affects the phenotypic character of interest [remembering that phenotypes are distinguished by interaction with the environment]. But the conventional geneticist defines "phenotypic effect" in such a way that X and Y and Z must all be confined inside one individual body wall. The extended geneticist recognizes that the cut-off is arbitrary, and is quite happy to allow his X, Y, and Z to leap the gap between one individual body and another. . . . Human red blood cells, for instance, have no nuclei, and must express the phenotypes of genes in other cells. So why should we not, when the occasion warrants it, conceive of the bridging of gaps between cells in different bodies? And when will the occasion warrant it? Whenever we find it convenient, and this will tend to be in any of those cases where, in conventional language, one organism appears to be manipulating another. . . . And how far afield can the phenotype extend? Is there any limit to action at a distance, a sharp cut-off, an inverse-square law? The farthest action at a distance I can think of is a matter of several miles, the distance separating the extreme margin of a beaver lake from the genes for whose survival it is an adaptation. If beaver lakes could fossilize, we would presumably see a trend toward increased lake size if we arranged the fossils in chronological order. The increase in size was doubtless an adaptation produced by natural selection, in which case we have to infer that the evolutionary trend came about by allele replacement. In the terms of the extended phenotype, alleles for larger lakes replaced alleles for smaller lakes. In the same terms, beavers can be said to carry within themselves genes whose phenotypic expression extends many miles away from the genes themselves. (1999:232–33)

I have quoted Dawkins at length because I think what he has said must be kept in mind in our discussion of biological and genetic characteristics of alcoholism, and in the range of phenotypic variation. The drinkers who, over time, changed the environment of drinking (over time but culminating, through frontier extension, in the period of the Alcoholic Republic, 1790–1840) were, on this showing, engaged in extended phenotypic variation not unlike the beavers building ever larger lakes. Of course, the timeline is much shortened, but the point remains. One point it may be advisable to make here. The extended phenotype may include partial contribution toward the construction of a society for particular expression of phenotypical or genotypical variants. Thus there may exist a society—or, more likely, societies—that are the extended phenotypes of berserks, druids, shamans, oracles, sibyls, bards, all those who especially have heard the "voices of the gods." But how would it be if the origin of consciousness spelled *finis* to the world of these bicameral men and women—to use the term suggested by Julian Jaynes (1982)—and yet the genotype continued true? Could this happen? Are there clues that it has happened with manic depression over the years, as the work of Kay Redfield Jamison (1993) suggests? Could this also help explain the existence of alcoholic genotypes? Was William James on the right track with the paean to drunkenness?

We will of course be looking at possible genetic components as part of our considering alcoholism as a (physical) disease (specifically, Alcoholism[2]) in Chapter 5, but we should look now more specifically at the genetics of alcoholism. We will touch on COGA, the Collaborative Study on the Genetics of Alcoholism (typology and results to date), and on QTLs for Alcohol-Related Behaviors, in this chapter. We will also look at the value of genetic studies for alcoholism traits, including twin studies and adoption studies, and Vaillant's findings on the natural history of alcoholism. These seem to us to be most properly a part of the discussion of the biochemistry of alcoholism. But now, before we get to COGA, we had best review some basic research in genetics, and how that research has been carried on, define some terms, and then perhaps look at implications.

MORE ON GENETICS

It all goes back to the monk of Brno, Gregor Mendel, whose breeding experiments with pea plants (*Pisum*), published in 1865, defined the early science of genetics. With his peas, Mendel could control pollination and develop highly inbred varieties that bred true and that had clearly defined and clearly observable traits (phenotypes). At the end of the nineteenth century, an American Mendelian, R. A. Emerson, using maize (Indian corn) as his experimental organism, began experimenting with Mendelian principles in plant breeding. (Each kernel on a cob of maize is the result of separate fertilization, enhancing the significance of Emerson's statistical data.) Emerson and E. M. East established the idea that "quantitative traits" result from the independent inheritance of several different genes and their alleles, and the consequent effect of each on the others.

By 1914, the common fruit fly, *Drosophila melanogaster*, had displaced maize as a more advantageous organism for genetic tests. The fly has a short reproductive cycle (ten days), abundant progeny (one hundred to four hundred per mating), and the odd quality that meiosis in males is not accompanied by the exchange of chromosome segments, making results of matings regularly interpretable. (Meiosis, you recall, is the form of cell division taking place in sexual reproduction, where half the offspring's DNA comes from the mother and half from the father.) These characteristics made it possible, in a few short years, for Thomas Morgan and his colleagues to show (1) that genes occur in linear arrays along each chromosome, (2) that pairs of homologous chromosomes exchange parts (cross over) in meiosis during maturation of eggs, and (3) that many genes—possibly, eventually, all—can be assigned to individual chromosomes and their positions mapped relative to one another.

Before this, in 1902, the British physician Archibald Garrod had noted that the inherited human defect *alcaptonuria* (black urine) had an odd pattern of inheritance, which William Bateson (who coined the term "genetics") recognized as being similar to a recessive Mendelian trait. By 1914, Garrod had extended the Mendelian paradigm to other Human metabolic maladies, eventually suggesting that each malady was the result of the loss of a different metabolic step, arguably because of a particular enzyme deficiency—thus arguably a deficiency in the gene, according to the "one gene–one enzyme" rule. But in those days most medical doctors did not care about genetics, and geneticists did not read medical literature.

It was not until almost midcentury that G. W. Beadle and others, working first with *Drosophila m.*, and then more successfully with bread mold (*Neurospora crassa*), then still more successfully with *E. coli* bacteria, finally developed a model for testing Garrod's hypotheses. In the meantime, the work with *Neurospora* had shown that each gene was responsible for one enzyme required for the synthesis of a particular cellular constituent. This is the one-gene/one-enzyme hypothesis, now known as the one-gene/one-polypeptide paradigm.

Since that time, *Drosophila* has come back into its own in a central position in biological research. The nematode (tiny worm) *Caenorhabditis elegans* has revealed unexpected attributes of the developmental process, and genetic analysis of the special aspects of vertebrate biology has the advantage of decades of work on mutant mice. But since the rediscovery of Mendel's work a century ago, nothing has contradicted the assumption that all genetic systems, regardless of organism, work in fundamentally the same way and through the same set of molecules. And that is why, when we discuss the genetics of alcoholism, we find ourselves talking about fruit flies and tiny worms and mutant mice. Humans are not *merely* living organisms like *Drosophila m.*, and *C. elegans*, and the mutant mice. But we *are* living organisms, subject to the laws of genetic systems, and Alcoholism(2), as we understand it, is a genetic condition. We have already spoken of *phenotype* and *genotype*. Before we go on, we should define three other terms, *allele, homozygote,* and *marker gene.*

Alleles, as we noted above, are different forms or variants of genes found at the same place, or *locus,* on a chromosome: they are assumed to arise by mutation. Homozygotes are nuclei, cells, or organisms with identical alleles for one or more specific genes. The word leads to an adjective, *homozygous* and noun *homozygosity,* contrasted with *heterozygous* and *heterozygosity.* Marker genes are genes that confer a readily detectable phenotype on cells carrying the gene: enzymic reporter genes, selectable markers conferring antibiotic resistance, or a cell membrane protein with a characteristic *epigote* (site on a large molecule against which an antibody is produced). When we make our genetic or genomic search to see possible indications of the heritability of alcoholism, we will be using these terms. We will also be using them in our discussion (1) of the relationship of alcoholism to other heritable conditions and (2) of the question of brain changes (and other "psychobiosocial" changes) in adolescence, and thus the possibility that what we call Zucker type 2 (Developmentally Limited Alcoholism) is a condition the "alcoholic" may grow out of.

The matter of chaotic ordering has a place in our discussion of genetics here, and in our discussion of the *koinonia* in the chapter on theology. Moreover, to the extent that alcoholism may be linked genetically with manic-depressive psychosis ("bipolar disorder"), the study of chaos theory as bipolarity may be additionally useful. And it is also possible that allergic threshold change may obey laws of chaotic ordering. Here we will begin by defining what we mean by *chaotic ordering,* and then go on to link it to our discussion of genetics. Other linkages come later.

CHAOTIC ORDERING

In chaos theory, the progress of certain values (which may include genetic values) is heavily dependent upon initial conditions, giving rise to a system (meaning a system described in nonlinear equations) where solutions determining the values can only be determined iteratively (that is, by repetition), and where there are multiple "correct" solutions. If we map our iterative findings logistically, we will come up with what is called a bifurcation diagram, whose net effect is to show us (1) that all outcomes cannot be predicted (which is the "chaotic" part), but (2) that the pattern of outcomes provides evidence of *scaling* in the system—that is, that in self-similar systems (which these are) an exact copy of the whole is reproduced again and again, becoming smaller and smaller (the "ordering" part). The pattern remains, though the scale changes. In other words, the system (the "pattern") is determined, even though the outcomes cannot be known. We can express probabilities, but we cannot predict specific events: that's part of this ordering, and it means that (among other things) individual stories may be more important than statistical averages. Before we go further in our discussion here, we should define *phase space*.

In Alan Dean's words, "Phase space gives a way of turning numbers into pictures, abstracting every bit of information from a system of moving parts . . . and making a flexible road map to all its opportunities" (1997:110–11). This means that it is possible to depict a dynamical system as being, at a given moment, the resolution of all the elements making up the system, which can be diagrammed as a single point. Your existence (or mine, or an alcoholic's) at any moment (say this one) may be considered an instantaneous resolution of all the components, biological, psychological, social, cultural, and historical, that comprise your life (or mine, or the alcoholic's). If it were possible to identify and depict each and every component in an n-dimensional matrix, what you are at one instant of time could be denoted by a single point within that n-dimensional matrix of your life—that is, you would have a unique n-dimensional address. At the next interval you will have moved to another point and thus acquired a new (also unique) n-dimensional address. The space in which this movement occurs is what is called n-dimensional phase space.

Now one would think it should be possible to move anywhere within the matrix that defines his or her life, but those who work with nonlinear systems have found that movement within phase space is in fact determined by specific characteristics called *attractors*. "That is" (again quoting Alan Dean), "particular non-linear dynamical systems display differing patterns of movement; they are attracted to certain kinds of motion" (ibid.). This means the point that describes the state of the system does not move at random, but instead describes specific forms of movement. The picture drawn to depict movement in *phase space* is called a *phase portrait*. There are four varieties of phase portraits: (1) sinks (steady-state attractors), (2) sources (steady-state "repellers"), (3) saddles (steady in one direction, unstable in another, like sitting in a saddle), and (4) limit cycles (which cover a region of phase space in which points "cycle"). Because points outside these features will have motion determined by the features (frequently toward the feature), the features are called attractors. There is one of these attractors whereby points follow an unpredictable complex trajectory, the one we call a *strange attractor*. The way we find strange attractors—which signal the presence of chaotic ordering—is by the iterative (repeating) process of trying out values and seeing what happens. If we map our iterative findings logistically, we will come up with a so-called bifurcation diagram.

In one of the simplest introductions to this chaos theory, talking about the swing of a pendulum, we may use one value x to calculate one value y, then replace our x with y and calculate a new resulting value, as with the swing of the pendulum. But suppose we were to take two values, w and x, to calculate two values y and z (using constants a and b in our calculation). We would now get a whole plane of resulting values, or rather of regions of values, where the (y, z) pairs cycled around a series of values, without ever diverging toward infinity. The regional boundaries (measuring the bounds of different behaviors) would be infinitely scaled and spiky, like a snowflake whose outlines are made up of the boundaries of an infinite number of smaller snowflakes of the same shape. Whatever governs this "infinite snowflake" result is now called a *strange attractor*. The *attractor* in the pendulum case would be a point in "phase space" of zero angle and zero speed. In the case of heritable characteristics, the *attractor* would be a point in phase space having to do with genetic coding. Quoting David Ruelle,

First strange attractors look strange: they are not smooth curves or surfaces but have "non-integer dimension"—or, as Benoit Mandelbrot puts it, they are fractal objects. [This mathematics of fractal objects, though interesting, and leading to some fascinating—and literally beautiful—constructs, is not our primary interest here.] Next, and more importantly, the motion on a strange attractor has sensitive dependence on initial conditions. Finally, while strange attractors have only finite dimension, the time-frequency analysis reveals a continuum of frequencies. (1991)

This point leads us to the matter of sensitive dependence on initial conditions, which must be considered of major significance here: the state of two (or more) systems will diverge if, at time 0 (zero), they have an asynchronous status—which will be the case in the presence of a strange attractor.

Now, biologically all persons but identical twins are different, and this gives us a first level of sensitivity to initial conditions. True, even greater dissimilarities may come from differences in experience, but what we are discussing here is the degree to which the principles of chaotic ordering affect not observable phenotypes but the underlying genotype. In the genetic progression of a human type (say, an alcoholic genotype), a very small genetic variation in the two parental lines, and in the age of conception (not to mention other possible variations), could lead to offspring closer to one prototype or another of alcoholism than either of the parents. A later-life child of a γ alcoholic and a δ alcoholic (or of two mixed-type alcoholics) might be γ, δ, or even ε, or another mixed type, and an earlier-life child be of a different type even from its same-sex sibling.

The ultimate conclusion drawn from our view of chaotic ordering in the genetics of alcoholism is given by Alan Dean:

> On balance it is probably the case that . . . each person has a different neuro-biological basis from which motivation or direction stems. In other words, the use of alcohol . . . arises differently for each person from genetic differences which determine the particular effects of given substances upon particular neurobiological sites. (1997:144)

Work with QTLs has shown that quantitative traits stem from the interaction of different QTLs. Same output from different inputs. This appears to be the case with quite a number of neuronal conditions or diseases (see *Science*, 31 Oct 2003:822–823 passim). And the more dimensions there are in a system above two, the higher is the likelihood of chaotic (and thus individually unpredictable) outcomes. This would seem to emphasize the importance of self-testimony in determining who is an alcoholic and of what kind, while still supporting the importance of FHP data. (We recall that Jellinek's types are the only ones based on self-testimony.) It would also seem to emphasize the complexity of our undertaking in this study, as though, with extended phenotypes, complex behaviors from simple alterations at one locus, and all the rest of modern genetics, lack of agreement on alcoholic type, even failures to distinguish between Alcoholism(1) and Alcoholism(2)—not to mention koinospheres and the idea of the adjacent possible—we needed further complexity.

BACK TO GENETICS

The status of research on genetic components in alcoholism through the mid-1990s was perhaps best given in a report by the National Institutes of Health (1997). It is advisable to review the suggestions of this report before going on. We have already looked at the question of human phenotypes (our types of alcoholics), which are included in the reportin the sections with the subheadings "Individuals at High Risk" (our Psa and Pca, perhaps Pea) and "Alcoholism Co-morbidity with Psychiatric Disorders" (Sda) under the general heading, "Human Phenotypes Associated with Alcohol Related Disorders." Our review here will thus concentrate on two remaining major subheadings in the report: (1) "Research on the Genetic Basis for Alcoholism in Humans" and (2) "The Collaborative Study on the Genetics of Alcoholism" (COGA).

Before looking at research on a genetic basis for alcoholism, it may be a good idea to enter a caveat: we should not expect to find either a single genetic marker or indeed any single etiology for alcoholism, as we have noted (see *Science*, 31 Oct 2003:822–823). In a recent paper, Ralph Tarter and Michael Vanyukov (1994) note that the population fitting the clinical definition of alcoholism or alcohol abuse (more exactly, of "Psychoactive Substance Use Disorder—alcohol abuse or alcohol dependence") includes both those with medical symptoms and those with psychological symptoms, as well as those who abuse and those who are dependent (see also Zucker 1994). It is therefore considered unlikely that etiological studies on this basis will find a single genetic marker for "alcoholism"—and particularly if defined to include "alcohol abuse." But if we put what Tarter and Vanyukov say together with what Zucker says, we may still conclude that *markers* (*marker genes*) may exist for certain types of alcoholism. I would go further: I would suggest that (despite Vaillant) the different types may well have different marker genes.

The Collaborative Study on the Genetics of Alcoholism (COGA) began a dozen and more years ago: it is a six-center study to detect and map susceptibility genes for alcohol dependence and related phenotypes (note: phenotypes, not genotypes). Probands (test subjects) were selected from inpatient and outpatient treatment units (that is, were not self-selected). They were selected if their families included sibship of at least three individuals and if parents were available for study. Test subjects were excluded if they were intravenous drug users (thus eliminating at least some alcoholics of Zucker type 1), had AIDS, or had a terminal non-alcohol-related illness. In other words, alcoholics who were not "pure" alcoholics were excluded. (According to the "Big Book," when A.A. tried this, it didn't work and compromised their mission.) Phenotypes of families including three or more affected relatives in the first degree with alcohol dependence were studied more intensely than others and were used for genetic linkage and association studies. Control families chosen "without respect to diagnosis" included two available parents and three offspring over the age of fourteen years.

Adult lifetime psychiatric status was assessed by direct interview with the Semi-Structured Assessment for the Genetics of Alcoholism (SSAGA). It was used to make diagnoses of alcohol dependence, alcoholism, alcohol abuse or harmful use, by Feighner, DSM-III, and DSM-III-R criteria. A close approximation to a diagnosis of alcohol dependence by DSM-IV and ICD-10 criteria was also possible. Semistructured interviewing for age-appropriate lifetime psychiatric diagnosis of children and adolescents (C-SSAGA, A-SSAGA) was also accomplished and accompanied by an interview for parents (P-SSAGA) for better assessment of symptoms of psychopathology in juveniles. A semistructured interview, Family History Assessment, was developed to assess the presence of psychiatric disorders in relatives.

Phenotypic assessment included measures that have been correlated with susceptibility to alcohol dependence. Biochemical assays were conducted for adenylate cyclase (AC) and monoamine oxidase (MAO) activity (see Chapter 5). Probands and relatives, including juveniles, completed both neuropsychological and neurophysiological tests. Personality traits were assessed using the Tri-dimensional Personality Questionnaire (TPQ) and the Zuckerman Sensation Seeking Scale. Heritable measures were studied as correlated quantitative phenotypic markers of susceptibility to alcohol dependence. An alcohol challenge protocol (procedure) was carried out at the San Diego COGA site to study effects of controlled exposure to alcohol in eighteen- to thirty-year-old offspring of alcohol-dependent probands.

Cooperative families that included three or more members with alcohol dependence were selected for more intensive phenotypic and genotypic study if they were *not* bilineal. Blood was drawn for the transformation of lymphocytes into lymphoblastoid cell lines that were cryopreserved (frozen) for adults and from which DNA was directly extracted for juveniles. Twelve hundred and seventeen families of alcohol-dependent probands (test subjects), including 7,847 adults (eighteen and over) and 1,047 juveniles (ages seven to seventeen), have been personally interviewed with the age-appropriate SSAGA. A random sample of 234 control families, each of two parents and with at least three children (fourteen and over) was selected and the SSAGA was administered. Everyone was also given the selected personality trait-assessment "tests" (TPQ and Zuckerman). Cooperative families with three or more interviewed alcohol-dependent first-degree members were accepted for more intensive assessment and for inclusion into the molecular genetics database (a total of 346 families with 4,164 individual members). Members of these families were recruited for a battery of neuropsychological tests, assessment of electroencephalograms (EEGs) and tests for event-related potentials (ERPs), blood samples for the production of cell lines (adults), DNA samples (adults and juveniles), and biochemistry tests. Members of the control families participated in the neurophysiology protocol and had blood drawn for DNA preparation. The assessment of the 263 (not 346) informative families was completed in the 1990s. An informative sample for genetic linkage and association studies of alcohol dependence, ERP phenotype, and personality traits (105 families) was selected for an initial genomewide linkage analysis. To test by replicating initial findings of genetic linkage and association, a secondary "replication" sample (157 families) was also selected for study.

Two hundred and ninety-one markers were genotyped, with an average heterozygosity of 0.72 and an average intermarker distance of 13.8 cM (a centiMorgan is equal to 1 percent recombination frequency: these are the measures commonly used for determining genetic linkages and associations). There were seven intermarker regions greater than 30 cM, and twenty-eight greater than 20 cM (higher than average recombination frequency is equal to greater linkage). Most markers were trinucleotide or tetranucleotide repeat polymorphisms (microsatellites), in keeping with the fact that linkage studies generally are dealing with multiallelic polymorphisms. Association studies focus on single nucleotide polymorphisms (SNPs).

The COGA criteria for alcohol dependence (alcoholism) require diagnosis of definite alcoholism by Feighner criteria and alcohol dependence by the DSM-III-R criteria. Two-point linkage analyses revealed that twenty-four loci provided evidence for linkage at the $p \leq 0.01$ level. Multipoint analysis identified chromosomal regions suggesting linkage with the alcohol-dependent phenotype on chromosomes 1, 2, and 7. Using the SIBPHASE program, the maximum lod (logarithm of the odds) score for a region on chromosome 1 was 2.93, on chromosome 7 was 3.49, and on chromosome 2 was 1.81. There was suggestive evidence for a protective locus on chromosome 4 near the alcohol dehydrogenase genes, for which protective effects have been reported in Asian populations (see the discussion in Chapter 5 of alcohol-metabolizing enzymes).

It is worthwhile here to define what a lod score is. Suppose we want to decide if two genes/markers are linked. (1) We examine a number of families informative for the loci in question. (2) For each family we find the genotype of each parent and of the offspring. (3) We try to deduce whether each child has the parental arrangement of *alleles* or is a recombinant: this effort is greatly helped if we know how the alleles at the loci we are considering entered the parents (the "phase"). (4) We decide—the tricky part—whether it is more likely that we have observed the particular progeny in that family (a) because the genes are linked and tend to be inherited together, or (b) through chance (Mendelian) *independent assortment* of alleles at the two genes. For this we use the statistic known as the lod score, which is $Z = \log_{10}$ of the probability of observing this family if the genes are linked divided by the probability of observing this family if the genes are not linked. We calculate this relative likelihood assuming that the two genes are tightly linked with no recombination occurring between them at all, i.e., the recombination fraction $g = 0$. Or we can calculate the relative likelihood of any other value of g we choose. The value of g for which Z reaches a maximum positive value is then our best estimate of the distance between the two loci, and the value of Z_{max} is a measure of our confidence in the result. If Z_{max} is greater than 3, we take the linkage to have been proved, if Z_{max} is less than –2, we take the linkage to have been disproved.

Using the ICD-10 typology for alcohol dependence, the study looked at linkages for Withdrawal from Alcohol and Severe Dependence criteria. Analysis with two-point methods provided evidence for linkage at the

$p \geq 0.01$ level on chromosomes 1, 7, 11, and 16, for regions that showed linkage to more than one phenotype. (Note that these phenotypes are *not* defined to bear any particular relation to our hypothetical Psa, Sda, and Pca—or Pea—phenotypes, or to the Zucker or Jellinek typologies.) Regions on chromosomes 1 and 16 showed evidence for linkage with alcohol dependence defined by both COGA and ICD-10 criteria.

However, the levels of significance for linkage with the withdrawal and latent-class phenotypes were greater than for either COGA or ICD-10 diagnostic criteria, over all the chromosomal regions identified. (This suggests, among other things, that there is not so far a good match between phenotypes and diagnostic criteria.)

Multipoint lod scores greater than 2 were observed for COGA-defined alcohol dependence on chromosomes 1 and 7, as noted, and with ICD-10-defined alcohol dependence on chromosomes 8 and 16. Evidence of linkage with the withdrawal phenotype was found on chromosomes 7, 10, 16, and 18. The highest lod score was 4.6 on chromosome 16 for severe alcohol dependence defined by latent-class analysis.

For ERPs, multipoint quantitative linkage analyses showed lod scores greater than 2—a level that is significant without proving a connection—on chromosomes 2, 5, 6, and 11. The strongest signals were found on chromosomes 2 (lod score 3.28) and 6 (lod score 3.41). Conventionally, these two linkages on chromosomes 2 and 6 should, on this showing, be considered proven, as well as there being proof for severe alcohol dependence at chromosome 16. But is this worth all the time we have spent on it—and if it is, why?

Not, certainly, because it is *these* two ERP linkages on chromosomes 2 and 6, or alcohol dependence on chromosome 16—at least, not yet. But it is significant, given a complexly ordered condition with possible inadequate specification of types, that we have *any* proven genetic links in any behavior pattern—even with only "statistical" proof. What it signifies (along with much else already noted), I believe, is that by whatever measures we come up with (and this is the strictest and fullest study yet carried out, to our knowledge), it is reasonable to consider Alcoholism(2) a genetic condition or precondition. Now, to be sure, we are perhaps not as certain as we used to be exactly what this means, and we should look now at a way of saying what it may mean.

THE CO-CONSTRUCTION OF ALCOHOLISM?

Let us note that it is a principle of modern investigation into heredities, as into the determination of life conditions generally—and much else—that "organisms, niches, and search procedures jointly and self-consistently co-construct one another" (Kauffman 2000:20) as part of a biosphere. As Kauffman has observed, the "strange thing about the theory of evolution is that everyone thinks he understands it. But we do not. A biosphere, or an econosphere, self-consistently co-constructs itself according to principles we do not yet fathom" (ibid.). Note: *co-constructs*. We do not yet know the principles (or laws) of agent co-construction that are relevant here. But we can suggest some of them, and they (with the idea of the extended phenotype) are relevant here. Here is a key passage from Kauffman: "Some wellspring of creation, lithe in the scattered sunlight of an early planet, whispered something to the gods, who whispered back, and the mystery came alive. Agency was spawned. With it, the nature of the universe changed, for some new union of matter, energy, information, and something more could reach out and manipulate the world on its own behalf" (ibid.:49). The reader should be cautioned that, compared to old established principles like those of chaos theory, this is new and even untried.

It builds on chaos theory, of course, and it may serve to link together what we will say on the development of the brain, biochemical genetics, and all of that, with the development of the mind. Other modes of explaining that linkage may be available: as with the Johannine theology of the Incarnation (in Chapter 6—and with which this may also be linked), this one is chosen as part of our scientific research program (1) because it is a known and accepted (if not widely accepted) view, (2) because it makes sense (to me at least), and (3) because it may help explain why the modes of treatment for a threefold illness (of mind, body, and spirit) are congruent, even affine, maybe even coterminous—that is, essentially, one and the same.

An autonomous agent, Kauffman suggests, must be an autocatalytic system able to reproduce and able to perform one or more thermodynamic work cycles. He draws a parallel between his work and that of Wittgenstein in his *Philosophical Investigations,* which he characterizes as presenting the hard-won view that *knowing* is in essence "living a language game" (Kauffman 2000:50), cognate to his own view that there is something going on in the universe that is not finitely prestatable: "Life and language games seem persistently open to radical innovations that cannot be deduced from previous categories and concepts" (ibid.). In fact, as a candidate for a kind of fourth law of thermodynamics (which is part of what he is investigating), Kauffman suggests:

> As an average trend, biospheres and the universe create novelty and diversity as fast as they can manage to do so without destroying the accumulated propagating organization that is the basis and nexus from which further novelty is discovered and incorporated into the propagating organization. (ibid.:85)

Life in a nonergodic (not-reproducing-identically) universe creates (or cocreates) change as rapidly as possible.

Recalling, as we noted above, that "organisms, niches, and search procedures jointly and self-consistently co-construct one another" (ibid.:20) we may now add several additional ideas. (1) First, the idea that "communities of agents will evolve to an 'edge of chaos' between over-rigid and over-fluid behavior" (ibid.:22); (2) second, the idea that "the concept of an agent is, inherently, a non-equilibrium concept" (ibid.:8) and that "there appears to be some positive relationship between the diversity and complexity of structures and processes and the diversity and complexity of the features of a non-equilibrium system" (ibid.:95); (3) third, the idea that the push into novelty may be formalized mathematically as an "adjacent possible" (ibid.:22); and (4) fourth, the idea "that the biosphere gates its way into the adjacent possible at just that rate at which its inhabitants can just make a living, just poised so that selection sifts out useless variations slightly faster than those variations arise" (ibid.).

This leaves us—where? Kauffman suggests (ibid.:160) it leaves us with a set of four laws for four apparently different phase transitions for coevolutionarily constructible communities of autonomous agents:

Law 1: Communities of autonomous agents will evolve to the dynamical "edge of chaos" within and between members of the community, thereby simultaneously achieving an optimal "coarse-graining" of each agent's world that maximizes the capacity of each agent to discriminate and "act without trembling hands."

Law 2: A coassembling community of agents, on a short timescale with respect to coevolution, will assemble to a self-organized critical state with some maximum number of species per community. In the vicinity of that maximum, a power law distribution of "avalanches of local extinction events" will occur. As the maximum is approached, the net rate of entry of new species slows down, then halts.

Law 3: On a coevolutionary timescale, coevolving autonomous agents attain a self-organized critical state by tuning landscape structure (ways of making a living) and coupling between landscapes, yielding a global power law distribution of extinction and speciation events, and even a power law distribution of species lifetimes.

Law 4: Autonomous agents will evolve such that causally local communities are on a generalized "subcritical-supercritical boundary" exhibiting a generalized self-organized critical average for the sustained expansion of the "adjacent possible" of the effective phase space of the community. We might say (perhaps with particular reference to the first and last of these, and to what we have said about the disequilibrium community of agents in a nonergodic universe, and the novelty and complexity involved in the push into the adjacent possible) that it leaves us with the outlines of a model of biospheric construction something like this:

(1) There are divergences in brain chemistry at some point in the progress from parents to children, as a result of the nonergodic (not-reproducing-identically) nature of the universe; some of these divergences, in families in the same generations, will be very similar, and this new diversity will increase in the next generations, if it is useful.

(2) The rapidity of this development will depend (perhaps critically) on the "edge-of-chaos" location of the local biosphere, and thus to the ease of gating into the adjacent possible.

(3) There will be a kind of quantum leap in the diversity and complexity of the biosphere as chaotic ordering "heats up" and entry into the adjacent possible speeds up, and we have the "emergence of novel functionalities in evolution" (Kauffman 2000:5) such as language (Kauffman's fourth example, after hearing, sight, and flight, and his first specifically human example). Two points to note here: First, this development is cocreated. Second, at the point where language comes in, it is possible for the agent to become conscious of agency: the adjacent possible here is the realm in which mind exists along with brain, and where cocreation can be conscious or, perhaps, in some sense, willed. Which brings us to the question of language.

It is an old saying that ontogeny recapitulates phylogeny—that is, the natural history of the individual recapitulates the natural history of the race or type. It was in a conversation with the philosopher Owen Barfield (1898–1997) that I first heard the punning statement that ontology (the study of being) recapitulates philology (the historical study of language), in other words that what we are (and what we think, and what we think we are) is all determined by our language. In fact, it may be argued—was to be argued, I think, by C. S. Lewis and J. R. R. Tolkien in their *Language and Human Nature*—that language ability (particularly language invention) is precisely what distinguishes human nature from the nature of other animals. Here is John McWhorter's statement on that point: "various indications suggest that human beings are at least genetically predisposed to acquire and use language" (2001:8)—and then,

> if this genetic instruction or predisposition for language is real, then it must have been created by a mutation. In this light, it is more economical [the economy of Occam's Razor, again] to reconstruct that such a mutation occurred once in the stem population of *Homo sapiens* 150,000-odd years ago and was then passed on to all descendants, rather than emerging at various later times in separate offshoot populations. . . . Some traits can mutate into existence separately throughout the world, such as the development of eyes or the power of flight. . . . [But] if language had emerged in separate populations at later dates, then we would expect there to remain pockets of human groups where this mutation had not occurred—or at least for there to be records of such in the past. (ibid.:8–9)

Myself, I'm not entirely convinced by McWhorter's argument that there was a once-and-for-all mutation 150,000-odd years ago. I am, rather, convinced that, with a community of agents on the edge of chaos or the subcritical-supercritical edge, if the development of language does not occur, there will be an avalanche of local extinction, and the community will cease to be. In one sense, I suppose, the distinction may not matter: predisposition to language remains the distinguishing mark of *Homo sapiens*, and it is a genetic mutation. But the timetable may matter very much. Our research program here is based on the separated development of languages at relatively recent times (say the Later Wisconsin Ice Age, possibly as a critical event), with the development beginning with interjections and winding up with the first development of proper nouns (names) perhaps ten thousand to twenty thousand years ago—separate development, not diffusion. We will briefly sketch some implications of this in the next chapter, and more in Chapter 9. In the meantime, we should note that the capacity or predisposition for language is proposed (hypothesized) as a genetic mutation, meaning that it should obey the laws we have already discussed. And it should in principle be possible to construct biogenetic connections between "speech genes" and the genes for predisposition to Alcoholism(2).

Given our present almost-naked nescience on the subject, and given the doubtless polygenic nature (actually, I suspect, multiple natures) of both speech capacity and alcoholic predisposition, we are a long way from knowing how to test for the connection. A few fragments of our knowledge may, however, be shored up here: (1) the speech areas of the brain are affected by ingestion of alcohol, and (2) there is (as we will see) some possible evidence of differential effect in alcoholics and nonalcoholics. Also (3) as Kay Redfield Jamison (1993) has shown, there are unquestionable connections between artistic creativity and manic-depressive psychosis (to which Jellinek type γ alcoholism is often connected). Also (4), research on extinction of languages suggests "fundamental links between human languages and cultures, non-human species, and the earth's ecosystems" with the extinction of languages tied in some way to the extinction of biospheres (Nettle and Romaine 2000:49, though Nettle and Romaine do not use the word *biosphere*): it also suggests a move away from one kind of complexity in language (it might be called the complexity of the small) toward another (it might be called the complexity of the large) as the biosphere or econosphere expands.

Perhaps we may use the word *koinosphere* here, and perhaps we should note that, in general, archaic languages as we have first discovered or experienced them are more complex than their successors in structure and meaning—as suggested quite a while ago by Owen Barfield (1928). What I am suggesting here, as the outline for this part of our scientific research program, and making use of Siegel's *Intoxication: Life in Pursuit of Artificial*

Paradise (1989), is that in protohuman communities on the supercritical-subcritical edge (would that be Adam and Eve on the edge of "creation"?), the realization of the goals of the "fourth drive" was in some way connected with the creation of language for that *koinosphere*. This linking of intoxication and the creation of language is scarcely a new point: as Siegel notes, "William James believed that the intoxication revealed the uniqueness of our species to contemplate the hidden meaning behind language and thought" (ibid.:214)—and it is only a step from contemplating the hidden meaning behind language to being part of the creation of that meaning. A step from perception to utterance (see Chapter 6).

In fact, if we formulate this in the terms suggested by Jaynes, or if we adopt the language of the theologians, it may not be a step at all. And lurking at the edges of our discussion here are phrases like "drunk with words" (or in the Gladstonian version, "inebriated with the exuberance of his own verbosity") and even the Latin *in vino veritas*. Those who heard the outburst of "tongues" at Pentecost simply thought the speakers were drunk, not inspired, but the linkage in behavior is still there. In Chapter 5 we will be looking at some suggestions on the evolution (or development) of consciousness.

Before summarizing what we have said in this chapter thus far, we should look briefly at—so that we may tie in with—the propositions advanced by Plomin and Edelman (1989), and the distinction between *primary* and *secondary* repertoires. First, Edelman argues (as briefly noted above), that the process of morphogenesis, based on cell division, cell movement, and cell differentiation, produces a species-dependent neuroanatomy variable at the individual level: groups of neurons in a specific brain region deriving from this process are known as *primary repertoires*. The genetic code is a template imposing constraints, but not imposing unanimity (I am tempted to put this in italics, to emphasize its importance). Second, through behavioral engagement with the external world, some synaptic connections are promoted through use and thus strengthened, others neglected and thus weakened, so that certain neural networks are self-selected from the diversity of those available: these are *secondary repertoires* (this also deserves italics for importance). In practice, primary and secondary repertoires may be overlapping. Finally, third, primary, and secondary repertoires link psychology and physiology, by forming maps: these maps are connected by the entrance and reentrance of neural linkages.

To summarize, what this means is what we have said already, albeit in different words and in a different context: that is, by our behavior in, with, and through the external world, we promote (even co-create) certain synaptic connections, self-selected (these are the *secondary repertoires*), in accordance with the templates imposed by the genetic code (these are the *primary repertoires*). To put it in terms of alcoholism and alcoholic behavior, the alcoholic has a genetic predisposition toward alcoholism and alcoholic behavior, but he or she chooses the behavior to engage in, thereby strengthening either alcoholic synaptic connections or those opposed to alcoholic behavior. The theological parallel would be original sin—we have a tendency to do wrong things, but we can choose not to—and our behavior constitutes and defines our choice. The *telos* of sobriety would thus parallel the *telos* of salvation. In the meantime, *we form our own neural linkage maps by our chosen behavior*.

We have thus far suggested that Alcoholism(2) is heritable; that it may be genetically connected with certain speech abilities may in fact have arisen as either an evolutionary byproduct or an evolutionary *desideratum* in a great shift (or set of shifts) to an adjacent possible of human speech sometime in the late Wisconsin Ice Age; that the genotypic condition may be phenotypically altered (even as part of an extended phenotype) through conscious synaptic alteration (more on the matter of consciousness in the next chapter); that the heritability of the condition is multigenic, possibly to the point of real differentiation in types (perhaps even cognate with language differentiations), and that laws of chaotic ordering seem to apply—this all, of course, as a very brief summary. Now to Chapter 4.

4 ~

Mind: The Psychology of Alcoholism

IF ALCOHOLISM IS A MENTAL ILLNESS—as Bill W. said it was, and as the *Diagnostic and Statistical Manual* says it is—we should be looking, among other things, at what exactly a mental illness is, and (since it is clearly in some sense an "illness of the mind") therefore at what the mind is. But that is, unfortunately, much more easily said than done. First off, we must decide whether we are talking about "the mind" or *Mind*. If, as in the Cartesian view (popularized if not invented by René Descartes in the seventeenth century), eternal, immaterial, incorruptible *Mind* is God's presence in humankind, it cannot be ill (nor, for that matter, do ill). The illness must lie in Mind's corporeal agent, the brain, or in the nervous system that feeds the brain. The effect of the Cartesian view would be—and was—to transfer "mental illness" into "brain-sickness"—and thus cast treatment, in effect, as getting the brain out of the way of Mind, so that the patient's irreducible innate "moral nature" could come through. But even with the Cartesian view, so long as we do not follow it as far as Mrs. Eddy followed it (I think, though I'm not always entirely sure we know exactly what she meant), we can at least look at the brain, taking it as the mind in the body (so to speak), and at least beginning there. In fact, however, we can do more. Once again, we turn to the founder of American "psychology"—the great man we have met in the three preceding chapters, William James.

James was greatly impressed by the work of Charles Darwin, who suggested that every physical characteristic that evolves in a species serves a purpose, performs a needed function. And if physical characteristics, James argued, then why not mental characteristics? James suggested that thinking, feeling, learning, remembering—all the processes of human consciousness—exist in present-day humankind because they have helped us survive as a species. This is the variety of psychology generally called *functionalism*. That we now speak of *cognitive process* rather than *function* does not alter the fact that many present-day psychologists and even psychotherapists have views going back directly to William James. And, on the grounds that it might be a good idea to look at *how* we got where we

129

are, before fully analyzing *where* we are, that is what we will try to do—switching the terms we use if not our goal. Perhaps we might begin with why this illness might come to exist. How did it evolve (if it did)? And (as a part of this, at least) what useful purpose can this special sensitivity to, and predisposition to uncontrolled use of, alcohol have served, so that it came down through the ages? (It will not escape attention that we have begun to do this in our last chapter.)

WHAT IS MIND, AND HOW DID IT GET THAT WAY?

Now, one may believe that there is one omnipotent Mind behind the process of "evolution"—a Mind that may occasionally intervene to maintain viable life forms despite the procession of diverse and unfriendly environments. One may believe there is such a Mind but that it is really only a kind of cosmic watchmaker that sets the evolutionary process in motion and establishes its rules. One may believe simply that there is no mind (or Mind) but only rules of natural selection (keeping away, for the moment, from the question, Who made the rules?). One may simply believe that the mind is a kind of interface between body and spirit. In all these variations on what constitutes the mind, if we are to look at mental illness, the question will remain, pretty much, how did we—humankind—get to where we are? In the end, we seem to have three alternatives: we can say that, in some sense, the mind itself is ill, and look toward psychiatry; we can say that the mind is ill because there are neurological and other neural ("brain") problems, problems essentially of the body; or we can say that what is really involved is a kind of spiritual malady that plays itself out in what we call mental illness. We can also say, as Bill W. said, that this is a strange illness of mind, body, and spirit, all together but in that order, suggesting that mind and body are the most closely linked of the possible pairs (mind/body, mind/spirit, body/spirit). This is what we will do, and we will ask, How did we get to where we are? And why? And particularly, where is this *where*? Suggestions on the road there will come later. And before we get *there*, we might suggest that even our mind—if not the Mind behind evolution—may itself evolve. Here we may adopt into our scientific research program the suggestions of Julian Jaynes (1982).

BEFORE PHILOSOPHY

To the question of where we are with this illness (or predisposition), there are four kinds of answers: (1) the historical/philosophical shading into the psychological (as with Jaynes), (2) the psychiatric, (3) the neurological, and (4) the theological. We will begin with the most controversial part of our model—if you like, of our scientific research program—that is, with the proposition that consciousness (in the sense we ordinarily use the word) is a new thing, coming into the world perhaps three thousand years ago, so that (inter alia) before this time there was—there *could be*—no philosophy. In one sense, of course, this is scarcely a new proposition: it is found implicit in Henri Frankfort (1897–1954) and others in the first half of the twentieth century, and indeed in Goethe (1748–1832), in Rudolf Steiner (1861–1925), and in Owen Barfield (1898–1997).

Frankfort's conclusions are worth noting:

> Even early man, entangled in the immediacy of his perceptions, recognized the existence of certain problems which transcend the phenomena. He recognized the problem of origin and the problem of *telos*, of the aim and purpose of being. He recognized the invisible order of justice maintained by his customs, mores, institutions; and he connected this invisible order with the visible order, with its succession of days and nights, seasons and years, obviously maintained by the sun. Early man even pondered the hierarchy of the different powers which he recognized in nature. . . . Natural phenomena, whether or not they were personified and became gods [this is not perhaps the best way to put this], confronted ancient man with a living presence, a significant "Thou," which, again, exceeded the scope of conceptual definition. (1949:17, 29)

This almost-Buberian "I and Thou" dichotomy will reappear in Chapter 6, as well as in our discussion of what we may call the ontogenic and phylogenic processes of alcoholism and sobriety in Chapter 9. And yes, we do suggest, in effect, that the ontogeny of the individual alcoholic recapitulates the phylogeny of alcoholism in the human race—and even perhaps, as Barfield has suggested, that ontology recapitulates philology (or the other way 'round).

In this connection, we may look at the remarks of Thorkild Jacobsen: "We must remember that in mythopoeic thought a name is a force within a person propelling him in a certain direction" (1949:172)—so that, as the name of the god *Á-zi-mu-a* ("the growing straight of the arm") suggests that, as *Á-zi-mu-a* operates within En-ki, it will be to straighten En-ki's arm—and then, discussing the time almost before time, quoting the words of the *Enuma Elish* (going back to the third millennium B.C.E.), "When a sky above had not yet even been mentioned / And the name of firm ground below had not yet even been thought of / . . . / When no god whosoever had appeared; / Had been named by name, had been determined as to his lot, / Then were gods formed within them" (ibid.:184). The *them* within whom the gods were formed were the primal forces of chaos: Apsu, the sweet waters, Mummu, the mist and cloud, and Ti'amat, the salt waters, the sea. But the point for us is that, at the very birth of the oldest literature we know, the naming of something is what brings it into existence (or immediately accompanies its being brought into existence) and the names of gods (or things) express their true nature. This is as close as mythopoeia comes to philosophy—and this is the worldview (or world-approach) that underlines Jaynes's view of the development of consciousness, of its origins in the breakdown of the bicameral mind, through which the gods (doubtless even *Á-zi-mu-a*) spoke in olden time.

BICAMERAL MINDS?

Though others got there first, it is in fact the version of the model proposed by Jaynes (1982) that has the strongest affinities and suggestiveness for our research program. Its importance lies in the (highly usable but not necessary) proposition that up until about three millennia ago, human beings did what they did in response to the "voices of the gods" and that half the mind (half the brain) was set aside, as it were, for that purpose, capable of receiving "voices" but silent as to their expression or sending. In *The Origin of Consciousness in the Breakdown of the Bicameral Mind,* Jaynes argues that schizophrenic hallucinations are similar to the guidances of the gods in antiquity, and suggests that the reason most of us do not undergo hallucinations under stress—unless it is extreme stress—is that the breakdown products of stress-produced adrenalin are passed rapidly through our kidneys. On the other hand, presumably for genetic reasons, in those individuals who do suffer hallucinations, these breakdown products do not pass with normal rapidity through the kidneys, and build up in the blood (ibid.:93). His paragraph on Achilles and Hector is worth quoting.

> So Achilles, repulsed by Agamemnon, in decision-stress by the grey sea, hallucinates Thetis out of the myths. So Hector, faced with the decision-suffering of whether to go outside the walls of Troy to fight Achilles or stay within them, in the stress of the decision hallucinates the voice that tells him to go out. The divine voice ends the decision-stress before it has reached any considerable level. (ibid.:94)

And this brings him to the question of voices, which, he argues, are the least resistible (because most intrusive) of all sense phenomena.

In what he calls bicameral men, those who are not subjectively conscious, he argues that "volition came as a voice that was in the nature of a neurological command, in which the command and the action were not separated, in which to hear was to obey" (ibid.:99). Since the bicameral mind is mediated by speech, the speech areas of the brain must be involved in some important way. In that 95 percent of the population that is right-handed, the left hemisphere contains the three speech areas: (1) the supplementary motor cortex, on the very top of the left frontal lobe; (2) Broca's area, lower down at the back of the left frontal lobe; and (3), the most important, Wernicke's area, chiefly the posterior part of the left temporal lobe with parts of the parietal area. But why only in the one hemisphere (except in some peculiarly ambidextrous people)? The areas exist in both hemispheres, but in one are undeveloped.

> Could it be that these silent "speech" areas on the right hemisphere had some function at an earlier stage in man's history that now they do not have? The answer is clear if tentative. The selective pressures of evolution which could have brought about so mighty a result are those of the bicameral civilizations. The language of men was involved with only one hemisphere in order to leave the other free for the language of gods. (ibid.:103–4)

In this connection, it is worth noting that recent work in anthropology, and particularly palaeoanthropology, suggests (as Jaynes suggests, ibid.: 128–37) that specifically *human* beings come with—and are defined by—the use of language, initially some time around forty thousand years ago. Jaynes has also suggested that in language development "calls, modifiers, and commands" came before nouns, and that names—"proper nouns"— were the last stage, coinciding with the ceremonial burial of the dead (after all, what *is* it that would be buried ceremonially if *it* didn't have a name?), about ten thousand years ago. (Myself, I think this may be too recent a date, by some few thousand years. I find the apparent personalizations implicit—and possibly announced—in the art at Lascaux suggestive here.) And here is Jaynes on "auditory hallucination" (ibid.:134) and on the "individualizing" or "personalizing" of "auditory hallucination" (ibid.:137).

> Let us consider a man commanded by himself or his chief to set up a fish weir far upstream from his campsite. If he is not conscious, and therefore cannot narratize the situation and so hold his analogue "I" in a spatialized time with its consequences fully imagined, how does he do it? It is only language . . . that can keep him at his time-consuming all-afternoon work. . . . Lingual man would have language to remind him, either repeated by himself . . . or, as seems more likely, by a repeated "internal" verbal hallucination telling him what to do. (ibid.:134)

And, "once a specific hallucination is recognized with a name, as a voice originating from a particular person, a significantly different thing is occurring. The hallucination is now a social interaction with a much greater role in individual behavior" (ibid.:137). We must, of course, remember that "hallucination" is a value-laden word chosen by Jaynes partly perhaps for argumentative purposes but more, I think, because we simply do not have a word for what might be called a "true hallucination"—for voices that are really there, even if (perhaps) from gods who are, in some sense, really there. Jaynes suggests that

> the astonishing consistency from Egypt to Peru, from Ur to Yucatan, wherever civilizations arose, of death practices and idolatry, of divine government and hallucinated voices [Egyptian *ka*, Mesopotamian *ili*, Hebrew *nabiim*], all are witnesses to the idea of a different mentality from our own. (ibid: 202)

With the advent of writing for civil purposes, the shift from the so-called Code of Hammurabi to the altar inscriptions of Tukulti-Ninurta I five centuries later, the coming of civil trade, the rise of prayer (and its shadowy partner, divination), the mythologizing of divine voices to angels and demons, we perceive the origins and signs of the breakdown of the bicameral mind, between the days of the *Enuma Elish* and the days remembered in *Genesis*. The "sons of the *nabiim*," the itinerant prophets, the Oracles and sibyls, even the druids and the bards, are (on this showing) remembrances or legacies or remnants of the bicameral mind. And Jaynes suggests there are biochemical and genetic forces here at work, as well as conscious adaptation to the very idea and nature (in the old sense, the "name") of consciousness.

All this may seem to combine biogenetics and biochemistry of the brain with an odd sort of theology of the mind, and be out of place in this chapter on psychology. This doesn't seem to be what is generally meant by *psychology*. After all, leaving aside the American institutional psychiatry of the nineteenth century to which we referred earlier, psychiatry (for most purposes) means (in most minds) Freudian psychiatry. We will of course look briefly at the rules of Freudian psychiatry, even while noting that not all the psychiatrists involved with Bill W. or Alcoholics Anonymous were Freudians. Nevertheless, most of the rest of this chapter will be devoted to the neurological answer (or at least the neurological program for determining an answer). Some, also, will—as what we have said so far will suggest—be devoted to the "theological" study of the mind, or, in Cartesian terms (or those of Mary Baker Eddy), of Mind, and we will take this up briefly before we come to the neurological, or, if you like, the study of the brain. The theology of alcoholism and sobriety itself is of course properly the subject of Chapter 6. The study of the brain, besides taking up most of this chapter, will conclude it and lead into our next chapter, on the physiology or neurology of alcoholism—thus into alcoholism as a genetic condition or precondition, what we are calling Alcoholism(2). And thus into the possible genetic development—or evolution—of alcoholism. But, as a reminder, the business of "narratization" plays a significant role not only in Jaynes, nor only in alcoholism and Alcoholics Anonymous, but also in current psycho-analytic process, especially in Attachment Theory and work connected with the name of John Bowlby, and we will be looking there also. But first, because it is what we generally think of a psychology or psychoanalysis, we should take a brief look at Freudian psychiatric theory.

SIGMUND FREUD AND OTHERS

Sigmund Freud (1857–1938) distinguished three levels of conscious awareness—the *conscious* mind, the *preconscious* mind, and the *unconscious* mind. The conscious mind is like the tip of the iceberg, while the impor-tant bulk of the mind's workings are below the surface. The preconscious mind holds the vast storehouse of easily accessible memories: its contents were once conscious and can be returned to consciousness when needed. The unconscious mind, further down, stores primitive instinctual motives, and also memories and emotions that are so threatening to the conscious mind that they have been unconsciously pushed down through the pro-cess of *repression*. These are not ordinarily accessible to the conscious mind and can be made accessible only through great effort.

This division of the conscious, preconscious, and conscious mind is the first of Freud's triads.

The second triad is Freud's division of the mind into the id, the ego, and the superego. The id (which at birth is the only part of the mind) is com-posed primarily of two sets of instincts, *life instincts* and *death instincts*. The life instincts give rise to motives that sustain and promote life, such as hunger, self-protection, and sexual instinct. Freud believed that, from birth on, everyone's life is governed by the sexual instinct and the instinct for aggression (that is, asserting and thus protecting oneself against one's environment). The id (which Freud sometimes called the beast) operates according to the pleasure principle, and satisfies its needs through pri-mary process thinking, which is really mental imaging. During infancy (when there is only the id), the child is protected by adults; thereafter, the id must find realistic ways of meeting its needs, thus creates the ego, a kind of personality executive, using its cognitive abilities to manage and control the id, holding it in check from time to time till its desires can be realisti-cally fulfilled. But neither id nor ego possesses any moral consciousness: that belongs to the superego. The superego, which develops temporally after the ego (which comes after the id), enforces moral restrictions and striving to attain a goal of "ideal" perfection. Parents serve to create the superego by creating a set of moral inhibitions (called *conscience*), and by rewards that set up a standard of conduct in the superego (called the *ego ideal*). By the divisions in the first triad, the id is at the base of the iceberg, the superego and ego higher up, so that both appear at the tip, but are certainly not confined to it.

In any case (according to Freud), mental health comes from the process of psychoanalysis, so that the therapist, and thus the patient, can see how things got to be the way they are, and (over the long recommended period of the analytical process) what therefore can be done about them. In other words, the end result of psychoanalysis is a kind of cognitive therapy. The claim has been made that Freudian psychiatry is in fact both mystical and religious, because it assumes away any problem of the interface between mind and body or mind and spirit. Or, it might be called a kind of differentiated Cartesian approach—not that we each participate in Mind, but that, somehow, there is a differentiated mind, or relation to Mind, in us all. The categories—conscious, preconscious, unconscious, or id, ego, superego—are all a kind of grand abstraction. Not for nothing did Freud turn to mythology for his analogues (as with the Oedipus complex) or to the Bible for his exemplars. But there is one other cardinal point to Freudian analysis that we should mention here: Freud's theory of personality is essentially a developmental theory.

The developmental stages, in his view, represent a shifting of the primary outlet for the energy of the id, particularly the sexual energy, from one part of the body to another. These *psychosexual* stages are (in order), the oral stage, anal stage, phallic stage, latency stage, and genital stage. In all stages, particularly the latter, there is *sublimation* of the sexual energy into useful and productive forms. Most psychoanalysts now seem to agree that Freud may have placed too much emphasis on sexuality (and psychosexuality), but at least he found, in human sexuality, a way—though not entirely explicit—of linking mind and body. Two other early psychiatrists, Alfred Adler of Vienna (1870–1937), who coined the term *inferiority complex,* and Carl Jung of Switzerland (1875–1961), whom we have already met, who coined the terms *extravert* and *introvert* and who believed in the collective unconscious, both rebelled against Freud's heavy emphasis on sexuality. So far, not so bad (in the minds of the psychoanalytic establishment—though the collective unconscious took a bit of swallowing). But then they fell away from "orthodoxy" in other ways, Adler into cognitive goal-development and Jung, as we have seen, into *spiritus contra spiritum,* echoing William James.

To these who severely modified or disagreed with Freud should be added the name of another American, Harry Stack Sullivan (1892–1949), the man who, above others, should be given credit for developing the idea of group therapy. His major importance for our purposes comes later in

Chapter 7, but we may note here that he bypasses the definition of mind, echoes Jung and Adler in the importance of interpersonal relationships, and in essence shows (as we will see) that it is not necessary to define the bounds of mind and body, or even the nature of mind, in striving to promote mental health. It is worth noting, I believe, that (though there is substantial difference in terminology) Sullivan anticipates a good bit of John Bowlby and his Attachment Theory, as we will also see, a little later on.

It is also worth noting that Sullivan's work with group therapy depended on consensual validation of the process of growing out of parataxic distortion into syntaxic thinking—in other words, in the process of growing up (see Chapman 1976:esp. 165–73). The importance of this in A.A. we will see in Chapters 7 and (to a lesser degree) 8. Its importance here—and we need not go immediately into Sullivan's special terms for now—is that it fits in with Freud (on "His Majesty the Baby"), with Sandór Radó and his ego-deflation (and his alcoholics as frozen in oral fixation), with the age-locus (and general emphasis) of Attachment Theory, and with Harry M. Tiebout and his treatment of alcoholics as children, following Radó—thus with Bill W. in the *12&12* (1952/53).

HOW DID IT GET THAT WAY: EVOLUTION OF MIND?

All of this, of course, deals with the psychology of the alcoholic as generally perceived. But how did the alcoholic get this way—or, to put the question on another level, why did the human race come to include alcoholics? We have been talking about the mind, and about the brain. Perhaps, at least briefly, we should talk about their development, not individually but in humankind generally, what some would call their evolution. On that account (speaking of the evolution of the brain), we should remind ourselves of two definitions introduced earlier. These are the definitions of *genotype* and *phenotype*. By a *phenotype* we mean the visible properties of an organism produced by the interaction of the genotype and the environment. By *genotype* we mean all or part of the genetic constitution of an individual or a group. The phenotype of an organism is contrasted with its genotype on the grounds that the *phenotype* concerns the organism's concrete existence in the observer's domain or domains, whereas the *genotype* concerns the genetic makeup which the organism inherited and that accounted for its embryogenesis and development. The following example (we use it more than once if only as a reminder) may help to make the matter a little clearer. There are different kinds of corn—niblet, shoepeg, white—and these are genotypes. Plant the corn and grow the crop, and you get specific examples according to the soil, rainfall, sunlight, amount of labor expended—in short, the corn's concrete existence in the observer's domain, determined by interaction of the genotype and the environment. These are the phenotypes. Genotypes are the principal—but not sole—subject of the study of evolution.

Since fossil records show, in general, that the older a species is, the less it is like contemporary species, it appears that over a very long time, the diversity as well as the complexity of species has increased. The work of the geologist Charles Lyell (1797–1875) established that *geological* evolution was sequential and progressive, but before that was established, the climate of ideas had made it possible for evolutionary ideas to be welcomed, in biology as well as in geology. The task for an evolutionary biologist would be to account for the great diversity of current species, and the disappearance of some species and appearance of others. After a false start by Lamarck (1774–1829), who argued that phenotypic characteristics acquired by parents in their lifetime could be passed to their children, a new twist was given by Charles Darwin in *The Origin of Species by Means of Natural Selection; or, The Preservation of Favoured Races in the Struggle for Life* (1859).

Darwin's twist from Lamarck brought us a system of evolutionary change based on three components of change: (1) overpopulation of the organism in terms of environmental support, (2) subsequent competition among offspring for survival, and (3) inheritable variations in phenotype—that is, the difference between Darwin and Lamarck was that Lamarck thought the phenotypic variations were created in the adult during its lifetime (because of their survival value), then passed to the offspring (because of the survival value), while Darwin thought the phenotypic variations were in a sense accidental (trying not to beg too many questions with that word), but that the offspring with the phenotypic variant most suited to survival were likely to be the offspring to survive. Hence the phrase "survival of the fittest"—meaning, of course, the survival of the survivors. What we have called the Darwinian twist is in the third component. Obviously, if all offspring were phenotypically identical, survival would be solely a matter of chance. But because of this third component, some of the offspring will be better suited to survival than others. And if the phenotypic variations arise from differences in genotype, then the advantages given by these characteristics would propagate through the species through better survival rates.

That is, to quote Alan Dean in *Chaos and Intoxication*, "those more suited to a specific environment by virtue of a phenotypic advantage which was grounded in a genetic change would have better rates of survival. Over time, the adapted variety would tend to increase in proportion to the non-adapted variety" (1997:34). Thus, to take modern examples, there are mosquitoes resistant to DDT, viruses resistant to penicillin, and so on. We will look later at the evolution of pattern in the brain, and specifically at Edelman's work. But before we get to that (quite a while before), we should make note of one particular point. The survival of a phenotype—still more of a genotype—suggests that its characteristics at one time had a survival value. Now, why would alcoholism have a survival value—or more exactly, why would genotypic characteristics revealed in current alcoholic phenotypes have a survival value?

INTOXICATION

This brings us to a discussion of the Fourth Drive. Here we make use the work of Ronald Siegel, *Intoxication: Life in Pursuit of Artificial Paradise* (1989). Now, Siegel suggests that his fourth drive—the drive to intoxication—is acquired rather than innate, but that it is still a "natural" drive. He finds it in goats, birds, cats, dogs, apes, flying insects, rodents of various sorts, horses, pigs, cattle, elephants—and I may have missed a few. His conclusions are that intoxication must have adaptive value in evolution, or else that "the pursuit of intoxication is a side effect of a beneficial gene or genes" (ibid.:211). This would, of course, connect with the openness to the voices of the gods in earlier men, though not exclusively to that. Note, however, that by intoxication, Siegel means not only alcoholic intoxication, but any form of intoxication—with stimulating, inebriating, tranquilizing, *or* hallucinogenic properties—even intoxication from playground swings, amusement park rides, or sports. Our nervous system (Siegel suggests) is arranged to respond to chemical intoxicants in much the same way it responds to rewards of food, drink, or sex. And there are so-called natural highs. How much this helps to explain alcoholism is not certain, and we may find that it is chiefly important in reaffirming the use of nonhuman subjects in alcoholism research. But it may have some additional importance, particularly in explaining what some have called juvenile pseudo-alcoholism, developmental alcoholism, or (less accurately perhaps) situational alcoholism.

Why the natural highs? Evidently because we are constructed so that we relish them. But what is it we relish? What *is* this Fourth Drive? The Fourth Drive "is not just motivating people to feel good or bad—it is [also] a desire to feel different, to achieve a rapid change in one's state" (ibid.: 217). (This would appear to be highly important, since we are talking about the attraction of altered states of consciousness.) The direction of the change, whether up or down, good or bad, Siegel argues, is of secondary importance only. This is his conclusion after studying the phenomenon of the attraction of phencyclidine (PCP), despite 100-percent negative effects (as against 60-percent temporary positive effects). But there is also an out-of-body feeling involved, and a sense of the unreality of one's physical surroundings. Of course, this is not original with Siegel. Consider the lead provided by William James, where he suggests that the alcoholic experience is a mystic door to perception ([1903] 1961:304). But before we pursue the similarities between intoxication and spiritual experience, we might want to pause a moment at the work of Eugene Marais (in Siegel 1989: 89–90).

Eugene Marais worked with a troop of three hundred wild chacma baboons in the early days of the twentieth century, and first proposed the theory that captured and caged primates will indulge in intoxicating substances (usually plants) that they would walk away from in the wild. The point, as I take it, is that any intoxicating substance, even a depressant, will stimulate by the very excitement of the physiological and psychological change it induces, and those whose lives were or should be full of change will turn to intoxicants if they are not. But note that Siegel is discussing intoxicants to which all users react in much the same way. A list of such intoxicants does not include alcohol. Whether this is a distinction without a difference is something we should be looking at. For the moment, let me say that (for various reasons) I think the difference is there.

Here is William James on the question of the "value" of alcohol and more specifically of intoxication by alcohol:

The sway of alcohol over mankind is unquestionably due to its power to stimulate the mystical faculties of human nature, usually crushed to earth by the cold facts and dry criticisms of the sober hour. Sobriety diminishes, discriminates, and says no; drunkenness expands, unites, and says yes. It is in fact the great exciter of the *Yes* function in man. It brings its votary from the chill periphery of things to the radiant core. It makes him for the moment one with truth. ([1903] 1961:304)

Only, I suggest, not all men (or women)—only those who have the gift of alcoholism. And James goes on to say this:

To the poor and unlettered [drunkenness] stands in the place of symphony concerts and of literature; and it is part of the deeper mystery and tragedy of life that whiffs and gleams of something that we immediately recognize as excellent should be vouchsafed to so many of us only in the fleeting earlier phases of what in its totality is so degrading a poisoning." (ibid.:305)

James remarks that he is convinced that

our normal waking consciousness . . . is but one special type of consciousness, whilst all about it, parted from it by the flimsiest of screens, there lie potential forms of consciousness entirely different. . . . Apply the requisite stimulus, and at a touch they are there in all their completeness, definite types of mentality *which probably somewhere have their field of application and adaptation.* (ibid., emphasis mine)

I would myself go further than *probably*—like Darwin, I would say this type of mentality would not have evolved if it were not valuable. Why it was valuable we may find out by following Jaynes.

EVOLUTION OF PATTERN IN THE BRAIN

This brings us to what we may call the evolution of pattern in the brain, and here we are looking primarily at the work of G. M. Edelman, in what is called (perhaps misleadingly) a Darwinian perspective on the brain.

For Edelman the brain is not a computer hardwired to process external stimuli, but is actively engaged in constructing the environment. That is, the mind is not a blank sheet [Locke's *tabula rasa?*] upon which the external environment writes a program from which to actively engage the world, but instead we are born with capacities for action which serve to construct and interpret the world. (Dean 1997:39–40)

This is a bit like Immanuel Kant's a priori categories of the mind, existing prior to experience. But Edelman takes us farther, arguing that the way the mind engages the world evolves—and if evolving, then subject to natural selection. Hence the use of the word "Darwinian" even though that is a red-flag word. At this juncture we should rehearse some points in Edelman's approach, which is based fundamentally on his idea of biological diversity at the individual level.

First, he suggests that in the morphogenesis (form-development) of the brain, certain topographical features, such as place and timing, are central. As a result, the actual configuration of microelements, such as the fine detail of neural networks, cannot be known at any given time. In other words, as I understand it, phenotypic variation in human microsystems can be very great, even with identical twins (after all, *one* of them must be born first, and they cannot experience their environment in completely identical ways). The theory of natural selection holds that evolved forms give relative survival advantage: evidently, a system of brain morphogenesis that imparts diversity in brain anatomy (and thus in mode of function) would conduce to producing more survivable forms than a system hardwired to one specific external world. The hardwiring would be a key to mass extinction when the external world changed. In the so-called mass extinction of the dinosaurs, those dinosaurs that could adapt to the changed environment survived—albeit as birds. But we note that alcoholics have not suffered mass extinction, even as external conditions have changed.

Edelman has called his theory of brain development the Theory of Neuronal Group Selection (TNGS). TNGS is complex, but based on three reasonably simple principles. First, this process of morphogenesis, based on cell division, cell movement, and cell differentiation, produces a species-dependent neuroanatomy variable at the individual level: groups of neurons in a specific brain region deriving from this process are known as *primary repertoires*. The genetic code is a template imposing constraints, but not imposing unanimity. Second, through behavioral engagement with the external world, some synaptic connections are promoted through use and thus strengthened, others neglected and thus weakened, so that certain neural networks are self-selected from the diversity of those available: these are *secondary repertoires*. In practice, primary and secondary repertoires may be overlapping. Finally, third, primary and secondary repertoires link psychology and physiology, by forming maps: these maps are connected by the entrance and reentrance of neural linkages. For the functions of the mind to be performed:

> Primary and secondary repertoires must form maps. These maps are connected by massively parallel and reciprocal connections. . . . Re-entrant signalling occurs along these connections. This means that, as groups of neurons are selected in a map, other groups in re-entrantly connected but different maps may also be selected at the same time. . . . A fundamental premise of the TNGS is that the selective coordination of the complex patterns of interconnection between neuronal groups by re-entry is the basis of behavior. Indeed, re-entry (combined with memory . . .) is the main basis for a bridge between physiology and psychology. (Edelman 1992:85)

MEMORY

Here it is appropriate to look briefly at the question of memory and it will be appropriate eventually to look at the question of the biochemistry of memory. We all know that there is something called short-term memory (STM) and something called long-term memory (LTM). These are stages two and three in the process of memory, the first stage being what is called the sensory register, which provides and encodes raw data for transfer to the short-term—and thence, we believe, to the long-term—memory. Information stored in the sensory register does not last long, but it is apparently a complete replica of the sensory experience. "Not last long" is perhaps an understatement—a famous experiment by George Sperling in the late 1950s suggests a length of time perhaps one-tenth of a second. Then, when a bit of information is selected for the STM (automatically simply by "paying attention" to it), it will last (unless it is rehearsed) perhaps a few seconds: moreover, the STM will hold only five to perhaps nine chunks of information even for that limited time.

Long-term memory is a different thing altogether, and the transfer from STM to LTM is different also (from the earlier automatic transfer from sensory register to STM). Briefly (1) LTM is indexed for retrieval; (2) LTM stores information by *semantic* codes, STM by *experiential* (particularly *acoustic*) codes; (3) LTM information is permanent (does not drop out of the system) so that "forgetting" is a retrieval problem, while STM information if not rehearsed or processed does simply drop out of the system; and (4) LTM is held in the hippocampus and then transferred to the areas of the cerebral cortex involved in language and perception, while STM primarily "resides" in the frontal lobes of the cerebral cortex. (Memory is a function of language, and language a function of memory.) Also, (5) there are three varieties of LTM, procedural memory (how to do things), semantic memory (what things are), and episodic memory (data on specific events at specific times and places). Both semantic and episodic LTM are connected with speech, though in different ways, and most LTM difficulties seem to reside in the episodic memory, which is apparently the most difficult of the three to access.

It can be made easier to access by enhancing any of the three modes of retrieval—recall, recognition, and relearning—all of which involve a species of narratization, and thereby involve speech. Forgetting occurs either through decay (in sensory-register or short-term memories) or through interference by other memories (in long-term memories). Thus, if one learns to emphasize certain sets of memories through narratization, others may decay and be forgotten. But just as episodic memories are likely to be episodic, so is episodic forgetting (that is, the forgetting of episodic memories is itself episodic). In all LTM cases, of course, memories may be repressed (Freud's term), and I believe there is evidence available suggesting that memories are somehow modified over time to enhance the pleasant and limit the unpleasant parts. (For the moment, this begs the question whether in the event, whatever it was, the original sensory register and STM exaggerated the unpleasant, so that the memory is in fact more accurate a representation of the event than was the first impression.) How the modification—and the organization—of memories take place in LTM is our next point.

Through selective reentry coordination, environmental factors act at various levels to select some configurations of neural cells over others. With primary repertoires it is a stochastic process, inasmuch as cell lines, in competition with others, either do or do not survive. With secondary repertoires, environmental selection of the specific synaptic pathways occurs in behavioral engagement with the outside world. Edelman's third component suggests how the primary and secondary repertoires combine to create maps, and how different maps are connected through synaptic cross-linkages. "The way we engage the world perceptually and behaviorally is selected for in terms of survival advantage" (Edelman 1992:85). We will go into some of the implications of this later. Here let us note two points. First, according to Henry Plotkin, on the nature of knowledge, "once intelligence has evolved in a species, then thereafter brains have a causal force equal to that of genes" (1994:177). Second, according to Alan Dean, "at each stage in the ontogenesis of the individual there occurs great uncertainty with respect to outcomes" (1997:57). And from this and what else we have said thus far, if alcoholic drinking

> is not simply present or absent, but is instead continuously variable, as work on QTLs [Quantitative Trait Loci] suggests, then predicting outcomes for individuals becomes extremely difficult if not impossible. As research on QTLs has shown, a specific quantitative trait can arise from a number of different QTLs on the genome. . . . There exists a dynamic equilibrium whereby environmental changes which affect gene expression may . . . change the action of a complex system of linked QTLs, which will in turn give rise to further changes in the state of the system. (ibid.:93)

The point here is that the state of a system at time = +1 cannot be known with certainty unless all the conditions at time = 0 can be specified—which, in the nature of things in this chaotic world, they cannot. But at least we can look briefly at the brain as a system, even if all we can do after that is make do with qualitative generalizations.

BRAIN AND BODY

Briefly, the brain communicates with the body through an intricate system of neurons, arranged either in what we call the somatic nervous system, which is the basis (we believe) of our conscious awareness and thinking, or in what we call the autonomic nervous system, which (we believe) regulates the internal body organs and activates primary motivation and emotion. In either system, the nerve cells (neurons) are made up of a cell body (nucleus) containing the cell's control center, branches called axons, which transmit messages to other neurons, and branches called dendrites that receive messages from other neurons. All told, the human body contains trillions of neural connections, most of them in the brain. All these neurons are sacs filled with one type of fluid on the inside and bathed with a different type of fluid on the outside: both fluids are soups of dissolved chemicals including ions, but the inner soup is largely made up of ions with a negative charge, while the outer soup (a kind of sodium soup) is largely made up of ions with a positive charge. The neuron is thus *polarized*. However, when the neuron is stimulated by an adjacent neuron, positively charged ions from the sodium soup can then enter the neuron, *depolarizing* it, sometimes sufficiently to trigger a chain of events known as the *action potential*.

During this action potential, a small section of the axon adjacent to the cell body becomes more permeable to the positive sodium ions, leading to dramatic depolarization in that part of the axon, which is then repolarized by sending the disturbance on down the chain, and so on, throughout the axon, and thence to another neuron. These neurons are not directly connected one to another: rather, where they are "joined" (the *synapse*) there is a small gap (the *synaptic gap*), across which the electrical action potential cannot jump, but must be carried by synaptic neurotransmitters, stored in tiny synaptic knobs at the ends of the axon.

There seem to be quite a number and variety of these neurotransmitters, as well as a number and variety of neurotransmitter-blockers. In our discussion in this book, we will be looking principally at three or four of the neurotransmitters—dopamine, epinephrine, norepinephrine, acetylcholine, a couple of neurotransmitter-receptors (or neuroreceptors)—GABA receptors, for example, and at least one set of neurotransmitter-blockers—the endorphins. The process of neurotransmission goes on throughout the system, though certain parts of the brain do different things with the transmissions—the hypothalamus, for example, having specific pleasure centers (including sexual pleasure) as well as being connected (along with the amygdala) with anger and fear.

Besides natural blockers, there are exogenous chemical blockers (that is, chemicals from outside the system). The effect any exogenous substance has on the system of neurotransmission (or, for that matter, the effect of any substance whatever) will largely depend on how the body processes the substance, and in particular on the endocrine system—that is, the system of glands that secrete chemical messengers called hormones into the system. Some of these hormones (epinephrine and norepinephrine, for example) are chemically identical with some of the neurotransmitters. Hormones aid the nervous (neural) system by activating bodily organs, influencing blood-sugar levels, determining levels of the metabolism, regulating the body's reactions to stress and its resistance to disease. We have here a link between the chemistry of the predisposition (Alcoholism[2]) and the chemistry of the resulting prolonged (and progressive) disease-state (Alcoholism[1]).

Discussion of neurotransmitters and endocrine systems comes mostly in the next chapter, after we have looked more at patterns of the mind and patterns of the brain. But it seemed worthwhile to look for a moment here at what the brain is (including how it relates to the body). In fact, since we have already introduced an attempt to categorize patterns of behavior according to the way the alcoholic mind seems to work, and since we are working within the hypothesis that there is a connection between mind and brain, it is certainly highly advisable that we have at least a fleeting idea of how both mind and brain work. At this point, perhaps, we might reasonably look at an alternative hypothesis, also Cartesian (though perhaps of an extreme variety), that the brain is a nonentity, and the only reality is Mind. This may be found in the set of doctrines proposed under the name of Christian Science by Mary Baker (Glover) Eddy (1821–1910).

MIND AND MRS. EDDY

Mrs. Eddy began her "discovery" of Christian Science (in the years 1866–1875) with efforts at mind-cure, initially asserting the supremacy of mind over matter (including the brain), and over time refining that into an assertion that "matter is mortal error" so that "Man is not material, he is spiritual" (1897:468, also 1908:21). As Eddy uses *Mind* and *Spirit* as synonyms (and both as synonyms for God), she appears to assert a unity of treatment for any illness of mind, body, or spirit, at the cost of denying any difference between the mind and the spirit (or *Mind* and Spirit) and denying the real existence of the body. Given the almost-Scholastic subtlety of her thought on substance and matter, and how she welcomed the advances in physical theory in the late nineteenth century, perhaps this is neither so extreme a Cartesian view nor so odd a doctrine as many have found it. For all that she repudiated Freud (in her repudiation of "Mesmerism"), her emphasis on testimony of life-experience, "scientifically" ordered according to the testifier's "study of Christian science," would appear to give her entry into more contemporary realms of therapy than are suggested by the peculiarly nineteenth-century phrase "mind-cure." And we shall note later the importance of what members of the Church of Christ, Scientist, refer to as "concordance work" (the concordances being to the Bible and the works of Mrs. Eddy) in using language formulae to order experience through a special version of "narratization."

Even so, and even though Christian Science may have represented the only real attempt at mind-cure of alcoholism in the later years of the nineteenth century, she is not really in our mainstream. And she would have had no interest in what has been called the natural history of alcoholism, wherein a kind of unity of mind and brain (and body) is assumed, but we are interested precisely in that. We have previously noted George Vaillant's study of this natural history of alcoholism, a kind of landmark work in the field, to which we now turn as a kind of *per contra* to Mrs. Eddy. (Vaillant's results were also summarized in an article in the *Archives of General Psychiatry* 1996b).

THE NATURAL HISTORY OF ALCOHOLISM

The subjects of the studies were 268 former Harvard University undergraduates and 456 nondelinquent inner-city adolescents who had been repeatedly studied in multidisciplinary fashion since 1940. At some point during their lives, fifty-five of the college sample (21 percent) and 150 of the core-city sample (33 percent) met DSM-III criteria for alcohol abuse. The college sample was followed until seventy years of age, the core-city sample only until sixty years of age. By sixty years of age, 18 percent of the college alcohol-abusers had died, 11 percent were abstinent, 11 percent were controlled drinkers (on their showing, which may beg more than one question), and 59 percent were still known to be abusing alcohol. By sixty years of age, 28 percent of the core-city alcohol-abusers had died, 38 percent were abstinent, 11 percent were controlled drinkers (on their showing), and only 28 percent were still known to be abusing alcohol.

But this is lumping together alcohol-abusers with those who are alcohol-dependent. If we restrict our analysis to the members of the sample populations adjudged alcohol-dependent—twenty-one of fifty-five college abusers and seventy-seven of 150 core-city abusers—we have somewhat a different picture. By age seventy, thirteen (62 percent) of the twenty-one college alcohol-dependent men were dead, as against 17 percent of the college non-alcohol-dependent men. Many members of the college sample spent the years from fifty to seventy alternating between periods of so-called controlled drinking and periods of alcohol abuse. None of the thirty-four college men who were alcohol-abusers but not alcohol-dependent ever met the criteria for stable abstinence: ten of the other twenty-one did. Alcohol-dependent core-city men were also more likely than the nondependent alcohol-abusers to achieve stable abstinence. Now, as the alcohol-abusers aged, the prevalence of alcohol abuse generally declined, partly because of early mortality of abusers, partly from achieving stable abstinence. Vaillant found that stable abstinence for five to six years was a good predictor of future stable abstinence, but any shorter period was not. His findings on recurring patterns of periodic alcohol abuse or even dependence echo Jellinek's problem with ε alcoholism as a progressive disease. None of either sample was apparently other than Caucasian, but the core-city sample showed significantly greater alcoholism among the English or Irish and other northern Europeans than among those of Mediterranean ancestry. The college sample had significantly higher IQs (130+ on average) than the core-city (about 100 on average), later onset of alcoholism, and greater difference in mortality between alcohol-abusers and non-alcohol-abusers. Also somewhat different drinking patterns, and greater difficulty in achieving stable abstinence. The longitudinal studies of these samples were not designed to study alcoholism, but because of two serendipitous factors, these samples have a particular value for us.

Both samples were selected as normal nondelinquent adolescents at a time and place when alcohol rather than drugs was the principal subject of abuse. Second, because of the similarity of time and place, the study in effect controls for federal and state law, cost structures, and drinking mores. Any recovery from alcoholism should be viewed as a function of the natural course of the disorder, including interaction with A.A., but not of any other interaction or any change in laws, drug availability, mores, or other treatments. In *The Natural History of Alcoholism Revisited* Vaillant discusses the etiology of alcoholism, suggesting that adult alcoholism is *not* correlated with such things as bleak childhood environments, personal instability in college, adult evidence of premorbid personality disorder, and depression or low self-esteem before alcoholism (1996a:52). One study showed prealcoholics to be more compulsive, gregarious, and nonconforming, another that in high school they tended to be "out of control, rebellious, pushing limits, self-indulgent, and assertive" (ibid.:51) but *not* with strong inferiority feelings. Nor are diagnosable biological differences good predictors of risk of adult alcoholism (ibid.:72), though alcoholics seem to be biologically different.

In his book, though not in his article, Vaillant goes on to discuss predictors of recovery and to review other studies of the natural history of alcohol abuse. Predictors of recovery have not worked any better than predictors of alcoholism. Here is Vaillant's suggestion why, on the basis of his own studies:

> On the one hand, socially disadvantaged men, in part as a function of the early onset of severe alcohol dependence, often become stably abstinent. However, because of poor health habits . . . they are also more likely to die. On the other hand, alcohol abusers with excellent social supports, high education, good health habits, and late onset of minimal alcohol abuse are more likely to survive and resume problem-free drinking, but such men also appeared more likely to maintain a pattern of lifelong intermittent alcohol abuse. (ibid.:248)

It is my view—but not his—that typological differentiation could well be the cornerstone of a new research program to improve both predictors of recovery and the process of recovery itself. Particularly if we could find support for the anecdotal evidence that ε drinking is correlated with artistry, intelligence, or intellectuality—and, as alcoholics might observe, therefore with difficulty in recovery.

MANIC DEPRESSION, ASPD, OTHER COMORBIDITIES, AND THE COUSINS EFFECT

Dr. Silkworth noted long ago the special classification of the manic-depressive alcoholic—a category that seems to make up a considerable portion of what we will be defining as our Sda phenotype. And more than one observer has noted the close connection between what is now called ASPD (antisocial personality disorder) and the (admittedly dubious) Cloninger type 1 (as in the previous chapter)—including, among those observers, Cloninger himself—as well as with Silkworth's "psychopathic" alcoholism, and (as we noted above) Jellinek's ε-type. Before we conclude this chapter, it may be well to look briefly at these two "disorders"—one of which, at least, was considered a *psychosis*—the closest technical term to the layman's (or nineteenth-century physician's) "mental illness." In our remarks on bipolar disorder (manic-depressive psychosis), we are greatly indebted to the psychologist Kay Redfield Jamison (1993), herself a sufferer from manic depression.

Jamison notes that cyclothymia (which is like manic-depressive psychosis except that it apparently leaves no permanent damage), manic depression, and major (or clinical) depression (which seems to have no true manic state) are closely related. All three are apparently hereditary: as early as the 1600s, Robert Burton (in *The Anatomy of Melancholy,* 1660) wrote that "I need not therefore make any doubt of Melancholy [that is, in our terms, Depression], but that it is an hereditary disease" (quoted in Jamison 1993:192). Certainly "the genetic [and thus chemical] evidence for manic-depressive illness is especially compelling, indeed almost incontrovertible" (ibid.:193). Early attempts to locate the gene (or genes) responsible for manic-depressive illness have not been especially successful, and Jamison remarks that there are "central questions about the interactions between genetic predisposition, the physical and physiological environment (including stress, alcohol . . . drugs, sleep loss, changing patterns of light, and psychological loss or trauma), and other protective or potentiating genes" (ibid.:194–95). In this connection, recent work on adult-onset neuropsychiatric disease may also have something of value to tell us:

The discovery of genes causing adult-onset neuropsychiatric diseases is both possible and informative. Indeed, knowledge of these genes has led both to the creation of robust animal models and to the design of therapeutic strategies. . . . However, it has also become apparent that families segregating [these diseases] as simple autosomal-dominant traits are the exception rather than the rule. The majority of cases . . . seem to have a more complex pattern of inheritance that does not fit the simple rules of classical Mendelian inheritance (one gene-one disorder that is transmitted as a dominant, codominant, or recessive trait). The same also seems to be true for schizophrenia and bipolar disease. (Kennedy [2003]:823)

It is worth noting that the diagnostic criteria for manic depressive illness include grandiosity, extreme talkativeness, racing thoughts, excessive involvement in pleasure-seeking activities with a potential for painful consequences—these alternating with depressed or irritable moods, diminished interest in doing anything, weight fluctuations, insomnia or hypersomnia, feelings of worthlessness, indecisiveness, recurrent thoughts of death (ibid.:261–63, quoting from DSM-III). These seem to have a certain congruence with some patterns of alcoholism or alcoholic behavior. The condition is manageable with treatment by lithium carbonate, leveling out the peaks and troughs at the cost of lowering the overall level of satisfaction with life and impairing both creativity and organization. It is worth noting also that manic-depressive artists have refused to take lithium, preferring, in the event, to kill themselves when conditions turn down.

Work on ASPD is more recent, partly because ASPD has not been uniformly accepted as a true mental disorder at all. Indeed, only within the last year or two has it been suggested that there is a physiological condition—reduced prefrontal gray matter—that is a statistically significant indicator of ASPD regardless of other conditions. The functions of the cerebral cortex are not well understood, but the prefrontal gray matter is part of the limbic system that includes the hypothalamus and the amygdala. Accordingly, we may hypothesize that ASPD may involve a rush of pleasure from committing antisocial acts, and be connected to certain characteristics of the immature brain common in adolescence (a subject on which there is also some recent research). Neural fibers—making possible neural transmissions—connect the frontal region of the cerebral cortex to the hypothalamus: as in the film, *One Flew Over the Cuckoo's Nest*, a frontal lobotomy, disconnecting the frontal and prefrontal matter with the hypothalamus, can eliminate antisocial behavior, at the cost of virtually eliminating human behavior. But, of course, psychosurgery, though discredited, bears witness to the fact that mental disorders are disorders of the brain. Because this book centers on alcoholism, we will not look much further at either of these disorders. But, before going on to the biology and genetics of alcoholism— that is, looking at alcoholism as a disease of the body—let us pause to remark on a clue given by Robert Burton back in 1660, and more recently by the late Norman Cousins (1979). After that, we will look briefly at one or two psychologists or psychiatrists involved with Alcoholics Anonymous, especially Harry Tiebout. And then to the biology and genetics of this disease or allergy or illness or predisposition.

In 1964, Norman Cousins, after a hectic trip to the Soviet Union, was diagnosed as suffering from a severe collagen illness—a disease of the connective tissue. His sediment rate rose to 115 (almost double the danger level). A specialist, called in, suggested a possible chance of recovery of one in five hundred (ibid.:31). In the hospital, Cousins "was astounded when four technicians from four different departments took substantial blood samples on the same day. That the hospital didn't take the trouble to coordinate the tests . . . seemed to me inexplicable and irresponsible" (ibid.:28). He refused to have more blood taken, but the hospital gave him medications to which he was severely allergic, woke him out of a sound sleep because it was time to give him his sleeping medicine, fed him processed food he believed nutritionally empty, and when the specialist gave his verdict, Cousins and his doctor (William M. Hitzig) got him out of the hospital, into a hotel room, and determined to try a regime of ascorbic acid and laughter—the patient's suggestion. "Dr. Hitzig said it was clear to him that there was nothing undersized about my will to live. He said that what was most important was that I continue to believe in everything that I had said. He shared my excitement about the possibilities of recovery and liked the idea of a partnership" (ibid.:39).

So Hitzig had Norman Cousins released from the hospital to a hotel room, for his treatment by laughter—but even before that, he had the nurses instructed in how to show the patient classics from "Candid Camera" and old Marx brothers films. "It worked. I made the joyous discovery that ten minutes of genuine belly laughter had an anesthetic effect, and would give me at least two hours of pain-free sleep" (ibid.:39). Moreover, with heavy doses of ascorbic acid to accompany the laughter, the connective tissue began to be restored. Norman Cousins returned to his job at the *Saturday Review*. Of course, it was suggested by doctors not on the case (ibid.:45) that this was nothing but a *placebo* effect:

> Two or three doctors . . . have commented that I was probably the beneficiary of a mammoth venture in self-administered placebos. Such an hypothesis bothers me not at all. Respectable names in the history of medicine, like Paracelsus, Holmes, and Osler, have suggested that the history of medication is far more the history of the placebo effect than of intrinsically valuable and relevant drugs. Such modalities as bleeding . . . purging through emetics, physical contact with unicorn horns, bezoar stones, mandrakes, or powdered mummies—all such treatments were no doubt regarded by physicians at the time as specifics with empirical sanction. But today's medical science recog-

nizes that whatever efficacy these treatments may have had—and the records indicate that the results were often surprisingly in line with expectations— was probably related to the power of the placebo. (ibid.:45–46)

Because, as he goes on to say, the power of the placebo is that it engages the chemistry of the will to live. And he notes that

William James said that human beings tend to live too far within self-imposed limits. It is possible that these limits will recede when we respect more fully the natural drive of the human mind and body toward perfectibility and regeneration. Protecting and cherishing that natural drive may well represent the finest exercise of human freedom. (ibid.:48)

Cousins observes that the placebo (the most common form is what used to be called *sugar pills*) triggers specific biochemical changes in the body— so long as the patient does not know the pill is a placebo. Belief in a higher power can trigger precisely the same biochemical reactions as belief in a pill—or perhaps even better ones than the pill can produce.

In a sense, "the doctor himself is the most powerful placebo of all" (ibid.:57). Among the processes and disorders favorably affected by placebos, as reported by Cousins are "severe postoperative wound pain, seasickness, headaches, coughs, and anxiety . . . rheumatoid and degenerative arthritis, blood-cell count, respiratory rates, vasomotor function, peptic ulcers, hay fever, hypertension, and . . . warts" (ibid.:58). Unfortunately, the placebo effect does not always work favorably: "The cerebral cortex stimulates negative biochemical changes just as it does positive changes" (ibid.:61). At the Cornell Conference on Therapy in 1946, H. Gold reported a finding that "the higher the intelligence [of the patient] the greater the potential benefit from the use of placebos" (ibid.:63). And Cousins quotes Albert Schweitzer: "Each patient carries his own doctor inside him. They come to us [doctors] not knowing that truth. We are at our best when we give the doctor who resides within each patient a chance to go to work" (ibid.:69).

HARRY TIEBOUT, SANDÓR RADÓ, HARRY STACK SULLIVAN

If we seem to have spent a little more than expected time and space on this, it is because this is testimony not from an alcoholic (not even from an alcoholism counselor) seeking to explain A.A., not from a mind-doctor or a Christian Scientist (for both of whom something like this may be taught belief), but from an intelligent man who came to believe, from his own experience, that a medical condition—a diagnosed medical condition—could be cured by the doctor within, with the help of laughter, which is of the mind, the body, and the spirit. Now let us consider an unorthodox mind-doctor, from the Blythewood Sanitarium in Greenwich, Connecticut, one of the first psychiatrists to describe alcoholism as a disease. His name was Harry Morgan Tiebout (1896–1966), the alcoholic patient whom he brought to the "Big Book" was a woman named Marty M., and he later treated Bill W. His writings on alcoholism (from the *Quarterly Journal of Studies on Alcohol*) have been recently republished in *The Collected Writings* (1999).

In many ways, Harry Tiebout was influenced by the work of one of Freud's less orthodox followers, the Hungarian Sandór Radó (a professor at Columbia University in New York), particularly in Radó's early study, "The Psychoanalysis of Pharmachothymia (Drug Addiction): The Clinical Picture" (1933)—but not only there. (It is, however, curious that Tiebout did not make more use of Radó's article "The Psychic Effects of Intoxicants: An Attempt to Evolve a Psychoanalytic Theory of Morbid Cravings," [1929].) Radó has been largely overlooked by historians of alcoholism and Alcoholics Anonymous, though his influence on Tiebout appears (and is acknowledged) in Tiebout's articles "The Ego Factors in Surrender to Alcoholism" (1954) and "Alcoholics Anonymous: An Experiment of Nature" (1961). The statement by Radó that Tiebout quotes extensively is this:

> Once it was a baby, radiant with self-esteem, full of belief in the omnipotence of its wishes, of its thoughts, gestures, and words. . . . But the child's megalomania melted away under the inexorable pressure of experience. Its sense of its own sovereignty had to make room for a more modest self-evaluation. The process, first described by Freud [in his discussion of His Majesty the Baby], may be designated the reduction in size of the original ego; it is a painful procedure and one that is possibly never completely carried out. (1999:58, 79)

It is in Radó's later article, "Narcotic Bondage" (1957), that we see his own later conclusions. First, "narcotic super-pleasure" (including alcoholic drinking) is a "derivative of alimentary orgasm," and second, the repressed tendencies that early psychoanalytic investigators found to be mobilized by alcohol were oral-dependent and might involve latent passive homosexual cravings (which themselves involve oral fixation). It is important here to take note of (1) Radó's work in *traumatophobia*—the idea that the traumatized ego tries to escape further traumatic experiences through avoidance reactions such as loss of consciousness, speech, locomotion, and coordination of movements (which "falling-down-drunk" blackout drinking will do), and (2) Radó's work in *adaptational psychodynamics*, coming from a concern that standard psychoanalysis fosters regression without supplying a counterforce toward progression. To quote Radó's article "Recent Advances in Psychoanalytic Therapy," "To overcome repressions and thus be able to recall the past is one thing; to learn from it, and be able to act on the new knowledge, another" (1953). (For much of this discussion of Radó I am indebted to Franz G. Alexander and Sheldon T. Selesnick, 1966:306, 327–29, 343 and *passim*.)

In 1949, Tiebout gave a talk to the American Psychiatric Association (published in the *QJSA* in 1951) in which he argued that "alcoholism is a symptom that has become a disease" (1999:8)—the symptom of Alcoholism(2) becoming the disease of Alcoholism(1), in our terms. He remarks that, in

> advancing this concept of the nature of alcoholism, there is no thought of denying or belittling the importance of psychotherapy on the deepest possible level. Such therapy, however, must aim at helping the individual to learn to live with his limitation, namely, that he cannot drink normally. The alcoholic must be brought to accept that he is the victim of a disease and that the only way for him to remain healthy is to refrain from taking the first drink. (ibid: 9)

In other words, psychotherapy, with all that it brings in the way of release from the unremembered past (once it is remembered), treats the symptom that becomes the disease earlier ages called inebriety: it does not, in Radó's terms, treat the disease condition through progress in learning from the past. That, as William James well knew, takes something more. To quote Tiebout once more,

> the psychotherapy that achieves this may require penetration into the unconscious defiance of, hostility toward, and rejection of reality, including the inability to drink normally, [but] this tapping of unconscious activity cannot and does not resolve the disease, alcoholism. At best, it helps the patient to live with his limitations. (ibid.:11)

Note that Radó was discussing alcohol *and* narcotics, not trying to explain, but accepting, the fact that some people have a particular (and group-idiosyncratic) reaction to alcohol. He was not trying to understand why some are alcoholics and some are not, but suggesting that therapy for alcoholics should concentrate on the alcoholic's failure to grow up beyond the almost infantile stage of oral fixation. He was a brilliant man and a close student of Freud—but his chief influence for our purposes was his influence on Tiebout. And it was Tiebout who brought his knowledge of Radó (and Freud) to meet with the early success of A.A. in treating—however unorthodoxly—this illness of the mind. We will talk more of how this treatment worked (and works) in Chapter 7. Meanwhile, we might mention a little more about the views of Harry Stack Sullivan, and especially his distinctions between and among *prototaxic, parataxic,* and *syntaxic* thinking, his views on language, and his idea of *consensual validation*.

Prototaxic thinking occurs during the first year of life and then recedes in the next two: the infant's life consists of an unending flood of brief vague sensations forming a seamless blur. This thinking may be likened to a confused perception of scenes of photographic slides projected in a random helter-skelter way on a blank screen, without continuity or relatedness of subject matter (Chapman 197:165–66). In parataxic thinking, dominant in the second year of life and receding (though sometimes very slowly thereafter), the child forms links between the fragmentary experiences, but the links are haphazard and nonrational. They do not follow rules of logic and cause-and-effect relatedness. Here the child frequently links together events happening close to each other in time, but not in fact logically related. Parataxic thinking is normal at this stage of the child's development, but it is in fact distorted thinking—Sullivan uses the phrase *parataxic distortion*. In healthy emotional development, the vast majority of these parataxic distortions are corrected during the subsequent syntaxic phase of experience and thinking, beginning in the third or fourth year of life and continuing thereafter. This is the time in which the child develops the capacity for logical and realistic thinking, for sound appraisals of himself or herself and others and of relationships. The basis for this syntaxic thinking is *consensual validation*, and the earlier distorted patterns of thinking that stand in the way of proper consensual validation are the *parataxic distortions*—those that are not corrected (because of anxiety or other emotional difficulties, perhaps reflecting biochemical distortions) persist into later childhood, adolescence, and adulthood (ibid.:166–69).

Sullivan believed that consensual validation—particularly that required to deal with embedded parataxic distortions—came from language (ibid.:171), inasmuch as syntaxic thinking, in the appropriate progression, begins with and accompanies the development of language. Hence the use of Sullivanite group therapy to develop both appropriate consensual validation and appropriate language to produce syntaxic thinking. Hence, also, perhaps, difficulties in "rehab" programs for alcoholics where consensual validation (through bonding) may come from fellow sufferers themselves with inappropriate language.

It has been observed that

> while the Freudian paradigm held fast (with some important deviations such as . . . Harry Stack Sullivan) for the first half of the [twentieth] century, resulting for some in a certain sterility of psychoanalytical thinking, the story of the latter decades is the break-up of the rigid Freudian paradigm. (Phillips 1999:31)

And one of the most interesting phenomena involved in that breakup is the gradual growth of Attachment Theory (connected with the name and work of John Bowlby) and the implications of the ways Attachment Theory and Narrative Theory work together.

Here let us very briefly recapitulate some of the principal points of Attachment Theory (from Bowlby 1980:39–41).

(1) Attachment behavior is conceived of as any form of behavior that results in a person attaining proximity to some other differentiated and preferred individual.

(2) As a class of behavior with its own dynamic, attachment behavior is conceived as distinct from feeding behavior and sexual behavior and of at least an equal significance in human life.

(3) During the course of healthy development throughout the life cycle, attachment behavior leads to the development of affectional bonds or attachments, initially between child and parent and later between adult and adult.

(4) Attachment behavior, like other forms of instinctive behavior, is mediated by behavioral systems, which early in development become goal-corrected: in such a homeostatic system, there is continuous feedback on instruction/performance discrepancies.

(5) An attachment *bond* endures, but the forms of attachment behavior that contribute to it are active only when required—"good at need" so to speak.

(6) Many of the most intense emotions arise from or during the formation, maintenance, disruption, or renewal of attachment bonds: the psychology and psychopathology of emotion is thus in large part the psychology and psychopathology of affectional bonds.

(7) Attachment behavior contributes toward the individual's survival, keeping him in touch with his caregivers and reducing risk of harm from cold, drowning, hunger, predators, and so on.

(8) Caregiving is the functional behavior complementary to attachment behavior.

(9) As attachment behavior is potentially active through life and has its vital biological function; its persistence in an adult is not indicative of either pathology or regression to immature behavior.

(10) If there is psychopathology, it is the result of the individual's having followed a deviant pathway.

(11) Disturbed patterns of detachment behavior can occur at any age as a result of following a deviant pathway: the two most common are anxious attachment behavior and the deactivation of attachment behavior.

(12) The principal pathway determinants occur in infancy, childhood, and adolescence, and the pattern of affectional bonds made during the individual's life turn on the way his attachment behavior becomes organized within his personality.

NARRATIVES

One can see here how neatly Sullivan's group therapy can be tied in with the theory of attachment. With the work of Mary Main in the development of the AAI (Adult Attachment Interview), four patterns have become evident: we may categorize them by looking at the way a one-year-old child may react to brief separation from and then reunion with his or her caregiver. A securely attached child will protest on separation, and then on reunion the protests are accepted, "metabolized," and soothed by the caregiver. Mirroring Tolstoy on happy and unhappy families, all securely attached children are alike in their security, while insecurely attached children are insecurely attached in their own different ways: these may be summarized under three headings—insecure-avoidant, insecure-ambivalent, insecure-disorganized. All protest on separation, but the insecure-avoidant hover nervously at the edge after reunion, the insecure-ambivalent cannot be pacified on the reunion but cling furiously to the caregiver, and the insecure-disorganized show no coherent pattern of response to reunion (Holmes 1999:53).

In adult narratives, the style may likewise be divided into four kinds: (1) secure-autonomous (equivalent to secure attachment in the child), (2) insecure-dismissive (equivalent to insecure-avoidant attachment), (3) insecure-preoccupied (equivalent to insecure ambivalent), and (4) insecure-unresolved (often punctuating the other two and equivalent to insecure-disorganized attachment behavior). Insecure-dismissive narratives are curt, unelaborated, unrevealing and uninformative; insecure-preoccupied narratives are rambling, inconclusive, painful (particularly in the sense that past pain is still present today). Insecure-unresolved narratives are frequently punctuated by broken and disjointed passages possibly indicative of past repression of traumatic memories (ibid.:54). The process of psychotherapy under attachment theory is the process of retelling the stories: "raw experience plus meaning equals narrative" (ibid.:57). Meaning is provided in the psychotherapy by stored or condensed stories provided by the therapist. Just as with the linguistic triad of signified, sign, and lexicon (from which the sign is drawn)—where the sign is linked to the referent via the world of language—so here the story is linked to "raw experience" through the world of meaning. And it seems likely that the capacity to make this link is a developmental link, mediated by early attachment experience. Those who are securely attached can distinguish between their own experience and that of others, represent and tell the story of their feelings, and if need be break up their stories and re-form them more in keeping with the flux of experience. Ambivalent individuals are so close to their feelings that they cannot objectify, externalize, or "mark" the events in the way needed for a working story. Avoidant people cling to a stereotyped version of themselves and their past and feel threatened by the need to update their narrative in the way characteristic of creative living. And the unresolved cannot find a narrative strong enough to contain their traumatic pain.

The process of therapy is then the process of constructing a narrative that when complete will mirror the correction of attachment-insecurities. If I seem to have spent an awfully long time on this—and perhaps I have—we will nonetheless spend a little more time to try to link it (perhaps more briefly) to the question of memory and forgetting, and the principal types of alcoholics noted above. It would be satisfying if we could suggest that our principal types of alcoholism—Zucker type 1 Revised (Jellinek γ) and Zucker type 3 Revised (Jellinek γ), Zucker type 4b (Jellinek ε Revised), and Zucker type 4c (Jellinek δ)—could each be connected with a different memory pattern and perhaps even a different pattern of neurotransmission. Specifically, we may wonder if episodic LTM could be connected with episodic drinking, and be mediated perhaps by pheromal or other sensory signals. After all, the only brain cells outside the brain are in the nose.

THERAPY: FREUD, SULLIVAN, KOHUT, AND THE NARCISSISTIC BABY

In extreme cases of episodic (or periodic) drinking, it has been reported that the drinker does not stop drinking once he starts, but that *on some occasions he cannot bring himself to start,* and on rare occasions can even take one or two drinks without going further. In other words, both drinking and not drinking would appear to be—at least possibly—triggered behaviors. This would seem to have some possible connections with unresolved narrative and insecure-disorganized attachment (obvious examples of parataxic distortion), possibly with literal allergies and neurotransmitter-blocking endorphins, and of course with idiosyncratic (or group-idiosyncratic) memory patterns. Extreme cases are, of course, the exceptions that "prove" (that is, test) the rule.

But what about the therapy based on other psychiatric or psychological models? And, to take it back a step further, what do other models (and most particularly the orthodox Freudian model and its offshoots) have to say about alcoholism—or, in Freud's case (he being a cocaine addict) about addiction? Freud's earliest comment on the subject is this: "It has occurred to me that masturbation is the one great habit that is a 'primary addiction,' and that the other addictions, for alcohol, morphine, etc., only enter into life as a substitute and replacement for it" (letter to Wilhelm Fleiss, [1897] 1985:287). Freud believed that adolescents (and perhaps children in earlier development) continue to resolve not to masturbate and continue to fall away from their resolution, then assuage their guilt by the pleasure of the "forbidden act," then feel guilt and resolve not to masturbate, . . . , and so on—this setting the pattern for all the replacement addictions. In later work (1926, 1928), Freud suggests that addiction serves as a means for punishment of the original "forbidden wish"—so that, for example, the drinker would punish himself for his addiction to drink by drinking. Also, Freud emphasized the narcissistic aspects of addiction (certainly true of his own for cocaine), so that, in the words of J. D. Levin, the "love object of the alcohol abuser becomes alcohol itself, which is experienced either as an extension of the self or as an omnipotent substance with which the drinker merges" (1995:195).

In the first psychoanalytic paper specifically on alcoholism, Karl Abraham ("The Psychological Relations Between Sexuality and Alcoholism," 1908) viewed alcoholism as a nervous and sexual perversion—by "perversion" referring to oral-regressive and homoerotic tendencies. In fact, he suggested that the camaraderie of men in beer halls was essentially homoerotic if not specifically homosexual. Twenty years later, Edward Glover (1928) emphasized the "oral rage" and "anal sadism" of drinking. Five years later, Sandór Radó, whom we have already met, linked alcoholism and manic-depressive psychosis, with elation during the high and depression during the hangover, mimicking the manic-depressive cycle.

In his paper in 1937, discussed in the previous chapter, Robert Knight of the Menninger Clinic distinguished between "essential alcoholics" and "reactive alcoholics"—the first being examples of borderline personality disorder, fixated at the oral stage, while the second are examples of narcissistic personality disorders, also fixated at the oral stage, but with children enraged against their (most often) alcoholic parents for not filling their oral needs, and then at themselves—thereby producing depression. Otto Fenichel (1945) likewise suggested that oral dependence and frustration result in chronic dependence in the alcoholic. He saw alcoholism (as Jerome David Levin has remarked, 1995:197) as a maladaptive defense mechanism used to resolve neurotic conflicts, especially conflict between dependence and expression of anger. It is to Fenichel we owe the comment that "the superego is that part of the mind which is soluble in alcohol" (ibid.:379). Thus, forbidden impulses can be indulged and id-superego conflicts resolved by the use of alcohol. Fenichel was the first to refer explicitly to narcissistic regression in alcoholism, with the deepening self-involvement accompanying alcoholic regression. (One notes a parallel here to the picture of the deepening self-involvement accompanying damnation, in Charles Williams's powerful novel, *The Descent into Hell* (1938)—casting some light, perhaps, on the link, or even identity, between sin and sickness.) More recent theorists have picked up on the adaptive function of addictions, including alcoholism.

On the other hand, Karl Menninger (1938) put major emphasis on alcoholism as chronic suicide, aggression against oneself as a punishment for hostile aggressive feelings against the parent: "Alcohol makes the conflict between passive, erotic dependence on the father and resentment of him manageable" (Levin 1995:197). Something of this insight, with those from before it, has gone into the work of Krystal and Raskin (1970), who have proposed a theory of affect regression in alcoholism, in which discrimination is lost and the predominant affect becomes diffuse dysphoria, a muddle of anxiety and depression—in which the alcoholic does not know what she or he is feeling, except that it isn't pleasant. Now, recognition of affect is at least partially learned. But affect labeling is an important object-relational experience. If it has been lost by the process of affect regression, it must be restored.

If indeed fixation/regression to pathological narcissism is a significant psychodynamic correlative of alcohol abuse or alcoholism—as it seems to be, using Freudian terms—that still does not tell us whether the alcohol abuse causes or is caused by the pathological narcissism. Here we may look at the work of Hans Kohut (1977). Kohut defines the self as a unit cohesive in space and enduring that is a center of initiative and recipient of impressions, possibly a mental structure superordinate to the agencies of the mind (id, ego, superego) or the content of those agencies. The infant develops a fragmented sense of self very early: the infant experiences *selves* but no *self*.

The stage of *fragmented self* is the stage at which psychotic persons are fixated. The next stage is the *archaic nuclear self*, cohesive and enduring but not well-established. This arises from the infant's experience of being related to as a self, rather than as a collection of parts and sensations (in other words, as the novelist Madeleine L'Engle would say, of being named). This self is prone to regressive fragmentation, nuclear in the sense of having a center, archaic in the sense of being the archaic (i.e., grandiose and undifferentiated) precursor of the mature self: it is also bipolar in that it includes the grandiose self and the idealized parental *imago*. There is a differentiated self, experienced as omnipotent, but not differentiated objects.

The internalization of psychic structure (i.e., the capacity to do things once done by parents and now a part of self) comes with and in the formation of the nuclear self. Failure to internalize functions originally performed by self-objects results in deficits in the self. A *self-object* is both the internal representation of an object perceived as an extension of the self and a person so experienced. Addiction—including alcoholism—is, in Kohut's view, a futile attempt to compensate for the failure in internalization. Pathological narcissism is the regression/fixation to the stage of the archaic nuclear self. It is characterized by

(1) the presence of an insecure but cohesive self that is threatened by regressive fragmentation;
(2) grandiosity (but of less than psychotic proportions) manifesting itself in arrogance, isolation, and unrealistic goals;
(3) low affect tolerance;
(4) feelings of entitlement;
(5) the need for omnipotent control;
(6) poor differentiation of self and object;
(7) deficits in the self-regulating capacity of ego (self);
(8) massive anxiety stemming from fear of annihilation (self-fragmentation); and
(9) empty depression (reflecting paucity of psychic structure and good internal objects).

The overt grandiosity of the alcoholic (in the words of Jerome David Levin in *Dynamic Therapies*) "is a manifestation of a false self that is isolated, both affectively and cognitively, from the more mature reality ego, which is itself enfeebled by its inability to integrate the archaic grandiosity—hence the coexistence of haughty arrogance and near-zero self-esteem in alcoholics" (1995:202). It is no accident, as Levin goes on to observe, "that the phrase 'His Majesty, the baby,' which comes from Freud's 1914 essay *On Narcissism: An Introduction*, plays such a prominent role in A.A. literature" (ibid.:202).

The body of empirical psychological findings on the clinical alcoholic personality shows elevated psychopathic deviancy (Pd) and depression on the Minnesota Multiphasic Personality Inventory (MMPI), field dependence (reliance on environmental clues rather than proprioceptive input in construing the environment, overdependence on external stimuli), ego weakness (impulsivity, lack of frustration tolerance, lack of self-concept differentiation), and stimulus augmentation (experience of stimuli as impinging on the self). These fit excellently with the concept of alcoholic regression/fixation to pathological narcissism. Because they experience others as extensions of themselves, the pathologically narcissistic are by definition dependent on those others for their very existence as integral selves. They can be neither independent nor interdependent, because there is no one apart from themselves from whom to be independent or with whom to be interdependent—hence the loneliness of the alcoholic. Also, because the very existence of the self is dependent on the object (experienced as a self-object), the dependency is fraught with primitive, massive, panic-level anxiety—hence the need for control.

It does not matter whether we accept the dependency conflict theory of alcoholism, or the need-for-personal-power theory, or the epistemological (or cognitive) error theory: all will fit with pathological narcissistic regression/fixation. In the first case, alcoholic drinking is a covert way of meeting unacceptable dependency needs (alcohol becomes an all-powerful parent who will "provide the goods"). In the second case, the alcoholic attributes omnipotent power (not parental power) to the alcohol, and the alcoholic drinking is driven by a wish to participate in the self-object's greatness and power. In the third case, the driving force behind alcoholism is seen as "an impossible misperception of reality that sets the alcoholic in opposition to the world and allows no meaningful interaction with that world" (Levin 1995:204). Rather than experiencing reality as "an infinite set of interrelationships, interactions, and feedback loops, the alcoholic experiences it as a reified subject, acting on a disjunctive world" (ibid.). This is exactly the phenomenology of the world as experienced by the pathologically narcissistic. The alcoholic in his or her pathological narcissism may experience the self as separate from the world, but he or she does not experience the world except in the self. There is thus a resounding imbalance or even contradiction at the heart of the alcoholic's world.

It is perhaps worthwhile to note here some of the implications of this psychological and psychotherapeutic analysis for sobriety (including recovery from the effects of alcoholism). Briefly (following Levin), we note that the

> neurochemical and neurophysiological effects of ethanol are profound. In effect, it induces a transient organic brain syndrome. On the cognitive side, . . . there are impairments in the ability to abstract, reason, and remember. . . . On the affective side, [this] syndrome manifests itself as emotional liability. The patient is up, down, and sideways. . . . Recovery from the effects of alcohol abuse takes a long time. . . . Anywhere from three months to two years must elapse before full neurochemical recovery takes place. . . . We are working with people who are not playing with a full deck. (1995:208)

Moreover, the

> regressive pull of addiction is overwhelmingly powerful, and forces of equal or greater weight pulling in the opposite direction must be put in place. . . . The patient is also desperately in need of an object to idealize. Alcohol had been the ideal object. Now it is gone and must be replaced. Generally

that replacement takes place through idealization of a therapist, an AA sponsor, an AA group, the AA program, or AA's "higher power." (ibid.: 208–10)

—so that the "formation of a self-object transference provides the patient with the stability and the security out of which growth from the stage of the archaic nuclear self into the stage of the mature self can take place" (ibid.:210).

PSYCHODYNAMIC NARRATIVE

The whole process

reduces anxiety by providing cognitive structure for chaotic experience; through providing tools for living, the psychic structure needed to deal with feelings and conflicts; through the reversal of affect regression; through internalization, transmuting and otherwise; through de-repression; and through the breakdown of defensive isolation through integration into a community of recovering persons. (ibid.:212–13)

There are indications in Levin's psychodynamic analysis that we have passed beyond—though not necessarily contradicted—Freud's original approach. These indications are borne out by the American James Phillips in his discussion of changes in the psychodynamic narrative from Freud to present practice, with some notice specifically of the work of Hans Kohut (Phillips 1999:27–48): "There is no longer one psychodynamic narrative, one developmental narrative, and one treatment narrative. There are now several of each" (ibid.:31). And also as the result of work by Roy Schafer and others, there,

is no longer a psychodynamic narrative of the patient's past and then a second narrative of the treatment itself. For Schafer the two are collapsed into one. The psychodynamic narrative is now a complex interwoven tale, told along psychoanalytical lines, that intertwines themes from the patient's past with themes from the treatment itself, *the emphasis falling on the latter rather than the former.* (ibid.:44, my emphasis)

Although (ibid.:45) Freud does not frame his case histories in the language of narrative, he comes (Phillips suggests) closer than our psychoanalytic contemporaries to making narrative central to the psychoanalytic process—with the exception of the narrative therapists and some others who accept the view of Alasdair MacIntyre that defines selfhood in terms of "a concept of a self whose unity resides in the unity of a narrative, which links birth to life to death as narrative beginning to middle to end" (quoted in ibid.:44). The therapeutic challenge, within narrative therapy (as Phillips reminds us), is to loosen the sense of inevitability carried by the narrative of one's past, so that the chapters that will extend into the future are more under the auctorial control of the narrator.

To put this together, the newly sober alcoholic will be engaged in a process of mixed mirror transference and idealizing transference (from alcohol as self-object to therapist or sponsor or group or "higher power" as self-object); this will be connected with modifications of the self-narrative that help organize the chaotic information of the past (in A.A. terms, "what it was like") and meld it with the process of therapy, including the A.A. program (in A.A. terms, "what happened"), and the alcoholic's present state (in A.A. terms, "what it's like now"). As I understand it, the sponsor in A.A. will provide his own story, or episodes from his or her own story, as an aid to the newly sober alcoholic in formulating his or hers. So far as theory is concerned, it does not really matter (in this context) whether the past is organized by Freudian constructs, with their heavy sexual basis—though, given the state of psychoanalytic theory, the probability is that it will be. So far as result is concerned, the Freudian emphasis on sex does not necessarily promise a high degree of utility.

But what matters for us here is that the story be told—that the life-experience be "narratized"—according to an accepted pattern and process of events that is also an explanation of events. In psychotherapy, of course, the establishment of pattern (and thus of explanation) is in the hands of the therapist, or in group therapy in the hands of the group as led, guided, and given cohesion and cohesiveness by the therapist. In Alcoholics Anonymous, I have heard it suggested, it is in the hands of the sponsor, or the experienced members of the group, or in the "Big Book" and its stories as exemplars and models, condensed life-narratives in the sense suggested by Jeremy Holmes in *Healing Stories* (1999). This, by the way, seems to use the "Big Book" in somewhat the same way as *Science and Health* is used as part of the weekly "lesson-sermon" in Christian Science, where the book is in a sense the pastor. I believe sponsors will sometimes suggest particular stories to those they sponsor, as guides to organizing their own experience. Moreover, some alcoholics, in telling their stories, will (according to what I am told) organize their experience in terms of the Twelve Steps of Alcoholics Anonymous, comprising the pattern of recovery into sobriety.

We have talked about narratization in attachment theory and in Freudian psychotherapy, about the elimination of parataxic distortions in Sullivanite group therapy, about mind-cure and the extreme Cartesianism of Mrs. Eddy. All of this speaks to roughly the same means of therapy, or arresting the "disease" of alcoholism. We should probably rehearse here, before going on to the next chapter, two parts of our model most closely related to the possibility of self-induced physiological (that is, neurophysiological) change.

The first part may be expressed in three propositions. First, as we recall from Edelman's work, morphogenesis produces a species-dependent neuroanatomy variable at the individual level: the neuron groups in a specific brain region deriving from this process are known as *primary repertoires*. The genetic code imposes constraints but not unanimity. Second, as we also recall from Edelman's work, through the individual's behavioral engagement with the external world, some synaptic connections are promoted through use and thus strengthened, others neglected and thus weakened. That is, certain neural networks are self-selected from the diversity of those available: these are *secondary repertoires*. Finally, again from Edelman, primary and secondary repertoires link psychology and physiology by forming maps that are connected by the entrance and reentrance of neural linkages.

QUANTITATIVE TRAIT LOCI, THE ALCOHOLIC VOICE—AND ON TO BIOCHEMISTRY

The second part of our model (which to some degree may be taken as a restatement of the first) has to do with *quantitative trait loci* (QTLs). As research on QTLs has shown, a specific quantitative trait can arise from a number of different QTLs on the genome, and it has been suggested that there exists a dynamic equilibrium whereby environmental changes that affect gene expression may change the action of a complex system of linked QTLs, which will in turn give rise to further changes in the state of the system. Environmental changes affect the action of linked QTLs through system-interaction with the environment, and we are proposing that it may be self-selected system-interaction (as with Norman Cousins). The fundamental point (made by Alan Dean 1997) is that, while we cannot alter our genotype, we can alter our extended phenotype, our system interaction with the environment, by our self-selection of secondary repertoires, thus altering our neural linkage as well as our cognitive maps. About our ability to alter our own cognitive maps there is little argument; about our ability to alter our own synaptic or neural-linkage maps there may be more—but the evidence seems sufficient to make this part of our scientific research program.

The other part of our scientific research program proposed here that may seem particularly controversial is our use of Jaynes's hypothesis to explain the observations recorded more than a half-century ago by Frankfort and

Jacobsen and others—and, more important for our program here, to suggest a point of origin for the preconditions for alcoholism (and most specifically for Jellinek type ε alcoholism). We are suggesting that a drive humans share with other animals (Siegel's Fourth Drive) came to be conceived of as a mode of opening the mind to the voices of the gods in the day before "consciousness" and therefore before philosophy (or psychology). Note—the *voices* of the gods. Note that the *Enuma Elish* views "authority as a power inherent in commands, a power which caused a command to be obeyed, caused it to realize itself, to come true" (Jacobsen 1949:189)—which is pretty much what Jaynes is talking about with commands in the bicameral mind that must be obeyed. Jaynes uses the word *hallucinations* in connection with the voices of the gods: it is, however, our contention here that these voices are no more hallucinatory than our view that we have something called our own free will, and can make our own decisions, can reasonably be described as hallucinatory.

We do, so far as we know, make our own decisions, though it may well be that the ancients did not. So far as they knew, they were commanded by the gods (or in the case of Abraham, with Isaac, perhaps by God), though we may well have lost the contact (or knowledge or consciousness of the contact). One thing, by the way, that we learn from the *Enuma Elish* and other ancient texts is that the gods did inexplicable things while drunk (or at least while "buzzed" on beer)—but apparently they were themselves periodics, ε drinkers. One wonders occasionally if periodic drinking is not the ancient norm, daily drinking the modern divergence. As we will see, there are hints that some of the more rundown oracles and sibyls of classical times may have been daily drunks, much to their contemporary discredit. That, however relevant in the longer run, is only by the way for the present discussion. And now, with our proposed psychological theory (or research program) suggested, and other theories noted, and some groundwork laid as to the types of alcoholics and alcoholism, it is time to look in more detail at the biology (or biochemistry) that marks the predisposition toward alcoholism, and may mark the *telos* of sobriety. We will come back to this material (and to all the rest of the material in Chapters 1 through 8) when we construct our working model in Chapter 9.

5 ~

Body: The Biogenetics and Biochemistry of Alcoholism

IN CHAPTER 3, WE LOOKED AT SEVERAL ROUTES OF SCIENTIFIC INQUIRY INTO ALCOHOLISM—typologies, genetics, and what may be called the mathematics of change, this last with particular attention to the origins of Alcoholism(2)—the heritable precondition—and of language. Now one reason for looking at both typologies and biogenetics is to look specifically at the biology, or biochemistry, of alcoholism. That is, by finding what genetic traits seem to cluster in alcoholics, as distinct from non-alcoholics, we can find out something of the biochemistry of alcoholics, and specifically that part of their biochemistry relevant to their alcoholism. For example, if we find (as we do) that alcohol-preferring mice exhibit a central serotonin deficiency connected with higher tryptophan pyrrolase activity—and if we then find (as we do) that FHP (Family History Positive = genetic?) alcoholics are serotonin-deficient in a way connected with the availability of circulating tryptophan pyrrolase to the brain—we may reasonably conclude (as we do) that the biochemistry of alcoholism involves serotonin and tryptophan pyrrolase.

Before going into further biochemical assays, we should perhaps look here in more detail at genetic questions, as a possible guide for further research—and to further understanding. The review in the *Report on Genetics* (National Advisory Council on Alcohol Abuse and Alcoholism [NACAAA] 1997) suggests that "additional development in genetic analytic techniques is required to accept multiple correlated qualitative, quantitative, and compound phenotypic measures that are produced in the multi-domain studies of alcohol-related phenotypes." It does not suggest, though I believe it should, that greater typological precision is needed before we can hope to identify different phenotypes for different alcoholisms, or at least for different development patterns (etiologies) of alcoholism. Like the *Report on Genetics* itself, we should turn now to laboratory (nonhuman) research, specifically research on QTLs for alcohol-related behaviors, mentioned in Chapter 3 but not discussed in detail.

LABORATORY RESEARCH

Since alcoholism is, so far as we know, a condition (or developmental process) with multiple biological origins, multiple precipitating environmental events, and complex processes maintaining the condition, it will be difficult to identify any individual phenotype for animal study that can capture all relevant dimensions. We are looking for an array of alcohol-related phenotypes, through selective breeding, specialized strains, and neoclassical congenic (genes-with-genes) methodology, using backcrossing wherein a monogenically (one-gene) controlled phenotypic variant is "moved" onto a background of another strain (typically an inbred strain). Marker-based breeding schemes involve a mapped QTL (quantitative trait locus) and can be used in the genetic analysis of alcohol-related phenotypes. With polymorphic flanking markers spaced closely enough to make recombination unlikely, it is possible to move a QTL onto another background.

Marker-assisted selection uses pairs of flanking polymorphic polymerase chain reaction (PCR)-identified markers to fix to homozygosity (same-allele genes). It would be possible to use short-term selection for alcohol-related phenotypes: employing mass selection, beginning typically with F2 (second filial generation) populations, where QTL mapping has already been accomplished and markers linked to the putative QTL are tracked through a few generations of selections, providing strong "verification" strategy for QTL regions. (Note that the P generation is the parents, of differing phenotypes and genotypes, F1 the next generation, and F2 the third generation.)

Selective breeding was used (NACAAA 1997:passim) initially to show that alcohol-related behavioral phenotypes were heritable, and that these heritable phenotypes can provide the material for our further biochemical assays. The major breeding programs in rodents (mice and more recently rats), fruit flies (*Drosophila melanogaster*), and nematodes (*Caenorhabditis elegans*) have established three principal alcohol-related phenotypes (biometrically determined), determined by (1) acute alcohol response, (2) alcohol tolerance/dependence withdrawal, and (3) alcohol preference. These (we hope appropriately defined) are the characteristics bred into the rats, flies, and nematodes: it is worth noting there are at least three of these, casting still further doubt on a simple dual typology for human alcoholics. (We would for our purposes prefer our four phenotypes, much differently defined, but relevant only to humans.)

There are some advantages in using selected lines with expected continued utility:

(1) Selected breeding provides a wide divergence of phenotypes beyond the range found in the base population, and the use of such phenotypes has resulted in new pharmacotherapies for excessive alcohol consumption.

(2) Selected lines catch most of the relevant genetic variation, which is usually derived from a wide array of progenitor strains of heterogeneous background.

(3) Large population sizes are available, permitting examination of multivariate correlation structure while controlling for the selected phenotype.

(4) Production of extreme populations can produce unexpected but informative outcomes.

(5) Selected breeding enables simpler comparisons as against characterizing batteries of inbred strains or large arrays of QTL-based marker-differentiated stocks, providing an ideal model system for tests of behavioral theories.

Selected breeding is also arguably an ideal strategy for gene mapping, with lower power required, considerable capability for generalization, and providing a control condition against which genotype-based selected QTL lines are compared. On the other hand, problems with selected breeding can arise from nonreplicated lines, low population sizes, and breeding bottlenecks. Replicated within-family bidirectional design may mitigate these difficulties. It has been suggested that the presence of genetic correlation is questionable unless selected lines differ by two or three phenotypic SDs on the correlated character.

A qualitative trait (QT) is one whose phenotypic variation is continuous rather than discrete, and is determined by the segregation of many genes. Most of the genetic variation in alcohol action is specified by several genes typically defined as QTLs. Mice are useful in this research because the genetic map of the mouse is covered with highly polymorphic loci, facilitating the mapping of QTLs. QTL mapping for alcohol-related phenotypes in one strain of recombinant inbred (RI) mouse has led to the identification of a number of provisional QTLs, but only two studies have reported QTLs that satisfy rigorous criteria for statistical significance. These studies involved whole-genome scans, mapping (1) preference for alcohol and (2) initial sensitivity to alcohol (NACAAC 1997:passim).

The degree of the detectable association between a marker and a phenotype is based on the size of the effect of the QTL on the phenotype and on the genetic distance between the QTL and the marker (measured in cMs, centimorgans, as noted in Chapter 3). If the QTL is close to the marker and has a large effect, then detection and mapping of the QTL can be done easily and accurately. If not, then recombination between the marker and the QTL will lead to lower association levels and a lower "effect size" for the QTL. Mice have provided the principal area for QTL animal studies on alcohol-related behavior. In addition to QTL study in mice, there have been "knockout" and "antisense" studies, both involving gene alteration. A transgenic (gene-altered) animal possesses a gene that has been specifically altered to over- or underexpress a particular gene product. Obviously, we cannot (or must not) thus alter human genes, but we have the mice.

The term *knockout* usually refers to a gene that has been altered in such a way that its function is entirely deleted. There has been only limited use of transgenic and knockout mice in alcohol research, but promising results have been claimed. (We will see what they are and what they promise later on.) In particular, male transgenic mice overexpressing human transforming growth factor a (TGFa) maintained elevated aggressive behavior in the presence of ethanol, except at the highest dose administered. Transgenic mice overexpressed for IGF-binding protein 1 (insulinlike growth factor 1) developed significantly higher ethanol tolerance than controls. There have been test results showing alteration in the $GABA_A$ (gamma-aminobutyric acid A) receptor function in the brain tissue of mutant mice for ethanol but not for flunitrazepam or pentobarbital, which would be expected to have effects like those of ethanol. In addition, it has been shown that mice lacking a functional copy of the gene coding for serotonin 1_B receptors drank twice as much ethanol in a free-choice drinking situation as wildtype controls (Bowers 2000). (We will look at this further a little later on, and note that xerotonin 1_A receptors also seem important. So, by the way, do both $GABA_A$ and $GABA_B$ receptors.)

In connection with research on *Drosophila melanogaster*, it should be noted that the natural environment for *Drosophila m.* includes fermenting plant materials, which often contain high levels of ethanol and other alcohols (3.0 percent). *Drosophila* is quite resistant to the toxic effects of alcohol and can degrade ethanol efficiently for use an energy source. The enzyme alcohol dehydrogenase (ADH) plays a key role in ensuring both metabolic use and detoxification from ethanol: it is encoded by a single structural gene, and heritable levels of ADH have been associated with increased ethanol resistance. (We will see the relevance of this for certain types of alcoholics.) *Drosophila melanogaster* larvae with high ADH activity prefer ethanol-supplemented agar, while larvae lacking ADH avoid agar containing 8 percent or more ethanol. Acetaldehyde is toxic to *Drosophila* larvae, and it has been suggested that ethanol avoidance correlates with both the relative rate of acetaldehyde production and relative aldehyde sensitivity, for fruit flies as, apparently, for humans. In other words, in alcoholic fruit flies as in alcoholic humans, high levels of ADH encourage alcohol consumption, and the ability to consume alcohol may be a marker for certain types of alcoholism.

The nematode *C. elegans* is an attractive organism for research on central nervous system function and behavior, having a simple nervous system with exactly 302 neurons, each of which can be identified in the live semitransparent (and tiny) animal, and the complete circuitry of the nervous system is known—but having an array of classical neurotransmitters similar to that found in vertebrate nervous systems. Several mutations have been isolated with altered sensitivity to volatile anesthetics, and a subset of these mutants having altered sensitivity to anesthetic effects of ethanol—though not all in the same direction. It is hard to avoid believing that the simplicity of tests on *C. elegans* and the ease and quickness of breeding mutant strains is not accompanied by useful results in the understanding of a genetic basis of alcoholism.

The value of studying laboratory genetic mutations for understanding the genetics of alcoholism—and, here, for understanding its biochemistry—is not dependent on finding precise markers or precise phenotypic variants within the test populations. The value lies in demonstrating some possible relationships for human study and particularly in assembling evidence that alcohol-related traits are genetic among alcoholics, and are thus defining traits. As we come closer and closer to understanding that precise markers may not really mark anything precisely, the simple demonstration of qualitative relationships becomes even more important. As we noted in Chapter 3, and will again in Chapter 9, it is also—indeed, especially—important that many conditions we recognize as genetic diseases are present in certain populations because, in the not-too-distant past, they actually conferred a survival advantage on their carriers (or, possibly, a condition to which the diseases are connected conferred such an advantage). In most cases the disease is manifested in the homozygote, whereas the heterozygote is at an advantage. (We noted that in tests marker-assisted selection uses pairs of flanking polymorphic PCR-identified markers to fix to homozygosity.) When there is both a dominant and a recessive allele at a locus, their frequencies in the population will remain relatively constant as the generations go by, in what is called Hardy-Weinberg equilibrium, from its discoverers in 1908.

GENOTYPES

Here we suggest our four principal genotypes, homozygotes for each of the alleles and the heterozygotes. Relative frequencies (which are sometimes called gene frequencies but are actually allele frequencies) will as noted ordinarily remain more or less constant from one generation to the next; and no matter what the relative frequencies of the genotypes in the starting population, in subsequent generations these too will be more or less fixed at values determined by allele frequencies. This is the Hardy-Weinberg equilibrium, and it holds in general for large populations, random mating, no exogenous preference on particular genotypes, low rate of mutation for introduction of new alleles, and no significant net migration of particular genotypes into or out of the population. That being the case, once a trait has been established with a certain frequency in the population, it will continue to show at approximately that frequency. But there is an area that renders the whole matter simultaneously more difficult in some respects and easier in others. This is the matter of chaotic ordering, which we have already touched on, which in turn is part of the change-conditions implied by action on the borders of the adjacent possible, as discussed in Chapter 3.

What is the value of studying the possible genetics of alcoholism? And why have the areas on which genetic studies on human subjects have concentrated been (1) the study of twins and (2) adoption studies? We study the possible genetics of alcoholism because an individual's genetic endowment (genotype) affects his or her physical form (phenotype). We study twins and adoptees because they provide the closest approximation we can reach to a laboratory situation—since we are unable, as noted, to breed alcoholics for laboratory study. First, let us look at the value of genetic studies.

If—as we believe—alcoholism is grounded in part in biological processes, and biological processes can be influenced greatly by the biochemistry that governs the inheritance of a genetic code from which biological development takes place, and if the genetic code has developed as a response to external conditions (as Darwin suggests) and represents a survival from a time when it conferred a survival value on the carrier (as noted and possibly modified above), then the various alcoholic phenotypes we have suggested (Psa, Sda, Pca, Pea) can be studied in connection with their putative causes back in time in the evolutionary process. By understanding how things got the way they are, we can see how they might be changed. Of course, once again (and this is the second point), since we cannot breed humans the way we breed mice and fruit flies and nematodes, we look at differences in genetic makeup between identical and fraternal twins, and we look at children of alcoholic parents adopted by nonalcoholic parents. These are the so-called adoption and twin studies, playing a major part in human research on the genetics of alcoholism.

In fact, the two major methods of studying the heritability of alcoholism have been twin studies and adoption studies. Twin studies compare the incidence of alcoholism in identical twins with the incidence of alcoholism in fraternal twins. In general, in these studies, no attention has been paid to types of alcoholism, except for Cloninger type I and type II, which are unfortunately open to question. It is argued that, if there is a genetic component in the risk for alcoholism, then identical twins, who have identical genes, would be expected to exhibit more similarities in alcoholic development than fraternal twins, who are genetically different individuals born at the same time. The expectations have generally held true.

TYPES AND GENOTYPES

For example, Pickens and his coworkers studied 169 pairs of same-sex twins of which at least one twin had sought treatment for alcoholism: they found greater concordance of alcohol dependence (DSM-III) in identical than in fraternal twins, and in identical male twins more than in identical female twins. Partanen and his coworkers, in studying 902 male Finnish twins, for less severe drinking patterns less heritable and more severe drinking patterns more heritable. Problems in evaluating these studies come from the question of whether identical twins grow up in more identical environments than those in which fraternal twins grow up. Apparently they do. Also, even the identical twins would need to grow up almost exactly synchronously for us to be sure—or reasonably sure—that we are escaping the effects of chaotic ordering in our analysis.

Adoption studies may employ a number of techniques. One is to compare the history of (1) children of alcoholics who are adopted by nonalcoholics and grow up in a nondrinking environment with (2) the children of nonalcoholics similarly raised or similarly adopted and raised. If genetic factors play a role, then children of alcoholics adopted by nonalcoholics should preferentially develop alcoholism as adults. Problems in the analysis here may include failure to distinguish by alcoholic typology and the simple lack of data on parents who give up children for adoption. Even so, in a pioneering study of adopted Danish children, Goodwin and his coworkers (1973) found some evidence of expected heritability. Then Cloninger and his team (1981), working with much more extensive Swedish data and using the type I/type II typology, found evidence that his type II alcoholics had a more heritable form of alcoholism than his type I alcoholics. Type II alcoholics, you will remember, were usually male early-onset drinkers displaying ASPD.

The fact that Marc Schuckit (1981, 1994) and others have suggested that the inheritance scenario is more complex, involving a mix of traits including ASPD, rather than simply "alcoholism itself" suggests a problem in defining alcoholism: the "traits" may in fact constitute the alcoholism. There is a saying in A.A., "My problem isn't alcohol—it's alcoholism," or (essentially along the same lines) "I'm a sober alcoholic." In fact, it would seem that for A.A., the traits (including ASPD) define the alcoholism. In his *Natural History of Alcoholism Revisited*, George Vaillant noted three questions yet (1995) to be answered by research:

> First, why does the prevalence of alcohol abuse decline sharply after age 50? Is the explanation for this decline stable abstinence [as, for example, in A.A.], return to asymptomatic drinking, high mortality, or poor case finding among the elderly? Second, how long must abstinence or return to controlled drinking persist before an individual's recovery can be considered secure? In cancer, remission must often last five years before relapse is considered unlikely. In treatment studies, however, investigators often speak of recovery after the alcohol-abuser has been symptom-free for six months or one year; two years of abstinence is considered an adequate criterion for candidacy for liver transplant. Is that long enough? Third, *why do smoking, depression, and alcohol abuse so often occur together* [my emphasis]? Each of these three conditions is associated with high mortality. *Only by studying individuals for a lifetime* is it possible to unravel the relative dangers and the etiological importance of each of these variables [again, my emphasis]. (1996a:12–13)

The answer to the first question seems to be, in effect, all of the above (except that return to asymptomatic [i.e., social] drinking is uncommon). The answer to the second question (ibid.:234–35) seems to be six years. (Rather than the three years suggested by Vaillant in his tests for success of alternative modes of treatment.) We do not have the answer to the third question—yet—and that is the one of particular importance here. Especially, what is the connection between depression and alcoholism? (The connection between nicotine addiction and alcoholism is certainly capable of supporting the same kind and degree of biogenetic and biochemical research, but what research I have seen on this connection has tended toward the sociological, particularly in adolescent studies, while research on alcoholism and depression has perforce tended toward the biochemical and biogenetic.) Here, in effect, we return to the question of whether the traits define the alcoholism.

That is, we are asking whether the depression—and probably the nicotine abuse (or, perhaps, addiction)—might be considered not a comorbid characteristic, but part of the alcoholism. (It may also, as we will see, be an aftereffect of alcoholic drinking.) Certainly Vaillant (ibid.:80–85 and passim) suggests significant linkage between depression and nicotine use: the conclusions on depression and alcoholism are less clear. What he does report is that alcoholics (in the "premorbid" stage) are likely to be passive-dependent, egocentric, latently homosexual, sociopathic, intolerant of psychic tension, lacking in self-esteem, and frightened of intimacy (ibid.:75). In other words, these are characteristics (traits) that fall under the umbrella of alcoholism. Vaillant reduces the question of depression and its relation to alcoholism to a dichotomy and notes that his "own interpretation of the data is that most alcoholics are depressed because they drink and not vice versa. But many disagree" (ibid.:270). This is in his discussion of how stably abstinent alcoholics resemble the general population more than they resemble drinking alcoholics. I think the dichotomy may itself be misleading—better to say that many alcoholics drink because their particular alcoholism includes depression, not because they are depressed: it may generally be better to say that alcoholics drink because they are alcoholics.

The point is that we need to study the biochemistry of depression and the biochemistry of alcoholism—ideally employing a typology of alcoholisms—to see what's under the umbrella. Vaillant recommends that we "learn to conceive of alcoholism as a disease that causes depression, marital breakup, and unemployment, not as a symptom that results from such events" (ibid.:362–63). That, I think, is more like it—though we should keep in mind Tiebout's remarks on the symptoms of our Alcoholism(2) that become the disease we are calling Alcoholism(1).

Let me reiterate that Alcoholism(1) is what the word *Alcoholismus* meant to the German speakers who coined the word (in 1848 by the Swede Magnus Hoff, and it appears in a German dictionary in 1852), a progressive state of diseased body resulting from chronic alcoholic drinking. In other words, alcoholism, in this sense, was cirrhosis and wet-brain and all that went with those conditions, and the alcoholic was (in 1930s terms) the bum under the bridge, drinking out of a bottle of cheap wine in a paper bag. But what we have been looking at much more in this chapter is Alcoholism(2), the illness of the body (and thus, through the brain, of the mind) that leads the alcoholic to drink alcoholically, thus producing the symptoms of Alcoholism(1) and leading, if not checked (in a phrase commonly heard in A.A.) to jails, institutions, or death. This Alcoholism(2) also—and this is Vaillant's point—leads to depression, perhaps marital breakup, unemployment, probably indeed before it leads to cirrhosis and wet-brain. Yet our understanding of natural selection strongly suggests that this Alcoholism(2) must either have had a survival value for those with this genetic inheritance, or that it accompanies and accompanied other genetic characteristics with such a survival value.

Or, possibly, we might find that different types of Alcoholism(2) would be attached to different genetic characteristics with such a survival value. This is an area where future research (and putting together the results of research already carried out) might well be useful. For the moment, let us suggest that in Celtic peoples, the "priestly" or "prophetic" orders of druids and bards might well have involved altered consciousness from intoxication.

Also, in Germanic or Nordic peoples (to the extent they are differentiated from the Celtic) a relative ease in attaining the *berserkr* rage of battle might have been related to alcoholic intoxication (perhaps with a premium on a periodic alcoholic pattern). In both these cases, the premium would be on the differential effect of alcohol on those with the relevant differential characteristics.

An interesting sidelight may come from considering two peoples with heavy concentrations of genetic alcoholism but no particular evidence of its potentiation until relatively modern times—the Finns and the Native American tribes. Here, possibly, genotypic characteristics remained quiescent until the environment again included strong drink, while in the meantime other modes of inducing altered consciousness (such as the sweat-lodge or sauna) were used. Or, it is possible that intermarriage also potentiated the genetic alcoholism. We will look at research that might be of value here in presenting our model in Chapter 9. With all this in mind (as an example, though wishing we had a Jellinek/Zucker typology for the FHP alcoholics), we will begin here with relatively recent (1990s) developments in pharmacogenetic and pharmacogenomic studies.

A paper in *Science* a few years ago (Kleyn and Vesell 1998) noted that the "methodology of genome-wide DNA genotyping as applied to pharmacogenomic studies evolved from linkage and association studies of complex diseases," and certainly alcoholism, if a disease, is by definition a complex disease (in fact, a private communication to me from the authors of the paper in *Science* suggests that it is the complex disease par excellence). In Chapter 3 we noted linkage studies that involve genotyping families with microsatellite markers (variable numbers of short tandem repeats), within a family; the shared regions are typically tens of millions of bases long, so that only a few hundred microsatellite markers evenly spaced throughout the genome will be sufficient to detect the relevant region. We can identify several regions determining "alcoholic" response to alcohol, so that alcoholism is not only a complex disease (or at least condition) but a complexly genetic (heritable) disease (or at least condition). Much more work remains to be done in this area, and work is in fact continuing.

We looked briefly in Chapter 3 at the matter of heritability. Here we will return to the definition of the "alcoholic" response to alcohol, once again regretting that we do not have proper data for the alcoholic response by types of alcoholics. We may note, however, that some material on adolescent "alcoholism" and ASPD may be helpful here, as FHP-positive adolescent alcoholism may be taken as an ε type, assuming ASPD is not an anterior comorbid disorder.

Of course, except for allergies and alcoholism, drug response data can rarely be obtained from multiple members of a family, so that, in general, linkage studies are impractical for pharmacogenomics. Association studies, on the other hand, correlate the presence of a chromosomal region and a trait (disease or chemical entity/biological entity response) in unrelated individuals, with much smaller shared chromosomal regions, and far more microsatellite markers required. As a result, association studies tend to look at single nucleotide polymorphisms (SNPs) rather than microsatellite markers. SNPs are simple pair-based substitutions that occur inside and outside genes. They are biallelic (two alleles involved) rather than multiallelic (like the markers), thus less polymorphic, but also more frequent and less mutable.

PHARMACOGENETIC MARKERS AND NEUROTRANSMITTERS

Among the pharmacogenetic markers noted by Kleyn and Vesell (1998) are the "slow acetylator" phenotype (in roughly half of all Caucasians) leading to slow clearance (and thus toxicity) of multiple drugs (including Procainimide) and to polymorphisms in the coding region for 5-HT2AT (a serotonin receptor), and for the polymorphic drug-metabolizing enzyme (PME) CYP2D6, a member of the cytochrome P450 superfamily. These could give us a starting place for discussing the "alcoholic" response to alcohol. (In this chapter, we will indeed be discussing both 5-HT and cytochrome P450 in more detail.) Because Procainimide has certain structural connections with cocaine (also involving certain neurotransmitters and neuroreceptors), it may be valuable evidence for us, as may the slow clearance involved with antihistamines (connected at least with norepinephrine/epinephrine).

Obviously, if the condition (or precondition) is heritable, what is inherited should be the biochemical (biogenetic) differences that mark alcoholics as different from nonalcoholics. We have gone into the genetics (and will be going further): from there we will be going into the differences. The *Report on Genetics* by the NACAAA (1997) of the NIH covers both biological and psychosocial phenotypes. For reasons connected with the presence of chaos in genetics, these may not be so different from each other as might be thought, but we will certainly preserve the distinction here.

In both cases, we are concerned with the contrast between FHP and FHN (Family History Negative) "alcoholics." We will review the current state of knowledge primarily on biological (biochemical) phenotypes, looking at (1) neurotransmitter-related systems, (2) enzyme systems, (3) cognition, response to stress, and electrophysiology, and (4) response to alcohol challenge, with some consideration of psychosocial phenotypes. Note that the areas of biological research fall into two broad categories: signal systems and breakdown systems, the way alcohol sends signals to the brain, and the way it alters the body, though these areas overlap in certain respects. The first seems principally to relate to Alcoholism(2); the second relates to both Alcoholism(1) and Alcoholism(2).

Work in this area has been done on endogenous opioids, serotonin and serotonergic functioning, GABA, epinephrine/norepinephrine, glutamate (but not much until quite recently), and dopamine, of the neurotransmitter-related systems, and some very recent work suggests the possibility of a connection between the P substance (a neurokinin discovered in 1933) and alcoholism. So far as I know, there has as yet been no research carried out on the connection between alcoholism and this neurokinin. Obviously, any such connection would most likely be with Sda alcoholism—which is arguably the case for some of the other neurotransmitters, though probably not the endogenous opioids, and perhaps not serotonin. I would note that Cloninger type II and Babor type B alcoholisms may include both Psa and Sda alcoholics (and probably Pea), making them—I should think—relatively inapplicable typologies for genetic study, including the study of neurotransmitter markers. It may be the case that different neurotransmitter markers would apply to different alcoholic phenotypes. It is certainly the case that serotonin seems to apply most widely.

Endogenous Opioids

There is considerable evidence on the interactions between alcohol and the endogenous opioid system (Froehlich 1993). Investigations have shown that rodent lines can be bred with very high or very low levels of voluntary alcohol drinking (ibid.:22), and that rat lines selected for high alcohol drinking can be used "to investigate the efficacy of pharmacological, behavioral, and environmental manipulations that have the potential to inhibit alcoholic drinking" (ibid.:24). In one sense, of course, these are manipulations of dubious applicability to humans—who are not actually rats, whatever the resemblances—but the biochemistry underlying the manipulations should still be of value to us. In what way? Well, many of the effects of alcohol and opiate administration are quite similar, and this raises the possibility of a common biochemical mechanism. (This possibility, apparently, if it holds true, may hold true only for alcohol and opiates, not for drugs other than opiates.) Administration to alcohol-choosing rats of naloxone, a nonspecific opioid receptor antagonist, by injection one hour prior to alcoholic fluid access, led to significantly suppressed alcohol consumption by the rats. Administration of a highly selective delta receptor antagonist, ICI 174864, also led to suppressed alcohol consumption, but not to the same degree—suggesting that both mu and delta opioid receptors are involved (ibid.:25–27).

It has been suggested that alcohol consumption may stimulate increased activity in the endogenous opioid systems, as—for example—the enkephalinergic system, and by potentiating the duration of the enkephalins might increase alcohol consumption. Enkephalins are generally short-lasting, being degraded rapidly by enkephalinase and aminopeptidase enzymes. It is possible that the genetics—which is to say, the biochemistry—of alcoholism would include the presence of a potent enkephalinase inhibitor, such as thiorphan. In one set of tests, administration of thiorphan to alcohol-drinking rats produced a 53 percent increase in voluntary alcohol consumption. In any case, "one might expect that a genetic predisposition toward alcohol drinking may be accompanied by an increase in responsiveness of opioid systems to alcohol" (ibid.:29). But the enkephalins are not the only opioids we may find involved in genetic predisposition toward alcoholic drinking.

Opioid peptides are synthesized (ibid.:29–30) as part of high-molecular-weight precursors. Beta-endorphin is derived from pro-opiomelanocortin (POMC); the enkephalins are derived from the precursor pre-pro-enkephalin A (PPENK). POMC and PPENK messenger ribonucleic acid (mRNA) levels in the brain reflect the biosynthesis of the precursor molecule before postmessage processing. Comparison of the activity of the beta-endorphin and enkephalinergic systems in alcohol-drinking rats showed that intragastric (in the stomach) infusion of alcohol (equivalent to drinking) produced a significant increase in POMC (beta-endorphin precursor) mRNA levels in rats from the P (alcohol-drinking) line but not from the NP line, and the same was true for PPENK (enkephalin precursor) mRNA levels. These results suggest that a genetic predisposition toward high alcohol drinking is accompanied by increased responsiveness of both the beta-endorphin and enkephalinergic systems to alcohol. Alcohol-induced activation of the endogenous opioid system may serve to enhance the reinforcing effects of alcohol and thereby increase the probability of subsequent drinking episodes. (In other words, alcoholics find alcohol more pleasurable than nonalcoholics find it.) Also, alcohol-induced activation of the opioid system may reduce aversion to high-dose effects of alcohol (in other words, emphasizing what we just said, make "being drunk" a more pleasurable experience than it would otherwise be, for the alcoholic).

Activation or blockade of the opioid system has been shown in other tests to alter alcohol consumption in animals (Reid and Hubbell 1990). In addition, lower beta-endorphin-like immunoreactivity has been reported in FHP individuals ("genetic" alcoholics) than in non-FHPs (Gianoulakis et al. 1996). Also, there is evidence of greater increase in beta endorphins following alcohol consumption in high-risk (of alcoholism) subjects than in lower-risk subjects (Peterson et al. 1996). There is also considerable anecdotal evidence from members of Alcoholics Anonymous suggesting abnormal endorphin-processing in some alcoholics.

Possible mechanisms suggested include differences in concentrations of opiate peptides (note that the P substance is a peptide), possible actions of opiate-producing neurons inhibiting corticotropin-releasing hormone (CRH) production, interactions between inherent levels of opiates and reactivity of the hypothalamic pituitary adrenal system, and innate activity levels. Note that CRH, which is secreted by the hypothalamus under stress, triggers release of hormones that raise the level of cortisol in the blood. Cortisol is itself a powerful hormone produced by the adrenal gland in times of stress and found in higher than normal levels in patients with AIDS, multiple sclerosis, and Alzheimer's—but possibly simply because of the stress involved in those conditions. Prolonged high levels of cortisol can throw the immune system into chaos. It has been shown that alcoholics have abnormal reactions to stress (see Vaillant 1996a:270). Would this perhaps suggest (I believe it might) that adrenal and cortisol releases in asthmatic children—for whom adrenalin and cortisone are anti-asthmatics—could potentiate heritable alcoholism in these children, and even perhaps, under chaotic ordering, vary the type of alcoholism?

In line with this, we should consider the effects, including differential effects, of alcohol on regulatory aspects of the stress axis—that is, primarily on the hypothalamic-pituitary-adrenal (HPA) axis and perhaps secondarily on the sympathoadrenal (SA) axis. Now, the primary and obligatory regulator of the corticotropin-derived POMC peptides (which we have met already), such as adrenocorticotrophic hormone (ACTH), is corticotropin-releasing factor CRF. ACTH is the primary regulator of glucocorticoid (GC is cortisol in humans and corticosterone in mice and rats).

Glucocorticoids

The actions of GCs are pervasive and there are major long-term potential consequences of even subtle alcohol-induced changes in basal plasma GC diurnal rhythms, inasmuch as GCs have inhibitory, stimulatory, or priming affects (or all of these) on virtually every organ system in the body, with accompanying influences on the HPA stress-axis hormones at every level (Eskay et al. 1993:3). It has also been shown that the neuroimmunoendocrine system, upon activation, modulates the HPA axis. That is, certain challenges are capable of activating mononucleated leukocytes, particularly macrophages, to produce a variety of cytokines and hormones, including POMC-derived peptides. These cytokines, through feed-forward and feedback, can modulate HPA-axis events at virtually every level, including the medullary cells of the adrenal gland (the primary source of epinephrine) and the catecholamines (including epinephrine/norepinephrine) from the cortical cells of the adrenal gland.

As synthesized epinephrine (ephredrine, adrenaline) is a specific against allergic reactions, including asthma, it may be that the old identification of alcoholism as an allergy is not entirely off the mark. (We shall see some other indications pointing this way shortly.) Also, and perhaps more to our present point, it was established as long ago as 1966 that alcohol administered to rats resulted in a dose-related change in plasma corticosterone (GC) levels and that ACTH replacement therapy after hypophysectomy activated corticosterone secretion from the adrenal gland: in other words, alcohol activates the brain-pituitary axis and the alcohol-induced rise in GC is *not* the result of a direct end-organ response (ibid.:8).

Briefly, acute and chronic alcohol consumption in animals (including humans) activates the stress axis, resulting in continuously or intermittently elevated GCs. If we consider the neuronal consequences of chronically elevated GCs, and the distribution of type II GC receptors, we may conclude that sustained high GC levels and possible disruption of GC diurnal rhythm could create a dangerous neuronal environment and weaken cellular structure and conditions, particularly in the hippocampus, which is vital to learning and memory (ibid.:17). It may be hypothesized that certain types of alcoholics (possibly not all types) may have lower-than-normal GC levels, so that they can function over a long term with GC levels (at least intermittently) elevated above their norm, without crossing the threshold levels implicated in memory loss and cell death. Here is a case where tests await accurate pretest typology. We might suggest that (FHP) ε-alcoholics would fit most easily into this classification, and their periodic (i.e., intermittent) drinking might represent a self-medicating bodily biochemical response to their condition. This, of course, says nothing about the genetic selection process leading to such a condition. (One might ask if it is significant that this is a glucosteroid, given the anecdotal connection between alcoholism recovery and blood sugars.)

SEROTONIN AND R-A SYSTEM ACTIVITY

Serotonin (5-HT) and Serotonergic Functioning

Increased serotonergic functioning (giving effect to serotonin release) generally accompanies decreased alcohol consumption, and decreased serotonergic functioning generally accompanies increased alcohol consumption. There are at least fourteen mammalian 5-HT receptors, and the relationships between them and alcohol consumption are complex. Several of the receptor subtypes have been reported to be altered in alcohol dependence, including 5-HT1B, 5-HT2, and 5-HT3. There is, however, no clear and present knowledge as to whether these receptor subtypes are altered in individuals at risk—partly because the applicability of mouse studies is unclear, partly because human studies lump alcohol abuse and alcohol dependence together, and partly because of problems with the assumed typology of alcoholisms. Nevertheless, serotonergic receptor functions appear to be a fruitful area for study. We have already mentioned, as an example, the possible connection of at least one type of alcoholism with tryptophan metabolism and brain serotonin synthesis. There is indeed an NIAAA study ("Effects of Acute Plasma Tryptophan Depletion on Serotonin Receptor Occupancy and Binding Affinity using PET [Positron Emission Topography] in Healthy and Alcoholic Human Subjects") currently under way on serotonin in alcoholism.

The hypothesis being tested is that neuronal 5-HT turnover and release is altered in alcoholic individuals, and that this plays a role in alcohol-seeking behavior. Tryptophan is an amino acid from which serotonin is made, and serotonin, as we know, is one of the chemicals (neurotransmitters) that allow brain cells to communicate. What is specifically being tested for is a four-part hypothesis:

(1) that there are differences in 5-HT turnover and release in alcoholic subjects, compared with healthy controls, before and after acute tryptophan depletion (ATD);
(2) that putative differences in 5-HT turnover are governed primarily by genetic variation in the 5-HT transporter (5-HTT) in alcoholics;
(3) that 5-HTT genetic variation correlates with [(18)F]-FCWAY/ 5-HT(1A) binding, and cerebrospinal fluid (CSF) 5-hydroxyindoleacetic acid (5-HIAA) concentration, before and after ATD (acute tryptophan depletion); and
(4) that regional cerebral blood flow (rCBF) differs at baseline and after ATD (acute tryptophan depletion) in both alcoholics and healthy controls (so that this is not a distinguishing mechanism).

Positron emission topology will allow indirect measurements of synaptic 5-HT concentration by measuring the binding of [18(F)]-FCWAY, a 5-HT(1A) receptor antagonist. While we do not yet know the results of this (my records show the study has just now—January 2004—gotten underway), the best opinions of those doing research are in accord with the hypotheses being tested.

Renin-Angiotensin System

In this connection, we should look at interrelations between alcohol and the renin-angiotensin (R-A) system. We know, for example, that rats subsensitive to 5-hydroxytryptamine (5-HT) agonists (compounds that mimic 5-HT, serotonin, in their effects) drink very large amounts of alcohol (Grupp 1993:57)—and, indeed, rats bred for a permanent suppression in R-A system activity, display "a robust predisposition to alcohol consumption" (ibid.:). Also, it has been shown that mice lacking a functional copy of the gene that codes for serotonin 1_B receptors (in other words, for serotonergic functioning) drank twice as much ethanol in a free-choice drinking situation as the wildtype controls (see below). And as far back as 1979, a study (Ballenger et al. 1979) showed that the level of 5HIAA in alcoholics twenty-eight to sixty-three days after their last drink was significantly lower than for a nonalcoholic comparison group and significantly lower than for alcoholics in the immediate postintoxication phase (within one to two days after their last drink).

> We may note here also that the R-A System activity which inhibits alcohol consumption is characterized by having events in the periphery set into motion central processes that eventually result in the inhibition of alcohol intake. This chain of events is quite typical of peptides and hormones that influence behavior and has been observed with respect to the actions of vasopressin, oxytocin, and aldosterone on memory processes, and of cholecystokinin on feeding. (ibid.:61)

It has been suggested that the bioactive peptide ANG II is itself activated in the R-A system by alcoholic intake (the R-A system itself being so activated) and then produces a satiety or stop signal at a point determined by emotional state, diet, environmental motivators, and individual predisposition (ibid.:63). The process is parallel to—and it seems likely is connected with—the process of memory. It may be worthwhile here to look briefly at a highly significant study coming out of Yale's Substance Abuse Center and having to do with cocaine, but with implications for any craving, including the craving for alcohol (Grant et al. 1996).

MEMORY

The findings that are principally of interest to us here are two in number: (1) The regional cerebral metabolic rate for glucose (cRMRglc, an index of local brain function) was measured for cocaine abusers and an otherwise similar nonuser control group on the presentation of cocaine-related stimuli, the results showing stimulus-responses in the dorsolateral prefrontal cortex and the medial temporal lobe—but also in the amygdala and cerebellum—all regions involved in either explicit or implicit memory. (2) It is not true that the same brain regions that mediate the direct pharmacological affects of the drug also generate responses to the drug-related stimuli. The activation of brain regions implicated in the several forms of memory (including episodic) is directly related to the cue-elicited craving. In this case the cues were visual and obvious, but with episodic memory involved, it may be suggested they need not be.

In any case, the "discrete distribution of activation produced by cocaine-related stimuli differs markedly from the response to acute cocaine administration, which involves widespread decreases [my emphasis] in rCMRglc in human volunteers" (Grant et al. 1996:12044, col. 2). The reasonable conclusion is that craving comes from cue-stimulated memory—working, episodic, and emotional—more than from the neural substrates of the direct experience with the substance involved. (This may have some connection with observed P3 abnormalities in prepubescent sons of alcoholics, in a positive deflection of the ERP wave-form thought to reflect attentional resources during memory update: we know of no existing test of this hypothesis nor are we expert enough to suggest one.)

In this connection, we may consider memory as a species of neuroadaptation (see Hoffman et al. 2000:91ff.). "Learning and memory, like tolerance and dependence, can be viewed as adaptive responses of the CNS [central nervous system] to external stimuli" (ibid.:91). Research on lower organisms (specifically the marine snail *Aplysia*) has provided evidence that the serotonin-induced activation of adenylyl cyclase (AC) and subsequent activation of protein kinase A (PKA) are critical factors in short-term and long-term sensitization, as precursor to memory. (Memory as ordinarily defined for human beings presumably does not exist in non-self-conscious organisms.) The structural alterations associated with the long-term sensitization in *Aplysia* are thought to be related to down-regulation of cell-adhesion molecules related to nerve-cell-adhesion molecules (ibid.:93). Investigation has also shown that a 3,5'-cyclic adenosine monophosphate (cAMP)-regulated transcription factor is involved, and the cAMP system has also been implicated in learning and memory in *Drosophila m.*

One further—perhaps highly indicative—finding in recent research should be noted. It has been reported that the rate of human brain serotonin synthesis (measured by PET and the tracer -[11C]methyl-L-tryptophan) has been found to be 52 percent higher in normal males than in normal females, and it has been suggested that this marked difference may be a factor in the lower incidence of major unipolar depression in males (Nishizawa et al. 1997). If this is the case, and given what we have said so far about the effects of alcohol on serotonin synthesis in alcoholics, it would follow that male nondrinking alcoholics could expect (recurrent?) episodes of unipolar ("major" or "clinical") depression. It might also follow, as we will suggest, that serotonergic function is linked to heavily male-dominated phenotype Psa.

GABA AND DOPAMINE

GABA

Gamma-aminobutyric acid (GABA) is an inhibitory neurotransmitter that has been demonstrated to mediate some of the effects of alcohol. (This is relevant to the association between teenaged ability to drink more without getting drunk and without being or becoming an alcoholic—and may be connected to differences in brain chemistry between adolescents and adults: I am reminded of the observer of student riots in the 1960s, "I say it's juvenile delinquency, and I say the hell with it!") The $GABA_A$ receptor system is responsive to the effects of alcohol at clinically relevant doses, and some studies have reported that alcohol-dependent individuals have lower levels of activity of this receptor. Alcoholics might well have an increased prevalence of the a-3e receptor gene, and there is some confirmatory evidence for reduced levels of the a-1 gene. But we have only limited GABA data on FHPs and FHNs, and what few data we have are contradictory. Moreover, the tests did not distinguish among types of alcoholics. And, of course, with chaotic ordering in heritability, there is no guarantee that FHPs will be positive for the same types of alcoholism, or inherit the same idiosyncratic neurotransmitter or neuroreceptor functions—though on average they may. In fact, the majority of naturally occurring neuroactive steroids possess selective effects at $GABA_A$ receptors, and increasing circumstantial evidence suggests physiological interactions between alcohol and these neuroactive steroids.

These neuroactive steroids alter neuronal excitability, regardless of their site of synthesis. (They are to be distinguished from neurosteroids, which are simply those steroids synthesized in the brain, many of which are, however, neuroactive). Evidence suggests that some neurosteroid binding sites on $GABA_A$ receptors are sensitive to barbiturates, benzodiazepines, and alcohol. Benzodiazepines include diazepam (Librium) and chlordiazepoxide (Valium). We are reminded that among "old-timers" or "long-timers" in Alcoholics Anonymous (I don't know the difference in meaning between those two terms for sure), Librium and Valium are sometimes referred to as "alcohol in a pill." (Note that Diazepam [Valium] is known to depress all levels of the central nervous system, possibly by increasing actions of $GABA_A$ inhibitory receptors, as we find when looking into monoamine oxidase inhibitors [MAOIs].)

Here, in essence, with GABA, we are looking at what might be called, in some instances, a neuroinhibitor rather than an ordinary neurotransmitter—an off-switch rather than an on-switch—but we are still looking at the products of the HPA axis and their relation to alcohol consumption and the predisposition to alcohol consumption. What would be of particular interest here would be some evidence that GABA receptor sites in adult (mostly or entirely male) Psa and Pea alcoholics are similar to GABA receptor sites in male adolescents, particular delinquent adolescents. We will look further at this subcategory of drinkers when discussing epinephrine/ norepinephrine, as well as looking at serotonergic functioning.

GABA transmitters represent an Na+ dependent system, voltage-dependent and responsible for electrical excitability in neurons, though occurring also in astrocytes and other so-called glial cells (which regulate system repair and immune responses, among other things, but are not as active as neurons). The glial cells, we believe, will turn out to have an importance in both Alcoholism(2) and Alcoholism(1). Note that there have been test results showing alteration in the $GABA_A$ receptor function in the brain tissue of mutant mice for ethanol but not for such cognate substances ("drugs") as flunitrazepam or pentobarbital. GABA receptor genes on chromosome 4 are near the region for which protective factors have been reported, though this is an uncertain indicator. What is certain is that, in a genome study, no evidence of linkage was found for GABA receptor genes on chromosome 5, and there was only weak evidence for linkage with two-point methods on chromosome 15 near the region that includes GABA receptor genes. No evidence for linkage was found on the X chromosome in the region of the monoamine loci (MAO-B). In short, not much has been found so far in genomic studies, particularly on GABA.

Recent studies have demonstrated ethanol (alcohol) action at the second transmembrane domain of glycine/$GABA_A$ receptor chimeras, suggesting that ethanol affects the conformation of ion channel receptors. It may stimulate the ion channel; it may act specifically on the membrane receptors; it may act on the gene promoters. Attempts to create an amethystine (anti-alcohol) drug in the form of a GABA-receptor agonist (mimic) have not been notoriously successful. One drug, acamprosate, turns out to reduce glutamergic rather than $GABA_A$-ergic action, and another drug, gamma-hydroxybutyrate (GHB), has turned out to have disastrous alcohol-like effects. Both of these, in fact, if connected to GABA receptors, may be aimed at the $GABA_B$ receptors.

Dopamine (DA)

Some aspects of the reinforcement of behavior involve the brain's DA pathways, with animal evidence suggesting the importance of DA activity in the rewarding effects of acute alcohol administration. Although there were initial reports of a population-based association between alcoholism and the dopamine D2 receptor locus (DRD2), evidence for this association, or for linkage of any alcoholic phenotype to allelic variation in DRD2, is a subject of controversy. It has been suggested that the nature of the control group may determine whether significant population-based associations are found. So also may—and will—the typology of alcoholisms, which determines the bounds of both control group and noncontrol group. In fact, only limited data regarding DA are available on FHPs and FHNs, which limits possible analysis of available data for genetic study. An increase in the DA metabolite homovanillic acid has been noted in the younger sons of substance-abusing fathers, but this study lumped drugs and alcohol together. A much earlier study noted no differences between FHPs and FHNs in dopamine beta hydroxylase, an enzyme that metabolizes DA. Note that research on dopamine speaks to signaling, but research on the enzyme metabolizing dopamine speaks to body response, so this is an area of overlap.

One older study (Brown et al. 1979) tested for correlation of aggressive behavior with the cerebral spinal fluid major central metabolites of serotonin (5HT), norepinephrine (NE), and dopamine (DA)—these central metabolites being, respectively, 5-hydroxyindoleacetic acid (5HIAA), 3-methoxy-4-hydroxy-phenylglycol (MHPG), and homovanillic acid (HVA). Independently scored history of aggressive behavior (a mark of Psa alcoholism, though sometimes present in others) showed no HVA correlation, significant negative correlation (-0.78) with 5HIAA, significant positive correlation (+0.64) with MHPG. Signaling effects of dopamine may be substituted for by other signals or triggers in the alcoholic's neuronal system, or changes in DA levels may come into play only as an effect of Hoff's *alcoholismus chronicus*. Some weak or contradictory evidence of dopamine connections with alcoholism has been noted, and we will return to this very briefly later on. Here, however, we may note that dopamine is connected with what is called positive emotionality.

In fact it has been remarked (Depue et al. 1994) that in animals, responsivity within an emotional system analog of positive emotionality (PE) is dependent on brain dopamine activity, and a human study (ibid.) was carried out using a specific DA D2 receptor agonist (agent-mimicking dopamine in effect). Results suggested strongly that agonist-induced reactivity was specifically associated with trait levels of PE. Now, as PE is based on sensitivity to signals of incentive-reward, and as there seems to be no characteristic alcoholic's dopamine level, it might reasonably be suggested (as we suggested above) that something characteristically substitutes for dopamine-related positive emotionality in the alcoholic.

We might note here that abnormal levels of the neurotransmitter dopamine are connected with brain abnormalities in schizophrenics. When the phenothiazine drugs were first introduced in the treatment of schizophrenia in the 1950s, it was found that they induced symptoms like those of Parkinson's disease, which is caused by deterioration of those parts of the system using the neurotransmitter dopamine—suggesting, in turn, that schizophrenia is the result of abnormal dopamine transmission. There are, one supposes, schizophrenic alcoholics—that is to say, alcoholics who are also schizophrenics—but, if so, any correlation with dopamine levels would be governed by the schizophrenia, not the alcoholism. The same is generally true in neuroimaging—brain profiles of schizophrenics and "schizophrenic alcoholics" are very similar to each other, and different from the brain profiles of nonschizophrenic alcoholics (Sullivan 2000:490–91). Lysergic acid diethylamide 25 (LSD), originally developed in part to mimic the inner life of a schizophrenic, was subsequently touted as an amethystine (that is, an anti-alcoholic), and experimented with in that context by Bill W.

Recent work on the phenomenon of craving in alcoholism has led to a new look at dopamine: all the results are not in yet, but early enthusiasm for the research seems to have cooled off (Swift 1999). It has been found that high levels of craving are associated with increased probability of relapse, particularly in the early stages of treatment for alcoholism (ibid.:207). Now there is a possible problem here. Craving is a subjective phenomenon, measured by the answers to questions such as "How much do you desire alcohol right now?" and is frequently considered to be the same thing as "obsessive-compulsive drinking" (ibid.:208). But craving in the neurophysiological sense is not the same thing as desire. Alcoholics seem to speak mostly of a compulsion to drink or a desire to drink, but not, like many drug addicts, of a craving.

The neurophysiological "craving" can be assessed by measuring certain physiological changes, such as changes in heart rate, blood pressure, salivation, and sweat-gland activity. There are also behavioral measurements, but they could equally well measure compulsion or desire, which are not necessarily the same thing as the neurophysiological craving. And there is another problem with craving studies in general, which is that they discuss the phenomenon in the context of AODs—which is to say, alcohol and other drugs. That is, not only do they fail to distinguish between and among types of alcoholics, but they fail to distinguish between and among alcohol and drugs such as opiates, Valium and Librium, cocaine, MDMA (and other forms of "Ecstasy"), LSD-25, methamphetamines, phenylcyclidine, methedrine, and so on. Amidst this field of red flags, we find that "reinforcement of AOD use is associated with the release of the neurotransmitter dopamine in a brain region called the nucleus accumbens" (from a study published by Roberts and Koob in 1997, quoted Swift 1999:208) and that "certain manifestations of counter-adaptation, presumably involving persistent dopamine dysregulation in the nucleus accumbens, can prolong vulnerability to craving long after the acute symptoms of withdrawal have subsided" (ibid.).

The only function assigned to dopamine in alcoholism is that it mediates reinforcement of alcohol consumption (ibid.:209). (Counteradaptation, like adaptation, is of course connected with memory processes.) Reinforcement or its equivalent may reasonably come through such memory reinforcers as caffeine that release epinephrine into the system, thereby triggering blood sugar increases. Likewise, levels of the epinephrine/ norepinephrine-linked neurotransmitter acetylcholine are reduced in Alzheimer's patients, suggesting again the link between epinephrine and memory—which, given a link between memory and alcoholism (a link we have already indicated), suggests that reinforcement of alcohol consumption might be tied more closely to epinephrine/norepinephrine than to dopamine. The genome survey carried out under NIAAA included markers in or near several candidate genes implicated in the etiology of alcohol dependence. No evidence was found for linkage with the dopamine D2 receptor gene (DRD2).

NOREPINEPHRINE AND ADOLESCENT DRINKING

We may now turn to the possible correlation of certain types of alcoholism with levels of this neurotransmitter norepinephrine. We have touched on this already in our discussion of serotonergic functioning, but the possible presence of our Psa phenotype presents us with an interesting backdoor approach here, using evidence on juvenile FHP alcoholism. The same kind of backdoor is also available in looking at our putative Sda phenotype, by looking at what (I am told) an old—and sober—alcoholic used to refer to as "ladies of the feminine gender." We will look at juvenile FHP alcoholism for additional clues on the biochemistry of Psa, as we will later look at female FHP alcoholism for additional clues on the biochemistry of Sda. A look at juvenile (primary sociopathic) alcoholism as our lead-in may be justified by the apparent results of quite a number of studies showing early onset of what we take to be Psa. First, we should remark that adolescence is a unique neurobehavioral stage during which certain brain regions—including the prefrontal cortex (PFC) and other forebrain dopamine projection regions—show marked alteration.

These areas have been implicated in mediating the reinforcing effects of alcohol (Spear 2000:315ff.). The absolute PFC volume of the brain declines in adolescence, substantial synapse elimination occurs (linked to developmental loss of glutaminergic excitatory input), and cholinergic innervation of the PFC likewise increases. The hippocampus produces greater amounts of norepinephrine release, as against that in older or younger individuals, accompanying the emergence of inhibitory 2-norepinephrine autoreceptors. A transient expression of DA (Dopamine) autoceptor-like DA synthesis modulation previously existing disappears during adolescence (ibid.:318). In short, adolescents find it harder to get the "highs" that used to come unforced, at the same time the hypothalamic-pituitary-gonadal (HPG) axis is greatly awakened, and there are other neuronal shifts in the body. We might therefore expect that those with alcoholism in their family backgrounds (FHPs)—who therefore may have certain hereditary reactions to alcohol and a certain hereditary ability to "outdrink" their nonalcoholic friends—will as continuously as possible engage in "risky" drinking and drink-related behavior. Because it makes them feel "really good"—and because the excitement of anticipation includes what they are going to do when they're drunk and they need to keep the excitatory effects going.

A study by Clark and Bukstein points out that "more than 80 percent of adolescents who were dependent on or abused alcohol also had some other form of psychopathology" (1998:117), with the common comorbid psychopathologies including ASPD in its juvenile form (that is, conduct disorder—the identification is almost exact) and major depressive disorder (negative-affect disorder characterized by severe bouts of depression). This information is not quite as useful as it might be, because the authors join alcohol abuse and alcohol dependence together. It is also not quite as useful as might be because the two major groups of disorders, antisocial and depressive, are not (in the article) linked to the gender of the drinker, though we know in general that one is predominantly male and the other predominantly female. Moreover, to the extent that conduct disorders (if not connected to ADHD) have not been subjected to pharmacological study, conduct disorder diagnosis is—unlike diagnosis of depression—biochemically not very helpful. But given the differentials in male and female serotonergic functioning, it does suggest a look at serotonergic functioning as a marker characteristic for alcoholism with ASPD, Zucker type 1 revised or type 4b, or what we have called Jellinek ε (modified), our Psa.

Before looking at women and Sda, we will continue our examination of the biochemistry of alcoholism by looking at intracellular signaling pathways and at enzyme action. First, we look at AC (the intracellular signaler adenylyl cyclase) and MAO (which inhibits serotonergic functioning); second, at alcohol-metabolizing enzymes; third, at stress and electrophysiological tests; fourth, at alcohol challenge. In a way, by examining the intracellular signaling, we are turning back toward serotonergic functioning, but we are looking at the pathway for the transmission rather than at the transmitter. One of the difficulties we face here is that we can rarely be sure whether specific problems in intracellular signaling derive from the effects of drinking (thus being part of Alcoholism[1]) or from predrinking conditions (thus being part of Alcoholism[2]). For example, in fruit fly tests, it has been found that genetic alterations in the cAMP pathway and pharmacological alteration of PKA activity both modulate ethanol sensitivity (Dohrman et al. 2000:58–59). If we find that alcoholics have certain biochemical characteristics, are these (1) the result of alcoholic activity, (2) part of the alcoholic precondition, or possibly (3) the result of a condition from which alcoholism also results?

ADENYL CYCLASE, MONOAMINES, ENZYMATIC ACTIVITY

AC and MAO

We begin with AC and MAO. Adenylyl cyclase is part of a complex biological system composed of at least three membrane-bound proteins, including cell-membrane receptors, G proteins (the G is for guanine nucleotide binding), and the AC enzyme. The G proteins operate by coupling with cell membrane receptors, resulting in changes in cAMP. There are two forms of G proteins, one stimulating (G_s) and one inhibiting (G_i). The cAMP is a "second messenger" that has numerous effects within the cell, including gene expression. The activity of AC can be measured by production of cAMP under baseline conditions or following chemical stimulation. Alcoholics have been shown to have reduced cAMP in platelets and lymphocytes after stimulation. It has been proposed that these findings may be the result of the presence of a G_{sa} protein. Greater activity levels of G_{sa} have been observed in red blood cells and lymphocytes of FHPsubjects, with no group differences on various measures of G_i.

What exactly is it that AC does and what is it? It is the enzyme that synthesizes cAMP from ATP. Cyclic AMP functions as a "second messenger" to relay extracellular (outside-the-cells) signals to intracellular (between-the-cells) effectors such as protein kinase A. Regulation of cyclic AMP is largely the result of controlling adenylyl cyclase. As to what it is—adenylyl cyclases are integral membrane proteins that consist of two bundles of six transmembrane segments: two catalytic domains extend as loops into the cytoplasm. There are at least nine isoforms of adenylyl cyclase. We noted in the preceding paragraph that binding of a stimulatory alpha (G_s) enhanced activity, while binding of an inhibitory alpha (G_i) inhibited cyclase activity. This is certainly the case in some situations: for example, the β-adrenergic receptor is coupled to AC via G_s and the binding of epinephrine to this receptor leads to increased cAMP synthesis. Also, when epinephrine binds to alpha-2 adrenergic receptors, AC activity is inhibited, because that receptor is coupled via G_i, an inhibitory G-protein. More recently, it has become clear that cyclase activity is regulated by multiple effectors, which include not only the alpha subunits of G_s and G_i proteins, but also the beta-gamma subunits of G proteins and protein kinase C. Of possible major significance, five of the nine adenylyl cyclases known are regulated by calcium, three being stimulated and two inhibited. It appears there is a tight integration between cAMP and calcium, the cell's two major internal signalers.

MAO is a mitochondrial enzyme responsible for the degradation of biological monoamines. (Note that in the next section we discuss the mitochondrial ALDH2, which is biologically active at low acetaldehyde levels and may be controlled by genes on chromosome 12: we do not yet know where genetic or genomic controls may be located for MAO.) There are multiple forms of MAO (A and B), with the levels of each under genetic control—at least in findings concerning male Chinese. In some studies, alcoholics were reported to demonstrate lower MAO-B activity, especially if the antisocial personality is present—these would be our Zucker type 1 revised or Jellinek ε alcoholics. Higher activity of MAO-B has been reported in the relatives of alcoholic women, but so earlier had lower activity in relatives (mostly) of alcoholic men. The studies did not control for smoking, nor are their definitions of alcoholism unassailable, but it may be that the women's study dealt largely with Sda alcoholics and the study of men and women dealt largely with Psa alcoholics. We should look here at these MAOs, and in particular, as a mode of approach, at MAO-inhibitors, used as medication against depression.

MAOIs (MAO-inhibitors) are used as second-line antidepressants: they increase catecholamine (dopamine, noradrenaline = norepinephrine/epinephrine) and serotonin concentrators at the synapse by inhibiting monoamine oxidase, the enzyme involved in their metabolism. Neurotransmitters (catecholamine, serotonin, GABA) are generally monoamines. When released into synaptic space, they are either reabsorbed into the proximal (near) nerve or destroyed in the synaptic "cleft" by monoamine oxidase. It has been suggested that clinical (i.e., major) depression is related to decreases in concentration of the excitatory neurotransmitters. Pharmaceutical research has therefore produced NCEs that can either block the reuptake (reabsorption) of neurotransmitters (as, for example, cyclic antidepressants or SSRIs, selective serotonin reuptake inhibitors) or interfere with the breakdown of the monoamines within the synaptic "cleft" (the MAOIs). We should take note of the fact that any drug releasing catecholamines may precipitate life-threatening events in those using MAOIs, as may alcohol, all serotonergic agents, and (by the way) any foods containing tyramine, among those foods being sauerkraut (Dawson et al. 1995). Catecholamines, serotonin, and (apparently) sauerkraut seem to serve the same function as alcohol to the alcoholic, or may potentiate the effects of alcohol. It is worth noting that in the early days of A.A., Bob S. treated newly sober alcoholic patients with sauerkraut. Also tomato juice, though that apparently had a different function, perhaps in scouring the system. Or perhaps it too promoted enzymatic action. Dr. Bob also administered paraldehyde to his newly sober patients.

Alcohol-Metabolizing Enzymes

The principal alcohol-metabolizing enzyme is alcohol dehydrogenase (ADH), with smaller amounts of alcohol broken down by cytochrome P450 as part of the microsomal ethanol oxidizing system (MEOS), especially at higher blood alcohol concentrations. The rest is metabolized by catalase and through additional enzymatic and nonenzymatic pathways. Each of these produces acetaldehyde, which is rapidly metabolized by the enzyme aldehyde dehydrogenase (ALDH). Both ADH and ALDH are under genetic control. In fact, there are at least seven different ADH-related genes producing at least eight forms of ADH, with ADH2 (for which there are at least three alleles) and ADH3 (for which there are at least two alleles) having the greatest clinical relevance.

Studies suggest different metabolic rates for Caucasians and Orientals. For example, some forms of ADH2 (ADH2-2) and ADH3 (ADH3-1) are associated with a faster metabolism rate for alcohol for a Japanese population. A negative relationship between ADH2-2 and alcohol consumption or the risk of alcoholism has been reported in Japanese and Israelis. The presence of ADH3-1 has been associated with a lower risk of alcoholism in the Chinese, along with increased risk of liver disease in English drinkers. At least one gene affecting the cytochrome P450 system has been reported to interact with the ALDH-2 allele in affecting the risk for liver disease. It has been proposed that variations in catalase might be related to alcohol consumption. This would seem particularly relevant to our Zucker type 1 revised or Jellinek ε alcoholics. There are some indications that low systemic levels of acetaldehyde may stimulate and reinforce alcohol consumption. High levels of acetaldehyde are known to produce skin flushing, rapidly changing blood pressure, nausea and vomiting, and a rapid pulse. There are at least two forms or isoenzymes of ALDH, the major mechanism for metabolizing the acetaldehyde produced from ADH action on alcohol. The mitochondrial ALDH2 is biologically active at low acetaldehyde levels: it has at least two variants controlled by genes on chromosome 12. ALDH2-1 codes for a functional form of this enzyme, while ALDH2-2 is biologically inactive. Individuals who are homozygotes for ALDH2-2 experience intense flushing after consuming alcohol, whereas heterozygotes flush, but not with great intensity. ALDH2-2 homozygotes represent about 5 to 10 percent of the Asian population with close to zero risk for alcoholism; heterozygotes represent 30 to 40 percent of Asians showing significantly lower risk of alcoholism than ALDH2-1 homozygotes.

The impact of the ALDH-2 heterozygote state is affected by environmental factors, including living in heavier drinking environments or exhibiting ASPD, which, of course, we have characterized in this chapter as part of Zucker type 1 revised (with some Zucker type 4-b) or Jellinek ε (modified) alcoholism. Note that the ALDH-2 heterozygote state may thus be considered part of the genotype, while its impact and that of the environment are expressed in the phenotype. ASPD may thus possibly be considered part of the alcoholic genotype. (The heavier drinking environments might, of course, in the Dawkins terminology, be considered part of the extended phenotype. Note, also from what Dawkins says, that ASPD would not be recognized until there is an appropriate social milieu in which the ASPD can be adjudged antisocial.)

In some studies, FHPs (that is, to repeat, subjects from "alcoholic" families) are more likely to demonstrate problems with attention, organizational skills, abstracting, planning, reflectivity, and impulsivity, while also showing increased evidence of motor activity or diminished standing steadiness. (Note that this searching for "inherited predisposition" suggests a parallel with studies of allergies and asthma.) Varieties of Attention Deficit Disorder (ADD) or Attention Deficit Hyperactivity Disorder (ADHD) would, of course, fit in with the suggested genotype for Zucker type 1 revised (with Zucker 4-b) or Jellinek ε alcoholism(modified). There is, however, a relatively large number of studies reporting a general absence of group differences in cognitive functioning. Similarly, there are no clear findings on FHP/FHN differences in IQ. (One wonders if the idiosyncratic reaction to Ritalin [methylphenidate] among ADHD children could be tied to a genotype for Zucker type 1 revised or Jellinek ε alcoholism modified. ADHD has been defined, not jokingly, as the condition marked by this idiosyncratic response to Ritalin—"if it speeds them up, they're not ADHD.")

The differences in the findings across studies might in fact be related to other characteristics of the specific populations evaluated. It has been suggested that the most fruitful area for future research would be in measures of planning, impulsivity, and abstracting abilities, but I would suggest that more certainly accurate typology would be useful here before further studies are undertaken. After all, if brain chemistry and neuropathology differ in different kinds of alcoholics, and we do not take this into account, we run a severe risk of condemning our studies to failure before we start them. This, particularly, is where tests according to our four suggested phenotypes, Pea, Pca, Psa, and Sda, would seem to be indicated, as impulsivity, ADHD characteristics, and the whole constellation of traits these suggest seem to be involved in what we have called Psa alcoholism, and can be examined from the perspective of early-onset alcoholism. This constellation may be further illuminated by looking at stress, electrophysiology, and alcohol challenge.

STRESS, STIMULI, AND DEPRESSION

Stress, Electrophysiology, and Alcohol Challenge

It has been suggested that FHPs might have an increased cardiovascular response to stress, along with the ability of alcohol to improve this condition. This idea has been corroborated in a limited number of studies, although there are inconsistent results. Presumably the positive results could be for Sda alcoholics (who are risk-averse) and, for them, use of alcohol would be self-medication for an anterior condition. It should, however, be noted that much more can be said on stress, alcoholism, and the HPA axis. In particular, it would appear that stress plays an important role in the onset and maintenance of alcoholism and alcohol abuse, perhaps through the HPA axis, though the mechanisms are not clear. Also, it appears that patients with increased vulnerability to alcoholism have a hypofunctional HPA axis. Tsigos and Chrousos have suggested that "genetically determined differences in the activity of the stress system . . . are responsible for vulnerability to alcohol abuse" (1995:118). Note that in this case the phrase "alcohol abuse" seems to be used as a catchall phrase that would apparently include alcoholism. Once again, we note a problem of possible inexact specification.

The work previously mentioned on the stress axis is relevant here. The response to stress is generated within two well-defined regions of the brain, the hypothalamus and the brainstem. We have looked at the hypothalamic center with corticotropin-releasing hormone (CRH): it also releases arginine vasopressin (AVP) neurons. The brainstem center includes the CRH neurons of the medulla, and other catecholaminergic neurons of the medulla and pons.

> Following perception of stress, the hypothalamus releases CRH, AVP, and other adrenocorticotropin (ACTH) secretagogues . . . resulting in the release of ACTH from the pituitary gland. In turn ACTH initiates the release of the adrenal androgens and glucocorticoids, [which] prepare the organism for stress by . . . increasing glucose and fatty acid availability for the central nervous system. (Wand 2000:398)

Also, the HPA interacts with the immune system. Inflammatory cyto-kines and other inflammation mediators stimulate the HPA axis, while the glucocorticoids inhibit cytokine production and more or less turn the immune system way down, preventing "an overwhelming and potenti-ally harmful immune response to stressors" (ibid.). It appears that reduced ACTH and cortisol responses to CRH activity are correlated with alcoholic activity, and "even acute ethanol exposure impairs the ability of the HPA axis to respond to physiological stressors" (ibid.:400).

Since part of that HPA response is the production of glucocorticoids that regulate the immune system, and part of the HPA response is the release of adrenal androgens, the inhibition of these by alcohol could be expected to have something of the effect of an allergic reaction, and something of the effect of a stress-response system generally out of control. What this means in behavioral terms is not entirely clear, but one thing is clear—this is far from being a suggestion that alcoholics drink because they are "stressed out," and much closer to being a suggestion that alcoholics drink because they are alcoholics, and the effect on the stress axis is to make their actions and reactions unpredictable in normal terms.

On the question of electrophysiology, it has been shown that detoxified alcoholics and FHP children have a reduced amplitude of the scalp-positive wave that peaks approximately 300 msec after a rare but anticipated event (P300). The relationship of a family history of alcoholism (FHP) to a reduced P300 amplitude was demonstrated in two small follow-up studies wherein increased rates of substance-related problems were observed in those FHP children with reduced P300 amplitudes. The heritability of P300 amplitude suggests that reduced-amplitude P300 could be transmitted from alcoholic parent to offspring, which would seem to tie in with Siegel's suggestion that the anticipation of the changed state, rather than the changed state itself, is a key to William James's "mystical" nature of alco-holism. That is, alcoholics do not react as strongly as nonalcoholics to a rare but anticipated event, so they build up their uncertainty and anticipation by drinking—particularly if, as with teenagers, the drinking itself is a for-bidden event, and thus a recognized "risky business."

The findings mentioned above, involving the P3 component of a visual ERP time-locked electrocorticol response to a visual stimulus, refer in this case to a late positive deflection of the ERP wave-form thought to reflect attentional resources during memory update. The mean amplitude of the P3 component of a visual ERP has, as noted, been reported to be signifi-cantly smaller among the prepubescent sons of male alcoholics, as com-pared to similarly aged sons ofnonalcoholics. This does not seem to hold for girls or postpubescent boys (Begleiter et al. 1984). It would seem that brain-wave amplitude in response to observations promising a rare but anticipated event reflects lowered response in the memory-update period (in other words, it sounds as though, in FHP male children, memory cues require less update and serve more easily to reinforce previous expectations than in other children—though there are other possible interpretations of the data).

In contrast to the consistency of results from P300 studies, the results of electroencephalogram (EEG) studies have been quite inconsistent. Those studies specifically addressing possible differences between FHP and FHN groups have been mostly negative. Three exceptions have noted an association of FHP with higher amounts of fast brain-wave activity or more fast alpha activity. Of course, these findings could be interpreted to support the view (sometimes heard in meetings of Alcoholics Anonymous) that alcoholics have racing brains. That, in turn, would suggest that some varieties of alcoholics might drink in order to "turn on, tune in, and drop out" in the Timothy Leary/LSD sense. (This would parallel ADHD reaction to methylphenidate, and suggest that ingestion of alcohol in "alcoholic" amounts represents—for some alcoholics—unconscious or subconscious self-medication.)

Alcohol Challenge

Alcohol challenge studies compare FHPs and FHNs on responses to alcohol as measured by subjective feelings, motor performance, and/or physiologic measures. Genetic factors appear to be involved in the level of response to alcohol, because identical twins are more similar here than fraternal twins, and because animals can be bred to show high or low alcohol reactions. The value of a low level of response to alcohol in predicting alcoholism is supported by the finding that low level of response to alcohol at age twenty significantly predicted increased likelihood for subsequent diagnosis of alcohol dependence in 453 men, and by a ten-year follow-up of about 100 men in Denmark.

We should look also at studies on women, when considering the biochemistry of alcoholism in more detail. We may begin with a suggestion that female alcoholics are more likely than male alcoholics to have a positive family history of alcoholism (see McGue and Slutsky 1996:65). This suggestion does not seem to us (any more than to McGue and Slutsky) to be supported by any evidence adduced, but there are some interesting and relevant points made in the discussion. The association of alcoholism with other psychiatric disorders appears to be stronger among women (65 percent) than among men (44 percent), the only exception being ASPD, more common among men.

Unfortunately, very little work has been done on the biochemistry of women's alcoholism, though there are suggestions that there may be menstrual cyclicality and perhaps (given possible links with manic-depressive psychosis) with other cyclicality, including lunar cycles. Here recent work on brain chemistry of such conditions as manic-depressive psychosis and schizophrenia may be of value to us. We find it interesting, by the way, that Emil Kraepelin, who gave us the term manic-depressive psychosis a century ago, did much of his original research on alcoholics (Andreasen 2001:esp. pp. 168ff.). On the question of depression, it has been suggested that

> there are several different forms of depression, one of which is characterized by abnormalities in the norepinephrine system and another of which is characterized by deficits in serotonin. Much more likely, however, is the possibility that these two neurotransmitters, in conjunction with others as well, such as acetylcholine and dopamine, work together to achieve an overall balance. (ibid.:244)

Tricyclic antidepressants are aimed at norepinephrine balances, while amitryptaline (Elavil) aims at serotonin and acetylcholine, and the generation of selective serotonin reuptake inhibitors (SSRIs, including Prozac) have their effect solely on serotonin. But what triggers the depression, of whatever type?

The answer seems to be that cyclical manic depression (bipolarity) does not need an evident trigger, though it may have one. But even if there is a trigger, the subject "may also carry an abnormal gene or two, which predispose to depression" (ibid.:245). Also, the "subjective experience of depression (of any kind) is the expression of the interplay between our brain regions that register and interpret our current emotional experiences in the light of our past emotional experiences" (ibid.). Psychiatrists who are also neuroscientists are currently engaged in trying to see how the various distributed regions in the "extended limbic system" link together past memories, present experiences, and the attribution of "feeling tones" to these. It is this complex set of interconnections that enables us to experience (subjectively) emotions such as sadness and (cognitively) attribute these figures to ourselves, as by saying, "Gee! I feel depressed today." Why women say this more often than men (except possibly nondrinking alcoholic men) almost certainly has something to do with serotonin, as we have seen. But SSRIs do not work on manic depression, which is bipolar and for which the preferred treatment is the natural salt lithium, one step away from sodium on the table.

It has been suggested that bipolar disorder may be related to the bipolarity of chaotic ordering, though it might be connected with lunar cycles and the tides. (A longtime member of A.A. has mentioned to me that when he came into the fellowship in the late 1940s there was a doctor who claimed that the tidal pull of the moon on brain fluids had something to do with periodic—Jellinek ε—drinking. The explanation need not be correct but the periodicity might be—as with *luna*tics or *luna*cy generally.) There are some indications that very rapidly cycling bipolarity might be a different condition (at least differently treatable) from the more common form. Now, bipolarity of either form is not unique to women, but it is heavily concentrated in women and highly creative men, particularly artists (schizophrenia seems more linked to highly creative mathematicians, as with John Nash and possibly even Einstein). Unless we suggest that highly artistic men "have more of the woman in them" (which was indeed a commonplace from Tiresias to Leonardo), and consider the possibility of male menstrual cycles, it is not clear where this leaves us. But we know there are gender differences in alcoholics, and gender concentrations in types of depression, so work on the biochemistry of manic depression may help us in any case.

After all, any cyclothymic disorder may reflect the influence of cyclic events on cortisol production (Andreasen 2001:236). If, as we suggested earlier in this chapter, alcoholics have lower than normal cortisol levels, it would mean that for self-preservation the alcoholic manic-depressive would need to be "up" more than her (or his) nonalcoholic counterpart—and we recall that one thing producing cortisol is stress. If we postulate an alcoholic (a young "born" alcoholic) who is a manic depressive with a first great depression ("triggered" perhaps by a parent's death, for example), say at age twelve or thirteen, we might expect that she (more likely than he) would either start to drink (possibly in a periodic pattern at first), or at least engage in other stress-producing behavior, or both, to ameliorate the depressive phases of the condition (and, being young, enjoy the manic). Of course, the swings might be so violent even so that thoughts of suicide would still occur, but drinking and stress-seeking would be a prime example of self-medication for the bipolar disorder.

There are a number of studies on the level of response to alcohol (alcohol challenge). A meta-analysis (analysis of analysis) on ten studies revealed a lower subjective response to alcohol in FHPs. This study also determined that the differences occurred only after active alcohol challenge, not placebo, and was seen at both rising and falling blood alcohol concentrations. Although some studies have not observed this phenomenon, they tended to use small samples, relatively low blood alcohol concentrations, or a prolonged multistep procedure for administering alcohol.

Most studies have, in fact, reported a lower level of alcohol-induced changes in body sway in FHPs, for example. Moreover, less persistent alcohol-related changes have been reported for P300 latency in FHPs than in FHNs in males, along with lowered rate of decrease in the fast alpha component of the cortical EEG. Other investigators have found greater EEG changes for FHPs, especially during rising blood alcohol concentrations.

These studies also concentrated on males. We note that the concentration on males may have had the effect of concentrating attention on Psa (or psa or PSA) or Pea (or pea or PEA) rather than on Sda (sda or SDA) alcoholics (which includes larger numbers of women)—accepting, for the moment, the separate existence of the Pea (pea or PEA) strain—Jellinek's type-ε alcoholics.

Differences among studies include analysis of different electrode positions, frequency bands, and levels of alcohol consumption. Some investigators have observed that the higher the density of alcoholism in families, the greater the decrease in alpha following alcohol consumption. But a lesser decrease in alpha with alcohol consumption at nineteen years of age predicted alcohol dependence ten years later, and this relationship was also observed for beta. In other words, insensitivity to alcohol reflected in the fast alpha component in the cortical EEG is indicative of an alcoholic predisposition—or, in yet other words, "if you can drink your friends under the table when you're nineteen, you're probably an alcoholic."

Decreased endocrine response to alcohol in male FHPs has been reported for cortisol, ACTH (adrenocorticotropic hormone), and prolactin, and FHPs appear to be resistant to the ability of alcohol to blunt the ACTH response to CRF, the corticotropin releasing factor. Although some studies have reported alcohol-associated increases in heart rate (that is a release of adrenaline or other anticipatory excitement) in FHP males, this has not been observed in females or in other studies. FHPs, especially with multigenerational family histories of alcoholism, are likely to show a greater stress-dampening effect after consuming alcohol and show greater increase in beta-endorphin-like material after alcohol consumption. In other words, to repeat what we have said already, alcohol does different (and immediately better) things for these alcoholics than it does for nonalcoholics.

Alcohol Challenge Response

The specificity of response to alcohol challenge has been examined by comparisons with those induced by intravenous (IV) diazepam (Librium). In contrast with alcohol consumption, FHPs demonstrated no diminished response to diazepam on subjective high, body sway, or several hormones. However, in another study, FHPs who were given logarithmically increasing doses of IV diazepam showed significantly higher levels of high and euphoric feelings, and decreased changes in memory, self-rating of sedation, and several biological factors. Note that these also are studies of males, which may (or may not) reduce their value for us. There is a study of older women early-onset alcoholics (FHP positive) suggesting that as many as one in six can undergo spontaneous (untreated) remission (quoted in

Pagliaro and Pagliaro 2000:119)—if this is true it suggests some fundamental differences between men and women alcoholics, and specifically in the duration of sustained dopamineregic dysfunction after abstinence (ibid.:281), though it might also be in the duration of HPA axis dysfunction (ibid.:282). On the other hand, there is suggestive—even strong—anecdotal evidence from members of A.A. that older women early-onset alcoholics claim "untreated" sobriety while taking Librium or Valium (or even Prozac and other SSRIs). The value of self-testimony to stable abstinence among males has been shown to be dubious (Vaillant 1996a), and we should be surprised to find a gender difference in this.

One area needing significant further research is the mode by which the genetic preconditions for alcoholism are "triggered" or potentiated or brought into play. We recall that in chaotic ordering, there is a sensitive dependence on initial conditions, and—as has been pointed out, taking one very simple example—twins may be identical (monozygotic), but one or the other of them must have come first, which may have a potentiating effect (or its contrary) throughout a lifetime. Triggers may be event-related, may be cognitive, may be disguised as the effects of "nurture" (as against "nature"), but it will still be worth something to find out how they work. Here, of course, research will run up against the difficulty that the first drink may be the trigger ("I was an alcoholic from the start"), or it may not ("I was a social drinker"), according to the conditions under which that first drink was taken. When acute quickly becomes chronic, we may have trouble disentangling the effects of Alcoholism(2) from those of Alcoholism(1). The area of neuroimaging of brain vulnerability to alcoholism, with specific reference to FHP adolescents, might be useful here.

One thing particularly we should remember. A theory postulating a single underlying pathway to alcoholism may offer a model for investigating vulnerability to alcoholism, through any single factor isolated in effect by the postulate. But as alcoholism is etiologically heterogeneous, with multiple interconnecting pathways implicated in alcoholic development, we will need careful and stepwise progress in the identification of those pathways. In this chapter, we have been looking at the biochemistry and biogenetics of alcoholism as the illness of the body, having looked already at alcoholism as an illness of the mind. Why mind before body? Essentially, that's the order Bill W. put them in when speaking to the U.S. Congress, and that's the order here (as also in Elwood Worcester's *Mind, Body, and Spirit*, 1930). We are not looking here at social factors beyond the possibility they may potentiate the genetic factors. We are incorporating into our research program the proposition that alcoholics drink because they are alcoholics.

Beyond mind and body, there is, of course, another way of looking at all this. We have remarked, all along, that this is, in Bill W.'s words, an illness of mind, body, and spirit. We briefly noted (in Chapter 4), that besides the question of the mind, there is the question of Mind (in the Cartesian sense). It is time to turn now to at least the rudiments of a theological view of what goes on in the spiritual program of Alcoholics Anonymous. One consolation I have, realizing how incomplete (even if overdetailed) this book is in discussing most of its topics, is that I do not think anyone will wish the next chapter (on the theology of alcoholism and sobriety) were longer.

But I could be wrong there. In any case, that is where we now turn.

6 ~

Theology of Alcoholism, Sobriety, and Alcoholics Anonymous

"THERE WAS A MAN SENT FROM GOD WHOSE NAME WAS JOHN." Actually, there were at least two of them, the John of whom this was said, and the John who said it. It is the second John who is of importance to our quest, because it is he who formulated the distinctive theology that bears his name (we call it Johannine theology), and that we are using here as part of our scientific research program. It may seem odd to shift from the latest research and discoveries in modern biochemistry and biogenetics to a theology mostly the better part of two thousand years old—but most of the great discoveries and experiments in theology are centuries old now, and this happens to be the one that fits in best with our modern science of the mind and of the body.

When we speak about theology in general, we are speaking about the investigation and study of the Being and Nature of God and His creatures (including us), the complex of the divine dispensation and its mediation to humankind (not necessarily the Christian mediation), including natural truths, the soul, moral law—everything accessible to reason enlightened by faith (*fidês quaerens intellectum*). The purpose of theology is the investigation of the contents of belief (including how it works) so far as that belief is accessible to analysis by this reason enlightened by faith. For those who wish to subdivide theology into its types, this chapter might be considered as a series of exercises in both historical and practical theology. Those who are not interested in theology may of course skip this chapter, but it is possible—and I believe—that by skipping it they will impoverish their understanding of what may be going on in Alcoholics Anonymous, if indeed (as Bill W. believed, and we accept his formulation) alcoholism is indeed an illness of the spirit.

When we speak about the theology of alcoholism, of sobriety, and of A.A. (Alcoholics Anonymous), we are of course speaking about three different but (also, of course) interrelated subjects. If, as we have suggested, alcoholism is a condition of the brain, where mind and body intersect—or, to put it in more recognizably theological terms, where the mind is in some sense incarnate in the body—we would therefore be well advised to look at the theology of incarnation. We should also examine the theology of sobriety, or of recovery—to use a word perhaps more frequently used these days (though not so good a word, I think). This might be called a study of the *telos* of sobriety. Finally, we should look at the theological underpinnings—and, to a considerable degree, the history of the theological underpinnings—of the society, or *koinonia*, of Alcoholics Anonymous, after we have looked briefly at what a *koinonia* is, and how it works.

To be sure, Alcoholics Anonymous is not a religious body—if by religion we understand "sect" or "denomination" or "organized religion" (albeit it is a religious society under the laws of the State of New York, where its General Service Board is incorporated). But it is by its own belief and acknowledgment a "spiritual" society, and, as we noted earlier, the present spiritual/religious distinction is not unlike the nineteenth century's religious/gospel distinction. The study of matters of the spirit is what has, over the centuries, come to be called theology, and that is why this chapter has the title it has. We will look first at a theology of incarnation, then at the *telos* of sobriety, then at the idea of the *koinonia* and at what we might call spiritual history. Or we might call it theological history. Or (my choice), we might call it the history of the Spirit, which had come to the point that was (in my view) the precondition for the "golden moment" when Alcoholics Anonymous was formed. One further note: because of the wide variety of beliefs likely to be present in any A.A. meeting, theology—discussion of the nature of God and of our relation to God—is doubtless inappropriate at such a meeting, or in A.A. literature. But this book is not A.A. literature, not even essentially literature for members of A.A. (though I hope some of them will read it), and I believe the discussion is appropriate and may even be necessary here.

A THEOLOGICAL RESEARCH PROGRAM

Knowing any theological underpinnings of our endeavor may not, of course, be necessary to our understanding of what is being done. But it is still important *sub specie aeternitatis,* and those who are not irremediably put off by theology should welcome an opportunity for better understanding of what may be going on. Underlying what we might call the spiritual part of our study is—I believe—a set of assumptions (perhaps a better word would be *understandings*) having to do with the relationship of Mind and matter. These understandings play a significant part in our study—though they may not be necessary to it, and in fact, alternative theological underpinnings may also work (though not, I think, as well). We should remember that Carl Jung, who spoke of the need for a spiritual experience, apparently did not believe—certainly did not proclaim his belief—in God as most understand Him. (Though, of course, there may have been reasons for this going back at least to the Clark Vigentennial, as we have noted in Chapter 1.) But if alcoholism, as A.A. says, is a mental, physical, and spiritual condition—a strange illness of mind, body, and spirit—we had better examine the relationship at least of mind and matter. We should at least suggest a theology of incarnation.

This is, as we have noted (in the sense of the phrase used by the late Imre Lakatos), a "scientific research program" and it could be restated in more technical theological terms than I have used here. I have chosen, however, to forgo as much of the technical language of theology as possible (some may not think enough), and to present the research program as an hypothesis adopted for the purposes of this book—as indeed it is. Let me explain what I mean by calling this a Lakatosian research program. Whatever explains things with the fewest "protective" assumptions made, fewest complications, greatest enlightenment, greatest ability to predict, that is our acceptable scientific research program, and may be used as true until it wears out (needs more protective assumptions, cannot predict, and so on). In essence, we are adopting a way of looking at things—a paradigm in the sense used by Thomas Kuhn—as a framework for scientific inquiry. I happen to believe that the way we have adopted is in fact the correct way of looking at things, but for our purposes here it is an hypothesis that can be used in making sense of observable phenomena.

That the way of looking at things we have adopted is the way implicit in the theology of John the Evangelist might be thought accidental—but I do not believe it is an accident. To those who wish to look further at this matter, I suggest John A. Sanford's *Mystical Theology: A Psychological Commentary on the Gospel of John* (1996), and especially his discussion of Carl Jung and this mystical theology. With this—including our disclaimer—for prologue, here is my understanding of the world, and the word, and specifically of the relation between spirit and matter, underlying our approach here.

Let me note that it is far from our intention here to develop a new hermeneutic (that is, method of biblical interpretation): I am making use of my general knowledge and of what I understand from commentaries on the Gospel of John the Evangelist, particularly those by Raymond Brown, John Sanford, and (perhaps unusually) Rudolf Steiner, whose perceptions according to the Goethean way of knowledge seem useful here, as elsewhere (in the discussion, particularly, in Chapter 9).

BUILDING A METAPHYSICAL UNIVERSE

We may begin, after the manner of a science-fiction writer, by suggesting an "invented" universe with a variety of "philosophic" beginning, in which Cosmic Mind becomes conscious of its difference from Matter (Creation)—mass and energy—and in that Consciousness was (is) aware of the organization, the form, of Matter (that is, of Creation). The form of this Matter, this mass and energy, is the way it is because that is the way the Mind perceived it (perceives it): the imprint of the Mind was (is) in the form of the Matter, like a software program embedded in the hardware of a magnificent and universal computer. The Mind wrote (writes) the program on and for the computer. The Mind wrote (writes) the program on and for the Matter.

Of course, the presence of energy, which can and does convert and reconvert to and from mass, and which can and does decay, in the process called entropy, means, in this universe, the necessity of Time. Time, so to speak, is in the Matter, not in the Mind. In the fullness of time, at the end of this universe, the Matter (the whole Creation) will reach the state that the Mind perceived (perceives) as already there, in the instant of perception, the first awareness, or first utterance, or creation. In the meantime, to the extent the Cosmic Mind is imprinted in the Matter (the whole creation), this Mind-in-Matter (or Mind-in-Creation), this sort of self-correcting and apparently self-conscious software, will perceive through the lens of Time. But it does perceive. There is some kind of two-way perception going back and forth between the Mind and the Mind-in-Matter. We might call this two-way perception, this kind of perceptual feedback loop, either Knowledge or Wisdom.

After all, we humans think in triads—that seems to be part of *our* programming (it was certainly part of Freud's), and what we have here is the traditional triad of Being, Creator, Cosmic Mind, *Nous*, as 1; Creation, Word, *Logos*, as 2; and Knowledge, or Wisdom, *Sophia*, or occasionally Intellectual Love, as 3 (but note that we are using our Early Christian understanding of the relationship between and among *Nous*, *Logos*, and *Sophia*). In this system, there are certain important implications of what we might call differential time for the parts of the Mind-in-Matter, or perhaps we might say the minds-in-Matter.

The creatures in this "invented" world in our example—call them humans—are developing through time, as they perceive it, toward that eventual state where they are as the Mind perceived (perceives) them in the instant of creation, or differential perception, or utterance, or programming, or whatever we call it. There is no reason why all the members of this human race should be at the same stage of development at the same time. Suppose one comes along, at a point in perceived time, who is already at the point where the Mind in him (or her, or whatever we postulate in our imagined world) fully perceives and is fully in touch with the Cosmic Mind, and thus in some sense unified with it. We would thus have a human being with incredible knowledge and what we would think were incredible powers, because they would be the powers of the final-stage Mind-in-Matter (Creation). An incredibly charismatic human being, by the way. He or she would appear to be ordering the matter (creation) to do his or her will, because he or she would be one with the Mind that imprinted or programmed the matter. We might think it was magic, but it would simply be a kind of superintelligent anticipation (or perception) of the eventual form of the matter (creation).

In other words, this human being wouldn't exactly change water into wine: instead, he or she would perceive that at some point in the natural order of things, through the process of grape-growing and harvesting and fermenting and all that, the water would be (or is) wine. Since time is not involved in the perceptions of the Cosmic Mind, this person embodying the Mind would perceive the water as wine, and everyone else would share the perception and see and taste wine. This seems to have happened at Cana of Galilee, and also, if we can believe the Venerable Bede, it happened with St. Cuthbert in the seventh century. And, of course, this all leaves room for the possibility of other Minds-in-matter very nearly approaching this perfection over perceived time. Gautama Siddhartha (Buddha) might be an example. So, I suppose, might be the gods, if they existed as the legends say (that is, as they say in our perceived time). The matter is obviously of interest to those inventing universes after the manner of a science-fiction writer, but not to our salvation, or anyone's "temporal salvation" in sobriety. Our salvation here—in Christian terms—would be defined as our perfect participation in the Perfect Mind-in-Matter (Mind-in-Creation), whom in His Incarnation in matter (one of them?) some call Yeshua bar-Joseph, or Jesus Messias, or Christ. Can one get there through Buddha? Or through other means besides the Christian? Not my department, not here, at least. (And— to reveal my own presuppositions, as I should—I'm not sure that, *sub specie aeternitatis*, the question has a meaning.)

The real challenge in determining how things work is in finding a way in which this traditional triad of Being, Word, and Wisdom— Mind, Program, and Knowledge—could be reproduced in the triad with the Mind, and the leader, and his followers. The answer, as we shall see, lies in the nature of the *koinonia*, and more exactly of what theologians would call the salvific *koinonia*. But why should we bother to try to reproduce the triadic form? That triadic form seems to be something in the way we humans think, perhaps part of the imprint or program of the Mind. Like chaos theory in mathematics, it really seems to describe "The Way Things Are." Perhaps the kind of interactive spirit that can animate a group of human beings—a kind of mysterious linkage like that formed in and with an undefeated athletic team—could be used as an analogue to this interactive both-ways perception, this dual feedback passing between Mind and Mind-in-Matter (or the Mind-in-Creation). And the fact that this Spirit exists could be a witness of the imprint of the Mind-in-Matter in the followers. The coming of this Witness, this Spirit, into the followers of the charismatic leader, who is the perfect form of Mind-in-Matter, is the testimony of the unity of Mind and Mind-in-Matter (or Mind-in-Creation).

Now because we are involved in process—change and decay and all that—we are in time. Time is the Lord of This World. Until the Mind is perfectly in us, we will still be seeing things through the lens of time. We will be everlastingly dying. The process of time will bring cosmic explosions, earthly fire and flood and famine, on the way to the final physical state of entropy, and we will be required to perceive them in time. I think this rather neatly gets over a problem I have had with the idea of hellfire and damnation. If we fail to achieve the necessary identification with the perfect Mind-in-Matter (Mind-in-Creation) in this life, then in some material form we will, in some time (though doubtless different from our present time, as our body will be different from our present body), necessarily go though the material experiences the universe goes through. (Both the fire of the traditional Hell and the cold and ice of Dante's would be part of this.)

In the perception of the Mind, we would be (indeed, we are) in the final state of unity, but in our perception in time (whatever time), we would be undergoing the tortures of Hell. Note, by the way, that the present equation for the formation of the universe includes "unused" timelike dimensions: different levels of being (as, for example, angels) could be linked to these unused dimensions of time. That's a bit by-the-way for us here, but we should at least remind ourselves of two reasonable corollaries to be drawn from this. First, God's time is not our time. Second, the testimony to the success of the salvific *koinonia* is that the Spirit working in its members is so strong as not only to convert the assembly into a church, but in the case of the Christian church (it is argued—though not by us here) to convert it into the Body of Christ itself.

In the Cosmic Mind, whatever we call it (John called it God, *hô Theos*, as many do even in 2004), all humans are perceived in the final (and also instant) state of unity with this God. That is, this is how they are perceived by God. Not by themselves, because they are in time. We could perhaps say that they are in their time, and God is in His time—exactly how we put it may not matter hugely, so long as there is a major difference between God's (final or instant) time and our perceived time. Maybe God's time approaches what we call eternity asymptotically, getting there in the fullness of time. The point is, for us, now, we see ourselves reaching that point only in our time, and the quicker we can do it, the better off we are. Before the fire and the entropy, before we die and our bodies decay in this world of matter. That is why we seek to reach the point. The motives of the perfect Mind-in-Matter (-Creation) must be different. The way the Mind-in-Matter triumphs over the change and decay that matter involves is through the coming of John's Paraclete, his Witness (from the Greek *parakalein*, to witness). When the Mind-in-Matter (Mind-in-Creation) in its first perfect example is perceived by His followers as fully united with the Mind, that perception will link the followers together in a way impossible before the perception. That is what this perfect example, the one we call the Christ, meant when He said He would have to go away before His disciples would possess this Spirit of Witness, this Paraclete.

Are the two triads, Creator/Word/Wisdom and that traditionally called Father/Son/Holy Ghost, really the same? And why? As to why, principle of parsimony—Occam's razor. Why multiply hypotheses needlessly? If God is the Creator and the Son is the Word, two points out of the three are the same, so by that principle, that razor, the Spirit or feedback loop or Love of the second triad would be the Wisdom of the first. And if the Spirit that links the Mind, the *Nous*, and the Mind-in-Matter, the *Logos*, is the same that links the Mind with this leader who is the first perfect Mind-in-Matter, the one called Jesus Christ, what happens when the leader goes back to being with the Mind—or, as John puts it, when He goes to the Father? The logic of the situation, as I see it, is that the followers must become the Christ, the incarnation of the *Logos*. The Mind remains the same, and the feedback link, the Spirit, remains the same, so (same principle, same razor) the Mind-in-Matter (Mind-in-Creation) must remain the same. The gospel story would be the attempts of the Mind-in-Matter person, the "anointed one" or Christ or Messiah, to bring his followers to that point, including the absolutely necessary step of his "going away" or "returning to the Father."

The group has been picked out by the leader, this perfect example of Mind-in-matter, from the people who "happened" to be there, the neighbors. You may recall the old Army draft notice—"Greetings: A Committee of your friends and neighbors has selected you . . ." And *friends and neighbors* is a legal doublet like *give and bequeath* or *let or hindrance*: the words mean pretty much the same thing, except neighbors are nearer, "neigh" meaning "nigh" meaning "near." It would be like a child or young adult picking a best friend, a "near friend"—the kind of child of which it is said "of such is the kingdom of Heaven" (which is, after all, within us). You would need to sense the spirit in the person who is going to be your "near friend"—your neighbor, the one so close to you that you will love him or her like yourself. Your group will be filling the role of the perfect Second Person of the Trinity, so that this closeness, this unity, is absolutely essential. (And this, of course, is implicit in the New Testament meaning of *koinonia*.)

John whom we call the Evangelist learned about the relationship of mind and matter, or Mind and Mind-in-matter (which we call the Incarnation), back in the days when Jesus of Nazareth was beginning to go around proclaiming the good news that He had the full Mind in Him, and that He could bring his followers into the same relationship with the Mind that He had. Somehow, because it had happened in Him—the first time it had happened with any human being, indeed any form of Matter, so far as we know (I must be careful not to say form of Creation here, so as not to trespass on the "begotten not created" of the Creed)—it was up to Him to bring as many as he could into that relationship. We sometimes call that relationship Love, because He sometimes called it Love, or called it by a word, *agapê*, that we sometimes translate as Love. I suppose the need for bringing others into that relationship had (has? will have?) something to do with winning out, triumphing, over the time implicit in matter. Love, as the modern playwright has said, is the bridge, the only bridge.

We have two triads—the Creator/Word/Wisdom triad and the Father/Son/Holy Ghost triad. If the Father is the Creator, *Nous*, and the Son is the Word, *Logos*, the Holy Ghost (Holy Spirit) must be the Wisdom, *Sophia* (feedback loop, *agapê*). If the Father is the Creator, and the Holy Ghost (Holy Spirit) is the Wisdom (feedback loop, *agapê*), and the Christ returns to the Father, then the place of the Christ must be taken by someone or something else, which is also the Word of the Creator/Word/Wisdom triad. The members of the church are it. Their body (the church) is the body of Christ, their spirit is the Spirit of God bestowed on John Evangelist by adoption, perhaps on James and Andrew and Peter and Bartholomew on Galilee, and all the church by the same adoption (joint heirs with Christ). (This should be kept in mind when we discuss Alcoholics Anonymous as a *koinonia*.)

TELOS OF RECOVERY, THEOLOGY OF SOBRIETY

This sketch is obviously not intended to be exhaustive. What is important here is not that it be an exact rendition of the full Johannine theory of the Incarnation, but that it is a reasonable approximation of that theory, that it is consistent with the documents, and most of all that it can be used as a fruitful way of looking at the relationship of mind and matter (or mind and creation), or Mind and Matter. Specifically, that it can be used as the basis for a scientific research program linking the *telos* of salvation, which is spiritual, with the *telos* of recovery—by spiritual means—from a physical and mental condition—that is, with the *telos* of sobriety. Remember, we are adopting it as an hypothesis, a kind of Lakatosian research program. If it leads nowhere that is equivalent, for the moment, to falsifying it. If it leads to useful results, that will do in lieu of verification (since verification may not be possible until the end of time, or thereafter).

We will here look first at the most recent attempt to suggest a theology of sobriety for Alcoholics Anonymous. This attempt is not entirely satisfactory, for reasons we will suggest. After suggesting reasons for its unsatisfactory nature, we will look at our understandings (or assumptions) on the relationship of mind and matter, and specifically at what I am defining as this essentially Johannine theology of Incarnation. This theology makes possible the essential theological argument in this book (though not essential to the book), which is that the *telos* of sobriety or recovery from active alcoholism is a model of the *telos* of salvation.

The recent study (Mercadante 1996) I mentioned on the theology of recovery in Alcoholics Anonymous (A.A.) seems to be from the Methodist (thus at least quasi-Arminian) point of view, though it is published by a Presbyterian publishing house. Let me note a few points raised in Mercadante's chapter, "The Nature of the Problem," and what I take to be one fundamental weakness. We begin with the weakness, and in order to explain why I think we are making steps here toward overcoming this weakness, it will be necessary to take a brief excursion into New Testament history. The weakness, quite simply, is that she devotes no attention to that book of the New Testament most fundamental to the thinking of the cofounders of Alcoholics Anonymous, Bob S. and Bill W. The book is the Epistle General of St. James, so important to the thinking of the cofounders that they suggested (not entirely tongue-in-cheek), with this epistle in mind—and William James's *The Varieties of Religious Experience*—that A.A. be called the James Club or (more humorously) the James Gang.

I believe (given that James of Jerusalem and John the Evangelist were coadjutors in the administration of the church immediately after the death of Jesus Christ) that this epistle is built on an essentially Johannine theology. (I have, in addition, reasons for believing that James of Jerusalem was one of the Twelve, making the ties even closer, but that—being contrary to received doctrine—must be the subject of another essay.) And I believe also that the understanding of the relationship of Mind and Matter implicit here is the understanding on which Alcoholics Anonymous is based, whatever may be the understanding of individual members. I gather (from its lack of mention in her book) that Mercadante does not believe this. She does not, indeed, discuss St. James. And yet the founders of Alcoholics Anonymous found virtually every word of that short epistle to be to the point.

Now, on some of the points Mercadante does raise. First, she argues that Alcoholics Anonymous took over the Oxford Group's emphasis on sin as moral illness (she is one of the very few commentators to notice this) and amplified it to include specifically physical illness. That is true, so far as I know, and is of course what lies at the root of our discussion of the theology of the Incarnation. Second, she argues that this emphasis on disease (and on individual sin) may have worked within the framework of the Oxford Group (where members shared a kind of theological bent)—and remember, the Oxford Group adopted what may be called the disease concept of sin—but she argues that it will not (does not) work in the anti-theological rooms of Alcoholics Anonymous. The truth of that assertion is beyond my ability to support or contradict. We may, however, note that the "anti-theological" bent of Alcoholics Anonymous seems to be part of what has been called the anti-intellectual bent of Alcoholics Anonymous. We may note also that reliance on experiential rather than intellectual knowledge is not necessarily a bad thing—at least for those who have the experience. And we may note that the sudden *bouleversement*, the revolution in paradigm, the spiritual realignment Jung suggested, James's passive conversion, are all experiential. But there is also *volitional* change, *volitional* conversion ([1903] 1961:172).

The closest thing to a full history of Alcoholics Anonymous is the book by Ernest Kurtz ([1979] 1991). Kurtz, as one might expect from a graduate of a Roman Catholic seminary, puts Alcoholics Anonymous in the context of the Augustinian search for the Other—for "Thee" (ibid.:178). This search, Kurtz suggests, may emphasize the human separation from the Other, salvation coming from outside the self, and in this mode may be called Pietist (if self-abnegating) or Evangelical (if joyful); or it may emphasize the human participation in the Other, salvation coming from inside and outside the self, and in this mode may be called Humanist or Liberal. Kurtz also suggests that the rise of neo-orthodoxy in the early 1930s, with a "sense of urgency and a demand for moral and intellectual humility" (ibid.:180)—the neo-orthodoxy of Unamuno's *Tragic Sense of Life*—also played a part in fashioning Alcoholics Anonymous. I daresay he's right, though speaking from my own experience in the Episcopal Church (and given Sam Shoemaker's importance, and the Calvary Mission, and the Emmanuel movement), I think he might look more at the traditions of the Episcopal Church, whose members—like those of A.A., it has been suggested—"get together to read to God out of a book he knows better than they do." One point where he is clearly correct—in my view—

is in his comparison of what he calls the "Evangelical Pietism" of A.A. with that of Jonathan Edwards (1703–58). Whatever we call it (there may be better choices), there is an Edwardsian cast to Alcoholics Anonymous. Edwards's point in his *Sinners in the Hands of an Angry God* (that God will not let sinners go, but keeps His hands under them, if they come to Him) is almost identical to the "Big Book's" insistence that alcoholics "have a daily reprieve contingent on the maintenance of [their] spiritual condition" ("Big Book" 1976:85).

Kurtz finds the spiritual (or religious?) success of Alcoholics Anonymous to lie, fundamentally, in what he speaks of as Word and Witness: "The individual member and the A.A. group itself had to engage in missionary works of Word and Witness; but the efficacy of the works lay in their effect on the *worker*, rather than in any external result" (1979, 1991:187–88). But surely, if there were *no* external result, ever, it would be difficult to call these missionary works at all. To be sure, alcoholics may think that by accepting themselves (including in that category others within the fellowship) as "not-God," they may be made whole by the acceptance of limitation (ibid.:197), and that, I suppose, is true: it makes good psychological sense, and it fits in with Kurtz's Pietist Evangelism meeting Humanism (or Liberalism). But I am wary that it may not be good theology because it is not theology at all. I think there is much more to be done with Word (*Logos*) and Witness (*parakalein* and thus *Paraclete*). How should this reading A.A.'s books and telling A.A. stories work? One problem here, as both Kurtz and Mercadante suggest, is that A.A. is not really interested in "How It Works" in any sense other than that of "using the tools in the tool kit"—this (Bill W. et al. 1939:Chapter 5) is "How It Works" in that sense, and asking further questions is counterproductive for those members of A.A. who will use it as an excuse for not working the Steps—but not necessarily for our inquiry. Certainly this attitude, which both Kurtz and Mercadante call "anti-intellectualism," has certain problems.

We recall the statement of John's (and Polycarp's) friend Ignatius (also called Theophoros), that the *mysterion* (the sacrament) is *pharmaokon athanasias*, the medicine of immortality. This is, as we have noted, an implied example of the consideration of sin as illness, which is part of the original Oxford Group disease concept of sin—and of alcoholism. Still, Mercadante suggests, this view has in fact led (in A.A.) to a downplaying of sin as a human condition and to a tension between (1) the view of alcoholism as spiritual disease and (2) the demonizing of alcohol as a physical substance, with its attendant view of alcoholics as fundamentally different from other people. (But the evidence indicates that *physically* or *genetically* alcoholics *are* different from other people.) Third, she argues that the anti-intellectual tendency of Alcoholics Anonymous (as in "utilize—don't analyze"), with its implicit warning against theology, confuses the issue on the fundamental problem of Grace. That may be, and therefore it may be well to look here briefly but generally at the question of Grace. (We will look at Grace in John Newton's context a little further on.) And because we are looking at the question of Grace, it may be advisable also to look (however briefly) at the question of the Sacraments as they relate to Grace. This may (in theological terms) help explain how it works—or why.

THERE BUT FOR THE GRACE OF GOD

I believe alcoholics in A.A. frequently quote (applying it to themselves), old John Bradford's line: "But for the Grace of God, there goes John Bradford" (said when he saw prisoners on their way to execution). But what exactly is meant by *Grace*? A common definition is that it is a free gift of God, but that is theologically incomplete, and some would say oversimplified to the point that it may be misleading. In fact, Christian theologians have divided Grace (1) into *prevenient* Grace and *subsequent* Grace (Augustine), (2) into *sufficient* Grace and *efficacious* Grace (Augustine), (3) into *habitual* Grace and *actual* Grace (Thomas Aquinas), and (4) into *irresistible* Grace and *congruous* Grace (Duns Scotus, and others, commenting on Augustine). Prevenient Grace is the free gift of God, antecedent to conversion. Subsequent Grace occurs if God and Man cooperate after conversion. Prevenient Grace might be—but is *not* in fact—adequate to (that is, sufficient for) salvation, while subsequent Grace is adequate to (sufficient for) salvation.

Efficacious Grace, on the other hand, is subsequent to conversion and depends on the congruity or appropriateness of the Grace, which is God's choice (according to Augustine). Habitual or sanctifying Grace is the gift of God inhering in the soul, by which men are enabled to perform righteous acts: it is held generally to be conveyed in the sacraments. Actual Grace, which may exist in the unbaptized and even the unbelieving, is a certain motion of the soul (toward God), bestowed by God ad hoc for the production of some good act. Prevenient Grace is the form of actual Grace, which leads men to sanctification before the reception of the sacraments: it is the free gift of God and entirely unmerited.

The English Franciscan scholar Alexander of Hales (1186–1245) (1) taught that even nonbelievers could, by initiating some movement toward virtue, merit congruous Grace, (2) identified prevenient Grace with the "general assistance" (*assistentia generalis*, meaning, in a sense, the general presence) of God, and (3) denied irresistible Grace, leaving free will open to all. If efficacious Grace—particularly in medieval theology—is conferred by the sacraments (as is generally held), it is important to note that the sacraments (the word "sacrament" originally means "oath") were considered by Augustine and by others, as late as Hugh of St. Victor (d. 1142), to be as many as thirty in number and to include *inter alia*, the Lord's Prayer, as well as other spoken formulae. A Christian theologian might well consider the prayer at the end of an A.A. meeting as a sacrament, especially if it were the Lord's Prayer.

The basic definition of a sacrament is "the outward and visible sign of an inward and spiritual grace given to us" (see the definition in the *Oxford Dictionary of the Christian Church*) or, more briefly, in Aquinas, "the sign of a sacred thing insofar as it sanctifies men" (*signum rei sacrae in quantum est sanctificans hominês*) (ibid.). Alexander of Hales, following Peter Abelard, counted the seven sacraments of the present Roman Catholic church (Baptism, Confirmation, Eucharist, Penance, Extreme Unction, Orders, Matrimony), but we should note that he apparently believed in the efficacy of actual (prevenient) Grace, as well as in "merited" congruous Grace—neither of which required one of these seven sacraments. All this—which may seem an unmerited excursion into the by-ways of medieval theology—is in fact important. It is important because it sets a framework for considering the process of sobriety in Alcoholics Anonymous as involving a formulaic sacrament of the Word, providing for the passage from prevenient Grace to efficacious (congruous) Grace, to habitual Grace. In other words, it may help us to see Alcoholics Anonymous as fitting squarely in the medieval tradition of the process of Grace, and thus of the *telos* of salvation. (It might be noted that the familiar A.A. statement that "we claim spiritual progress rather than spiritual perfection" is to assert the *telos*, the goal toward which we progress, but not yet the *teleios*, the perfection, the "having progressed.")

Now, this is not the only theology that can be found implied in Alcoholics Anonymous, though it seems to us to be one that would explain theologically why Alcoholics Anonymous would work (which is part of the purpose of theology). There seems to be a lot said these days in A.A. to the effect that "Alcoholics Anonymous is a spiritual program, not a religious program." If this means (as it may) that A.A. "is not allied with any sect, denomination . . . or institution," especially with any religious sect, denomination, or institution, then it may be true—and certainly should be true, from A.A.'s point of view (this quotation is from the Preamble that is read at the beginning of A.A. meetings, defining what A.A. is and what meetings are for).

But one implication of the dichotomy of *spiritual* and *religious* is more troubling theologically, though it is possible to construct a workable—albeit somewhat Manichaean—theology that would justify it. The implication is that organized *religion* is more concerned with *material* things—

rituals, vestments, petitionary prayers for material outcomes, wealth—while A.A. is more spiritually pure. "I learned more about my Higher Power [or God] in church basements [where A.A. meetings are frequently held] than in the churches upstairs." That is doubtless a statement of fact for most (perhaps all) of those making it, though one might be tempted unworthily to inquire how much they have learned about God in either location. I believe also that it is not uncommon to hear members talk about their "spirituality" in A.A. meetings, the implication seeming to be that they are becoming more "spiritual" and less—what? (Never mind, for the moment, the definition that "religion is the method we establish for contact with God; spirituality is the method God establishes for contact with us"—which would mean that "my" spirituality" would not be *mine*, but *His*.)

Now, spirituality is generally defined as the fact or quality of being *spirit*—spirit being the intelligent and immaterial part of man or the human soul in general, and especially that aspect of it concerned with religious truth and action and directly susceptible to divine influence (see the definition of spirit in *Oxford Dictionary of the Christian Church*). Here again, one opposite of *spiritual* (which is *immaterial* as well as *intelligent*) would seem to be *material*. One is reminded of a pamphlet published by the Christian Science Publishing Company, arguing for—not twelve steps but—one step (Christian Science) to sobriety. Those who believe, with Mrs. Eddy, that Matter is a species of Error (though her definitions of Matter sometimes may seem to challenge the Scholastics in their subtlety), have a consistent theology, and we would be far from denying the value of Christian Science to some heavy drinkers, especially those who have been brought up in—and then fallen away from—Christian Science. After all, there were recoveries into sobriety before A.A., and there have been those since that did not come through A.A.—though how many of those who recovered were alcoholics may be open to question.

It turns out that, with everything else it is, this book may also (as we have hinted) be considered a study in a particular realm of philosophy called teleology, from the Greek *telos*, meaning end in the sense of goal or purpose. To be more exact, by *telos* we mean an ultimate goal toward which a system—whether the whole universe or an individual human being or a group of human beings—is moving. In Christian theology, this is generally taken as the fulfillment of God's plan. The teleological (goal-seeking) aspect of Christianity and of the Judaism from which it came distinguishes them from a number of other faiths, though not all. Zoroastrianism and Northern Paganism both have something of this same teleological character. As we have already remarked in Chapter 4, a linear teleological character also inheres in the Jungian psychology of individuation—a point worth at least a brief mention here—and it may not be accidental that Jung occupies his unique place in the annals of Alcoholics Anonymous. And here I ask your indulgence for adding to the discussion two more terms from technical Johannine theology, which seem to me of importance—*theosis* and *theopoiesis*. The *telos* implicit in the matter of *theosis* or *theopoiesis* brings us straight to the Johannine world.

The process of *theosis* means that the human soul is saved (from its fallen state of sin) through a mystical union with Christ (part of the Christian *mysterion*), through death and rebirth, meaning the infusion of the life of Christ into the soul, through prayer, through struggle against the egocentricity of sin, and through the increasing awareness of the soul that the temporal things of this world are reflections of the eternal things in the realm of the spirit. The important point in the process of this *mysterion*—for our study—is what the Incarnation of Christ signifies: in the words of Athanasius, "He was made Man so that we might be made God" (*theopoiethomen*). Or, in the words of Gregory Nazianzen, "We become like Christ, since Christ also became like us: we become gods on his account, since he also became man for our sake" (*Ox. Dict. Chr. Church* [ODCC] 1975).

We should note here that the Biblical injunction, "Be ye therefore perfect" (Matthew 5:48), uses the word *teleios*, meaning "perfected" or "brought to one's completion or end state"—what we have spoken of as the way in which all humans are perceived in the final (or instant) state of unity with God, or, in other words, salvation. This process of *theosis* or *theopoiesis* is the process toward the *telos* of salvation. We might briefly note here the statement by Irenaeus, foster-son or adopted son of Polycarp, who was in turn foster-son or adopted son of John: "Jesus Christ became what we are [Man] in order that we might become what he himself is [God]" (ODCC loc. cit.)—another reference to the *teleios* of *theopoiesis*. And remember again the statement of John's friend Ignatius (Theophoros), that the *mysterion* (the sacrament) is *pharmaokon athanasias*, the medicine of immortality. This is, I repeat, one of the first examples I have found (albeit an implied example) of the consideration of sin as illness, which is part of the original Oxford Group "disease concept" of sin—or of alcoholism, and therefore (I have heard it argued) of alcoholism *as* sin.

MORE JOHANNINE THEOLOGY

Perhaps we should look back briefly at the way the words *Nous, Logos,* and *Sophia* were used in the days John was writing, though for the first of these I believe we must direct our consideration to the writings of Irenaeus. The *Nous* is, as Irenaeus tells us, the Father Himself. The *Logos*, which we translate as Word in John's Gospel, is, I believe, akin to the "reason" of Heraclitus and the immanent divine Mind of Anaxagoras, as well as Aristotle's "spark"—remembering that Aristotle's prime mover or unmoved mover, God, is immanent in matter as the form of the matter: the Hebrew word (in Deuteronomy 30:11) is *dabar*. It has been suggested that this is virtually equivalent to *Sophia* (wisdom) in the Old Testament (and Apocryphal) "wisdom literature"—in which, however (as a kind of red flag to our speculations), the Hebrew word translated by the Greek *Sophia* is in fact *chokmah*.

This *chokmah* is the divine power dwelling within the human heart, represented by fire, which is also, of course, the representation of the Holy Spirit. The clear implication of the writings of those closest to the Johannine tradition, is indeed that the triad of *Nous, Logos*, and *Sophia* is the triad we know as Father, Son, and Holy Spirit. Note again that I am using the writings of the early church fathers in the Johannine tradition not because I believe they guarantee the truth of the framework suggested for our scientific research program, but because they help define that framework as it was understood by John, who first proposed it. It is adopted for its pragmatic value (though also for its historical value), as we look to William James's *The Varieties of Religious Experience* for its pragmatic value (though also for its historical value). Of course, as we have noted, if it works in our inquiry, if it is in fact a progressive rather than a degenerating research program, that is at least evidence against its being untrue. Some of our readers, seeing how the argument of this book is progressing, will, of course, make note of the fact that Logos means Word, and that we have spoken of God's "utterance" of creation.

The Oxford Groups spoke of a return to first-century Christianity (which we have just now been examining theologically). What first-century Christianity was particularly involved in doing practically was creating a church, as an assembly of the faithful with a common language (*koinonia*), as an assembly of the faithful (*ekklesia*—though this also refers to a building), and as something *belonging* to the Lord (*kyriakon*) The separation of Alcoholics Anonymous from the Oxford Groups may be read, in large part, as the determination of the alcoholics not to be part of the organization of the faithful (*ekklesia*)—not a church in (the second part of) that sense. But there is little doubt in my mind that they constitute a *koinonia*, an assembly of men and women speaking a common language (*koinê*) and seeking common goals.

Koinonia

The word *koinonia* may be used in two senses, as a subsystem within a human social system—along with the market (*agora*) and the voting system (*polis*), or as a church or religious assembly (these being the original

Greek senses, though distinguished from *ekklesia*, the church "establishment"). We will be looking at both, but before we do, we should take a look at what we mean by systems and subsystems. Briefly, a system is a complex set of parts in interaction: the parts may be what we will call components (persons or institutions) or what we call properties. These properties may be material or immaterial—by which I mean ideas and beliefs. Systems are of three kinds, defined by the way they react to new diversity introduced into the system. A mechanical system rejects the new diversity—the picture is that of sand in the gears. A biological system adapts to new diversity in a kind of once-and-for-all adaptation—the picture is of mosquitoes and DDT. But the developmental system adapts to new diversity by incorporating it and introducing still newer diversity in the process: the motto is "change or die." Social systems are developmental systems.

Now, what I am calling a social system, and others might for preference call a society, contains, and is largely coterminous with, three subsystems. These subsystems are generally considered to be the proper subjects of the disciplines of economics, political science, and sociology. When the subsystems are not coterminous with the system as a whole, there ensues a tension that may be either constructive or destructive. Of that, more later. What are the three subsystems in our social system? We have already suggested them above. One is the subsystem that comprises the people engaging in marketlike activities *or other modes of exchange of goods and services,* buying and selling, trucking and bartering, getting and spending, potlatch or present-giving—and in gathering rosebuds or capital assets while they may: this was the *agora* of Greek times, and it is the subsystem that is the subject of the discipline of economics. A second is the subsystem that comprises the people engaging in political activities, voting or choosing not to vote, bribing or choosing not to bribe (or so I would argue), ruling or choosing neither to rule or be ruled: this is the *polis* of Greek times. We generally speak of this as the political system, and it is the subsystem that is the subject of the discipline of political science.

The third is the subsystem that comprises the people meeting in groups in discourse with one another, neither chaffering nor electioneering, but worshiping, philosophizing, going to sporting events, reminiscing—the thousand natural diversions that flesh is heir to: to this we give the Greek word *koinonia* (again, from *koinē*, meaning the common language). We generally speak of this as the social system (though that word is better reserved for the system as a whole) and it is the subsystem for which our best current word is *community*, though it may also be called a *society*—as opposed to *Society*. There are, obviously, dual definitions of *koinonia*, and A.A. can satisfy them both. As a spontaneously ordered social system based neither on markets or hierarchies (or votes) it is a *koinonia* rather than *agora* or *polis*. As a meeting or assembly that is essentially aimed at appeal to a "Higher Power," it is a *koinonia* in the sense of church-meeting or assembly.

In Chapter 8, we will look at the ways in which the *koinonia* of A.A. (church-meeting sense) obeys the rules of order of the *koinonia* (social-systems sense), as well as at the ways in which A.A. conforms to both types of *koinonia*. We note that one of the key points is that single-peaked preferences implied by the existence of a *koinonia* in the church-meeting sense are necessary for the ordering of the *koinonia* in the social-systems sense. We will also be looking to see how A.A. has gone about attempting to preserve both versions of *koinonia* by the use of the Twelve Traditions. For the moment, let us look a little more at the two varieties of *koinonia*. It will not have escaped the attentive reader that both are based on a common *speech*.

First, the *koinonia* is a traditionary social subsystem. The component part that is its ground is tradition or custom; the component part that is its (transmission) code is particularity (individuality); and the component part that is its binding force is law. (Those wishing to examine this set of distinctions more fully may do so in my forthcoming—but as yet incomplete—sociological study which I have tentatively entitled *The Old Custom: The Nature and Decline of our Formerly Conservative Social System*.) When we say that the binding force of the *koinonia* is law, we do not mean law imposed from outside but from inside—what in fact the *koinonia* of Alcoholics Anonymous accepts as law or rules (while denying that any such thing exists) are what the members, following Bill W., call the Twelve Traditions. These rules frequently (in any *koinonia*) include a statement of purpose (in A.A., it is called the *Preamble*), as well as governing the relationships between and among the human components within the institutions and between and among the institutions.

Second, the *koinonia* is a church, though that is not the most common Greek word—which, again, is either *ekklesia* (from which is derived both Latin *ecclesia* and French *église*) or *kyriakon* (from which our *church* is derived, and the German *Kirche*, Scottish *kirk*, and so on). The reason for using *koinonia* (which may also be translated as "community"—a community with a common language—or even as "communion") is precisely that it emphasizes the *koinê*, the common tongue. We should note that in I John 1:3,6,7, the word *koinonia* is translated (in the Authorized Version) as the "fellowship"—which is, of course, precisely the way Alcoholics Anonymous generally defines itself. It has been suggested that this originally reflects the Qumran *yahad* or "unity"—unity being, as we will discover, what the Traditions, which are A.A.'s "law" as a *koinonia* (systems sense), are all about (see Brown 1966:776–77). Perhaps we might look a little at the history of the "church"—*koinonia*—Christian fellowship—Christian church—through the ages.

THE QUALITY OF DISBELIEF?

About the time Alcoholics Anonymous was producing its "Big Book," there was published in England a very curious volume from an equally curious man by the name of Charles Williams (1886–1945), longtime editor at Oxford University Press, book reviewer, friend of C. S. Lewis and J. R. R. Tolkien, poet and theologian. The volume is *The Descent of the Dove: A Short History of the Holy Spirit in the Church* (1941). The chapters that are to our particular point are Chapter 8, "The Quality of Disbelief," which covers the years from the Protestant Reformation to Voltaire, and Chapter 9, "The Return of the Manhood," which covers the years from John Wesley to 1939. Briefly, Williams argues that, in the sixteenth century,

> something general and very deep in Man awoke to revolt. . . . It may have been mere exhaustion, or perhaps mere humanitarianism, . . . which gave it an opportunity. . . . It was a quality of spirit, not clarity (though it may involve clarity), not charity (though it may lead to charity). It is a rare thing, and it may be called the quality of disbelief. . . . It is a qualitative mode of belief rather than a quantitative denial of dogma. (ibid.:189–90)

That is, the quality of disbelief is an attitude—a "Show me!" attitude, if you like—rather than a specific disbelief in *this* proposition or *that*.

Williams remarks on the case of Lorenzo Valla, who was charged with heresy and protested that he believed all that the holy church believed, but added with a scholar's accuracy, that the church *believed*, which meant that she did not *know*. He mentions—indeed concentrates on—Michel de Montaigne (1533–92), who remained orthodox all his life, as a matter of deliberate choice. "He believed in the old human *pietas* of religion, the religion of custom, of good tradition, 'of my king and my nurse.' But he made a point of *believing* in it; he grew into some state of mind through it" (ibid.:193). It was chiefly Montaigne's style that made his writings fashionable, but "as so often happens, the minds of his readers were not the equal of his own . . . his ambiguity was reduced to irony, and the quality of unbelief with which he believed was extracted and congealed" (ibid.:194). "Ritual became nothing more than ritual, and the *pietas* of the Gascon gentleman was mechanized into official custom" (ibid.). And then came Blaise Pascal (1623–62), who saw around him "a society already cutting its fashionable coat in Montaigne's manner, but not wearing it at Mass with Montaigne's air" (ibid.:195).

Pascal saw that "we have an incapacity of proof, insurmountable by all dogmatism; we have an idea of truth, invincible to all skepticism" (quoted in ibid.:196). Also, "all the principles of stoics, skeptics, atheists, etc. are true. But their conclusions are false, because the opposite principles are also true" (ibid.). And (his version of incarnation), "our soul is cast into the body, where it finds number, time, dimension. Thereupon it reasons, and calls this nature necessity, and can believe nothing else" (ibid.). Now Pascal was a friend and intimate of those Jansenists and Quietists whose reputation clouded that of Brother Lawrence (1614–91), his longer-lived contemporary. He had himself known the workings of something like a mystical experience. He was also a mathematician, a scientist, and he strove to write, as it were, an *apologiã* for the world as he found it. He did not live to complete it. He did set before the ages the terms of what has come to be called Pascal's gamble: "The finite to stake . . . the infinite to win." He allowed his imagined opponent the objection, "The true course is not to wager at all." And crushed him with the answer, "You must wager: it is not optional" (ibid.:199). As Williams points out, he was right: it is no more optional than death. To fail to wager is to wager: in the last analysis, we must choose belief and not any quality of belief.

In the next century, Voltaire chose disbelief, because he saw the evils of organized religion, and cried *"Écrasez l'infame!"* But, even as that cry echoed over Europe, there came—from regions of Europe scarred by the Thirty Years' War, from the Quietists of England, from a young priest of the Church of England (where the quality of disbelief was raised almost to the status of belief)—a new beginning, a next step, the "return of the manhood." There came what Williams has called "one of the last and sincerest efforts to base religion on actual experience, and not on formal belief" (ibid.:206). But no sooner had this attempt begun, than it released—one might say unleashed—a new mysticism, with its new theology, a new sacramentalism even: what Williams calls the Way of the Affirmation of Images (that is, essentially, of the Incarnation). And side by side with this (he uses Kierkegaard's example), there was real doubt as to the quality of doubt that the world (in Voltaire's image) seemed to admire. "It was not the doubt which Pascal had combated and Montaigne had encouraged; it was something of which men were proud, and therefore it was not real experience: that happens. One can never be anything but humble about that" (ibid.:217). (One can, of course, see how A.A. may be defined in Williams's paradigm.)

I believe it is said from time to time in Alcoholics Anonymous—as elsewhere—that God has a sense of humor. It is also said [in one of the stories in the back of the third and fourth editions of the "Big Book" (1976, 2001)] that there are no accidents in God's world (understood, in this context, to refer inclusively to the world of Alcoholics Anonymous). So a member of A.A. might say it is unlikely to be accidental that this discussion brings us back, once again, perhaps ironically (God's humor?), to the figure of William James and his uneasy balance between disbelief and conversion—between Voltaire and Wesley. The "conversions" recounted in *The Varieties of Religious Experience*, including those from alcoholism, are "based on actual experience rather than formal belief," in the words of Charles Williams (*v. supra*). As an aside (but not entirely an aside), one of the famous eighteenth-century conversions (from experience rather than formal belief) is that of John Newton. When William Wilberforce, the man who forced the end of the British slave trade, was seized by a strong conviction of guilt (because he had not opposed the trade), he was "recovered from this state by the Reverend John Newton, once a slave-trader, then an evangelical clergyman [and hymn-writer]," who brought Wilberforce from his misery into that "'serenity, tranquillity, composure which is not to be destroyed'" (ibid.:210).

AMAZING GRACE—AND PRAGMATISM

But what of Newton's own conversion: he put his experience in a hymn that seems to grow stronger over the years, "Amazing Grace," whose words set out the process clearly. Oddly (in my view), Newton (1725–1807) is not so far as I know mentioned in *The Varieties of Religious Experience*, though his own experience is strongly suggestive. In his early twenties, while living a dissolute (read *drunken*?) and scoffing life (he was a lukewarm Deist), he read Thomas à Kempis, *The Imitation of Christ*, and asked himself, what if those things should be true? (Note the parallel to the stories of Jim B. and Fitz M. in Chapter 2). For the next six years, he says, his spiritual growth was gradual (no irresistible Grace?), and indeed, his most famous hymn appeared in the *Olney Hymns* (written with William Cowper) in 1779, when he was fifty-four. The hymn gives something of the quality of his conversion (*Olney Hymns*, first with its tune in Carrell and Clayton, *The Virginia Harmony*, 1831: his account of his life is principally in his *Out of the Depths*). The words are well known in these days:

Amazing Grace—how sweet the sound that saves a wretch like me.
I once was lost but now am found, was blind but now I see.
'T was Grace that taught my heart to fear, and Grace my fear relieved;
How precious did that Grace appear, the hour I first believed.
The Lord has promised good to me, His word my hope secures;
He will my shield and portion be, as long as life endures.
Through many dangers, toils, and snares, I have already come;
'T is Grace has brought me safe thus far, and Grace will lead me home.
Yea! when this heart and flesh shall fail and mortal life shall cease
I shall possess within the veil a life of joy and peace.
The earth shall soon dissolve like snow, the sun forbear to shine,
But God who called me here below shall be forever mine.
When we've been there ten thousand years, bright shining as the Sun,
We've no less days to sing God's praise than when we first begun.

I call particular attention to the opening stanza with its "sound" of Grace, and in this connection, to the words of William James:

> [It is] not conceptual speech, but music rather, [that] is the element through which we are best spoken to by mystical truth. Many mystical scriptures are indeed little more than musical compositions. . . . Music gives us ontological messages which non-musical criticism is unable to contradict. ([1903] 1961: 330)

Though William James himself had the quality of mystical vision, though he supported the Emmanuel movement as well as giving academic credence to the varieties of religious experience (and sometimes seems to have envied not only healthy-mindedness—that, certainly—but also religious conversion), he had also the quality of disbelief. Not perhaps so much as his pragmatic heir—or should we say, the heir to his pragmatism—John Dewey; but even so, James is considered one of the founders of Pragmatism. Pragmatism? What determines the value of an idea, a program, a society or fellowship? Does it work? It does? Then tell me how it works. And it has been suggested that perhaps an uneasy tension (including a "theological" tension) at the heart of Alcoholics Anonymous comes from the uneasy tension in James himself, who strove, in at least one sense (as we noted), to follow both Voltaire and Wesley.

It was James who denied the intrinsic authority of mystical revelations—after he had summarized the mystical experience in these words:

> Only when I become as nothing can God enter in, and no difference between his life and mine remain outstanding. This overcoming of all the usual barriers between the individual and the Absolute is the great mystic achievement. In mystic states we become one with the Absolute and we become aware of our oneness. This is the everlasting and triumphant mystical tradition, hardly altered by differences of clime or creed. In Hinduism, in Neo-Platonism, in Sufism, in Christian mysticism, in Whitmanism, we find the same recurring note. (pp. 328–29)

But not a note necessarily to be relied upon by those who have not had the experience. (In this context, it may be worth noting that in the early 1950s—perhaps before—some members of A.A. in the New York City area were strongly encouraged to read Martin Buber's *I And Thou*, [1937] 1958.)

And what says James's pragmatic heir? In his *A Common Faith*, Dewey asks "what conception of unseen powers and our relation to them would be consonant with the best achievements and aspirations of the present?" (1934). In other words, not *Is it in some sense true?* but *Will it work?* Moreover, Dewey rejected James's idea that religious experience was a separate and identifiable kind of experience, and said that psychological accommodation to the world ("living life on life's terms" in A.A. parlance) could occur as well without religious (or spiritual) terminology and practice as with them. Since Dewey, when he applied the word *God* at all, applied it to an active relation between the ideal and the actual, and since he saw in mystical states a passive relation, he considered mysticism in effect an escape from God. (This view, by the way, seems to have echoes both in Christian Science and in some severe forms of Anabaptist Protestantism today.) In short, there is more than a hint in Dewey of Voltaire's "If God did not exist, it would be necessary to invent Him," and James's uneasy personal reconciliation of Voltaire and Wesley found its true heir not in Dewey, whom he had met, but in Bill W., who was a fourteen-year-old Vermont schoolboy when James died. Yet the line from James to Carl Jung through Rowland H. and Ebby T. to Bill W. makes clear the passage of the Jamesian ambiguity enshrined in Alcoholics Anonymous.

MYSTERION AND THEOPOIESIS

Theologically speaking (in Johannine terms), Alcoholics Anonymous is a fellowship using the sacrament (*mysterion*) of the Word in community of common speech (*koinonia*) to create the progress toward perfection (*teleios*) implicit in the process of *theopoiesis* (surrender of the human will to God so as to make the human divine, which may be considered, for our purposes, pretty much the same thing as *theosis*, the surrender of the human will to God so as to make the human one with God). The word—the testimony, even the meeting of Alcoholics Anonymous—is the *pharmaokon athanasias* (the medicine of immortality, or, if you like, of salvation from the sickness that is sin).

Because, through twenty centuries, the ancient unities have been shattered, because there is no single *koinonia* as there is no single *koinê*, it is important that throughout the *koinonia* (in this case, Alcoholics Anonymous) there should be a set of agreed-upon words and readings—to that extent, a new *koinê*. Before the days of the "Big Book," readings were from the Bible or devotional literature. Now they are from the "Big Book," the "Twelve and Twelve" (*Bill W.* 1952/53), a relatively new (1990) collection of *Daily Reflections*, and in many cases from a book neither published nor approved by A.A., *Twenty-Four Hours a Day* (Richmond W. 1954), to which we shall turn shortly.

It should also be considered important that the meeting, the assembly, begins in many cases with prayer (frequently the so-called Serenity Prayer) and ends with prayer (frequently the Lord's Prayer, though sometimes the Serenity Prayer). Obviously, at least those who founded Alcoholics

Anonymous believed in some way in the efficacy of prayer. Whether they realized that they were establishing a kind of sacrament of the Word, and thus that their prayers were liturgical, is not clear (though there seems to be some evidence, from Ohio at least, that they did)

THE MATTER OF PRAYER

In any case, because it is part of the theology of A.A., as well as of sobriety, we ought to be looking here at the matter of prayer. What, exactly, does the church (meaning, generally, Christian churches) understand by prayer? And what (since we have already used the word) does the church understand by liturgical prayer?

Briefly, petition, invocation, and adoration—widely practiced in all world religions—are practiced in Christian spirituality under two dominant ideas: (1) submission to the divine will and (2) recognition of the direct relationship of every creature to God. They are therefore acts directed to God either through Jesus Christ or "in the Spirit" (Epistle of Jude, v. 20). The theology of the Incarnation discloses "a congruity of humanity with deity," supplying a new basis for the human search for God in prayer, leading to a vision of God and union with and likeness to Him (s.v. *prayer* in *Oxford Dictionary of the Christian Church*). These are types of vocal prayer: there is also mental prayer (which verges on but is not entirely the same as what is frequently called meditation): the distinction between *vocal* and *mental* is not the same as that made between *prophetic* prayer and *mystical* prayer, though it bears some relation to that. Indeed, in Protestant churches, as in Judaism, vocal prayer and prophetic prayer are much the same thing—although it has been remarked that "to the Hebrew requirement of holiness as a precondition of true prayer, Christianity adds the converse that true holiness comes only of prayer" (ibid.).

Moreover, vocal prayer may be either common or private, and if common, may be either liturgical or informal (including extemporaneous prayer as informal). By liturgy we mean the written texts—including prayer texts—providing the order for a service held in public (that is, for example, a meeting of a religious or spiritual group, a *koinonia*). In the New Testament, prayer is an art to be learned—hence the pattern given as an instruction in the Lord's Prayer. There seems to be a certain degree of controversy in Alcoholics Anonymous over the use of the Lord's Prayer, and Narcotics Anonymous, which is an offshoot of (but of course not affiliated with) A.A., seems generally to use the Serenity Prayer for both opening and closing meetings. The Lord's Prayer may be well enough known not to need quoting here: the Serenity Prayer is, however, much less known, at least outside of Alcoholics Anonymous and its offshoots, and may reasonably be quoted here, in its short form.

"God grant me the serenity to accept the things I cannot change, courage to change the things I can, and wisdom to know the difference." The prayer came to Bill W.'s attention in a funeral or memorial notice in the *New York Herald Tribune* in 1941, in a version later traced to the Protestant theologian Reinhold Niebuhr, but it has been suggested that it is at least as early as the middle of the eighteenth century. It may have first appeared in Germany (and obviously in German), credited—as the "Soldier's Prayer"—to the German Pietist minister, Friedrich Ötinger, whose life spanned much of the eighteenth century (or else, it has been recently claimed, it may be traced to a modern theologian writing under Ötinger's name, who in fact lifted the prayer from Niebuhr). If it is from the original Ötinger, one supposes—given the pacifist nature of the Pietists—that the soldier in question was praying for serenity to accept being a soldier. In any case, it may be noted that the version of the prayer given here, which is the version printed and distributed by A.A. World Services in New York, apparently asks for only so much serenity as is needed for the specified acceptance, while asking without limit for courage and wisdom (though mentioning the particular benefit derived from each). We come back to this in Chapter 9.

Ötinger was connected—how closely I do not know—with Zinzendorf and his Moravians (and thus Wesley) on one hand, and on the other (it is believed) with such extreme mystics (both of these in America) as Kelpius of Wissahickon and Beissel of the Ephrata Cloister. It was suspected (before the question of the pseudonym came up) that the prayer (in German) made its way to North America (perhaps to Ephrata) long before it was called to Bill W.'s attention in the *Herald Tribune*. What is particularly important for our point is that this Serenity Prayer is vocal and even (by its use in the "ritual" of A.A. meetings) liturgical, but it comes out of the mystical tradition—regardless of whether it existed in the eighteenth century in anything like its present form. Also, it is in that German mystical tradition in the 1600s and earlier 1700s, out of the lands ravaged by the Thirty Years' War of Religion, that there comes revitalized the idea of the mystical spiritual brotherhood, the *Unitas Fratrum.* The Greeks had a word for it: *koinonia.*

We mentioned the "meditation" book, *Twenty-Four Hours a Day* (Richmond W. 1954). Far from being "Conference-approved" A.A. literature, we believe the book was specifically rejected when submitted to Alcoholics Anonymous when it was first completed between 1948 and 1951. But it has been sufficiently widely used by members of A.A. as to suggest that its theology—implicit and explicit—must be in accordance with the personal beliefs of a considerable number of the members of A.A., to the extent, at least, that they know what these beliefs are. When we look at the history of the book, certain points stand out, and the first of these is that the author, Richmond W., first got (temporarily) sober through the Oxford Groups, in Massachusetts in 1940–41 (when he may also have been in contact with Emmanuel's Courtenay Baylor), then was "taken drunk" again, then returned to sobriety through Alcoholics Anonymous in Florida, in his fifties. (He died in 1965 at the age of seventy-two, whether sober or not we cannot say, though we have no reason to believe not.) Richmond W. came from a stratum of Massachusetts and Rhode Island society similar to that from which came Rowland H., but I have been unable to find any direct connection between them.

The book has a reading, a meditation, and a brief prayer for every day of the year. The reading frequently quotes the "Big Book," though it also makes considerable use of earlier Oxford Groups material—the "five C's" and the "Four Absolutes," for example. The meditation is mostly (though not always) based on—but modified from—a curious book coming out of the Oxford Groups, *God Calling*, by Two Listeners (Russell 1938). I know very little of the Two Listeners except that they were two elderly women, possibly of what has been called "the Governess class," who tried to see whether they "could get such guidance as A. J. Russell reported" in his *For Sinners Only*, one of the guiding books of the Oxford Groups. One of them could (Russell 1932); the other writes that

> with my friend a very wonderful thing happened. From the first, beautiful messages were given to her by our Lord Himself, and every day from then these messages have never failed us. . . . The tender understanding of some of our Lord's messages was at times almost heart-breaking: but His loving reproofs would leave no hurt. Always, and this daily, He insisted that we should be channels of Love, Joy, and Laughter in His broken world. . . . I found this command very difficult to obey. . . . To laugh, to cheer others, to be always joyful when days were pain-wracked, nights tortured by chronic insomnia, when poverty and almost insupportable worry were our daily portion, when prayer went unanswered and God's face was veiled and fresh calamities came upon us? Still came this insistent command to love and laugh and be joy-bringers to the lives we contacted. (Russell 1938:11–12)

As the brief prayers suggested each day are based on the meditations (and even some of the readings are based on Oxford Groups material), three things are clear.

First, *Twenty-Four Hours a Day*, like *God Calling* from which it largely comes, is essentially based on private revelation, and, though it quotes the "Big Book" from time to time in the readings, is as much an Oxford Groups document as an A.A. document. (The direct personal faith of *God Calling* is, however, toned down, and references to Jesus omitted.) Second, since the primary lesson of both prayers and meditations is the need for substituting spiritual things (which the Two Listeners had, or were striving to have) for material things (which they did not), the book plays to the antimaterial (in essence, Manichaean) definitions of spirituality. Third, to the degree that there is a real connection between the readings (which have to do with sobriety) and the meditations and prayers (which have to do with salvation), the book—Manichaeanism to the contrary notwithstanding—implicitly supports an identification of the *telos* of sobriety with the *telos* of salvation. We have now twice referred to Manichaeanism, and it occurs to me that a brief definition may be in order.

By Manichaeanism we mean the doctrine, given in its full form by Mani (Manes) or Manichaeus (ca. 216–76 C.E.), that the dualities of soul and body, spirit and matter, light and dark, mind and brain, are in essence one duality, so that the more austere and ascetic one's life—the further from the life of the body—the closer one comes to releasing the light that Satan (evil) has imprisoned in our brains (what Mrs. Eddy might call Mortal Mind) and bodies. The doctrine is the most elaborately worked out early version of (Gnostic) dualism, and the word *Manichaean* is thus frequently used to describe the whole collection of beliefs involving the goodness of spirit set against the evil of the body or of material things—a collection including the beliefs of the Albigensians, Bogomils, Cathars, even the Shakers.

Technically speaking, Manichaeanism also included a significant element of astrology. There seems to be considerable anecdotal evidence, if no more, that astrology and antimaterial spirituality—the Way of the Rejection of Images, as Charles Williams would call it—are today combined in New Age "spirituality," and may thus be found in present-day A.A. meetings. Angels are likewise a presence in Manichaean, as in Christian theology. Because of the quasi-Manichaeanism of such documents as *Twenty-Four Hours a Day*, the fuller Manichaeanism of the New Age has made its way into A.A.—but we should emphasize that it was *not* implicit in A.A. from the beginning—quite the contrary, I think.

One implication of this whole discussion of the theology of alcoholism, sobriety, and A.A. is that, in some sense, the meetings of Alcoholics Anonymous may be considered meetings for the purpose of worship. As we will see in the next chapter, an early A.A. (pre-Conference and thus not Conference-approved) document (*Table Talk*, A.A. no date [ca. 1940]) implies that the original idea of an A.A. meeting was that it was a kind of worship service, defining religion as the form of the worship and spirituality as the worship. Moreover (as we shall see in Chapter 8), the long form of Tradition Three reads as follows:

Our membership ought to include all who suffer from alcoholism. Hence we may refuse none who wish to recover. Nor ought A.A. membership ever depend upon money or conformity. Any two or three alcoholics gathered together for sobriety may call themselves an A.A. group, provided that, as a group, they have no other affiliation.

It would seem to be highly unlikely that the "two or three gathered together" is an accidental phrase, since Bill W. called Sam Shoemaker, an Episcopal clergyman, one of the founders of A.A., and this phrase echoes the Episcopal *Book of Common Prayer* (1928). Moreover, in one of his early addresses to the General Service Conference of A.A., Bill W. used the phrase "sorts and conditions of men," echoing again the Episcopal *Book of Common Prayer*.

In the *Book of Common Prayer* (following the Prayer for All Sorts and Conditions of Men), we find the prayer of St. Chrysostom, used daily in Morning and Evening Prayer:

> Almighty God, who hast given us grace at this time with one accord to make our common supplications unto thee; and dost promise that when two or three are gathered together in thy Name thou wilt grant their requests; Fulfil now, O Lord, the desires and petitions of thy servants, as may be most expedient for them; granting us in this world knowledge of thy truth; and in the world to come life everlasting. *Amen.*

I think it more likely that this was the inspiration of the "two or three alcoholics gathered together" than that it was the underlying passage in Isaiah (which led to the revision of this prayer in the 1979 *Book of Common Prayer* to read "When two or three are gathered together in thy Name thou art in the midst of them"). But in either case, the implied reference to religious text or religious ritual supports the view implied by *Table Talk* and by the origins of Alcoholics Anonymous in the Oxford Groups. The early A.A. meetings were conceived of as meetings for worship, not entirely unlike meetings at the Calvary Mission, or at Jerry McAuley's Mission fifty or sixty years before.

It must be made clear that none of this means that a member of Alcoholics Anonymous must accept this theology in order to benefit from meetings of Alcoholics Anonymous. There is anecdotal evidence that members have selected as their "Higher Power" a doorknob (because it opened the door to sobriety?), a dead chicken, a tree, their sponsors (we'll get to what that means later on), and—more reasonably, I would think— the A.A. group. One A.A. member with more than twenty years' sobriety is reported to have spoken of his "Higher Power" as Charley. Substitutions of this sort for God (except the substitution of a believing group) are, of course, theological nonsense—or are they? Rationally, yes, they are. But one recalls a statement of mystical theology used as a kind of *mantra* by Charles Williams, of all things in relation to God: "This also is Thou; neither is this Thou." The dead chicken I would suggest might be taken as a kind of rebelliousness against the necessity of conversion (but then, I wasn't there). There is perhaps a clue to be found in the passage in the "Big Book" that gives rise (if indirectly) to the phrase "Higher Power"—in Step 2, "Came to believe that a power greater than ourselves could restore us to sanity." The word to look at here is *ourselves*—or, more briefly, *self*.

One of the A.A. prayers (see Chapter 7) refers to the bondage of self. Traditionally, for the mystic of any kind, the self—as an ontological spiritual entity separate from but associated with the physical body—has always been something to overcome. The strength of Manichaeus (though I think he was wrong) was that he linked this self more firmly with the physical and material than was the case with Christian theology generally: it is easier simply to deny the body than deny the self. (Mrs. Eddy comes in here also, though on the other side—there being, she says, no physical body, the self is necessarily spiritual, and, Spirit being a synonym of God, is necessarily a reflection of God.) Cartesian dualism separated the self from other ontological entities, but Descartes did not invent Cartesian dualism. The mystical answer to escaping Cartesian dualism was and is the achieving of a temporary religious or philosophic state of mind (or soul) that leaves one psychically and spiritually changed—and the less temporary the better. The Deweyite (Pragmatic) answer was and is to proclaim the self an illusion, an intellectual rather than an ontological stumbling-block. The Freudian answer is to deny, in effect, that there are other ontological entities, affirming the multifaceted self. (We must be careful, however, to make sure that we do not assume all A.A. references to the ego are to the Freudian ego.)

PRACTICING THE PRESENCE

This is beginning to sound more like psychology than theology. But the point must be made, and made again, that the keynote of the A.A. program, as we will see in the next chapter, is the search for spiritual experience (or mystical experience)—an experience that will transform the alcoholic. The end, the *telos*, of the mystical journey is the end found by Brother Lawrence, or by Kierkegaard's Knight of Faith, or by John Newton or Samuel Hopkins Hadley (or Dr. Bob S. or Bill W. or Fitz M. or Clarence S. or Jim B.)—that is, to live enlightened in the practical or physical world, passing through the universal to live in the concrete world that is ontologically superior to the spiritual. In other words, like the Lady Julian, one has a "shewing" (or "shewings") of God (in 1373 in her case) and then lives on day by day, counseling, praying, doing "the next thing" (the phrase is her contemporary Chaucer's) for the rest of one's life (in her case nearly fifty years).

The practice and process of mystical life never concludes: "maintenance activities," continued growth, and passing the message to others fill the days of mystical lives. That holds true even outside the central Christian tradition—in Zen Buddhism, certainly (so far as we can tell) in Manichaeanism. The destructive Freudian concentration on the Self is replaced by the mystic's concentration on the Other. (We repeat that one of the books recommended for reading by certain A.A. members in New York in the 1950s was Martin Buber's *I and Thou*.) The path, it has been said, becomes the destination: by concentration on the Other, one lives a spiritual life in the physical world, which, for the alcoholic, is sobriety.

It is sometimes argued that Alcoholics Anonymous steals the *experience* out of the religious or spiritual experience, saying that the alcoholic may not be aware of it when it comes: this is a way of saying that the path becomes the destination. I would argue that this presupposes something like the Johannine theology of the Incarnation we have discussed, so that alcoholics (or anyone similarly ill in mind, body, and spirit), being creatures of mind, body, and spirit, can recover by bringing their part of the Mind-in-Matter (Mind-in-Creation) more strongly into alignment with the Mind— that is, by *theosis* or *theopoiesis*. Moreover, to assert that those who are alcoholics can recover through the *koinonia*, through liturgical prayer and liturgical readings, interspersed with personal witness (*parakalein*)—in other words, through meetings of their fellowship, encouraged thereby to take the steps toward their redemption—is clearly to assert pretty much what the early Christian church asserted: the church militant brings its members to the church triumphant, indeed *is* the church triumphant viewed through the material lens of time. The church of the Spirit viewed through the lens of created being, if you like.

We should return here, for a moment, to the theology of the Oxford Group, out of which Alcoholics Anonymous came (both in Akron and in New York—and Johnny L. recalls that the first A.A. meeting he went to in Philadelphia was chaired by an Oxford Grouper, a fact to which he, as a Presbyterian elder, strongly objected). Mercadante has noted (1996:56–57) that the Oxford Group got its start on college campuses (and especially the "rough heavy drinking" campus at Penn State, where Frank Buchman was a YMCA collegiate evangelist): alcoholic drinking was indeed one of the principal concerns of the early Buchmanites.

Now

a key method of the Oxford Group movement was to intrigue the imagination before appealing to the will. To that end, nearly every gathering featured the personal stories of individuals, formerly beset by intractable sins, who had become "changed" by submitting to Christ. . . . A grouper who had overcome a problem such as drunkenness would sit alongside a newcomer known to have the same difficulty. At other times, Groupers would be sent out to confront, through the sharing of stories, a notorious troublemaker at a school or university. (p. 56)

The difference from A.A. (as A.A. developed) was not so much that the Oxford Group opposed concentration on drinking as that they opposed concentration on any one specific sin (or disease condition) to the exclusion of others—and, of course, that they believed this was a problem of the will. What brought hope to Dr. Bob when the Oxford Group approach had not worked was the idea that, because of a physical condition (alcoholism)—an illness, if you like—his will was powerless over alcohol (which is Step 1).

We ought to look here again—briefly—at the matter of Grace. The phrase "there but for the Grace of God" has come to mean, apparently, something like "but for the providence of God"—somehow God provided an answer, or kept the alcoholic safe from harm. That this happens (if we accept the testimony of the alcoholics themselves) is undoubtedly true. But I do not think this is what the phrase "but for the Grace of God" originally conveyed. Remember John Bradford, who had committed a capital crime and was brought to confess and make restitution by an evangelical sermon preached by Bishop Latimer. He suddenly saw the truth. The Grace of God rushed in upon him. That was the reason he was not being hauled away to execution like the unfortunates whose situation occasioned his use of the phrase. It has been pointed out to me that there is a description of this kind of blinding Grace in the Book of Daniel (10:vii–x) in the Old Testament (as well, of course, as with Saul on the road to Damascus, but this is fuller):

> And I Daniel alone saw the vision; for the men that were with me saw not the vision; but a great quaking fell upon them, so that they fled to hide themselves. Therefore I was left alone, and saw this great vision, and there remained no strength in me; for my comeliness was turned in me into corruption, and I retained no strength. Yet heard I the voice of his words: and when I heard the voice of his words, then was I in a deep sleep on my face, and my face toward the ground. And behold, an hand touched me, which set me upon my knees, and upon the palms of my hands.

This is, I believe, what Augustine called *prevenient* Grace: it is also apparently what Duns Scotus, commenting on Augustine, called *irresistible* Grace. It is the free gift of God, and, as we noted, it is *not*, by itself, generally *sufficient* for salvation (or, in our case here, sobriety). It can become *efficacious* Grace (sufficient for sobriety) if the recipient works to convert it into *habitual* or *sanctifying* Grace (the Thomistic distinction is from *actual* Grace, which in this case would be both *prevenient* and *irresistible*): the mode for this conversion would be through the sacrament of the Word (through meetings and reading the "Big Book" liturgically). It would then be a *congruous* Grace.

The Oxford Group approach—we may argue—did not permit the conversion into *sanctifying* and *congruous* (and *subsequent*) Grace, but the exercise of the Twelve Steps does. Of course, it is not necessary for any alcoholic or observer of Alcoholics Anonymous to accept this medieval theology of Grace, but if one is interested in the theology of sobriety in Alcoholics Anonymous, this puts it into traditional theological terms. What is important for our concerns here is that this seizure by Grace is toward the self-surrender end of the Jamesian spectrum—and, more immediately, that the Oxford Group idea of "intriguing the imagination before appealing to the will" is generally, at best, irrelevant to this process.

I am aware that this begs an important question. The Oxford Group, the Washingtonians, Alcoholics Anonymous, all use personal testimony to involve—if not always precisely to intrigue—the imagination of the person coming in. Doesn't this work? There is an A.A. saying (not a slogan) that Alcoholics Anonymous is for people who want it, not for people who need it. Recall the medieval Franciscan Alexander of Hales, who defined prevenient Grace as the general presence of God. That is enough to start the process. The process involves the sacrament of the Word, and it also (and this is Bill W.'s gift—and partly Dr. Bob's) involves the practice of the presence of God (Brother Lawrence's phrase)—in the Twelve Steps of Alcoholics Anonymous.

JOYOUS COMPANIONS IN CONVERSION AND GRACE

Before we look at these Steps, there is one further point that ought to be emphasized. Because we are using, as part of our scientific research program, a form of the Johannine theology of the Incarnation, we may be saying, in effect, that the hereditary predisposition toward alcoholism— that is, Alcoholism(2)—is a material and temporal analogue, or even a material and temporal equivalent, to humankind's hereditary predisposition toward sin. Now, humankind's hereditary predisposition toward sin is what is known, in the study of theology, as the condition of Original Sin. The sacrament of Baptism was regarded by virtually all Christians (up to the time of the Anabaptists) as making it possible for infants to begin their temporal lives freed from the burden of punishment for that sin, but not freed from the condition.

As soon as a human being reaches the age of reason, the condition begins to assert itself and requires continuing action: there is no once-and-for-all single action that ends it. Instead, what is needed is other sacramental action, including, particularly, the sacrament of the Eucharist or Holy Communion. There are other sacraments, as we have noted, that were accepted up to the Protestant Reformation—and still more, including the sacrament of the Word, that were accepted in the early church. The parallel to the process of Alcoholics Anonymous, in the Twelve Steps, would seem to be apparent. Admission to Alcoholics Anonymous, in the early days, was very much like adult baptism, or like the ceremony of knighthood.

This brings up a matter that—I think—might reasonably be mentioned here. There is a passage, frequently quoted by members of Alcoholics Anonymous, to the effect that recovered (or even recovering) alcoholics should be "happy, joyous, and free." The middle word of the three is uncommon, and I believe it may have at least a quasi-religious connotation. There are places where Bill W. refers to Alcoholics Anonymous as a company (also, of course, as a society), and of course the French word for a company (like our "X and Y, Inc.") is Société Anonyme (the Société Anonyme of Alcoholics, for example?) It is purely speculation, and there may be another reason (or even several) for the use of the word, but *joyous* is a French-sounding word (as in *Joyeux Noel*), and the most common reference for joyous in English, for those in Bill W.'s generation who were brought up on King Arthur and the Round Table, would be to the Company of Joyous Garde, the castle from which the knights went out to seek the Holy Grail. And then came back to tell their stories. I suggest there may have been, in Bill W.'s mind, a certain religious (or spiritual) aura around the word *joyous*.

On the basis of our model, the *telos* of sobriety in Alcoholics Anonymous would parallel (and might of course be a part of) the *telos* of salvation in the church. Alcoholics Anonymous, like the church (but also like the Company of Joyous Garde), would then precisely be a salvific ("saving") *koinonia*. How does the salvation come about? That is, after all, the theological question. The sacrament of the Word may bring the alcoholic to freedom from his continuing burden of being an alcoholic in the Alcoholism(2) sense, his precondition; it certainly makes him free from the burden of past alcoholic behavior (Alcoholism[1]). A.A., with its Pietist leanings, seems to claim only the second. But the sacrament of water and the Spirit (Baptism), in Catholic (including Episcopal) doctrine, makes the sinner free from the burden of Original Sin, the precondition. Let us look once more, briefly, at the matter of Grace, summarizing what we said before, and then briefly and specifically link them with what goes on in A.A.

Prevenient Grace is the free gift of God, entirely unmerited, antecedent to conversion: it is that form of *actual* Grace that leads men to sanctification before the sacraments. *Subsequent* Grace occurs if God and humankind cooperate after conversion. *Prevenient* Grace is not sufficient for salvation, while *subsequent* Grace is sufficient for salvation. *Efficacious* Grace is *subsequent* to conversion. Whether it is efficacious (that is, whether it works) depends on the congruity of the Grace, which is God's choice: it is conferred by the sacraments, including (as late as the twelfth century) the Lord's Prayer—and even other written (and therefore spoken) formulae.

Habitual or *sanctifying* Grace, we remember, is the gift of God inhering in the soul, by which men are enabled to perform righteous acts: it is conveyed in the sacraments (or a sacrament). *Actual* Grace, which may exist in the unbaptized and even the unbelieving, is a motion of the soul toward God, bestowed by God ad hoc for the production of some good act. Thirteenth-century followers of St. Francis suggested that even the unbelieving could, by initiating some movement toward virtue, merit *congruous* Grace; they identified *prevenient* Grace with the "general assistance" (*assistentia generalis,* the general presence) of God; and they denied *irresistible* Grace, thereby leaving free will open to all. (Is this perhaps the "free" of "happy, joyous, and free?")

So what happens—using these distinctions and definitions of Grace—when an alcoholic is brought into the *koinonia* (company or fellowship or society or communion) of Alcoholics Anonymous? We may say he has received the *actual* Grace to bring him there ("a motion of the soul toward God, bestowed by God for the production ad hoc of some good act"); by that *actual* Grace he may stay in the general presence of God, and there by the same Grace cooperate with God so that he continues in *subsequent* Grace, which by a sacrament (or sacraments) is *efficacious,* because *congruous* (by God's choice); then it will grow (or he will grow), through practice, into *habitual* or *sanctifying* Grace. The Franciscans, following Francis's contemporary, Alexander of Hales, would have us believe that the individual might himself initiate the first movement toward Grace—but it might even so be Grace that brought him to that.

All this, of course, is a progress of the soul, but (in the words of the Athanasian Creed, perhaps the best statement of the Johannine doctrine of the Incarnation), "the reasonable soul and flesh is one man" as "God and man is one Christ"—one altogether, not by confusion of substance, but by unity of person. Which is why Grace, which is spiritual, is likewise of the flesh, and the *telos* of sobriety is of mind, body, and spirit. One point emphasized by the distinction and definition of the various types of Grace is that there is always room for choice along the way. One may—but one need not—pass from *actual* to *subsequent* Grace. One may—but one may not—receive the sacrament of the Word by which the Grace is *efficacious.* One may—but one may frequently decide not to—practice the presence of God into *habitual* Grace.

One other point. We have mentioned the matter of witness. If the Johannine doctrine is applicable, then by the spirit that exists between and among members of the *koinonia* is witness to (*parakalein*) the fact that the body of the fellowship is engaged toward the *teleios* of *theopoiesis*, as with the phrase of Athanasius (again)—"He was made Man so that we might be made God" (*theopoiethomen*). But that Man has already gone to the Father, and as we have noted, the logic of the situation is that the followers (in any *koinonia* so dedicated, so consecrated, so hallowed) must themselves become the incarnation of the Logos. The witness, so to speak, testifies to the presence of the Word.

Let me reemphasize that it is not necessary that anyone reading this book accept Johannine theology, or my conjectures on Joyous Garde—or even, as we remarked, that they read this chapter. But the model presented here makes theological sense of what goes on—especially both the liturgical and the ritual reading (they are not the same)—in a meeting of Alcoholics Anonymous, as well (I think) as making sense of the program generally. And since the cofounders (and their colleagues) believed that belief in God was a necessary ground for the program—in fact, that God *was* the ground for the program—and that the Twelve Steps were spiritual exercises, an acceptable theology (beyond a kind of "not-God" psychology) would seem to be a good idea.

And it is time now to turn to those Steps.

7 ~

The Twelve Steps of Alcoholics Anonymous

WE MAY BEGIN OUR DISCUSSION OF THE WAY A.A. IS PERCEIVED AS WORKING—and, especially, was perceived in its early years—with the often-heard injunction, "Don't drink and go to meetings!" There have been, I believe, many changes in what might be called unessential A.A. ritual: for example, at the end of many A.A. meetings now, those present link hands and stand in a circle to say the Lord's Prayer (or sometimes the Serenity Prayer). The Lord's Prayer for closing the meeting has been a part of A.A. from the very beginnings, and might even be considered essential (apparently was, in the view of the cofounders), but the linking of hands seems to be a California custom, passed to the rest of A.A. at the 1975 International Convention in Denver. The addition (with swinging hands) of "Keep coming back! It works if you work it!" is believed by most I have asked to have come in from rehabilitation centers and not really to be part of A.A. Some members occasionally vary this with "Don't drink and go to meetings!" Members of long sobriety I have spoken with regard this whole ritualistic incantation as resembling the vain repetitions of the heathen inveighed against in Matthew 6:7, which may (or may not) cast some doubt on the antiquity (in A.A. terms) of the phrase "Don't drink and go to meetings!" But it seems to be a widely quoted summary of what A.A. is about.

Indeed, I have heard it said in meetings of Alcoholics Anonymous that the underlying message of A.A.'s First Step—"We admitted we were powerless over alcohol—that our lives had become unmanageable"—is precisely "Don't drink and go to meetings!" I am not able to trace with any certainty the connection between this message and the actual words of the First Step. The pamphlet *Table Talk* (published in Akron very early in the 1940s and widely circulated, though having no official force within A.A.) does, however, make these suggestions: (1) that attending "the regular Group meeting each week without fail" is part of the decision—to drink or not to drink—that all alcoholics must make as part of their admission that they are alcoholics, and (2) that it "is the experience of A.A. that once a person becomes a pathological 'alcoholic' drinker" the only alternatives are total abstinence or continued chronic active alcoholism.

If full data were available, we might be able to trace the exact historical connections between the First Step and "Don't drink and go to meetings!" Here it would seem that "Go to meetings!" was a part of "Don't drink!" very early on, though perhaps not the most important part (it is fifth on a list of twelve resolutions "to do something about it" in the pamphlet). This interpretation of the First Step as meaning primarily "Don't drink and go to meetings!" would now appear (on my very limited experience) to be virtually ubiquitous—which may suggest that there have been significant changes in Alcoholics Anonymous over the years. But this book does not deal, except tangentially, with those changes: that is the business of another book and almost certainly another author. The phrase, so far as I can determine, does not appear in A.A.'s printed literature, although a contrasting summary heard in some meetings does appear in the literature, "Trust God [or "trust in God"] and clean house!" (Bill W. et al. 1976:98).

This brings up a matter of some importance. Our inquiry, as I said, does not deal with the ways in which the A.A. of today represents a significant shift from the A.A. of 1939 (when the "Big Book" was first published). What we are principally looking at here is the A.A. created by Bill W. and his confrères, just after Repeal of Prohibition, and guided and shepherded by Bill W. until his death in January 1971 at the age of seventy-five. All social systems necessarily change and grow through the incorporation of new diversity (which produces new diversity within the system). It may be that A.A. has gone wrong, as some members suggest. It may be that it has not. As of 2004, we have new genetic knowledge and new biochemical knowledge and even new knowledge of the invention of tradition and of the modes of operation of a *koinonia*. But what we have learned—and the scientific research program formed from it here—fundamentally supports what Bill W. knew in his vision and what he created.

What Bill W. created in the golden moment was not only Alcoholics Anonymous in 1935 and the "Big Book" in 1939, but also and specifically the Twelve Steps in the "Big Book" in (1938-)1939. What he created not long thereafter (1946) was the Twelve Traditions that are designed for the continuance of the fellowship—and eventually the *Twelve Concepts for World Service* (1962) that are designed to amplify and explain the practical use of the Twelve Traditions and the so-called service structure of A.A. Both the Traditions and the Concepts (though these latter very briefly and incompletely) come in the next chapter. Now, with all this—and all that we have discussed in earlier chapters—for background, let us take a look at these Twelve Steps of Alcoholics Anonymous. These are the means for the "conversion" that Alcoholics Anonymous seeks in its members. What are they and what do they mean?

SIX STEPS AND TWELVE STEPS

In the beginning, there were six steps, perhaps belonging to the Oxford Groups, though not, to my knowledge, in the Oxford Group literature, at least in this form. In the form developed by Dr. Bob S. in Akron in the period 1935–37, the six steps were these:

(1) Complete deflation;
(2) Dependence and guidance from a Higher Power;
(3) Moral inventory;
(4) Confession;
(5) Restitution;
(6) Continued work with other alcoholics. ("Big Book" 1976:292)

(There is another version of the Six Steps, from New York and in the hand of Bill W.—we shall come to these momentarily.) By 1938–39, when the "Big Book" was published, these Akron six steps had become twelve (taken from Chapter 5 of the "Big Book"):

(1) We admitted we were powerless over alcohol—that our lives had become unmanageable.
(2) Came to believe that a Power greater than ourselves could restore us to sanity.
(3) Made a decision to turn our will and our lives over to the care of God *as we understood Him.*
(4) Made a searching and fearless moral inventory of ourselves;
(5) Admitted to God, to ourselves, and to another human being the exact nature of our wrongs.
(6) Were entirely ready to have God remove all these defects of character.
(7) Humbly asked Him to remove our shortcomings.
(8) Made a list of all persons we had harmed, and became willing to make amends to them all.
(9) Made direct amends to such people wherever possible, except when to do so would injure them or others.
(10) Continued to take personal inventory, and when we were wrong, promptly admitted it.
(11) Sought through prayer and meditation to improve our conscious contact with God *as we understood Him*, praying only for the knowledge of His will for us and the power to carry that out.
(12) Having had a spiritual awakening as the result of these steps, we tried to carry this message to alcoholics, and practice these principles in all our affairs. (1939, 1955, 1976, 2001:59–60, reprinted by permission)

Now these twelve expand the original six Akron steps in an interesting way. Clearly, Step 1 is (and part of new Step 2 may be) a version of old Step

1 (deflation), Step 4 a version of old Step 3 (moral inventory—but Step 10 is moral inventory also), Step 5 a version of old Step 4 (confession—which may also include a little of Step 10), Steps 8 and 9 a two-part version of old Step 5, and Step 12 an expanded version of old Step 6. But old Step 2 (dependence and guidance from a Higher Power) has its new counterparts in Step 2 (in part), Step 3, Step 6, Step 7, and Step 11. On the question of dependence, deflation (the old Step 1) includes an acknowledging of dependence, while the old Step 2 involves *accepting* (or *welcoming*) that dependence. (And welcoming that dependence, as we will see later, is part of humility, in at leasts its more Protestant definition.)

Whether the line between old Step 1 and old Step 2 is the same as the line between new Step 1 and new Step 2 is not clear. What is clear is that, wherever the line between Step 1 and Step 2 in either version, the *acceptance* of dependence and of guidance from a Higher Power spreads out through the new Steps 2, 3, 5 (in the confession to God), 6, 7, and 11. The Twelve Steps do not simply break each of the old six into two parts—make the decision and then do it, though this is the pattern for Steps 8 and 9 of the Twelve Steps (from the old Step 5). Instead, in this case, they break dependence on and guidance from a Higher Power (i.e., God) into five steps and part of a sixth, and then include its result (a "spiritual awakening") in Step 12. Why?

Before we look toward an answer for that question, we may note another version of the Six Steps, this one coming from Bill W. in New York. This New York version (I have a xerographic copy of an original in Bill W.'s handwriting) appears in an article by one Ray R. published on the Internet by Bill C. in September 1995:

- We admitted we were licked.
- We got honest with ourselves.
- We talked it over with another person.
- We made amends to those we had harmed.
- We tried to carry this message to others with no thought of reward.
- We prayed to whatever God we thought there was.

(Taken from the website www.recovery.org/aa/misc/oxford.html by the author on 9 March 1998.)

An alternative version, also from Bill's papers, is found in Dick B.:

(1) Admitted hopeless;
(2) Got honest with self;
(3) Got honest with another;
(4) Made amends;
(5) Helped others without demand;
(6) Prayed to God as you understand him. (1998)

In either form, these may well be considered the agnostic's six steps, and they seem to come from a time when Bill W. had withdrawn from his very early heavily evangelistic attitude and was playing down God's participation in the whole business. We could, however, take these as roughly equivalent to the Akron six steps in a different order, and without God involved till the end: in other words, the New York six are roughly the Akron six in the order 1, 3, 4, 5, 6, 2.

This may reflect what Bill W. had been told early on in his attempts to help other alcoholics, that he was too much the preacher and evangelist: here are Dr. Silkworth's comments to Bill when Bill said he couldn't get his "pigeons" to stay sober:

> You're preaching at these fellows, Bill, although no one ever preached at you. Turn your strategy around. Remember, Professor [William] James insisted . . . "deflation at great depth" is the foundation of most spiritual experiences like your own. Give your new contacts the medical business. (as reported by Sam Shoemaker's assistant, Irving Harris 1978:207–8)

Giving the new contacts the medical business was precisely what Bill W. did with Dr. Bob.

GOD AND THE "HIGHER POWER"

Be that as it may, there is no doubt some of the early members of A.A. had a great deal of trouble with identifying the "Higher Power" with some idea of God. Particularly this was true of Hank P. (whose story is in the first edition of the "Big Book" but who apparently did not stay sober) and Jim B. As we noted above, the story Jim B. told is that he was responsible for adding the salvo "as we understood him" to Steps 3 and 11. It is partly for that reason that one of the early members we looked at in Chapter 2 was Jim B. We also looked briefly at Clarence S., a Roman Catholic who was apparently in part responsible for the separation of A.A. (at least in Cleveland) from the Oxford Groups.

We propose to look first at the Jim B. salvo, before going on to see what these Twelve Steps are and were intended to be. After looking at what they are or were intended to be, we will try to see how they may be (1) a usable manual for cognitive psychotherapy, (2) an order or rule (in the sense of the Benedictine rule) for the conduct of improved spiritual life, (3) guides to clearing the decks for more effective mutual help in a mutual-help society, or (4) a perhaps indifferently understood but occasionally internalized guide to putting the plug in the jug (not drinking)—or a combination of any or all of these. Before doing that, I would call attention to the fact that Carl Jung advised Rowland H. in the early 1930s that the only hope for his release from alcoholism was a spiritual experience (see Chapter 2 and the text of the letters, most conveniently in "The Bill W.–Carl Jung Letters;" Bill W. 1989:276–81). But Jung himself denigrated the need for specific faith, thought that "union with God" was simply the medieval language for "oneness of the self" or *individuation*—and in fact, by most present-day standards, could not be said to believe in God, though he most emphatically did believe in a Higher Power. (Perhaps, as his letter to Bill suggests, he did believe in God, or came to, but was being careful about what he said.)

Interestingly, when Bill W. was reflecting on the purposes of the Twelve Steps (and of the Twelve Traditions, as we will see in Chapter 8), in 1948, he wrote these lines: "The recovery steps would make each individual AA [abbreviation for a member of Alcoholics Anonymous] whole and one with God; the Twelve Points of Tradition would make us one with each other and the world around us" ([1948] 1989:94). It would seem that making us "whole" and making us "one with God" are in Jung's terms simply two ways of saying the same thing—"union with God" would be the medieval way of saying "oneness of the self" so that this is a doublet like "friends and neighbors" or "let and hindrance." God as Bill W. understood him, at this time, was pretty much still the same God his friend, Ebby T., had brought him in the late fall of 1934:

> My friend suggested what then seemed a novel idea. He said, *"Why don't you choose your own conception of God?"* That statement hit me hard. It melted the icy intellectual mountain in whose shadow I had lived and shivered many years. I stood in the sunlight at last. *It was only a matter of being willing to believe in a Power greater than myself. Nothing more was required of me to make my beginning.* (1939, 1955, 1976, 2001:12)

Ebby T. had his conversion from Rowland H., who had his, in essence, from Carl Jung.

Interestingly also, A.A. literature, including *The Grapevine*—the A.A. journal or newsletter—lists these steps as Copyright 1939 by A.A. World Services, although they appear in the first (1939) edition of the "Big Book," now out of copyright. They are quoted in this book by permission of A.A. World Services. These steps, as we have remarked, were expanded from a preliminary list—or more than one list—of six steps (not the same as the six steps coming from the Oxford Group), partly (but not mostly) by breaking apart the decision to take a step from taking the step. The Twelve Steps are the basic A.A. process of recovery, and are sometimes the focus of special meetings or special groups discussing the Steps (or the Steps and

Traditions). Some sponsors tell their "pigeons" that they should go to at least one step meeting a week (though this seems to have been more common thirty or forty years ago than now.) The process of taking these Steps, whose goal is a "spiritual awakening," is often called "working the Steps," in some cases (I have heard) with the addition "till the Steps work you." These Twelve Steps have become so ubiquitous in the "recovery world," that they are the model for quite a number of other "Twelve Step" groups.

There are therefore quite a number of commentaries and guides to these Twelve Steps, but very few of them are recognized by Alcoholics Anonymous. Bill W.'s book, *Twelve Steps and Twelve Traditions* (hereafter abbreviated as the *12&12*), represents (1952/53:5–9, 21–125) the surviving cofounder's thinking on the Twelve Steps around 1950–52, but it is really a set of historical sketches and meditations rather than a guide. The material in the "Big Book" Chapter 5, "How It Works," Chapter 6, "Into Action," and Chapter 7, "Working With Others," can serve—I believe some members say, *should* serve—as guide to taking these steps: Steps 1–4 are in Chapter 5, Steps 5–11 in Chapter 6, Step 12 in Chapter 7. These chapters have been unchanged since 1939, and while it is certainly not clear to me to what degree current processes in A.A. reflect the cofounders' experience or belief, we can certainly set out what apparently those beliefs and that experience may have been. Here we may be aided by *Table Talk: A Guide to the Twelve Steps of Alcoholics Anonymous* (A.A., Akron, no date). The version I have is taken from the Internet (*www.twistedserpent. com/archives/tabltalk.htm*, downloaded 10 March 1998); the text is not guaranteed, but it will help us see what the Steps meant in Akron around 1940. The *12&12* gives a good clue as to what they meant in New York in the later 1940s.

THE FIRST THREE STEPS

It is apparently quite often said in A.A. that the First Step is the only one that "we have to work perfectly every day"—a point made by Bill W. in the "Big Book" (1976:82). It is sometimes also said that the First Step has not two but at least *three* main parts—not only *powerlessness* over alcohol and *unmanageability* of life, but also the key word *admission* (and, some say, the word *we*). The admission, I take it, is the thing that must be done, that must be worked perfectly every day. Bill W. summarized his discussion of the First Step in the *Twelve Steps and Twelve Traditions* as follows: "Who cares to admit complete defeat? Admission of powerlessness is the first step in liberation. Relation of humility to sobriety. Mental obsession plus physical allergy. Why must every A.A. hit bottom?" (1952/53:5). In the "Big Book,"

the first two steps are summarized in the "a-b-c" of A.A. as "three pertinent ideas": "(a) That we were alcoholic and could not manage our own
lives, (b) That probably no human power could have relieved our alcoholism, (c) That God could and would if he were sought" (1939, 1955, 1976,
2001:60). As (b) and (c) are clearly a divided form of Step 2, the original
summary form of Step 1 was "[we admitted] that we were alcoholic and
could not manage our own lives."

The *Table Talk* pamphlet spends considerable time suggesting ways in
which the "prospect" can find out what an alcoholic is and whether he
qualifies. I believe some drug and alcohol counselors with A.A. experience (possibly particularly in the Midwest) tell their clients to write a narrative of their drinking life as part of their preparation for the First Step, or
as part of working the First Step, and sponsors there tell their "pigeons"
the same. The chief requirements for taking this Step have been said to be
willingness, honesty, and open-mindedness (W.H.O.), though Narcotics
Anonymous (possibly reflecting A.A. culture from the 1970s) makes it
honesty, open-mindedness, and willingness (H.O.W.), and the early *Table
Talk* pamphlet makes it willingness, open-mindedness, and honesty, which
provides no useful acronym.

In the "Big Book," Bill W. briefly recounts the life of the alcoholic as Step
1 forces him to realize what it has been: this is the "unmanageable" life:

> Each person is like an actor who wants to run the whole show; is forever try-
> ing to arrange the lights, the ballet, the scenery and the rest of the players in
> his own way. If his arrangements would only stay put, if only people would
> do as he wished, the show would be great. . . . What usually happens? The
> show doesn't come off very well. He begins to think life doesn't treat him
> right. He decides to exert himself more. He becomes . . . still more gracious
> or demanding, as the case may be. Still the play does not suit him. . . . He is
> sure that other people are more to blame. He becomes angry, indignant, self-
> pitying. . . . Our actor is self-centered, ego-centric, as people like to call it
> nowadays. . . . Selfishness—self-centeredness! That, we think, is the root of
> our troubles. . . . They arise out of ourselves, and the alcoholic is an extreme
> example of self-will run riot. ("Big Book" 1976:60–62)

(I have been told that in the late 1940s and early 1950s, the phrase "self-
will run riot" was so well-known to members of A.A. in and around New
York City that it was abbreviated S.W.R.R. and sometimes referred to
when outsiders were present as "riding the South Western Rail Road"—
also that there was an A.A. member in New Jersey who was a model rail-
roader, whose layout was the S.W.R.R.)

Note that there is in this summary no reference to powerlessness over
alcohol, except to suggest that (if this powerlessness over alcohol is equivalent to alcoholism) it combines with egocentricity to produce the *extreme*

case. This should be put beside the fact that, according to Bill W., it was knowledge of the alcoholic's *physical* powerlessness over alcohol that was the *spiritual* key in his approach to Dr. Bob, as he recounts in the story he told over the years, including telling it to the U.S. Congress.

Bill W. continues the stage-manager metaphor in discussing Step 2:

> First of all, we had to quit playing God. It didn't work. Next, we decided that hereafter in this drama of life, God was going to be our Director. He is the Principal; we are His agents. . . . When we sincerely took such a position, all sorts of remarkable things followed. . . . Established on such a footing we became less and less interested in ourselves, our little plans and designs. . . . As we felt new power flow in, as we enjoyed peace of mind . . . as we became conscious of His presence, . . . we were reborn. (ibid.:62–63)

This Second Step as listed in the "Big Book" is "Came to believe that a Power greater than ourselves could restore us to sanity" (ibid.:59). We have noted the two-part summary of this in the "a-b-c" in the "Big Book": "That probably no human power could have relieved our alcoholism; that God could and would if he were sought" (ibid.:60). And we have noted the summary of the ongoing process of Step 2 in Bill W.'s words quoted in the last paragraph. In the *12&12*, Bill W. gives a summary of his later (1952) comment and meditation on this step:

> What can we believe in? A.A. does not demand belief; Twelve Steps are only suggestions [comment reported from more than one A.A. meeting, "like pulling the ripcord on the parachute when you jump—that's only a suggestion"]. Importance of an open mind. Variety of ways to faith. Substitution of A.A. as Higher Power. Plight of the disillusioned. Roadblocks of indifference and prejudice. Lost faith found in A.A. Problems of intellectuality and self-sufficiency. Negative and positive thinking. Self-righteousness. Defiance is an outstanding characteristic of alcoholics. Step Two is a rallying point to sanity. Right relation to God. (1952/53:5)

This idea of the rallying point suggests a comment heard at an A.A. meeting:

> The first time I read Step 2, I thought it said "*Only* a Power greater than ourselves could restore us to sanity"—but it doesn't say that: it says "a Power greater than ourselves *could* restore us to sanity." It's a message of hope, not of limitation.

To this may be added the comment on Step 2 from *Table Talk*, remembering that this pamphlet (which is not Conference-approved A.A. literature) is quoted only as an indication of the way the steps were interpreted in Akron in the early days of A.A., around 1940:

Our drinking experience has shown that (1) as we strayed away from the normal social side of life, our minds became confused and we strayed away from the normal mental side of life; (2) an abnormal mental condition is certainly not sanity in the accepted sense of the word. We have acquired or developed a mental illness. Our study of A.A. shows that (a) in the mental or tangible side of life we have lost touch with, or ignored, or have forgotten the spiritual values that give us the dignity of man as differentiated from the animal. We have fallen back on the material things of life and these have failed us. [Note the almost Manichaean view here, and the similarity to *God Calling* (Russell 1938).] We have been groping in the dark; (b) no human agency, no science or art, has been able to solve the alcoholic problem, so we turn to the spiritual for guidance. Therefore, we "Came to believe that a Power greater than ourselves could restore us to sanity." We must believe with great faith. Faith will sustain us when we do not understand.

It sounds like Bill's mentor Sam Shoemaker: "Surrender to Him, if necessary, in total ignorance of Him. Far more important that you touch Him than that you understand Him at first" (1934:128). We will come back to this in discussing Step 3. One point we might mention here: Step 2 uses the phrase "restore us to sanity" and the commentary in *Table Talk* remarks that "an abnormal mental condition is certainly not sanity"—also, in the commentary by Bill W. in the text of the *12&12*, he writes "Sanity is defined as 'soundness of mind.' Yet no alcoholic, soberly analyzing his destructive behavior . . . can claim 'soundness of mind' for himself . . . and every A.A. meeting is an assurance that God will restore us to sanity if we rightly relate ourselves to Him" (1952/53:33). But in no place in Conference-approved A.A. literature (or even what we might call the pseudoepigraphical literature from the early days, like *Table Talk*) have I been able to find the word *insanity* used, though I have heard at open meetings a definition of *alcoholic insanity*, as consisting in continuing to do the same thing (drink) and expecting different results. In other words, alcoholic thinking is not sane, but it was not regarded by the cofounders or in the early days as insane. Rather, simply, as unsound or not sane. A personality somewhat out of kilter, but not a psychosis.

The difference might well be that personality problems, even those which reflect a heritable (or genetic) condition, would not be primarily treatable by medication, whereas psychotic conditions (psychoses) resulting from chemical imbalances might be. In Chapter 5 of the "Big Book," Bill W. writes, "Resentment is the 'number one' offender. It destroys more alcoholics than anything else. From it stem all forms of spiritual disease, for we have been not only mentally and physically ill, we have been spiritually sick" (1939, 1955, 1976, 2001:64). Note that alcoholism is here defined as mental and physical illness, and spiritual disease or sickness. To be sure, Bill W. had a habit of multiplying synonyms (see Step 5 ["wrongs"], Step 6 ["these defects of character"], Step 7 ["our shortcomings"]), but I think it may be important that only the spiritual man is described as having a sickness (disease), and, as we have noted already, the Oxford Groups, following the ante-Nicene fathers of the church, spoke of sin as spiritual disease.

If the spiritual disease of alcoholism is, quite precisely, the spiritual disease called sin, then it would follow that the principal manifestations of this disease in action would be the so-called seven deadly sins, pride, greed, lust, anger, gluttony, envy, and sloth. And when Bill W. discusses the process of making a "searching and fearless moral inventory of ourselves" in his summary on Step 4 in the *12&12* (1952/53:46), it is significant that he chooses, as appropriate categorizations of the alcoholic's defects, precisely this list. We will come to this point again when we discuss Step 4 below, but for the moment this can be taken at least as an indication that one of the cofounders (the *less* religious one) thought of the spiritual disease (or "malady") of alcoholism as the disease of sin. In case there should be any doubt about this in light of Bill's word "reborn" (ibid.:63), we might note that he recommends at least certain of the seven virtues as the ground for the fight against alcoholism, at least prudence and fortitude among the four cardinal virtues, and faith, hope, and charity, the three theological virtues.

Getting back to the mental part of the equation, we believe it is important that the alcoholic (1939, 1955, 1976, 2001:64) is said to be *mentally ill* with alcoholism. Not insanity, but mental illness. As we noted, not a *psychosis*, but a personality condition not necessarily to be treated with medication—indeed, as some A.A. members might say, at least in the beginning, necessarily *not* to be treated with medication. In this it would differ from, say, manic depressive psychosis (now usually called bipolar affective disorder), which might be properly treated with lithium carbonate, thus righting an imbalance in what used to be called the body's "essential salts." More recent psychotropic pharmaceuticals would seem to be much more an open question here. One longtime A.A. member, Clancy I., speaking at open A.A. meetings, has said that he would tell anyone he sponsored in A.A. that he "would need to find a new sobriety date" if he had used Prozac. This assertion has apparently been the subject of quite considerable debate within Alcoholics Anonymous. I have tried to find out what the cofounders might have thought about this. It turns out that this is relevant to Steps 1–3.

According to the A.A. biography of Bill W. (A.A. 1984), the cardinal point about using drugs to combat alcoholism was this: if the drug specifically aided (and was designed to aid) in ego deflation, thereby promoting a spiritual experience, it might be considered an adjunct to the work of A.A., while if it was simply an amethystine (anti-alcohol drug) or a substitute (like Valium), taking it might (amethystine) or would (substitute) be contrary to the A.A. program, and most particularly to Steps 1–3 and the "a-b-c" of Chapter 5 in the "Big Book" (ibid.:370–76, my summary). Bill himself experimented with LSD in the mid- to late 1950s, with ego deflation and bypassing the ego in mind. He did not believe it compromised his sobriety. I quote from a letter to Sam Shoemaker in June 1958:

> [There is] the probability that prayer, fasting, meditation, despair, and other conditions that predispose one to classical mysticism do have their chemical components. These chemical conditions aid in shutting out normal ego drives, and to [that] extent, they do open the doors to a wider perception. If one assumes that this is so—and there is already some biochemical evidence of it—then one cannot be too concerned whether these mystic results are encouraged by fasting or whether they are brought on by [other means]. (ibid.:375)

But within a year of writing that letter, Bill had withdrawn from the LSD experiments—principally because his position as the surviving cofounder of A.A. made him uniquely vulnerable to having what he did confused with what A.A. believed. Whether LSD was a suitable vehicle for ego deflation within A.A. is not the point here: the point here is the distinction between chemical help in being able to get started on the Twelve Steps, and chemical help essentially designed to replace reliance on the Twelve Steps. (Even Mrs. Eddy wrote that a practitioner may take a painkiller if the pain is so great as to preclude the practice.) The same distinction would seem to apply when a manic depressive takes lithium carbonate—though it might well not apply when the same manic depressive takes a mood-elevating drug. Moreover, taking LSD as a recreational drug would also seem to fall on the wrong side of the fence (though, once again, this is *my* extrapolation from what Bill W. said in the letter to Sam Shoemaker). The point is that it is unnecessary to replace alcohol medically if it can be replaced by spiritual means—*spiritus contra spiritum*. Doing so, in fact (in medical terms), would be strongly contraindicated.

Bill W.'s views on drugs do not have any formal value in determining A.A.'s views on drugs, since there is no such thing as A.A.'s views on anything except alcoholism, not even on drunk driving or underage drinking. That is part of A.A.'s Tenth Tradition, which we will come to somewhat later, in Chapter 8. The important point for us here (looking at what Bill W. set up) is that what is involved in these Twelve Steps is clearly spiritual, and medicinal aids (if any at all) are to support the spiritual experience that often begins the Steps and the spiritual awakening the Steps should bring about—not to replace these. From this point, we can go on to Step 3, noting that the "Big Book" begins its discussion of Step 3 immediately after Bill W.'s statement, "We were reborn":

We were now at Step Three. Many of us said to our Maker, *as we understood Him*, "God, I offer myself to Thee—to build with me and do with me as Thou wilt. Relieve me of the bondage of self, that I may better do Thy will. Take away my difficulties, that victory over them may bear witness to those I would help of Thy power, Thy Love, and Thy Way of Life. May I do Thy will always!" [In A.A., this is known as the Third Step Prayer: we will come later on to the Seventh Step Prayer and the Eleventh Step Prayer.] We thought well before taking this step[,] making sure we were ready; that we could at last abandon ourselves utterly to Him. We found it very desirable to take this spiritual step with an understanding person. . . . But it is better to meet God alone than with one who might misunderstand. The wording was . . . optional so long as we expressed the idea, voicing it without reservation. ("Big Book" 1976:63)

In the *12&12*, Bill's meditations and comment on this step are summarized in these words:

Step three is like opening of a locked door. How shall we let God into our lives? Willingness is the key. Dependence as a means to independence. Dangers of self-sufficiency. Turning our will over to Higher Power. Misuse of will-power. Sustained and personal exertion necessary to conform to God's will. (1952/53:5–6)

What is the outline for study of the Third Step in *Table Talk* (which, as noted, is not "A.A. literature"—but which can be used to suggest understanding of the Third Step as in Akron in the early 1940s)?

In the first step, we learned that we had lost the power of choice and had to make a decision. (1) What decision could we make better than to (a) turn our very will over to God, realizing that our own use of our own will has resulted in trouble; (b) As in the Lord's Prayer we must believe and practice "Thy will be done!" (2) God as we understand Him. (3) Religion is a word we do not use in A.A. We refer to a member's relation to God as the spiritual. A religion is a form of worship—not the worship itself. (4) If a man cannot believe in God, he can certainly believe in something greater than himself. If he cannot believe in a power greater than himself he is a rather hopeless egotist. (A.A. no date)

The word to which I would particularly call attention is *hopeless*.

At this point, since it seems to be pretty central in A.A., we should look at what is meant by "God as we understood Him"—frequently quoted in A.A. meetings as "God as I understand Him." In 1934, the Rev. Mr. Shoemaker published a collection of his 1933–34 sermons under the title, *The Gospel According to You*, and in that collection, talking about self-surrender, he wrote:

The true meaning of faith is self-surrender to God. . . . Surrender to whatever you know about him or believe must be the truth about him. Surrender to Him, if necessary, in total ignorance of Him. Far more important that you touch Him than that you understand Him at first. Put yourself in His hands. Whatever He is, as William James said, He is more ideal than we are. (1934:128)

The same note is sounded in a Shoemaker sermon on June 30, 1935, "The Way to Find God," where Shoemaker says "We need to know little about his nature . . . to make the initial step towards Him. Understanding will come later; what is wanted first is relationship." Many years later, not long before Sam Shoemaker died, I heard him speak of turning oneself over to God—"as much of God as you understand," which I take to be something like his meaning of "God as you understand him." It is worth noting here that I have been told by some A.A.s that in the phrase, "God as we understood Him," the *we* is of paramount importance, and the specific reference is to the Higher Power to which A.A.s turn over their alcoholism and its problems. (This, they say, is a "we" program.) What is important for the alcoholic here would seem to be A.A.'s understanding of God as the Higher Power on whom alcoholics unload their alcoholism, rather than the alcoholic's own understanding of God.

The distinction between religious and spiritual has come down to the present day in Alcoholics Anonymous apparently in the phrase we have already mentioned, "This is a spiritual program, not a religious program." This will be seen to have certain "organizational" implications when we come to the decision not to organize the *koinonia* of A.A. as a church—in other words, not to follow in the steps of Mary Baker Eddy. In our discussion of the theological underpinnings of the process toward sobriety in A.A., we have looked at this distinction between religious and spiritual— not in its effect on the practical matter of providing for the continuance of A.A. after Bill W.'s death (what we might call the Mary Baker Eddy problem—which comes in the next chapter), but in the matter of its theological implications. We noted the statement in *Table Talk* that religion is the form of worship, not the worship itself. The clear implication, to me (as we noted in Chapter 6) is that Alcoholics Anonymous *was* (or was believed to be) a form of worship, a point supported by Bill W.'s Third Tradition, as originally set out in 1946.

STEPS FOUR AND FIVE

Step 4 set out in detail in the "Big Book," in Chapter 5, "How It Works" ("Big Book" 1976:64–72). There is an extensive commentary in the *12&12*

(1952/53:42–54). There are innumerable unapproved pamphlets and guides to taking Step Four, which is simply "Made a searching and fearless moral inventory of ourselves"—but which seems to invite endless interpretation. In what follows I am relying almost entirely on the "Big Book" and the *12&12*, with some personal communications. For Step 4, I have been told that the important words are *searching* and *fearless*. I have also been told that the important words are *searching, fearless,* and *moral*. This second set appears to me to be more in keeping than the first with what I understand of the basic nature of A.A., but in any case, we should look at the steps, so to speak, that go into Step 4. Here they are, as I have found them (under guidance from A.A. members) in Chapter 5 of the "Big Book" (1976:64–72). I have been told that if I looked and found fewer than fifteen, I wasn't looking hard enough, and if I found more than thirty-five, I was looking too hard.

(1) We searched out the flaws in our make-up which have caused our failures.
(2) We set our resentments down on paper.
(3) We listed people, institutions, principles, with whom we were angry.
(4) We asked ourselves why we were angry.
(5) We set our injuries opposite each name on our "grudge list."
(6) Was it self-esteem, security, ambition, personal or sex relations, that were interfered with?
(7) We went back through our lives, thoroughly and honestly.
(8) When we were finished, we considered the list carefully.
(9) We knew that, if we were to live, we had to be free of anger.
(10) We realized that people who wronged us were spiritually sick.
(11) We asked God that we show them the tolerance, pity, patience we would show the sick.
(12) When offended, we said "This is a sick man. How can I help? God save me from anger."
(13) We avoided retaliation or argument.
(14) We looked again at the list.
(15) Putting others' wrongs out of our minds, we resolutely looked for our own mistakes.
(16) When we saw our faults, we listed them in black and white.
(17) We admitted our wrongs honestly and were willing to set them straight.
(18) We reviewed our fears thoroughly.
(19) We put our fears down on paper, even if we had no resentments in connection with them.
(20) We asked ourselves why we had them.
(21) We trusted God rather than ourselves, realizing we are here to play the role He assigns.

(22) We reviewed our own conduct over the past: selfishness, dishonesty, inconsiderateness.

(23) Whom had we hurt? With whom had we aroused jealousy, suspicion, bitterness? Where at fault?

(24) In this way, we tried to shape a sane and sound ideal of our future sex life.

(25) We subjected each relation to this test: was it selfish or not?

(26) We asked God to mold our ideals and help us live up to them.

(27) In meditation, we asked God what we should do about each specific matter.

(28) To sum up on sex, we prayed for right ideals, guidance, sanity, and strength to do right.

That's twenty-eight, divided—as I see it—into the overall statement of the process (1), anger and resentments (2 through 8 with an answer in 9 through 13), listing the wrongs committed in these cases and becoming willing to set them straight (14 through 17), listing and analyzing fears and turning to God with them (18 through 21), reviewing and analyzing conduct with regard to sex and personal relationships and turning to God about them (22 through 28). Remember that this listing of twenty-eight "steps" is simply my summary of what I read there. The matter can be much more briefly summarized as the "Big Book" summarizes it, saying that

we have written down a lot. We have listed and analyzed our resentments. We have begun to comprehend their futility and their fatality. We have commenced to see their terrible destructiveness. We have begun to learn tolerance, patience and good will toward all men, even our enemies, for we look on them as sick people. We have listed the people we have hurt by our conduct, and are willing to straighten out the past if we can. ("Big Book" 1976:70)

And, we

have been trying to get a new attitude, a new relationship with our Creator, and to discover the obstacles in our path. We have admitted certain defects; we have ascertained in a rough way what the trouble is; we have put our finger on the weak items in our personal inventory. Now these are about to be cast out. (ibid.:72)

The casting out is in the next Steps (5 through 9). Let us, before going there, see what Bill W. has to say about this Fourth Step in the *12&12*. Here he emphasizes our instincts run riot.

Creation gave us instincts for a purpose. Without them we wouldn't be complete human beings. . . . these desires—for the sex relation, for material and emotional security, and for companionship—are perfectly necessary and right, and surely God-given. Yet these instincts, so necessary for our existence, often far exceed their proper functions. . . . Our desires for sex, for material and emotional security, and for an important place in society often tyrannize us. . . . Step Four is our vigorous and painstaking effort to discover what these liabilities in each of us have been, and are. We want to find out exactly how, when, and where our natural desires have warped us. We wish to look squarely at the unhappiness this has caused others and ourselves. By discovering what our emotional deformities are, we can move toward their correction. Without a willing and persistent effort to do this, there can be little sobriety or contentment for us. Without a searching and fearless moral inventory, most of us have found that the faith which really works in daily living is still out of reach. To borrow Santayana's line, those who will not study the past (which in this case, as in his, means using it to change the future) are doomed to repeat it.

Here is the summary of Step 4 in the beginning of the *12&12*:

How instincts can exceed their proper function. Step Four is an effort to discover our liabilities. Basic problem of extremes in instinctive drives. Misguided moral inventory can result in guilt, grandiosity, or blaming others. Assets *can* [my emphasis] be noted with liabilities. Self-justification is dangerous. Willingness to take inventory brings light and new confidence. Step Four is beginning of lifetime practice [of taking self-inventory]. Common symptoms of emotional insecurity are worry, anger, self-pity, and depression. Inventory reviews relationships. Importance of thoroughness. (1952/53)

This would seem to be a good summary of the process of Step Four as it appears in the "Big Book," but there are some parts of Bill W.'s explanatory commentary (in the *12&12*) that seem to be particularly relevant to our inquiry on how A.A. works—meaning, in this case, how its Twelve Steps work. The first passage may in fact describe Bill W.'s own experience: if he was indeed a manic depressive, he would be both "on the depressive side" and "inclined to self-righteousness or grandiosity." But the passage is quoted because of its warning as to what the inventory is not or ought not to be, and what the goal ought not to be, followed by the second passage, which describes what it is, or (in Bill W.'s view) ought to be:

The minute we make a serious attempt to probe [our instincts on rampage], we are liable to suffer severe reactions. If temperamentally we are on the depressive side, we are apt to be swamped with guilt and self-loathing. We wallow in this messy bog, often getting a misshapen and painful pleasure out of it. As we morbidly pursue this melancholy activity, we may sink to such a point of despair that nothing but oblivion looks possible as a solution. . . . This is not a moral inventory at all; it is the very process by which the depressive has so often been led to the bottle and extinction. If, however, our natural disposition is inclined to self-righteousness or grandiosity . . . we shall point with pride to the good lives we thought we led before the bottle cut us down. We shall claim that our serious character defects, if we think we have any at all, have been *caused* . . . by excessive drinking. That being so, we think it logically follows that sobriety—first, last, and all the time—is the only thing we need work for. (ibid.:44–45)

In fact, what is needed is a fair appraisal. The depression is a form of pride in reverse (as Bill W. points out, ibid.:45), and the grandiose or self-righteous reaction is likewise pride. It has been said by Christian theologians over the years that pride is the sin against the Holy Ghost, the unforgivable sin—because, I gather, it cannot or will not seek forgiveness. This can serve here as our introduction to the second passage:

Now let's ponder the need for a list of the more glaring character personality defects all of us have in varying degrees. To those having religious training, such a list would set forth serious violations of moral principles. Some others will think of this list as defects of character. Some others will call it an index of maladjustments. Some will be quite annoyed if there is talk about immorality, let alone sin. But all who are in the least reasonable will agree upon one point: that there is plenty wrong with us alcoholics about which plenty will have to be done if we are to expect sobriety, progress, and any real ability to cope with life. To avoid falling into confusion over the names these defects should be called, let's take a universally recognized list of major human failings—the Seven Deadly Sins of pride, greed, lust, anger, gluttony, envy, and sloth. It is not by accident that pride leads the procession. For pride, leading to self-justification, and always spurred by conscious or unconscious fears, is the basic breeder of most human difficulties, the chief block to true progress. . . . When the satisfaction of our instincts for sex, security, and society becomes the sole object of our lives, then pride steps in to justify our excesses. (ibid.:48–49)

And then, all these feelings "generate fear, a soul-sickness in its own right. Then fear, in turn, generates more character defects" (ibid.:49).

This puts the matter pretty clearly. Alcoholism is the specific mental and physical form for alcoholics (those with alcoholism[2]—predisposition for alcoholic drinking) of the spiritual disease condition we call sinfulness or sin. And the disease is grounded in fear. The commentary in this chapter of the *12&12* goes on to talk about the other deadly sins, showing their connection with instincts run riot, with fear, with this worst of sins, pride. We will not be surprised if we find that the next Steps (like this, and like the first three) are designed to replace fear with courage, pride with humility, the seven deadly sins, perhaps, with the seven virtues. We turn now to Step 5. We will find that the division between Step 4 and Step 5 does not always seem quite as clear-cut as it might be, and we will also find that it may be more clear-cut than it seems. We begin with Step 5 as it appears in the list of the Steps in Chapter 5 of the "Big Book."

Step 5 reads, "Admitted to God, to ourselves, and to another human being the exact nature of our wrongs." I have heard it said that this Step, if not in fact misquoted, is frequently misread. It is read (with emphasis on the words italicized) as "Admitted to *God,* to ourselves, and to *another human being* the exact nature of our *wrongs.*" It is suggested that the proper reading is, "*Admitted* to *God,* to *ourselves,* and to *another human being* the *exact nature* of our wrongs." The differences are obvious. In the first case, what is important is that another human being hear a confession to God of wrongs done. That is the ancient practice of auricular confession: there is nothing wrong with it, and it is indeed part of what is recommended here. But the second reading emphasizes the *admission* to *oneself*—as well as to God and another human being—of what one has done, and not only what one has done, but the *patterns* of what one has done, which seems to be what is meant by *exact nature.* It is, in other words, part of the process of knowing oneself (*gnothi seauton*) and learning the extent of one's own patterns of sin. The other human being is frequently, but not always, the alcoholic's A.A. sponsor, though it may be a priest or even an alcoholic other than one's sponsor. This may be the place to discuss the matter of sponsorship—very briefly.

Essentially, a sponsor was initially an "experienced" sober A.A. who could guide the newcomer into the program, answer for him somewhat as a Godparent (sponsor at baptism) answers for the person baptized—and then guides him toward confirmation in the church, till he has learned enough to speak for himself. Initially, of course, Alcoholics Anonymous functioned as a kind of secret fellowship, and one had to be sponsored to be present at the meeting of the existing fellowship (*koinonia*). Dr. Bob, with his huge vocabulary of outdated slang, his ready laughter, and his gentle self-mockery, called those he sponsored his *pigeons*—like homing pigeons, they came home to roost; like any pigeons they made a lot of noise and not a little mess. They have been called *babies* (which preserves something of the original idea of sponsorship), and they are now frequently called either *sponsees* or *sponsorees*—which latter sounds to me like some kind of a Scout outing.

The word *sponsee* sounds French, but is not (the French word for baptismal sponsor is *parraine* or *marraine* and for the person sponsored *filleul* or *filleule*). It appears rather to be a kind of short-hand neologism for "the person I sponsor" in Alcoholics Anonymous), and I have heard it suggested that the creation of such a term is an indication of how much Alcoholics Anonymous has changed since its early days. Sponsorship seems originally to have been a one-on-one relationship established to get the newcomer through the Steps (at least the first time) and fully into the fellowship, like the godparent guiding the godchild into full membership in the church. One can, of course, go for moral guidance to one's godparent (or godparents) long after one is confirmed into the church, but their formal function is gone. But I am told that now, in Alcoholics Anonymous, there are those with ten or twelve (or more) "sponsees" whom they gather together for purposes of bonding, and who are in some kind of permanent student/mentor relationship with the sponsor. In fact, *sponsor* seems to have slid into *mentor*. Whether this is good or bad I cannot say—nor is it my place to. What I can say is that the idea and purpose of the sponsor seems to have changed, and what to call the person being sponsored seems to be an open question.

But that is by way of being at least a seeming digression (though we will come back to it later). The summary of Step 5 at the beginning of the "Big Book" reads this way:

> Twelve steps deflate ego. Step 5 is difficult but necessary to sobriety and peace of mind. Confession is an ancient discipline. Without fearless admission of defects, few could stay sober. What do we receive from Step Five? Beginning of true kinship with man and God. [note—not *of* man and God]. Lose sense of isolation, receive forgiveness and give it; learn humility; gain honesty and realism about ourselves. Necessity for complete honesty. Danger of rationalization. How to choose the person in whom to confide. Results are tranquillity and consciousness of God. Oneness with God and man prepares us for the following Steps.

Beside this, let us set the brief discussion of the Fifth Step in the "Big Book" (I have stripped the section down and have omitted that part which deals with the difficulty of finding someone to confide in or confess to, since it is now very largely—I believe—the function of the sponsor to be the confidant, or confessor):

> We think we have done well enough in admitting these things to ourselves. There is doubt about that. In actual practice, we usually find a solitary self-appraisal insufficient. . . . If we skip this vital step, we may not overcome drinking. Time after time newcomers have tried to keep to themselves certain facts about their lives. . . . They took inventory all right, but hung on to some of the worst items in stock. . . . We must be entirely honest with somebody if we expect to live long or happily in this world. . . . When we have decided who is to hear our story, we waste no time. We have a written inventory and we are prepared for a long talk. . . . We pocket our pride and go to it, illuminating every twist of character, every dark cranny of the past. Once we have taken this step, withholding nothing, we are delighted. We can look the world in the eye. We can be alone at perfect peace and ease. Our fears fall from us. We begin to feel the nearness of our creator. We may have had cer-

tain spiritual beliefs, but now we begin to have a spiritual experience. . . . We feel we are on the Broad Highway, walking hand in hand with the Spirit of the Universe. Returning home we find a place where we can be quiet for an hour, carefully reviewing what we have done. We thank God from the bottom of our heart that we know Him better. . . . Carefully reading the first five proposals [i.e., Steps], we ask if we have omitted anything, for we are building the arch through which we shall walk as a free man. . . . If we can answer to our satisfaction, we then look at *Step Six*. ("Big Book" 1976:72–76)

This is a description of the result of a true and thorough confession—not necessarily specifically of a Fifth Step but of any true and thorough confession. The point of the other human being is that he or she guarantees (by very presence) that the confession will be true and thorough. The point of the *exact nature* is that it will, if achieved, provide both detail and organization (thus self-understanding) by the person making the confession. Also, in the text of the *12&12*, Bill W. observes that "people of very high spiritual development almost always insist on checking with friends or spiritual advisors the guidance they feel they have received from God" (1952/53:60). The presence of another human being is a kind of "reality check" for the person taking Step Five. Also, in the text of the *12&12*, Bill W. makes this observation, echoing what he said earlier in the "Big Book."

Before long, your listener may well tell a story or two about himself which will place you even more at ease. Provided you hold back nothing, your sense of relief will mount from minute to minute. The dammed-up emotions of years break out of their confinement, and miraculously vanish as soon as they are exposed. As the pain subsides, a healing tranquillity takes its place. And when humility and serenity are so combined, something else of great moment is apt to occur. Many an A.A., once agnostic or atheistic, tells us that it was during this stage of Step Five that he first actually felt the presence of God. And even those who had faith already often become conscious of God as they never were before. This feeling of being at one with God and man, this emerging from isolation through the open and honest sharing of our terrible burden of guilt, brings us to a resting place where we may prepare ourselves for the following Steps toward a full and meaningful sobriety. (ibid.:62)

In the second (1955) and following editions of the "Big Book," in Appendix II, "Spiritual Experience," Bill W. writes that

it is true that our first printing gave many readers the impression that these personality changes, or religious experiences, must be in the nature of sudden and spectacular upheavals. Happily for everyone, this conclusion is erroneous. In the first few chapters a number of sudden revolutionary changes are described. Though it was not our intention to create such an impression, many alcoholics have nevertheless concluded that in order to recover they must acquire an immediate an overwhelming "God-consciousness" [an Oxford Group term] followed at once by a vast change in feeling and outlook. Among our rapidly growing membership of thousands of alcoholics such transformations, though frequent, are by no means the rule. Most of our experiences are what the psychologist William James calls the "educational variety," because they develop slowly over a period of time. ("Big Book" 1976:569)

(I have been unable to find the place where William James uses the phrase *educational variety* or even the word *educational* in this context.)

But the words in which Bill W. has described the Fifth Step experience, in both the "Big Book" and the *12&12*, are precisely a description of the sudden and overwhelming "God-consciousness," of the immediate vast change in feeling and outlook. No one I have spoken with doubts that this was indeed Bill W.'s experience—but what of the alcoholic whose experience is both "volitional" and educational, rather than instantaneous conversion through the mystical self-surrender involved in profound conversion? Can this alcoholic go on with the next Steps without having had this immediate vast change? The answer implicit in this appendix is yes, but the procedure is not fully worked out in the literature I have examined, though there is no doubt that all alcoholics in A.A. are expected to continue with the Steps. That is certainly the implication of the appendix, of Bill W.'s statement that "we begin to have a spiritual experience," and of the questions (self-analysis) he suggests as the preparation for Step 6.

One other point. We remarked that what happens is the coming of a sense of true kinship *with* (not *of*) man and God. That is, the alcoholic, in Step 5, realizes that (in John Donne's words) "No man [least of all he himself] is an island, entire of itself; every man is a piece of the continent, a part of the main." (Whether he also internalizes the latter part of that same Meditation XVII, to the effect that pain, given by God, is good coin or treasure only if it is used profitably is another question.) The alcoholic also realizes that he (or she) has a kinship with God. The alcoholic is *involved* (Donne's word) with humankind and with the divine. The realization may be—apparently frequently is—no more than that, a realization, a kind of knowledge by learning. In such cases (the "volitional" or "educational" cases), it will be necessary for the alcoholic to continue taking the Steps, putting one foot in front of the other, until the summit is reached. Evidence suggests that Dr. Bob's experience was something like this. Evidence suggests that the experience of Marty M. (in "Women Suffer Too" 1976:222–29) was something like this. It appears they both were brought to understand that their situation was not hopeless by learning that their alcoholism was an illness of the mind and body, and they went on from there—Dr. Bob till he died sober fifteen years later, Marty M. till she died sober (but possibly not straight through) more than forty years later. They carried on, doing what they knew they had to do, without a "white light" experience. One can go back to John Newton (and earlier, I think, to Brother Lawrence) to see the same thing, though both of them grew into the mystical vision (it took John Newton the better part of a quarter-century). In any case, whatever the alcoholic's experience with Step 5, Step 6 comes next, and cannot be bypassed.

STEPS SIX AND SEVEN

The summary of the Sixth Step in the front of the *12&12* is relatively brief:

> Step Six is necessary to spiritual growth. The beginning of a lifetime job. Recognition of difference between striving for objective—and perfection. Why we must keep trying. "Being ready" is all-important. Necessity of taking action. Delay is dangerous. Rebellion may be fatal. Point at which we abandon limited objectives and move toward God's will for us.

This seems to take us back to the "educational" process, indeed to "volitional" conversion. The *Step* itself reads, "Were entirely ready to have God remove all these defects of character." This seems to be saying, "*Became* entirely ready to have God remove all these defects of character," as though the conversion experience of the Fifth Step was necessary but might not be sufficient. But what does Bill W. say about the Sixth Step in the "Big Book"? The discussion there is only one paragraph long. It comes after he has concluded the discussion of Step Five with a list of questions to be asked on completion of Step Five. The questions are

> Is our work solid so far? Are the stones [of the arch through which we will walk a free man] properly in place? Have we skimped on the cement put into the foundation? Have we tried to make mortar without sand?

> If we can answer to our satisfaction, we then look at *Step Six*. We have emphasized willingness as being indispensable. Are we now ready to let God remove from us all the things which we have admitted are objectionable? Can He now take them all—every one? If we still cling to something we will not let go, we ask God to help us be willing. ("Big Book" 1976:75)

That's it. That's *all* of what Bill W. says in the "Big Book" about Step Six. At this point (1938–39), he seems to be taking it pretty much as the checkpoint for going on from Step Five to Step Seven.

But that was before he met Father Edward Dowling, S. J., on a rainy night in 1941. Father Dowling had come to New York from St. Louis, via

Akron (where he had talked to Dr. Bob, but probably not sufficiently to Dr. Bob's colleague, Sister Mary Ignatia Gavin). He had apparently been struck, in hearing about Alcoholics Anonymous, and in reading the "Big Book," with similarities between the Twelve Steps and the *Spiritual Exercises* of Ignatius Loyola. I can't say I see a very close relationship myself, and the *Exercises* are in a way a handbook for leaders of what we would call retreats. But, whatever the cause for Father Dowling's appearance in Bill's life, he changed and enlarged Bill's understanding. Dr. Tiebout came into the ambit of A.A. through an alcoholic patient at Blythewood, wound up as Bill W.'s own therapist—and helped link A.A. and psychiatry. Father Dowling came into the ambit of A.A. through looking in it for Ignatian (and thus Roman Catholic) spirituality, wound up as Bill W.'s own spiritual counselor—and helped link the Twelve Steps with spiritual tradition since the first century. It is, I believe, to him that we owe the great expansion of Step Six from the "Big Book" to the *12&12*.

> "This is the Step that separates the men from the boys." So declares a well-loved clergyman who happens to be one of A.A.'s greatest friends. He goes on to explain that any person capable of enough willingness and honesty to try *repeatedly* [my emphasis] Step Six on all his faults—*without any reservations whatsoever* [Bill W.'s emphasis] has indeed come a long way spiritually, and is therefore entitled to be called a man who is sincerely trying to grow in the image and likeness of his own Creator.

Bill W. goes on to reconcile what he is saying here in the *12&12* with what he said earlier in the "Big Book." He provides a generic statement ("heard daily," he says, "in A.A. meetings all over the world") about the experience of A.A.s in having their obsession to drink vanish when they "became willing to clean house" and then asked God to give them release (1952/53:63). "It is plain for everybody to see that each sober A.A. member has been granted a release from this very obstinate and potentially fatal obsession. So in a very complete and literal way, all A.A.s have 'become entirely ready' to have God remove the mania for alcohol from their lives" (ibid.:64). In short, willingness to clean house provides readiness for God's removal of the defects of character (flaws, sins, shortcomings). The linchpin is that to be willing is to do—the willingness is shown, if I may coin a word, in the doingness. Not in the doing simply of one thing or another, but in the constant doing that is Brother Lawrence's "practice of the presence of God"—a state of doing that is a spiritual state. This is in the Epistle of James and it is in the *Spiritual Exercises*, as well is in Brother Lawrence's *Practice of the Presence of God* (Herrmann [1692] 1996). It is arguably what the author of the epistle is talking about when he talks about looking into the perfect law of liberty and remembering what kind of creature one is.

In his discussion of Step Six in the *12&12*, Bill goes down the list of the instincts run wild—the seven deadly sins. He remarks that

> Step Six . . . is A.A.'s way of stating the best possible attitude one can take in order to make a beginning on this lifetime job. This does not mean that we expect all our character defects to be lifted out of us as the desire to drink was. A few of them may be, but with most of them we shall have to be content with patient improvement. The key words "entirely ready" underline the fact that we want to aim at the very best we can know or learn. How many of us have this degree of readiness? In an absolute sense practically nobody has it. The best we can do, with all the honesty we can summon, is to *try* to have it. . . . No matter how far we have progressed, desires will always be found which oppose the grace of God. (1952/53:65–66)

Note that this cannot be *irresistible* Grace, which cannot be opposed. But all *prevenient* Grace, or *actual* Grace, is not *irresistible* Grace. What Bill W. seems to be talking about here is the process of conversion from *actual* to *habitual*, and in essence a conversion that is volitional—not the absolute self-surrender to the (irresistible) Grace that Daniel felt, or John Bradford received from Latimer's sermon, that came to Bunyan or Alline or S. H. Hadley, or that (and this is a curious case) built up in John Newton over more than a quarter-century—finally coming irresistibly through poor mad William Cowper, who put together the *Olney Hymns*.

And then, after discussing sins or defects many alcoholics do not want to be rid of, he summarizes: "the difference between 'the boys and the men' is the difference between striving for a self-determined objective and for the perfect objective which is of God. Many will at once ask , 'How *can* we accept the entire implication of Step Six? Why—that is *perfection!*" (ibid.:68). He responds that Steps Two through Twelve "state perfect ideals. They are goals toward which we look, and the measuring sticks by which we estimate our progress. Seen in this light, Step Six is still difficult, but not at all impossible. The only urgent thing is that we make a beginning, and keep trying" (ibid.). So Step Six has grown from a checkpoint on the effects of a variety of religious experience in Step Five, to a spiritual exercise in its own right. In ordinary speech, there is a difference between *ready* and *willing*. One thinks of the phrase "ready, willing, and able" or the old "ready—get set—go!" with its counterpart "on your mark—get set—go!" To be ready is to be on the mark, prepared, the "ducks in a row"—the gun loaded and "at the ready."

What Bill W. seems to me to be saying is that complete willingness makes one ready—the implication being that the hole that will be left in one's life if one's sins and flaws are removed will itself be filled by God (and A.A.), if one is completely willing. But one must keep up the readiness, the preparedness. Eternal vigilance is the price of liberty. Of course, unless—or rather, except—"the Lord build the house, they labor in vain that build it: except the Lord keep the city, the watchman waketh but in vain" (Psalm 127, first verse). But the house must be ready, swept clean, for the new tenant—"redded up" in the old Ulster expression. Readiness, in essence, seems to include willingness and in some sense depend on it, and willingness without readiness is not true (or useful) willingness. The two are complementary—but not the same. Nevertheless, one senses, on reading about Step Six in the "Big Book," and then in the *12&12*, that Bill W. himself may have come to understand Step Six better over the years, perhaps under Father Dowling's tutelage (for all that Bill W. wrote the Step in the first place). This brings us to Step Seven.

The summary of Step Seven in the front of the *12&12* is also brief:

> What is humility? What can it mean to us? The avenue to true freedom of the human spirit. Necessary aid to survival. Value of *ego-puncturing* [my emphasis]. Failure and misery transformed by humility. Strength from weakness. Pain is the admission price to new life. Self-centered fear chief activator of defects. Step Seven is a change in attitude which permits us to move out of ourselves toward God.

But brief as it may be, it is as long as the entire section on Step Seven in the "Big Book." In fact, what the "Big Book" does for Step Seven is simply to provide the Seventh Step prayer. "When ready [that is, ready to let God remove our defects, which is Step Six], we say something like this:

> "My Creator, I am now willing that you should have all of me, good and bad. I pray that you now remove from me every single defect of character which stands in the way of my usefulness to you and my fellows. Grant me strength, as I go out from here, to do your bidding. Amen." We have then completed *Step Seven*. ("Big Book" 1976:76)

The discussion of the Seventh Step in the text of the *12&12* begins with a kind of paean to humility.

> Since this Step so specifically concerns itself with humility, we should pause here to consider what humility is and what the practice of it can mean to us. Indeed, the attainment of greater humility is the foundation principle of each of A.A.'s Twelve Steps. For without some degree of humility, no alcoholic can stay sober at all. Nearly all A.A.s have found, too, that unless they develop much more of this precious quality than may be required just for sobriety, they still haven't much chance of becoming truly happy. Without it, they cannot live to much useful purpose, or, in adversity, be able to summon the faith that can meet any emergency. (1952/53:70)

Very well, but what is humility? From what follows, we can deduce an answer, at least as to what humility was in Bill W.'s mind, though he never specifically defines the word. He observes that "humility, as a word and as an ideal, has a very bad time of it in our world. Not only is the idea misunderstood; the word itself is often intensely disliked" (ibid.:70). It is intensely disliked, apparently, because it is confused with *humiliation*. But what *is* humility?

Bill W. begins by telling us what it is not. It is *not* the view that "a man-made millennium lies just ahead" (ibid.:70). It is *not* the belief that material satisfactions are the purpose of living (and by implication *is* the view that "character-building and spiritual value" must come first—ibid.:71). It is *not* the view that "we could live exclusively by our own individual strength and intelligence" (ibid.:72). It is *not* self-centeredness (ibid.:73). "Where humility had formerly stood for a forced feeding on humble pie [which sounds suspiciously like *humiliation*], it now begins to mean the nourishing ingredient which can give us serenity" (ibid.:74). Then Bill W. goes back to the praise of humility.

> Everywhere we saw failure and misery transformed by humility into priceless assets. We heard story after story of how humility had brought strength out of weakness. . . . Refusing to place God first, we had deprived ourselves of his help. But now the words "Of myself I am nothing, the Father doeth the works" began to carry bright promise and meaning. We saw we needn't always be bludgeoned and beaten into humility. It could come quite as much from our voluntary reaching for it as it could from unremitting suffering. (ibid.:75).

In other words, in William James's terms, humility—whatever it is— could be on the volitional end of the conversion spectrum as well as coming from self-surrender under pain.

> The Seventh Step is where we make the change in our attitude which permits us, with humility as our guide, to move out from ourselves toward others and toward God. The whole emphasis of Step Seven is on humility. It is really saying to us that we now ought to be willing to try humility in seeking the removal of our other shortcomings, just as we did when we admitted we were powerless over alcohol, and came to believe that a Power greater than ourselves could restore us to sanity. *If that degree of humility could enable us to find the grace by which such a deadly obsession could be banished* [emphasis mine], then there must be hope of the same result respecting any other problem we could possibly have. (ibid.:76).

So humility is what enables us to find Grace, what can give us serenity, what enables us to move out from ourselves toward God. But what *is* humility? Lexicographically, humility is the recognition of the littleness of man. Theologically, it has traditionally been defined (my summary) as (1) the recognition that the goodness of good work is in the work, not the worker, and (2) the joyful acceptance in doing what God wills, rather than what we will. The first of these is more or less considered to be the Roman Catholic view, the second the Protestant view, though of course they are complementary. The first of these says "If the job is well done, it doesn't matter whether you did it or someone else: the point is that it is well done." The second says "We will do what God would have us do, and we will be happy."

The distinction is drawn in the *Oxford Dictionary of the Christian Church* (see *humility;* 1977:677) between the Roman Catholic view of humility and the Protestant view. Thomas Aquinas teaches (*Summa CG.*:iv, 55) that humility consists in keeping oneself within one's own bounds, not reaching out to things above or beyond one's proper sphere: it is part of the cardinal virtue of temperance inasmuch as it represses inordinate ambition and inordinate self-esteem without allowing the opposite error of exaggerated or hypocritical self-abjection, and it thus subjects will and reason to God.

Now Bill W.'s spiritual mentors were, first, Sam Shoemaker (an Episcopalian) and, then, Father Edward Dowling, a Jesuit (Roman Catholic). This is, I think, pretty much what Bill W. eventually had in mind when he talked about humility. On the other hand, Frank Buchman, who founded the Oxford Group movement (of which Sam Shoemaker was part), was a Lutheran, and Martin Luther's definition of humility was that it was the joyful acceptance of God's will, and certain nineteenth-century Protestant theologians (as, for example, Albrecht Ritschl of Göttingen) identified humility as complete acceptance of unconditional dependence on God. The two definitions are not, in the end, very different, but there is a suggestion on the Catholic side that this is to be worked for (as a matter of *volition*?), on the Protestant side that this comes from a profound overturning of the self (such as is involved with *self-surrender*).

This introduces the question of the relationship of humility and grace. The Catholic definition of humility concentrates on a process of bringing the gift of *prevenient* Grace into a state of *subsequent* Grace, *sufficient* Grace into *efficacious* Grace, *actual* Grace into *habitual* Grace, even *irresistible* Grace into *congruous* Grace (Duns Scotus, and others, commenting on Augustine). Remember that *prevenient* Grace is the free gift of God, antecedent to conversion, while *subsequent* Grace occurs if God and man cooperate after conversion. *Sufficient* Grace is sufficient for the initial conversion, while *efficacious* Grace, on the other hand, is subsequent to conversion and depends on the congruity or appropriateness of the Grace, which is God's choice (here we see Augustine as the forefather of Luther and even Calvin). *Actual* Grace, which may exist in the unbaptized and even the unbelieving, is that certain motion of the soul (toward God), bestowed by God ad hoc for the production of some good act. *Habitual* or *sanctifying* Grace is the gift of God inhering in the soul, by which men are enabled to perform righteous acts. *Prevenient* Grace is the form of *actual* Grace, which leads men to sanctification before the reception of the sacraments (or, in this case, attendance at and membership in A.A.): it is the free gift of God and entirely unmerited. It is what Alexander of Hales identified with the "general assistance" (*assistentia generalis,* meaning, in a sense, the general presence) of God.

The Protestant definition, on the other hand, concentrates on the initial gift, and even considers (with Augustine) that *efficacious* or *congruous* Grace, like *prevenient* or *irresistible* Grace, is the free unmerited gift of God. The fact of "ego-puncturing," back in the summary of the Seventh Step in the front of the *12&12,* would thus be itself a gift, though the phrase, of course, comes from psychology (whether Sandór Radó or William James). As a result, we might fairly conclude, the Protestant (and thus the Oxford Group) idea of humility as joyful total acceptance of God's will, sees it as a result of the ego-puncturing event or series of events, which is itself part of unmerited Grace. This was held to be the original Pauline idea—after all, the Oxford Group was originally the First-Century Christian Fellowship—and in some ways assumes a kind of "road to Damascus" (or "white-light") experience. But the process of the Twelve Steps suggests volitional conversion, more in tune with the Catholic view of humility. Is this important? Yes. And it is one of the gifts, I believe, from Father Dowling to Bill W., and explains the difference in what is written about the Sixth and Seventh Steps between the "Big Book" in 1939 and the *12&12* in 1952–53.

STEPS EIGHT AND NINE

The summary of Step 8 in the front of the *12&12* links it with Steps 9 and 10.

> This and the next two Steps are concerned with personal relations. Learning to live with others is a fascinating adventure. Obstacles: reluctance to forgive; non-admission of wrongs to others; purposeful forgetting. Necessity of exhaustive survey of the past. Deepening insight results from thoroughness. Kinds of harm done to others. avoiding extreme judgments. Taking the objective view. Step Eight is the beginning of the end of isolation.

What is clear from this summary is that Step 8, as Bill W. viewed it in 1952–53, was an extension—or rather, perhaps, a deepening—of Step 4, as he viewed it in 1938–39. What is implied, since he speaks in the *12&12* (1952/53:62) of Step 5 as producing the "emerging from isolation," is that Step 8 is an extension—perhaps a deepening—of Steps 4 and 5 together, as he viewed them then. I believe that alcoholics have been frequently told by their sponsor to keep their Fourth-Step lists ("we have listed the people we

have hurt by our conduct" ["Big Book" 1976:70]—which are also the people on the "grudge lists"). Why? Because they will be at the top of
the Eighth-Step list. Pretty clearly, Step 8 builds on Steps 4 and 5—after the
alcoholic has gone through the spiritual exercises in Steps 6 and 7.

In the "Big Book" (pp. 76–84), Step 8 is firmly linked with Step 9. Only
a couple of paragraphs are specifically devoted to the Eighth Step
(ibid.:76), part of one to the list, the rest of that one and the beginning of
the next to the willingness to make amends. On the list, what Bill W. says
is a simplified form of the sponsor's advice noted above. Having given the
Seventh Step prayer, Bill W. goes on to say,

> Now we need more action, without which we find that "Faith without works
> is dead" [*James*]. Let's look at *Steps Eight and Nine*. We have a list of all per-
> sons we have harmed and to whom we are willing to make amends. We
> made it when we took inventory. We subjected ourselves to a drastic self-
> appraisal. Now we go out to our fellows and repair the damage done in the
> past. (ibid.)

(which brings the reader to Step 9). Here it would appear that the Fourth
Step list is the same as the Eighth Step list: but it would seem that in the
past fifty years the Eighth Step has come to be used as the time for expanding and deepening the list. And, I would suggest, for expanding and deepening the willingness to make amends. From an historian's view, I suggest
that Bill W. may have come to realize that the Steps he (and others) created
had taken on a life of their own. Certainly that was the case with Steps 6
and 7 (probably in part under Father Dowling's influence): it seems to be
the case here. Let's look a little more fully at what the text of the *12&12* says
specifically about Step 8—or what Bill W. discusses under the rubric of
Step 8 (1952/53:77–82). We have already looked at the brief summary from
the front of the book.

> Steps Eight and Nine are concerned with personal relations. First, we take a
> look backward and try to discover where we have been at fault. . . . Learning
> how to live in the greatest peace, partnership, and brotherhood with all men
> and women, of whatever description, is a moving and fascinating adven-
> ture. Every A.A. has found that he can make little headway in this new
> adventure of living until he first backtracks and really makes an accurate and
> unsparing survey of the human wreckage he has left in his wake. *To a degree*
> [my emphasis], he has already done this when taking moral inventory, but
> now the time has come when he ought to *redouble his efforts* [my emphasis
> again] to see how many people he has hurt, and in what ways. (p. 77)

Certainly Bill W. came to see that the inventory in Step 4 needed to be
expanded and deepened—"*to a degree*" and "*redouble his efforts*" show that.

He mentions several obstacles to carrying out Step 8, some of which deal with the first part ("Made a list of all persons we had harmed"), some with the second ("and became willing to make amends to them all"). Those dealing with the first part are essentially two in number.

First is

> forgiveness. The moment we ponder a twisted or broken relationship with another person, our emotions go on the defensive. To escape looking at the wrongs we have done another, we resentfully focus on the wrong he has done us. This is especially true if he has, in fact, behaved badly at all. (ibid.:78)

But, if "we are now about to ask forgiveness for ourselves, why shouldn't we start out by forgiving them, one and all?" It is not accidental, perhaps, that many A.A. meetings end (and in the early days virtually all ended) with the Lord's Prayer (in the Prayer Book version), "Forgive us our trespasses as we forgive those who trespass against us." Bill W. asks it as a question, but theologians over the years have made it pretty clear that forgiving is the key to being forgiven. Now, what—we may ask here—*is* this forgiveness? Essentially, it is (as I understand it) to "give-through" (in the Latin, *per donare*)—to renounce anger and resentment against—to pardon (in fact, the Old English *forgiefan* is a direct translation of Middle Latin *perdonnare*). That is, the person who forgives treats the person who wronged him (or her) as though the wrong had not been done. "Forgive and forget" is thus, as has been noted, a doublet like "let or hindrance" or "friends and neighbors."

Second is the attitude that

> when drinking, we never hurt anybody but ourselves. Our families didn't suffer because we always paid the bills and never drank at home. Our business associates didn't suffer, because we were usually on the job. . . . A lively bender was only a good man's fault. What real harm, therefore, had we done? . . . This attitude, of course, is the end result of purposeful forgetting. (ibid.:79)

As a response to this attitude, Bill W. defines "harm" and goes on to show (ibid.:79–81) that the harms done by alcoholics are many in number and kind, not to be denied by this purposeful forgetting. These include being irritable, critical, impatient, humorless, dominating, controlling, or wallowing in depression and self-pity, inflicting them on those around (ibid.:81). This purposeful forgetting is to be combated by "a deep and honest search of our motives and actions" (ibid.:)—in other words, by a deepening of Step 4, in fact a spiritual exercise.

Those dealing with the second part are likewise two in number. First is the difficulty of being willing

to make a face-to-face admission of our wretched conduct to those we had hurt. . . . The prospect of actually visiting or even writing the people concerned now overwhelmed us, especially when we remembered in what poor favor we stood with most of them. (ibid.:78–79)

The second is the requirement

to ransack memory for the people to whom we have given offense. To put a finger on the nearby and most deeply damaged ones shouldn't be hard to do. Then, as year by year we walk back through our lives as far as memory will reach, *we shall be bound to construct a long list of people who have, to some extent or other, been affected* [my emphasis]. . . . We should avoid extreme judgments, both of ourselves and of others involved. We must not exaggerate our defects or theirs. (ibid.:81–82)

Note especially the *bound to construct* and the *long list*.

The implication of the first is that coming to be willing to make amends itself requires significant spiritual effort. The implication of the second—and I have had this confirmed in conversations—is that the list should include *all* those the alcoholic has harmed (whether during the drinking life or before). The clear statement on the second is that the alcoholic *must* (*is bound to*) have a long list. It appears that the ransacking of the memory, the creation of the long and complete list, is likewise a spiritual exercise, a significant deepening of the exercise in Step 4. Before we go on to the next Step—which seems to be the crux of the matter—there is one further thing we ought to do. We ought to define *amends*. This does not turn out to be so easy as it would seem.

What are *amends*, or what is *amendment*? The origin of the word in Modern English is the Middle English *amendes*, plural of the Old French *amende*, meaning *reparation*. The word *amendment* generally means a *correction*, sometimes the formal statement of such a correction (as in an *Amendment* to the Constitution. The word *amende* in the singular is now seen (if at all) in the phrase *amende honorable*, which may mean a formal *open* statement of fault, sometimes accompanied by payment in reparation. The word *amendment* occurs in the (1928) Episcopal *Book of Common Prayer* in the short form of the "Declaration of Absolution or Remission of Sins" said by the priest after the General Confession at Evening Prayer. "The Almighty and merciful Lord grant you Absolution and Remission of all your sins, true repentance, amendment of life and the grace and consolation of His Holy Spirit."

In the sense used in A.A., neither *amend* nor *amendment* is a common word, and I see Sam Shoemaker's influence at work here as I see it elsewhere—particularly since I have been informed that this was the form of the Absolution he preferred, and since Evening Prayer was the service he conducted at the Calvary Mission, using this Prayer Book, in the days when Bill W. came there. Indeed, Bill W. wrote that "moral inventory, amends for harms done, turning wills and lives over to God," came straight from "association from the Oxford Groups, as they were then led in America by that Episcopal rector, Dr. Samuel Shoemaker" ([1948] 1989:198). The ideas came from Shoemaker, but diligent search by A.A. member Dick B. has failed to find the word *amends* in Shoemaker's writings (except his paper on the Twelve Steps published posthumously in *A.A. Grapevine*, long after the word was taken up in the Steps). Yet the word *amendment* was there in virtually every evening service he held at Calvary Mission. And it goes with repentance, grace, and spiritual consolation.

The front-of-the-book summary of the Ninth Step in the *12&12* reads as follows:

> A tranquil mind is the first requisite for good judgment. Good timing is important in making amends. What is courage? Prudence means taking calculated chances. Amends begin when we join A.A. Peace of mind cannot be bought at the expense of others. Need for discretion. Readiness to take consequences of our past and to take responsibility for well-being of others is spirit of Step Nine.

Note the word *readiness*. Note also the words *courage* and *prudence*, and that the variety of *courage* involved is surely *fortitude* rather than *daring* (or *audacity*). Given that "taking consequences" and "responsibility for the well-being of others" are in essence part of the cardinal virtue of *justice*, and that tranquillity of mind and good timing are characteristics of the cardinal virtue of *temperance*, what in fact do we have here? We have a requirement that the person taking Step 9 be in possession of the "natural" (or "cardinal") virtues of prudence, temperance, justice, and fortitude. It's an interesting summary.

The "Big Book" emphasizes Step 9—in fact, one of the most important of the "liturgical" readings at A.A. meetings seems to be what are sometimes called the Ninth Step Promises, more often simply the Promises. They come in a passage (concluding the discussion of Step 9) that is frequently read either at the beginning or end of the meetings.

> If we are painstaking about this phase of our development [Step Nine], we will be amazed before we are halfway through. We are going to know a new freedom and a new happiness. We will not regret the past nor wish to shut

the door on it. We will comprehend the word serenity and we will know peace. No matter how far down the scale we have gone, we will see how our experience can benefit others. That feeling of uselessness and self-pity will disappear. We will lose interest in selfish things and gain interest in our fellows. Self-seeking will slip away. Our whole attitude and outlook upon life will change. Fear of people and of economic insecurity will leave us. We will intuitively know how to handle situations which used to baffle us. We will suddenly realize that God is doing for us what we could not do for ourselves. Are these extravagant promises? We think not. They are being fulfilled among us—sometimes quickly, sometimes slowly. They will always materialize if we work for them. ("Big Book" 1976:83–84)

Some groups prefix these with a brief statement from a preceding paragraph, "The spiritual life is not a theory. *We have to live it*" (ibid.:83, emphasis in the original).

The discussion of the Ninth Step that leads up to this is about what happens when the alcoholic makes amends, which apparently should always involve some kind of direct contact with the person wronged. Obviously the contact with those who are dead is unlikely to be made face-to-face. And, as the "Big Book" points out, there are some (husbands or wives wronged by extramarital affairs, for example) who are not to be the recipient of direct amends, because those amends might harm them or others. Who are to be the recipients of direct amends is, it seems, to be determined by the alcoholic's sponsor or other spiritual counselor (this is an argument for doing Step 5 with the sponsor or, in rare cases, a spiritual counselor not the sponsor—and against doing it with some random member of the fellowship or *a fortiori* a nonmember who is not a spiritual counselor).

How are the amends to be made to those who are dead? I have been given answers ranging from prayer to writing a letter and burning it, or reading it in a graveside visit, or graveside prayer and communication with the dead. These fit in with the emphasis in A.A. on the fact that amends are made not to benefit the recipient but the maker of the amends. Let's look briefly at the fuller discussion of Step 9 in the *12&12* (1952/53:83–87). It is interesting, by the way, that the discussion of Step 9 in the *12&12* is shorter than the discussion of Step 9 in the "Big Book" (1976:77–84), being a little less detailed and a little more meditative—and at the same time less an exhortation and more an explanation.

It begins, "Good judgment, a careful sense of timing, courage, and prudence—these are the qualities we shall need when we take Step Nine" (1952/53:83). Courage, presumably (as we have noted), in the sense of *fortitude*, rather than in the sense of *audacity* or *daring*—and thus at the outset (as we have also noted) two of the four cardinal virtues are recognized as *necessary* for this Step. I have heard of at least one alcoholic who had— as he and his sponsor both believed—gotten successfully through Steps 1 through 8, only to be turned back by his sponsor to 4, because he clearly lacked *justitia* ("good judgment"), *temperantia* ("timing"—connected with the Latin *tempus*, time), *fortitudo* (courage, fortitude), and *prudentia* (prudence). What seems to be the lesson here, in traditional theological terms, is that the first eight Steps (or at least the first seven) must bring the alcoholic back to the spiritual starting point, the possession of the natural (or "cardinal") virtues. The seal on this is doing Step 9. It is an interesting theological question whether the theological virtues (faith, hope, charity or love) can come in the absence of the natural virtues. The answer might come from a more detailed theological inquiry than we have time for here.

One thing is very clear in reading Bill W.'s meditation on this Step: he sees the Step in one sense as beginning at the very beginning—at the moment of the alcoholic's entry into A.A.

> Most of us begin making certain kinds of direct amends from the day we join Alcoholics Anonymous. The moment we tell our families that we are really going to try the program, the process has begun. . . . After coming from our first meeting, or perhaps after we have finished reading the book *Alcoholics Anonymous* [reading the "Big Book" originally came *before* "joining" A.A.], we usually want to sit down with some member of the family and readily admit the damage we have done by our drinking. Almost always we want to go further and admit other defects that have made us hard to live with. (pp. 83–84)

And a cautionary note, "While we may be quite willing to reveal the very worst, we must be sure to remember that we cannot buy our own peace of mind at the expense of others" (p. 84).

After approaching the family, the alcoholic may want to wait "several weeks or longer" (ibid.) before approaching those "at the office or factory" or those outside the family "who know all about our drinking, and who have been most affected by it." Then, with this part of the process concluded, "We will want to rest on our laurels. The temptation to skip the more humiliating and dreaded meetings that still remain may be great. . . . Let's not talk prudence while practicing evasion" (ibid.:85). And then Bill W. reflects (ibid.:86) on making direct amends for illegal activities, concluding that "there is no pat answer which can fit all such dilemmas. But all of them do require a complete willingness to make amends as fast and as far as may be possible in a given set of conditions" (ibid.:87).

The parts of the process, in Bill W.'s experience, are clear: (1) the conversion by self-surrender that makes possible a virtually instantaneous embarking on the process of amendment apparently out-of-order in the Steps; (2) amendment to the family; (3) amendment to others with whom the alcoholic is currently in close contact; (4) amendment to those harmed (perhaps greatly) in the past. The progression from (2) to (3) to (4) is, I should say, sound psychology, and does not depend on (1): it would presumably work also for volitional (or "educational") conversion. But not so swiftly, I would think, as for the convert (like Bill W.) with the white-light experience: I believe the phrase "The Steps are in order for a reason" is frequently heard in A.A., and bears witness to the fact that most A.A. conversions are not of the white-light or burning-bush kind.

STEPS TEN AND ELEVEN

This brings us to Step 10. In the summary at the front of the *12&12*, Bill W. begins by asking a difficult question, and then goes on to give the parameters of the answer.

> Can we stay sober and keep emotional balance under all conditions? Self-searching becomes a regular habit. Admit, accept, and patiently correct defects. Emotional hangover. When past is settled with, present challenges can be met. Anger, resentments, jealousy, envy, self-pity, hurt pride—all led to the bottle. Self-restraint first objective. Insurance against "big-shot-ism." Let's look at credits as well as debits. Examination of motives.

It is instructive to put this beside the discussion of Step 10 in the "Big Book." Obviously, the two books are talking about the same Step, but consider some of the differences in *nuance* and implication:

> We have entered the world of the Spirit. Our next function is to grow in understanding and effectiveness. . . . Continue to watch for selfishness, dishonesty, resentment, and fear. When these crop up, we ask God at once to remove them. We discuss them with someone immediately and make amends quickly if we have harmed anyone. Then we resolutely turn our thoughts to someone we can help. . . . We have ceased fighting anything or anyone—*even alcohol* [my emphasis]. For by this time sanity will have returned. We will seldom be interested in liquor. If tempted, we recoil from it as from a hot flame. . . . We will find that this has happened automatically. We will see that our new attitude toward liquor has been given us without any thought or effort on our part. . . . The problem has been removed. (Bill W. et al. 1939:84–85)

But, it

> is easy to let up on the spiritual program of action and rest on our laurels. We are headed for trouble if we do, for alcohol is a subtle foe. We are not cured of alcoholism. What we really have is a daily reprieve contingent on the

maintenance of our spiritual condition. Every day is a day when we must carry the vision of God's will into all of our activities. "How can I best serve Thee—Thy will (not mine) be done." (ibid.:85)

In the "Big Book," this leads neatly into Step 11, but here we need to pause to see what exactly is being said, in the "Big Book" and in the *12&12*. The first thing that may come to mind is that the outline of Step 10 in the front of the *12&12* emphasizes the regular self-searching, the problem of balance, the problem of emotional hangovers, the admission, acceptance, and correction of defects, the keeping watch for "anger, resentments, jealousy, envy, self-pity, hurt pride." In the "Big Book," the alcoholic will "continue to watch for selfishness, dishonesty, resentment, and fear"—a somewhat different list, perhaps, but then Bill W. liked to avoid repetitions (as in his use of *wrongs*, *defects*, and *shortcomings* in Steps 5 through 7).

The important thing in the "Big Book" is that Step 10 is a single-day version of Steps 4 and 5—inventory and sharing it with someone else—and this is what is necessary for the maintenance of the alcoholic's spiritual condition. And the "Big Book" makes it very clear that this Step is about alcohol, from which there is a daily reprieve based on spiritual condition, which is a subtle foe, which requires the alcoholic to keep watch. Those statements are, in a way, in the great tradition—the daily reprieve carries us back to Jonathan Edwards and his "Sinners in the Hands of an Angry God" (was there perhaps alcoholism in his wife's family? Coming out in his grandson Aaron Burr? As it did in another Hopkins descendant, Samuel Hopkins Hadley?); the subtle foe takes us back to the words of the late medieval Scots poet William Dunbar ("the flesche is brukle, the fend is slee"); and the true nature of the watch to Psalm 127. Alcohol is the fiend, the tempter, and the watchman keeps our watch, or else we watch in vain. In a word, there is a little more *apocalypse* in Step 10—and more *irresistible* Grace—in the "Big Book" than in the summary in the *12&12*.

What of the fuller discussion (1952/53:88–95) in the *12&12*? Here, as in Steps 6 and 7, the advice is essentially practical. The spiritual exercises are laid out in some detail. There are various types of inventory-taking: the spot-check inventory, taken at any time of day; the end-of-day inventory; the periodic inventory with the sponsor or spiritual adviser; the annual or semiannual housecleaning. After making these distinctions, Bill W. goes on to one of the hardest places in the *12&12*: "It is a spiritual axiom that every time we are disturbed, there is something wrong with *us*" (ibid.:90). The quick inventory is aimed at the alcoholic's daily ups and downs, "especially those where people or new events throw us off balance" (ibid.:91). The first objective is the development of self-restraint ("Count ten and do the Tenth Step!")—and then, Bill W. points out that disagreeable or unexpected problems "are not the only ones that call for self-control. We

must be quite as careful when we begin to achieve some measure of importance at a time and material success" (ibid.)—in other words, here we are
again at the cardinal virtue of temperance. But how is it to be practiced?

We find, Bill W. says,

> that we still need to exercise special vigilance. . . . We can often check our-
> selves by remembering that we are today sober only by the grace [pro-
> vidence?] of God. . . . Finally we begin to see that all people, including
> ourselves, are to some extent emotionally ill as well as frequently wrong, and
> then we approach true tolerance and see what real love for our fellows actu-
> ally means. It will become more and more evident, as we go forward, that it
> is pointless to become angry, or to get hurt by people who, like us, are suf-
> fering from the pains of growing up. Such a radical change in our outlook
> will take time, maybe a lot of time. . . . We can't stand it if we hate deeply. The
> idea that we can be possessively loving of a few, can ignore the many, and
> can continue to fear or hate *anybody*, has to be abandoned, if only a little at a
> time. (ibid.:92–93)

How?

> We can try to stop making unreasonable demands upon those we love. We
> can show kindness where we had shown none. With those we dislike we can
> begin to practice justice and courtesy. . . . Whenever we fail any of these peo-
> ple, we can promptly admit it. . . . When in doubt we can always pause, say-
> ing "Not my will, but Thine, be done." And we can often ask ourselves, "Am
> I doing to others as I would have them do unto me—today?" When evening
> comes . . . many of us draw up a balance sheet for the day. . . . As we glance
> down the debit side of the day's ledger, we should carefully examine our
> motives in each thought or act that appears to be wrong . . . Having so con-
> sidered our day . . . and having searched our hearts with neither fear nor
> favor, we can truly thank God for the blessings we have received, and sleep
> in good conscience. (ibid.:92–94)

In short, every time the alcoholic finds himself with a problem (especially an unexpected problem), the first thing to do is self-examination.
The same thing is true in a moment of success. The problems in particular
should be the occasion of being less demanding, more kind, more just,
more courteous, realizing all human beings are fallible.

The alcoholic should promptly admit error, also should say frequently,
"Not my will, but Thine, be done!" and practice self-examination in light
of the Golden Rule. All this should become habitual. And at the end of the
day, there should be a more searching self-examination, with thankfulness
to God for blessings bestowed. There is, as Father Dowling claimed, some
resemblance to the *Spiritual Exercises* of Ignatius Loyola (see Dulles) but
also to our point here is that—resemblance to the founder of the Jesuits

or not—this is evidently a process of spiritual exercises toward habitual grace.

The summary of the Eleventh Step in the front of the *12&12* conceals the fact that it is in this Step in this book that Bill W. introduces the "prayer of St. Francis of Assisi" as the Eleventh Step prayer. Here's the summary:

> Meditation and prayer main channels to Higher Power. Connection between self-examination and meditation and prayer. An unshakable foundation for life. How shall we meditate? Meditation has no boundaries. An individual adventure. First result is emotional balance. What about prayer? Daily petitions for understanding God's will and *grace* [my emphasis] to carry it out. Actual results of prayer are beyond question. Rewards of meditation and prayer.

(The St. Francis prayer is concealed under the phrase "an individual adventure.") It is worth noting that the Third Step and Seventh Step prayers are in the "Big Book"—indeed, the Seventh Step Prayer takes up just about the entire space the "Big Book" allots to Step Seven. But the "Big Book" has no Eleventh Step prayer, though of course its discussion of the Eleventh Step is largely devoted to prayer.

> We shouldn't be shy on this matter of prayer. Better men than we are using it constantly. It works, if we have the proper attitude and work at it. . . . [We] believe we can make some definite and valuable suggestions. When we retire at night, we constructively review our day [but this is, of course, Step Ten]. . . . After making our review we ask for God's forgiveness and inquire what corrective measures should be undertaken. On awakening . . . [we] consider our plans for the day. Before we begin, we ask God to direct our thinking, especially asking that it be divorced from self-pity, dishonest or self-seeking motives. . . . In thinking about our day . . . we ask God for inspiration, an intuitive thought or a decision. We relax and take it easy. We don't struggle. . . . Being still inexperienced and having just made conscious contact with God, it is not probable that we are going to be inspired at all times. . . . Nevertheless, we find that our thinking will, as time passes, be more and more on the plane of inspiration. ("Big Book" 1976:85–87)

This time of "listening for God" is, of course, a part of the Oxford Group routine. Bill W. goes on to say,

> We conclude the period of meditation with a prayer that we be shown all through the day what our next step is to be, that we be given whatever we need to take care of such problems. We ask especially for freedom from self-will, and are careful to make no requests for ourselves only. . . . If circumstances warrant, we ask our wives or friends to join us in morning meditation. If we belong to a religious denomination which requires a definite morning

devotion, we attend to that also. If not members of religious bodies, we some-times select and memorize a few set prayers which emphasize the principles we have been discussing. (ibid.:87)

Bill W. wrote a prayer that he and Lois used in their morning prayer and meditation for many years:

> Oh Lord, we thank Thee that Thou art, that we are from everlasting to ever-lasting. Blessed be Thy holy name and all Thy benefactions to us of light, of love, and of service. May we find and do Thy will in good strength, in good cheer today. May thy ever-present *grace* [my emphasis] be discovered by fam-ily and friends—those here and those beyond—by our Societies throughout the world, by men and women everywhere, and among those who must lead us in these troubled times. Oh Lord, we know Thee to be all wonder, all beauty, all glory, all power, all love. Indeed, Thou art everlasting love. Accord-ingly, Thou hast fashioned for us a destiny passing through Thy many man-sions, ever in more discovery of Thee and in no separation between ourselves. (A.A. 1984:265)

This prayer, composed some time around 1941, might be considered Bill W.'s own Eleventh Step prayer, before he borrowed a much older prayer for the *12&12*.

Just as Step 10 suggests spot-check inventory, Step 11(1952/53:88) sug-gests spot-check prayer. That suggestion, along with asking God to direct one's thinking, carries over into the text of the *12&12*. But there are several significant differences in emphasis between the discussion of Step Eleven in the *12&12* and the discussion of Step 11 in the "Big Book." First is the specific use of the prayer of St. Francis. Here is the version in the *12&12*:

> Lord, make me a channel of thy peace—that where there is hatred, I may bring love—that where there is wrong, I may bring a spirit of forgiveness—that where there is discord, I may bring harmony—that where there is error, I may bring truth—that where there is doubt, I may bring faith—that where there is despair, I may bring hope—that where there are shadows, I may bring light—that where there is sadness, I may bring joy. Lord, grant that I may seek rather to comfort than to be comforted—to understand, than to be understood—to love, than to be loved. For it is by self-forgetting that one finds. It is by forgiving that one is forgiven. It is by dying that one awakens to Eternal Life. Amen. (ibid.:99)

This prayer is both petitionary and (in the last three sentences) medita-tive. This is important, but what is more important for our purpose is that it is a prayer to put the person praying into a condition where God's grace is present and working. Gone is what some might consider the easy optimism of the "Big Book"—the relaxing and taking it easy and stopping the struggle, and then the answer comes. Just as Step 6 and Step 7 expanded (and Step 10—all perhaps under Father Dowling's influence), so in a way did Step 11, and in the same direction—toward becoming a formal spiritual exercise.

This brings us to a second difference in emphasis. The "Big Book" seems to be saying that by opening oneself to God in prayer, one will be directed ("guided" was the Oxford Group word) how to do God's will—if one relaxes sufficiently. That remains true, but the *12&12* makes it clear that one of the things to be relaxed is one's insistence on defining the terms of the problem:

> Our immediate temptation will be to ask for specific solutions to specific problems, and for the ability to help other people as we have already thought they should be helped. In that case, we are asking God to do it *our* way. (ibid.:102)

And also,

> We have seen A.A.s ask with much earnestness and faith for God's explicit guidance. . . . Quite often, however, the thoughts that *seem* to come from God are not answers at all. They prove to be well-intentioned unconscious rationalizations. (ibid.:103)

In other words what the person praying wanted to do all along. And, similarly, Bill W. remarks,

> We form ideas as to what we think God's will is for other people . . . and we pray for these specific things. Such prayers, of course, are fundamentally good acts, but often they are based upon a supposition that we know God's will for the person for whom we pray. (ibid.:104)

So that side by side with the prayer there is presumption and conceit in the person praying.

A third difference in emphasis comes toward the end of the chapter on Step 11 in the *12&12*:

> All of us, without exception, pass through times when we can pray only with the greatest exertion of will. Occasionally we go even further than this. We are seized with a rebellion so sickening that we simply won't pray. When these things happen we should not think too ill of ourselves. We should simply resume prayer as soon as we can, doing what we know to be good for us. (ibid.:105)

I do not believe the word *sickening* is purely metaphorical. I call this a difference in emphasis because in the "Big Book" the emphasis is primarily on the fact that prayer works, while here, though prayer works (to be sure), the alcoholic may sicken, may fall into a fit of "antiprayer" (what was called *accidie* in the Middle Ages). Our common name for this sin is sloth, but the kind of *accidie* Bill W. experienced (particularly in 1944–45) we would call depression, and it unquestionably had a physical component. In fact, when Bill W. began his plunge into depression in 1944–45, his friends wanted to get him out to the camp in Minnesota where Dr. Bob and Earl T. and Archie T. and others met for rest and relaxation in the summers (Camp Karephree in 1945 and 1946). Joe F. of Montclair, New Jersey (who brought A.A. to Vermont) was willing to charter a plane to fly Bill and Lois out, but Bill's doctor said he was not physically capable of sustaining the trip. The point to be emphasized is that prayer really does link the person praying with God's power, and indeed God's grace. (Of course, Bill may have been giving Joe F. that answer because he really didn't want to go—which would speak to the depression.)

THE TWELFTH STEP

The Twelfth Step reads "Having had a spiritual awakening as *the* result of these steps [emphasis mine], we tried to carry *this message* [emphasis mine] to alcoholics, and to practice *these principles* [again, my emphasis] in all our affairs." The summary in the front of the *12&12* is long (as the chapter on the Step itself is long):

> Joy of living is the theme of the Twelfth Step. Action its keyword. Giving that asks no reward. Love that has no price tag. What is spiritual awakening? A new state of consciousness and being is received as a *free gift* [my emphasis]. Readiness to receive gift lies in practice of Twelve Steps. The magnificent reality. Rewards of helping other alcoholics. Kinds of Twelfth Step work. Problems of Twelfth Step work. What about the practice of these principles in *all* our affairs? Monotony, pain, and calamity turned to good use by practice of Steps. Difficulties of practice. "Two-stepping." Switch to "twelve-stepping" and demonstration of faith. Growing spiritually is the answer to our problems. Placing spiritual growth first. Domination and overdependence. Putting our lives on give-and-take basis. *Dependence upon God necessary to recovery of alcoholics* [my emphasis]. "Practicing these principles in *all* our affairs": Domestic relations in A.A. Outlook upon material matters changes. So do feelings about personal importance. Instincts restored to true purpose. Understanding is key to right attitudes, right action key to good living.

In the Step itself, we have singled out five words—*the* in "the result" and *this message* and *these principles*. It is clear (to me, at least) from my reading and inquiry that "this message" is the message that the Twelve Steps work, that they are the answer to alcoholism, and that they produce a spiritual awakening. Given Bill W.'s tendency to make use of synonyms to reinforce his message (one wonders about the influence of Mary Baker Eddy here), I believe that "these principles" and "this message" are pretty much the same thing. What seems to me to set Alcoholics Anonymous apart from a number of other "Twelve-Step" programs is—as suggested in an earlier chapter—the little word *the*. The Narcotics Anonymous version of the Twelfth Step, for example, reads "Having had a spiritual awakening as *a* result of these Steps." But Bill W. is clear: *the* result of the Twelve Steps, summarized in Step Twelve, for any alcoholic who puts these Steps into practice, is a spiritual awakening. Note also the line I have italicized in the *12&12* summary: "Dependence upon God [is] necessary to recovery of alcoholics." Not "my Higher Power is a door-knob" or even "my Higher Power is the group"—but dependence on *God*, and not *advisable* or *desirable* but *necessary*. Old-timers (long-timers?) in meetings have been known to say, when someone talks about "the spiritual part of the program," that "for myself, there isn't a spiritual part, it's a spiritual program." This seems to go back to this matter of the spiritual awakening as *the* result of the program, and the *necessity* of dependence on God.

In the "Big Book," the Twelfth Step takes an entire chapter (Bill W. et al. 1939:89–103). In the *12&12*, the chapter (1952/53:106–25) is sufficiently long that many Step and Tradition meetings discuss it in two parts (frequently from p. 106 to the bottom of p. 115, and from the bottom of p. 115 to p. 125). Part of the reason for the length of the discussion in the *12&12* is the summary of Steps 1 through 11 (1953/53:107–9). But the chief part of the reason is that the communal life of Alcoholics Anonymous (the life of the *koinonia*) *is* the Twelfth Step, the working with others, and the carrying on from day to day as a member of the fellowship. The conclusion—is sometimes read at the end of meetings:

> God will constantly disclose more to you and to us. Ask Him in your morning meditation what you can do each day for the man who is still sick. The answers will come, if your own house is in order. But obviously you cannot transmit something you haven't got. See to it that your relationship with Him is right, and great events will come to pass for you and countless others. *This is the Great Fact for us.* ("Big Book" 1976:164; emphasis mine)

Once again, the emphasis of the Twelfth Step discussion in the "Big Book" is a little different from the emphasis in the *12&12*. In the "Big Book," Bill W. is telling the new members of A.A. how to do what is still today called Twelfth-Step work. The chapter ("Big Book" 1976:89–103) begins by saying that "our twelfth *suggestion*" is simply, "Carry this message to other alcoholics!" Discover a prospect; learn all you can about him; if it looks like he might want to stop drinking, talk to his wife; wait till he goes on a binge, then when he's in bad shape, talk to him; approach him not through his family but through a doctor or institution; see him alone if possible (that is, without his family, doctor, nurses); tell him about your own drinking career; make sure he's willing to believe in a power greater than himself; outline the program of action; if he's interested, give him the "Big Book" and tell him to read it; after he's read it, if he's prepared to go through the steps; if he is, make yourself available to hear his story—and, here's the fundamental point: "Burn into the consciousness of every man that he can get well regardless of anyone. The only condition is that he trust in God, and clean house" (ibid.:98). And the chapter ends with these words: "*After all, our problems were of our own making. Bottles were only a symbol. Besides, we have stopped fighting anybody or anything. We had to*" (ibid.:103, emphasis in the original).

By the time Bill W. wrote the *12&12*, things had changed. Much of the chapter on Step 12 in the later book (1952/53:106–25) is devoted to a summary of the first eleven steps, and how they have brought the alcoholic to his spiritual awakening. And much of the rest is devoted to the matter of practicing "these principles [meaning the Steps] in all our affairs." The difference in emphasis is in part explained in a passage in the *12&12* (ibid.:113) on "two-stepping"—that is, coming into the program and then carrying the message, without bothering to work the steps. It would appear that this was a significant problem in the 1940s—not least, one suspects, because in the beginning the Steps were all taken in pretty quick order. In the *12&12*, the emphasis is on having overcome fear (and the reverse side of the coin, false pride), and having had our distorted drives "restored to something like their true purpose and direction" (ibid.:124). This is in part the language of psychology, but the ultimate conclusion is unquestionably in the language of the spirit (perhaps with even a slight suggestion of the Buddha): "Understanding is the key to right principles and attitudes, and right action is the key to good living; therefore the joy of good living is the theme of A.A.'s Twelve Steps" (ibid.:125).

And then the return to a Christian hope and the language of a Christian prayer:

> With each passing day of our lives, may every one of us sense more deeply the inner meaning of A.A.'s simple payer: "God grant us the serenity to accept the things we cannot change, courage to change the things we can, and wisdom to know the difference." (ibid.)

It is interesting that in the version (translation?) Bill W. preferred, it asks courage and wisdom in full measure, but serenity only enough to accept what cannot be changed. We said before that Alcoholics Anonymous has something about it of the church militant, and so it does here. But Bill W. chose not to make it into a church—perhaps with the contrary example of Mary Baker Eddy and Christian Science in mind—and it is to what he did instead that we must now turn. How could he ensure A.A.'s continuance?

8 ~

The Twelve Traditions of Alcoholics Anonymous

FROM THE POINT OF VIEW OF A STUDENT OF "GOVERNANCE"—or order, or spontaneous order, or a "functioning anarchy"—the Twelve Traditions are by far the most interesting aspect of A.A. They represent an attempt by Bill W., as the longer-lived cofounder, to provide for the functioning of a social system without statute law (rules) and without *avowedly* giving lawlike effect to custom or tradition. Originally (in 1945–46), they were called Twelve Suggested Points of A.A. Tradition, and appeared in an early form under that name in an article in the *A.A. Grapevine* in April 1946. Of course, Alcoholics Anonymous as a functioning society was only slightly more than ten years old then, and its first real growth period (outside Cleveland) was only five years old, so what Bill W. was doing was suggesting on the basis of five years' experience how appeal to that experience could be organized and highly recommended, if not imposed.

After Dr. Bob's death in 1950, and with Dr. Bob's possibly reluctant last-year consent, Bill W. used his position as the surviving cofounder to establish—one might in a technical sense say "invent"—these traditions. The A.A. General Service Office and Conference and Board of Trustees in New York are called the guardians of the Traditions, and apparent disregard of the Traditions is supposed to be referred by individual members, through groups (by the group's General Service Representative), through Districts (by the District [Area] Committee Member, who meets at regular intervals with the District's GSRs), through Areas (by the Area Delegate, who meets at regular intervals with the District [Area] Committee Members), to the General Service Conference (which meets yearly in April in New York), and thence to the Board of Trustees—or individual members may write directly to the permanent General Service Office in New York and after some time receive a letter sketching applicable past experience with the disregard of the Traditions. This may be compared to the kind of process established in the Church of Christ, Scientist, where all questions are answered, essentially, by appeal to the Bible and Mrs. Eddy's *Science and Health With Key to the Scriptures*—except those on church governance, which are settled by appeal to the *Church Manual*. But the problem is older by far than Mrs. Eddy or Bill W. The creation of the Christian church in the first century is an answer to precisely this kind of problem. Here, briefly, are the Traditions in their final form (reprinted by permission):

(1) Our common welfare should come first; personal recovery depends upon A.A. unity;

(2) For our group purpose there is but one ultimate authority—a loving God as he may express Himself in our group conscience. Our leaders are but trusted servants; they do not govern;

(3) The only requirement for A.A. membership is a desire to stop drinking;

(4) Each group should be autonomous except in matters affecting other groups or A.A. as a whole;

(5) Each group has but one primary purpose—to carry its message to the alcoholic who still suffers;

(6) An A.A. group ought never endorse, finance, or lend the A.A. name to any related facility or outside enterprise, lest problems of money, property, and prestige divert us from our primary purpose;

(7) Every A.A. group ought to be fully self-supporting, declining outside contributions;

(8) Alcoholics Anonymous should remain forever non-professional, but our service centers may employ special workers;

(9) A.A., as such, ought never be organized; but we may create service boards or committees directly responsible to those they serve;

(10) Alcoholics Anonymous has no opinion on outside issues; hence the A.A. name ought never be drawn into public controversy;

(11) Our public relations policy is based on attraction rather than promotion; we need always maintain personal anonymity at the level of press, radio, and films;

(12) Anonymity is the spiritual foundation of all our traditions, ever reminding us to place principles before personalities. (*12&12* 1952/53:passim)

So, with these Traditions, A.A. is a nonorganized organization ("spontaneously ordered society" with a nonbinding Court of Appeal), whose members use the Twelve Steps to attain and maintain sobriety. The "Big Book" makes little mention of A.A. meetings—not surprising since the "Big Book" was first published in 1939, just about the time the first A.A. group was formed. (Meetings from 1935 through 1939 were either unofficial or unnamed or under the auspices of the Oxford Group.) There has been considerable controversy over whether meetings are in fact a form of group therapy, and the present majority view seems to be that they are—though we have suggested in Chapter 6 an alternative interpretation. We will find that there were attempts in the first fifteen or twenty years of A.A. to divorce meetings from group therapy sessions, although A.A. history here is quite fragmentary. (The name of Marty M. comes in here, as the first long-term member of A.A. who came in through a psychiatric sanitarium, under Dr. Harry Tiebout.) Also, there seems to be confusion between A.A. as a mutual-help society (which it pretty clearly is) and A.A. as a self-help society (which would seem to be a misleading definition).

KOINONIA AND KOINONIA

A.A. does, as we have noted, satisfy the dual definitions of *koinonia*. As a spontaneously ordered social system based neither on markets nor hierarchies (or votes) it is a *koinonia* rather than *agora* or *polis*. As a fellowship speaking a common language, it is a *koinonia* rather than *ekklesia* or *kyriakon*. We will begin here by looking at how a *koinonia* ("social-systems" sense) functions, or can be made to function, before we look at how A.A. has gone about attempting to preserve both versions of *koinonia* by the use of the Twelve Traditions.

But before we look at how the *koinonia* functions, we should perhaps take another look at types of social systems—not the typing by *agora, polis,* and *koinonia,* but at another way of classifying or categorizing social systems that cuts across these, is relevant to all three, and therefore to our discussion. Of social systems in the larger sense we may distinguish three types, utopian, conservative, and the *tertium quid* that shows sometimes as pragmatic, sometimes under the name utilitarian.

These types are defined by their basis for choice. Do we seek perfection, whether by reason or revelation (but almost certainly by revelation), looking to the future, whether heaven on earth or pie (presumably apple) in the sky? We are utopians, and the system we will (if we can) set in effect is utopian. We might also call it a system based on revelation. It is true that some have claimed an origin for perfection in reason, but I take this claim to be dubious. (Note that A.A. claims *progress* rather than *perfection,* thus seeking to remove itself from the utopian to the pragmatic—and note, *pragmatic* rather than *entrepreneurial*). Do we build our system on the common knowledge and experience of humankind, pygmies (or even giants) standing on the shoulders of giants? We are conservatives, and our system is conservative. It is true that traditionalist or "traditionary" might be a better name for the "conservative" system as a whole, but the tradition need not be a conservative tradition, and indeed, in all three subsystems, frequently is not. Do we build our system on what works? Then if we introduce new diversity into the system for our profit (whether material or even spiritual), we are entrepreneurs, and if we try to manage the system (avoiding new diversity to the extent possible), we are pragmatists. In either case, we are the *tertium quid*, neither utopian nor conservative—the name utilitarian being sometimes used in this case.

All three types have this in common: If new diversity cannot be handled by the creation of still newer diversity within the system (as, for example, by hiving off personal properties to some mediating structure), the system will fragment. That would be a case of too much new diversity. If there is too little new diversity, the system will atrophy. All developmental systems—including social systems—must change or die. But they can also die through too much change. Since change can best be handled by systems with sufficient freedom for adjustment at the individual level, the more rigid (or bureaucratic) a system, the less likely it is to absorb change—that is, to integrate new diversity into the system. It must be emphasized here that the more decentralized the making of decisions in the system, the more freedom at the individual level, then the more flexible the system, and the more readily it can respond to new diversity. This is the root of the pragmatic argument for freedom within the system, and against bureaucracy. As we will see, it is what Bill W. tried to create in the Society of Alcoholics Anonymous.

SOCIETIES, TRADITION, AND TRADITIONS

Societies exist in time and conserve images of themselves as continuously so existing. An essential feature of society is tradition—the handing on of formed ways of acting. Traditions of this kind are, as Edmund Burke taught, immemorial, prescriptive, and presumptive. What stands outside tradition is charismatic, whether postulating timeless existence or sacred origin (which includes creative origin). The criticism—but thus the affirmation—of tradition is history. All classical (as opposed to romantic) social systems are of this traditionalist sort. But because societies necessarily—in order to be societies—conserve images of themselves as existing (and acting in a certain way) *nemo meminisse contradicente* (the memory of man runneth not to the contrary), there is necessary conservatism in the very idea of a society, or what I am calling a social system. Social systems appeal to tradition and are thus traditional. They conserve tradition and are thus conservative, even if the tradition they conserve is not a conservative tradition. In recently formed societies, the immemorial quality will come down to later generations from the time of the charismatic founder—immemorial, one might say, in a limited sense. The memory of members of A.A. runneth not to the contrary.

What Bill W. did, to provide this immemorial quality, to bind this society together, was to "invent" these Traditions. The term "invention of tradition" is a technical one. Nearly twenty years ago there appeared a collection of seven essays, originally conference papers, by six authors (the first and last essays being by one of the collection's editors, Eric Hobsbawm), bearing the title *The Invention of Tradition* (Hobsbawm and Ranger 1983). I quote from Hobsbawm's introduction:

> "Invented tradition" is taken to mean a set of practices, normally governed by overtly or tacitly accepted rules and of a ritual or symbolic nature, which seek to inculcate certain values or norms of behaviour by repetition, which automatically implies continuity with the past. . . . The historic past into which the new tradition is inserted need not be lengthy, stretching back into the assumed mists of time. . . . However, insofar as there is such reference to a historic past, the peculiarity of "invented" traditions is that the continuity with it is largely factitious. In short, they are responses to novel situations which take the form of reference to old situations, or which establish their own past by quasi-obligatory repetition. (ibid.:1–2)

He goes on to say that invented tradition (which is generally invariant) must be distinguished from custom (which changes, if slowly, over time) as well as from convention and routine (which are technical rather than ideological). Inventing traditions is a process of formalization and ritualization, characterized by reference to the past, if only by imposing repetition (ibid.:4)—and these formalizations occupy a significant place in modern societies.

Why? For three interrelated (or overlapping) reasons: (1) they establish or symbolize the social cohesion or the membership of groups; (2) they establish or legitimize institutions, status, or relations of authority; (3) they provide "socialization" and inculcate beliefs, value systems, and conventions of behavior (ibid.:9). We note that when Hobsbawm is speaking about these invented traditions, he is mostly talking about such things as national song festivals, the Boy Scouts, Nuremberg rallies, the enacting of behavior in accordance with the invented tradition. But he is also talking about the creation of tradition in words as well as acts and things—the poems of Ossian in the Celtic revival and the Boy Scout oath being examples. Even so, the words must be said. Bill W. created the Twelve Traditions, but they will not inculcate belief (or value system), they will not legitimize any institution, they will not establish the social cohesion (or even the membership) of the groups, *unless they are read*—preferably read, marked, learned, and inwardly digested, but at least read, and at that, *read aloud*.

The Twelve Steps (whether or not as part of the whole "How It Works" passage from the "Big Book"), as we remarked in Chapters 6 and 7, are essentially read liturgically; the Twelve Traditions are, as part of Bill W.'s " invention of tradition," read as part of the tradition he invented, and thus, we might say, ritually. What are these Twelve Traditions, and how are they designed to carry the load Bill put on them? (We should, as analysts, make no mistake: the invention of tradition to serve the purposes of governance or maintaining or promoting spontaneous order in a functioning anarchy is—if it works—Bill W.'s greatest achievement within the realms of systems theory and political science. Though not, of course, in the affairs that presumably matter much more to alcoholics.)

BOUNDED RATIONALITY

Here let us take what may seem to be a digression, but is not. In Milwaukee, back in the 1930s, two rational men, each with the best interests of the community at heart, and both apparently agreeing on the objectives of a recreation program, were in a state of "continual disagreement and tension . . . with respect to the allocation of funds between physical maintenance, on the one hand, and play supervision on the other" (Simon 1982:481). A young college student, Herbert Simon, working for the city, came to the conclusion that this was a case of *subgoal identification*: "When the goals of an organization cannot be connected operationally with actions . . . then decisions will be judged against subordinate goals that can be so connected"(ibid.). In this lies the kernel of Simon's theory of bounded *procedural* rationality: the two men in question had adopted simplified models of the real situation, to permit them to work with goals that could be operationally connected to actions. The principle of bounded rationality is that the capacity of the human mind for formulating and solving complex problems is very small compared with the size of the problems whose solution is required for "objectively rational" behavior in the real world, or even for a reasonable approximation of such behavior. The consequence is that the "intended rationality of an actor" requires him to construct a simplified model of the "real situation" in order to deal with it (Simon 1957:241–43, 256).

To predict the actor's behavior (as, for example, the behavior of Simon's two men, or the members serving as "trusted servants" in Alcoholics Anonymous, or even members at a meeting, including a group's business meeting), we must understand the way in which the simplified model is constructed, and we know its construction will be related to—if not fully determined by—the actor's properties as a perceiving, thinking, and learning animal. Thus the principle of bounded rationality lies at the very core of organization theory, and also (as Simon specifically points out) at the core of any theory of action that purports to treat human behavior in complex situations—including the complex situations involved in A.A. committee (and other service structure) actions, or group actions.

Simon's two men in Milwaukee were the head of the school board and the head of the public works department: their subgoals were formed in accordance with their roles (Simon 1982:481). In Simon's terms, the specification of a role is in fact the specification of some subset of the premises that are to guide the decisions of the actor as to the correct course of behavior (decision premises, in short). The principle of bounded rationality tells us that many or most of the premises of rational choice will be determined by the social and psychological environment of the subject making the choice. The "role hypothesis" asserts that many of these premises will be obtained from the socially defined role in which the actor (in our case the committee member) is placed.

Hence, if we take the premise as the unit for role description, we can accept both the idea that behavior is rational and the idea that it is, to a considerable extent, role-determined. It is, however, necessary that roles (so as to be enacted) be specified in such a way as to bring them within the actors' computational capabilities. The two men in Milwaukee could not conceive of their roles as "making economic decisions at the margin" (that is, acting as that grand abstraction, Economic Man), because the computation—indeed the whole computational framework—which that required was beyond their capabilities.

We must therefore take into account the simplifications made by (in Simon's term) the "choosing organism" so as to bring his or her model of the situation within the range of the organism's computing capacity. The environment in which decisions are made thus lies in part within the skin of the organism: constraints that must be taken as givens in the equation for choice may be the organism's physiological and psychological limitations. Most important among them are likely to be limitations on computational choice. These limitations require simplifying decision processes by adopting—in accordance with one's role (one might say, *as* one's role)— certain subsets of decision premises that are thereafter left unexamined, and that must be left unexamined if work is to be done. But to the degree that the same subsets are adopted by more than one member of a group, there will tend to be factions (cliques, subgroups) within that group: this will lead to unstable activity and questionable output.

Different decision premises lead, as in our Milwaukee example, to different, even diametrically opposed, conclusions on important issues. If, in

our original A/B/C model, we were to have three three-person cliques
rather than three single persons, the model would still hold: indeed, inasmuch as there would be activity within cliques, lowering the level of the
group activity as a whole, the preferences of the cliques might be even
more intractable than individual preferences would be. It would appear,
from A.A.'s own literature, that there is a problem of *cliques*. The answer to
this problem, perhaps unique to A.A., lies in the spontaneous order which
the Twelve Traditions demand, and in the theory of committees. The spontaneous order comes in part *from* the Twelve Traditions, once came from
the charismatic presence of Bill W. (and in Akron and its environs, of Dr.
Bob), and comes through the World Service organization also created by
Bill W. For A.A. as *koinonia*, as we remarked in Chapter 5, the ground is tradition, the transmission code is individuality, and the binding force is a
kind of "law" governing the relations between A.A. and the rest of the
world. This law (which is in part spontaneous order) partakes of both
the Traditions and the General Service Structure, which is a structure of
committees—of both the Articles of Incorporation (a legal document) and
the Conference Charter (not a legal document). The committee structure,
as we shall see, is ordained (so to speak) by the Ninth Tradition. We should
look here at the question, How do committees make decisions? Fortunately for our purposes, in the 1960s, a considerable degree of attention
was being given to the problems of "committees" (in part as a form of the
problem of "legislatures").

COMMITTEE DECISIONS

This grew out of at least two sets of attempts (which we need not go into
here) to apply economic rules and economic reasoning to political problems. One set, called public choice theory, is particularly, in its origins, connected with the name of Duncan Black (Grofman 1981:11–46). Another,
bearing the more wide-ranging name of social choice, is connected particularly with the work of Kenneth Arrow (Arrow 1951). Both trace their
putative origins to the work of the Marquis de Condorcet in the eighteenth
century and that of Charles Lutwidge Dodgson (who was better known as
Lewis Carroll) in the nineteenth. Both deal with the question of the way in
which a decision-making body comes to conclusions, and whether those
conclusions represent the will of the body or of the constituents it represents. Of them, the public choice approach seems the more valuable tool
for our purposes (Grofman 1981:41).

Now what Duncan Black saw in a flash of inspiration (and has since been
systematically proven) was that, if committee members—indeed any per-

sons involved in joint decision-making in a committee-like structure—have preference rankings that rise steadily to a single peak and then fall steadily away from it, then there is one (unique) outcome capable of receiving a majority in pairwise competition with other alternatives: *this unique outcome will always be the median voter's most preferred alternative* (ibid.:19–20). The rule can be generalized to multidimensional issue spaces—that is, the "property of the median optimum" (the fact that the outcome will be what the median voter most wants) will hold even if more that one issue is at stake, but only if there are single-peaked preferences on every issue. It turns out that the greater the number of issues, the less likely this is. In other words, the more A.A. "sticks to its last" (dealing only with basic problems of alcoholism), the more likely it is to function smoothly, and the same holds for any committees created within the A.A. structure.

The problem that gives rise to the literature on committees has been set out in a three-person three-alternative example. Suppose person no. 1 prefers alternative A to alternative B to alternative C (1: ApBpC). Suppose person no. 2 prefers alternative B to alternative C to alternative A (2: BpCpA). Suppose person no. 3 prefers alternative C to alternative A to alternative B (3: CpApB). Now if all we have are these ordinal rankings, without any cardinal values attached, a committee consisting of these three persons (1, 2, and 3) and faced with these alternatives (A, B, and C) will vote 2–1 for A over B (ApB: 2–1), 2–1 for B over C (BpC: 2–1), but 2–1 for C over A (CpA: 2–1). That is, the preference for A over B and B over C will not produce (transitively) a preference for A over C. Indeed, as noted, C will be preferred over A, 2–1. This is known as the "impossibility" or "intransitivity" theorem.

This is very much a simplified case, but it presents the difficulty in no uncertain terms. What Duncan Black did was to show that the difficulty was not always insuperable. Under some conditions, there can be a stable equilibrium solution, and when there is, it is the most preferred alternative for the median voter. Various criteria (Grofman 1981:passim) for determining "majority will" had been proposed by Condorcet ("any alternative which is preferred by a majority to each and every other alternative"), Jean-Charles de Borda ("assigns to each alternative for each committee member one point for each alternative to which it is preferred by that committee member"—with the alternative that gains the highest point total being selected, rather like voting for the Most Valuable Player in Major League Baseball), and Charles Lutwidge Dodgson ("choose the element that would become maximal with the fewest changes to existing preference orderings"). None of these classical criteria can solve the intransitivity problem presented above, nor is there any median voter, which is why the median optimum solution cannot hold—unless we have in A.A., as we are suggesting, the exception that proves (i.e., tests) the rule.

Suppose, in our A/B/C case above, that person no. 1 would give any-thing to defeat alternative C, while person no. 3 would give anything to defeat alternative B: person no 2, on the other hand, prefers B to C to A, but does not really care very much. A minor change in no. 2's preferences can be assured by no. 1 or no. 3 or even possibly both, at low cost, provided there is another issue available for trade (an issue in which no. 2 is perhaps more involved). In fact, trading (log-rolling) of this type might produce de Borda, Condorcet, or median optimum solutions from the revised prefer-ence schedule. It might not, however, produce an advantageous outcome by anyone's standards.

We have not yet considered one highly important point in the public choice literature, the "agenda" question. It has been widely agreed that he who sets the agenda (in this imperfect world) determines the outcome. What is not agreed is whether there exists any reasonable way around this. Controlled (laboratory) experiments have shown that groups of decision-makers do not, in fact, act in such a way as to produce a lack of stable equilibrium in their decision-making. But they still seem to show that equilibrium, whether real or apparent, is a function of agenda-setting. At present, it appears that restrictive agenda-setting can assure equilibrium—that is, an agreed-upon decision—but cannot assure a "best" equilib-rium—that is, in economists' terms, Pareto-optimality. To take our A/B/C case, if the agenda-setter stops after the second pairwise vote, we have a solution (ApB and BpC, with the false implication that ApC). But the equi-librium is only apparent, since in fact, if we voted, C would be preferred to A.

Now we are arguing (via Simon) that committees will perforce seek "satisficing" solutions (that is, they will at some point adopt as recom-mendations the best-looking alternative to come along, without looking to see if there exists a better yet), which means we are accepting the absence of Pareto-optimality (that state in which no one can be made better off without someone's being made worse off). The question for us then becomes the restrictiveness of the agenda-setting and the question of who sets the internal order of the agenda: to this question we have, except by inference, no answer, but we can set out a general principle: To the degree that the same person (or body) appoints the members and sets the agenda, the members ought to be such that the agenda is suited to them, and to the goal of the body, unless the person (or body) making the appointments has failed to match them because of computational or information bounds. The exception would occur under conditions of insincere appointment or agenda-setting with concealed goals. One other point we should note before going on. Unanimity of role—that is, agreed-upon decision prem-ises (at least so far as the "role" subset is concerned)—is no guarantee of a best solution, only that a solution will be agreed upon.

THE FIRST TRADITION AND THE UNITY OF A.A.

With this for background, we may turn to Bill W.'s Twelve Traditions. Like the Twelve Steps, the Twelve Traditions of Alcoholics Anonymous did not spring full-grown from the mind of Bill W. They—and his commentary on them in the *12&12*—came in several stages, which are documented in Bill W.'s *The Language of the Heart: Bill W.'s Grapevine Writings* (1989) and his *Alcoholics Anonymous Comes of Age: A Brief History of A.A.* (1958). It seems to be commonly believed in the fellowship of Alcoholics Anonymous that the Traditions come much later in A.A. history than the Steps, which was arguably true in Bill W.'s lifetime (he died when A.A. was thirty-five years old), but is not really true now, when A.A. is almost sixty-nine. Both are in fact creations of A.A.'s youth: the Steps appear in the "Big Book" in 1939, while Bill W. began drafting the Traditions (or "Points of Tradition") for A.A.'s ordering in 1945.

In 1962, he found it necessary not so much to modify the Traditions as to correct what he apparently considered to be some misinterpretations (in his *Twelve Concepts for World Service*). Also, scattered through his miscellaneous writings collected in *As Bill Sees It* (1967) are some additional corrective interpretations. Some of Bill's original work on the Traditions owes a debt to Alexis de Tocqueville's great survey of *Democracy in America* (1835, 1840) in the 1830s, and the *Concepts* make this debt more evident and more explicit. But we will come to that (though not at all in detail) a little later on. It is time now to get directly at the Twelve Traditions.

In this discussion, we face a problem, in particular with the Third, Fourth, and Sixth Traditions. It is very difficult to find out how the Traditions were interpreted, if at all, when formulated. We can, however, see how they seem to be interpreted now. And for these three in particular, present interpretation does not seem to support what I would take to be the plain meaning of the Traditions. The best I could do in evaluating Bill A.A.'s structure and its success, is to set out what seem to be paradoxes and contradictions and leave the matter there.

The First Tradition, in its present (short) form, reads "Our common welfare should come first; personal recovery depends upon A.A. unity." In its so-called long form, it reads "Each member of Alcoholics Anonymous is but a small part of a great whole. A.A. must continue to live, or most of us will surely die. Hence our common welfare comes first. But individual welfare follows close afterward" (*12&12* 1952/53:189). Its first publication, in the *Grapevine* in April 1946, is in precisely this form ([1948] 1989:22). A commentary in the *Grapevine* in December 1947 opens with the following:

Our whole A.A. program is securely founded on the principle of humility—
that is to say, perspective. Which implies, among other things, that we relate

ourselves rightly to God and to our fellows; that we each see ourselves as we really are—"a small part of a great whole." Seeing our fellows thus, we shall enjoy group harmony. That is why A.A. Tradition can confidently state, "Our common welfare comes first."

Note the word "confidently"—the point is that Bill W. is *confidently* saying that A.A. is *already acting in accordance with this Tradition*—that this Tradition is *already* an ordering principle in Alcoholics Anonymous. In his commentary summarizing the Twelve Traditions, Bill W. summarizes this First Tradition as "Tradition One asks us to place the common good ahead of personal desire" ([1948] 1989:93). Note that this specifically defines the Traditions as minatory—as warnings—though Bill has said that this one is already being followed.

In *Alcoholics Anonymous Comes of Age* (1958), there is a gloss on this Tradition which is of some interest. Apparently, when Bill W. put this book together after the 1955 International Convention, he printed, in the section on the Traditions ("Unity" in "The Three Legacies of Alcoholics Anonymous," ibid.:97–137), an earlier (1948?) form of the material included on the Traditions in the *12&12* (1952/53:129–87). Because the earlier form was published *after* the later form, and in a book less widely read, it seems to be to some extent overlooked by members of Alcoholics Anonymous, even though, like the "Big Book" and the *12&12*, *Alcoholics Anonymous Comes of Age* is "Conference-approved literature. Here is the gloss on the First Tradition:

> The next big scare [in A.A.'s history] was the out-of-bounds romance, the well-known triangle. In the cases of more than half of our membership the family relation had been distorted. Drinking had turned the husband into the household's bad boy and the wife into his protective and possessive mother. When this relation persisted after A.A., the husband sometimes got the wandering eye. Alcoholic women whose husbands had long since cast them off put in an appearance. . . . Like other societies, we soon found there were forces among us that could threaten us in ways that alcohol and sex could not. These were the desires for domination, for glory, and for money. (pp. 97–98)

These therefore are the drives—sex, power, glory, money—that the First Tradition is designed to warn against. The Tradition seems to be saying, at least at the beginning of the Traditions, "Our common welfare *as alcoholics* comes before our welfare as individuals"—not before "our welfare as individual alcoholics" in effect because "we are *never* individual alcoholics in A.A." The individual drives are normal—but "because we are all alcoholics together, we must sublimate them for the sake of our group well-being."

THE SECOND TRADITION

The Second Tradition has the odd characteristic of being longer in its so-called short form than it is in its so-called long form. In its short or final form, it reads this way: "For our group purpose there is but one ultimate authority—a loving God as he may express Himself in our group conscience. Our leaders are but trusted servants; they do not govern." In the long form, it reads this way: "For our group purpose there is but one ultimate authority—a loving God as he may express Himself in our group conscience."

Note that in both cases, Bill W. is writing about "group purpose" and "group conscience." Before we go on to look more at the differences between the short and long form of this Second Tradition, it would be advisable to consider what exactly is meant by group conscience. Here we may call the A.A. *Service Manual* (1998–99) and an A.A. pamphlet, *The Group* (1995), for witness. The *Service Manual* includes a section on the group, which refers to the matter of the group conscience, but it is the pamphlet, *The Group*, that discusses the question of what makes an "informed group conscience." In *The Group* is this statement:

> The group conscience is the collective conscience of the group membership and thus represents substantial unanimity on an issue before definitive action is taken. This is achieved by the group members through the sharing of full information, individual points of view, and the practice of A.A. principles. To be fully informed requires willingness to listen to minority opinions with an open mind. On sensitive issues, the group works slowly— discouraging formal motions until a clear sense of its collective view emerges. Placing principles before personalities, the membership is wary of dominant opinions. Its voice is heard when a well-informed group arrives at a decision. The result rests on more than a "yes" or "no" count—precisely because it is the spiritual expression of the group conscience. The term *"informed* group conscience" implies that pertinent information has been studied and all views have been heard before the group votes. (A.A. 1995:34–35)

By contrast, the *Service Manual* (1998–99) says very little about what constitutes an "informed group conscience." But it points out (ibid.:S22) that the only authority in A.A. is that which is first expressed in the group conscience, and it devotes considerable attention to the question of selecting officers at the Area level (that is, the level which sends delegates to the annual conference: there are ninety-three of these areas). Since election to an area office requires a two-thirds vote (ibid.:S42), it would appear that a "group conscience" cannot be declared with less than two-thirds approval.

Now, the pamphlet *The Group* uses the interesting phrase, "a consensus, or informed group conscience" (1995:41) in a way suggesting that the two are the same, the phrase "or informed group conscience" defining the word "consensus"—the two being, in other words, the same thing.

The "informed group conscience" would thus seem a closer approximation to the ideal of having consensus rather than a vote, and here it may be useful to consider the idea of consensus as expressed early in this century by the philosopher Rudolf Steiner (1861–1925), the "spiritual scientist" who taught that consensus is *not* the result of voting (which is divisive), but occurs when the individual belief of any member of an assembly agrees with the individual view of every other member of the assembly—even a vote *nemine contradicente* not guaranteeing consensus in this sense. I am told by persons with long experience in A.A. that consensus is rarely if ever understood in this sense (it usually means a vote of two-thirds plus one), but I am not convinced that Bill W. understood it in any other way.

The old form of this Tradition—the shorter long form—does not have the final sentence: "Our leaders are but trusted servants; they do not govern." In the original form of the Traditions this is in the Ninth Tradition, which deals with rotation in office. We will look at this again when we come to our discussion of the Ninth Tradition: for the moment, its importance here is that its shift to the Second Tradition shows more fully the implication of reliance on "a loving God as He may express Himself in our group conscience." That is, A.A. trusts its "servants" (those who hold positions of leadership) because God speaks through the group conscience; God speaks through the group conscience because it is a consensus rather than majority rule; and consensus occurs (so far as I can tell—but this is apparently not "official" A.A. doctrine) when God brings every member of the group to an agreeing conclusion on a proper course of action.

This does not require anything more than a Jamesian or even a Jungian conception of God. Indeed, as we have already observed, this Jamesian or Jungian conception may lie behind the view that A.A. is a spiritual program, not a religious one. That is, the collective consciousness of the group may spiritually inform the individual consciousness of its members, or the mystical experience (or *conversion*) may be collective, as indeed the use of *we* in the Steps seems to suggest. I have heard members of A.A. say that they can "sense" the "spirit" of a group when they walk into the room where the group is meeting, even before the meeting begins, and that a "good group" is one where they can sense this spirit. (This would seem to have an obvious tie-in with the *koinonia* as *Logos*.) Moreover, on a more mundane level, we know that collective (or "committee") decision-making—the form of decision-making appropriate to a *koinonia*—is made easier when the members of the group have single-peaked preferences, and the property of the median optimum can obtain. We will come back to this again, later on.

THE THIRD TRADITION

The Third Tradition in the short form reads: "The only requirement for A.A. membership is a desire to stop drinking." In its long form it reads:

> Our membership ought to include all who suffer from alcoholism. Hence we may refuse none who wish to recover. Nor ought A.A. membership ever depend upon money or conformity. Any two or three alcoholics gathered together for sobriety may call themselves an A.A. group, provided that, as a group, they have no other affiliation.

We have already noted that it is highly unlikely that the "two or three gathered together" is an accidental phrase, and suggested its implication for the A.A. meeting as a form of worship, but there is, I think, something more to be said here, especially on the "provided, as a group, they have no other affiliation." Here the discussion of the Third Tradition in the *A.A. Grapevine* in February 1948 is revealing:

> Our membership Tradition does contain, however, one vitally important qualification. That qualification relates to the use of our name, Alcoholics Anonymous. We believe that any two or three alcoholics gathered together *for sobriety* [my emphasis] may call themselves an A.A. group, provided that, as a group, they have no other affiliation. Here our purpose is clear and unequivocal. For obvious reasons we wish the name Alcoholics Anonymous to be used only in connection with straight AA activities. One can think of no AA member who would like, for example, to see the formation of "dry" AA groups, "wet" AA groups, Republican AA groups, communist AA groups. Few, if any, would wish our groups to be designated by religious denominations. We cannot lend the AA name, even indirectly, to other activities, however worthy. If we do so, we shall become hopelessly compromised and divided. (reprinted in Bill W. 1989:79–80)

Now Bill's political examples (an odd couple) are Republican and communist—one of them the name of a political party, the other (with the lowercase c) a political doctrine. One may assume he picked one example of each. (Note, however, that in a similar passage in *Alcoholics Anonymous Comes of Age* [1958:105], Bill capitalizes *Communist*—note also, for what it's worth, that this passage is discussing the *Fourth* Tradition.) The party affiliation is an obvious point, and there are not many political parties in the United States, nor is anyone likely to be interested in setting up Republican

A.A. groups or Democratic A.A. groups. The matter of doctrine (verging at one end into the matter of religious denominations) is capable of greater extension: one thinks of feminism and wonders about groups restricted to women; one thinks about its converse (whatever that is) and wonders about groups restricted to men. On the matter of other affiliation, one notes that a group of doctors (with allegiance to the Hippocratic oath and affiliation to a medical society) would seem to be barred from calling themselves an A.A. group. (I am told that there is an organization of doctors and other medical professionals joined together for sobriety, and that they call themselves by another name—*Caduceus* is one that has been suggested to me, though they may also call themselves IDAA.)

Also, of course, there is a question about groups dedicated to other purposes besides (or in addition to) sobriety through A.A.'s Twelve Steps. It would appear that members of A.A. should be careful about banding together (with any announced connection to A.A.) for largely social purposes—dances, dinners, ice-cream socials, for example—and even (or perhaps especially) for conducting spiritual retreats. I believe there are questions, also, about members of A.A. banding together in any kind of fellowship with allegiance to or affiliation with any particular age cohort of the population—and then suggesting or announcing in any public way that they are *part* of A.A. This is certainly done: there appear to be a number of organizations whose acronyms end with AA, for example, YPAA—standing apparently for Young People in Alcoholics Anonymous.

That would appear to suggest that they are indeed *part* of A.A. (as opposed to their members being also members of A.A.), and would—from my vantage point though apparently not A.A.'s—appear to contravene the design of the Third Tradition, still more because some of them apparently hold open fundraising events, and thus may accept non-A.A. money, while using the acronym with A.A. in it. Whether this is conducive to the continuance of A.A. is not, of course, to be decided here, and I would suppose the "powers that be" in A.A. must have a reason for what appears to be a contravention of their own tradition. (See also our discussion below on the Sixth Tradition.) But, speaking as a political sociologist acquainted with the nature and "governance" of a *koinonia*, I can say that, if the continuance of A.A. as *koinonia* would be adequately ensured by following the Traditions—which I gather is what they're for—it is unlikely that not following them would help.

Of course, this particular case would seem to be a reflection of the quantum shift in the population of the United States that began with the baby boom, introducing new diversity into the entire social system, and thereby into its subsystems and their subsystems. We know that the preservation of the *koinonia* (any *koinonia*) will require the generation of new diversity within the *koinonia* in response to the new diversity introduced from outside (as with the age-shift in the population). We know that the great advantage of nonbureaucratic structure and spontaneous order is that it can allow for this. We also know that too much new diversity will splinter (and kill) the system, as too little will stultify (and kill) it. And we know that there is no mechanism for preventing members from acting against the design of the Twelve Traditions. Quite simply, the Traditions assume that everyone in A.A. accepts Ben Franklin's dictum: "If we do not hang together, we shall assuredly all hang separately." And that everyone making decisions that affect A.A. as a whole is essentially among the converted. This brings us to the Fourth Tradition.

THE FOURTH TRADITION

The Fourth Tradition, in its present form, reads as follows: "Each group should be autonomous except in matters affecting other groups or A.A. as a whole." The longer form is much more detailed:

> With respect to its *own* affairs [emphasis mine], each A.A. group should be responsible to no other authority than its own conscience [meaning, I take it, the "informed group conscience"]. But when its plans concern the welfare of neighboring groups also, those groups ought to be consulted. And no group, regional committee, or individual should *ever* take *any* action [again, my emphasis] that might greatly affect A.A. as a whole without conferring with the trustees of the General Service Board. On such issues our common welfare is paramount.

In his explanatory remarks on the Fourth Tradition in the *A.A. Grapevine* in March 1948, in regard to the "other groups" provision, Bill goes on to say, "An AA group need not be coerced by any human government over and above its own members. Their own experience, plus AA opinion in surrounding groups, plus God's prompting in their group conscience, would be sufficient." Furthermore, "we AAs have universally adopted the principle of consultation. This means that if a single AA group wishes to take any action that might affect surrounding groups, it consults them. Or, it confers with the intergroup committee for the area, if there be one" (1989:81). (In this context, we might note that since 1948, A.A. has created a General Service structure, involving Districts, Areas, Regions, and the Conference that meets in New York each year: these entities have essentially replaced the intergroup committees on questions relating to the Twelve Traditions.)

"Likewise," Bill goes on further to say, "if a group or regional committee [in present-day terms, a group, district committee, or area committee] wishes to take any action that might affect AA as a whole, it consults the trustees of the Alcoholic Foundation [now the General Service Board], who are, in effect, our overall general service committee. For instance, no group or intergroup [or district or area] could feel free to initiate, without consultation, any publicity that might affect AA as a whole. Nor could it assume to represent the whole of Alcoholics Anonymous by printing and distributing anything purporting to be AA standard literature" (ibid.). An example of a violation of this Tradition may be found in a card circulated in A.A. purporting to provide the "Twelve Principles of Alcoholics Anonymous." This card, which apparently derives from a presentation given at an intergroup meeting in Texas fifty years ago, masquerades as "standard A.A. literature"—to the point, I believe, that members of A.A. have referred to it as published by A.A. World Services, which I am told (by A.A.'s General Service Office) it is not.

Examples of actions "affecting other groups" that have been pointed out to me (and these are from a very limited time period—a month—in a small area surrounding the place where I live) include such things as (1) a "women's group" setting up a meeting devoted to A.A.'s literature, including the *Twelve Steps and Twelve Traditions*, on a Wednesday night competing with the Wednesday night meeting of another group in town as well as the weekly meeting of an established "Step and Tradition" group in the same town the night before (these being the only two such meetings in the town); (2) groups that advertise closed meetings (where only members may attend) voting *at the meeting* to change to an open meeting so a member's boyfriend or girlfriend may be there "for support"—which leads both those members and their friends to expect other groups to do the same; (3) groups (especially, in this case, intergroup associations) holding special meetings on the same day at the same time within half an hour's drive of each other.

None of these (if the Traditions are to be followed) should have been done without consultation, under the Fourth Tradition, and the second probably affects not only "other groups" but also "A.A. as a whole"—thus presumably requiring an appeal (seldom if ever made) to the Trustees for judgment. In none of these cases, I am told, was there any consultation of the kind envisioned by the Fourth Tradition. It may be, by A.A.'s prescription, that none of them should have been done at all, with or without consultation. It may, on the other hand, be that these are very minor and unimportant. These are mentioned here not because they are particularly egregious examples of Tradition violation (they may be—I simply don't know), but because they seem to be common, and thus suggest that perhaps the emphasis in the Tradition, if it is read aloud for effect, should be on the *except*.

That is, far from being a universal charter for unilateral action by the groups, what this Tradition seems to be saying is that, except for freedom from "coercion from any human government over and above its own members," the A.A. group should be bound (1) by the expressed will of God (wow! as we used to say in the 1960s) as determined by a consensus in the group (not majority voting) of those who are well informed on both fact and Tradition (which is probably a smaller subset of those who have accepted the A.A. program and are working the steps and staying sober); (2) by a consensus established through consultation with neighboring groups; and (3) by direct appeal to the guardians of the Traditions—that is the Trustees of the General Service Board in New York. Here is Bill W.'s conclusion (discussing the Fourth Tradition) on the "ultra-liberty" (his word) of the A.A. groups—including the fact that a group of alcoholics "could disagree with any or all of A.A.'s principles and still call themselves an A.A. group"—a matter which from time to time, I believe, causes some heart-burning and soul-searching in A.A.:

> Other societies have to have law and force and sanction and punishment, administered by authorized people. Happily for us, we found we need no human authority whatever. We have two authorities which are far more effective. One is benign, the other malign. There is God, our Father, who simply says, "I am waiting for you to do my will." The other authority is named John Barleycorn, and he says, "You had better do God's will or I will kill you." And sometimes he does kill. So, when all the chips are down, we conform to God's will or perish. . . . There is authority enough, love enough, and punishment enough, without any human being clutching the power. . . . For us, it is do or die. But that is not the whole story. As our individual and group development progress, we begin to obey the A.A. Traditions for other reasons. We begin to obey them because we think they are right for us. We obey these principles because we think they are good principles, even though we still resist somewhat. Then comes the final obedience, best of all. We obey A.A.'s Steps and Traditions because we really want them for ourselves. (1958:105–6)

The point is clear. The groups will obey the Traditions (and it may be worthwhile to emphasize that the word is *obey*) because if they don't, the group will fragment and the members get drunk. (This seems to assume that members belong to one group only—which is a point for another time, place, and author.) They will begin by obeying the Traditions more or less out of the fear that this will happen—and evidence for the reasonableness of that fear comes in the history of groups that have failed to obey them. They will go on to obey the Traditions because they increasingly seem right (a point perhaps on the borderline between the rational and the mystic)—the groups work more smoothly, there is less discord, members do better at staying sober. Finally they will obey the Traditions because, in essence (as with the Steps), they freely choose to do what they must do, for the pleasure of doing it. This may be called, as by the philosopher, *willing necessity*. It may be called (as it would by James or Jung) the result of the process of *conversion* or *a higher education of the mind beyond mere rationalism*.

It may be summarized (if we seek words away from mysticism) by quoting Charles Reade, "Sow an act, and you reap a habit. Sow a habit, and you reap a character. Sow a character and you reap a destiny." But always, for Bill W., it is the sowing and reaping in a field watched over by God, and it is God who establishes Reade's paradigm. Perhaps the difficulty some may find in holding Bill W.'s view could be summarized by the famous opening verse of Psalm 127: "Except the Lord build the house, they labor in vain that build it; except the Lord keep the city, the watchman waketh but in vain." Unless the members of an A.A. group really *know* this—or unless they simply accept as true the words of those who have gone before, and especially of Bill W.—their group is apparently likely to go its own way, unfettered by this Tradition. Rather (some in A.A. would say) like being unfettered from one's parachute when one jumps out of a plane.

THE FIFTH TRADITION

As Bill remarks, his discussion of the reasons for obeying the Traditions (and specifically, in this context, the Fourth) "leads straight to Tradition Five, which states: 'Each group has but one primary purpose—to carry its message to the alcoholic who still suffers'" (1958:106). This is sometimes known as the *primary purpose* or *singleness of purpose* statement. In its longer form (but not much longer), it reads "Each Alcoholics Anonymous group ought to be a spiritual entity *having but one primary purpose* [emphasis in the original]—that of carrying its message to the alcoholic who still suffers." The difference between the two is that the longer (and earlier) form specifically describes the group as a spiritual entity—which is, of course, as we have seen, implicit in everything we have said thus far about the first four of the Traditions. Two things should perhaps be remarked here.

First, there is also a *primary purpose* statement in the A.A. Preamble: "Our primary purpose is to stay sober and help other alcoholics to achieve sobriety." This statement apparently refers to individual alcoholics more than (or even rather than) the group: these individual alcoholics have two purposes (staying sober and carrying the message)—but the group has one. Second, what's this about "the alcoholic who still suffers"? Don't all alcoholics suffer (and everyone else, too)? Here we may turn to the discussion of Fifth Tradition in April 1948: "And may we reflect with ever deepening conviction, that we shall never be at our best except when we hew only to the primary spiritual aim of AA. That of carrying its message to the alcoholic who still suffers *alcoholism* [my emphasis]" (ibid.:83). In other words, as I understand it (members of A.A. may understand it differently), the group exists to carry the message of Alcoholics Anonymous to those who haven't yet got the message ("still suffer alcoholism").

This brings us to a discussion of the apparent present view that A.A. meetings are a kind of group therapy (even self-help therapy, since there is no therapist), where people "dump" their problems, or "air" them or "vent" them—the idea being that saying what's bothering you is what the meetings are for. At many A.A. meetings, statements are read that "we do not give advice to each other" but also that "we share our experience, strength, and hope with each other" (this one is from the Preamble)— everything I have read strongly suggests that the experience to be shared is of the same kind as the strength and hope, that is, experience *of sobriety*. Not giving advice, but sharing experience (of sobriety), strength (in Alcoholics Anonymous) and hope (at least of the alcoholic's temporal salvation) *in lieu of* giving advice. One would think, emphatically *not* airing one's grievances and resentments, venting one's displeasures, dumping the waste and refuse of one's life on the group.

It is worth remarking that group therapy for alcoholics was tried during and immediately after the Second World War, in New Haven, Connecticut, in connection with the Yale School and Yale Center. The therapist (as we noted in Chapter 1) was Raymond McCarthy, a Peabody lay therapist. The transcripts of a number of these sessions appeared in the *Quarterly Journal of Alcohol Studies*: I have skimmed (but not thoroughly read) them, and my first (unfair) reaction was that they must have been hard up for material to print. But despite their repetition, general aridity, and inconclusiveness (or in part because of it), they do make two things clear. First, it would seem that group therapy (of this kind, at least) could never by itself be a generally effective path to sobriety. Second, this group therapy was designed (even as early as 1943) to be a supplement to, not a substitute for, Alcoholics Anonymous. It may be that this shows the hand of Marty M., whose psychiatrist, Harry Tiebout, gave her a copy of the "Big Book" in 1939. Perhaps we can find some kind of confirmatory evidence for this idea that group therapy was considered a part of therapy for alcoholics separate from (though perhaps supplemental to) the therapy of A.A. meetings. I have found a little such evidence, but it is diffuse, highly anecdotal, and, of course, anonymous.

It is in the late 1940s in New York City. There is a Sullivanite psychoanalyst by the name of Frank Hale, with an office at 167 E. 82nd Street in Manhattan. To him are directed (I believe by Marty M.) a number of women from the city and from suburban New Jersey, Westchester County, New York (where Bill W. lives), and even Fairfield County, Connecticut (where Dr. Tiebout practices). These women are new in sobriety. They go to their group therapy sessions with Dr. Hale (he is also recommended by Dr. Ruth Fox, who founded the group later to become the American Society for Addiction Medicine, as well as being involved in the founding of Al-Anon). After the sessions, they go to the nearby Schrafft's together for dessert (something with chocolate, possibly a hot fudge sundae), before dispersing to their respective homes by public transportation. They call themselves Hale's Hearties. And what is a Sullivanite psychoanalyst?

We have already considered (very briefly in Chapter 4) the views of Harry Stack Sullivan, founder of modern group therapy, and his tripartite distinction of the prototaxic, parataxic, and syntaxic phases of experience. You will recall that we linked these to Harry Tiebout, Radó's 1933 paper, and Freud's "His Majesty, the Baby." Tiebout suggested that "ego-deflation" (in the popular parlance adopted by A.A.) translated in Freudian terms to the reduction of the narcissistic component of the Freudian *ego*. What a Sullivanite therapist would be doing in his group therapy is attempting, through the group dynamics with the therapist as a participant observer, to establish consensual validations by which parataxic distortions and thus unhealthy interpersonal patterns in action, habit, and character could be corrected. The members of Hale's Hearties went to their own A.A. meetings (not all of them to the same meetings, since they were scattered throughout the New York metropolitan area), but they also went to their weekly sessions with Dr. Hale.

They also had their own individual sponsors (though I believe Marty M. sponsored several of them at least briefly). The Sullivanite group therapy involved leading questions from Dr. Hale and guided conversation (guided by Dr. Hale). He was a guileless-looking round-faced man, in his forties at the time (I am told), with round glasses and an engaging manner. He also worked in individual therapy with adolescents, perhaps because of the dangers of consensual peer-group validation in any process of adolescent group therapy. The key point in the guided Sullivanite group was that the consensual validation came originally from the therapist, then from the *guided* group—because, in essence, the members of the group all suffered from parataxic distortions. In other words, they hadn't "grown up" to the point where their consensus would be of any value without guidance. This was not at all the same thing as the acting-out of encounter groups, or the "dumping" and "venting" of groups in "rehabs" or the same as intensive outpatient therapy in groups meeting with counselors (unless, of course, in this latter case, the counselor should improbably be a trained Sullivanite psychotherapist).

This may help us see the way in which, at least at the time the Traditions were being written, group therapy was considered to be different from— and supplemental to—A.A. meetings. Since consensual validation (even guided by the therapist) produces a certain degree of *bonding* among the members of the group, it may suggest that the whole group process could represent a two-edged sword. Hale's Hearties bonded together (indeed, this may be one of the earliest examples of bonding from outpatient therapy for alcoholics), but (anecdotal and anonymous) evidence suggests that those of them who did best in A.A. were those who kept up their bonds by attending at least some A.A. meetings with each other. There would always be the chance that, once out of therapy, the bonding might have negative effects and even countervail against involvement in A.A. It is worth noting that, once there were enough women (in this case) with long enough sobriety to serve as sponsors and to play a significant part in A.A. groups and meetings, the perceived need for this kind of Sullivanite therapy seems to have declined. With the vitamins fully available, so to speak, the vitamin supplement was shelved.

THE SIXTH TRADITION

The Sixth Tradition, in its short form, reads "An A.A. group ought never endorse, finance, or lend the A.A. name to any related facility or outside enterprise, lest problems of money, property, and prestige divert us from our primary purpose." That is, no group should endorse or finance a "recovery" facility or ("rehab" or hospital), nor lend the name of Alcoholics Anonymous (or the initials A.A.) to such a facility. Now that's pretty clear and is to some degree an extension and explanation of Tradition Four as well as of Tradition Five ("primary purpose"). If an A.A. group starts worrying about raising money, keeping up the building, or having a better facility than the one down the street or in the next town, that obviously works against the group as a spiritual entity having but one primary purpose. The words "outside enterprise," however, are not perhaps quite so clear as the rest of the Tradition. What is an "outside enterprise" as distinct from a "related facility"? As a matter of fact, what is an "enterprise" as against a "facility"—never mind the "related" or "outside"? Will the long form of the Tradition help us here?

In the long form, the Tradition seems very long indeed:

Problems of money, property, and *authority* [my emphasis] may easily divert us from our primary spiritual aim. We think, therefore, that any considerable property of genuine use to A.A. should be separately incorporated and managed, thus dividing the material from the spiritual. An A.A. group, as such, should never go into business. Secondary aids to A.A., such as clubs or hospitals, which require much property or administration, ought to be incorporated and so set apart that, if necessary, they can be freely discarded by the groups. Hence such facilities ought not to use the A.A. name. Their management should be the sole responsibility of those people who financially support them. For clubs, A.A. managers [meaning, managers who are A.A.s] are usually preferred. But hospitals, as well as other places of recuperation, ought to be well outside A.A.—and medically supervised. While an A.A. group may cooperate with anyone, such cooperation ought never to go so far as affiliation or endorsement, actual or implied. *An A.A. group can bind itself to no one* [my emphasis].

This certainly provides some additional insight into what Bill W. intended in this Sixth Tradition—but not, alas! on the definition of "outside enterprise." The discussion in the *12&12* does make it clear that some members of A.A. in the early days saw themselves "getting married to all kinds of enterprises, some good and some not so good" (1952/53:156–57). Among those mentioned are reform efforts in alcohol education (ibid.:156), the criminal justice system and legal reform or political reform (ibid.:157)—but these are then summarized under the statement that "in no circumstances could we endorse any related enterprise, no matter how good" (ibid.). It looks as though *related* enterprises and *outside* enterprises were pretty much the same thing in Bill W.'s mind—and we recall that he had a propensity for synonyms rather than exact verbal repetition (as with "wrongs" in Step 5, "defects" in Step 6, "shortcomings" in Step 7). Is there any additional help on this, perhaps, in *A.A. Comes of Age*?

Yes. In the discussion there of the Sixth Tradition, there is a passage which makes pretty clear what kind of enterprise Bill W. had in mind when he wrote the Tradition:

Long afterward [in context, less than ten years] we saw something else. We saw that the more A.A. minded its own business, the greater its general influence would become. Medicine and religion and psychiatry began to borrow some of our ideas and experience. So did research, rehabilitation, and education. All sorts of therapeutic groups began to spring up. They dealt with gambling, divorce, delinquency, dope addiction, mental illness, and the like. They, too, borrowed from A.A., but they made their own adaptations. They worked their own fields, and we did not have to endorse them, or tell them how to live." (1958:109)

So the outside enterprises (which are also related enterprises) are Twelve-Step groups, research programs, religious retreats, education, rehabs (which could also be considered related facilities), religion, psychiatry, and medicine—the scope of this Sixth Tradition is very broad indeed. Also, in the brief discussion of the Sixth Tradition in the *A.A. Grapevine* in May 1948 (Bill W. 1989:83), there is a passage where quotation marks may be taken as commentary.

"Tradition Six also enjoins the group never to go into business or ever to lend the AA name or money credit to any 'outside' enterprise, no matter how good. Strongly expressed is the opinion that even clubs should not bear the AA name." The quotation marks on "outside" suggest strongly that *outside* enterprises are indeed *related* enterprises—though perhaps not all related enterprises are outside. A.A. money (if any) and the A.A. name must not go for anything other than the primary purpose of A.A., and group money must not go for purposes other than carrying the message to the alcoholic who still suffers (alcoholism). As we will see in the discussion of the Seventh Tradition, there are highly recommended ways in which groups distribute their money.

Before getting to that, we should perhaps pick up from our discussion of the Third Tradition, whose "long form" notes that an A.A. group should not, as a group, have any other affiliation. We remarked that there are a number of groupings of A.A. members with names ending in "-CYPAA" that seem (despite age affiliations) to be considered *part* of A.A. I have recently (January 2004) been informed that these entities, and specifically the International Conference of Young People in A.A., are in fact considered by A.A.'s General Service Office to be *affiliated* with A.A., in apparent contravention of this Sixth Tradition. My informant has also called to my attention widespread references to "A.A. retreats," "A.A. clubhouses," and the like. Once again, it is not for me to tell A.A. how to conduct its affairs—but once again, also, if the Traditions are meant to preserve A.A., violating them seems to me an unlikely way of assuring that preservation.

Two further points in particular in the long form of the Sixth Tradition are worth a minimal discussion. First is the matter of *authority*. Second is the statement, "An A.A. group can bind itself to no one." Why did Bill W. replace *authority* in the older version with *prestige* in the newer (but both appear in Conference-approved literature, so both are Conference-approved formulations)? And what is the effect of the "can" in that statement that an A.A. group can bind itself to no one. Since it is part of the same long form of the Tradition that denies the appropriateness of problems of authority—and since, as we know, A.A.'s "leaders" do not govern—it cannot be the case that this is a legal proscription. It would be my guess that *prestige* replaced *authority* because Bill W. was already beginning to see problems with spontaneous order—the problems that led to the creation of the Twelve Concepts in 1962—and he simply needed a word to complete the triplet. But I still do not believe that the "can" is precisely a legal prohibition, though it might have legal effect. It would seem to be a part of the view that the group is a spiritual fellowship, and that it would lose this quality if it bound itself to anyone.

In other words, by a kind of natural (or spiritual) law, it would cease to be *a group*, as Bill W. would understand *a group*. Then, I presume, if it were to seek recognition by A.A. as an A.A. group, there would be a problem.

An example (again taken from the area near where I live) may be found in a pioneering group (dating back to the early 1940s) that in the early 1950s established a clubhouse. The group became principally—perhaps entirely—involved in running the clubhouse, holding all its meetings there and having its officers as the officers of the corporation running the house. It found out some six or seven years later, possibly to its chagrin, that it was no longer counted as a group by the General Service Office in New York (though a splinter group that had split off so as not to move to the clubhouse was counted). A new group was promptly formed that had its meetings at the house, and was accepted as a group—but the original group had in fact ceased to exist.

The way Bill W. set this out may be flawed, but he was dealing with a fundamentally difficult (if not intractable) problem. And note the tenor of what he is doing. An A.A. group is "a spiritual entity"—but in his revision of the Fifth Tradition he eliminated that phrase. An A.A. group should act in a way "dividing the material from the spiritual"—but in his revision of the Sixth Tradition he eliminated that phrase (and a lot of others also). As we noted before, these Traditions may be considered natural guidelines for those who are part of the koinonia in the church-meeting sense: the trick is to make them work for those who are part of the koinonia only (or principally) in the social-systems sense. And part of that trick comes in downplaying the spiritual nature of the "governance" or spontaneous order of A.A. for those who do cannot yet accept it. (He could not, of course, downplay the spiritual nature of the Steps.)

And yet they must accept the Traditions if the Traditions are to hold A.A. together. It would appear that Bill "invented" these Traditions, and apparently the tradition of their ritual reading, so as to inculcate in all the members a kind of acceptance of the Twelve Traditions as a kind of law, even if primarily iconic law. (As with, for example, the Pledge of Allegiance—another invented tradition of another koinonia—which likewise has no legal force while remaining both icon and lawlike statement.) We remember that the ground of the koinonia (in the social-systems sense) is custom or tradition, the transmission code is individuality or particularity, and the binding force must in some sense be law. There are no laws in A.A., except in the sense that it is a law that "if we don't hang together, we shall assuredly all hang separately." Yet Bill W. provides a lawlike binding force in the Traditions.

In A.A. Comes of Age, Bill W. does not pause between his discussion of the Sixth Tradition and his discussion of the Seventh Tradition. Recall his conclusion that "the more A.A. minded its own business, the greater its general influence would become" (1958:109)—or, as he puts it in summary two paragraphs later, "The more A.A. sticks to its primary purpose, the greater will be its helpful influence everywhere." Then there is a passage that reflects, among other things, one theological definition of humility that we may remember from our discussion in Chapter 6:

> After a while we awoke to the pleasant fact that A.A. as such was not going to require much money after all. When we got rid of our grandiose ideas about hospitals, research, rehabilitation, and education, not much of a bill was left to pay. Other enterprises needed large sums, but we did not. We could be spared that headache. (ibid.:110)

The theological definition of humility involved (the more Protestant definition, we recall) is that humility is the state in which one joyfully accepts God's direction of one's life. The grandiose ideas about hospitals, research, rehabilitation, and education, were almost certainly Bill's ideas—though doubtless others shared them. There may indeed be something slightly rueful about this paragraph. But the fundamental point is that Bill and his colleagues "found that God was doing for us what we could not do for ourselves" (Bill W. et al. 1976:83–84) and they realized that they were happy about having been put back on the right road.

THE SEVENTH TRADITION

From here he goes (without noting any break) into the discussion of the Seventh Tradition. In the short (and final) form, "Every A.A. group ought to be fully self-supporting, declining outside contributions." In the long form, it reads as follows:

> The A.A. groups themselves ought to be fully supported by the voluntary contributions of their own members. We think that each group should soon achieve this ideal; that any public solicitation of funds using the name of Alcoholics Anonymous is highly dangerous, whether by groups, clubs, hospitals, or other outside agencies; that acceptance of large gifts from any source, or of contributions carrying any obligation whatever, is unwise. Then, too, we view with much concern those A.A. treasuries which continue, beyond prudent reserves, to accumulate funds for no stated A.A. purpose. Experience has often warned us that nothing can so surely destroy our spiritual heritage as futile disputes over property, money, and authority.

Here is the mention of *authority* again, in a way which makes it clear that the "can" of the Fifth Tradition does not involve proscriptive authority. Also, here is confirmation that the word "outside" (though *agencies* rather than *enterprises*) can refer even to clubs or hospitals.

In the *12&12* Bill W. observes:

Probably no A.A. Tradition had the labor pains this one did. In early times we were all broke. When you add to this the habitual supposition that people ought to give money to alcoholics trying to stay sober, it can be understood why we thought we deserved a pile of folding money. (1952/53:160)

But then came a change. In *A.A. Comes of Age*, Bill W. puts it this way, in linking his discussion of the Sixth Tradition and of the Seventh:

A big factor in our thinking at the time was the philosophy of St. Francis of Assisi. *His also began as a lay movement* [my emphasis], one man carrying the good news to the next. In his day it was common enough for individuals to pledge themselves to poverty. But it was unusual, if not unique, for a whole organization or fellowship to do the same thing. For the purpose of his society, Francis thought corporate poverty to be fundamental. The less money and property they had to quarrel about, the less would be the diversion from their primary purpose. And just like A.A. today, his outfit did not need much money to accomplish its mission. Why be tempted and diverted when there was no need for it. Therefore A.A. adopted the wisdom of Francis as its own. Not only would we have the least possible service organization; we would use the least possible money. (1958:110–11)

Of course, A.A. was helped to accept this view by John D. Rockefeller, Jr., who told Bill and the other early members that money would spoil Alcoholics Anonymous. Bill remarks that there were three great temptations for A.A. to depart from the Franciscan principle. The first was when they went to Rockefeller for money. He loaned enough to get the "Big Book" published and gave enough to Bill and Dr. Bob (personally) to make it possible for Bill and Lois to live and for Dr. Bob to pay off the mortgage on his house—but no more. The second was the temptation to spend too little, "half-refusing to support A.A.'s simple but essential area-and-over-all services" (ibid.:111). The third was the temptation to accept large bequests. A.A. avoided the temptations of seeking outside money, of restricting necessary services because there was no money in the pot (thus denying what is sometimes called the spiritual principle of supply), and of accepting large sums from the dead. (And of accepting any sums from those, dead or alive, who were not members). They did not, of course, see their original appeal to Rockefeller as succumbing to temptation. It was Albert Scott, chairman of the trustees for the Riverside Church, who, on hearing Bill's telling what this as yet nameless "group of drunks" was doing, said "Why, this is first-century Christianity!" (A.A. 1958:148). It was Scott who first asked whether money wouldn't spoil this thing. (This was in December 1937 at the RCA Building in New York, more than two years before the Union League dinner on February 8, 1940, where the "Rockefeller interests" firmly established the principle of corporate A.A. poverty.) Only with the Rockefeller meetings did the nature of the temptation begin to become apparent.

The remark about "first-century Christianity" reminds us that the First-Century Christian Fellowship was the early name of Frank Buchman's movement, before it was the Oxford Group(s), before it was Moral Re-Armament, before it was whatever it is now. It would need someone more adept than I in the theological currents of the first third of the twentieth century (and the theological position of the Rockefeller interests) to know exactly how far-reaching Scott's comment was. Did he recognize the influence of Buchman (or, more accurately, Sam Shoemaker) on Bill? Did he see the resemblance between the meetings of these drunks and the Oxford meetings? Did he simply recognize the "Faith without works is dead" principle of the Epistle of James? One thing is very clear. A movement whose founder likens it to the Franciscans, while it may be a lay movement, is certainly not a secular one. And when the chairman of the Rockefeller church likens the same movement to the Christian church in the Apostolic Age, he is not talking about a secular movement.

By A.A.'s self-denials, the fellowship (*koinonia*) came to the point where "the irresponsible had become responsible, and . . . by making financial independence part of its tradition, Alcoholics Anonymous had revived an ideal that this era had almost forgotten" (ibid.:114). There is some amount of subsidiary A.A. literature, including pamphlets, directly concerned with the Seventh Tradition, "where money and spirituality meet." These, I suppose, are principally of interest to A.A. members. The same is true of Bill W.'s remarks on the Seventh Tradition in the *A.A. Grapevine* in June 1948 ([1948] 1989:85–86), which is almost entirely practical advice for the groups on a day-to-day basis. What is most of interest to us here is the continuing emphasis on the A.A. group as a spiritual entity, and the way in which this serves—and is apparently designed to serve—to create what we have called single-peaked preferences.

In other words, once again Bill is giving practical advice under the guise of tradition (which is part of the invention of tradition). Once again he is trying to make possible some degree of order (or "governance") in accordance with what we have since discovered are the principles of committee (or group) decision-making. Once again he is simplifying structure. Once again he is reiterating the spiritual nature of A.A., while trying to avoid any specific religious connection. It becomes apparent, to me, as we go along, that the Twelve Traditions are to some degree a (possibly artificial) separation of one piece of proscriptive advice into twelve parts. We turn to the Eighth Tradition.

THE EIGHTH TRADITION

The Eighth Tradition, in its short form, is, "Alcoholics Anonymous should remain forever nonprofessional, but our service centers may employ special workers." It would seem that this Tradition, at least in this form, may have spoken more to problems in the 1940s than it does to problems today, since the discussion in the *12&12* is mostly on whether secretaries or other office staff can be paid. This would appear, at first glance, to be more relevant to the people running the General Service Office in New York than to the average A.A. around the country or around the world. The longer form of the Tradition not only makes the matter clearer, but also points out its continued relevance:

> Alcoholics Anonymous should remain forever nonprofessional. *We define professionalism as the occupation of counseling alcoholics for fees or hire* [my emphasis]. But we may employ alcoholics where they are going to perform those services for which we might otherwise have to engage nonalcoholics. Such special services may be recompensed. *But our usual A.A. Twelfth Step work is* never *to be paid for* [again, emphasis mine].

When Bill W. wrote his first brief commentary on the Eighth Tradition, in the *A.A. Grapevine* in July 1948, he began by saying,

> Throughout the world, AAs are Twelfth-Stepping with thousands of new prospects a month. Between one and two thousand of these stick on our first presentation; past experience shows that most of the remainder will come back to us later on. Almost entirely unorganized, *and completely nonprofessional* [my emphasis], this mighty spiritual current is now flowing from alcoholics who are well to those who are sick. One alcoholic talking to another; that's all. Could this vast and vital face-to-face effort ever be professionalized or even organized? Most emphatically it could not. The few efforts to professionalize straight Twelfth Step work have always failed quickly. ([1948] 1989:86–87)

In his remarks on the Eighth Tradition in *A.A. Comes of Age* (1958:116–17, see also 1989:168–69), Bill W. confronts the problem as it was in the late 1940s. He lists as jobs that might be—but are not—violations of the prohibition on paid Twelfth Step work, alcohol and alcoholism education (college level), employee assistance program management, managing a "state drunk farm," social work with the families of alcoholics, research for a state alcohol commission. He remarks that "A.A. members have bought farms or rest homes where badly beat-up topers could find needed care" (ibid.), suggesting that this too is appropriate.

What he does not talk about is the member of A.A. employed as a paid counselor in, or paid for supervising paid counselors in, a recovery facility, rehab, or halfway house. The applicable remark might appear to be his reference to the farms or rest homes. But the implication of that remark, as I read it (and as we look back at the 1940s), is that this is a not-for-profit enterprise, and that the only professional care would be a doctor (medical or osteopathic) for detoxification and subsequent physical care. The A.A. would not be making money out of the process (except, perhaps, enough to recompense him—or her—for devoting full time to running such a facility—the "running" not including paid counseling).

This would therefore seem not to apply in the present-day case of members of A.A. who work in rehabs or other similar facilities as alcoholism (or alcoholism and addiction or even addiction) counselors. Nor would it speak to the case of those who have supervisory capacities in such facilities, even (or especially) if they use A.A. as part of the rehabilitation process. These people are being paid, or otherwise receiving financial benefits, for counseling alcoholics on how to be sober. And counseling alcoholics on how to be sober (through A.A.) was and is part of Twelfth Step work. Moreover, it would seem that there might be a strong temptation for such persons to use A.A. as part of the referral network for their facilities (after all, it works and they know it works)—though this would imply violation of the Sixth Tradition (and the Seventh), as well as and perhaps more than the Eighth.

In other words, times change. We know that systems must change with the times (that's part of systems theory). We also know that too much new diversity, inadequately absorbed into the system (which creates its own new diversity for the absorption process), will break the system apart. We know (from our discussion of the Twelfth Step in the previous chapter) that the nature of Twelfth Step work has altered: that has already happened. What has happened with this Tradition—and the Ninth, to which we now turn—is that the changing times have presented a situation that apparently leaves A.A. with two alternatives: (1) A.A.s may achieve or maintain an apparent unity by "going with the flow," even though (it would appear) the flow is destabilizing and divisive, or (2) A.A.s may fight against the change, because it is in fact destabilizing and divisive, and risk possibly greater disunity implicit in fighting a long drawn-out rearguard action.

It is interesting that those of whom I have inquired to find out which is better have suggested two answers—disagreeing, but both based almost entirely on spiritual arguments. First (the answer I am told is favored by the General Service Office in New York), take no action beyond prayer. Second (the answer given by some "elder statesmen" of whom I have inquired), take your stand—*Ich kann nicht anders*—and serve as the "saving remnant" or the "just men" for whose sake God will preserve A.A.

There is of course a third position taken by some A.A.s, that the matter really isn't important enough to do anything about, if indeed it's important at all. I cannot say whether these A.A.s are right. I can only say that, looking at the Traditions, I find considerable concern on anything—especially money—possibly interfering with the spiritual current flowing from alcoholics who are well to those who are sick, that is, still suffer alcoholism. But this book, fortunately, is not about telling A.A. what it should do. It is about what A.A. is, and why it worked and (if it does) continues to work. If members of A.A. want to make use of any insights it produces, that is for them to do; they are welcome to, but it is not why the book is written.

THE NINTH TRADITION

The Ninth Tradition, in its short form, reads, "A.A., as such, ought never be organized; but we may create service boards or committees directly responsible to those they serve." As it stands, this is (1) a reaffirmation of spontaneous order (implicitly of A.A. as a spiritual entity or sets of spiritual entities) and (2) a way of preserving the opportunity for this guided spontaneous order by creating committees or boards to maintain guidance, replacing the cofounders in this respect. Committees or boards are the appropriate mechanism for ordering the social system called *koinonia*, in part because they function best (perhaps, in the end, only) with single-peaked preferences, and single-peaked preferences are closely related to the possession of a *koinê* or common speech (common language patterns implying common ways of looking at things). But in its long form, it does more. In fact, it does so much (or tries to do so much) that parts of what was the Ninth Tradition in 1948–50 became part of the Second Tradition by 1952. Here's the long form of the Ninth Tradition (modernized by substituting "General Service Board" for "Alcoholic Foundation"):

> Each A.A. group needs the least possible organization. Rotating leadership is the best. The small group may elect its secretary, the large group its rotating committee, and the groups of a large metropolitan area their central or intergroup committee, which often employs a full-time secretary. The trustees of the General Service Board are, in effect, our A.A. General Service Committee. They are the custodians of our A.A. Tradition and the receivers of voluntary contributions by which we maintain our A.A. General service office at New York. They are authorized by the groups to handle our overall public relations and they guarantee the integrity of our principal newspaper, the A.A. Grapevine. All such representatives are to be guided in the spirit of service, for true leaders in A.A. are but *trusted and experienced servants* [my emphasis] of the whole. They derive no real authority *from their titles* [again, my emphasis]. Universal respect is the key to their usefulness.

The General Service Structure of Alcoholics Anonymous was created in 1951, after the traditions were accepted by voice vote at A.A.'s first international convention in Cleveland in 1950. The group has a guiding committee, chosen annually or (in some cases) every two years (in some, even, every six months) by those members of the group who choose to come to the group's regularly scheduled business meetings. One of these "trusted servants" is the General Service Representative or GSR. These GSRs meet (usually monthly) with other GSRs from their district (a geographical entity ideally including fifteen or twenty groups, but in some cases more than fifty). Every two years these GSRs choose a member (usually a GSR) to represent the district on the Area Committee (the Area being a larger geographic entity, sometimes a whole state): this representative from the district on the Area Committee is called a District Committee Member (DCM), though the District Committee Member is in fact a voting member of the Area Committee, not the District Committee. A specimen Area Committee might have six officers and perhaps as many as fifty DCMs. The officers would likely include the Delegate (who represents the Area at the Annual General Service Conference in New York), the Alternate Delegate (in case he or she can't), the Chairman (to chair Area Committee meetings), the Vice-Chairman (for backup; in some cases this may be an Area Officer-at-Large who backs up not only the Chairman but the Secretary and the Treasurer), a Secretary, and a Treasurer.

The officers are generally elected every two years, but not by the DCMs—instead at a kind of Convention/Assembly where the DCMs and GSRs all vote. In some cases, only DCMs and current Area officers are allowed to stand for the positions. In such a case, it would be possible (perhaps even likely) that a member might serve fourteen consecutive years on the Area Committee (counting two as a DCM, with two in each of the six officer positions). At first glance, this might be taken as a violation of the principle that a rotating leadership is best, but this may not be the only apparent problem with present practice, as I understand it. We will come back to some of these apparent problems, after looking for further enlightenment on what Bill W. meant when he wrote out the Ninth Tradition.

First, in the *A.A. Grapevine* in 1948, we find this statement:

> If . . . an AA group elects a secretary or rotating committee, if an area forms an intergroup committee, if we set up a foundation [read, General Service Board], a general office or a Grapevine, then we are organized for service. The AA books or pamphlets, our meeting places and clubs, our dinners and regional assemblies—these are services, too. Nor can we secure good hospital connections, properly sponsor new projects, and obtain good public relations just by chance. People have to be appointed to look after these things, sometimes paid people. Special services are performed. *But by none of these special services has our spiritual or social activity, the great current of AA, ever been really professionalized or organized* [emphasis mine]. . . . As such facts and distinctions become clear, we shall easily lay aside our fears of blighting organization. (1989:88–89)

From what I have been told, I wouldn't go so far as *easily* myself, but the point is clear. Not only is "the great current of A.A.," its activity in the Spirit and in the society (fellowship or *koinonia*), not professionalized (which is taken care of in the Eighth Tradition), it is not to be organized either, which is taken care of here in the Ninth.

The discussion of this Ninth Tradition in *A.A. Comes of Age* (1958:118–23), better than the shorter form of the discussion in the *12&12* (1952/53: 172–75), makes two things abundantly clear. First,

> Every nation, in fact every form of society, has to be a government adminis-
> tered by human beings. *Power to direct and govern is the essence of organization*
> *everywhere* [my emphasis]. To this rule Alcoholics Anonymous is a complete
> exception. It does not at any point conform to the pattern of a government.
> Neither its General Service Conference, its General Service Board, nor the
> humblest group committee can issue a single directive to an A.A. member,
> let alone hand out any punishment. (1958:118)

And second,

> In the spirit of Tradition Nine, we old-timers [meaning, specifically, Bill W.]
> will step aside, leaving with you only the offer of our advice if and when you
> want it. *We shall no longer direct and govern, nor will anybody else* [emphasis
> mine]. A.A. as such should always remain unorganized. (ibid.:123)

In short, organization implies a power to direct and govern. No one in A.A. will have this power, after Bill W. gives it up. He turns over his responsibilities as cofounder to a committee or set of committees whose only power is, in effect, to provide information—besides, of course, their power to direct and govern in the very limited sphere of providing services (publications, for example) that help guide the flow of the great current.

Before going on to the Tenth Tradition, we should remind ourselves of two passages we have especially noted in the long form of the Ninth Tradition. No authority is derived from titles (except in a very limited and specific way within a committee, where the chairman chairs, the secretary takes notes, the treasurer handles the books). And, in that portion of the Ninth Tradition (early version) largely taken over into the Second Tradition (final version), the leaders of A.A. are but "trusted servants." Well, yes, and the Pope of Rome is *servus servorum Deî*—the "servant of the servants of God." Given Bill's general theological awareness, his close connection with Father Ed Dowling, the fact that he took Roman Catholic instruction (although married in a Swedenborgian church and received into the Episcopal Church by Sam Shoemaker), I do not believe the Roman Catholic connotation is irrelevant.

Bill faced essentially the same problem encountered in the first-century Christian church (and by the churches generally thereafter), by Islam after Mohammed, by Mary Baker Eddy. He could not, in his anonymous twentieth-century fellowship, take the path taken by the early churches, with Apostolic Succession (in some cases by direct adoption, in some by ordination and consecration)—still more because he did not claim to have the powers necessary to ordain such a succession. He could not take the paths taken by the two major branches of Islam, either through the secular authority (originally of the Prophet's family) or of the succession of one Imam to another. He chose not to take the path of Mary Baker Eddy, who ordained the Bible (AV) and her textbook, *Science and Health With Key to the Scriptures* (1875 *et seq.*), as "pastor" over the Church of Christ, Scientist—though he followed her in creating boards and committees to oversee the details of support services for the fellowship. Hers, by the way, may be found in the *Manual of the Mother Church, The First Church of Christ Scientist in Boston, Massachusetts* (1908), which is "authorized literature of the First Church of Christ, Scientist, in Boston, Massachusetts," and which includes, in its front matter, the statement that the provisions in the *Manual* "sprang from necessity, the logic of events,—from the immediate demand for them as a help that must be supplied to maintain the dignity and defense of our Cause." A detailed account of Bill W.'s answer, set beside that by Mrs. Eddy, awaits its historian.

This Tradition concludes what we might call the positive or "expansionary" portion of the Traditions—which are still further expanded in Bill W.'s *Twelve Concepts of World Service* (1962). That is (principally, in Traditions 6 through 9), he is setting out what A.A. may do, in order to keep going, setting bounds admittedly (or trying to set them), but wrestling with the need for some form of organization and direction. In the Tenth Tradition, and the two following, he is principally looking at the proscriptive or "limiting" portion.

THE TENTH TRADITION

The Tenth Tradition, short form, reads, "Alcoholics Anonymous has no opinion on outside issues; hence the A.A. name ought never be drawn into public controversy." That seems pretty clear, though we note the word *outside*, which we discussed at some length under the Sixth Tradition. The long form of the Tenth Tradition reads:

> No A.A. group or member should ever, in such a way as to implicate A.A., express any opinion on outside controversial issues—particularly those of

politics, alcohol reform, or sectarian religion. The Alcoholics Anonymous
groups oppose no one. *Concerning such matters they can express no views whatever* [my emphasis].

This is the Tradition under whose rubric Bill W. discusses the Washingtonians (*12&12* 1952/53:178–79).
Here is the central point of the discussion:

Instead, the Washingtonians permitted politicians and reformers, both alcoholic and nonalcoholic, to use the society for their own purposes. Abolition
of slavery, for example, was a stormy political issue then. Soon, Washingtonian speakers violently and publicly took sides on this question. (ibid.:178)

Well, no, so far as I can tell. The Washingtonians disappeared behind the
veil of the church and the locked doors of fraternal orders pretty much
before the Free-Soil Party was created, before the Fugitive Slave Law
was ever passed, before Harriet Beecher Stowe wrote *Uncle Tom's Cabin*.
Whatever the tempests that tore the fabric of the Washingtonians might
have been (and Milton Maxwell [1950] finds no evidence of pro- or anti-
slavery agitation among them), one should look to some reason other than
agreed-upon historical fact for this remark. And the answer is not hard to
find. First, Bill is writing at the dawn of the Civil Rights era, when the same
tempests are beginning to grow. Second, he is emphasizing the point that
no cause, however good, not religious, not political, not even in alcohol
reform, can be allowed to splinter A.A.'s unity. I daresay one of his sources
on the Washingtonians (I haven't found it yet) may have mentioned sec-
tional agitation, which he translated (in the end, correctly) as agitation
over slavery. But his picture is exaggerated for effect—which is part and
parcel of the invention of tradition, particularly tradition to be used both
as ground and as binding force.

In Bill W.'s September 1948 *Grapevine* discussion of the Tenth Tradition
([1948] 1989:89–90), there is no mention of the Washingtonians, though
there had already been a *Grapevine* article on them (in 1946). Instead, Bill
propounds a question:

Though God has bestowed on us great favors and though we are bounded
by stronger times of love and necessity than most societies, is it prudent to
suppose that automatically these great gifts and attributes shall be ours forever? If we are worthy, we shall probably continue to enjoy them. So the real
question is, how shall we always be worthy of our present blessings? (ibid.)

And answers it,

Our best defense? This surely lies in the formation of a Tradition respecting
serious controversy so powerful that neither the weakness of persons nor the

strain and strife of our troubled times can harm Alcoholics Anonymous.
. . . May God grant us the wisdom and fortitude ever to sustain an unbreakable unity. (ibid.)

Note that this language, about being *worthy of our present blessings,* if suitable for anyone, would be suitable only (or chiefly) for a *koinonia* dedicated to divine service. Note also that Bill W. is here speaking of "the formation of a Tradition . . . so powerful that neither the weakness of persons nor the strain and strife of our troubled times can harm Alcoholics Anonymous." Strong stuff—and note the Prayer Book echoes in the language.

The reference to the Washingtonians also appears (in almost exactly the same words as in the *12&12*) in the section on Tradition Ten in *A.A. Comes of Age* (1958:124–25). But there is a surprise to come. After discussing the Washingtonians, Bill adds a passage presumably written between the *12&12* (1952/53) and the publication of *A.A. Comes of Age* (1958). The central point is the stand taken by the General Service Conference on the proposal by the trustees that A.A. seek a Congressional charter along the lines of the charter for the American Red Cross. The question was not whether the General Service Board (formerly the Alcoholic Foundation) should be incorporated—it was and is—or A.A. World Services or the A.A. Grapevine, which are subsidiary service organizations under the expansionary terms of the Ninth Tradition. The question was whether Alcoholics Anonymous—the fellowship—should be federally chartered or incorporated. Even now, the Conference Charter is not a legal document: apparently, New York is the only part of the A.A. General Service structure to be incorporated—though clubs in general seem to be, and some intergroup associations, presumably because they (and not their individual members) hire employees for pay. Here is what Bill W. calls the moving resolution by which the Conference rejected the Trustees' proposal to charter or incorporate Alcoholics Anonymous:

We have reviewed all of the arguments pro and con on this subject, have discussed it with many members of A.A. within the Conference and outside of it, and we have come to these conclusions; (1) the evils which caused the question to rise [a negative movie to be called *Mr. and Miss Anonymous*] have largely abated. (2) A Congressional incorporation would create by law a power to govern which would be contrary to, and violative of, our Traditions. (3) It would implement the spiritual force of A.A. with a legal power, which we believe would tend to weaken its spiritual strength. (4) When we ask for legal rights, enforceable in Courts of law, we by the same act subject ourselves to possible legal regulation. (5) We might become endlessly entangled in litigation which, together with the incidental expense and publicity, could seriously threaten our very existence. (6) Incorporation of A.A. could conceivably become the opening wedge that might engender politics and a struggle for power within our own ranks. (7) Continuously since its beginning, and today, A.A. has been a fellowship and not an organization. Incorporation necessarily makes it an organization. (8) We believe that "spiritual faith" and a "way of life" cannot be incorporated. (9) A.A. can and will survive so long as it remains a spiritual faith and a way of life open to all men and women who suffer from alcoholism. Therefore, keeping in mind the high purpose of the General Service Conference as expressed by the Chairman last year when he said, "We seek not compromise but certainty," your Committee unanimously recommends that Alcoholics Anonymous does not incorporate. (1958:127)

This resolution Bill W. calls the final foundation for the Tenth Tradition (ibid.:128). One could argue that, being proscriptive against proscription, this too is expansionary—in rather the same sense, perhaps, as the Eleventh Tradition, to which we now turn.

THE ELEVENTH TRADITION

In its short (final) form, the Eleventh Tradition reads, "Our public relations policy is based on attraction rather than promotion; we need always maintain personal anonymity at the level of press, radio, and film" (which, as I understand it, now includes television). In its longer (and earlier) form, it reads,

> Our relations with the general public should be characterized by personal anonymity. We think A.A. ought to avoid sensational advertising. Our names and pictures as A.A. members ought not be broadcast, filmed, or publicly printed. Our public relations should be guided by the principle of attraction rather than promotion. There is never need to praise ourselves. We feel it better to let our friends recommend us.

It would be easy to say that this is not a Tradition that greatly affects most A.A. members, since most A.A. members are unlikely to have their names or pictures as A.A. members printed or broadcast, but quite obviously it spoke to a perceived problem, and apparently a problem with at least three parts. Two of these are clear. First, the public reputation of Alcoholics Anonymous should not be tied to specific individuals—they may drink and harm A.A. This might be particularly true of celebrities who were famous before they stopped drinking and who have had only short sobriety—but even John B. Gough, one of the leading Washingtonian circuit speakers, slipped, and the slip was far from going unnoticed in the public press of that day. Or they may not drink—but still take A.A. where it does not want to be. Second, the limelight is not spiritually a very good place for those of whom Bill W. wrote, "By temperament, nearly every one of us had been an irrepressible promoter [this may have been true especially in the early days and especially in New York] . . . We knew we had to exercise self-restraint" (1952/53:181). Such people, in the limelight, may drink—and harm themselves. Or they may not drink—but still be harmed by being a center of attention.

The third part of the problem is implicit in the concluding lines of Bill W.'s discussion of the Eleventh Tradition in the *A.A. Grapevine* in October 1948:

> To the million alcoholics who have not yet heard our AA story, we should ever say, "Greetings and welcome. Be assured that we shall never weaken the lifelines which we float out to you. In our public relations, we shall, God willing, keep the faith." (1989:92)

To quote the *12&12* on the Eleventh Tradition, "each member becomes an active guardian of our Fellowship" (ibid.:183)—by keeping his own anonymity intact outside the fellowship, and therefore not weakening, indeed strengthening, the lifelines to those coming in to Alcoholics Anonymous. So it turns out that, while most members of Alcoholics Anonymous were not celebrities before coming in, are not celebrities after coming in, and are not trying to make money by giving a public series of "Twelve Lectures on Alcoholics Anonymous" over a national network (that story is in *A.A. Comes of Age* 1958:130–31), nevertheless, by guarding their public anonymity, they can show new and prospective members that *their* anonymity will be guarded.

Even so, the most important aspect of anonymity (from Bill W.'s point of view) comes not in the Eleventh Tradition, but in the Twelfth.

THE TWELFTH TRADITION

In the short and final form, the Twelfth Tradition reads, "Anonymity is the spiritual foundation of all our traditions, ever reminding us to place principles before personalities." In the earlier (and longer) form, it reads,

> And finally, we of Alcoholics Anonymous believe that the principle of anonymity has an immense spiritual significance. It reminds us that we are to place principles before personalities; that we are actually to practice a genuine humility. This to the end that our great blessings will never spoil us; that we shall ever live in thankful contemplation of Him who presides over us all.

The discussion of the Twelfth Tradition in the *12&12* makes it clear that this is another case where Bill W. seems to have subdivided his "invented tradition" into what appear to be slightly arbitrary parts. Under the rubric of the Twelfth Tradition, in the *12&12* (1952/53:186–87), Bill W. discusses early media publicity—Jack Alexander's *Saturday Evening Post* article (1941), Elrick Davis's series of articles in the Cleveland *Plain-Dealer* (1939), even the desire of certain entertainers who have benefited from sobriety to do A.A. a good turn. This is more or less an amplification of the fact that anonymity is good both for the recovering alcoholic and for A.A. I suppose it could be said that the discussion of anonymity under the Eleventh Tradition emphasizes the practical side, but the discussion under the Twelfth Tradition, the spiritual side. Here is Bill W.'s discussion of the Twelfth Tradition in the *A.A. Grapevine* in November 1948:

> One may say that anonymity is the spiritual base, the sure key to all the rest of our Traditions. It has come to stand for prudence and, more importantly [!], for self-effacement. True consideration for the newcomer if he desires to be nameless; vital protection against misuse of the name Alcoholics Anonymous at the public level; and to each of us a constant reminder that principles come before personal interest—such is the wide scope of this all-embracing principle. In it we see the cornerstone of our security as a movement; at a deeper spiritual level it points us to still greater self-renunciation. . . . The recovery steps would make each individual AA whole and one with God; the Twelve Points of Tradition would make us one with each other and whole with the world about us. Unity is our aim. Our AA Traditions are, we trust, securely anchored in those wise precepts: charity, gratitude, and humility. Nor have we forgotten *prudence*. May these virtues ever stand clear before us in our meditations; may Alcoholics Anonymous serve God in happy unison for so long as he may need us. ([1948] 1989:92–94)

Note the use of the word *unison* and recall William James's—and John Newton's—linking of the musical and the mystical. In *A.A. Comes of Age* (1958:136), Bill W. tells about the mausoleum A.A.s wanted to build for Dr. Bob (who was then still alive, though barely) and his wife, Anne (who had just died). He quotes Dr. Bob's remark: "God bless 'em. They mean well. But for heaven's sake, Bill, let's you and I get buried just like other folks." All this is a tribute to Bill W.'s (and Dr. Bob's) view of Alcoholics Anonymous as a spiritual fellowship.

The Twelfth Tradition summarizes the spiritual Why? of the Traditions, rather as the Twelfth Step summarizes the spiritual Why? of the Steps. It is of fundamental importance, obviously, to Alcoholics Anonymous. For our purposes here its primary value is in its assertion that Alcoholics Anonymous is a spiritual *koinonia*. On A.A. as a *koinonia* in the social-systems sense it has less to say. Only the short form of the Twelfth Tradition is regularly read at meetings, though the longer (and much more overtly "religious") form is read occasionally. So far as I know, the statement in the *A.A. Grapevine* for November 1948 is not read at A.A. meetings at all. In general, what we have called the *ritual* (but not *liturgical*) reading of the Twelfth Tradition is restricted to the latest and shortest form. At (relatively rare) A.A. "Tradition" meetings, it is the relevant section of the *12&12* that is read, which indeed mentions the "spiritual substance of anonymity" (1952/53:184) and concludes that "humility, expressed by anonymity, is the greatest safeguard that anonymity can ever have" (ibid.:187)—but this is deliberately low-key and (by comparison with earlier texts) understated. One might see this as Bill W. deemphasizing the degree to which A.A. is a spiritual fellowship, trying to provide guidance through historical examples tied to his invented tradition, rather than as spiritual advice. As we noted, the criticism, but thus the affirmation, of tradition is history. The Traditions, we recall (in Hobsbawm's words), should provide "responses to novel situations which take the form of reference to old situations, or which establish their own past by quasi-obligatory repetition" (Hobsbawm and Ranger 1981:3). The key words are *old* and *past*.

But for all that we have said here, it is obvious that, however brilliantly (in our analysis) Bill W. handled the "social-systems" problem of creating Alcoholics Anonymous, he believed he was creating—or "subcreating"?— a spiritual fellowship, a "company" in the same sense the Round Table was a company. We know he learned something from Alexis de Tocqueville's *Democracy in America* (1835,1840). So far as we know he did not specifically study social-systems theory beyond that. Even his references to the "Society of Alcoholics Anonymous" have made me wonder (as noted in Chapter 6) if he did not have in his mind a kind of pun on the French word for company in the ordinary business sense—*société anonyme*—with collective not individual responsibility for actions (and, of course, limited personal liability).

The emphasis on committee consensus rather than majority vote may be seen as a way of avoiding the pitfalls of intransitivity of social choice. The emphasis on the primary purpose or singleness of purpose may be seen as a way of ensuring single-peaked preferences so as to permit Condorcet solutions and avoid the necessity for mechanistic De Borda solutions or the "argle-bargle" of Dodgson solutions. Whether or not he knew what he was doing in the terms we would use now, I believe he knew what he was doing. Not for nothing did Aldous Huxley call him the greatest social engineer of the twentieth century. Not for nothing did *Time* magazine's end-of-the-century poll rank him in the top hundred men and women of the century. But in the end, the social engineering was based on a spiritual insight, and with all the safeguards of the Twelve traditions, it looks as though A.A. will function well as a *koinonia* in the social-systems sense pretty well to the degree it functions well as a *koinonia* in the spiritual-assembly sense. That would appear to be the lesson in particular of the Twelfth Tradition, but it is in fact the lesson of all the Twelve Traditions.

There is an interesting example of this in the shuffling of material from the Ninth Tradition to the Second, in 1948–49, which shows Bill W.'s increasing consciousness of the spiritual nature of the Traditions. The early form of the Second Tradition was, as we have remarked, missing the phrase, "Our leaders are but trusted servants; they do not govern." In essence, as we have noted, that part of the Tradition was brought in from the Ninth Tradition, where it was part of what was pretty much a practical discussion of the principle of rotation. The transfer to the Second Tradition, tying it in with the idea that God really is the force behind (or the grounding of) the group, appears to represent a shift from a practical principle of leadership to a spiritual principle of dependence on God. Similarly, the practical recommendations on anonymity in the Eleventh Tradition lead into the spiritual principle (and spiritual value) of anonymity in the Twelfth. Now, with this in mind, and then looking at Bill W.'s next "set of twelve" (the *Twelve Concepts for World Service* 1962), an outside observer might reasonably conclude that Bill W. eventually found reliance on the "spirituality" of the A.A. structure he had created perhaps a little on the overenthusiastic side. Be that as it may, the Twelve Concepts provide a set of guidelines for how the committees and boards of A.A. are to get anything done on a day-to-day basis. The Twelve Concepts are now included in the fourth edition of the Big Book (2002), as well as being printed with the *Service Manual* (but still under the separate 1962 title, *Twelve Concepts for World Service*). In a sense, they seem to represent Bill W.'s continuing argument with those who would essentially oppose any formal order in A.A.

THE TWELVE CONCEPTS

We are certainly not going to go into them in any detail, though that would be advisable for advanced students of the structure of "spontaneous order" in a nongoverned fellowship. But simply by quoting them (in their short form) we can guess at some of the problems Bill W. found in relying upon the Twelve Traditions for the "ordering" of A.A. Here the Concepts are presented in three groups. Concepts 1 through 5 are procedural, relating to rights of decision, participation, and appeal. Concepts 6 through 9 summarize the relationship between the Conference and the Trustees. Concepts 10 through 12 (mixing a metaphor) are reminders of pitfalls in the structure.

(1) Final responsibility and ultimate authority for A.A. world services should always reside in the collective conscience of our who fellowship; (2) The General Service Conference of A.A. has become, for nearly every practical purpose, the active voice and the effective conscience of our whole society in

its world affairs; (3) To insure effective leadership, we should endow each element of A.A.—the Conference, the General Service Board and its service corporations, staffs, committees, and executives—with a traditional "Right of Decision;" (4) At all responsible levels, we ought to maintain a traditional "Right of Participation," allowing a voting representation in reasonable proportion to the responsibility that each must discharge; (5) Throughout our structure, a traditional "Right of Appeal" ought to prevail, so that minority opinion will be heard and personal grievances receive careful consideration.

(6) The Conference recognizes that the chief initiative and active responsibility in most world service matters should be exercised by the trustee members of the Conference acting as the General Service Board; (7) The Charter and Bylaws of the General Service Board are legal instruments, empowering the trustees to manage and conduct world service affairs. The Conference Charter is not a legal document; it relies upon tradition and the A.A. purse for final effectiveness; (8) The trustees are the principal planners and administrators of overall policy and finance. They have custodial oversight of the separately incorporated and constantly active services [A.A. World Services and the A.A. Grapevine], exercising this through their ability to elect all the directors of these entities.

(9) Good service leadership at all levels is indispensable for our future functioning and safety. Primary world service leadership, once exercised by the founders [I think this means "cofounders" but am not sure], must necessarily be assumed by the trustees; (10) Every service responsibility should be matched by an equal service authority, with the scope of such authority well defined; (11) The trustees should always have the best possible committees, corporate service directors, executives, staffs, and consultants [this last looks like it might open several cans of worms]. Composition, qualifications, induction procedures, and rights and duties will always be matters of serious concern; (12) The Conference shall observe the spirit of A.A. Tradition, taking care that it never becomes a seat of perilous wealth or power; that sufficient operating funds and reserve be its prudent financial principle; that it place none of its members in a position of unqualified authority over others; that it reach all important decisions by discussion, vote, and, whenever possible, by substantial unanimity; that its actions never be personally punitive nor an incitement to public controversy; that it never perform acts of government, and that, like the Society it serves, it will always remain democratic in thought and action. (A.A. 2000–1:front matter)

Now, that's a mouthful! In 1937, the Akron and New York groups (the only two existing at the time) gave Bill W. and Dr. Bob the authority to "create over-all services which could spread the A.A. message worldwide" (*ibid.*:10), thus providing a "grandfather" clause that held until, in 1955, "the groups confirmed the permanent charter for their General Service Conference [created in 1951]" (ibid.)—I believe at the 1955 International Convention in St. Louis. The relative complexity of the Twelve Concepts— in contrast to the relative simplicity of the Twelve Steps and even the

Twelve Traditions—may of course reflect (as has been suggested to me) the fact that they were written by Bill W. without consultation with Dr. Bob. But it is my guess that they are more complex because they deal with the problem of how to make a widespread enterprise actually run, while preserving as much as possible of the primitive simplicity of the old days—a very difficult problem. Apparently Bill W. recognized (between 1952 and 1962?) that in fighting a battle, it is necessary not only to trust in God, but also to keep your powder dry, and these (so to speak) are the engineering and logistical provisions for keeping the powder dry. In essence, they are Bill W.'s last major contribution to keeping A.A. going—necessarily so, since the problem was to keep A.A. going after his death, and by the time one might be able to judge whether the Concepts would work, he was necessarily dead. The Steps were developed in 1938–39, the Traditions between 1946 and 1952, the Concepts in 1961–62—say, 1938, 1950, 1962 (Bill W. thought in twelves). By 1974 he was dead. But his creation lives on—we believe. Why?

THE SURVIVAL OF ALCOHOLICS ANONYMOUS— ON TO CHAPTER 9

In the first two chapters, we brought the story up to 1940. In Chapter 3 we made a slight scientific *excursus* preparing for Chapters 4 and 5. In Chapters 4 through 6 we looked at present understanding of alcoholism as an illness of mind, body, and spirit (Bill W.'s formulation), supporting his formulation and setting up what we hope can serve as a scientific research program for understanding what might be going on in Alcoholics Anonymous and might be expected to work in bringing about sobriety there or elsewhere. (Chapter 9 suggests some next steps in that scientific research program.) In Chapter 7 we looked at the Twelve Steps, and primarily at how they were understood by their creators, and in Chapter 8 at Bill W.'s invention of tradition and at the rules for the functioning of a *koinonia* and of a committee structure. But we ventured only tentatively and occasionally into the last fifty years of A.A.'s history (or the history of sobriety).

To do that was not our purpose—but available (albeit largely anecdotal) data suggest it might appropriately be someone's purpose (perhaps ours), in another book. At the end of our next and final chapter, we will turn briefly to the question, Where do we go from here? But before that, we will draw together our model, our paradigm, the basis of our scientific research program. In other words, we will try to tie together everything we have said thus far.

9 ~

Paradigm Regained: Suggestions from Our Scientific Research Program

IT WOULD, OF COURSE, BE ABSURD TO CLAIM that we have come up with a "unified-field" theory of alcoholism and its treatment (particularly in connection with A.A., where unity is important, but theory is not). That is, with a way of explaining how and why alcoholism began, why it has been passed on, why it comes in *types*. A way also of explaining why there is a treatment for the mental (psychological) condition, the physical (biochemical and biogenetic) precondition and thereby its symptoms, and the spiritual condition (or precondition)—and why it is essentially the same treatment for all three. And a way also (in the course of this) of explaining why and how Alcoholics Anonymous has worked and should continue to work. All this in terms more or less set out in Bill W.'s vision. Yet, though it would seem to be absurd, I am not entirely sure. Perhaps we are doing it— or coming close to doing it—after all.

We began our history, back in Chapter 1, with a brief look at a few suggestive items in the history of alcoholism and treatment for alcoholism— treatment of mind, body, and spirit—going back at most a few thousand years. Then, in Chapter 2, we came up to 1935 and took a look at Bill W. and his paradigm for the threefold illness of alcoholism and its threefold treatment. But some of what we said in Chapters 3 and 4 (particularly) may enable us to carry our story back, at least by suggestion, into prehistory, ten times as far back. And although what we have to say here is not susceptible of proof (though it might be of falsification), I think it makes sense, both of the heritable precondition of alcoholism and of the congruency of the threefold treatment.

Perhaps it might be thought that (Miltonic pun and associations apart) "Paradigm Retained" would be better for this chapter title than "Paradigm Regained." But my sense of the course of treatment for alcoholism in the past thirty years is that Bill W.'s paradigm has, indeed, been lost. And yet, the more we have looked into the frontiers of scientific inquiry, the more

(I believe) we have seen some fundamental truths in what he saw—his threefold paradigm—and in the treatment A.A. was designed to provide. Treatment mostly designed by Bill W. And not at all the same thing as the "Twelve-Step treatments" in jails, institutions, and rehabs, which we apparently owe largely to the Hazelden Foundation. Perhaps unfortunately, there seems to be some confusion between the Twelve Steps of Alcoholics Anonymous and "Twelve-Step treatment" generally, though I suspect much of that confusion may be outside the walls of A.A. Now, back to (pre-)history.

BACK TO (PRE-)HISTORY

As I read it, there was a fundamental change in humankind some thirty-five thousand or so years ago, during one of the intervals in the Wisconsin Ice Age, when our ancestors, or some of them, began to speak and began to paint or draw. This was not the great transformation of fifty thousand or so years ago that "produced the fully modern ability to invent and manipulate culture" (Klein and Edgar 2002:24), but the evident outcome of that great transformation. Humankind was, I believe, poised on the supercritical/subcritical edge we discussed in Chapter 3, and whether the great leap forward was taken all at once and then diffused or (as I think more likely) taken in some cases and not others, over a relatively compact period of time (relative to geological ages), and a relatively compact space (relative to the whole world), we cannot say. A description of the process of its happening (in Stuart Kauffman's terms) may, however, be given briefly here, backing up to the molecular level, then jumping forward to the human.

We begin with autonomous agents in that biosphere which is their self-consistent co-construction (Kauffman 2000:110), there being no autonomous agent who knows how the whole self-constructing system works. For exemplary purposes, using a lowest common denominator, we conceive (ibid.:111) a system in which an incoming molecular species arriving in the interior of an autonomous agent is (1) food, (2) poison, (3) a signal, (4) neutral, or (5) something else: this, however much an LCD, brings us to the edge of semantics. As Kauffman observes, the

> incoming molecule is "yuck" or "yum." I think the major conceptual step to yuck or yum is unavoidable, once there is an autonomous agent. And I think we have roughly the Darwinian criteria in mind. If yum, there will probably be more of this type of agent, offsprings of the first. If yuck, it is not so likely this lineage will prosper. Once yuck and yum, we are not far from C. S. Peirce's meaning-laden semiotic triad: sign, signified, significans. (ibid.:111)

Then Kauffman goes on to discuss what happens if the recipient of the signal is an autonomous bacterium (ibid.:113), and pictures the bacterium telling a story to its mate, promising to return in his next chapter "to discuss such stories, for I will say we cannot pre-state the configuration of a biosphere and, therefore, cannot deduce that which will unfold. Thus, among other things, we must tell stories to understand the oriented actions of agents in their worlds" (ibid.). This process, in one way or another, characterizes all living things—but because of the great transformation in humankind in the Pleistocene, it began to happen with us in a way it had never happened before, in something we may reasonably call a mind. It is more than merely tempting to find the explanation for that great change—that great transformation—using the Darwinian criteria.

Recall the construction set out by Henri Frankfort (1949:17, 29) and quoted in Chapter 4, that early man recognized the existence of problems transcending his immediate perceptions—the problem of origin and the problem of *telos*, of the aim and purpose of being, the invisible order of justice maintained by customs, mores, institutions, connected with the visible order, obviously maintained by the sun, confronting him with a living presence, a significant "Thou," outside him. We noted that this "I and Thou" dichotomy would reappear in our discussion of the ontogenic and phylogenic processes of alcoholism and sobriety in this chapter and we quoted Thorkild Jacobsen, how that in mythopoeic thought a *name* is a force within a person propelling him in a certain direction (1949:172).

In the words of the *Enuma Elish* (going back to the third millennium B.C.E.), there was a time "When no god whosoever had appeared; / Had been named by name, had been determined as to his lot, / Then were gods formed within them [within the primal forces of chaos]." Here, five millennia ago, it is an established truth that the naming of something is what brings it into existence (or immediately accompanies its being brought into existence) and that the names of gods (or things) express their true nature. This is the world-approach beneath Jaynes's (1982) view of the development of consciousness, of its origins in the breakdown of the bicameral mind, through which the gods spoke in olden time. We suggest that from the first days of names (say 8000 B.C.E.) until about three millennia ago, in some sense (if not necessarily in Jaynes's) human beings did what they did in response to the "voices of the gods," half the mind (brain) being set aside, as it were, for that purpose.

Jaynes suggests that—for reasons having to do with the fact that the breakdown products of stress-produced adrenalin are passed rapidly through the kidneys of some human beings and not of others—there are some who are genetically tuned to these "voices of the gods." Of Achilles and Hector:

So Achilles, repulsed by Agamemnon, in decision-stress by the grey sea, hallucinates Thetis out of the myths. So Hector, faced with the decision-suffering of whether to go outside the walls of Troy to fight Achilles or stay within them, in the stress of the decision hallucinates the voice that tells him to go out. The divine voice ends the decision-stress before it has reached any considerable level. (ibid.:94)

These voices are the least resistible (because most intrusive) of all sense phenomena. In bicameral men, who are not subjectively conscious, "volition came as a voice that was in the nature of a neurological command, in which the command and the action were not separated, in which to hear was to obey" (ibid.:99).

The bicameral mind is mediated by speech. In that 95 percent of the population that is right-handed, it is the left hemisphere that contains the three speech areas: (1) the supplementary motor cortex, on the very top of the left frontal lobe; (2) Broca's area, lower down at the back of the left frontal lobe; and (3) (the most important) Wernicke's area, chiefly the posterior part of the left temporal lobe with parts of the parietal area. The areas exist in both hemispheres, but are undeveloped in one.

Could it be [Jaynes asks] that these silent "speech" areas on the right hemisphere had some function at an earlier stage in man's history that now they do not have? The answer is clear if tentative. The selective pressures of evolution which could have brought about so mighty a result are those of the bicameral civilizations. The language of men was involved with only one hemisphere in order to leave the other free for the language of gods. (ibid.: 103–4)

We quoted the passage earlier, but it is worth quoting again here:

Let us consider a man commanded by himself or his chief to set up a fish weir far upstream from his campsite. If he is not conscious, and therefore cannot narratize the situation and so hold his analogue "I" in a spatialized time with its consequences fully imagined, how does he do it? It is only language . . . that can keep him at his time-consuming all-afternoon work. . . . Lingual man would have language to remind him, either repeated by himself . . . or, as seems more likely, by a repeated "internal" verbal hallucination telling him what to do. (ibid.:134)

(That is, the *I* involves consciousness of self, involving self-memory and self-narratization.) And then, "once a specific hallucination is recognized with a name, as a voice originating from a particular person, a significantly different thing is occurring. The hallucination is now a social interaction with a much greater role in individual behavior" (ibid.:137). We should remind ourselves again that *hallucination* is a value-laden word chosen by Jaynes partly perhaps for argumentative purposes but more because we simply do not have a word for what might be called a "true hallucination"—for voices that are really there, even (perhaps) from gods who are, in some sense, really *there*. But "really there" or not, "sons of the *nabiim*," itinerant prophets, Oracles and sibyls, druids and bards, are to be taken as remembrances or legacies or remnants of what Jaynes defined as the bicameral mind. We believe, with Jaynes, that there are biochemical and genetic forces here at work, as well as conscious adaptation to the very idea and nature (in the old sense, the "name") of consciousness.

A point of origin for our prehistorical inquiry may be given by the cave paintings at the Chauvet caves (Klein and Edgar 2002:258)—more exactly the paintings in the caves discovered in 1994 by Jean-Marie Chauvet, Éliette Brunel Deschamps, and Christian Hillaire, in the Ardèche region of south-central France—and perhaps by the ivory figurines in the (contemporaneous or even earlier) caves at Vogelherd (Stetten), Geissenklösterle, and Hohlenstein-Stadel, in southwestern Germany. Both of these are works of art (or sets of works) connected with the hunt and thus arguably religious in nature. These are perhaps twice as old as the paintings at Lascaux, dating to about 35,000 B.C.E. This point, in the late Pleistocene, is precisely the point at which, a quarter-century ago, Jaynes centered his hypothesis on the development of vocal qualifiers or modifiers, which fits with but does not require the rest of his hypothesis (1976). Here is what he says, in summary, in his *The Origin of Consciousness in the Breakdown of the Bicameral Mind*:

> The first real elements of speech were the final sounds of intentional calls differentiating on the basis of intensity. For example, a danger call for immediately present danger would be exclaimed with more intensity, changing the ending phoneme. . . . The next step was when these endings . . . could be separated from the particular call that generated them and attached to some other call. . . . The crucial thing here is that the differentiation of vocal qualifiers had to precede the invention of the noun which they modified. . . . What is more, this stage of speech had to remain for a long period until such modifiers became stable. This slow development was also necessary so that the basic repertoire of the call system was kept intact to perform its intentional functions. . . . The next stage might have been an age of commands, when modifiers, separated from the calls they modify, can now modify men's actions themselves. Particularly as men relied more and more on hunting in the chilled climate, the selective pressure for a group of hunters controlled by vocal commands must have been immense. (1982:132–33)

This could have taken place, Jaynes suggests, from 40,000 up to 25,000 B.C.E.—that is, at a time centering on Chauvet and the figurines. It is possible to consider these ivory figurines as the nouns of a spoken language that as yet had only verbs or interjections. A parallel (at the risk of falling into the easy identification of ontogeny and phylogeny) would be with little boys playing with soldiers, telling the story by moving the soldiers (and the trucks, tanks, guns, and planes) and speaking with interjections and perhaps occasional verbs. It is possible to consider the paintings as verbs and nouns of a full narrative, for a people using only interjections (perhaps with dependent modifiers). They would represent adjuncts to language (perhaps even most *of* the language) for peoples in very early language-states. It would not be accidental that the earliest language scripts are pictographic, then hieroglyphic, then syllabic, then alphabetic—alphabetic scripts being the child of conscious man. (Note that the paintings and figurines are in some sense "religious"—at a point in human development where religion and speech must be inexplicably intertwined.) And perhaps the great changes in language and consciousness had something to do with the climate—relatively but not impossibly cold. Perhaps the advent of writing (which came later) had to do more with the availability of materials for writing, better than scratches on a stone, than with changes in consciousness (though its development from pictographic to alphabetic does relate to those changes).

Perhaps, since the brain chemistry that has to do with speech has strong links to the brain chemistry having to do with at least some types of alcoholism, the "Fourth Drive" was linked to the changes forty thousand years ago. We know that alcohol affects exactly those parts of the neuronal systems that are involved with speech. We know that it also affects those parts of the neuronal systems that are connected with memory. We also know that other animals besides humans (*animales rationales*) have a drive to intoxication (the "Fourth Drive"). We also know that full anticipation of altered states of mind requires memory of previous altered states of mind, and we have hypothesized (with Jaynes) that this must involve either the separation of the self acting one way from the self acting another way (in other words, consciousness of the self), or else it involves hearing voices of the gods in the chamber of the bicameral mind reserved for that function.

And we know that the ancient oracles—and perhaps the sibyls—used intoxication to provide these voices, when, as we believe, the old bicameral mind was already breaking down (ibid.:321–32). We believe that Ptolemy Philopator (for example), as *dévoté* of Bacchus, twenty-two centuries ago (and a little more), was hearkening back to that more ancient bicameral day of the voices of the gods, as the story told of him in Third Maccabees suggests. The connection between Philopator's violence and his alcoholic worship is interesting—alcohol has, after all, been sufficiently used in connection with war to have provided us with a term ("Dutch courage") for alcohol-induced warlikeness. But the connection between the voices of the gods and the altered states of consciousness that came to the sibyls or the bards and that come (from drinking) particularly to those drinkers we now call alcoholics is perhaps of more primary interest here. Or perhaps they are both of equal interest, as representing two different types of alcoholism, with two different (but related) origins. Whatever the case, the leap over the subcritical/supercritical edge may well have involved conceptualization, altered consciousness, through intoxication—making use of a basic drive, already existing in animals, which became an instrument of survival for bicameral man.

Here it may be suggested that certain alcoholic genotypes actually are attendant on particular genetic *haplotypes*—an area of research where we have scarcely begun to begin. The *haplotype* represents a distinct mitochondrial lineage defined by mutations in the DNA of the mitochondria (singular *mitochondrion*, tiny "battery-packs" in our cells, running into the trillions in each human being, but all identical in each human being). Mitochondria are maternally transmitted, and it has been estimated that the mitochondria of a single human female about one hundred thousand years ago were the ancestors of all existing human mitochondria, though there are quite a number of distinct haplotypes by now (see Olson 2002: 24–25, 35–37, and passim). A number of haplotypes have been identified so far: one of the most interesting is haplotype X, present in Finnish, Italian, Druze, and North American Woodlands Algonquian populations. I'm not sure about the Druze, but all the rest have sweat-lodges or the equivalent as part of their extended phenotype—and if possibly sweat-lodges for X, what about other extended phenotypes for other genetic haplotypes, including alcoholic drinking.

Recall that a *phenotype* is defined by the interaction of the genotype and the environment, and may be substantially *extended*. A *genotype* is the genetic constitution of an individual or a group. The *phenotype* concerns the organism's concrete existence in the observer's domain or domains, whereas the *genotype* concerns the genetic makeup that the organism inherited. The different kinds of corn are genotypes. Plant the corn, grow the crop, and you get specific examples according to the soil, rainfall, sunlight, labor expended—in short, the corn's concrete existence in the observer's domain, determined by interaction of the genotype and the environment. These are the phenotypes. Genotypes are the principal—but not sole—subject of the study of evolution. Gene frequencies—allele frequencies—ordinarily remain more or less constant from one generation to the next; and no matter what the relative frequencies of the genotypes in the starting population, in subsequent generations these too will be more or less fixed at values determined by allele frequencies. With large populations, random mating, no exogenous preference on particular genotypes, low rate of mutation for introduction of new alleles, and no significant net migration of particular genotypes into or out of the population, it happens that, once a trait has been established with a certain frequency in the population, it will continue to show at approximately that frequency. Past is, in a way, present.

MENTAL ILLNESS AND NARRATIVE

When the authors of the DSM categorized alcoholism as a mental illness, the figure in the background was, of course, Sigmund Freud. Early twentieth-century attempts to place alcoholism as a disease of the mind reflect Freudian analysis, Freudian triads—the *conscious* mind, the *preconscious* mind, and the *unconscious* mind, the id, the ego, and the superego. The preconscious mind holds the vast storehouse of easily accessible memories: its contents were once conscious and can be returned to consciousness when needed. The unconscious mind, further down, stores primitive instinctual motives, and also memories and emotions that are so threatening to the conscious mind that they have been unconsciously pushed down into the unconscious mind through the process of *repression*. They can be accessed by the conscious mind only through great effort.

According to Freud, mental health comes from the process of psychoanalysis, so that the therapist, and thus the patient, can see how things got to be the way they are, and (over the long recommended period of the analytical process) what therefore can be done about them. In other words, the end result of psychoanalysis is a kind of cognitive therapy. Freud's developmental stages represent a shifting of the primary outlet for the energy of the id, particularly the sexual energy, from one part of the body to another. Now, although Freud does not frame his case histories in the language of narrative, he comes pretty close, and we may consider Freudian psychoanalysis in terms of narrative theory. The therapeutic challenge, within narrative therapy, is to loosen the sense of inevitability carried by the narrative of one's past, so that the chapters that will extend into the future are more under the auctorial control of the narrator.

To put this together, we may suggest that the newly sober alcoholic will be engaged in a process of mixed mirror transference and idealizing transference (from alcohol as self-object to therapist, sponsor, group, or higher power as self-object); this will be connected with modifications of the self-narrative helping organize the chaotic information of the past (in A.A. terms, "what it was like") and meld it with the process of therapy, including the A.A. program (in A.A. terms, "what happened"), and the alcoholic's present state (in A.A. terms, "what it's like now"). In this quasi-Freudian context, we may repeat our summaries of the work of Tiebout and Sullivan.

Harry Tiebout was influenced by the work of one of Freud's less ortho-dox followers, the Hungarian Sandór Radó. Recall Radó's statement, quoted extensively by Tiebout:

> Once it was a baby, radiant with self-esteem, full of belief in the omnipotence of its wishes, of its thoughts, gestures, and words. . . . But the child's mega-lomania melted away under the inexorable pressure of experience. Its sense of its own sovereignty had to make room for a more modest self-evaluation. The process, first described by Freud [in his discussion of His Majesty, the Baby], may be designated the reduction in size of the original ego; it is a painful procedure and one that is possibly never completely carried out. (quoted in Tiebout 1999:58, 79)

Radó's conclusions (1957) may be briefly summarized. Alcoholic drink-ing is a "derivative of alimentary orgasm"—and the repressed tendencies that early psychoanalytic investigators found to be mobilized by alcohol were oral-dependent and might involve latent passive homosexual crav-ings (which themselves involve oral fixation). Also, Radó suggested that the traumatized ego tries to escape further traumatic experiences through avoidance reactions such as loss of consciousness, speech, locomotion, and coordination of movements (which "falling-down-drunk" blackout drink-ing will do), and also that standard psychoanalysis fosters regression with-out supplying a counterforce toward progression. "To overcome repressions and thus be able to recall the past is one thing; to learn from it, and be able to act on the new knowledge, another" (Radó 1953).

In Tiebout's talk to the American Psychiatric Association, he argued that "alcoholism is a symptom that has become a disease" (1999:8)—that is, the symptoms resulting from Alcoholism(2) become the disease of Alco-holism(1). The alcoholic must be brought to accept that he is the victim of a disease and that the only way for him to remain healthy is to refrain from taking the first drink. That is, psychotherapy, with all it brings in the way of release from the unremembered past (once it is remembered), treats the symptom that becomes the disease earlier ages called inebriety: it does not, in Radó's terms, treat the disease condition through progress in learning from the past.

Meanwhile, we have Harry Stack Sullivan, and his distinctions between and among *prototaxic, parataxic,* and *syntaxic* thinking, his views on lan-guage, and his idea of *consensual validation.* Although there is substantial difference in terminology, in fact Sullivan anticipates a good bit of John Bowlby and his Attachment Theory. (And Attachment Theory is worth looking at, given the old statement that an alcoholic is one who can neither give nor receive love easily.) Moreover, Sullivan's work with group ther-apy depended on consensual validation of the process of growing out of *parataxic* distortion into *syntaxic* thinking—the process of growing up. This fits in with Freud on "His Majesty, the Baby," with Sandór Radó and his ego-deflation (and his alcoholics-as-frozen-in-oral-fixation), with the age-locus (and general emphasis) of Attachment Theory, and with Harry M. Tiebout and his treatment of alcoholics as children, following Radó—thus with Bill W. in the *12&12*.

Prototaxic thinking occurs during the first year of life and then recedes in the next two: the infant's life consists of an unending flood of brief vague sensations forming a seamless blur. This thinking may be likened to a con-fused perception of scenes of photographic slides projected in a random helter-skelter way on a blank screen, without continuity or relatedness of subject matter. In *parataxic* thinking, dominant in the second year of life and receding (though sometimes very slowly) thereafter, the child forms links between the fragmentary experiences, but the links are haphazard and non-rational. They do not follow rules of logic and cause-and-effect relatedness. Here the child frequently links together events happening close to each other in time, but not in fact logically related. *Parataxic* thinking is normal at this stage of the child's development, but it is in fact distorted. In healthy emotional development, the vast majority of these *parataxic* distortions are corrected during the subsequent *syntaxic* phase of experience and thinking, beginning in the third or fourth year of life.

This is when the child develops the capacity for logical and realistic thinking, for sound appraisals of himself or herself and others and of rela-tionships (here is a link to Attachment Theory). The basis for this *syntaxic* thinking is *consensual validation,* and the earlier distorted patterns of think-ing that stand in the way of proper consensual validation are the *parataxic distortions*: those that are not corrected (because of anxiety or other emo-tional difficulties, perhaps reflecting biochemical distortions) persist into later childhood, adolescence, and adulthood. Sullivan believed that con-sensual validation—particularly that required to deal with embedded *parataxic* distortions—came from language, as *syntaxic* thinking, in the appropriate progression, begins with and accompanies the development of language. Hence the use of Sullivanite group therapy to develop both appropriate consensual validation and appropriate language, to produce *syntaxic* thinking.

It has been observed that, while the Freudian paradigm pretty much held fast for the first half of the twentieth century, the story of the latter decades is the breakup of rigid Freudianism. One of the most interesting phenom-ena involved in that breakup is the gradual growth of Attachment Theory, connected with the name and work of John Bowlby, and the ways Attach-ment Theory and narrative theory work together. In Attachment Theory, four principal patterns are evident: we may categorize them by looking at the way a one-year-old child may react to brief separation from and then reunion with his or her caregiver. A securely attached child will protest on separation, and then on reunion the protests are accepted, "metabolized," and soothed by the caregiver. All securely attached children are alike in their security, while insecurely attached children are insecurely attached in their different ways: these may be summarized as insecure-avoidant, insecure-ambivalent, insecure-disorganized. All protest on separation: the insecure-avoidant hover nervously at the edge after reunion, the insecure-ambivalent cannot be pacified on the reunion but cling furiously to the caregiver, and the insecure-disorganized show no coherent pattern of response to reunion.

In adult narratives, the style may likewise be divided into four kinds: (1) secure-autonomous (equivalent to secure attachment in the child), (2) insecure-dismissive (equivalent to insecure-avoidant attachment), (3) insecure-preoccupied (equivalent to insecure-ambivalent), and (4) insecure-unresolved (equivalent to insecure-disorganized attachment behavior). Insecure-dismissive narratives are curt, unelaborated, unrevealing, and uninformative; insecure-preoccupied narratives are rambling, inconclusive, and painful (particularly in the sense that past pain is still present today). Insecure-unresolved narratives contain broken and disjointed passages perhaps indicative of past repression of traumatic memories. The process of psychotherapy under Attachment Theory is the process of retelling the stories: "Raw experience plus meaning equals narrative." Meaning is provided by stored or condensed stories provided by the therapist. Meaning may be provided in Alcoholics Anonymous by the stored and condensed stories in the back of the "Big Book," or by stories told at speaker's meetings of A.A., or I believe by the alcoholic's sponsor. Just as with the linguistic triad of signified, sign, and lexicon (from which the sign is drawn)—where the sign is linked to the referent *via* the world of language—so here the story is linked to "raw experience" through the world of meaning.

It seems likely that the capacity to make this link is itself a developmental link, mediated by early attachment experience. Those who are securely attached can distinguish between their own experience and that of others, represent and tell the story of their feelings, and if need be break up their stories and re-form them more in keeping with the flux of experience. Ambivalent individuals are so close to their feelings that they cannot objectify, externalize, or "mark" the events in the way needed for a working story. Avoidant people cling to a stereotyped version of themselves and their past and feel threatened by the need to update their narrative in the way characteristic of creative living. And the unresolved cannot find a narrative strong enough to contain their traumatic pain.

The process of therapy is then the process of constructing a narrative that when complete will mirror the correction of attachment-insecurities. We recall here the definition of an alcoholic as one incapable of giving or receiving love. On the question of healing narrative, we note the work of Hans Kohut (quoted in 1999:27–48): "There is no longer one psychodynamic narrative, one developmental narrative, and one treatment narrative. There are now several of each" (ibid.:31). Also, as the result of work by Roy Schafer (ibid.:40–42) and others, there is no longer one psychodynamic narrative of the patient's past and then a second narrative of the treatment itself: the two are collapsed into one. Psychodynamic narrative is now a complex interwoven tale, along Freudian lines, intertwining themes from the patient's past with themes from the treatment itself, the emphasis falling on the treatment.

We have talked about narratization in Attachment Theory and in Freudian psychotherapy, about the elimination of parataxic distortions in Sullivanite group therapy. All of this speaks to roughly the same means of therapy, or arresting the "disease" of alcoholism. We should probably rehearse here two parts of our model most closely related to the possibility of self-induced physiological (that is, neurophysiological) change. As a link to get us into the illness of the body, we should recall that, the "regressive pull of addiction is overwhelmingly powerful, and forces of equal or greater weight pulling in the opposite direction must be put in place. . . . The patient is also desperately in need of an object to idealize" (Levin 1995:208).

Alcohol had been the ideal object. Now it is gone and must be replaced. Generally that replacement takes place through idealization of a therapist, an AA sponsor, an AA group, the AA program, or AA's higher power— and so the "formation of a self-object transference provides the patient with the stability and the security out of which growth from the stage of the archaic nuclear self into the stage of the mature self can take place" (ibid.:210). The process

> reduces anxiety by providing cognitive structure for chaotic experience; through providing tools for living, the psychic structure needed to deal with feelings and conflicts; through the reversal of affect regression; through internalization, transmuting and otherwise; through de-repression; and through the breakdown of defensive isolation through integration into a community of recovering persons. (ibid.:212–13)

This is largely speaking to counteracting—gaining a reprieve from—the symptoms of Alcoholism(2). But what is it about the neuronal inherited aspects of Alcoholism(2), as we understand them, that makes this work. Here we return to Gerard Edelman, the evolution of pattern in the brain, and the matter of primary and secondary repertoires.

NEURONAL GROUP SELECTION AND MEMORY

For Edelman, as we have noted, the brain is not a computer hardwired to process external stimuli, but is actively engaged in constructing the environment. That is, the mind is not a blank sheet upon which the external environment writes a program from which to actively engage the world, but instead we are born with capacities for action that serve to construct and interpret the world. This is a bit like Immanuel Kant's a priori categories of the mind, existing prior to experience. But Edelman takes us farther, arguing that the way the mind engages the world evolves—and if evolving, is then subject to natural selection.

In the morphogenesis of the brain, certain topographical features, such as place and timing, are central. As a result, the actual configuration of microelements such as the fine detail of neural networks cannot be known at any given time. That is, phenotypic variation in human microsystems can be very great, even with identical twins (after all, *one* of them must be born first, and they cannot experience their environment in completely identical ways). The theory of natural selection holds that evolved forms give relative survival advantage: evidently, a system of brain morphogenesis that imparts diversity in brain anatomy (and thus in mode of function) would conduce to producing more survivable forms than a system hardwired to one specific external world. The hardwiring would be a key to mass extinction when the external world changed. In the so-called mass extinction of the dinosaurs, those dinosaurs that could adapt to the changed environment survived—albeit as birds.

Edelman's theory of neuronal group selection (TNGS) may be summarized in three parts. First, this process of morphogenesis, based on cell division, cell movement, and cell differentiation, produces a species-dependent neuroanatomy variable at the individual level: groups of neurons in a specific brain region deriving from this process are known as *primary repertoires*. The genetic code is a template imposing constraints, not imposing unanimity. Second, through behavioral (extended phenotypic) engagement with the external world, some synaptic connections are promoted through use and are thus strengthened, others are neglected and are thus weakened, so that certain neural networks are self-selected from the diversity of those available: these are *secondary repertoires*. In practice primary and secondary repertoires may be overlapping.

Finally, third, primary, and secondary repertoires link psychology and physiology, by forming maps connected by the entrance and reentrance of neural linkages. For the functions of the mind to be performed it will be recalled that "primary and secondary repertoires must form maps connected by massively parallel and reciprocal connections. . . . Re-entrant signalling occurs along these connections" (Edelman 1989:92). That is, as groups of neurons are selected in a map, other groups in reentrantly connected but different maps may also be selected at the same time. A fundamental premise of the theory of neuronal group selection is that the selective coordination of the complex patterns of interconnection between neuronal groups by reentry is the basis of behavior. "Indeed, re-entry (combined with memory . . .) is the main basis for a bridge between physiology and psychology" (ibid.).

Through selective reentry coordination, environmental factors act at various levels to select some configurations of neural cells over others. With primary repertoires it is a stochastic process. With secondary repertoires, *environmental selection of the specific synaptic pathways occurs in behavioral engagement with the outside world*. Edelman's third component suggests how the primary and secondary repertoires link psychology and physiology by forming maps connected by the entrance and reentrance of neural linkages—that is, through synaptic cross-linkages. "The way we engage the world perceptually and behaviorally is selected for in terms of survival advantage" (Edelman 1992:84). We will go into some of the implications of this later. Here let us again note that, according to Henry Plotkin, "once intelligence has evolved in a species, then thereafter brains have a causal force equal to that of genes" (1994:177).

Here also it is appropriate to look briefly at the question of memory and of the biochemistry of memory. We all know that there is something called short-term memory and something called long-term memory. These are stages two and three in the process of memory, the first stage being what is called the sensory register, which provides and encodes raw data for transfer to the short-term—and thence, we believe, to the long-term—memory. Information stored in the sensory register lasts perhaps one-tenth of a second, but it is apparently a complete replica of the sensory experience. When a bit of information is selected for the short-term memory (automatically simply by "paying attention" to it), it will last (unless it is rehearsed) perhaps a few seconds: moreover, the short-term memory will hold only five to perhaps nine chunks of information even for that limited time.

Long-term memory is a different thing altogether, and the transfer from short-term to long-term memory is likewise different from earlier automatic transfer from sensory register to short-term memory. Briefly (1) LTM (long-term memory) is indexed for retrieval; (2) LTM stores information by *semantic* codes, STM (short-term memory) by *experiential* (particularly *acoustic*) codes; (3) LTM information is permanent so that "forgetting" is a retrieval problem, while STM information if not rehearsed is impermanent; and (4) LTM is held in the hippocampus and then transferred to areas of the cerebral cortex involved in language and perception, while STM primarily "resides" in the frontal lobes of the cerebral cortex. Also, (5) there are three varieties of LTM, procedural (how to do things), semantic (what things are), and episodic (specific events at specific times and places).

Both semantic and episodic LTM are connected with speech, though in different ways, and most LTM difficulties seem to reside in the episodic memory, which is apparently the more difficult to access. It can be made easier to access by enhancing any of the three modes of retrieval—recall, recognition, and relearning—all of them involving a kind of narratization, and thereby involving speech. Forgetting occurs either through decay (in sensory-register or short-term memories) or interference by other memories (in long-term memories). Just as episodic memories are likely to be episodic, so is episodic forgetting (that is, the forgetting of episodic memories is itself episodic). We may, in fact, consider memory as a species of neuroadaptation—learning and memory, like tolerance and dependence, can be viewed as adaptive responses of the central nervous system to external stimuli.

Research on lower organisms (specifically the marine snail *Aplysia*) has provided evidence that the serotonin-induced activation of adenylyl cyclase (AC) and subsequent activation of protein kinase A (PKA) are critical factors in short-term and long-term sensitization, as precursor to memory. (Memory as ordinarily defined for human beings presumably does not exist in non-self-conscious organisms, like marine snails.) Structural alterations associated with long-term sensitization in *Aplysia* are thought to be related to down-regulation of cell-adhesion molecules related to nerve-cell-adhesion molecules. A cyclic adenosine monophosphate (cAMP)-regulated transcription factor is involved, and the cAMP system has also been implicated in learning and memory in *Drosophila melanogaster*.

BIOCHEMISTRY AND GENETIC CODE

Alcoholism, we believe, is grounded at least in part in biological processes, and biological processes can be influenced greatly by the biochemistry of the genetic code from which biological development takes place. If the genetic code has developed as a response to external conditions (as Darwin suggests) and represents a survival from a time when it conferred a survival value on the carrier, then the various alcoholic phenotypes we have suggested (Psa, Sda, Pca, Pea) can be studied in connection with their putative causes back in time in the evolutionary process. By understanding how things got the way they are, we can perhaps see how they might be changed.

Once we have the genotypes, the hereditary alcoholics (those with heritable Alcoholism(2), we can examine them to see what they have in common biogenetically that may define their precondition. We have looked particularly at neurotransmitters, pathways for neurotransmission, and especially the hypothalamic-pituitary axes. We began with neurotransmitters, noting that some of what has been discovered comes not from human studies but from alcoholic nematodes, fruit flies, and mutant mice, bred for the purposes over hundreds and thousands of laboratory generations (and we are suggesting that Alcoholism [2] as we know it has grown up over a thousand generations).

Work in this area of neurotransmission has been done on endogenous opioids, serotonin and serotonergic functioning, GABA (gamma-aminobutyric acid), epinephrine/norepinephrine, glutamate, and dopamine. It has been suggested that alcohol consumption may stimulate increased activity in the endogenous opioid systems, as—for example—the enkephalinergic system, and by potentiating the duration of the enkephalins (possibly in an analogue of memory) might increase alcohol consumption. Enkephalins are generally short-lasting, being degraded rapidly by enkephalinase and aminopeptidase enzymes. It is possible that the genetics—which is to say, the biochemistry—of alcoholism would include the presence of a potent enkephalinase inhibitor, such as thiorphan. In any case, we might well expect that a genetic predisposition toward alcohol drinking may be accompanied by an increase in the responsiveness of opioid systems to alcohol." And the enkephalins are not the only opioids we may find involved in genetic predisposition toward alcoholic drinking.

Among the opioid peptides, beta-endorphin is derived from pro-opiomelanocortin (POMC); the enkephalins from the precursor pre-pro-enkephalin A (PPENK). Comparison of the activity of the beta-endorphin and enkephalinergic systems in alcohol-drinking rats showed that alcohol produced a significant increase in POMC (beta-endorphin precursor) mRNA (messenger ribonucleic acid) levels in rats from the P (alcohol-drinking) line but not from the NP line, and the same was true for PPENK (enkephalin precursor) mRNA levels. A genetic predisposition toward high alcohol drinking is accompanied by increased responsiveness of both the beta-endorphin and enkephalinergic systems to alcohol. Alcohol-induced activation of the endogenous opioid system may serve to enhance the reinforcing effects of alcohol and thereby increase the probability of subsequent drinking episodes. (In other words, alcoholics find alcohol more pleasurable than nonalcoholics find it, partly for reasons of memory.) Alcohol-induced activation of the opioid system may reduce aversion to high-dose effects of alcohol (increasing the pleasure of "being drunk").

It was established as long ago as 1966 that alcohol administered to rats resulted in a dose-related change in plasma corticosterone (GC) levels and that ACTH replacement therapy after hypophysectomy activated corticosterone secretion from the adrenal gland. In other words, alcohol activates the brain-pituitary axis and the alcohol-induced rise in GC is not the result of a direct end-organ response. Acute and chronic alcohol consumption in animals (including humans) activates the stress axis, resulting in continuously or intermittently elevated GCs. It may be hypothesized that certain types of alcoholics (possibly not all types) may have lower-than-normal GC levels, so that they can function over a long term with GC levels (at least intermittently) elevated above their norm, without crossing the threshold levels implicated in memory loss and cell death. We might suggest that (FHP) ε-alcoholics would fit most easily into this classification, and their periodic (i.e., intermittent) drinking might represent a self-medicating bodily biochemical response to their condition. This, of course, says nothing about the genetic selection process leading to such a condition. (One might ask if it is significant that this is a glucosteroid, given the anecdotal connection between alcoholism recovery and blood sugars.)

Increased serotonergic functioning (giving effect to serotonin release) generally accompanies decreased alcohol consumption, and decreased serotonergic functioning generally accompanies increased alcohol consumption. There are at least fourteen mammalian 5-HT (serotonin) receptors, and the relationships between them and alcohol consumption are complex. Several of the receptor subtypes have been reported to be altered in alcohol dependence, but there is no clear and present knowledge as to whether these receptor subtypes are already altered in individuals at risk (and therefore in those who are dependent)—partly because the applicability of mouse studies is unclear, partly because human studies lump alcohol abuse and dependence together, partly because of problems with typology. Still, serotonergic receptor functions appear to be a fruitful area for study.

In Chapter 5, we mentioned, as an example, the possible connection of at least one type of alcoholism with tryptophan metabolism and brain serotonin synthesis. Tryptophan is an amino acid from which serotonin is made: what is specifically being tested for is

(1) that there are differences in 5-HT (serotonin) turnover and release in alcoholic subjects, compared with healthy controls, before and after acute tryptophan depletion;

(2) that putative differences in 5-HT (serotonin) turnover are governed primarily by genetic variation in the 5-HT transporter in alcoholics;

(3) and that 5-HT Transporter genetic variation also correlates with cerebrospinal fluid concentration of serotonin metabolite 5-hydroxyindoleacetic acid (5-HIAA), before and after acute tryptophan depletion. The current best opinions of those doing research are in accord with these hypotheses.

We look also at the interrelations between alcohol and the renin-angiotensin (R-A) system. We know, for example, that rats subsensitive to serotonin agonists (compounds that mimic serotonin in their effects) drink very large amounts of alcohol—and rats bred for a permanent suppression in R-A system activity display "a robust predisposition to alcohol consumption"(Zakaria 1993:57). Also, mice lacking a functional copy of the gene that codes for serotonin 1_B receptors (in other words, for serotonergic functioning) drank twice as much ethanol in a free-choice drinking situation as the wildtype controls. A 1979 study showed that the level of 5HIAA in alcoholics twenty-eight to sixty-three days after their last drink was significantly lower than for a nonalcoholic comparison group and significantly lower than for alcoholics in the immediate postintoxication phase (within one to two days after their last drink).

We may note here also that the R-A system activity that inhibits alcohol consumption is characterized by having events in the periphery set into motion central processes that eventually result in the inhibition of alcohol intake. This chain of events is quite typical of peptides and hormones that influence behavior and has been observed with respect to the actions of vasopressin, oxytocin, and aldosterone on memory processes. It has been suggested that a bioactive peptide is activated in the R-A system by alcoholic intake (the R-A system itself being so activated), then produces a satiety or stop signal at a point determined by emotional state, diet, environmental motivators, and individual predisposition, in a process parallel to—and likely connected with—the process of memory.

The implications of a study coming out of Yale's Substance Abuse Center, having to do with cocaine, are interesting. Regional cerebral metabolic rate for glucose (cRMRglc, an index of local brain function) was measured for cocaine abusers and an otherwise similar nonuser control group on the presentation of cocaine-related stimuli. The results showed stimulus-responses in the dorsolateral prefrontal cortex and the medial temporal lobe—also in the amygdala and cerebellum—all regions involved in either explicit or implicit memory. The activation of memory regions in the brain is directly related to the cue-elicited desires. Allowing for some possible problems with the definition of *desires* (are they the same as *craving*?), this seems indicative. We repeat from Chapter 5 that the "discrete distribution of activation produced by cocaine-related stimuli differs markedly from the response to acute cocaine administration, which involves widespread *decreases* [my emphasis] in rCMRglc in human volunteers" (Grant et al. 1996:12044). The reasonable conclusion is that desires or craving come from cue-stimulated memory more than from the neural substrates of direct experience with the substance involved—in other words, from physical addiction.

Activation or blockade of the opioid system has been shown to alter alcohol consumption in animals. In addition, lower beta-endorphin-like immuno-reactivity has been reported in FHP individuals ("genetic" alcoholics) than in non-FHPs. Also, there is evidence of greater increase in beta-endorphins following alcohol consumption in high-risk (of alcoholism) subjects than in lower-risk subjects, and considerable anecdotal evidence from members of Alcoholics Anonymous suggesting abnormal endorphin-processing in some alcoholics. Possible mechanisms suggested include differences in concentrations of opiate peptides, possible actions of opiate-producing neurons inhibiting CRH (corticotropin-releasing hormone) production, interactions between inherent levels of opiates and reactivity of the hypothalamic pituitary adrenal system, and innate activity levels. Note that CRH, which is secreted by the hypothalamus under stress, triggers release of hormones that raise the level of cortisol in the blood.

The primary and obligatory regulator of the corticotropin-derived POMC peptides (which we have met already), such as adrenocorticotrophic hormone (ACTH), is the corticotropin-releasing factor CRF. ACTH is the primary regulator of glucocorticoid (GC is cortisol in humans and corticosterone in mice and rats). It is known that the neuroimmunoendocrine system, upon activation, modulates the HPA axis. That is, certain challenges can activate mononucleated leukocytes to produce a variety of cytokines and hormones. The cytokines, through feed-forward and feedback, modulate HPA-axis events at virtually every level, including the medullary cells of the adrenal gland (primary source of epinephrine) and catecholamines (including epinephrine/norepinephrine) from the cortical cells of the adrenal gland.

Following perception of stress, the hypothalamus releases CRH, AVP, and other ACTH secretion analogues, resulting in the release of ACTH from the pituitary gland. In turn ACTH initiates the release of the adrenal androgens and glucocorticoids, which prepare the organism for stress by increasing glucose and fatty acid availability for the central nervous system. Also, inflammatory cytokines and other inflammation mediators stimulate the HPA axis, while the glucocorticoids inhibit cytokine production and more or less turn the immune system way down, preventing overwhelming and potentially harmful immune response to stressors. It appears that reduced ACTH and cortisol responses to CRH activity are correlated with alcoholic activity, and even acute (one-time) ethanol exposure impairs the ability of the HPA axis to respond to physiological stressors. Since part of that HPA response is the production of glucocorticoids, which regulate the immune system, and part of the HPA response is the release of adrenal androgens, the inhibition of these by alcohol could be expected to have something of the effect of an allergic reaction, and something of the effect of a stress-response system generally out of control.

What this means in behavioral terms is not entirely clear, but one thing is clear—this is far from being a suggestion that alcoholics drink because they are "stressed out," and much closer to being a suggestion that alcoholics drink because they are alcoholics, and the effect on the stress axis is to make their actions and reactions unpredictable in normal terms. Also, and important particularly here, memory processes are implicated in these reactions. What we need to do in future research, I believe, is link the HPA axis research to specific alcoholic types, and most specifically to the types that apparently involve ASPD—what we might call Psa or perhaps "fighting" alcoholism—and then, for confirmation, to link the whole to the process of memory patterning, which it resembles.

With GABA, we are looking at what might be called, in some instances, a neuroinhibitor rather than an ordinary neurotransmitter—an off-switch rather than an on-switch—but we are still looking at the products of the HPA axis and their relation to alcohol consumption and the predisposition to alcohol consumption. One study tested for correlation of aggressive behavior with the cerebral spinal fluid major central metabolites of serotonin (5HT), norepinephrine (NE), and dopamine (DA). Independently scored history of aggressive behavior (a mark of Psa alcoholism, sometimes present in others) showed no correlation with dopamine metabolite HVA, significant negative correlation (–0.78) with serotonin metabolite 5HIAA (see above), and significant positive correlation (+0.64) with norepinephrine metabolite MHPG. Signaling effects of dopamine may be substituted for by other signals or triggers in the alcoholic's neuronal system, or changes in DA levels may come into play only in chronic alcoholics. A human study carried out using a specific $D_A D_2$ receptor agonist (agent mimicking dopamine in effect) suggested agonist-induced reactivity specifically associated with trait levels of PE (positive emotionality), itself based on sensitivity to signals of incentive-reward, which are valueless without some form of (even Pavlovian) "memory." As there seems to be no characteristic alcoholic's dopamine level, it might reasonably be suggested that something substitutes for dopamine-related positive emotionality in the alcoholic.

The primary function assigned to dopamine in alcoholism is that it mediates reinforcement of alcohol consumption. Counteradaptation, like adaptation, is of course connected with memory processes. Reinforcement or its equivalent may reasonably come through such memory-reinforcers as caffeine that release epinephrine into the system, thereby triggering blood-sugar increases (I believe meetings of Alcoholics Anonymous almost universally serve coffee—though sometimes decaffeinated, which would not make a great deal of sense in this context). We may note, likewise, that levels of the epinephrine/norepinephrine-linked neurotransmitter acetylcholine are reduced in Alzheimer's patients, suggesting again the link between epinephrine and memory. This, given a link between memory and alcoholism (a link we have already indicated), suggests that reinforcement of alcohol consumption might be tied more closely to epinephrine/norepinephrine than to dopamine.

On the question of electrophysiology—relevant to anticipation of altered states—we recall that detoxified alcoholics and FHP children have a reduced amplitude of the scalp-positive wave that peaks approximately 300 msec after a rare but anticipated event (P300). The relationship of a family history of alcoholism (FHP) to a reduced P300 amplitude was demonstrated in two small follow-up studies wherein increased rates of substance-related problems were observed in those FHP children with reduced P300 amplitudes. The apparent heritability of P300 amplitude suggests that reduced-amplitude P300 could be transmitted from alcoholic parent to offspring, and that would seem to tie in with Siegel's suggestion that the anticipation of the changed state, rather than the changed state itself, is a key to William James's "mystical" nature of alcoholism. That is, alcoholics do not react as strongly as nonalcoholics to a rare but antici- pated event, so they build up their uncertainty and anticipation by drink- ing—particularly if, as with teenagers, the drinking itself is a forbidden event, and thus a recognized "risky business."

The findings (mentioned above) involving the P3 (or P300) component of a visual ERP time-locked electrocortical response to a visual stimulus refer in this case to a late positive deflection of the ERP wave-form thought to reflect attentional resources during memory update. The mean ampli- tude of the P3 component of a visual ERP has, as noted, been reported to be significantly smaller among the prepubescent sons of male alcoholics, as compared to similarly aged sons of nonalcoholics. This does not seem to hold for girls or postpubescent boys. It would seem that brain-wave amplitude in response to observations promising a rare but anticipated event reflect lowered response in the memory-update period. In other words, it sounds as though, in FHP male children, memory cues require less update (may not, perhaps, be susceptible to updating) and serve more easily to reinforce previous expectations than in other children.

ALCOHOLIC CONSCIOUSNESS AND
ALCOHOLIC PATTERNS

The absolute PFC volume of the brain declines in adolescence, substantial synapse elimination occurs (linked to developmental loss of glutaminergic excitatory input), and cholinergic innervation of the PFC likewise increases. The hippocampus produces greater amounts of norepinephrine release, as against that in older or younger individuals, accompanying emergence of inhibitory norepinephrine autoreceptors. In short, adolescents find it harder to get the "highs" that used to come unforced, at the same time the HPG (hypothalamic-pituitary-gonadal) axis is greatly awakened, and there are other neuronal shifts in the body. We might therefore expect that those with alcoholism in their family backgrounds—who therefore may have certain hereditary reactions to alcohol and a certain hereditary ability to "outdrink" their nonalcoholic friends—will as continuously as possible engage in "risky" drinking and drink-related behavior. Because it makes them feel "really good"—and because the excitement of anticipation (based on memory) includes what they are going to do when they're drunk and they need to keep the excitatory effects going. One way they do this is by remembering in communal speech previous excitatory effects. ("Hey! Do you remember how out-of-control we were that night?")

We are constructed so that we relish natural highs, but what exactly are we relishing? The Fourth Drive (going back to Siegel) "is not just motivating people to feel good or bad—it is [also] a desire to feel different, to achieve a rapid change in one's state" (1989:217)—which, of course, suggests being *consciously* on the subcritical/supercritical edge. The direction of the change, whether up or down, good or bad, Siegel argues, is of secondary importance only. Of course, this is not original with him. Consider the lead provided by William James in *The Varieties of Religious Experience,* where he suggests that alcoholic experience opens the mystic doors of perception. Here he is, on the question of the "value" of alcohol and more specifically of intoxication by alcohol:

> The sway of alcohol over mankind is unquestionably due to its power to stimulate the mystical faculties of human nature, usually crushed to earth by the cold facts and dry criticisms of the sober hour. Sobriety diminishes, discriminates, and says no; drunkenness expands, unites, and says yes. It is in fact the great exciter of the *Yes* function in man. It brings its votary from the chill periphery of things to the radiant core. It makes him for the moment one with truth. ([1903] 1961:304)

But, I suggest, not all men (or women)—only those who have the gift of alcoholism. And James goes on to say this:

> To the poor and unlettered [drunkenness] stands in the place of symphony concerts and of literature; and it is part of the deeper mystery and tragedy of life that whiffs and gleams of something that we immediately recognize as excellent should be vouchsafed to so many of us only in the fleeting earlier phases of what in its totality is so degrading a poisoning. (ibid.:305)

But the earlier whiffs and gleams are recited and thus engraved in communal memory, which is one reason adolescents drink to get drunk in self-reinforcing groups.

James remarks that he is convinced that

our normal waking consciousness . . . is but one special type of consciousness, whilst all about it, parted from it by the flimsiest of screens, there lie
potential forms of consciousness entirely different. . . . Apply the requisite
stimulus, and at a touch they are there in all their completeness, definite
types of mentality *which probably somewhere have their field of application and
adaptation.* (ibid.:305, emphasis mine)

I would myself go further than *probably*—like Darwin, I would say this
type of mentality would not have evolved if it were not valuable. Therefore, either this Alcoholism(2) at one time conferred a survival value on
those that had it, or else it is the natural accompaniment of other characteristics that confer such a survival value. Just possibly, different types of
Alcoholism(2) would confer or accompany genes that conferred different
survival values. Future research here (if we had an accurate or agreed-
upon typology) would appear to be desirable: we might even be able to
make some advance by examining data already available.

Thus, for example, altered consciousness for the Celtic druidic or bardic
orders, or a different altered consciousness for the Germanic or Nordic
warriors (especially the *berserkr* rage of battle), might well make use of
intoxication. The pattern would presumably be periodic: not even Germanic warriors were always fighting, nor were druids always exercising
their priestly functions, nor bards their poetic. In both these cases, as we
noted, the premium would be on the differential effect of alcohol on those
with the relevant differential characteristics—the more strongly, for the
druids and bards, if we accept Jaynes's hypothesis on the bicameral mind.
In any case, those times are long gone: what was valuable for CuChulainn
or Harald Baresark is not valued by today's society.

If we put together what Plotkin and Edelman have said with what we
have learned about the connections of serotonergic and other neurotransmitter functioning in the alcoholic, and the linkage of these neurotransmitters with memory (and speech), we can see that the biochemical
key to alcoholism may lie not in chemical entities like Naltrexone or
Naloxone—but in training reentrant signaling along the pathways and
from the axons of neurotransmission. Whether, with Norman Cousins, we
speak of the placebo effect, or with Bill W. of a "spiritual" reprieve from
alcoholism—however we put it—the linkage of memory and speech,
memory and neurotransmission, with the alcoholic's special reactions
(even special allergies) to kinin and kinase, monoamines and monoamine
oxidases, serotonin and norepinephrine, corticosteroids and enzymes, and
above all (I suspect) to beta-endorphins, suggest this: By altering phenotypic reaction, by training memory *through both speech and abstinence,* the
alcoholic predisposition, Alcoholism(2), may be permanently held in
check—and, as a bonus, its effects in Alcoholism(1) at least partly reversed.

So much, temporarily and briefly, for mind and body. Now, what modern science of the spirit—what "theology"—fits in best with our modern science of the mind and of the body. Theology in general, we have said, is the investigation and study of the being and nature of God and his creatures (including us), the complex of the divine dispensation and its mediation to humankind, including natural truths, the soul, moral law—everything accessible to reason enlightened by faith. Its purpose is the investigation of the contents of belief (including how it works) so far as that belief is accessible to analysis by this reason enlightened by faith.

THEOLOGY OF ALCOHOLISM AND SOBRIETY

If, as we have suggested, alcoholism is a condition of the brain, where mind and body intersect—or, to put it in more recognizably theological terms, where the mind is in some sense incarnate in the body—we are well advised to look at the theology of Incarnation. We are looking also at the theology of sobriety and the *telos* of sobriety. Finally, we are looking at the theological underpinnings—and the history of the theological underpinnings—of the society, or *koinonia,* of Alcoholics Anonymous. Underlying this "spiritual part" of our study is a set of *understandings* having to do with the relationship of mind and matter.

We humans think in triads—that seems to be part of *our* programming (it was certainly part of Freud's), and the traditional theological triad is that of (1) Being, Creator, Cosmic Mind, *Nous*; (2) Creation, Word, *Logos*; and (3) Knowledge, or Wisdom, *Sophia*, or occasionally Intellectual Love. The clear implication of the writings of those closest to the Johannine system that we are following here is that the triad of *Nous, Logos,* and *Sophia* is the Triad we know as Father, Son, and Holy Spirit. That is, we have two triads—the Creator/Word/Wisdom triad and the Father/Son/Holy Ghost triad. If the Father is the Creator, *Nous*, and the Son is the Word, *Logos*, the Holy Ghost (Holy Spirit) must be the Wisdom, *Sophia*, (feedback loop, *agapê*). If the Father is the Creator, and the Holy Ghost (Holy Spirit) is the Wisdom (feedback loop, *agapê*), and the Christ returns to the Father, then the place of the Christ must be taken by someone or something else, which is also the Word of the Creator/Word/Wisdom triad. The members of the church (*koinonia*) are the replacement. Note again that I am using the writings of the early Church Fathers in the Johannine tradition not because I believe they guarantee the truth of the framework suggested for our scientific research program, but because they help define that framework as it was understood by John, who first proposed it. It is adopted for its pragmatic value (though also for its historical value), as we look to William James's *The Varieties of*

Religious Experience for its pragmatic value (though also for its historical value). If it works in our inquiry, if it is in fact a progressive rather than a degenerating research program, that is at least evidence against its being untrue. Some of our readers, seeing how the argument of this book is progressing, will, of course, make note of the fact that *Logos* means Word, and that, earlier, in Chapter 6, we spoke of God's "utterance" of creation.

Theologically speaking (in Johannine terms), Alcoholics Anonymous is a fellowship using the sacrament (*mysterion*) of the Word (*Logos*) in community of common speech (*koinonia*) to create the progress toward perfection (*teleios*) implicit in the process of *theopoiesis* (surrender of the human will to God). The word—the testimony, even the meeting of Alcoholics Anonymous—is the *pharmaokon athanasias* (the medicine of immortality, or, if you like, of salvation from the sickness which is sin). How should reading A.A.'s books and telling A.A. stories work in this?

Theologically, the process of sobriety in Alcoholics Anonymous may be considered as involving a formulaic sacrament of the Word, providing for the passage from prevenient Grace, to efficacious (congruous) Grace, to habitual Grace. The basic definition of a sacrament is "the outward and visible sign of an inward and spiritual grace given to us" or, more briefly, in Aquinas, "the sign of a sacred thing insofar as it sanctifies men." In other words, we may see Alcoholics Anonymous as fitting squarely in the medieval tradition of the process of Grace, and thus of the *telos* of salvation. (And we are noting that the familiar A.A. statement that "we claim spiritual progress rather than spiritual perfection" is to assert the *telos* (the goal toward which we progress) but not yet the *teleios* (the perfection, the "having progressed"). We also note here that the biblical injunction, "Be ye therefore perfect" (Matthew 5:48), uses the word *teleios,* meaning "perfected" or "brought to one's completion or end state"—what we have spoken of as the way in which all humans are perceived in the final (or instant) state of unity with God (also the instant of "utterance")—that is, salvation.

This process of *theosis* or *theopoiesis* is the process toward the *telos* of salvation (or, for alcoholics, of sobriety). We mentioned before (with examples from the Knight of Faith to Jim B.) that the goal of the mystical journey (the *telos* whose achievement is the *teleios*) is to live in the concrete world. We mentioned also that this concrete world is ontologically superior to the spiritual world. What this means, in our context, is that we come through our spiritual exercises to live better in this world, or the alcoholic comes through his spiritual exercises (the Twelve Steps) to practice the presence of God (the principles of the Twelve Steps) in all his affairs. However much she was part of her current world, there in the church and churchyard, Lady Julian nonetheless lived as an anchoress, a hermit within the world. The alcoholic, however, must live fully in the world, not in the anchoress's cell. It is done, it is said, by the Grace of God.

Alcoholics in A.A. frequently say, "There, but for the Grace of God, go I." Here we return to the question, what is *Grace*? A common definition is that it is a free gift of God, but that is theologically incomplete. In fact, as we have noted in Chapter 6, Christian theologians have divided grace (1) into *prevenient* grace and *subsequent* Grace, (2) into *sufficient* Grace and *efficacious* Grace, (3) into *habitual* Grace and *actual* Grace, and (4) into *irresistible* Grace and *congruous* Grace. Prevenient Grace is the free gift of God, before conversion. Subsequent Grace occurs if God and man cooperate after conversion. Prevenient Grace might be—but is *not* in fact—sufficient for salvation, while subsequent Grace is sufficient for salvation. Efficacious Grace comes after conversion and depends on the congruity or appropriateness of the Grace, which is God's choice. Habitual or sanctifying Grace is the gift of God inhering in the soul, by which men can perform righteous acts: it conveyed in the sacraments. Actual Grace, which may exist in the unbaptized and even the unbelieving, is a motion of the soul (toward God), bestowed by God ad hoc for the production of some good act. Prevenient Grace is the form of actual grace leading men to sanctification before the reception of the sacraments: it is the free gift of God and entirely unmerited. (These sorts and conditions of Grace are reflected in John Newton's hymn, "Amazing Grace.")

There is a description of Bradford's kind of blinding Grace in the *Book of Daniel* 10:vii–x (as well, of course, as that of Saul on the road to Damascus, but this is fuller):

> And I Daniel alone saw the vision; for the men that were with me saw not the vision; but a great quaking fell upon them, so that they fled to hide themselves. Therefore I was left alone, and saw this great vision, and there remained no strength in me; for my comeliness was turned in me into corruption, and I retained no strength. Yet heard I the voice of his words: and when I heard the voice of his words, then was I in a deep sleep on my face, and my face toward the ground. And behold, a hand touched me, which set me upon my knees, and upon the palms of my hands.

And here, from Bill W., is a description of the same kind of thing. This is Bill ostensibly writing about Fitz M., but as it does not entirely agree with Fitz's story as he tells it, we may reasonably suspect that it recapitulates Bill's own experience.

> In a few seconds, he was overwhelmed by a conviction of the Presence of God. It poured over and through him with the certainty and majesty of a great tide at flood. The barriers he had built through the years were swept away. He stood in the Presence of Infinite Power and Love. He had stepped from bridge to shore. For the first time, he lived in conscious companionship with his Creator. Thus was our friend's cornerstone fixed in place. (Bill W. et al. 1939:56)

This is *prevenient* and *irresistible* Grace. It is the free gift of God. It can become *efficacious* Grace (sufficient for sobriety) if the recipient works to convert it into *habitual* or *sanctifying* Grace: the mode for this conversion would be through the sacrament of the word (through meetings and reading the "Big Book" liturgically). It would then be a *congruous* Grace. The Oxford Group approach—we may argue—did not permit the conversion into *sanctifying* and *congruous* (and *subsequent*) Grace, but the exercise of the Twelve Steps does. Whether we have *efficacious* Grace depends on the congruity of the grace, which is God's choice: it is conferred by the sacraments, including (as late as the twelfth century) the Lord's Prayer—and other spoken formulae. *Habitual* or *sanctifying* Grace, we repeat, is the gift of God inhering in the soul, by which men are enabled to perform righteous acts: it is conveyed in the sacraments, including the sacrament of the Word. A Christian theologian might well consider the prayer at the end of an A.A. meeting as a sacrament, especially the Lord's Prayer. Sacraments, in the early church, were administered only to the baptized. A parallel to the process of Alcoholics Anonymous, in the Twelve Steps, and involving a sponsor, is apparent. (The godparent in the rites for baptism is called a sponsor.) Admission to Alcoholics Anonymous, in the early days, was very much like adult baptism, or like the ceremony of knighthood.

KOINONIA AND KOINÊ

So what happens—using these distinctions and definitions—when an alcoholic is brought into the *koinonia* (speech-linked company or fellowship or society or communion) of Alcoholics Anonymous? We may say he has received the *actual* Grace to bring him there; by that *actual* Grace may stay in the general presence of God, there by the same Grace cooperate with God so that he continue in *subsequent* Grace, which by sacrament (or sacraments) is *efficacious*, because *congruous* (by God's choice); then it or he will grow, through practice, into *habitual* or *sanctifying* Grace. The Franciscans, following Francis's contemporary, Alexander of Hales, would say that the individual might himself initiate the first movement toward grace—but it might be that Grace brought him to that.

On the basis of our model, we have concluded that the *telos* of sobriety in Alcoholics Anonymous would parallel (and might of course—in fact, will—be a part of) the *telos* of salvation in the church. Alcoholics Anonymous, like the church, would then precisely be a salvific ("saving") *koinonia*. How does the salvation come about? That is, after all, the theological question. The sacrament of the Word may bring the alcoholic to freedom from his continuing burden of being an alcoholic (in the alcoholism[2] sense), his precondition; it certainly makes him free from the burden of past alcoholic behavior (alcoholism [1]). A.A., with its Pietist leanings, seems to claim only the second. But the sacrament of water and the spirit (baptism), in Catholic (including Episcopal) doctrine, makes the sinner free from the burden of original sin, the precondition.

We know that the practice and process of mystical life never concludes: "maintenance activities," continued growth, and passing the message to others fill the days of mystical lives. That holds true even outside the central Christian tradition—in Zen Buddhism even, certainly (so far as we can tell) in Manichaeanism. The destructive Freudian concentration on the Self is replaced by the mystic's concentration on the Other. The path, it has been said, becomes the destination: by concentration on the Other, one lives a spiritual life in the physical world, which, for the alcoholic, is sobriety. To assert that those who are alcoholics can recover through the *koinonia*, through liturgical prayer and liturgical readings, interspersed with personal witness (*parakalein*)—in other words, through meetings of their fellowship, encouraged thereby to take the steps toward their redemption—is clearly to assert pretty much what the early Christian church asserted: the church militant brings its members to the church triumphant, indeed *is* the church triumphant viewed through the material lens of time—the church of the Spirit viewed through the lens of created being. Through liturgical prayer, as I said. And what do we mean by prayer?

Briefly, petition, invocation, and adoration—widely practiced in all world religions—are practiced in Christian spirituality under two dominant ideas: (1) submission to the divine will and (2) recognition of the direct relationship of every creature to God. A theology of Incarnation discloses "a congruity of humanity with deity," supplying a new basis for the human search for God in prayer, leading to a vision of God and union with and likeness to Him. These are types of vocal prayer: there is also mental prayer, which verges on but is not entirely the same as what is frequently called meditation. The distinction between *vocal* and *mental* is not the same as that made between *prophetic* prayer and *mystical* prayer, though it bears some relation. Moreover, vocal prayer may be either common or private, and if common, may be either liturgical or informal (including extemporaneous prayer as informal). By liturgy we mean the written texts—including prayer texts—providing the order for a service held in public (that is, for example, a meeting of a religious or spiritual group, a *koinonia*). In the New Testament, prayer is an art to be learned—hence the pattern given as an instruction in the Lord's Prayer. There seems to be a certain degree of controversy in Alcoholics Anonymous over the use of the Lord's Prayer, and Narcotics Anonymous, an offshoot of (but of course not affiliated with) A.A., seems generally to use the Serenity Prayer (in an "I" form and a "we" form) for both opening and closing meetings.

I do not suppose it would be very popular in the rooms of Alcoholics Anonymous these days to assert that A.A. meetings are—or rather, were fundamentally considered to be—worship meetings, though that is the burden of the pamphlet *Table Talk,* as well as of the "as-told-to" autobiography of Clarence S., *How It Worked.* We noted that, in the Akron view, meetings were indeed a kind of worship service, religious in form and spiritual in nature, concluded with the Lord's Prayer. The reminiscences of Episcopal Evening Prayer in "any two or three alcoholics gathered together" or in Bill's talk one year to the Conference about "all sorts and conditions of men" (and there are other echoes also) strongly suggest the influence of Sam Shoemaker and his Evening Prayer services at Calvary Mission. The similarities to the services fifty years before at Jerry McAuley's Water Street mission are not coincidental.

Not only would it be an unwelcome intrusion into the affairs of A.A. for any scholar to tell the fellowship that it is really conducting religious services, it well might be inaccurate, and it would certainly be counterproductive. Counterproductive, at the very least, because it would confuse and alarm and suggest the possibility of dangerous entangling alliances in contravention of the A.A. Preamble and Traditions. Inaccurate, perhaps, because the purpose, nature, and conduct of the meeting have evidently changed since 1939—which is appropriately the subject of another book, if indeed it is an appropriate subject for analysis at all. Evidently, as we said before, there is no necessity for any A.A. member to accept the theology we have set out, in order to benefit from meetings of Alcoholics Anonymous. And some, as we just noted, might be driven away by being told they were at something originally conceived as a worship service—in Ernie Kurtz's term, for "Word and Witness." But, all this to the contrary notwithstanding, it is still worth our while to look at the prayers most widely used in these putative nonservices, and especially at the Serenity Prayer.

It has very recently (October 2003) been argued—by Niebuhr's daughter—that the Serenity Prayer was composed by Reinhold Niebuhr for a church service in New England in 1943 (Sifton 2003), and that the attribution to Friedrich Ötinger is disastrously off course. With due respect to Mrs. Sifton, I do not see any reason to change much of what I have written in Chapter 6. There is sufficient evidence that the prayer was known before 1943 to make it clear that this was not a first writing, and while the old attribution to Ötinger may have come from the work of a modern writer using his name (as though we were to attribute *The Money Game* to Adam Smith of Kirkcaldy), it remains true that the pseudonym was well chosen (like Adam Smith's) and the prayer (*pace* Mrs. Sifton) is in the Pietist tradition. Subjectively, it seems to me (after some study of Zinzendorf and Kelpius of Wissahickon and Beissel of Ephrata) that the germ of this prayer is indeed firmly in this German mystical tradition, with its emphasis on the mystical spiritual brotherhood, the *Unitas Fratrum,* the *koinonia.*

Note that if the prayer was written substantially by Reinhold Niebuhr in English, then there is an interesting corollary: the presence or absence of the definite article for *serenity, courage,* and *wisdom* then becomes more important than if the prayer were translated from the German. If there is a definite article ("the") only for *serenity* (the "official" A.A. version), then the prayer requests a limited amount of serenity only, for this one purpose ("to accept the things I cannot change"), unlimited courage (with the effect of having courage to change the things that can be changed), and unlimited wisdom (with the effect of having wisdom to know the difference). If there is a definite article ("the") for both *serenity* and *wisdom* (the version quoted in Mrs. Sifton's book), then there is a limitation on the amount of wisdom desired, which leaves it agreeable to Zinzendorf and the Moravians, but further from the extreme mystics.

Be that all as it may, the dichotomy in certain forms of mystical thought—the "I/"Thou" dichotomy—of Ernie Kurtz's *Not God* ([1979] 1991) is that he clearly shows how (to a former Roman Catholic seminarian, which he is) A.A. exemplifies the Augustinian search for the Other, as over against the Self, the "Thou" as over against the "I." This may emphasize salvation coming from outside the Self to be Pietist, as he notes (if it is self-abnegating), or Evangelical (if it is joyful); it may emphasize salvation inside the Self as well, and to be Humanist or liberal.

In any case, Kurtz finds the spiritual (or religious?) success of Alcoholics Anonymous to lie, fundamentally, in what he speaks of as "Word and Witness" (ibid.:186ff.). "The individual member and the A.A. group itself had to engage in missionary works of Word and Witness; but the efficacy of the works lay in their effect on the *worker*, rather than in any external result" (ibid.:187–88). But as we say, if there were *no* external result, ever, it would be difficult to call these missionary works at all. And yes, alcoholics may think that by accepting themselves as "not-God," they may be made whole by the acceptance of limitation: that makes good psychological sense, and it fits in with Kurtz's locus where Pietist Evangelism meets humanism (or liberalism). But finally this good psychology may not be good theology because—though relevant and valuable—it is not theology at all.

It is, however, as I said, good psychology, and good medicine—not, perhaps, good enough to keep away some of the problems that seem to have grown up since the 1940s. If the meetings of Alcoholics Anonymous are not meetings of the *koinonia* in the church sense, if they are not (as *Table Talk* suggests they are) worship meetings, if they are "only" group therapy (or even meetings for comparing progress notes), there may be something missing in the scheme of things. Sullivanite sessions or McCarthy's sessions at Yale (or comparisons in Dr. Saul's office) had this undoubted quality: there was a doctor, a leader, to whom the patients could look for interpretation, to make sense out of—to validate—their experience. Not a "prescription doctor," but a learned man (*hakim* in the Arabic) who could make sense out of the blooming, buzzing confusion (William James again) of an alcoholic life.

In the early days, that making sense of the blooming, buzzing confusion was what we might consider the "baptized and confirmed" members of A.A. did for the catechumens, the newcomers, the "babies," or "pigeons"—the unbaptized and unconfirmed. And when he wrote the "Big Book," here is what Bill W. had to say on this:

> Still you may say: "But I will not have the benefit of contact with you who write this book." We cannot be sure. God will determine that, so you must remember that your real reliance is always upon Him. He will show you how to create the *fellowship* [my emphasis] you crave. (1939:164)

And then, a little further down the page, "Give freely of what you find and join us. We shall be with you in the *Fellowship* [again] of the Spirit, and you will surely meet some of us as you trudge the Road of Happy Destiny." If the new members do not have the benefit of listening to the early members (who "wrote the book"), the book will at least show them how to create the fellowship in which they will hear others (and read these), and in some sense they will meet at least some of those who went before (in the "communion of saints" one might think).

When Frank Buchman spoke of his movement (in its original incarnation) as First-Century Christianity, he had in mind not only a return to first-century "simplicity" but to first-century (or "primitive") church organization. And if he did not specifically have in mind first-century theology, he was looking to emulate a church based on precisely that theology. In the first century, as we have noted, the Christians were creating the church—*Koinonia*, the assembly of the faithful with a common language; *Ekklesia*, the assembly of the faithful, with its building; *Kyriakon*, something belonging to the Lord, including the building. The separation of A.A. from the Oxford Group(s) was in part, as we noted, a determination not to be part of Frank Buchman's faithful (his *ekkklesia* or his *koinonia*). But A.A. remained a fellowship, a *koinonia*, speaking a common language and seeking common goals. It is not, of course, a *kyriakon*, though its members frequently meet in the basements of *kyriaka*.

Here we remind ourselves of what was said earlier about the two meanings of *koinonia*, and particularly about the *koinonia* in the social-systems sense. Let us also remind ourselves of some of the implications of a systems approach to anything. Systems theory, developed in the 1950s, is a body of theoretical constructs used to search for general relationships in the empirical world. In systems theory, any unit is seen as being a subsystem of a larger and more complex system. The subsystems within the larger system interact with and affect one another. To understand a system or even subsystem as a whole, we must study the smaller units (subsystems, components, properties) and the interactions among them (based on a rather neat summary in Brian Fagan's *From Black Land to Fifth Sun: The Science of Sacred Sites* [1998]).

Our (social-systems-sense) *koinonia* (like the *agora* and the *polis*) is a subsystem in which members of the social system organize themselves in a particular way of interaction for a particular set of purposes. The parts of the system are not limited to persons or institutions (components); they also include both ideas and beliefs (immaterial properties) or things (material properties). All of these operate in complex interaction according to the mode appropriate to the particular system or subsystem. Because the *koinonia* has neither market transactions nor political order (by hierarchy or vote), its "rule" of order (or ordering) lies in tradition and in the operation of committees. Committees operate best when their members have single-peaked preferences (as, for example, staying sober). They function best when they have some agreed-upon "rules of order"—but that is another story, for another time. Single-peaked preferences should be common, if not guaranteed, in any *koinonia* in the church-meeting sense; they are virtually necessary in any *koinonia* in the systems sense if it is not to turn into a political subsystem (*polis*).

A.A. has of course, as a result of Bill W.'s original insight, and of his efforts at social engineering, established its Twelve Traditions as the binding force for the *koinonia*. They must therefore be—and as we have seen, they are—part of the common speech (*koiné*) of the fellowship. Likewise, the committee structure Bill W. set up for his *koinonia* operates best when it operates, so to speak, under the aegis of those Traditions. And here we come up against (or to) a question, about the way of establishing—in the technical critical sense "inventing"—a new tradition, or traditions. And here it is where we turn to J. G. A. Pocock, on the characteristics of societies, inasmuch as what we have been calling a social system may also and equally well be called a society.

Perhaps we should here review the characteristics of societies in Pocock's formulation. The first point, we note, is that societies exist in time and that they "conserve" whatever represents their continuously existing from time past—preferably long past. They thus must have traditions, not only in the sense of stories but also and particularly in the sense of handing on through stories and instruction those formed ways of acting that characterize society and its modes of operation. These traditions (in the Burkean triad) are immemorial, prescriptive, and presumptive. Outside the tradition, though sometimes seen at (or as) its sacred origin, is the charismatic (and frequently, though not with A.A., this is the timeless). The society—in this classical formulation—affirms its tradition even as it criticizes it. Even if the society's traditions are not themselves what we consider as being conservative, the very idea of a society involves the conserving of its representations of the past and its representations of continuity. There is thus what we have called a necessary conservatism in the very idea of a society or social system, or a social subsystem.

The Burkean triad applies especially when the representations of past and continuity come specifically from the time—and even more if from the hands—of the charismatic founder. Some observers seem to have misunderstood the charismatic foundation of immemorial quality as the hallmark of a charismatic "cult"—but to say this is to betray ignorance of Pocock's work on the nature of social systems—societies, communities, fellowships—generally. As we have said, Bill W. provided the necessary immemorial quality—and the prescriptive quality and the background of the presumptive—through the Twelve Traditions. Remember that invented tradition (Hobsbawm and Ranger 1983:1–2) is a set of practices governed by tacitly accepted rules and seeking to inculcate values and norms of behavior by repetition, thus implying continuity with the past. These invented traditions establish cohesion among group members, legitimize institutions and authority, and inculcate beliefs, value systems, and conventions of behavior. The liturgical, or at least ritual, repetition of the Twelve Traditions at meetings, their posting on roll-down sheets at some meeting-places, sometimes the reading-aloud of the "Traditions" section of the *12 &12* at "Traditions" meetings are all part of the attempt to establish behavior norms by reference to the past and continuity with the past, by Bill W.'s invented tradition. (On the whole, though I have certainly not attended enough A.A. meetings to have any fully-formed opinion, it would seem to me that the Twelve Steps or the whole "How It Works" section of the "Big Book" are read liturgically, while the reading of the Twelve Traditions may be liturgical or simply ritualistic.)

In light of what seems to be a strong and constant (if limited) seeking for still greater contact with A.A.'s past, as the years go by since Bill W.'s death in 1971, it might be asked whether Bill's efforts with the Traditions were entirely successful. Members make an annual pilgrimage to Akron for Founders' Day (June 10); there are seminars held at Bill W.'s childhood home in Vermont; the Gratitude Dinner he established in New York in the 1940s is still held each year; the picnic he and his wife Lois started at their home in Bedford, New York, is still held each year, and year-round there are pilgrimages to their house in Bedford, as to Dr. Bob's in Akron. There are constant (if limited) efforts to return the supposedly purer and more effective A.A. of older days (when admission, as I understand it, was essentially by examination). We take no position on any of these developments—they are not germane to our thesis here—but we believe they may be reasonably looked at in future research. It may be that there may be a need to establish a new A.A. narrative, as there is a need for alcoholics to establish their own new narratives in their recovery.

NARRATIVES, LITURGY, RITUAL

The Steps are read as a schema for organizing experience. That is, they are a model for the narrative that gives meaning to the A.A. member's life and sobriety, what in some forms of therapy might be called narratization for recovery. (This should not, I believe, be considered the same thing as rote repetition of catch-phrases as a kind of ornament to such a narrative.) Some members of A.A., particularly at speaker's meetings of "Step and Tradition" groups or "Step" groups or "Step-study" groups, will, I believe, be asked to tell their stories "in terms of the Twelve Steps." Just as the medieval (or "dark ages") Christian church seems to have turned to Saint's lives as exemplars of the process of sanctification, so Alcoholics Anonymous turns to "sober lives" as exemplars of the process of sobriety. Just so there were Washingtonian narratives in the 1840s, and narratives by such as Samuel Hopkins Hadley fifty years later.

But it is necessary to be careful in looking at this narratizing for the process of sobriety. There is some considerable difference between the Saint's life in the Longfellow mode—"Lives of all great men remind us / We can make our lives sublime"—on the one hand, and the cautionary (or "war-story") temperance narrative, on the other. But there is an even greater difference between both of these and the "healing narrative." This healing narrative combines psychodynamic narrative(s), developmental narrative(s), and treatment narrative(s)—in short, to use a formulation we see as common in A.A., what it was like, what happened, what it's like now. The psychodynamic narrative of the patient's past and the narrative of the treatment itself are collapsed into one complex interwoven tale, intertwining themes from the patient's past with themes from the treatment itself, the emphasis falling on the latter rather than the former.

The therapeutic challenge, within narrative therapy, as we noted, is to get away from the sense of inevitability that marks the narrative of the alcoholic's progressive decline, and toward a sense that the alcoholic (with the help of Higher Power, *koinonia*, sponsor) is rewriting his life story: in that rewriting, ideally, what was before seen as inevitable is now seen as the result of wrong choices, and the putative chapters of the future life are under greater auctorial—or is it Auctorial?—control. This new narrative, when complete, will mirror the correction of what John Bowlby calls the attachment insecurities. Those who are securely attached can distinguish between their own experience and that of others, represent and tell the story of their feelings, and if need be break up their stories and re-form them more in keeping with the flux of experience. Ambivalent individuals are so close to their feelings that they cannot objectify, externalize, or "mark" the events in the way needed for a working story. Avoidant people cling to a stereotyped version of themselves and their past and feel threatened by the need to update their narrative in the way characteristic of creative living. And the unresolved cannot find a narrative strong enough to contain their traumatic pain. In short, by developing the narrative, the patient overcomes attachment-insecurities.

The purpose of Sullivanite group therapy lies in the process of developing *syntaxic* speech through consensual validation—which is, to put it another way, growing up through learning to speak like a grown-up, and thus to think like a grown-up. The therapist, then, is the grown-up that one emulates. If the process of Alcoholics Anonymous is to be considered as involving group therapy (in the Sullivanite sense), then it is through the sponsor and the other experienced members of the group acting as (joint or communal) group-leader. It is their consensual validation that is necessary. This also seems to have been the case with Raymond McCarthy's "Emmanuel" therapy groups at Yale in the mid-1940s. If one reads the transcripts in the *Quarterly Journal,* one can see the therapist gently nudging the members of the group (as I have been told Hale nudged Hale's Hearties) toward group consensual agreement on what he wanted them to agree on. Much more gently than anecdotal evidence suggests for "old-style" A.A. meetings, where older members are said to have growled at loquacious newcomers, "Take the cotton out of your ears and put it in your mouth!"

A group-therapy approach in which experienced members at an A.A. meeting act like McCarthy at Yale or Hale at 82nd Street would appear to be miles removed from the "dumping" that is part of rehab discussion groups and A.A. meetings whose style is affected by them. I have no indication that any such Sullivanite or Emmanuel-based system exists anywhere in A.A. today, though something like it might be in accordance with the earliest form of the Fifth Tradition, wherein the groups exist so that those who have made progress in the process can guide those who "still suffer from alcoholism." In Sullivanite terms, by telling their stories, in the appropriate framework using appropriate words—that is, in *syntaxic* language—the senior members provide the template for the junior members. But recall that Marty M. wanted group therapy kept separate from meetings.

One A.A. member with longer than average sobriety has observed that the injunction to tell what it was like, what happened, and what it's like now is an injunction to tell "how I formulated things then, how I learned a better way, and how I formulate things now." Asked if hearing the problems of newcomers helped him, he replied,

> Sometimes it helps me understand how I misformulated things in the beginning, and, though I don't like the phrase, in that sense it "keeps it green" for me. But I can't tell you the number of times I've heard a newcomer "dump" his problems (as he understands—or misunderstands—them), his accumulated grievances, misunderstandings, and sheer incomprehension at a meeting, and then either leave or obviously be paying no attention to what anyone else says. I don't believe that's what a meeting is supposed to be about.

This comment seems to be emblematic of a fundamental divergence on what an A.A. meeting is. Is it a rehab meeting where everyone, especially the newcomer, should share what's bothering him (or her), to get rid of the burden? Is it a guided session in which those who have experience in living the A.A. way of life share that experience? Anecdotal historical evidence suggests that this problem is not new, though greatly aggravated by the rise of the rehabs in the 1970s, and virtually institutionalized by the more recent rise of intensive outpatient therapy (IOP). Alcoholics, it is said, are supposed to share their "experience, strength, and hope" at meetings. It seems to be generally, if decreasingly, understood that this is experience and strength and hope *in getting sober*, not in drinking. Old-timers have been heard to say, "If you're telling your story in forty-five minutes, you ought to be sober after fifteen—if not before." The implication is that the principal sharing at a meeting—whatever the "topic" of the meeting— is not to be experience in drinking, weakness in sobriety, and fear. If it is, then there is neither true group therapy nor worthwhile narratization.

This is not a point that seems to need future research, and indeed it is difficult to see how research could be carried out, given requirements of anonymity and confidentiality—though it may be indicative of changes in technique (changes in how meetings work) that early A.A. claimed a 75 percent success rate (or sometimes more), while current estimates run as low as 10 percent (or sometimes even less). The area where research seems to be needed now is in the biogenetic and biochemical nature of Alcoholism(2)—the precondition—and its different types. The problem is that while we have some idea of why we have Alcoholism(2), why we have people on whom alcohol works the way it does, and some indications of the biochemistry, we do not have enough (and not enough knowledge of neuronal group selection) to be sure what should work, and whether what should work differs from type to type. Kurtz's "Word and Witness" is essentially a statement of what works psychologically, though expressed in religious terms. We have suggested more exact formulation in psychological terms and a theological explanation in theological terms: there appears to be virtually full congruence between treatment of the mind and treatment of the spirit. But this leaves uncovered the treatment of the body, and here there has been substantial disagreement on the proper modes of this treatment: indeed there have been at least two substantial (if reinforcing) disagreements.

DISAGREEMENTS

One lies in an attack on what the attackers believe is the "disease concept of alcoholism" (using the interpretation of that concept common in "Twelve-Step-based" treatment facilities); the other lies in what has been called the *medicalization* of treatment, deemed appropriate if alcoholism is indeed a disease or an illness of the body (Naltrexone is the most recent *panacea* here, based on an identification of compulsion to drink with physiological "craving"). We, on the other hand, have been suggesting a redirection of neuronal transmission channels, concentrating on the channels involved in memory, making use of recent theoretical work by Edelman (1989) and Plotkin (1994). Passing for the moment over the "Clockwork Orange" difficulty, where we can "cure" a problem involved in moral choice at the cost of denying the exercise of free will, it would appear the fundamental area of conflict lies in what is meant by the "disease concept of alcoholism."

One set of critics suggests that the disease concept is designed to give the alcoholic a kind of out, so that he or she can say "I'm not a bad person trying to get good; I'm a sick person trying to get well"—and the concept has even been defended on the grounds that, though possibly untrue, this view liberates the alcoholic from guilt and shame. ("Believe this not because it is true but for some other reason.") The other set of critics suggests that the way to treat a physical illness is with physical medicine: this view is, of course, the child of advances in physical medicine since the time A.A. was founded, so that it has become pretty much a truism. It was not always so, of course. And it would almost seem that the two sets of critics would offset each other. But they can be combined to say, roughly, that (1) the disease concept neglects—in fact denies—the matter of moral choice, and (2) that if this is a physical condition, the thing to do is to cure it (or ameliorate it, or hold it in abeyance) by medicines. To this formulation we see two objections, though increased scientific knowledge might work to remove some of our difficulties. In fact, we believe we should seek this increased knowledge.

ADDITIONAL RESEARCH

Unfortunately, perhaps, the first area for an advisable general increase in scientific knowledge is in theology, recalling that the disease concept of alcoholism comes out of the disease concept of sin. We have already discussed this, and it is unlikely that additional research will lead to additional knowledge. But the second is an area where research can be expected to yield results. The locus of the studies we suggest (making allowances for different genetic types of alcoholism) is defined by glucocorticoids and glucose, electrocortical event reactions, epinephrine/norepinephrine, serotonin, and dopamine, all essentially as they are related to memory processes, but not as limited to that, and including the hypothalamic-pituitary-adrenal axis generally and the renin-angiotensin system. We may briefly sum up what we have said thus far.

We know that acute and chronic alcohol consumption in animals (including humans) activates the HPA stress axis, resulting in continuously or intermittently elevated glucocorticoids (GCs). It may be that certain types of alcoholics may have lower-than-normal GC levels, so that they can function over a long term with GC levels (at least intermittently) elevated above their norm, without crossing the threshold levels implicated in memory loss and cell death. In reaction to stress, the hypothalamus releases adrenocorticotropin (ACTH) secretion analogues, resulting in the release of ACTH from the pituitary gland. In turn ACTH initiates the release of the adrenal androgens and glucocorticoids, which prepare the organism for stress by increasing glucose and fatty acid availability for the central nervous system. Also, the HPA interacts with the immune system. The GCs inhibit cytokine production and more or less turn the immune system way down, preventing overwhelming and potentially harmful immune response to stressors.

In the Yale test we mentioned before, the measurement of the regional cerebral metabolic rate for glucose (an index of local brain function) was taken for cocaine users and a control group of nonusers. There were user stimulus responses (metabolic rate increases) in the dorsolateral prefrontal cortex, the medial temporal lobe, the amygdala and cerebellum—all regions involved with memory. The cue-elicited desires (here for cocaine) came through memory: on the other hand, when cocaine was administered, there were decreases in the regional cerebral metabolic rate for glucose. The desires seem to come from cue-related memory, rather than from neural substrates of direct experience—which is to say, from physical addiction. This pattern would seem to carry over into alcohol use by at least some types of alcoholics.

We noted a study in the late 1970s that tested for a correlation of aggressive behavior with the major cerebral spinal fluid metabolites of serotonin

(5HT), norepinephrine (NE), and dopamine (DA). Aggressive behavior, as we also noted, is a mark of our Psa alcoholism and present in others. There was no correlation between aggressive behavior history with the dopamine metabolite (HVA), significant negative correlation with the serotonin metabolite (5HIAA), and significant positive correlation with the norepinephrine metabolite (MHPG). More recently, as we reported, it has been suggested that differences in serotonin turnover are governed by genetic variation in the serotonin transporter in alcoholics—and that the genetic transporter variation correlates with the concentration of the serotonin metabolite (5HIAA) before and after acute tryptophan depletion. Certain (genetic) types of alcoholics appear to have low levels and slow manufacture of serotonin.

Since dopamine metabolites are not correlated with aggressive behavior history, it has been suggested that (at least in these alcoholics) the signaling effects of dopamine may be substituted for by other signals or triggers in the alcoholic's neuronal system—though it has also been suggested that dopamine levels are significant only in the chronic alcoholic and thus may be a measure of Alcoholism(1) rather than Alcoholism(2). In this context we note again that tests of a dopamine agonist (mimic) suggested induced reactivity associated with levels of positive emotionality. Positive emotionality is based on reward-signals requiring memory, and the one function that has been assigned to dopamine in the alcoholic's system is the mediation of reinforcement of "alcoholic" alcohol consumption, through adaptation or counteradaptation—both of them associated with memory. But since there is no characteristic alcoholic's dopamine level (except maybe the chronic alcoholic's), it looks as though this may be a needed area for study.

Reinforcement or its equivalent may reasonably come through such memory-reinforcers as caffeine that release epinephrine into the system, thereby triggering blood-sugar increases. We may note, likewise, that levels of the epinephrine/norepinephrine-linked neurotransmitter acetylcholine are reduced in Alzheimer's patients, suggesting again the link between epinephrine and memory. This, given a link between memory and alcoholism, suggests that reinforcement of alcohol consumption might be tied more closely to epinephrine/norepinephrine than to dopamine.

Here is another subject for study. To repeat what we have said before, if we put together what Plotkin and Edelman have said with what we have learned—and hope to learn—about the connections of serotonergic and other neurotransmitter functioning in the alcoholic, and the linkage of these neurotransmitters with memory (and speech), we can see that the biochemical key to alcoholism may lie in training reentrant signaling along the pathways and from the axons of neurotransmission. We note here also that the renin-angiotensin system activity that inhibits alcohol consumption is characterized by having events in the periphery set into motion central processes that eventually result in the inhibition of alcohol intake. This chain of events is typical of peptides and hormones that influence behavior and has been observed in the actions of vasopressin, oxytocin, and aldosterone on memory processes. It has been suggested that bioactive peptides are themselves activated in the R-A system by alcoholic intake (the R-A system itself being so activated) and then produce a satiety or stop signal at a point determined by emotional state, diet, environmental motivators, and individual predisposition, a process parallel to—and likely to be connected with—the process of memory.

The heritability of reduced P300 amplitude might come into play here. The Yale cocaine study suggested the importance of memory in cocaine use—memory, we think, of the changed state of and particularly the process of change from one state to another. We also bring into play Dr. Siegel's suggestion that anticipation of the changed state is the key, rather than the changed state itself. And we bring into play the ERP (event-related potential) P3 component in time-locked electrocorticol response to a cue promising a rare but anticipated event—here is where we found that, in FHP male children, memory cues require less update and serve more easily to reinforce expectations than is generally the case. Juvenile FHP drinkers would appear to learn their lesson of the greatness of alcohol early and well, and if banded together (or even if not), may go on expecting the insight of the druids, the poetry of the bards, the violence of the baresarks, and most especially the fellowship of Dionysios, as a people apart. Because they are a different people, an atavistic remnant, a stark anachronism. But even they may be able to take steps into change, if they want to.

This is simply a brief recapitulation of one set of suggestive findings from recent studies, with a note as to what they suggest for future research. The fundamental point is, taking Edelman's work into account, with the biogenetic types defined by neuronal transmissions, that in extended phenotypic engagement with the world, in some sense consciously determined, the phenotype can be altered, whatever the genotype remains. It would seem to us that the use of CEs such as Naltrexone (or Valium) does not represent a conscious co-constructive phenotypical alteration but something else, an anticraving short-circuit in the case of Naltrexone, a substitute "alcohol in a pill" for Valium, and a kind of finger in the dyke, perhaps, for both. This is not to say that Naltrexone does not reduce craving for alcohol: apparently (certainly in some cases) it does. On the other hand, our research (particularly into the results of others' research) suggests that not all alcoholic drinking is the result of physiological "craving" (a technical term), and treatments based on dopamine-centered hypotheses (like Naltrexone) may not be extensively applicable. That's by the way here, of course, since we are really concerned with conscious co-constructive phenotypical alteration involving neurotransmission and memory systems.

It may be the case that for this process to work well the alcoholic should be consciously on the subcritical/supercritical edge. Note also that the whole process may be subject to chaotic ordering, with sensitive dependence on initial conditions. It has been suggested to me that what I am told is a frequently heard saying (especially in Midwestern A.A.) that "it gets different before it gets better" is designed to enhance both consciousness of the edge and the greatest possible introduction of new diversity into the alcoholic's mind, to increase the likelihood of shift to a new attractor. Whatever the case, we can begin to see how the "scientific" treatment of alcoholism may be expected to work, and while it does not necessarily agree with Bunky Jellinek's "science-and-society" approach back in 1943–44, it would seem to us not so far removed as we would perhaps expect at a distance of sixty years. This is, however, an area where there would seem to be opportunities for research possibly sufficiently detailed for a whole new book—though it may be that book will never—in fact, can never—be written. Here's what we mean.

ANOTHER BOOK?

We have sketched the system as designed and set up by Bill W. in the 1930s and 1940s, and in the course of doing that we have noted from time to time changes that have apparently come to pass—as, for example, with the rise of rehabs in the 1970s and of IOP treatments in the 1990s—fundamental changes in the understanding of what an A.A. meeting is about, as well as fundamental changes in the understanding of what medicine is about. We have also noted some apparent changes in the understanding of the Traditions.

We do not have the time and space here to study the changes in A.A. in the last half-century, and perhaps unfortunately it does not look as though A.A. is likely to make that study: their concentration seems, quite properly, we suppose, to be on the golden moment, the pioneers, the giants in the earth. There is a study by Leach and Norris (1977; the latter a Class A—non-alcoholic—trustee), covering the years from 1952 (or thereabouts) up to 1977, and appendices in two editions of Kurtz's *Not-God* ([1979] 1991), bringing the story institutionally up to about 1990. But the difficulties in answering the questions, Does A.A. work as intended in 1935–1940? and What should (or should not) be done to change things? are legion. For one thing, no member is likely to take on the responsibility of replacing Bill W., who pretty much wrote the history of A.A. up to the last few years of his life, even if that member were allowed to—and no nonmember in his or her right mind would try to do so (or so it seems to me now). And yet, it may be that the alternative could be persistence in action deleterious to the cause and purpose of A.A.—unless, of course, one accepts the premise that the Higher Power will always act to preserve A.A., whatever the members do.

One thing that could be done is to look at any available records on what A.A. members have thought about changes, and at whatever objective evidence exists on what the changes are. I suspect that, institutionally, something can be done along these lines, though there may still be problems of anonymity and confidentiality. I am not sure I would care to spend my time steering between Scylla and Charybdis here. One fruitful area for study may be found in the changing stories in the four editions of the "Big Book" (1939, 1955, 1976, 2001). Another (more difficult to carry out, because of problems of availability) may be in a comparison of stories from the *A.A. Grapevine* over the years. Another may lie in a comparison of the attitudes in *Twenty-Four Hours a Day* (Richmond W. 1954), *Day By Day* (Hazelden:1974), and (Conference-approved) *Daily Reflections* (A.A.:1990). We believe a comparison between Bill W.'s writings and *Living Sober* (the first post-Bill W. Conference-approved book), though possibly revealing, might be invidious and would in any case have only limited value as reflecting attitudes in the mid-1970s that are well enough set out in the Norris-Leach report.

We have suggested in Chapter 8 a few points where the fellowship's observance of the Twelve Traditions seems a trifle problematical, but further discussion of these (if any) must await further detailed work. Comparisons of current General Service Office pamphlets and guidelines (and other service literature) with materials such as the 1944 sponsorship pamphlet produced in Cleveland can provide some guidance. So can studies of the pioneers—though, of course, A.A. preaches "principles before personalities" and that is sometimes taken to preclude studies of individual persons in A.A. (difficult in any case because they are anonymous). So can local studies of service structure within A.A., though these may run afoul of the problem that nonmembers may not be able to write them, and members may not want to (since staying sober is their most important concern), and the author—if they are written—may not in any case wish to reveal which he is. (See our brief essay on this point in Lobdell 2003.)

Finally, one other point. We have thus far avoided any significant consideration of the debate on total abstinence vs. moderate drinking, except to note that the word *temperance* has at one time or another meant both. Alcoholics Anonymous is, of course, based on the total-abstinence model, while other treatment modalities—especially outside the United States—

aim toward controlled or moderate drinking. As we understand the matter, alcoholic drinking is by definition not controlled and not (usually) moderate, so that these modalities are in fact aimed toward curing alcoholism, leaving the "former alcoholic" able to take one or two drinks and be sure of stopping. This "drinking normally" seems to have been a desire in the early days of Alcoholics Anonymous. Observation at open meetings of Alcoholics Anonymous suggests it may be a less frequent goal now, with "getting wasted" to have increasingly been considered a positive goal among young drinkers. The Zucker and Jellinek typologies both allow for such cases—Jellinek type-β and Zucker developmental alcoholics—as do those who consider the possibility of "situational alcoholism." These β-alcoholics or developmental alcoholics or situational alcoholics may or may not be "true" alcoholics, but it would appear to us that the whole discussion— beyond what we have said here—has produced much more heat than light. We have defined success as abstinence, but it does not seem to us that our inquiries depend on that definition. We believe it is the more intelligible goal, and probably the easier to achieve, in all three areas, and that, as part of our scientific research program, is enough for us.

When all this is said, the fact remains that, however tentative our research program, and even more tentative our conclusions, we believe we have reasonably sketched out a first attempt at understanding what goes on in the process—the *telos*—of sobriety, in congruent treatment of the threefold illness of mind, body, and spirit, as set out by Bill W. We have suggested that Alcoholism(2), the precondition, goes back more than a thousand generations; that it has its roots in the great advances in mind and speech that made possible the development of human beings; that with the origins of consciousness the need first became less and then much less, until what was necessary is now an "illness"—to be treated by mind and speech as it first arose in conjunction with them. We believe—at least, we have adopted as our scientific research program the belief—that the syntaxic development of psychotherapeutic narrative, the reentrant extended phenotypic training of neuronal group selection, and the sacrament of the Word (in accordance with the Johannine doctrine of the Incarnation), are congruous, indeed congruent, indeed joined together in Bill W.'s formulation—which no one had put together before, and which is the gift of Alcoholics Anonymous as he set it up.

Along the way, we have met quite a number of interesting people— Ptolemy Philopator, William Shakespeare and his character Michael Cassio (both alcoholics, we think), Nicholas Herrmann, John Bunyan, Henry Alline, Jerry McAuley, Samuel Hopkins Hadley, Washingtonians and ex-inebriates, Leslie Keeley, Mary Baker Eddy, Charlie Towns, William James, Sigmund Freud, Carl Jung, Sandór Radó, Harry Tiebout, Bunky Jellinek,

Jim B., Johnny L., Fitz M., Clarence S., Sam Shoemaker, Dr. Bob S.—but we believe the necessary, indeed the indispensable, connecting thread is provided by one man, the man who in the golden moment brought something new—and something real and true—into the world.

And that is Bill W.

References

A.A. Grapevine. 2001. Interview with Robert S., Jr. September.

Abraham, Karl. [1908] 1958. "The Psychological Relations Between Sexuality and Alcoholism." In *Clinical Papers and Essays on Psychoanalysis.* London: Hogarth.

Alcoholics Anonymous, Akron. No date. *Table Talk.* Akron, OH: Author.

Alcoholics Anonymous. 1984. *Pass It On: The Story of Bill Wilson and How the A.A. Message Reached the World.* New York: Author.

Alcoholics Anonymous. 1990. *Daily Reflections.* New York: Author.

Alcoholics Anonymous. 1995. *The Group* (rev. ed.). New York: Author.

Alcoholics Anonymous. 1998–99. *The A.A. Service Manual.* New York: Author.

Alcoholics Anonymous. 2000–1. *The A.A. Service Manual Combined with Twelve Concepts for World Service.* New York: Author.

Alexander, Franz G. and Sheldon T. Selesnick. 1966. *The History of Psychiatry.* New York: Harper and Row.

Alexander, Jack. 1941. "Alcoholics Anonymous" *Saturday Evening Post,* March 1.

Alline, Henry. 1806. *The Life and Journal of Mr. Henry Alline.* Boston: Gilbert and Dean.

American Bicentennial Song Book. 1975. Volume I, *The First Hundred Years.* Washington, DC: USGPO.

American Psychological Association. 1952. *Diagnostic and Statistical Manual of Mental Disorders: DSM-I.* New York: Author.

American Psychological Association. 1968. *Diagnostic and Statistical Manual of Mental Disorders: DSM-I* (2d ed.). New York: Author.

American Psychological Association. 1980. *Diagnostic and Statistical Manual of Mental Disorders: DSM-II.* New York: Author.

American Psychological Association. 1987. *Diagnostic and Statistical Manual of Mental Disorders: DSM-III-R.* New York: Author.

American Psychological Association. 1994. *Diagnostic and Statistical Manual of Mental Disorders: DSM-IV.* New York: Author.

Amit, Z., et al. 1980. "Acetaldehyde: A Positive Reinforcer Mediating Ethanol Consumption." In *Biological Effects of Alcohol,* edited by H. Begleiter. New York: Plenum Press.

Andreasen, Nancy. 2001. *Brave New Brain: Conquering Mental Illness in the Era of the Genome.* New York: Oxford University Press.

Arrow, Kenneth. 1951. *Social Choice and Individual Values.* New Haven, CT: Yale University Press.

Author Unknown. 1934. *Story of the Christian Science Church Manual.* New York: Author.

Aston, C. E. and S. Y. Hill. 1990. "A Segregation Analysis of the P300 Component of the Event-Related Brain Potential." *American Journal of Human Genetics* 47.

Attaway, J. N., et al. 1991. "Familial Drug Allergy." *Journal of Allergy and Clinical Immunology* 87.

Aquinas, Thomas. 1993. *Summa Contra Gentiles.* Chicago: University of Notre Dame Press.

Ayensu, W., et al. 1996. "Insulin-like Growth Factor I Expression Alters Acute Sensitivity and Tolerance to Ethanol in Transgenic Mice." *European Journal of Pharmacology* 305.

B., Dick. 1998. *New Light on Alcoholism: The A.A. Legacy from Sam Shoemaker.* Kihei, HI: Paradise Press.

B., Jim. [1968] 1999. "Sober for Thirty Years." *The Grapevine* 24 (March 1968).

B., Jim. 1946. "History of A.A. 1934–1941." Typescript in Eastern Pennsylvania Archives, Bensalem, PA.

B., Jim. No date. "History of A.A. in Philadelphia." *Valley Views*(supplementary issue:1–2). Bethlehem, PA: Allentown-Bethlehem-Easton Intergroup Association.

Babor, Thomas. 1986. "The Classification of Alcoholics." *Alcohol Health and Research World* 20:10–12.

Babor, T. F., et al. 1992. "Types of Alcoholics, I: Evidence for an Empirically-Derived Typology Based on Indicators of Vulnerability and Severity." *Archives of General Psychiatry* 49.

Ballenger, J. C., et al. 1979. "Alcohol and Central Serotonin Metabolism in Man." *Archives of General Psychiatry* (February, 2):224–27.

Barber, Jacques and Paul Crits-Christoph (Eds.). 1995. *Dynamic Therapies for Psychiatric Disorders.* New York: Basic Books.

Barfield, Owen. 1928. *Poetic Diction.* London: Faber.

Bauer, L. and V. Hesselbrock. 1993. "EEG, Autonomic and Subjective Correlates of the Risk for Alcoholism." *Journal of Studies on Alcohol* 54.

Baumohl, J. and R. Room. 1987. "Inebriety, Doctors, and the State." Pp. 135–75 in *Recent Developments in Alcoholism* (edited by Marc Galanter), Vol. 5. New York: Plenum.

Baylor, Courtenay. 1919. *Remaking A Man.* Boston: Houghton Mifflin.

Beecher, Lyman. 1825. *Six Sermons.* New Haven, CT: Author.

Begleiter, H., et al. 1984. "Event-Related Brain Potential in Boys at Risk for Alcoholism." *Science* 225:1493–96.

Belknap, J. K., et al. 1997. "Short-Term Selective Breeding as a Tool for QTL Mapping: Ethanol Preference Drinking in Mice." *Behavioral Genetics* 27.

Bennett, B., et al. 1997. "Quick Method for Confirmation of Quantitative Trait Loci." *Alcohol: Clinical and Experimental Research* 21.

Berman, S., et al. 1993. "P300 in Young Boys as a Predictor of Adolescent Substance Use." *Alcohol* 10.

Blum, K., et al. 1990. "Allelic Association of Human Dopamine D_2 Receptor Gene in Alcoholism." *Journal of the American Medical Association* 263.

Bowlby, John. 1980. *Attachment and Loss,* Vol. 3. London and New York: Vintage/ Ebury (A Division of Random House Group).

Bowman, K. M. and E. M. Jellinek. 1941. "Alcohol Addiction and Its Treatment." *Quarterly Journal of Studies on Alcohol* 2:98–176.

Brown, G. L., et al. 1979. "Aggression in Humans Correlates with Cerebrospinal Fluid Amine Metabolites." *Psychiatry Research* 1(October): 131–39.

Brown, Raymond (Ed.). 1966. *The Gospel According to John* [Anchor Bible, Vol. 29A]. New York: Doubleday/Anchor.

Brown, Sally. 2001. The Biography of Mrs. Marty Mann: The First Lady of Alchoholics Anonymous. Center City, MN: Hazelden Information Education.

Browne, Lewis. 1929. *This Believing World.* New York: Simon Publications.

Buber, Martin. [1937] 1958. *I And Thou.* New York: Harcourt and Brace.

Bunyan, John. 1666. *Grace Abounding to the Chief of Sinners.* London: Author.

Burton, Robert. 1660. *The Anatomy of Melancholy.* London.

Bunyan, John. [1678] 1684. *The Pilgrim's Progress.* London.

Chapman, A. H. 1976. *Harry Stack Sullivan: His Life and Work.* New York: Putnam.

Clark, Duncan and Oscar Bukstein. 1998. "Psychopathology in Adolescent Alcohol Abuse and Dependence." in *Alcohol Research and Health* 22(2):117–21.

Cloninger, C. R., et al. 1981. "Inheritance of Alcohol Abuse: Cross Fostering Analysis of Adoptive Men." *Archives of General Psychology* 38:861–68.

Cohen, H., et al. 1993. "The Effects of Ethanol on EEG Activity in Males At Risk For Alcoholism." *Encephalography and Clinical Neurophysiology* 86.

Conrod, P. J., et al. 1997. "Biphasic Affects of Alcohol on Heart Rate Are Influenced by Alcoholic Family History and Rate of Alcohol Ingestion." *Alcohol: Clinical and Experimental Research* 21.

Cousins, Norman. 1991. *Anatomy of an Illness as Perceived by the Patient.* New York: Bantam.

Cowley, D. S., et al. 1992. "Response to Diazepam in Sons of Alcoholics." *Alcohol: Clinical and Experimental Research* 16.

Cowley, D. S., et al. 1994. "Eye Movement Effects of Diazepam in Sons of Alcoholics and Male Control Subjects." *Alcohol: Clinical and Experimental Research* 18.

Cowley, D. S., et al. 1996. "Effect of Diazepam on Plasma Gamma-aminobutyric Acid in Sons of Alcoholic Fathers." *Alcohol: Clinical and Experimental Research* 20.

Crabbe, J. C., et al. 1996. "Elevated Alcohol Consumption in Null Mutant Mice Lacking 5-HT$_{1B}$ Serotonin Receptors." *Nature Genetics* 14.

Darwin, Charles. 1859. *The Origin of Species by Means of Natural Selection; or, The Preservation of Favoured Races in the Struggle for Life.* London.

Davis, Elrick B. 1939. *Cleveland Plain-Dealer* [articles on Alcoholics Anonymous], various dates.

Dawkins, Richard. [1982] 1999. *The Extended Phenotype: The Long Reach of the Gene* (rev. ed.). New York: Oxford University Press.

Dawson, J. K., et al. 1995. "Dangerous MAOI Interactions Are Still Occurring in the 1990s." *Journal of Accidents and Emergency Medicine* 12(1, March):49–51.

Day, C. P., et al. 1991. "Investigation of the Role of Polymorphisms at the Alcohol and Aldehyde Dehydrogenase Loci in Genetic Predisposition to Alcohol-Related End-Organ Damage." *Hepatology* 14.

de Tocqueville, Alexis. 1835. *Democracy in America,* vol. 1, New York: G. Dearborn & Co.

de Tocqueville, Alexis. 1840. *Democracy in America,* vol. 2, New York: J. & H.G. Langley.

Dean, Alan. 1997. *Chaos and Intoxication: Complexity and Adaptation in the Structure of Human Nature.* London and New York: Routledge.

Deperieux, E., et al. 1985. "Larval Behavioral Response to Environmental Ethanol in Relation to Alcohol Dehydrogenase Activity Level in *Drosophila melanogaster.*" *Behavioral Genetics* 15:.

Depue, R. A., et al. 1994. "Dopamine and the Structure of Personality." *Journal of Personal and Social Psychology* 67: 485–98.

DeShazo, R. D. and S. F. Kemp. 1997. "Allergic Reactions to Drugs and Biologic Agents." *Journal of the American Medical Association* 278(22, December 10).

Devaud, Leslie and Leslie Morrow 1995. "Interactions Between Neuroactive Steroids and Alcohol and GABA$_A$ Receptors: Effects of Alcohol Withdrawal." In *Stress, Gender, and Alcohol-Seeking Behavior*, NIAAA Research Monograph 29, edited by W. A. Hunt and Sam Zakari. Bethesda, MD:NIAAA.

Dewey, John. 1934. *A Common Faith*, New York.

Dictionary of Cell Biology, <www.mblab.gla.ac.uk/~julian/Dict.html>

Dohrman, D. P., et al. 2000. "Ethanol-Induced Translocation of Protein Kinases." Pp. 58–59 in *Ethanol and Intracellular Signaling*, NIAAA Research Monograph 35. Bethesda, MD: NIAAA.

Dudek, B. and T. Phillips. 1989. "Genotype-Dependent Effects of GABAergic Agents on Sedative Properties of Ethanol." *Psychopharmacology* 98.

Dudek, B. and T. Tritto. 1995. "Classical and Neoclassical Approaches to the Genetic Analysis of Alcohol-Related Phenotypes." *Alcohol: Clinical and Experimental Research* 19.

Dulles, Cardinal Avery, S. J. (Ed.). 2000. *Spiritual Exercises*. New York: Anchor.

Eddy, Mary Baker. 1875. *Science and Health, with Key to the Scriptures*. Boston: The Christian Science Publishing Co.

Eddy, Mary Baker. 1897. *Miscellaneous Writings*. Boston: The Christian Science Publishing Co.

Eddy, Mary Baker. 1908. *Manual of the Mother Church, The First Church of Christ Scientist in Boston, Massachusetts*. Boston: The Christian Science Publishing Co.

Edelman, Gerald. 1989. *The Remembered Present*. New York: Basic Books.

Edelman, Gerald. 1992. *Bright Air Brilliant Fire*. London: Penguin.

Edwards, Jonathan. 1741. "Sinners in the Hands of an Angry God." In *Collected Works*, I. New Haven, Connecticut.

Edwards, G. and M. M. Gross. 1976. "Alcohol Dependence: Provisional Description of a Clinical Syndrome." *British Medical Journal* 1.

Emmanuel Church, 1916. *Yearbook 1916*. Boston: The Church.

Emmanuel Church, 1924. *Report of the Department od Community Since 1924*. Boston: The Church.

Ehlers, C. and M. Schuckit. 1991. "Evaluation of EEG Alpha Activity in Sons of Alcoholics." *Neuropsychopharmacology* 4.

Eskay, R. L., et al. 1993. "The Effects of Alcohol on Selected Regulatory Aspects of the Stress Axis." In *Alcohol and the Endocrine System*, NIAAA Research Monograph 23. Bethesda: NIAAA.

Fagan, Brian. 1998. *From Black Land to Fifth Sun: The Science of Sacred Sites*. Reading, MA: Perseus Book Group.

Feighner, J. P., et al. 1972. "Diagnostic Criteria for Use in Psychiatric Research." *Archives of General Psychiatry* 26(1).

Fenichel, Otto. 1945. *The Psychoanalytic Theory of Neurosis*. London.

Finn, P. and R. Pihl. 1987. "Men At High Risk For Alcoholism: The Effect of Alcohol on Cardiovascular Response to Unavoidable Shock." *Journal of Abnormal Psychology* 96.

Fox, Emmet. 1926. *The Sermon on the Mount*. New York.

Frankfort, Henri (Ed.). 1949. *Before Philosophy: The Intellectual Adventure of Ancient Man*. Chicago: University of Chicago Press and Hammondsworth, Middlesex: Pelican.

Freud, Sigmund. 1914. *On Narcissism: An Introduction*.

Freud, Sigmund. 1926. "Inhibitions, Symptoms, and Anxiety." In *Collected Works*.

Freud, Sigmund. 1928. "Dostoevsky and Parricide." In *Collected Works*.

Freud, Sigmund and Wilhelm Fleiss. [1897] 1985. *The Complete Letters of Sigmund Freud to Wilhelm Fleiss*. London.

Froehlich, J. C. 1993. "Interactions between Alcohol and the Endogenous Opiate System." Pp. 21–35 in *Alcohol and the Endocrine System,* NIAAA Research Monograph 23. Bethesda: NIAAA.

Gabel, S., et al. 1995. "Homovanillic Acid and Monoamine Oxidase in Sons of Substance-Abusing Fathers" in *Journal of Studies on Alcohol* (56, 1995).

Gabrielli, W., et al. 1982. "Electroencephalograms in Children of Alcoholic Fathers." *Psychophysiology* 19.

Geer, B. W., et al. 1989. "Alcohol Dehydrogenase and Ethanol Tolerance at the Cellular Level in Drosophila melanogaster." *Journal of Experimental Zoology* 250.

Geer, B. W., et al. 1993. "The Biological Basis of Ethanol Tolerance in *Drosophila.*" *Compendium of Biochemical Physiology* 105B.

Gelerntner, J., et al. 1993. "The A1 Allele at the D_2 Dopamine Receptor Gene and Alcoholism: A Reappraisal." *Journal of the American Medical Association* 269.

George, D., et al. 1997. "Behavioral and Neuroendocrine Responses to m-Chlorphenylpiperazine in Subtypes of Alcoholics and in Healthy Comparison Subjects." *American Journal of Psychiatry* 154.

George, S. R., et al. 1991. "Endogenous Opioids Are Involved in the Genetically Determined High Preference for Ethanol Consumption." *Alcohol: Clinical and Experimental Research* 15.

Gianoulakis, C., et al. 1996. "Enhanced Sensitivity of Pituitary β-Endorphin to Ethanol." *Archives of General Psychiatry* 53: 250–57.

Glover, Edward. 1928. "The Aetiology of Alcoholism." *Proceedings of the Royal Society of Medicine* 22.

Goodwin, D. W. et al. 1973. "Alcohol <word?> in Adoptees <words?> from Biological Parents." *Archives of General Psychiatry* 28:128–43.

Grant, K. A. 1995. "The Role of $5\text{-}HT_3$ Receptors in Drug Dependence." *Drug and Alcohol Dependence* 38.

Grant, S., et al. 1996. "Activation of Memory Circuits during Cue-Elicited Cocaine Craving." *Proceedings of the National Academy of Sciences* 95(October): 12040–45.

Grofman, Bernard (Ed.). 1981. *Essays Presented to Duncan Black.* Blacksburg, VA: VPI.

Grupp, L. A. 1993. "The Renin-Angiotensin System as a Regulator of Alcohol Consumption." In *Alcohol and the Endocrine System,* NIAAA Research Monograph 23. Bethesda, MD: NIAA.

Hadley, S. H. No date. *Rescue Mission Work.* New York: Old Jerry McAuley Water Street Mission.

Hadley, S. H. 1902. *Down in Water Street.* New York: Simon & Schuster.

Haggard, H. W. and E. M. Jellinek. 1942. *Alcohol Explored.* New York.

Harris, Irving. 1978. *The Breeze of the Spirit: Sam Shoemaker and the Story of Faith-at-Work.* New York.

Harris, R. A., et al. 1995. "Mutant Mice Lacking the Gamma Isoform of Protein Kinase C Show Decreased Behavioral Actions of Ethanol and Altered Function of Gamma-Aminobutyrate Type A Receptors." *Proceedings of the National Academy of Sciences* 92.

Harrison, Brian, et al. 1969. "Drink and Sobriety in an Early Victorian Country Town: Banbury 1830–1860." *English Historical Review,* Supplement no. 4 (London).

Heath, A. and N. Martin. 1994. "Genetic Influences on Alcohol Consumption Patterns and Problem Drinking." *Annals of the New York Academy of Sciences* 708.

Herrmann, Nicolas (Brother Lawrence of the Resurrection). [1692] 1996. *Practice of the Presence of God* (rev. ed.). New York: Anchor.

Hesselbrock, V., et al. 1991. "Neuropsychological Factors in Individuals At High Risk For Alcoholism." In *Recent Developments in Alcoholism*, Vol. 9, edited by M. Galanter. New York: Plenum Press.

Higuchi, S., et al. 1996. "Alcohol and Aldehyde Dehydrogenase Genotypes and Drinking Behavior in Japanese." *Alcohol: Clinical and Experimental Research* 19.

Hilakivi-Clarke, L., et al. 1993. "Effects of Alcohol on Elevated Aggressive Behavior in Male Transgenic TGF*a* Mice." *Neuro Report* 4.

Hill, S. Y., et al. 1995. "Eight-Year Follow-Up of P300 and Clinical Outcome in Children From High Risk For Alcohol Families." *Biological Psychiatry* 37.

Hiller-Sturmhofel, S. 1996. "Jellinek's Typology Revisited." *Alcohol Health & Research World* 20.

Hobsbawm, Eric and Terence Ranger (Eds.). 1981. *The Invention of Tradition.* Cambridge: Cambridge University Press.

Hodge, C. W., H. H. Sampson, et al. 1994. "Effects of Intraaccumbens Injections of Dopamine Agonists and Antagonists on Sucrose and Sucrose-Ethanol Reinforced Responding." *Pharmacological and Biochemical Behavior* 48.

Hoffman, P. L., and B. Tabakoff. 1996. "Alcohol Dependency: A Commentary on Mechanisms. " *Alcohol and Alcoholism* 31.

Hoffman, P. L., et al. 2000. "Neuroadaptation to Ethanol at the Molecular and Cellular Levels." In *Review of NIAAA's Neuroscience and Behavioral Portfolio*, NIAAA Research Monograph 34. Bethesda, MD: NIAAA.

Holmes, Jeremy. 1999. "Defensive and Creative Uses of Narrative in Psychotherapy: An Attachment Perspective." Pp. 49–66 in *Healing Stories: Narrative in Psychiatry and Psychotherapy*, edited by G. Roberts and J. Holmes. Oxford: Oxford University Press.

Hsu, Y. P., et al. 1996. "Association of Monoamine Oxidase A Alleles With Alcoholism Among Male Chinese in Taiwan." *American Journal of Psychiatry* 153.

Jacobsen, Thorkild. 1949. "The Cosmos as a State." In *Before Philosophy: The Intellectual Adventure of Ancient Man*, edited by Henri Simon. Chicago: University of Chicago Press and Hammondsworth, Middlesex: Pelican.

James, William. [1903] 1961. *The Varieties of Religious Experience.* Cambridge, MA: Harvard University Press / New York: Collier.

Jamison, Kay Redfield. 1993. *Touched with Fire: Manic-Depressive Illness and the Artistic Temperament.* New York: Free Press.

Jaynes, Julian. 1976. "The Evolution of Language in the Late Pleistocene." *Annals of the New York Academy of Sciences* 280.

Jaynes, Julian. 1982. *The Origin of Consciousness in the Breakdown of the Bicameral Mind.* Princeton, NJ: Princeton University Press.

Jellinek, E. M. 1960. *The Disease Concept of Alcoholism.* New Haven, CT: HRAF.

Kauffman, Stuart. 2000. *Investigations.* New York: Oxford University Press.

Keeley, Leslie. 1881. *The Morphine Eater, or, From Bondage to Freedom.* Dwight, IL: C. E. Palmer.

Keeley, Leslie. 1896. *The Non-Heredity of Inebriety.* Chicago: Palmer.

Kennedy, James L. et al. 2003. "The Genetics of Adult-Onset Neuropsychiatric Disease: Complexities and Conundra?" *Science* 302(October 2003):822ff.

Kitson, K., and H. Weiner. 1996. "Ethanol and Acetaldehyde Metabolism: Past, Present, and Future." *Alcohol: Clinical and Experimental Research* 20.

Klein, Mitchell. 1999. *How It Worked: The Story of Clarence H. Snyder and the Early Days of Alcoholics Anonymous in Cleveland, Ohio.* Washingtonville, NY: The AA Big Book Study Group.

Klein, Richard and Blake Edgar. 2002. *The Dawn of Human Culture.* New York: John Wiley & Sons.

Kleyn, P. and E. Vesell. 1998. "Genetic Variation as a Guide to Drug Development." *Science* 281(5384, 18 September):1820–21.

Knight, Robert. 1937. "The Dynamics and Treatment of Chronic Alcohol Addiction." *Bulletin of the Menninger Clinic* 1:233–50.

Koechling, U. M., et al. 1995. "Family History of Alcoholism and the Mediation of Alcohol Intake by Catalase: Further Evidence for Catalase as a Marker of the Propensity to Ingest Alcohol." *Alcohol: Clinical and Experimental Research* 19.

Kohut, Heinz. 1971. *The Analysis of the Self*. New York: International Universities Press.

Kohut, Heinz. 1976. *The Restoration of the Self*. New York: International Universities Press.

Kramer, M. S., et al. 1998. "Distinct Mechanism for Antidepressant Activity by Blockade of Central Substance P Receptors." *Science* 281(5383).

Krystal, H. and H. A. Raskin. 1970. *Drug Dependence: Aspects of Ego Function*. Detroit, MI: Wayne State University Press.

Kurtz, Ernest. 1999. *The Collected Ernie Kurtz*. Wheeling, WV: The Bishop of Books.

Kurtz, Ernest. [1979] 1991. *Not God: A History of Alcoholics Anonymous*, expanded edition. Center City, MN: Hazelden.

L., John P. Undated (1970s). Letter to Nell Wing (sender's copy). Eastern Pennsylvania Archives. Bensalem, PA: Area 59 Archives.

Leach, Barry, and John L. Norris. 1977. "Factors in the Development of Alcoholics Anonymous." Pp. 441–553 in *The Biology of Alcoholism*. Volume 5, *Treatment and Rehabilitation of the Chronic Alcoholic*, edited by B. Kissen and H. Begleiter. New York: Pergamon.

Lender, Mark and James Kirby Martin. 1982. *Drinking in America: A History*. New York: Free Press.

Leuba, James H. 1896. "Studies in the Psychology of Religious Phenomena." *American Journal of Psychology* 7.

Levenson, R., et al. 1987. "Greater Reinforcement from Alcohol for Those At Risk: Parental Risk, Personality Risk, and Gender." *Journal of Abnormal Psychology* 96.

Levin, Jerome David. 1995. Chapter in *Dynamic Therapies for Psychiatric Disorders, Axis I*, edited by Jacques Barber and Paul Crits-Christoph. New York: Basic Books.

Lewis, C. S. and Ronald Tolkien. *Language and Human Nature*. Unpublished.

Lex, B., et al. 1993. "Platelet Adenylate Cyclase and Monoamine Oxidase in Women With Alcoholism or a Family History of Alcoholism." *Harvard Review of Psychiatry* 1.

Lobdell, Jared C. 2003. "The Lieutenant, the Captain, and the Colonel, or, The Beginnings of A. A. in the Lehigh Valley: A Problem in Writing Local A.A. History." *Culture, Alcohol, and Society Quarterly* 1(2, January):6–9.

Lobdell, Jared C. Forthcoming. *The Old Custom: The Nature and Decline of our Formerly Conservative Social System*.

London, John Griffith "Jack." [1913] 2001. *John Barleycorn*. New York: Modern Library Classics.

Loyola, Ignatius. 2000. *Spiritual Exercises*, edited by Avery Cardinal Dulles, S.J. New York: Anchor Books.

Mann, Marty. 1950. *Primer on Alcoholism*. New York: Rinehart and Co.

Markey, Morris. 1939. "Alcoholics and God." *Liberty* (magazine).

Maxwell, Milton A. 1950. "The Washingtonian Movement." *Quarterly Journal of Studies on Alcohol* 14:410–51.

McCarthy, Katherine. 1984. "Early Alcoholism Treatment: The Emmanuel Movement and Richard Peabody." *Journal of Studies on Alcohol* 45:45–59.

McGue, M. and W. Slutsky. 1996. "The Inheritance of Alcoholism in Women." Pp. 65–91 in *Women and Alcohol,* NIAAA Research Monograph 32. Bethesda, MD: NIAA.

McKechnie, S., and P. Morgan. 1982. "Alcohol Dehydrogenase Polymorphism of *Drosophila melanogaster." Australian Journal of Biological Sciences* 35.

McWhorter, John. 2002. *The Power of Babel: A Natural History of Language.* New York: W. H. Freeman.

Menninger, Karl. 1938. *Man Against Himself.* New York.

Mercadante, Linda. 1996. *Victims and Sinners: Spiritual Roots of Addiction and Recovery.* Louisville, KY: John Knox Press.

Mitchel, Dick. 2002. *Silkworth: The Little Doctor Who Loved Drunks the Biography of William Duncan Silkworth, M.D.* Center City, MN: Hazelden Information Education.

Morgan, George H. 1858. *Annals, Comprising Memoirs, Incidents and Statistics of Harrisburg.* Harrisburg, PA: Author.

Munson, Carlton. 2001. *The Mental Health Diagnostic Desk Reference* (2d ed.). New York: Haworth Press.

Murray, Jerome. 1879. *Ruminations of an Ex-Inebriate.* Toledo, OH.

Musto, David. 1980. *The American Disease.* New York: Oxford University Press.

Moss, H. B., et al. 1990. "Plasma GABA-like Activity in Response to Ethanol Challenge in Men at High Risk for Alcoholism." *Biological Psychiatry* 27.

National Institutes of Health. 1997. *Report of a Subcommittee of the National Advisory Council on Alcohol Abuse and Alcoholism on the Review of the Extramural Research Portfolio for Genetics.* Bethesda, MD: Author.

National Council on Alcohol and Drug Dependence. No date. *Definitions.* See http://www.ncadd.org/defalc.htm.

Neiswanger, K., et al. 1995. "Association and Linkage Studies of the TaqI A1 Allele at the Dopamine D_2 Receptor Gene in Samples of Female and Male Alcoholics." *American Journal of Medical Genetics* 60.

Nettle, D. and S. Romaine. 2000. *Vanishing Voices: The Extinction of the World's Languages.* New York: Oxford University Press.

Neumark, Y. D., et al. 1998. "Association of the ALDH2*2 Allele With Reduced Ethanol Consumption in Jewish Men in Israel." *Journal of Studies on Alcohol* 59.

New Oxford Annotated Bible. 2001. 3d ed. New York: Oxford University Press.

New Oxford English Dictionary on Historical Principles. 1921–1933. New York: Oxford University Press.

Nishizawa, S., et al. 1997. "Differences between Males and Females in Rates of Serotonin Synthesis in Human Brain." *Proceedings of the National Academy of Sciences* 94(May):5308–13.

Ober, Carole, Nancy: J. Cox, et al. 1998. "Genome-wide Search for Asthma Susceptibility Loci in a Founder Population." *Human Molecular Genetics* 7(9, September).

O'Connor, S., et al. 1994. "Heritable Features of the Auditory Oddball Event-Related Potential." *Encephalography and Clinical Neurophysiology* 92.

Olson, Steve. 2002. *Mapping Human History: Discovering the Past Through our Genes.* Boston: Mariner Books.

Oxford Dictionary of the Christian Church. 1975. Second edition. New York: Oxford University Press.

Pagliaro, A. M. and L. A. Pagliaro. 2000. *Substance Use Among Women: A Reference and Resource Guide.* Philadelphia: Brunner-Routledge.

Pandey, S., et al. 1996. "Serotonin 2C Receptor-Mediated Phospoinositide Hydrolysis in the Brain of Alcohol-Preferring and Alcohol Non-Preferring Rats." *Alcohol: Clinical and Experimental Research* 20.

Parsian, A., et al. 1996. "Platelet Adenylyl Cyclase Activity in Alcoholics and Subtypes of Alcoholics." *Alcohol: Clinical and Experimental Research* 20.

Parsian, A., et al. 1997. "Human GABA$_A$ Receptor á$_1$ and á$_2$ Subunit Genes and Alcoholism." *Alcohol: Clinical and Experimental Research* 21.

Partenan, J. and K. Brown. 1966. *Inheritance of Drinking Behavior.* Helsinki: The Finnish Foundation for Alcohol Studies.

Peabody, Richard. 1931. *The Common Sense of Drinking.* Boston: Little, Brown and Co.

Penick, E. C., B. J. Powell, et al. 1990. "Examination of Cloninger's Type I and Type II Alcoholism with a Sample of Men Alcoholics in Treatment." *Alcoholism: Clinical and Experimental Research* 14.

Peterson, B., et al. 1996. "Ethanol-Induced Change in Cardiac and Endogenous Opiate Function." *Alcohol: Clinical and Experimental Research* 20:1542–52.

Phillips, James. 1999. "The Psychodynamic Narrative." Pp. 27–48 in *Healing Stories: Narrative in Psychiatry and Psychotherapy,* edited by G. Roberts and J. Holmes. Oxford: Oxford University Press.

Phillips, T., and B. Dudek. 1983. "Amphetamine and Caffeine Effects on Ethanol Response in Long- and Short-Sleep Mice." *Behavioral Genetics* 13.

Pickens, R. W. et al. 1991. "Heterogeneity in the Inheritance of Alcoholism." *Archives of General Psychiatry* 48:19–28.

Plotkin, H. 1994. Darwin Machines and The Nature of Knowledge. Cambridge, MA: Harvard University Press.

Pocock, J.G.A. 1989. *Politics, Language, and Time: Essays on Political Thought and History.* Chicago: University of Chicago Press.

Porter, R. 1985. "The Drinking Man's Disease." *British Journal of Addiction* 80:385–96.

Powell, Lyman. 1930. *Mary Baker Eddy: A Life Size Portrait.* New York: Macmillan.

Radó, Sandór. 1929. "The Psychic Effects of Intoxicants: An Attempt to Evolve a Psychoanalytic Theory of Morbid Cravings." *International Journal of Psycho-Analysis.*

Radó, Sandór. 1933. "The Psychoanalysis of Pharmachothymia (Drug Addiction): The Clinical Picture." *Psychoanalysis Quarterly* 2.

Radó, Sandór. 1953. "Recent Advances in Psychoanalytic Therapy." *Psychiatric Treatment* 31.

Radó, Sandór. 1957. "Narcotic Bondage." *American Journal of Psychiatry* 114.

Randin, D., et al. 1995. "Suppression of Alcohol-Induced Hypertension by Dexamethasone." *New England Journal of Medicine* 332.

Raphael, Matthew. 1999. *Bill W. and Mr. Wilson: The Legend and Life of A.A.'s Cofounder.* Amherst, MA: University of Massachusetts Press.

Reid, L. and C. Hubbell. 1990. "Opioids Modulate Rats' Propensities." Pp. 121–34 in *Novel* Pharmacological *Interventions for Alcoholism,* edited by C. Naranjo and E. Sellers. New York: Springer Verlag.

Roberts, A. J., et al. 1996. "Intra-Amygdala Muscimol Decreases Operant Ethanol Self-Administration in Dependent Rats." *Alcohol: Clinical and Experimental Research* 20.

Roe, Anne. 1945. "Children of Alcoholic Parents Raised in Foster Homes." Pp. 115–26 in *Alcohol, Science, and Society: Twenty-Nine Lectures with Discussions, as Given at the Yale Summer School of Alcohol Studies* (reprinted). Westport, CT: Greenwood Publishing Press.

Roizen, Richard. 1991. *The American Discovery of Alcoholism 1933–1939*. Ph.D. dissertation, University of California, Berkeley. See www.roizen.com/ron/disshome/htm.

Roizen, Richard. 1993. "Paradigm Sidetracked: Explaining Early Resistance to the Alcoholism Paradigm at Yale's Laboratory of Applied Physiology 1940–1944." See www.roizen.com/ron/sidetracked.htm.

Rorabaugh, W. J. 1981. *The Alcoholic Republic: An American Tradition*. New York: Oxford Press.

Rosenzweig, Saul. 1994. *The Historic Expedition to America 1909: Freud, Jung, and Hall the King-Maker* (2d ed. rev.). St. Louis, MO: Diane Publishing Co.

Russell, A. J. 1932. *For Sinners Only*. London: Hodder & Stoughton.

Russell, A. J. (Ed.). (1938) 1989. *God Calling* by Two Listeners. London: Barbour & Co.

S., Clarence. 1999. *How It Worked*. Washingtonville, NY: The AA Big Book Study Group.

Sanford, John A. 1996. *Mystical Christianity: A Psychological Commentary on the Gospel of John*. New York: Crossroad/Herder & Herder.

Schuckit, M. 1994. "Low Level of Response to Alcohol as a Predictor of Future Alcoholism." *American Journal of Psychiatry* 151.

Schuckit, M., et al. 1981. "Dopamine-β-Hydroxylase Activity in Men at High Risk for Alcoholism." *Biological Psychiatry* 16.

Schuckit, M., et al. 1982. "Platelet Monoamine Oxidase Activity in Relatives of Alcoholics: Preliminary Study with Matched Control Subjects." *Archives of General Psychiatry* 39.

Schuckit, M., et al. 1990. "Examination of Cloninger's Type I and Type II Alcoholism with a Sample of Men Alcoholics in Treatment." *Alcoholism: Clinical and Experimental Research* 14.

Schuckit, M., et al. 1991. "Subjective Feeling and Changes in Body Sway Following Diazepam in Sons of Alcoholics and Control Subjects." *Journal of Studies on Alcohol* 52.

Schuckit, M., et al. 1996. "Alcohol Challenges in Young Men from Alcoholic Pedigrees and Control Families: A Report from the COGA Project." *Journal of Studies on Alcohol* 57.

Schuckit, M., T. Smith, et al. 1995. "An Evaluation of Type A and Type B Alcoholics." *Addiction* 90.

Sellers, E. M., et al. 1994. "Clinical Efficacy of the 5-HT$_3$ Antagonist Ondansetron in Alcohol Abuse and Dependence." *Alcohol: Clinical and Experimental Research* 18.

Shoemaker, Samuel M. 1934. *The Gospel According to You*. New York.

Shoemaker, Samuel M. 1935. "The Way to Find God," sermon June 30. *Calvary Evangel* (August).

Shoemaker, Samuel M. [1964] 1986. "Those Twelve Steps as I Understand Them." Pp. 125–34 in *The Best of the Grapevine*, vol. 2. New York: A.A.

Siegel, Ronald N. 1989. *Intoxication: Life in Pursuit of Artificial Paradise*. New York: Pocket Books.

Sigvardsson, S., M. Bohman, and R. C. Cloninger. 1996 "Replication of the Stockholm Adoption Study of Alcoholism: Confirmatory Cross-Fostering Analysis." *Archives of General Psychiatry* 53.

Silkworth, William. (1939). "The Doctor's Opinion." In Bill W., et al., *Alcoholics Anonymous*. New York: Alcoholics Anonymous.

Simon, Henri (Ed.). 1949. *Before Philosophy: The Intellectual Adventure of Ancient Man*. Chicago: University of Chicago Press and Hammondsworth, Middlesex: Pelican.

Simon, Herbert. 1957. *Models of Man.* New York: John Wiley and Sons.

Simon, Herbert. 1982. *Collected Essays.* Cambridge, MA: MIT Press.

Smith, Gerrit. 1833. "Letter from Gerrit Smith to Edward C. Delavan, Esq., on the Reformation of the Intemperate." In Lydia H. Sigourney, *The Intemperate and the Reformed: Shewing the Awful Consequences of Intemperance, and the Blessed Effects of the Temperance Reformation.* Boston.

Spear, L. P. 2000. "Adolescent Period: Biological Basis of Vulnerability to Develop Alcoholism." In *Review of NIAAA's Neuroscience and Behavioral Portfolio,* NIAAA Research Monograph 34. Bethesda, MD: NIAAA.

Stewart, R. B., et al. 1993. "Comparison of Alcohol Preferring P and Non-Preferring NP Rats on Tests of Anxiety and for the Anxiolytic Effects of Ethanol." *Alcohol* 10.

Sullivan, E. V. 2000. "Human Brain Vulnerability to Alcoholism." In *Review of NIAAA's Neuroscience and Behavioral Portfolio,* NIAAA Research Monograph 34. Bethesda, MD: NIAAA.

Swift, R. M. 1999. "Medications and Alcohol Craving." *Alcohol Research & Health* 23: 207–13.

Tanaka, F., et al. 1997. "Polymorphism of Alcohol-Metabolizing Genes Affects Drinking Behavior and Alcoholic Liver Disease in Japanese Men." *Alcohol: Clinical and Experimental Research* 21.

Tarter, Ralph and Michael Vanyukov. 1994. "Stepwise Developmental Model of Alcoholism Strategy." *The Development of Alcohol Problems,* edited by the U.S. Dept. of Health and Human Services. Rockville, MD: NIAAAA.

Teune, Henry and Zdravko Mlinar. 1979. *The Developmental Logic of Social Systems.* Long Beach, CA:Sage.

Thomasson, H. R. et al. 1991. "Alcohol and Aldehyde Dehydrogenase Genotypes and Alcoholism in Chinese Men." *American Journal of Human Genetics* 48.

Tiebout, Harry. 1954. "The Ego Factors in Surrender to Alcoholism." In *The Collected Writings.* Center City, MN: Hazelden.

Tiebout, Harry. 1961. "Alcoholics Anonymous: An Experiment of Nature." In *The Collected Writings.* Center City, MN: Hazelden.

Tiebout, Harry. 1999. *The Collected Writings.* Center City, MN: Hazelden.

Towns, Charles. 1915. *Habits That Handicap: The Menace of Opium, Alcohol, and Tobacco, and the Remedy.* New York: The Century Co.

Tsigos, C. and G. Chrousos. 1995. "Neuroendocrinology of the Stress Response." Pp. 103–24 in *Stress, Gender, and Alcohol-Seeking Behavior,* edited by W. A. Hunt and Sam Zakari. NIAAA Research Monograph 29. Bethesda, MD: NIAAA.

Turner, A., et al. 1997. "Frequency of the A1/A2 Alleles of the D2 Dopamine Receptor (DRD2) Gene in a British Caucasian Control Group Screened to Exclude Alcoholism and Heavy Drinking." *Addiction Biology* 2.

Vaillant, George E. 1983. *Natural History of Alcoholism.* Cambridge, MA: Harvard University Press.

Vaillant, George E. 1996a. *Natural History of Alcoholism Revisited.* Cambridge, MA: Harvard University Press.

Vaillant, George E. 1996b. "A Long-Term Follow-Up of Male Alcohol Abuse." *Archives of General Psychiatry* 53(March): 243–49.

Volavka, J., et al. 1996. "The Electroencephalogram After Alcohol Administration in High Risk Men and the Development of Alcohol Use Disorders 10 Years Later." *Archives of General Psychiatry* 53.

W., Richmond. 1954. *Twenty-Four Hours a Day.* Center City, MN: Hazelden Education Information.

W., Bill. [1952/53] 1994. *Twelve Steps and Twelve Traditions*. New York: Alcoholics Anonymous.

W., Bill. [1957–58] 1989. "Let's Be Friendly with Our Friends." *A.A. Grapevine*. Reprinted as pp. 171–90 in Bill W., *The Language of the Heart*. New York: Alcoholics Anonymous.

W., Bill. 1958. *Alcoholics Anonymous Comes of Age: A Brief History of A.A.* New York: Alcoholics Anonymous.

W., Bill. 1962. *Twelve Concepts for World Service*. New York: Alcoholics Anonymous.

W., Bill. 1967. *As Bill Sees It*. New York: Alcoholics Anonymous [originally published as *The A.A. Way of Life*].

W., Bill. 1969. Testimony before the Special Subcommittee on Alcoholism and Narcotics of the U. S. Senate Committee on Labor and Public Welfare, July 24.

W., Bill. 1989. *The Language of the Heart: Bill W.'s Grapevine Writings*. New York: Alcoholics Anonymous.

W., Bill. 2000. *Bill W. My First 40 Years*. Center City, MN: Hazelden.

W., Bill. No date. *Three Talks to Medical Societies by Bill W.* New York: Alcoholics Anomymous.

W., Bill, et al. 1939. *Alcoholics Anonymous*, 1st ed. New York: Works Publishing Co.

W., Bill, et al. 1955. *Alcoholics Anonymous*, 2d ed. New York: Alcoholics Anonymous.

W., Bill, et al. 1976. *Alcoholics Anonymous*, 3d ed. New York: Alcoholics Anonymous.

W., Bill, et al. 2001. *Alcoholics Anonymous*, 4th ed. New York: Alcoholics Anonymous.

W., Lois and Bill. 1998. *Diary of Two Motorcycle Hobos*. Herndon, VA: Online Recovery Resources.

Waltman, C., et al. 1994. "Adrenocorticotropin Responses Following Administration of Ethanol and Ovine Corticotropin-Releasing Hormone in the Sons of Alcoholics and Control Subjects." *Alcohol: Clinical and Experimental Research* 18.

Wand, G. S. and A. S. Dobs. 1991. "Alterations in the Hypothalamic-Pituitary-Adrenal Axis in Actively Drinking Alcoholics." *Journal of Clinical Endocrinology and Metabolism* 72.

Wand, Gary. 2000. "The Hypothalamic-Pituitary-Adrenal Axis." In *Ethanol and Intracellular Signaling*, NIAAA Research Monograph 35. Bethesda, MD: NIAAA.

Washington Temperance Society. 1842. *Washingtonian Pocket Companion, Containing a Choice Collection of Temperance Hymns, Songs, etc.* Utica, NY.

White, William L. 1998. *Slaying the Dragon: The History of Addiction Treatment and Recovery in America*. Normal, IL: Chestnut Health System.

Williams, Charles. (1938) 1965. *The Descent into Hell*. London: Wm. B. Eerdmans Publishing Co.

Williams, Charles. (1941) 1995. *The Descent of the Dove: A Short History of the Holy Spirit in the Church*. London: Regent College Publishing.

Wing, Nell. 1992. *Grateful to Have Been There: My 42 Years with Bill and Lois, and the Evolution of Alcoholics Anonymous*. Park Ridge, IL: Parkside Publishing Corp.

Witmer, Lightner. 1909. "Mental Healing and the Emmanuel Movement." *Psychological Clinic* 1.

Wolfe, Jonathan. No date. "Chemistry of the Cell and Genetics," Genetics Lecture 10: Genes in Populations. See www.ucl.ac.uk/~ucbhjow/bmsi/bmsi_10.html

Woodward, Samuel. 1838. *Essays on Asylums for Inebriates*. Worcester, MA.

Workman-Daniels, K. and V. Hesselbrock. 1997. "Childhood Problem Behavior and Neuropsychological Functioning in Persons at Risk for Alcoholism." *Journal of Studies on Alcohol* 48.

World Health Organization. 1992. *The ICD-10 Classification of Mental and Behavioural Disorders: Clinical Descriptions and Diagnostic Guidelines,* 10th revision.

World Health Organization. 1903. *Manual of the International Statistical Classification of Diseases, Injuries, and Causes of Death.*

Yalisove, Daniel. 1998. "The Origins and Evolution of the Disease Concept of Treatment." *Journal of Studies in Alcohol* 59.

Zucker, Robert. 1987. "The Four Alcoholisms." Pp. 27–83 in *Nebraska Symposium on Motivation. Alcohol and Addictive Behaviors,* edited by P. C. Rivers and R. Dienstbier. Lincoln, NE: University of Nebraska Press.

Zucker, Robert. 1994. "Pathways to Alcohol Problems and Alcoholism." Pp. 255–90 in *The Development of Alcohol Problems: Exploring the Biopsychosocial Matrix of Risk,* NIAAA Research Monograph 26. Rockville, MD: NIAAA.

Zug, John. 1842. *The Foundation, Progress and Principles of the Washington Temperance Society of Baltimore.* Baltimore, MD: Author.

Index